American Government in Action

Principle, Process, Politics

Ryan J. Barilleaux
Miami University, Ohio

Prentice Hall
Upper Saddle River, New Jersey 07458

For my wife, Marilyn,
and our children—
Gerard, Madeleine, Christine,
Paul, Thomas, and Michael

Library of Congress Cataloging-in-Publication Data

Barilleaux, Ryan J.
   American government in action : principle, process, politics /
Ryan J. Barilleaux.
      p.   cm.
   Includes bibliographical references and index.
   ISBN 0-13-078924-0
   1. United States—Politics and government.   I. Title.
JK271.B344   1996
320.473—dc20   95-20352
                                                         CIP

Acquisitions editor: *Michael Bickerstaff*
Development supervisor: *Virginia Otis Locke*
Development editor: *Leslie Carr*
Editorial/production: *Serena Hoffman*
Design supervisor: *Anne Bonanno Nieglos*
Interior design: *Lorraine Mullaney*
Buyer: *Bob Anderson*
Copy editor: *Linda Pawelchak*
Photo supervisor: *Lorinda Morris-Nantz*
Illustrations: *Moore Electronic Design*
Photo researcher: *Rhoda Sidney*
Cover design: *Tom Nery*
Cover art: *Elena Dorfman*

 © 1996 by Prentice-Hall, Inc.
Simon & Schuster/A Viacom Company
Upper Saddle River, New Jersey 07458

Printed in the United States of America
10 9 8 7 6 5 4 3 2 1

ISBN: 0-13-078924-0

Prentice-Hall International (UK) Limited, *London*
Prentice-Hall of Australia Pty. Limited, *Sydney*
Prentice-Hall Canada Inc., *Toronto*
Prentice-Hall Hispanoamericana, S.A., *Mexico*
Prentice-Hall of India Private Limited, *New Delhi*
Prentice-Hall of Japan, Inc., *Tokyo*
Simon & Schuster Asia Pte. Ltd., *Singapore*
Editora Prentice-Hall do Brasil, Ltda., *Rio de Janeiro*

Brief Contents

Contents

v

3   The Constitution in Action: Federalism, Nationalism, and Democracy 58

PART 2: Politics and the People

4   Citizen Rights and Liberties   85

5   The Public's Role in American Politics   118

12   Unelected Representatives   327

PART 4: Domestic and Global Policy

13   Domestic Policy   352

14   Foreign Policy and America's Global Context   377

Appendixes

Glossary   442

Notes   451

Photo Credits   458

Index   459

Boxed Features

Preface

Daily we are bombarded by television and radio reports of the activities of our government. At work or at home we learn of American trade negotiations with Japan, a new ruling by the Supreme Court in the area of civil rights, the results of a local election, the latest news of war in Bosnia, Rwanda, Sri Lanka. And the evening news brings us the major stories of the day: the tragic explosion of a bomb in Oklahoma City and the government's response to this act of terrorism; the president's address before Congress on the "state of the union"; the Republican effort in Congress to reduce our expenditures on welfare. These stories come to us at an amazing rate, reminding us that our government is an anthill of activity, but sometimes overwhelming us with information that we are hard put to decipher.

I wrote this textbook to help citizens and voters make sense of American government in action. A brief survey of how our government is structured and how it works, *American Government in Action* will help students acquire the knowledge and skills they need to play their part in the governing of the United States. As each chapter of this book makes clear, *citizens are the basis of American government,* its reason for being, and the ultimate judges of its performance. Our political system depends on its citizens, and thus we all have a role to play in the political life of the nation.

Unique Organizing Format

American Government in Action offers a format that is unique among textbooks yet also familiar to most professors who teach survey courses in American government. Each chapter begins by introducing its main topic and overviewing the entire discussion. Then, under the three major organizing rubrics of *principle, process, and politics,* it helps students understand the motivating ideas, the concrete nature, and the dynamics of a particular component of government.

Principles. The first major section of each chapter examines the *assumptions and values* that underlie the American political system—our ideas of what we want government to do and how we want it to operate. In these initial sections students come to understand *why* the U.S. government is structured as it is and what *motivates* the continuation of some aspects of government as well as the changes in others. In Chapter 4, for example, we see how the American political system gives a privileged place to citizen and liberties.

Process. The second major section of each chapter examines the way these beliefs and values have shaped the structures of our political system, as well as the rules, guidelines, and specific procedures by which the government functions on a day-to-day basis. In Chapter 11, for example, we see how judicial review has given the courts a central role as "guardians of the Constitution" in our checks-and-balances system.

Politics. In the third major section of each chapter, we explore the dynamics of the American system—the way individuals and groups attempt to accomplish their aims within the system. Although the structure of American government makes large-scale policy change infrequent, we will see in Chapter 6, for example, how interest groups use lobbying, campaign contributions, and other techniques to promote their political goals.

Important Themes

Ideas matter, and they have political consequences. One of the most distinctive features of this text is the way it explores and explains the ideas that form the foundation of American politics. Examining the principles behind our governmental system helps us understand how day-to-day political events are linked to these fundamental values and beliefs.

American politics often involves competition and conflict among different values. The text examines such struggles as freedom versus equality, liberty versus order, and democracy versus republicanism. Each chapter focuses on important questions that remain at issue and may not be capable of resolution.

The Constitution is fundamental to the operations of American politics. The U.S. Constitution plays a role in shaping every aspect of the American political system. Sometimes that shaping is explicit; the concept of the separation of powers embodied in the Constitution largely determines the relationship between the president and Congress. At other times the Constitution's role is more subtle, or even unintentional; the broad freedom accorded the press by the Constitution allows the contemporary media to act frequently as *unelected representatives* of the people, as we see in Chapter 13.

Citizens can be active participants in local, state, and national politics. Citizens need not be spectators; knowledge and effort can make them serious actors on the political scene. This textbook provides many examples of active citizenship as well as specific and detailed advice on how to get involved.

Special Features

Innovative Chapters. Several unique chapters help students understand the current state of American politics. Chapter 3, Constitutional Practice: Federalism, Nationalism, and Democracy, not only shows how our nation's charter has changed and developed since its adoption but makes the often "dry" subject of federalism come alive for students. Chapter 13, Unelected Representatives, not only explores the role of the media in federal and local politics, but it also presents a unique discussion of the important role played by staff members of all three branches of the government in influencing the actions of the officials for whom they work and even in making policy. Chapter 14, Foreign Policy: America's Global Context, discusses American foreign policy in a comparative analysis of other major powers and their systems of government.

Boxed Features. *Current Issues* boxes focus on topics at the forefront of current political controversies, such as abortion versus the right to life, the line-item veto, and the Balanced Budget Amendment. *Citizens in Action* boxes highlight the actions of ordinary citizens—and some better known individuals—whose seizing of initiative has effected lasting change in our government or in the way we live. *Participate!* boxes not only encourage the reader to emulate citizens who have gotten involved but supply detailed information on how to do this: addresses, telephone numbers, and how to go about using these means to make your voice heard. (Students will find a list of additional resources in Appendix F.)

"Open Questions." Open Questions sections, which conclude the chapters, offer students the opportunity to think critically about some of the unresolved issues that perplex government officials and the general citizenry. For example, in Chapter 5, The Public's Role in American Politics, the student is asked to consider the advantages and disadvantages of multiculturalism in American education.

Key Terms. Key terms are defined both in the text and in a running glossary in the margins of the book for quick reference and better understanding. All definitions are also collected in an alphabetized glossary at the back of the text.

Important Reference Documents. The complete texts of the Declaration of Independence, the U.S. Constitution, and *The Federalist Papers*, No. 10 and No. 51, are included in appendixes at the back of the book.

Supplements

Instructor's Manual. For each chapter of the book, the *Instructor's Manual* provides chapter summaries, reviews of major concepts, lecture and discussion suggestions, topic outlines, and additional materials.

Test Item File. Thoroughly reviewed to ensure the accuracy, clarity, and significance of each item, the *Test Item File* consists of 1300 questions in multiple-choice, true/false, and essay formats.

Prentice Hall Custom Test. Prentice Hall's new testing software program permits instructors to edit any or all items in the *Test Item File* and add their own questions. Other special features of this program, which is available for both IBM and Macintosh computers, include random generation of an item set, scrambling question sequence, and test preview before printing.

Study Guide. Students will find the *Study Guide* helpful in reinforcing and enhancing what they have learned from the text. The *Guide* includes chapter outlines, study notes, a glossary, and quizzes for each chapter of the book.

American Government Transparencies, Series IV. This set of 100 four-color transparency acetates reproduces illustrations, charts, graphs, and maps from a variety of sources.

American Government Simulation Software. This interactive software, available in IBM, Mac, and CD-ROM formats, permits students to assume a variety of roles—the president of the United States, a reporter covering a particular bill in Congress, the secretary of state, a Supreme Court justice—to achieve a better understanding of the complexities and the excitement of participation in government.

 **ABC News/Prentice Hall Video Libraries.** Prentice Hall and ABC News offer the instructor a collection of timely video segments that focus on many topics and issues covered in American government courses. These video libraries feature segments from such award-winning programs as "Nightline," "20/20," "World News Tonight," "The American Agenda," "Primetime Live," and "This Week with David Brinkley."

Themes of the Times. Prentice Hall and *The New York Times* offer a useful collection of articles from recent issues of the *Times* to help students expand their knowledge beyond the classroom and into the real world of government and politics. This collection, presented in newspaper format, is offered gratis to users of *American Government in Action*. Featuring the excellence in reporting and journalistic integrity for which the *The New York Times* has long been known, the articles both illustrate and update the text material, providing real-world applications of topics discussed throughout the text.

Acknowledgments

Every textbook carries the name of its author or authors, but every book is truly the effort of a team of people, and it benefits from the help and advice of many more. I am deeply indebted and grateful to the many people who have helped me in this project, whether they have contributed directly or offered information or advice.

I owe endless thanks to my family, who inspired this book and to whom it is dedicated. My wife, Marilyn, has been my constant support and encouragement. She shouldered many tasks to make the book possible, and I thank her with love. My children—Gerard, Madeleine, Christine, Paul, Thomas, and Michael—not only endured hours with Dad bent over his computer ("He's writing—*again*"), but made my hours away from the project joyful. Now they can see what it was all about.

Many colleagues have contributed to making this book better. Gary Gregg read the entire manuscript and provided much constructive criticism. Both Steven DeLue and Susan Kay, who served as my departmental chairs while I was working on this project, offered continual encouragement. Randall Adkins, Andrew Dowdle, Richard Forgette, Robert Gump, Walter Huber, Augustus Jones, Ilsu Kim, William Mandel, Michael Pagano, John Rothgeb, Phillip Russo, and Douglas Shumavon all helped by answering questions, lending resources, exploring fine points, and clarifying issues for me. I also want to thank two teachers whose example has provided me with inspiration over the course of my career: Herbert M. Levine and Bruce Buchanan.

I also want to thank the outside reviewers who pored over various versions of the manuscript. Having served in the same capacity myself, I have always wondered just how useful (or infuriating) an author found my comments to be. I can now attest that these anonymous reviews are most helpful, and I appreciate all the effort the following individuals put into them: Stephen G. Dale, Texas A&M University; Scott J. Hammond, James Madison University; Dwight Kiel, Florida Atlantic University; Doris R. Knight, Holyoke Community College; Leonard Meizlish, Mott Community College; Don Melton, Arapahoe Community College; Max Neiman, University of California, Riverside; Richard Pacelle, University of Missouri-St. Louis; Laura A. Reese, Eastern Michigan University; Leonard Ritt, Northern Arizona University; Pamela Rodgers, University of Wisconsin, LaCrosse; and J. David Woodard, Clemson University.

The staff at Prentice Hall has shown remarkable professional skill and good humor throughout the project. Michael Bickerstaff has been unfailingly encouraging and responsive. Virginia Otis Locke made the whole effort seem effortless. Leslie Carr did an outstanding job of challenging me to make each chapter the best it could be. Serena Hoffman skillfully coordinated the entire production. Nicole Signoretti and Anita Castro answered all my questions, and everyone else at Prentice Hall has been most helpful and gracious.

Finally, I want to thank all the students in all the American government classes I have taught over the years whose reactions to my ideas and presentations have helped to refine my thinking about our political system. Their contributions are a part of this book.

The chapters that follow are my own. In the end, all the comments and suggestions from others had to be filtered through my own abilities as a teacher and writer, and thus I take full responsibility for any shortcomings the book may have. I hope that both the professors and students who use this book will feel free to write to me with their opinions, criticisms, or comments.

Ryan J. Barilleaux

About the Author

Ryan J. Barilleaux is professor of political science at Miami University, Oxford, Ohio, where he is also director of graduate studies and the recipient of a number of awards for teaching excellence. Professor Barilleaux's broad experience as a teacher and researcher, as well as his work as a Washington aide to Louisiana's Senator J. Bennett Johnston, imbue this textbook with scholarly expertise and a deep commitment to the importance of citizen participation in government.

Professor Barilleaux, who earned his doctorate in political science at the University of Texas at Austin, is the author of four books on the American presidency: *The President and Foreign Policy, The Post-Modern Presidency, The President as World Leader,* and *Leadership and the Bush Presidency.* Widely known for this scholarship, Professor Barilleaux is a member of the Executive Committee of the Presidency Research Group. He also recently served as chair of the American Political Science Association's E. E. Schattschneider Award Committee.

Understanding American Politics

I n the past several years, voters in about half of America's states have enacted limits on the terms of office of public officials. In Ohio, Colorado, and Oregon, for example, they limited the tenure of the state legislature and representatives and senators in the United States Congress. Many observers attributed these limits to a national mood of anger against professional politicians. But term limits are nothing new in American politics. The issue has roots in the very origins of the United States.

At the time of the writing of the Constitution, some commentators argued that term limits would ensure rotation in public office, thus preventing the emergence of an elite class of rulers. Opponents of such plans saw the desire for reelection as the best check on officials, who would have to behave themselves in order to win popular support. The original Constitution imposed no limits on office, but presidents observed an unofficial two-term limit from Washington's retirement in 1796 until Franklin Roosevelt's 1940 election to a third term. Over the past two centuries the proposal has surfaced and resurfaced with regularity. The Twenty-second Amendment (1951) limited the president to two terms. The limits on congressional terms imposed during the 1990s reflect continued interest in the idea.

Restricting the number of years representatives could serve in government seems to many a simple and obvious solution to political problems such as massive federal deficits, check-bouncing scandals in the House of Representatives, and the collapse of the savings-and-loan system. But term limits raise a host of questions about the wisdom of restraining voters' choices and about what people want from their government. Do the states have the power to restrict how many years individuals may serve in the United States Congress? If so, does this mean that states can put other limits on the national government? Is it wise to limit whom voters may choose to represent them? Is it wise to allow officeholders to become entrenched in their jobs and out of touch with the people? How will limits on legislative terms affect the way government functions?

All of these questions illustrate a fundamental fact about government in the United States and elsewhere: Politics is not merely about what happens today and tomorrow or some specific event. The everyday issues of politics often involve far more important questions than just how high taxes will be or whether motorists must wear seatbelts while driving. Politics frequently, indeed usually, involves questions about what we create government to do, what we expect of it, how we want it to operate, and who gets to influence those decisions and how. Term-limit proposals seem simple enough: Do voters want to restrict the careers of legislators? Yes or no?

As simple as these initiatives may seem, they touch on the very definition of good government and the meaning of democracy in our political system. Which is more democratic: allowing voters unlimited choice in elections (no term limits), or setting restrictions on who may be chosen for office (using term limits to keep long-time incumbents off the ballot)? Should we emphasize experience in government (no limits on legislative terms), or the continual infusion of new voices brought on by frequent turnover in office (as a result of term limits)? At first glance term limits seem to present a simple choice, but when we look more closely we see that they involve deeper issues.

In the United States, citizens are often called upon to cast votes on an array of ballot proposals, from term limits and product labelling to bond issues and English-only rules for elections and public records. They must also regularly choose the individuals who will fill public offices, from sheriffs and school boards to Congress and the presidency. How are citizens to make an informed choice in each of these cases? One thing they should do is to learn about the questions they will be asked, the issues, and the candidates. To make sound judgments on the issues of the times, citizens should understand how the questions of the moment relate to the fundamental values and ideas at stake in public choices. For example, is the term-limit proposal merely a simple restriction on incumbency, or does it affect how representatives will serve their constituents? How would such limits alter the constitutional balance of power between the presidency and Congress? Do term limits advance or undermine democratic goals?

To examine the issues before them and to participate in the public affairs of the United States, citizens would do well to understand the principles and structures that underlie the unfolding events of war, peace, inflation, recession, elections, and policy making. The most fundamental concept that an American ought to understand is the meaning of politics.

Politics refers to struggles over power and claims to authority in society.[1] That is a broad definition, but a necessary one: Politics covers a large area of human activity. As we shall see, the struggles that constitute politics make more sense when we understand what power means and why authority is important.

"Politics" is a term that has noble beginnings but has acquired a bad reputation among Americans. Indeed, in our society it is often used in a negative way to explain why things go wrong in life. When a person is passed over for a promotion at work because it was given to someone else, he or she may blame the slight on "politics" rather than performance. Likewise, if public officials do not make what one observer is convinced is the correct choice in the location of a new City Hall, or the awarding of a contract, or appointment to high office, that critic might disparage the bad decision as the result of "politics."

Is politics what happens when things go wrong? Common use of the term might suggest such a definition, but it is far from a satisfactory one. What word would we use to describe the situation when our preferred candidate wins an election, or when the government pursues a policy that is exactly what we think it should be? Aren't these also examples of politics? Americans may not always like what happens in politics, but that does not mean that politics is only the wrong outcome.

How can we make more sense out of politics? The answer lies in the terms that we used previously in our definition: *power* and *authority*.

What Is Politics?

politics The struggle over power and claims to authority in society.

Power and Authority

Power exists in private life as well as in public affairs. It is the ability to influence events, to exert one's will, to command or prevent action, or to achieve desired outcomes.[2] Power is, of course, something of a universal phenomenon in society. Parents have power over children, officials have power over citizens, bosses have power over subordinates, professors have power over students.

Power can be used for good or ill, whether to teach students, build roads, or enslave a people. Power provides the ability to do something, but not the thing itself. Governmental power is a particularly good example of this fact. In the twentieth century, political power has been used at various times to send millions of innocent people to their deaths and to educate and protect millions of others. Because it is instrumental, power cannot be fully understood without some idea of why authority is important.

Authority refers to the legitimate possession and/or use of power. Those who possess authority are those who we recognize as having the right to power and who are using it in a legitimate fashion. Individuals generally obey those who they believe have the right to make rules for them and give instructions (such as a boss over subordinates), and whose directions are appropriate to the power they hold. For example, bosses can tell their employees when to report to work but not how they should vote in a presidential election.

Authority is particularly important to politics, because individuals and groups want to be governed by those who they believe have the right to wield power and do so appropriately. Few people are willing to accept without complaint the rule of institutions or people they regard as illegitimate, nor do they like it when even good rulers make decisions they find unjust. That is why political leaders around the world, even if they have acquired power by sheer force, will go to great lengths to associate themselves with symbols representative of legitimacy. Military dictators may surround themselves with national symbols, such as the country's flag, or even democratic symbols, such as an election (even if the results are fixed). Likewise, even elected leaders use flags, seals of office, invocations of the national constitution, and other signs that they have a right to be in power.

Power and authority are significant to our understanding of politics because so much of what we consider "political" involves these concepts. We have defined politics as the struggle over power and claims to authority in society. Certainly, politics involves struggle, even if it is a peaceful and orderly competition. It is a struggle ultimately about claims to power and authority—the power to direct and also the right to wield power.

The Study of Politics

Even with a good definition of politics in hand, we must make further distinctions. The foregoing use of the term "politics" includes many of the activities of private life—"office politics," the struggles over control of corporations or other

power The ability to exert one's will, to command or prevent action, or to achieve desired outcomes.

authority The legitimate possession and/or use of power.

private groups, even informal contests for control over a club or association. This text and this course concern *public politics,* struggles over claims to power and authority in public affairs.

Political scientists are those who study public politics. **Political science**[3] is a field of knowledge in which those things termed "political"—and that area is broadly defined—are studied in a *systematic* fashion. It is not a science in the same sense as is chemistry, in which there are specific fundamental laws upon which all complex actions are based and that lend predictability and precision to the work of chemists. Political science involves the study of political ideas, institutions and structures, political behavior, and public policies. It borrows research methods from fields such as philosophy, history, law, statistics, sociology, anthropology, psychology, geography, economics, and even literature. What unites political scientists is not so much a common outlook on their subject or a common method of analysis as a shared interest in whatever can be loosely termed "politics."

Most of public politics in the world takes place within the confines of some kind of formal political system. This means that it occurs within a set of institutions and rules, as well as a political culture, that make politics in one system somewhat distinct from what occurs elsewhere. As we shall see, politics in the United States is different from that of other political systems in several ways. The most significant aspects of a political system are its regime and government.

Regimes and Governments

Politics is a distinctively social activity. Throughout history, groups of people have formed political entities that set rules by informal (customs) or formal (laws) means. These entities may be independent of other systems, such as a country, or they may be subordinate to a larger political system, such as a city or province. Political scientists identify these systems as regimes.

What Is a Regime?

A **regime** is a set of institutions and laws through which the dynamics of public politics in a society or group is organized and formalized. It is the fundamental political organization of the group in question—whether that group is large or small, independent or subordinate to another. Since the world is not joined together in a single political entity, regimes large and small have been created to organize public politics in different places.

The term "regime" may seem a bit alien at first. It brings to mind images of regalia, royalty, and regiments. All of these words are related to regime because they all share a common root that means "to rule." No doubt you are familiar with terms such as "political system," "state," or "governmental structures." These terms often are used interchangeably with regime, but they do not really mean the same thing. For example, consider the term "political system." The essential meaning of this term is the same as that of regime—the set of rules and structures that govern a political community—but "political system"

political science A field of knowledge in which those things termed "political" (defined very broadly) are studied in a systematic fashion.

regime A set of institutions and laws through which the dynamics of public politics in a society or group are organized and formalized.

has been used to mean both much more and much less than that. On one hand, the term has been applied to all political activity in a community—that is too much. On the other hand, political system has been used to mean only the formal constitutional arrangements of a society—that is too little.

Political scientists use the term "regime" to refer to the formal and informal rules and structures by which a political community is governed (or *ruled*). They do so in order to distinguish the regime from something broader (politics) and something narrower (those who currently hold office, which party has a majority, and so on). The term "regime" makes no judgments about the desirability of those structures or the distribution of power; it is a term that captures a particular concept in the understanding of politics. For the sake of convenience, this text may occasionally use the term "political system," but only in reference to its original meaning—the same as regime.

A regime may encompass an entire country or only a county. We refer to countries or nation-states in our discussions of world affairs, but a country is not the same as a regime. France is a country composed of a particular geography, people, and culture, but it has had several regimes over the course of its history. For centuries, it was a feudal monarchy. Then, in 1789, the French Revolution overthrew the king, and a series of regimes followed, each lasting only briefly until Napoleon I seized control. He created first a dictatorship and then an empire. His defeat led to the temporary restoration of the old monarchy; France then experienced a series of different monarchies, republics, the empire of Napoleon III, and then republics again. Since World War II, France has had two different constitutions, each establishing a different regime. The current regime, known as the Fifth Republic, organizes and formalizes public politics in France in ways quite distinct from what preceded it. But at each turn in the

Residents of Paris live among evidence of France's many changes of regime in the past two centuries. Here, the triumphal arch that is a monument to the Napoleonic empire of the nineteenth century contrasts with the commercial life of the democratic Fifth Republic.

story, the country called France remained essentially the same, while the regime changed.

In contrast, the reunification of Germany presents a different story. Germany, too, has had a history of different regimes over the centuries: feudalism, an empire, a republic after World War I, the Nazi dictatorship, and the post–World War partition. The division of the country (land, people, culture) in 1945 created two regimes: a democratic one in the west, a communist dictatorship in the east. When the country was rejoined in 1990, the eastern regime ceased to exist, while the western regime remained the same (its fundamental law and political structures were not altered). So, Germans in the eastern *laender* (provinces) experienced a change of regime, while those in the west experienced only an alteration of their country's size and population.

Within those regimes that encompass countries are smaller regimes: governing regions (provinces, states, departments in France), cities, rural areas (counties, townships), and any other kind of group (for example, school districts). Each of these smaller regimes organizes public politics in its own jurisdiction, whether as a general government (such as an American state) or for a specific public purpose (such as a local school board).

One thing that makes the United States somewhat distinctive among the major industrialized nations of the world is that it has had so few national regimes in its history. Before they achieved independence, the American colonies were part of the British imperial regime, with royal governors and local legislatures ultimately subject to Parliament and the king in London. Upon declaring independence, the Americans established a regime under the Articles of Confederation (1777). The confederation lasted only about a decade, its weak association of the states ultimately giving way to the regime created by the U.S. Constitution in 1789. For the rest of American history, that constitutional regime has remained in force.

Regimes do more than order the rules of the political game and create the basic structures of government. They also embody underlying values and choices of the society being governed. The creation of the U.S. Constitution was shaped by fundamental ideas about what government is for (for example, the protection of liberty), how it should operate (through representative democracy), and even about how the new regime should be adopted (by conventions in the states).

What Is the Government?

Within a regime there is the government. Political scientists use the term **government** to mean the people who hold formal positions of responsibility within the regime and wield political power on behalf of the state. In other words, the government consists of the people who run the regime. In most political systems, governments come and go over time while the regime remains relatively constant. For example, following the election of 1992, the United States got a new government—president, executive officers, members of Congress, and so on.

government The people who hold formal positions of responsibility within a regime and wield political power on behalf of the state.

America experiences regular changes of government; each election brings new officeholders to power. What endures is the regime—the Constitution and institutions—that officials serve.

In a parliamentary system, where the executive is drawn from the majority party in the legislature, the government is always unified by party ties. One distinct characteristic of the American regime is that the separation of powers system, with the presidency and Congress elected independently, raises the possibility of a *divided government*—each branch can be controlled by different parties. Divided government has been a common (but not continuous) feature of our politics since the end of World War II. For example, the 1994 elections brought Republican majorities to Congress, while Democrat Bill Clinton held the White House.

This distinction between regime and government is relevant because it separates the fundamental structures of the political system from those who run it and the policies they pursue. In most political systems, and certainly in the United States, there is generally broad acceptance of the regime but disagreement over the personnel and policies of the government. Usually, political campaigns and issues are about the government: which candidate or party should run things, what should be the official policy on taxes or foreign affairs, and related matters. The nature of the regime is frequently not discussed at all. Indeed, while the structure of the regime may influence government policy in powerful ways, as in the American regime's requirement of compromise between the White House and Capitol Hill to make laws, it is often taken for granted in the give-and-take of daily politics.

The Sources of American Ideas about Politics

What is the nature of the American regime? The answer to that question is not immediately apparent. Americans often use terms like "democracy" or "republic" to describe their political system, although they may not know what these terms really mean. To fully understand how our own system came to be the way it is, it helps to have a sense of the variety of regimes that have been created.

Aristotle's Scheme: The One, the Few, and the Many

Many writers have attempted to identify the various kinds of regimes in the world, but one classification that remains compelling is also one of the earliest works of analytical political science. In his examination of the regimes of his day, the philosopher Aristotle (384–322 B.C.) developed a scheme that distinguishes different systems by two basic issues: (1) who governs—one, the few, or the many in society; and (2) whether those who govern do so in consideration of the public interest or for some personal interest.[4] With this approach, he was able to classify regimes into six types (see Figure 1.1).

Rule by One. Rule by one, if for the public interest, Aristotle termed *monarchy*. Throughout history, government by a member of a royal family or some other single ruler has been common, although these monarchs have not always wielded power in the public interest. Nevertheless, for a good part of history this form of regime was regarded as a legitimate (and indeed a superior) one, usually because of a prevailing philosophy that saw the monarch or

FIGURE 1.1 Aristotle's Classification of Regimes

FOR WHOSE BENEFIT?	WHO GOVERNS?		
	The Many	*A Few*	*One*
Public Interest	**POLITY** Athens under Pericles; United States, Canada, & other Western democracies	**ARISTOCRACY** Roman Republic, Venetian Republic	**MONARCHY** Carolingian Empire under Charlemagne; Saudia Arabia and Nepal today
Selfish Interest	**DEMOCRACY** Athens under the assembly that condemned Socrates; France during the Revolution	**OLIGARCHY** South Africa before 1994; People's Republic of China	**TYRANNY** Russia under Ivan the Terrible; Iraq under Saddam Hussein

other sovereign (emperor, shah) as deputized by God to rule on earth. In Western civilization, this idea, known as the "Divine Right of Kings," underlay the monarchy in France, England, and elsewhere. Even the sovereigns of Poland, who were elected for life, were held by law and custom to be responsible only "to God and to history."[5] Few monarchies of this sort survive today, although the rulers of Nepal, Bhutan, and Saudi Arabia still claim nearly absolute power to rule in the public interest (as they see it).

Aristotle distinguished monarchy from a system in which the single ruler is motivated by personal interest. He called this *tyranny*—wherein the ruler treats citizens as a master treats slaves.[6] There are probably more examples of this form in history because of corrupt rulers, who have been called dictators. In recent history, many countries have existed under such regimes: the Soviet Union under Stalin, Iraq under Saddam Hussein, the Philippines under Ferdinand Marcos, and Cuba under Castro.

Rule by the Few. For Aristotle, a regime in which political power resides in the hands of a few who pursue the public interest was an *aristocracy*. The term literally means "government by the best citizens." Historically, there have been a number of attempts at aristocracy, from the ancient Roman Republic to the Venetian Republic of the Renaissance. In each of these, the government consisted of those selected from a particular class of citizens given special privileges and rank. More common are regimes in which power is held by a few who exercise it for their own interest. Aristotle called a system of this type an *oligarchy*. Under oligarchy, government policy is employed to protect the power of the few rulers, while most citizens suffer. China (under the rule of the communist elite) has an oligarchic regime. So did South Africa under white minority government before 1994.

Rule by the Many. Aristotle's *polity* was a regime in which the body of citizens exercised power in the public interest. In a polity, the mass of citizens respect justice and the rule of law. A large middle class of citizens lend stability and a sense of moderation to the community. A polity may actually be a kind of "mixed" regime; that is, it may contain elements of other systems, in order to achieve a balance and stability in the government that will advance the public interest. For example, Aristotle discusses the Spartan regime, which combined popular elections (rule by many) with certain kinds of power being vested in a few.[7] Today's industrial democracies are polities or "mixed" regimes in Aristotle's sense of the term.

Aristotle did see danger in one type of mass rule. If the lower classes in society (in his day, the majority) wielded state power in their own interest and at the expense of the middle and upper classes, he called this *democracy*. As we will see shortly, in its modern use this term is more synonymous with the philosopher's idea of a polity. What Aristotle was discussing was something probably closer to mob rule, in which the mass of people abandon respect for law and justice in order to expropriate the wealth of others.

Of course, Aristotle's scheme is somewhat problematic, for it requires that we be able to discern whether a regime is established for the public interest or the self-interest of rulers. Indeed, it is not always easy to identify the public interest. James Madison has provided what is probably the most succinct definition, describing the public interest as "the permanent and aggregate interests of the community."[8] But his summary does not always give clear guidance in analyzing a regime. As Madison himself pointed out during the deliberations of the Constitutional Convention in 1787, it is nearly impossible to separate self-interest from politics. Nevertheless, Aristotle's scheme provides a useful method for examining regimes and illuminating important ideas about American politics and the creation of the American regime.

Evolving Ideas about Democracy

Aristotle's negative use of the term "democracy" is at first surprising, but it points to a problem that concerned political philosophers for centuries and played a role in the writing of the U.S. Constitution. That problem is how to construct a regime that will serve the public interest while at the same time dealing with the reality of self-interest. Aristotle's teacher, Plato, had wrestled with the problem of the public interest and proposed that it could be promoted only if kings became philosophers and philosophers became kings. Following in this tradition and Aristotle's own teachings, political thinkers sought a solution in the "good ruler," that is, a monarch or body of aristocrats who could, by the study of philosophy and statecraft, educate themselves to be wise and virtuous governors. Aristotle himself served as the tutor of the young Alexander the Great and attempted such a task.

Democracy was often disparaged as inevitable mob rule because the masses were believed incapable of governing wisely. These views are reflected, for example, in the works of Shakespeare, who wrote during a time in which the absolutist royal regime of the Tudors was considered superior to the supposed anarchy of popular government. His virtuous kings, such as Henry V, are contrasted with tyrants, such as Richard III and Lear. What Shakespeare does not consider a realistic alternative is democratic government in which the uneducated "groundlings"[9] of his audience would have dominant power.

Over time, however, the notion of political power being held in the larger body of citizens began to gain greater acceptance. In England, in particular, the idea of a legislature with democratic elements became significant. From medieval times, Parliament had served as an institution for bringing together the aristocracy (in the House of Lords) and the "commons." But for most of English history, the "commons" represented in the House of Commons was the landed gentry and middle class, not the poorer masses of people. A certain amount of democracy was acceptable, but not too much. Likewise, in Holland, a system of more popular government, based in the middle class and gentry, gained ascendancy in the seventeenth and eighteenth centuries.

American Views of Democracy

In the American colonies, where no aristocracy existed and the king was far away across the ocean, ideas of democracy were more readily accepted. But even in this environment, notions of popular government were still largely restricted to those productive (landed and/or taxpaying) citizens who contributed to society and had the greatest stake in social stability. Nevertheless, the Americans came to value democracy as an alternative to royal rule and a check on the power of tyrants, an attitude that became more intensely held during the events leading to revolution and the war for independence. This shift was bolstered among the educated classes of the colonists by the influence of Enlightenment thinking, which stressed the importance of liberty.

The Enlightenment of the eighteenth century gave prominence to the thought of writers such as John Locke (1632–1704), an English philosopher whose two *Treatises on Government* laid out a theory of politics that profoundly influenced the leaders of the American Revolution and early Republic.[10] Locke based his ideas on the concept of *natural law,* which he argued gave individuals inherent rights to life, liberty, and property. People in the "state of nature" (that is, society without government) were unable to enjoy these values because people's rights were only as extensive as their own power to defend themselves. Therefore, Locke maintained that government was necessary to protect human rights. People entered into civil society (society with government) through consent to a *social contract* (whether formal or informal) that set limits on the state but also obligated citizens to obey it. If government exceeded its limits and denied citizens their natural rights, they could reform the regime. Locke's writings were taken as justification for the political reforms of England's Glorious Revolution (1688), in which Parliament deposed the Catholic and autocratic King James II in favor of a more limited monarchy under the Protestant King William and Queen Mary. The Americans used these ideas in the Declaration of Independence as justification for their separation from London, because they believed that the British government had become tyrannical in its treatment of the colonies.

By the time of the American Revolution (if not sooner), the term "democracy" had lost much of its negative connotation. Of course, most leaders of the Americans still held serious doubts about "rabble rule," for their reading of philosophy and history made them suspicious of too much democracy. Moreover, as men of the Enlightenment, they placed primary value on *liberty*. Liberty had to be protected against danger from above (the monarchy) and below (the masses). Rulers could become tyrants and the masses could endanger the rights of property and speech as well as other liberties. The masses were seen as especially vulnerable to their self-interest and to passion, which as Madison was to write "never fails to wrest the scepter from reason" (*The Federalist,* No. 55).

At the same time, the American leaders saw popular government as a bulwark against tyrants. Representative assemblies, in particular, served to check the power of executives. Parliament had done so at several times in English history, and colonial legislatures had battled royal governors in the events that led to the American Revolution. Thus the Americans faced a paradox: They valued popular government but feared its dangers. Many of Aristotle's disciples over the centuries had looked for an answer in the good ruler, but American leaders had been the subjects of royal government too long to accept that solution.

James Madison believed that he had arrived at a better answer to the problem of self-interest versus the public interest. He explained it in two essays published in 1788, part of a larger group of newspaper editorials written to explain and defend the U.S. Constitution. In an effort to convince the citizens of New York to adopt the proposed Constitution, Madison had joined with Alexander Hamilton and John Jay to present a case for the new regime. Writing under the collective pseudonym "Publius," the three published in New York newspapers a set of 85 essays known as *The Federalist*. In *The Federalist,* No. 10 and No. 51, considered the most significant of these works, Madison (as Publius) articulated his solution to the age-old problem. (The text of these papers is included in Appendix C.)

The answer was to be found in the very structure of the regime. If the political system could be designed in such a way as to mitigate the influence of self-interest—indeed, to put it at the service of the public interest—then that regime offered the best chance of achieving good government in a world where everyone was vulnerable to the attraction of personal interest. Liberty, order, justice, and the public interest could be promoted if the regime joined a particular kind of democracy with certain features of republicanism.

democracy According to Aristotle, rule by the lower classes; in modern times, the doctrine of rule by the mass of people in a society.

direct democracy Any system of government or device for direct majority control over public policy decisions, such as the initiative and referendum.

referendum An election in which voters are asked to make substantive governmental decisions directly, such as deciding on tax levies, policy questions, or proposed constitutional amendments.

Modern Ideas about Democracy and Republicanism

Over time, the term "democracy" has acquired a meaning that is more positive than just "rabble rule." **Democracy** has come to mean a system of government in which political power is derived from popular election. Indeed, it has gained such positive meaning that even nondemocratic and antidemocratic political systems have expropriated the term for their own purposes. That is why such countries as the German Democratic Republic, the Democratic Republic of Czechoslovakia, and the Democratic Republic of Roumania all used the term while their regimes were oligarchies under the control of the Communist Party. When each of these countries adopted a more truly democratic regime, it dropped the word "Democratic" from its title.

Direct Democracy

Democratic regimes are not all alike. There are two major forms of democracy: direct and representative (Figure 1.2). **Direct democracy** is a system in which citizens make their own governmental and policy decisions. Proponents of this method often call it "pure democracy." Citizens may exercise direct rule by meeting together in some sort of citizen assembly, such as the town meetings in some small New England towns. In these meetings, all the citizens determine the laws, taxes, and the town budget by majority vote.

Another form of direct democracy is the **referendum,** in which a specific question is put to voters in an election and majority rule decides the outcome.

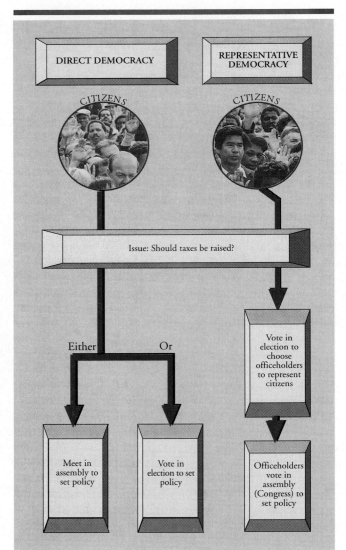

FIGURE 1.2
Direct versus Representative Democracy.
Under direct democracy, citizens decide directly on all matters of public policy by meeting to discuss and decide them or by voting on them. Under representative democracy, citizens elect other citizens to represent them on a regular basis, discussing and deciding or voting on policy issues.

initiative A device for direct democracy through which a petition with a sufficient number of signatures of registered voters may place a policy question on a ballot to be decided by popular vote in a referendum.

The question might involve raising taxes, instituting a new law, issuing public obligation bonds, or amending a constitution. The referendum is widely used in American state and local governments as a means of making governmental decisions. It is also used in a number of foreign democracies as a way to settle controversial political issues, even if the voters' choice is legally only advisory to government officials. In 1992, Canada held a referendum on whether to change its constitution to give special status to the province of Quebec and certain aboriginal groups.

Still another form of direct democracy is the **initiative,** in which citizens may by petition put questions on a ballot to be settled by referendum. California is one American state that provides for this device and in each election voters are called upon to decide questions regarding English-only rules for state records, insurance-law reforms, and any other proposal for which supporters can gain enough petition signatures. In 1994, this device was used to place Proposition 187—a plan to deny all nonemergency state services to illegal immigrants—on the ballot. The controversial proposal was approved by voters but is being challenged on its constitutionality.

Representative Democracy

Representative democracy is a system in which voters choose those who will occupy positions of governmental power, who in turn rule on behalf of citizens. This system, also known as *indirect democracy,* may take different forms.

One of the most common means of employing representative democracy is through a *parliamentary system.* In such a system, voters elect representatives to a legislative body called a *parliament* (structured differently in various regimes). Representatives belong to political parties or may be independent, but whichever party or coalition of parties can form a majority in the parliament makes up the government. The executive officers, usually a prime minister and ministers of state, are the leaders of the majority. Collectively, they are known as the cabinet or the government.

Laws and policy decisions are made by the parliament at the initiative of the government, with the legislature usually operating under strict party discipline (party members are expected to vote according to the party's position on an issue). As long as the government can win the support of a majority in the parliament, or until an election is required by the constitution (usually four or five years), it can continue to govern. If the government loses the confidence of the majority of the parliament, new elections must be held. Parliamentary systems can be found in Great Britain, Israel, Germany, Japan, and several other industrial democracies.

Another type of representative democracy is a *presidential system.* In this system, a chief executive (the president) is elected separately from the legislature and wields power both in conjunction with it and independently as well. The president is typically given broad control over foreign relations, a veto over laws passed by the legislature, and the power to make legislative proposals. Rather than being accountable to the legislature, as is a prime minister and cabinet, the president is responsible to the general public. In France, a popularly elected president enjoys broad political power and can name a prime minister from the majority in the legislature. In the United States, the president and Congress are structurally and operationally separate, even if they are controlled by members of the same party. Many parliamentary regimes also feature an elected figurehead president who is a ceremonial officer and has no real political power. The presence of such a figure does not make a regime a presidential system. The central issue is who holds political power.

As this contrast indicates, the term "democracy" does not imply one particular set of political arrangements. All governmental power may be vested in the

representative democracy A system of government in which voters choose officeholders to govern on their behalf.

mass of citizens, who meet and decide issues, or it may be embodied in representatives. At a minimum, democracy requires popular rule, majority rule, and free and fair elections. It does not put limits on popular rule. Putting limits on rulers is what republicanism is all about.

Republicanism

Republicanism refers to a system of government in which power is *distributed* among various officers and institutions in order to prevent tyranny. A republic is often defined in dictionaries as a system of government without a monarch, but that description leaves out the most important points of the story. The term "republic" was originally conceived by the Romans to distinguish the system they created when they deposed their last king, Tarquinus Superbus. Instead of concentrating political power in the crown, the Romans decided to distribute power among various state officers (consuls, tribunes, aediles, censors) and institutions (the aristocratic Senate, the Popular Assembly). Since that time, the term "republic" has been frequently adopted by regimes that do not have a king, emperor, or other royal figure at their head, regardless of how power is distributed within the state. Hence the confusion about the meaning of a republic.

A deliberative assembly is one key feature of republicanism, because this body will provide for due consideration of proposed laws and policies. Likewise, the rule of law prevails, to prevent government by the caprice of rulers. Historically, many republics—the Roman and Venetian ones in particular—have been aristocratic in nature. Although a certain share of political power was given to the mass of citizens, a class of aristocrats was ensured special privileges and influence over state policy. The Roman Senate, for example, was made up of heads of major families and others of the patrician class that held dominant economic power in the society.

In The Federalist, *James Madison explained how self-interest and the public good can be balanced. Two of his essays (See Appendix C) are considered among the greatest American contributions to political philosophy.*

The framers of the United States Constitution wanted to create a republic, but not an aristocratic one. Indeed, they chose to combine a number of republican features with those of representative democracy. (Publius and others from the founding period often use the term "republic" to mean representative democracy, but the two concepts are quite distinct.) They limited and distributed power through a written constitution, separation of governmental powers, constitutional rights and liberties (protected against majorities), the rule of law, an unelected judiciary (to enforce laws and the Constitution), and federalism (to allow each state considerable autonomy). But they filled the central offices of the government—the presidency and Congress—through election. In this way, they hoped to achieve a mixed regime that could deal with the problem of self-interest illuminated by Aristotle.

Madison's Solution: The American Democratic Republic

What, then, was Madison's answer to the problem of self-interest and the public interest? It was to create a large, complex, compound, democratic republic. No simpler solution was possible.

Madison began his analysis with a review of the goals of government, which were to promote the public interest, protect liberty, establish justice, and maintain order. But the reality of self-interest meant that he could not assume that political actors would necessarily serve these ends. Those in government might very well serve their own interests, and citizens could do so as well.

The Problem of Factions. Madison was most concerned about groups in society he called **factions:** "a number of citizens, amounting to a majority or minority of the whole, who are united and actuated by some common impulse of passion, or of interest, adverse to the rights of other citizens or to the permanent and aggregate interests of the community" (*The Federalist,* No. 10). In other words, factions are groups of people (whether formally organized or not) who cooperate to promote their interests at the expense of others or of the public interest. Madison did not suggest that every group in society was a faction, only those willing to damage others' rights or the public interest. Therefore, his notion of factions is different from our idea of interest groups, because not all interest groups necessarily act as factions. But the problem of factions is what makes democracy potentially dangerous, for if such a group constituted a majority of citizens, it might use majority rule as a means to get its way.

Madison argued that the best way to deal with this problem was to decrease the likelihood that majority factions would occur. This could be accomplished by enlarging the community to make it more diverse and thus more likely to be composed of many minority factions: "Extend the sphere and you take in a greater variety of parties and interests; you make it less probable that a majority of the whole will have a common motive to invade the rights of other citizens" (*The Federalist,* No. 10). These groups could be kept in check by majority rule.

Separation of Powers. Madison advocated dividing governmental power in several ways, an idea that had been promoted by John Locke and the French philosopher Baron de Montesquieu. Separating the executive, legislative, and judicial functions of the state among different branches would further complicate the task of factions seeking to influence government and restrain those officials who might use public power to serve their self-interest. The American contribution to the notion of separation of powers was to insist that the three branches of government check and balance one another, because "Ambition must be made to counteract ambition" (*The Federalist,* No. 51). The different divisions of the government would not operate in isolation, but under the watchful eye of one another and of the people. In addition, by creating a regime based on *federalism*—having both a strong national government and strong state governments—political power would be further divided. In the end, Madison believed that this complex, compound republic offered the best opportunity to solve the age-old problem, because the policies that would emerge from such a system would be more likely to serve the public interest.

What Madison supported, and what the American framers adopted, was a regime that could best be described as a democratic republic or a constitutional

factions According to Madison, groups in society "who are united and actuated by some common impulse of passion, or of interest, adverse to the permanent and aggregate interests of the community" (*The Federalist,* No. 10).

polity. It attempts to create the sort of mixed regime that Aristotle discussed, but it does so through a written constitution that combines elements of popular rule and restraints on the power of majorities.

Uncovering Ideas at the Root of the American Regime

The creation of this regime did not merely lay down the rules and structures for our political system. It also had an even more subtle effect on American politics, one that influenced the way we look at our political affairs. As the historian Daniel Boorstin has explained, the movement from colonial status to independence to the constitutional regime in a short span of years imparted to the people of the United States an attitude of "givenness" about their regime and political values that is not reflected in most other countries. "Givenness" provides an important link in understanding the operations of the American political system and illuminates how ideas play a central role in shaping our politics.

Givenness refers to "the belief that values in America are in some way or other automatically defined: *given* by certain facts of geography or history peculiar to us."[11] In other words, Americans take certain political values for granted. This concept helps to explain how ideas play a poorly understood role in our politics and why we often do not stop to consider the fundamental choices and values that underlie our political processes.

Givenness is the product of three aspects of the regime's founding and of American history: (1) the idea that our values are a gift from the past, in essence "preexisting" at the time of the founding of the Republic; (2) the idea that our values are also a product of our everyday experience, in essence a gift of the landscape; and (3) the continuity of American history, which merges together past and present and reinforces our sense of "preexisting" values continually validated by our national experience.

Values Given by the Past

Americans tend to see their political values as formed *in toto* at the time of our Republic's founding. Few nations have had an experience similar to our own, in which the birth of the country and its regime can be pinpointed to a relatively brief moment in history. Our own understanding of American history is that the founders sought independence from Great Britain because they wanted—as the Declaration of Independence put it—"life, liberty, and the pursuit of happiness." They then set about creating a regime that promotes and protects those values. Thus, the purposes for which we came into being and the ideas that informed our political system were consistent, identifiable, and well articulated by the people who participated in its creation.

The circumstances of our Republic's creation mean that we see our political values as preformed at the time of the founding. This distinguishes us from most other societies, in which the origins of the country are lost in the prehistoric past, and national history is a record of several different regimes with different political values over the centuries.[12] This experience is certainly typical of European nations, Japan, and most industrial democracies. Even the nations of

givenness The belief that values in America are in some way automatically defined— "given" by the special nature of national history and geography— articulated by historian Daniel Boorstin.

Part 1/Constitutional Foundations

Africa and Latin America have had experiences with a variety of regimes and value systems. The United States, in contrast, was created at a specific moment in time and its central values enshrined in the Declaration of Independence, the Constitution, and related documents of the time.

The fact that our national history is based on a clearly definable moment does not mean that there is unanimity on the question of how best to implement our values in practice. The Preamble to the U.S. Constitution states that the document's purpose is to "provide for the common defense, promote the general welfare, and secure the blessings of liberty," but it does not offer a blueprint for exactly how those goals will be reached. There is almost universal agreement that these values are the right ones for our nation and that the constitutional regime is the correct means to promote them.

Values Given by the Landscape

While Americans can point to their founding documents and the noble sentiments expressed in them, they also see the political values of their country as arising as much from everyday experience as from theories and institutions. We accept the idea that the very landscape of the United States supports a set of political values based on liberty, individualism, equality, and democracy.[13] In other words, the values of American political culture seem to us as much nat-

As this Albert Bierstadt painting of Yosemite National Park reminds us, wide open spaces are part of the American vision. Liberty seems a natural condition in a country where there is always more room in which to expand.

ural phenomena as they are political phenomena. In our land of plentiful space, abundant resources, and a social structure that holds "self-made" individuals as typical heroes, the values embodied in the Declaration of Independence and the Constitution seem to be natural outgrowths in what we call the "land of the free."[14]

This sense that our landscape promotes the same values as our founding documents makes it all the more likely that Americans will see their political ideas as given. When we read the ringing phrases of these documents, we do not react to them as if they represent some alien idea of society. Rather, the cause for which the founders fought seems consistent with our own understanding of what is important in politics.

The Continuity of American History

American history further affirms our sense of givenness. Consider the situation of Europe, where there is not only a long and diverse history but also physical evidence of the different civilizations that have waxed and waned over the centuries. Yet in the United States, we have a history that predominantly consists of our civilization and the various contributors to it (for example, the different cultures that blended to make American society).

The course of our national experience has served for most Americans to confirm our values rather than call them into question. One good example is the Civil War—certainly the most divisive conflict in our history. In that dispute, both sides claimed allegiance to the principles of the Constitution and accused the other side of distorting them. Likewise, in the civil rights struggles of the 1960s, Martin Luther King invoked the Declaration of Independence and the Constitution as the basis for providing equal rights to all Americans. He argued that civil rights were a fulfillment of the promise of the United States, not a challenge to the political order.

The consequence of this sense of givenness is that as Americans we tend to underestimate the importance of ideas in our politics. We tend to overlook the ideas that affect the way in which we pragmatically go about the business of resolving political issues. Yet values and choices shaped the American regime and our political culture. Americans have embodied their political principles in processes and institutions that, in turn, underlie our everyday politics. Yet because we take these values and processes as given, we often overlook how changes in our political system, perhaps an issue such as term limits, raise questions that are not merely mechanical in nature but involve the very principles on which the regime is based. This book and this course are designed to highlight the ideas underlying American government and our political processes.

In addition, givenness helps to explain why the United States has a more constitutionally oriented politics than any other country. Beginning with the next two chapters, we shall see how many of our political controversies are fought in constitutional terms. We regard the Constitution as the presumed starting point for political questions, and we see it as the embodiment of the values given by the past and confirmed by the present.

As citizens observe the American political system at work, it is not always easy to see how the ideals debated by James Madison, George Washington, and others of the founding generation continue to shape national politics. Certainly, nearly all Americans agree that the principles of "life, liberty, and the pursuit of happiness" are important, but just how do they play a role in the latest battle over the federal budget deficit or U.S. involvement in Bosnia?

The answer is that ideas and values provide the foundation on which politics is built. The daily give-and-take that is recorded by the newspaper or evening news—on the progress of the health care or handgun control bills, for example—takes a particular form based on the institutions and laws involved. Where did these structures come from? They were created by the Constitution. Congress is not a natural phenomenon, nor are political parties, though they may seem so to Americans. These institutions were created because people had ideas about what government is for and how it should work. If we want to make sense of the day's news, it helps to know something about the principles that provide the roots for budget battles between the White House and Capitol Hill.

The Plan of This Book: From Principles to Process to Politics

How Can We Make Sense of American Politics?

In order to understand American politics, we can take either of two approaches: work *down* to the roots or *up* from them. The first method works down to the roots of an issue from the events of the moment. Take the example of the politics of health care reform in the Clinton years. All Americans are aware of a high-profile effort by President Clinton, First Lady Hillary Rodham Clinton, and hundreds of other officials to construct a major health care reform program. These efforts were accompanied by much public debate on the issues on news programs, radio talk shows, or the street. Then Congress got into the act, with several alternatives to the president's plan offered by both Democrats and Republicans; congressional committees passed no less than four different schemes for health care reform. By the end of 1994, Congress had not acted on any of these proposals.

Why such a complex system for making policy? Why don't we just round up the best experts on health care, have them create a plan, and have the president put it into effect? The answer to these questions lies in the principles embodied in the Constitution, ideas that placed justice, deliberation, and other values ahead of efficiency. As we shall see in later chapters, the American political system was designed to be inefficient, in order to protect principles such as liberty.

As mentioned, it is possible to observe the daily unfolding of politics and work backward to discern the roots of contemporary events. That approach has its merits; it helps us to understand why the issue of abortion has been addressed in the courts as well as in legislatures, or why the president and Congress engage in an annual battle over the federal budget. Nevertheless, this uprooting of a current issue to find the principles at its base does not tell us all we might need to know if we want to be informed and active citizens. Each week, the news brings a long list of stories that have deep roots. If we learn something about the roots first, then we can better understand the issues that have grown up and why they take the shape that they do.

Three Steps to Understanding American Politics

This book offers a "roots-first" approach to understanding American politics. It shows that American politics is more than what occurs each day in Washington and around the nation. It shows citizens how to make sense of national politics by looking, first, at the values and choices underlying our political arrangements, then proceeding to examine the rules and structures that grow out of these ideas, and then describing how the dynamic interactions of American politics are influenced by these ideas and structures.

This book presents a survey of American politics that is unlike others you might encounter in a basic text. It covers all the standard topics, from the Constitution to interest groups and parties to the institutions of government, but it does so in a manner that is unique. Each chapter contains a three-step analysis of the subject at hand, showing how *principles* influence *processes* that shape *politics*.

Principles, Process, Politics. As we have seen, politics involves questions that frequently—indeed, usually—have their basis in ideas. To obtain a good understanding of American politics, we must begin with these ideas. Thus, the first stage in our three-step analysis is to examine the *principles* that underlie the subject at hand. For example, the discussion of the presidency begins not with the powers of the chief executive, but with the fundamental values that are embodied in the office (the desire for an independent executive, a unitary executive, a competent executive, and a republican executive). These values help us to see why the presidency was constructed with a particular set of powers and responsibilities.

Our discussion then turns to *process,* the formal and informal rules and structures of the subject at hand. In the case of the presidency, the discussion focuses on some implicit rules of behavior by which American presidents have operated over time, the roles that the president plays in our political system, and the structures that have grown up around the chief executive to enable presidents to do their job.

Finally, we turn to *politics,* the dynamic struggle for power and claims to authority in society. With regard to the presidency, we see that the president attempts to govern in a system marked by separated powers, separate levels of government, and separated parties; that presidents exercise power through a mix of command, persuasion, and public appeals for support; and that the malleability of presidential power means that different interpretations of executive power and differing circumstances affect what presidents are able to accomplish. Citizens who have seen this progression from ideas through structures to dynamics will have a sense of why in 1994 Bill Clinton had so much trouble trying to win passage of his health care reform plans and yet had his way on issues such as democracy in Haiti and keeping Iraq's forces out of Kuwait. They will also understand why the elections of November 1994 made such a difference to politics in Washington, because they reordered the relationship between the White House and Congress, between Democrats and Republicans, and between Bill Clinton and his own party.

Step-by-Step with Health Care. The example of the presidency provides only a brief look at how the approach of this book can illuminate the workings of American politics. The three-step approach is not just useful for understanding a political institution; it also helps to explain the headlines from the morning paper. We can see this by examining the fate of health care reform in 1994.

Health care reform was the centerpiece of President Clinton's domestic policy initiatives. It involved a large task force to construct a plan, several speeches by the president, a coordinated lobbying effort by the administration, the congressional policy-making process, intense interest-group activity, considerable media attention, and a combination of public confusion and interest. How can our three-step analysis help us to make sense of this episode in national policy making?

Principles are relevant in several ways. First, it is important to understand that the Constitution is chiefly concerned with the process rather than the substance of policy making; moreover, the American political system favors the status quo and incremental change. Add to these constitutional values a political culture that emphasizes compromise and consensus. The result is that the American regime favors a slow pace of policy change and values stability over action.

Process: These ideas have produced a complex and messy policy-making process. First, an issue must become part of the policy agenda. Bill Clinton was able to make health care reform a high priority on the congressional agenda, but that fact does not guarantee action. Next, the process requires that policy choices be made. As we shall see, Congress has a highly structured machinery for considering legislative proposals, involving several committees in the House and Senate (remember, the Constitution focuses on procedure, not substance of policy making). The Clinton health care reform plan eventually became the responsibility of four congressional committees, two in each chamber. Each committee issued its own version of the plan, after lengthy public hearings and ample opportunity for all interested parties to make themselves heard. The White House was one voice in this process—certainly a very important one—but not the only voice. As part of the congressional process, the impact of health care reform on the federal budget had to be considered.

Politics: The politics of health care reform in 1994 can be traced directly to the preceding two steps. Not surprisingly, in a regime that favors stability over change, major innovations in policy are rare. Moreover, the federal budget has become a major factor affecting policy making: With large budget deficits as a common occurrence over the past 15 years, programs involving significant increases in federal spending are difficult to enact into law. Health care is an issue over which Congress has more direct power than the president; therefore, any significant change in national policy had to be approved by the legislature. Congressional opponents of change in this area—most Republicans and some Democrats—were able to erect obstacles to any action on health care proposals before the congressional elections of 1994. Legislative decision making in Congress is open to media and public scrutiny, thus enabling a wide array of interest groups to lobby for their positions. Groups favoring inaction were likely to have greater success than those favoring change.

The fate of the Clinton proposal cannot be explained solely by blaming someone's shortcomings as a politician (the president, Hillary Rodham Clinton, Senate Majority Leader George Mitchell, and various presidential aides were all blamed at one point or another), nor by blaming unfair opposition (such as the Republicans or Rush Limbaugh), nor by focusing just on the amount of money spent to defeat reform plans (by interest groups). Any and all of these factors were significant, but to explain health care politics without reference to the principles and process underlying domestic policy making creates a distorted view of what happened in 1994.

Even without knowing anything about who was for or against the president's plan, a citizen who understands American politics would have known that a major domestic policy change would have been extremely difficult to pass in 1994. Certainly, the outcome of the health care debate was not determined at the beginning: Politics is full of surprises. It was not inevitable that Congress would do nothing about health care in 1994, but certainly it was unlikely that any major actions would occur. Our three-step analysis provides a means for cutting through the confusion of everyday political events to grasp the ideas and processes at work. In doing so, our principles-process-politics approach helps us to understand how the events of the day fit into larger patterns in national affairs.

What Should a Citizen Know?

The point of this method is to show how the daily events of politics are shaped and influenced by fundamental choices Americans have made about their government. But why should you care? Because politics affects your life—in the taxes you pay, the way business is run, the products you buy, and whether or not there is a war—and as a citizen of the United States you have a role in directing the government.

The American political system does not require that everyone be an Aristotle or a James Madison, but it does assume that each citizen will possess the kind of basic knowledge that this book provides. The framers of the U.S. Constitution presumed that self-government was possible because citizens could understand the structures of the regime and the principles on which it is based. Two facts make this point: (1) the Constitution places citizens at the heart of the political system as those who choose officials; and (2) it establishes a complex network of political institutions competing for power in three branches of government. Such an arrangement makes sense only if the source of political power and legitimacy—the people—are willing and able to play their role in the system.

Citizens can be effective when they understand how their political system works and how they can influence it.

To play your role as a citizen, whether it is in voting or some other action, you need to understand more than just what happened in Washington or your state capital this week. Indeed, you need to know the ideas and structures that create a system in which battles between Congress and the White House are a normal part of life. It is difficult to make an intelligent decision about whether to join a political party or what party to join if you do not know what parties are and why American politics has only two major ones. Likewise, it is nearly impossible to make sense of the elaborate mechanics of the judicial system in a case such as that of O.J. Simpson without some basic understanding of how ideas about justice and due process of law led to the evolution of rules of criminal law that are at work in that particular case. For that reason, this book will not just give you names, dates, and details; it will show you connections between the facts that will help you to make sense of them.

Open Questions about American Politics and Government

Our political system works best if citizens understand it and take part in it, but informed citizens are not just experts in political trivia. Many issues are never completely settled; rather, even basic issues such as the nature of representation are continually reexamined. That is why each chapter concludes with a section on "Open Questions," to illuminate controversies that still surround each subject explored in the text.

In every election, citizens are called upon to make decisions on important questions. Most of the time, it is through our vote for one candidate over another that we participate in governmental decision making; that candidate then takes office and proceeds to make decisions on our behalf. On other occasions, we make decisions directly, casting votes on tax levies, bond issues, state constitutional amendments, and other ballot questions. Between elections, we can express our opinions to policy makers through a variety of means. The point of examining open questions in American politics is to consider what kinds of choices lie before us as a nation, to examine the kinds of issues that politics involves, and to engage in the most basic form of political participation found in a democracy—discussing politics. Each chapter's "Open Questions" section allows you—as student and as citizen—to apply the tools that the chapter has given you through the principles-process-politics analysis.

Summary ▍

Politics is more than just disputes over who will hold office or what the policies of the government will be. To understand American politics requires knowledge of the principles that shaped our political system.

Politics, Political Science, and Government. Politics is the struggle over power and claims to authority in society. Two key concepts are needed to understand politics: (1) power—the ability to "exert one's will with more or less predictable results" and (2) authority—the legitimate holding or use of power. Political science is a field of knowledge in which all things considered "political" are studied systematically. This book is concerned with public politics (political struggles over public affairs).

Throughout history, people have formed political entities that set rules by both informal and formal means. A regime is a set of institutions and laws through which public politics in a society is organized and formalized. A regime may be as big as a country or as small as a village. Within a regime is the government, the people who hold formal positions of responsibility and wield political power.

Regimes and Governments. One way to classify regimes was designed by the philosopher Aristotle, who asked two questions: (1) Who governs? and (2) Is governing done in the public interest or the interest of those in power? Using these questions, Aristotle defined six types of regimes. *Rule by One:* Monarchy is rule by one in the public interest; tyranny occurs when the single ruler treats citizens the way a master treats slaves. *Rule by the Few:* Aristocracy is government by the few best citizens in the public interest; oligarchy occurs when a few govern to protect their own interests. *Rule by the Many:* A polity exists when the mass of citizens rules in support of the public interest; democracy (as the term was used by Aristotle) refers to the equivalent of "mob rule." Over time, the term "democracy" lost this negative meaning.

Modern Ideas of Democracy and Republicanism. Democracy is a political system in which political power is derived from popular elections. Direct democracy is a system in which citizens make their own governmental and policy decisions. In representative democracy, citizens choose representatives to govern for them. The two main forms of representative democracy are the parliamentary system (in which a majority in the legislature sets policy, as in Great Britain) and the presidential system (in which there are separate executive and legislative institutions that divide and share political power, as in the United States).

Republicanism refers to a system of government in which power is distributed among officers and institutions. Key features of a republic include a deliberative assembly and the rule of law. The founders of the United States wanted to create a democratic republic, combining representative democracy with republican features (a written Constitution, checks and balances, an independent judiciary, and so on).

James Madison's solution to the problem of the public interest and self-interest was to create a big, diverse republic in which there would be many minority factions (groups opposed to the public interest). The public interest would be promoted by majority rule through a complex set of institutions, so no one group could seize all power.

Uncovering Ideas at the Root of the American Regime. A good way to understand how ideas shape American politics is through Daniel Boorstin's notion of "givenness," which refers to a sense among Americans that their political values are "given" (that is, taken for granted). Americans adhere to a set of "values given by the past," the ideas of the Declaration of Independence and the Constitution. We see those values confirmed by our current circumstances and the landscape in which we live, and our history helps to enhance our commitment to the values given by the past. The concept of "givenness" helps us to understand why for Americans the Constitution is often at the center of political controversies.

The Plan of This Book. It is much easier to understand American politics if you understand the values and ideas on which the political system was founded. Therefore, each chapter of this book begins with a discussion of principles, then examines how those ideas and values are embodied in a process (rules and structures), which in turn shapes the way in which politics (the struggle over claims to power and authority) is conducted. Seeing politics this way will enable citizens to take a more active role in their political system. The book will also look at various open questions that are still controversial.

ARNHARDT, LARRY. *Political Questions: Political Philosophy from Plato to Rawls.* New York: Macmillan, 1987. Good introduction to political ideas and thinkers, with attention to how those ideas relate to American politics.

BARONE, MICHAEL. *Our Country: The Shaping of America from Roosevelt to Reagan.* New York: Free Press, 1990. Readable survey of American national politics 1930–88. A good way to catch up on major figures, trends, and events.

BOORSTIN, DANIEL. *The Genius of American Politics.* Chicago: University of Chicago Press, 1953. Articulates "givenness" in American political culture.

DAHL, ROBERT A. *A Preface to Democratic Theory.* Chicago: University of Chicago Press, 1956. Challenges Madison's analysis of the Constitution.

KIRK, RUSSELL. *The Roots of American Order.* Malibu, Calif.: Pepperdine University Press, 1977. Places the American political system within the context of the evolution of Western civilization.

LIPSON, LESLIE. *The Great Issues of Politics: An Introduction to Political Science,* 9th ed. Englewood Cliffs, N.J.: Prentice Hall, 1993. Well-organized and comprehensive introduction to political science.

RAVITCH, DIANE, ED. *The Democracy Reader.* New York: HarperCollins, 1992. Explores democracy through original writings and speeches.

Suggested Readings

America's Constitutional Design

M uch of the reason for Americans' sense of "givenness" about the underlying values and institutions of the regime is the role of the Constitution in our political system. To a greater extent than is found elsewhere, ours is a constitutional polity. Our news does not just concern the latest election campaign, debates over economic policy, or whether to employ our military abroad. Just as often the stories of the day are about a battle between the White House and Congress over a trade bill, new judgments from the Supreme Court, arguments over displays of religious symbols in public places, a state legislature banning doctor-assisted suicide, or whether the president has the authority to dispatch troops to fight in a foreign conflict. As commentator A. M. Rosenthal once put it, "There is no other country so involved in talking about fundamental law, its limits and flexibility."[1] This interplay has its roots in the relationships set down in the Constitution.

In order to make sense of American politics, one needs an understanding of the U.S. Constitution. The document is not just an interesting historical artifact; it is the fundamental charter that shapes our politics on a daily basis. This chapter is the first half of a two-part sequence on the Constitution in the American regime. It explores the background and origins of the charter, the convention that drafted it, and the principles and structures it embodies; Chapter 3 examines how the Constitution has actually been used as a basis for government in the United States.

The Constitution is one of the most successful creations that has ever been produced by a committee. Over the course of the hot summer of 1787 in Philadelphia, 55 delegates from 12 states gathered to consider the problem of building an effective regime for the young United States. These men—and they were only men because women lacked the vote and the right to hold office—had been charged by their respective states with the task of examining the current regime and how it might be improved. Their work, conducted in secret and through a deliberative process of debate and vote, ultimately resulted in the document that became the foundation for a new American regime.

Prelude: American Independence and Early Self-Government

The Road to Independence

The framing of this new constitution might be seen as the culmination of a long series of events that had begun in the American colonial era. The 13 British colonies in North America, peopled primarily by immigrants and the descendants of immigrants from Great Britain, had been particularly fortunate for the subjects of an imperial government. For a good part of their history, these settlements enjoyed a broad degree of self-government, a situation made possible because Parliament in London was more concerned with profitable enterprises elsewhere (such as in the West Indies or India) than with the American colonies. Colonists had grown accustomed to a political order in which they elected representatives to the lower houses of their colonial legislatures, enjoyed public order and rights enforced according to the mandates of English common law, saw great economic opportunities for the industrious, and paid little in the way of taxes.[2]

Following the end of the French and Indian Wars in 1763, however, the situation began to change. The British government had spent considerable amounts of its money and troops to defend the colonies and now wanted to recover some of its expenses. To do so, it altered the relationship between London and the Americans. New taxes were levied; a large body of troops was assigned permanently to America; and greater imperial control over the colonies was asserted. The famous events of American history that occurred in this period—from the Stamp Act Congress (1765) to the Boston Tea Party (1773) to the convening of the First (1774) and Second (1775) Continental Congresses—eventually came to a head with the outbreak of a war for American independence in 1775. The following year the Americans declared their separation from the mother country and defended it in an elegant Declaration of Independence from Great Britain.

The Declaration of Independence

The American **Declaration of Independence** (see Appendix A) was a political document that stated the former colonists' case in philosophical and legal terms. In its introductory passages, it invoked such principles as the God-given right to "life, liberty, and the pursuit of happiness." Then it listed grievances against King George III (that is, the British government) for such offenses against English law as imposing taxes without consent of the colonies, manipulating judges, and failing to respect elected legislatures. It represented the conviction among American leaders that they were now a people distinct from those of the country of their heritage. They wanted self-government and the sorts of liberties they had in the past, but which they now believed they could obtain only if free from London's control.[3]

The Declaration may have stated the Americans' case for independence, but they had to win their separation on the field of battle. After a difficult struggle, they were able to do so in 1781 when Lord Cornwallis—the British commander in America—surrendered to George Washington near Yorktown, Virginia. The following year England signed the Treaty of Paris recognizing American independence.

The Articles of Confederation

With independence came the need for a new political order, however. Each of the former colonies was now a state (in title and in the sense of a regime), with no formal association between them. Therefore, in 1777 the Second Continental Congress drafted a constitution for limited union among the American states. This document, the **Articles of Confederation,** created a weak association in which each state maintained its nearly absolute sovereignty, and the Continental

Declaration of Independence 1776 document in which the Continental Congress proclaimed and defended the decision of the American colonies to declare their independence from Britain.

Articles of Confederation America's first constitution, adopted in 1777. It created a weak association of states, each retaining absolute sovereignty. Its Continental Congress had little real power.

Congress lacked the power to levy taxes or regulate commerce. Each state had one vote in the Congress. In spite of these limits on the power of the central government, states such as Maryland and Rhode Island feared that even the weak association created by the Articles could threaten their sovereignty. In consequence, the Articles did not take effect until all states finally accepted them in 1781.

For six years the Articles provided a regime, but it was an impotent one at best. The Continental Congress was the only permanent institution of government. There was no judiciary, and the only executives were officers appointed by the Congress. Important actions required the vote of nine of the thirteen states, while amendments to the Articles were possible only with unanimous agreement. The weaknesses of the Confederation led to a crisis that alarmed a growing number of leaders in the new country. As historian Catherine Drinker Bowen summarized the state of things in the 1780s:

> The war debt still hung heavy; states found their credit failing and small hope of betterment. Seven states had resorted to paper money. True, the postwar depression was lifting. But prosperity remained a local matter; money printed in Pennsylvania must be kept within Pennsylvania's own borders. States and sections showed themselves jealous, preferring to fight each other over boundaries as yet unsettled and to pass tariff laws against each other. New Jersey had her own customs service; New York was a foreign nation and must be kept from encroachment. States were marvelously ingenious at devising mutual retaliations; nine of them retained their own navies. . . . The shipping arrangements of Connecticut, Delaware and New Jersey were at the mercy of Pennsylvania, New York and Massachusetts.[4]

Shays's Rebellion

Finally, fear of a breakdown in public order began to spread across the states.[5] In Massachusetts in 1785, Governor John Hancock made himself popular with creditors by arranging generous funding of state war debts, then made himself equally popular with taxpayers by failing to collect the taxes levied to pay for his debt funding. When his successor attempted to collect those taxes in order to right the state's finances, a taxpayers' revolt broke out. Captain Daniel Shays, a Revolutionary War veteran, organized about three thousand men into militia companies to fight the tax. The ultimate goal of **Shays's Rebellion** (1786) was unclear—it was crushed by a volunteer army raised in and around Boston—but it sent shock waves through the 13 states. General Henry Knox, the Confederation's secretary of war, erroneously informed George Washington that Shays had assembled between twelve and fifteen thousand men and was planning to assault Boston and eventually redistribute all property in the state. Although inaccurate, his report served as the basis for newspaper and other accounts of the incident. It induced leaders in several states to support calls for a meeting to discuss revisions to the Articles of Confederation.

Shays's Rebellion
1786 anti-tax uprising in Massachusetts that sent shock waves around the young United States, contributing to fears of impending anarchy if the *Articles of Confederation* were not revised. Helped build support for the Constitutional Convention of 1787.

While in reality not much of a threat to law and order, Shays's Rebellion frightened many leading citizens into believing that the Articles of Confederation no longer constituted an effective political system.

Creating a New Regime: The U.S. Constitution

The first attempt to revise the Articles of Confederation was a failure. A convention called by the Virginia General Assembly was to meet in Annapolis, Maryland, in September 1786. Only five states sent representatives. These delegates adopted a resolution calling for a meeting the following spring in Philadelphia. By that time, all states except Rhode Island agreed with the need for a convention and sent delegates.

The Constitutional Convention

The Federal Convention (or Constitutional Convention) convened in May 1787. Soon after they began their deliberations, the delegates concluded that they would not labor over revising the Articles of Confederation. They proceeded to debate the nature of government and the problem of constructing a new regime. Their deliberations were influenced by the intense reflection on political questions that occupied many leading Americans of the time. While they certainly did not all arrive at the same conclusions, politicians and other prominent citizens of the new nation had been stimulated by the events surrounding independence to think seriously about what kind of political order they wanted and how it could be achieved.

These individuals studied philosophy and contemplated the histories of ancient Rome and Greece, as well as that of Britain. They also reflected upon the struggles and constitution making they had undertaken in creating 13 newly independent states. Many of these men had also learned common law from William Blackstone and the "science of politics" from the works of David Hume,

TABLE 2.1 Major Events of the Constitutional Convention, Philadelphia, 1787

May	
14	Official opening—only Pennsylvania and Virginia in attendance.
25	A quorum is reached; George Washington elected to preside.
29	The Virginia Plan is introduced by Edmund Randolph (but James Madison is regarded as its chief author). It calls for a national government with a two-chamber legislature, an executive, and a judiciary. It forms the basis for most of the debate over the rest of the summer.
31	The Convention decides "that the national legislature ought to consist of two branches."
June	
1	James Wilson of Pennsylvania proposes a single executive; his suggestion is met with "a considerable pause."
7	The Convention decides that the upper legislative house (Senate) will be appointed by state legislatures.
15	The New Jersey Plan is introduced by William Paterson as a challenge to Virginia's proposals. It seeks to amend the Articles of Confederation, protect state sovereignty, and provide a plural executive.
19	The New Jersey Plan is rejected, but the Convention remains deadlocked over the issue of representation in Congress.
July	
16	The Great Compromise breaks the deadlock; states will have equal representation in the Senate and be represented in the House according to population.
26	The Convention appoints a Committee of Detail to bring its decisions into a workable arrangement, then adjourns while the committee labors.
August	
6	The committee presents its report; the rest of the month is consumed with debate on a variety of issues.
September	
8	The Convention appoints a Committee of Style to draft a Constitution.
12	George Mason of Virginia proposes that a bill of rights be included in the Constitution. His idea is rejected.
15	The Convention adopts the draft Constitution, as amended.
17	The Constitution is signed by those delegates remaining in Philadelphia, although Mason and Randolph of Virginia and Elbridge Gerry of Massachusetts refuse to sign. The Convention adjourns.

Locke, and Montesquieu. Some exhibited the Enlightenment's confidence in the power of reason to sort out political issues, while others relied on more traditional and biblical understandings of humanity to warn of human frailty.[6]

From May through September 1787, they took up issues as abstract as what motivates individuals and as practical as the appropriate size of a legislative body. They drew upon the experience of history as they understood it; upon moral, economic, and political philosophy; upon the interests of their own states and of the emerging United States; and upon a determination to produce a workable political system. They became the framers of the Constitution of the United States (Table 2.1).

The Virginia Plan: The Case for a National Government

One of the key questions that divided the delegates was who Congress would represent: the people or the states? The Articles provided for equal representation

The Constitutional Convention recognized that it had to create a new regime if America was to be governed effectively.

of states, as did the procedures of the Convention, and it was clear that several states would never accept a new regime that did otherwise. On the other hand, some delegates, including James Madison and James Wilson, wanted the more populous states to have a larger voice in legislative decisions.

On May 29 Edmund Randolph introduced to the Convention the **Virginia Plan,** a set of proposals—written largely by Madison—that called for a new national government. It proposed a two-chamber national legislature in which seats would be distributed according to population. It provided as well for an executive and a judiciary. The plan became the basis for most of the debate during the remainder of the Convention.

Of course, such a proposal sparked considerable controversy, as delegates divided over the issue of representation in Congress. This controversy is often simplified into a large state/small state division, because proportionate representation favored large states such as Virginia and New York, while equality of the states favored small states such as Delaware and Rhode Island. But that characterization is misleading, since some large-state delegates such as George Mason favored equality of the states, while some small-state delegates endorsed proportionality. The issue was not just one of conflict between competing state interests. Rather, it involved competing visions of the very nature of the new regime.

Virginia Plan Scheme presented at the Constitutional Convention of 1787 that called for replacement of the Articles of Confederation by a national government with three branches.

34   PART 1/CONSTITUTIONAL FOUNDATIONS

The States and the Central Government

Those favoring the Virginia Plan wanted a truly *national* regime, in the sense that they wanted a unified political system. Those who favored the existing equality of state power wanted the new regime to be essentially *confederate* in nature, even if the central government institutions had greater power than under the Articles. Several proposals were discussed to deal with the question of representation.[7] Charles Pinckney of South Carolina suggested that the country be divided into four equal regions for the purpose of selecting senators. Some delegates even went so far as to suggest that state boundaries be redrawn to roughly equalize populations (an idea that even Benjamin Franklin tended to favor); however, George Read of Delaware declared that he would rather abolish the states entirely than see large states overwhelm the small.

The issue for the framers was where "supreme power" would be located in the new regime. They were conversant with *unitary political systems,* in which supreme power resides in the central government, and all other governmental units are creations of that center. Such was the British system then, and so it remains today in Great Britain, France, China, and a host of other countries. The delegates also knew about *confederations,* not only the one in which they lived but others in Switzerland and various historical examples. These are regimes in which the component units retain supreme power and the association that binds them is created by and answers to them. Summing up the view of many thinkers of the time, at the end of May Gouverneur Morris told his colleagues that he could not imagine a government "in which there could exist two supremes."[8]

To counter the Virginia Plan, on June 15 the **New Jersey Plan** (drafted by William Paterson) was introduced. It proposed a Congress in which all states enjoyed equal representation. It protected state sovereignty, provided for a plural executive (a committee of executives), and generally did little more than amend the Articles of Confederation. While the Convention rejected the New Jersey Plan only four days later, the delegates still could not agree on representation in Congress.

The Great Compromise

The issue stymied the Convention for weeks. Finally, at the initiative of Roger Sherman of Connecticut, on July 16 an agreement was reached to settle the dispute. Congress would consist of two houses, one representing the people directly and the other giving each state an equal vote. The lower chamber, the House of Representatives, thus draws its membership from districts that are roughly equal in population, guaranteeing at least one representative to each state but apportioning all seats according to population. The upper chamber, the Senate, gives each state two votes regardless of population. (Until the Seventeenth Amendment was ratified in 1913, senators were chosen by state legislatures.) This **Great Compromise** not only broke the impasse but created a **bicameral** (two-chamber) **legislature** that would incorporate the two versions of representation.

New Jersey Plan Proposal at the Constitutional Convention that called for revisions to the Articles of Confederation rather than a national government.

Great Compromise Agreement on representation in Congress that broke the deadlock at Constitutional Convention. Called for a legislature in which representation in one house is based on population (House of Representatives), and the other is based on representation of the states (Senate).

bicameral legislature A legislative body that is divided into two chambers, as in the U.S. Congress and many state legislatures.

Establishing a National Executive

Another issue that divided the framers was that of the form and powers of the executive in the new regime. The delegates labored considerably over who should choose the president, because they understood that officials would be most loyal to those who placed them in office. Some delegates wanted Congress to choose the executive, but this was rejected out of concern for making the president a counterweight to the legislature. Others suggested a presidency beholden to the states. In June, James Wilson proposed a president elected directly by the people—a suggestion that was greeted with a shocked silence. Few members of the Convention were prepared for a popularly elected leader, because they feared such an officer could become a demagogue (that is, a rabble-rouser).

Most delegates wanted an executive who could be a counterweight to the power of the legislature. At the same time, they did not want the executive to become a dictator. So they compromised and created a president who would be powerful but restrained. After lengthy deliberation, in July they decided that the president would be chosen by a group of special officials—electors—chosen solely for that purpose. Then over the course of several weeks, the framers invested the presidency with a veto over legislation passed by Congress, a fixed term of office (four years), and an indefinite opportunity for reelection (no term limits). These measures stood as a compromise between the kinglike "Gouvernor" that Alexander Hamilton suggested early in the Convention and the weak executive committee proposed in the New Jersey Plan.

The Issue of Slavery

No question divided the Convention as starkly as that of ownership and trading in human beings. Several of the delegates, including Washington, Mason, and Madison, were slave owners. Others, including Alexander Hamilton, not only did not own slaves but opposed the very idea. Some slaveholders had mixed feelings about the "peculiar institution" but like Washington only freed their slaves in their wills. But for delegates from places like South Carolina, the right to own slaves was an economic imperative and an article of faith. Any attempt to outlaw slavery in the Constitution would have wrecked the Convention. Because of these disagreements, the Constitution treats slavery in a peculiar way. Unlike nearly anything else, it is singled out in the document for special provisions, for example, how to count slaves for the purposes of apportioning representation in Congress. For this purpose, slaves (who are mentioned only as "all other Persons" in Article I) are counted as three-fifths of their total number.

The **Three-Fifths Clause** has often been misunderstood in American history. Some critics have used it as evidence that the framers did not consider blacks to be people of equal worth with whites, but the origins of the clause belie that conclusion. (Certainly that was the view of many delegates, but it was not an assumption built into the Constitution.) The Three-Fifths Clause was created as a compromise between southern slave owners, who wanted all of their servants counted in distributing seats in the House of Representatives, and

Three-Fifths Clause A provision of the U.S. Constitution that embodies a compromise over slavery. Under it, only three-fifths the number of slaves in any state were counted toward the state's population for purposes of determining the apportionment of seats in Congress.

others who saw that proposal as having the effect of rewarding slaveholding in the legislature. Counting a fraction of slaves gave the slave owners some of what they wanted but denied them full "credit" for owning humans.

Another example of the special case of slavery is the **Slave Trade Clause.** Article I, Section 9 bars Congress from limiting or abolishing the importation of slaves before the year 1808, thus allowing that enterprise to continue for almost two decades. But it did pave the way for the national government to halt one of the most gruesome aspects of slavery, since the mortality rate on slave transport vessels was often as high as 50 percent. Again, the demands of the slave owners were accommodated to win acceptance of the new regime.

Of course, these provisions did not settle anything. Slavery would eventually become one of the dominant issues confronting the constitutional system. The spirit of compromise could carry the document only so far.

Slave Trade Clause
Constitutional provision that authorizes Congress to outlaw the importation of slaves only after 1808.

The U.S. Constitution

The ultimate product of the Convention's deliberations was the U.S. Constitution. By early September 1787, most issues had been resolved, and the delegates had sketched the major provisions of the new national charter. As a draft of the new Constitution was being prepared, George Mason of Virginia rose on September 12 to propose that a bill of rights be included in the document. Mason made an impassioned case for a statement of rights, but the Convention disagreed with him. As we shall see, the Convention's decision not to include a bill of rights became an issue in the debate over adopting the Constitution.

The final product provides a concise outline for the new regime (Table 2.2). It opens with a brief Preamble, or statement of purpose, then proceeds through seven articles that describe the organization and powers of Congress, the structure and powers of the president, the judiciary, divisions of power between the national government and the states, a process for amending the document, a provision making the Constitution the nation's supreme law, and the procedure for ratifying the new charter.

The document is brief, but that is the nature of a constitution (see Appendix B for the complete text of the Constitution). Its purpose is to set down a fundamental law and create institutions for governing a country. The framers of the Constitution understood that politics is ultimately an activity carried on by human beings. The national charter would establish rules and structures; people would have to do the actual governing.

Writing the Constitution was only part of the process of creating a new regime. The document then had to be adopted as the fundamental law in place of the Articles of Confederation. Accordingly, in September 1787 it was sent to the states for consideration.

Before long, an enormous nationwide debate was underway. The new Constitution provided that elected conventions in each state were to debate and vote on the document, with agreement by nine of the thirteen sufficient to ratify the charter. Therefore, the new regime was created by an act that was simultaneously

The Debate Over Ratification

TABLE 2.2 Outline of the U.S. Constitution

Article I: Legislative Power
Section 1: Legislative power vested in a Congress made up of a Senate and a House of Representatives.
Section 2: The House of Representatives—qualifications, election, term of office, apportionment of seats, the Speaker as presiding officer, power to impeach.
Section 3: The Senate—qualifications, election, terms, vice-president to preside, the president pro tempore, the method of hearing impeachment trials.
Section 4: Elections and meetings of Congress.
Section 5: Each house given control over its internal affairs.
Section 6: Pay and privileges of members; members prohibited from holding executive offices.
Section 7: The process for making laws.
Section 8: The powers of Congress, including power to "make all Laws which shall be necessary and proper" for performing the enumerated powers of Congress.
Section 9: Restrictions on the power of Congress, including ban on titles of nobility, *ex post facto* laws, and spending of money without an act of Congress.
Section 10: Restrictions on powers of states.

Article II: Executive Power
Section 1: Executive power vested in a president of the United States. Qualifications, election, term, and oath. Establishment of office of vice-president.
Section 2: Powers and responsibilities of the president.
Section 3: Further responsibilities.
Section 4: All civil officers of the United States subject to impeachment.

Article III: Judicial Power
Section 1: Judicial power vested in a Supreme Court and inferior courts to be established by Congress.
Section 2: Jurisdiction of federal courts and of the Supreme Court.
Section 3: Rules governing treason.

Article IV: The National Government and the States
Section 1: State records; Congress given power to set standards for state records.
Section 2: Citizens of each state entitled to privileges and immunities of citizens in the several states.
Section 3: Admission of new states; Congress given power over territories.
Section 4: Each state guaranteed a republican form of government.

Article V: The Amendment Process
Article VI: The Constitution as Supreme Law of the Land
Article VII: Ratification Process

Federalists Name adopted by those who favored ratification of the U.S. Constitution. Later adopted as the name of the political party formed under the leadership of Alexander Hamilton.

Antifederalists The name given to those who opposed ratification of the U.S. Constitution.

democratic and illegal. It was democratic because delegates to the conventions were elected representatives of the people of each state; it was illegal because the process sidestepped the methods already established for altering the Articles of Confederation—a unanimous vote of all states in the Continental Congress. The fight was to be long and at times bitter.

Contenders in the debate came to be grouped in two opposing camps. Proponents of the new charter called themselves **Federalists,** adopting as their label a term that at the time implied support of states' rights. Opponents of the proposed regime, a more disparate group, thus came to be known as **Antifederalists.**[9]

In state after state, Federalists pressed the case for the document, while their adversaries attacked it. The Federalist case rested on three key arguments: (1) that the Articles of Confederation were ineffective as a basis of government because they provided for no executive or judiciary; (2) that the Articles threatened chaos in newly independent America, as was seen in episodes such as Shays's Rebellion; and (3) that without a stronger central government to defend Americans, there was a good chance that the young United States might be subject to attack from Great Britain (which was still unhappy about American independence) or some other foreign power.

The Antifederalists made many charges against the new Constitution, and there was certainly much disagreement among them, but the main points of their position can be summarized as follows:

1. The Convention violated its charge, which was to propose amendments to the Articles, so its actions in writing and proposing the new Constitution were illegal, and all thirteen states would have to accept the new charter, not just nine.
2. They criticized the Federalists for being too willing to upset the fragile political stability of the United States at a time when that stability needed nurturing.
3. They attacked the Federalists for abandoning the ideals of the Revolution, especially individual rights.
4. They criticized the Constitution for not preserving the equality of the states.
5. Many Antifederalist thinkers also contended that small republics were superior to large ones, so they objected to the Constitution for undermining the civic virtue of their states in the name of union.

The Federalists realized that not just any nine states would do to ratify the Constitution. Large and powerful states like New York and Virginia were crucial to the success of the new regime. Therefore, prominent Federalist thinkers gave particular attention to New York, with Alexander Hamilton assembling the team of himself, Madison, and John Jay to write 85 essays laying out the case for the new Constitution. These essays, known collectively as *The Federalist,* appeared in New York newspapers from October 1787 through March 1788. Moreover, the arguments of those essays were distributed widely and used by supporters of the Constitution in several state ratifying conventions (see Appendix C for the texts of the two most important of these papers, No. 10 and No. 51).

Ultimately, the Federalists were successful in their cause, although they did make one major concession to their opponents. Antifederalist leaders had made a strong case that the Constitution did not go far enough to protect individual and state rights. In Massachusetts, for example, the ratifying convention endorsed the new charter, but only after Federalist leaders promised to press for a bill of rights to be added to the document. The vote in Virginia was also close, as it was in New York. By the time New Hampshire became the ninth state to ratify the Constitution—on June 21, 1788—an understanding had been reached that the new government would draft a bill of rights to be added as amendments to the new charter.

The debate over ratification ended, but it marked only the beginning of the long story of the Constitution. Before too long, a sense of givenness about the document would take hold in American politics. There might be serious dis-

CITIZENS IN ACTION

WOMEN FOR AND AGAINST THE CONSTITUTION

In the founding period, most women could not vote. But that did not stop many women from participating in the debate over ratifying the U.S. Constitution. Abigail Adams corresponded with her husband John, with Thomas Jefferson, and with other leading men of the period. While she favored the new Constitution, she was emphatic that women's rights should be protected by government. Mercy Otis Warren, a contemporary of Adams, wrote a widely read Antifederalist pamphlet, *Columbian Patriot.* Published anonymously in 1787, Warren's essay attacked the proposed Constitution for violating republican principles (by giving too much power to the executive and the national government) and for its lack of a bill of rights. Her arguments were used by Antifederalists in the New York convention to press for adding a bill of rights to the new charter.

agreement about its application in practice, but it would come to enjoy widespread support. Part of the reason for that change was the process by which the new regime was adopted. Although the Convention had acted in secret and certainly beyond the scope of its charge, the method of ratification was public, deliberative, and representative. Moreover, the arguments of Federalists and Antifederalists were usually disagreements "within the family" between two groups who shared many common political values.[10] As the course of American constitutional history would demonstrate, there would always be division over the meaning and application of the Constitution, but broad underlying support for it as the proper basis for government.

The Constitution soon became the law of the land in spirit as well as in fact. It became the measure of political legitimacy, such that the term "unconstitutional" would become a powerful charge to level against many governmental actions. What did this document contain that gave it such a central role in American politics? The answer can be found by examining the *principles* that are woven into the charter, the *processes* it establishes for the American regime, and the style of *politics* it encourages in our country.

Constitutional Principles: A Set of Values to Build on

The Constitution undertakes an artful balancing act: to create a regime that has sufficient power to achieve its ends but cannot become tyrannical; to promote competing objectives of liberty and order; and to advance certain political values as democracy while accommodating the realities of American society at the time of the founding. Of course, it is left to us as citizens to consider how that balance is to be pursued in practice. Let us now examine the principles underlying the nation's fundamental law.

The Goals of Government

The Preamble serves as a sort of statement of purpose for the Constitution, yet it does not provide a complete picture of the goals and values that infuse the document. Rather, several major political principles are woven into the Constitution, some quite openly and others beneath the surface. First, the document reflects a set of *goals for government*. The Preamble provides a lengthy list, but these can be summarized as four grand objectives: to establish justice, protect liberty, maintain order, and promote the public interest.

By *justice* the document means the traditional notion, taken from Aristotle, Judeo-Christian culture, and English common law, of giving to each person what is his or her due. James Madison stated the framers' view that "Justice is the end of government. It is the end of civil society."[11]

Liberty was identified in the Declaration of Independence as one of humanity's natural rights, and the Constitution proposes to defend that right. The framers understood liberty to mean a large measure of personal freedom in political, economic, religious, and social behavior. The Preamble states that to "secure the Blessings of Liberty to ourselves and our Posterity" is one of the chief goals of the new regime.

liberty The concept of personal freedom in politics, economics, religion, and social behavior. The Declaration of Independence refers to it as one of humanity's natural rights, and the Preamble of the Constitution declares the protection of liberty as one of the charter's goals.

Order—political and social stability—is the goal that conditions the others. The Constitution proposes to "insure domestic Tranquility" and "provide for the common defense." The framers feared social instability that could descend into anarchy and violence, which in turn could undermine justice and liberty. As a result of the crisis caused by the Articles and events like Shays's Rebellion (even if it was misunderstood), the Constitution aims at establishing a stable public order.

The *public interest* was that fundamental objective that had concerned political thinkers at least since Aristotle. To a great extent, the Constitution's overall purpose is to provide a means for promoting that interest. But the framers also saw a tension inherent in these goals: pursuit of one might not advance another. The very liberty that the framers desired threatened the public interest because it allowed factions—groups opposed to the public interest—to flourish. Therefore, the framers concluded that only a complex regime would allow society to promote and reconcile the competing goals of government.

The Principles of a Good Regime

Beyond these goals, however, the Constitution further embodies a set of values regarding the nature of a good regime. One of the most important of these is **popular sovereignty,** the idea that all political power is derived from the people and that a legitimate regime is one that establishes "government by the consent of the governed." Closely related to this sovereignty are the ideas of *limited government* and *popular self-government*. The Constitution embraces the values of restraint in the government and the assumption that individuals and communities ought to be able to govern themselves. Again, the document undertakes a balancing act: The national government is strong but not unlimited; it has broad reach but is designed for a society in which states and local communities had been (and would continue) taking care of their own affairs.

Another value implicit in the Constitution is its insistence on *responsible government,* in the sense that public officials and the regime itself are to be held accountable for their actions. Elections are one device for keeping officials in line, because they must face voters from time to time and be responsible for their actions in office. Another is impeachment, by which executive and judicial officers can be removed for "Treason, Bribery, or other high Crimes and Misdemeanors." Finally, the Constitution does not put the regime beyond the reach of responsibility. It anticipates that public officials, states, or even the national government may be parties to cases in court, thus suggesting (along with the rule of law) that government actions are challengeable by citizens.

Many of these ideas were ancient ones, such as the concern for justice and the public interest. Others, such as liberty, had their roots in older ideas but were given prominence only in the decades preceding American independence. Still other values that the framers wanted to incorporate in the Constitution were quite recent in origin; these were the principles about good government derived from seventeenth- and eighteenth-century studies of the "science of politics."

popular sovereignty
The idea that all political power is derived from the people and that a legitimate regime is one that establishes "government by the consent of the governed."

The "Science of Politics"

One of the most striking ways in which the Constitution embodies the political thought of the founding period is in its incorporation of ideas and choices from what the authors of *The Federalist* called "the science of politics." In *The Federalist,* No. 9, Alexander Hamilton notes that this science, "like most other sciences, has received great improvement. The efficacy of various principles is now well understood, which were either not known at all, or imperfectly known to the ancients." Two principles from the science of politics provide an example of how the Convention attempted to apply the lessons from that science.

A Government with Sufficient Power to Govern. One idea from the science of politics is giving government *competent*—that is, sufficient—powers to meet its responsibilities. In *The Federalist,* No. 31, Hamilton states as an "axiom" that "A government ought to contain in itself every power requisite to the full accomplishments of the objects committed to its care." The unspoken implication of his point is that the Articles of Confederation are flawed because they violate so fundamental a principle.

Separation of Powers and Checks and Balances. The more significant principle for shaping the Constitution was the doctrine of *separation of powers and checks and balances.* In *The Federalist,* No. 9, Hamilton identifies this principle as the best example of progress in the science of politics. A number of political thinkers of the time recommended a political system in which governmental power would be divided, although each writer had somewhat different prescriptions for exactly how to do so.

The U.S. Constitution created a political system with three distinct branches of government: legislative (Congress), executive (presidency, vice-presidency, and federal administrative agencies), and judiciary (the Supreme Court and lower courts). While these institutions of government were to be separate, they would share certain key powers—lawmaking, treaty making, the appointment of high officials, taxing and spending, determination of whether each was acting in a constitutional fashion—in order to *check and balance* one another. The framers of the Constitution did not want the three branches to work in isolation, but in relation to one another. As we see in Figure 2.1, the Constitution created a regime in which no one branch of government would have unrestrained power. Indeed, each branch is to some extent dependent on the others.

Ideas of Political Economy

Although the purpose of the Constitution was to create a new political order, it also embodied ideas of political economy that have been significant in the history of the United States. For example, there was broad agreement among the framers about the need to protect *property rights*. They were concerned about proposals from some of the more radical Americans who wanted to redistribute property (as was feared in Shays's Rebellion).

	SEPARATION OF POWERS	EXECUTIVE BRANCH Enforces laws	LEGISLATIVE BRANCH Makes Laws	JUDICIAL BRANCH Interprets Laws
CHECKS AND BALANCES	Over Executive		• Approves federal budget • Can override presidential veto by 2/3 vote • Can impeach president, other federal officials • Tries all impeachments • Approves senior federal appointments & treaties	• Reviews executive acts • Issues injunctions • Can declare executive actions unconstitutional
	Over Legislative	• Proposes laws • Can veto laws • Can call special sessions of Congress • Can appeal directly to the public		• Reviews legislative acts
	Over Judicial	• Grants pardon • Nominates judges	• Can propose constitutional amendment to counter Supreme Court ruling • Determines number, location, and jurisdiction of federal courts	

FIGURE 2.1 The Separation of Powers and Checks and Balances in the United States

Property meant more than just ownership. In English and American law it referred to a complex web of rules that governed many relationships between individuals, communities, and the state.[12] For example, rules of inheritance—important in a time when so many people were engaged in agriculture on farms that were handed down over generations—were key elements of the law of property. While the original text of the Constitution does not explicitly guarantee property rights (although such a guarantee was added in Amendment V), running through the text is the presumption that ownership and property will be maintained. Article III refers to cases "in Law and Equity," which means the document presumes maintenance of English common law as it was evolving in the states.

The original text of the Constitution contained several provisions that sought to protect the individual citizen's property rights, including a clause designed to prevent states from intervening in contracts between ordinary citizens and a provision that Congress regulate the declaration of bankruptcy by citizens and small business owners.

Does this concern for property rights mean that the framers were interested only in protecting the privileges of a few against the needs of the many? Some critics have charged that the delegates to the Constitutional Convention and others who supported the new regime did so in order to protect their personal wealth against redistribution to the masses.[13] The case for such a charge is weak, however, because it overlooks the realities of the founding period. For example, many of the leaders of the Convention—including George Washington himself—had as much to lose as to gain from the more powerful regime created by the document.[14] Moreover, there was considerable disagreement among supporters of the Constitution on many economic questions, thus undermining the notion of a unified group acting in concert. Nevertheless, because individuals such as Hamilton spoke openly about the need to protect society from the "levelling" spirit, the question of economic motives underlying the Constitution has not been completely settled.

The founding period was marked not only by turmoil and inquiry into politics and the science of government, but also by upheavals and innovation in economic ideas that are reflected in the Constitution. Several different economic philosophies competed for dominance in late eighteenth-century America, and old, even medieval, ideas of economics often shaped government policy.[15] Leaders in many of the American states adhered to such ideas as the notion that economic growth was not really possible. They believed that the amount of wealth in society was fixed for all time and that one person's prosperity could be achieved only at the expense of someone else's. In consequence, state legislatures prevented the emergence of commercial banking and would not charter business corporations, because many people believed that "paper wealth" was stolen from those who did "honest" work (such as farming).

Many people held to an ancient idea that every item had a "natural" value, so prices for many common items were fixed by law. For example, the price of bread was regulated in most American cities, while the rates charged by millers, ferrymen, keepers of inns and taverns, and operators of other "public utilities" were often fixed by law.[16] Furthermore, legislatures often interfered in buying, selling, and lending even after deals had been made. In Virginia and South Carolina, for example, planters who had made contracts to purchase goods from abroad were allowed by law to avoid paying their debts.[17] Unlike today, when one party to a contract can go to court to make the other party meet the obligations of the contract, many state governments held the view that public officials could change or void a legal contract if they did not approve of it.

Prior to the Constitution, governments often regulated what people could wear or eat or even their public behavior. These kinds of laws were known as *sumptuary legislation* and were usually adopted to prevent people from indulging in excessive luxury or to promote certain goods over others. For example, the Confederation Congress attempted to outlaw spending on luxury items (like jewelry) and immoral behavior (like attending the theatre). States routinely legislated to promote what the Massachusetts Bills of Rights described as "piety, justice, moderation, temperance, industry and frugality."[18]

The Constitution breaks with these ideas and endorses important elements of the emerging market-based economics preached by a variety of thinkers in the founding era, but expressed most effectively by Adam Smith in *The Wealth of Nations* (1776).[19] For example, the Constitution does not authorize Congress to enact sumptuary laws. The power to pass such legislation was proposed by Virginia's George Mason at the Constitutional Convention, but it was rejected. This omission in the powers of the new regime meant that government regulation of individual economic decisions would be more limited than in the past.

Perhaps more important was a concept that the Constitution actively promotes, the idea of free contract. Article I, Section 10 includes a **Contract Clause** that specifies that "No State shall . . . pass any . . . Law impairing the Obligation of Contracts." This clause sets American law firmly on the side of an economic system in which the price of goods and services would be determined primarily through the operations of the marketplace, rather than government direction. Contracts form the heart of a market economy, because buyers and sellers—rather than official lists—determine how much something costs.

The Principles of the Constitution: An Assessment

The principles of the Constitution are less—and more—than meet the eye. They are less in the sense that much of the universal language of the Preamble, such as "We the People . . . ," was not understood at the time of the founding to really mean everyone. Most delegates to the Convention did not interpret this

Contract Clause Article I, Section 10 of the U.S. Constitution, which specifies: "No State shall . . . pass any . . . Law impairing the Obligation of Contracts."

Take Part in the Constitutional System

When we see the U.S. Constitution enshrined under glass at the National Archives or gaze upon its image in a textbook, it may seem that the national charter is of historical interest but distant from our lives. Indeed, citizens may think that they are left out of the document, which concentrates on government institutions and officials. But the Constitution does affect how we live and one need not be an officer of the U.S. government to be a part of the constitutional system. You will be given specific names, addresses, and suggestions for ways you can make your ideas and concerns known in Washington in future chapters. Here are some basic things that every citizen can do to prepare to be active citizens.

1. Study the Constitution: To be an effective citizen, one need not be a constitutional expert. But those who understand the document and the political system it creates enjoy a decided advantage over those who do not. Even if one wants to make changes in American politics, the place to begin is at the beginning: at the fundamental law.

2. Study the rest of the political system: As important as it is for citizens to understand the Constitution, the political system has evolved in important ways since 1787. This book is designed to provide a good survey of American government in action, but the reader is also encouraged to read the various works suggested at the end of each chapter.

3. Be an active citizen: The Constitution's use of representative democracy and its checks and balances can seem intimidating, but citizens still have many opportunities to influence the direction of national affairs. Voting is important, but so are communicating with public officials, knowing and guarding one's rights, and staying informed on public issues. Politics can be a fascinating spectator sport, but the citizen's role is to do more than merely watch the show. The philosopher Albert Camus once observed that "not to choose is to choose." This observation has a moral for citizens: Those who are passive leave the direction of politics to those who are active.

phrase to include women or blacks, nor did they all regard their love of liberty as inconsistent with slavery. But that does not mean that they used these terms cynically. Americans of the twentieth century must remember that the eighteenth century was a different era with different standards. Its view of political equality was far more restrictive than that of today, but the Constitution established the most democratic regime ever known for its time.

Because the Constitution speaks in universal language—of persons, not particular ethnic or religious groups—it provided a means by which the protections and promises of the founding could with time come to apply to a larger and larger share of the population. For example, in the 1960s, Martin Luther King Jr. would frame the goals of the civil rights movement not as a challenge to American ideals but as a logical fulfillment of them. The creation of our contemporary social order, in which all men and women are protected by fundamental law, was achievable within the framework of the principles of the original text. In this sense, the principles are more than meet the eye.

None of this is to suggest that the Constitution created some sort of perfect system. The men who wrote it did not believe that such a feat would be possible, nor did they defend it as such. Rather, they argued that the document offered the best instrument for promoting the ideals they shared. As citizens of the regime they created, we are in a position to assess their work only if we understand those values and how the Constitution attempted to translate them into a process for governing.

The Constitution establishes a set of political institutions and processes that are designed to "preserve and protect" (to borrow one of the phrases in the text) the values embodied in the Preamble and elsewhere in the document. Moreover, the Convention had to do more than find ways to turn ideas into institutions; the delegates had to find ways to accommodate the political realities of late eighteenth-century America.

Making a Virtue of Necessity: Dynamic Processes Born of Compromise

Much of the success of the Convention can be explained by its ability to reconcile broad goals with many (although certainly not all) of the tough practical problems facing it. The framers were able, in effect, to make a virtue of the necessities imposed by the political circumstances of their time. Three key compromises reached during the deliberations achieved this reconciliation.

1. *Structures for Representative Democracy:* The Great Compromise provided for a bicameral legislature that embodied two different forms of representation. The Senate incorporates equal representation for each state, while the House embodies the idea of proportional representation. Article I provides that no bill can become law until it has been adopted in identical form by these two bodies. In effect, this means that the laws of the United States must be acceptable to a majority of the states (through the Senate) and to a majority of the population (through the House). This requirement increases the likelihood that the laws and policies that emerge from Congress will serve the larger public interest.

2. *Balancing National and State Interests:* In order to reconcile the need for national power and state self-government, the document establishes a federal system. **Federalism** means a system in which there is a strong and permanent central government uniting self-governing permanent units. The framers invented it in order to achieve a national government that could promote the goals of the regime, empowering the central authority to provide for defense and foreign policy, regulate interstate commerce, and take care of other national affairs. At the same time the Constitution protects those preexisting realities called the states, guaranteeing them equal representation in the Senate, territorial integrity, a "republican form of government," and broad power over elections. As we shall see later, the compromise was one that worked only with a considerable amount of tension, but it did establish a new way of distributing power between the center and component units of government (Figure 2.2).

3. *Selecting the President:* The framers disagreed over who should choose the president because they understood that the chief executive would be beholden to those who participated in presidential selection. Some delegates wanted the president to be chosen by state governments, others

federalism System of government in which there is a strong and permanent central authority (in the United States, the federal government) and strong and permanent subnational authorities (in the United States, states).

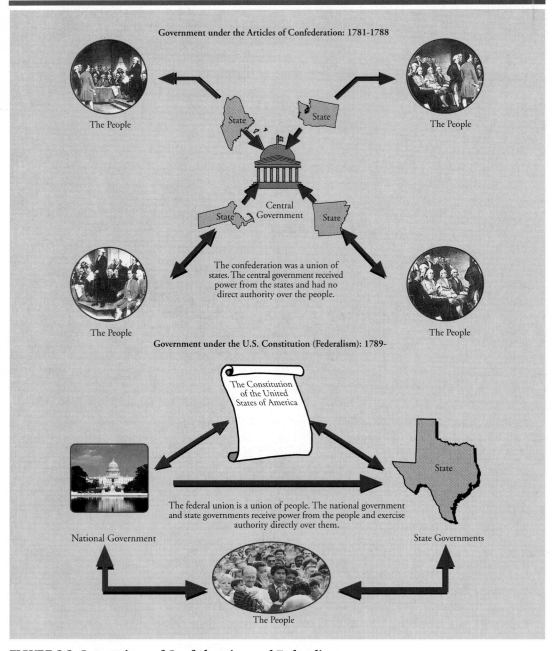

Government under the Articles of Confederation: 1781-1788

The People

The People

State

State

State

Central Government

State

The confederation was a union of states. The central government received power from the states and had no direct authority over the people.

The People

The People

Government under the U.S. Constitution (Federalism): 1789-

The Constitution of the United States of America

State

The federal union is a union of people. The national government and state governments receive power from the people and exercise authority directly over them.

National Government

State Governments

The People

FIGURE 2.2 Comparison of Confederation and Federalism

by Congress, still others by the people. All of these proposals met with objections. In the end, the Convention decided to create a new body of officials—the **Electoral College**—who would perform one function: to meet to select the president. The framers expected the Electoral College to serve as a body of eminent persons, selected by voters, who would assemble in each state to cast ballots for the president and vice-president. Electors would be allocated to each state on the basis of its representation in Congress. This process was intended to employ a kind of representative democracy in the choice of the chief executive, while making the president independent of other governmental officers.

The Supremacy of the Constitution

In order to help ensure that the principles embodied in the Constitution and the practical compromises that the Convention reached would be protected in the future, the framers made the document itself part of the process for governing the United States. The charter provides the foundation for the regime by mandating *constitutional supremacy*. Article VI declares that "This Constitution . . . shall be the supreme Law of the Land," thus tying government action and national politics to the structures and processes laid out in the document. All officers of national government and "Judges in every State" (Article VI) are bound to support the Constitution. Strong national and state governments are balanced by the power vested in the document itself.

The supremacy of the Constitution also shapes the process for governing through a set of *grants* and *limits* regulating the regime. Most of the Constitution involves grants of power to the three branches of the national government, from the lengthy list of congressional powers in Article I, Section 8 to investing the president with a veto, command of the armed forces, and authority in foreign affairs. At the same time, restrictions on both the national and state governments are spread throughout the text, including prohibitions on granting titles of nobility, passage of *ex post facto* laws, use of religious tests for office, or impairment of contracts. As the ultimate arbiter of these grants and limits, the Constitution becomes part of the process for governing.

Finally, the written constitution affects the regime by its *adaptability*. The document is not only amendable (Article V), but it is also interpretable. Rather than being a detailed rulebook for government, it is a framework for the regime. Several of its key phrases and provisions require interpretation in the course of operating the government: the conclusion of Article I, Section 8, granting Congress the power to do what is "Necessary and Proper" to fulfill its responsibilities; the commander in chief role of the president; the Contract Clause; the Interstate Commerce Clause; the Treason Clause; and many others.

The consequence of this adaptability is that the Constitution has guided the evolution of American politics over time, but the regime has not remained static. It also means that Americans spend a lot of time and effort debating the meaning of the charter in specific cases—such as the extent of power vested in Congress through the Commerce Clause or whether capital punishment is "cruel

Electoral College The mechanism for electing the president by which voters in each state select electors, who in turn meet and cast votes for president and vice-president. Electoral votes are allocated to the states according to their representation in Congress.

and unusual"—and continually speculating on the need to alter it. One factor in the death of the Articles of Confederation was that document's inflexibility; adaptability has probably been important for keeping the written constitution at the center of our politics.

Features of the Regime

The political order created by the Constitution is clearly that of a **democratic republic**—a regime in which the people elect representatives to govern in a system of divided power. The framers made a conscious choice in favor of representative democracy, providing for all important public decisions to be made by representatives of the people. There are no provisions for the public to vote on public issues or even for direct popular votes on constitutional amendments (as state constitutions and many foreign constitutions require). Instead, government is conducted through elected delegates of the public: members of Congress, presidential electors, and state legislatures. There are also ratifying conventions in the states; these were used to adopt the Constitution itself and provide one device for adopting amendments (see Articles V and VII, as well as the next chapter). The Constitution even provides the means for calling another constitutional convention (Article V).

The Constitution also contains elements that serve as safeguards against tyranny. One of these is its insistence on the *rule of law*. Article VI makes the charter the "supreme Law of the Land," and at 11 points throughout the various sections of the text provision is made for certain details left unspecified in the Constitution to be settled "by Law." Furthermore, the president is directed to "take Care that the Laws be faithfully executed," while the courts are given broad jurisdiction over matters of law. These requirements help to prevent tyranny by requiring that government officials act only in a lawful fashion; in turn, laws must be constitutional in order to be legitimate.

Another constitution element is **tripartite government**—a government with three branches. Creating three branches of government denies any one institution permanent dominance of the political system, which was a situation the framers clearly feared. They were particularly concerned about the legislature unilaterally dictating national policy and interfering in the operations of the system of justice. As James Madison explained this point in *The Federalist,* No. 51, "Ambition must be made to counteract ambition"—the ambition of officials in one branch offsetting the ambitions of those in another. That is why the idea of separation of powers and checks and balances was a central principle of the Constitution and one of the ideas contributed to the nation's charter by the "science of politics" as the framers understood it. Madison and his colleagues reasoned that if the skillful and ambitious individuals in the different parts of the regime could be put into competition with one another, liberty and the public interest would be more likely to flourish. The Current Issues box explores the effects of divided government.

The net effect of these structures and institutions is to make the American regime one of the most process-oriented political systems in the world. Few other regimes spend as much time and effort arguing over the rules by which

democratic republic
The joining together of popular rule (democracy) with divided governmental power and other limits on majority rule (republicanism), as in the American regime.

tripartite government
The kind of republicanism adopted in the United States in which governmental power is divided among three branches (legislative, executive, judicial).

Separated Powers, Divided Government

current issues

The Constitution divides governmental power through separation of powers among three branches—legislative, executive, and judicial. For much of American history, this separation has been bridged by political parties. Indeed, some observers of American politics contend that *divided government*—having the presidency and at least one house of Congress controlled by different parties—results in a kind of stalemate between the branches. According to this view, divided government creates "gridlock," which is best remedied by putting the White House and Congress in the hands of one party.

Nevertheless, American voters have made divided government a common feature of our politics since the end of World War II. During most of this period, Republicans have been presidents, and Democrats have been the majority party in Congress. The 1994 elections continued divided government, but with a new twist: Republicans now control Congress, and Democrats now control the White House.

Divided government has occurred under every president of the postwar period except Kennedy, Johnson, and Carter. Has it meant gridlock, as many critics have charged? The evidence is mixed. On one hand, sweeping policy changes such as occurred in President Lyndon Johnson's Great Society programs—rapid expansion of federal welfare and education spending and major civil rights laws—are probably possible only in an environment of unified government (one party in charge of both branches).

On the other hand, however, major legislation has been passed during times of divided government. Under President Truman, divided government produced the Marshall Plan to aid Western Europe after World War II and American entry into the North Atlantic Treaty Organization (NATO). During the Eisenhower years, the federal interstate highway system was created and a major civil-rights law was passed. Under Richard Nixon, federal revenue sharing with the states became law. Under Ronald Reagan, the Tax Reform Act of 1986 changed budget priorities.

In 1787, the framers of the U.S. Constitution chose to create a regime in which ambition would counteract ambition. Divided government has ensured that the competing ambitions of America's two major political parties intensify the separation between elected branches of government.

politics is to be conducted. Just as our sense of givenness leads Americans to accept as correct the values underlying the document, it also leads us to accept without surprise the struggles between the branches of government to direct national policy. For example, as a result of the 1994 elections, control of Congress passed into the hands of the Republican Party, which was determined to change public policy and advance its "Contract with America." This aggressive new majority created a challenge for the Democratic Clinton Administration, which had previously been able to work with a more congenial Democratic majority in Congress. Certainly, Americans are often frustrated by the battles that presidents and Congress wage up and down Pennsylvania Avenue, but we tend to see them as a somewhat inevitable part of our system.

The Constitution shapes American politics in ways that are both obvious and subtle. The document itself is often in the news, whenever the Supreme Court delivers a ruling on its meaning, the president invokes it to authorize sending troops abroad, Congress accuses the chief executive of violating it, or some activist in a public forum admonishes the nation to change it. Proposals to amend the charter to end abortion, safeguard abortion, stop the death penalty,

America's Constitution-Centered Politics

The Constitution acts as an "invitation to struggle" between the president and Congress over who shall direct foreign policy and military affairs. In 1991, Congress authorized President Bush to conduct a war to push Iraq out of Kuwait, a plan the president had threatened to carry out with or without the legislature's approval.

balance the budget, or ban flag burning remind us of its role in the political system.

The central relationship in American government, that between Congress and the president, is the result of the Constitution. Congress has law-making powers, but the chief executive can recommend legislation and sign or veto bills sent to the White House from Capitol Hill. The president needs the legislature to make treaties or appoint government officials, as well as to authorize and fund many policies the chief executive wants to pursue. As political scientist Richard Neustadt has put it, in practice the separation of powers system really means "separate institutions sharing power."[20]

Also sharing in power, albeit in a different way, is the independent judiciary established by the document. Unlike the situation in several other countries, where courts are subordinate to the political institutions of government or even part of the executive (France), the judiciary in this regime is co-equal with the other branches of government. It does not engage in the daily battles over the budget or trade policy, but it is intimately involved in deciding questions of constitutional interpretation, deciphering the meaning of laws, reviewing the actions of public officials and institutions, and probing the extent and limits of citizen rights. Courts in every regime make decisions on the evidence brought before them, whether in criminal cases or civil suits, but in no other system are they so often involved in interpreting and defining the rules of government. This fact has made the very appointment of judges a political event. The latest presidential nomination to the Supreme Court is not just a routine matter, but a public event carefully scrutinized for what it portends about the complex enterprise of constitutional interpretation.

All these events take place in the national government, but the Constitution also establishes a federal system. Even though they have lost some power in recent decades, the states continue to play a large role in the lives of Americans. Many of the laws that govern our daily lives, including those governing traffic, marriage and divorce, contracts, education, inheritance, and injury, are shaped primarily by state governments. The complex relationship between the states and the national government is yet another part of the politics of the constitutional regime.

"Not to worry, Ben . . . after all we went through, would people be stupid enough not to vote?
Cartoon by Paul Szep.

The Equal Rights Amendment, which to date has failed to get the necessary approval from the states, would make gender equality a constitutional right. Advocates see it as a long-needed guarantee of fairness to women, but critics see it as denying needed protections to women.

open questions

Should Equality Be a Constitutional Goal?

Despite the general sense of givenness that characterizes American attitudes toward the Constitution, many questions have been raised over the years regarding certain features and the principles of the document, the most significant of which concern whether the Constitution embodies the correct principles.

Several critics of the regime have observed that the principle of *equality* is missing from the Constitution. They charge that the Constitution is an "elitist document" and should value equality over liberty.[21] One school of thought holds that a political system is legitimate only to the extent that it promotes and protects equality among citizens. According to this view, the United States should alter its political and economic system in order to advance the condition of "equal freedom" among all persons in the nation. These alterations would include public funding of all electoral activities, proportional representation in the legislature, guarantees of material sufficiency for all, more equal distribution of wealth and resources in society, worker control over industry, reorganization of all institutions along egalitarian rather than hierarchical lines, guarantees of educational opportunities for all, and reducing barriers to majority rule in the state.[22] It is not immediately apparent what constitutional changes would be required to make "equal freedom" a reality, and introducing equality would have clear implications for the structure of the American regime.

Would the inclusion of equality be beneficial? Skeptics are unconvinced. They argue that the cost of making equality a central constitutional goal would be far too high.[23] First, a constitutional pursuit of equality would require breaking down the elaborate and well-conceived structure of checks and balances built into the regime. Second, and just as important, these skeptics maintain that the pursuit of equality will lead ultimately to demands not just for the right to pursue happiness but for the right to achieve it. Securing a right to happiness would require government to declare war on human nature. Those citizens who have been endowed by nature with intelligence, energy, beauty, or talent could not be permitted to benefit from nature's "injustice."[24]

Should equality be added to the goals of the Constitution? There is no easy answer. The document was built through an elaborate process of compromises and represents neither revealed wisdom nor merely base self-interest. It can be changed but is designed to be altered only when there is broad agreement in the nation about the need for change. Adding equality as a goal would involve costs and benefits to the regime that, like all proposed constitutional changes, need to be weighed carefully.

Even without such alteration, the Constitution remains the foundation of the American regime. As the main instrument for translating principles into the processes of politics, it is the central fact of our national political life. It shapes our politics in ways as subtle as the tension between the time perspectives of the White House (four years) and the House of Representatives (two years) and as obvious as prohibiting titles of nobility. Whatever we think of its strictures and grants of power, it gives us a political system that is driven by and continually debates the scope and meaning of its own fundamental law.

▎Summary

Understanding the Constitution is essential to understanding American politics. This chapter is the first of two on the constitutional system.

The Framers and Their Work. The Constitution reflects both the experiences of the founding generation and important principles that the authors of the document (the framers) held dear. The Declaration of Independence (1776) outlined the case for separation from Great Britain, asserting God-given rights to "life, liberty, and the pursuit of happiness." The Articles of Confederation (ratified 1781), America's first constitution, established a weak association of the 13 states, but rivalries between the states led to disorder, depression, and a sense of crisis. After a debtors' uprising in Massachusetts in 1786—Shays's Rebellion—a move to amend the Articles gained momentum. A Federal Convention was called to revise the Articles. This assembly, also known as the Constitutional Convention, met in Philadelphia in 1787. The delegates decided that the only way to make an effective political system was to scrap the Articles and write a new constitution.

Creating a New Regime. The Constitutional Convention met from May through September 1787. Its 55 delegates deliberated on the principles and features of the new political system and considered many different proposals. In May, the delegates considered the Virginia Plan, which called for a national government composed of a legislature apportioned according to population, an executive, and a judiciary. This plan became the focus of debate for the remainder of the Convention. Issues considered included the form of representation to be used in the new government (equality of states or proportional to population), the relationship between the central government and the states, and the nature of the executive. The main rival to the Virginia Plan was the New Jersey Plan, which called for little more than amendments to the Articles of Confederation.

The Great Compromise broke the impasse over representation in Congress, calling for a bicameral (two-chamber) legislature in which one chamber would represent all states equally (Senate) and the other would be apportioned according to population (House of Representatives). This agreement opened the way for other compromises on the executive and on slavery. A proposal for a bill of rights was rejected. The final product of the Convention was the Constitution of the United States.

Ratification. The Constitution was ratified by conventions called in each state. The Federalists were those who supported the new plan, while Antifederalists opposed it. To help win ratification, the Federalists promised to add a Bill of Rights to the Constitution after it was adopted. Because the opposing sides agreed on many principles, the Constitution gained wide acceptance after it was ratified in 1788.

Principles. The Constitution embodies key political values. The framers believed that government should advance four central goals: justice, liberty, order, and the public interest. They also believed that a good regime would embody a certain set of values: popular sovereignty, limited government and popular self-government, and responsible government. The framers also incorporated ideas from the "science of politics," including separation of powers and checks and balances. In addition, they wanted to protect property rights and commerce through contracts. One issue that divided the Convention was the question of slavery.

Process. The Convention made a "virtue of necessity" in devising the Constitution, as three examples illustrate: (1) representation—Congress was created with two houses (bicameralism), one apportioned according to state population and the other representing all states equally; (2) federalism—power was divided and shared by the national and state governments; and (3) presidential selection—the Electoral College selected the president independent of Congress, the states, or any other permanent governmental institutions.

Having a written constitution as the basis for the American regime has several important consequences: constitutional supremacy, a set of grants and limits regulating the power of the government, and constitutional adaptability. The regime created by the Constitution is a democratic republic that operates through the rule of law and includes tripartite government (government in three branches). Compromise provisions attempted to deal with slavery but were able only to delay but not resolve the controversy.

Politics. The Constitution shapes American politics in many ways. It creates a system in which the continual give-and-take between Congress and the president shapes public policy, while a powerful and independent judiciary plays a large role in constitutional interpretation and reviewing actions of government. The use of federalism means that many aspects of our daily lives are governed at the state or local level.

Suggested Readings

BECKER, CARL. *The Declaration of Independence.* New York: Random House, 1958. A widely respected analysis of the meaning of the Declaration.

BOWEN, CATHERINE D. *Miracle at Philadelphia.* Boston: Little, Brown, 1966. The most readable of many books available on the Convention of 1787.

CAREY, GEORGE. *The Federalist: Design for a Constitutional Republic.* Urbana: University of Illinois Press, 1989. Careful analysis of the main themes in the essays, by a distinguished scholar.

The Federalist. Various editions and editors. Essential reading for understanding the Constitution.

GOLDWIN, ROBERT A., AND WILLIAM A. SCHAMBRA, EDS. *How Capitalistic Is the Constitution?* Washington, D.C.: American Enterprise Institute, 1982. Essays on the economic ideas and features of the Constitution.

———. *How Democratic Is the Constitution?* Washington, D.C.: American Enterprise Institute, 1980. Essays address this question from several different points of view.

JENSEN, MERRILL. *The Articles of Confederation.* Madison: University of Wisconsin Press, 1948. Presents a sympathetic view of America's first constitution.

McDonald, Forrest. *Novus Ordo Seclorum.* Lawrence: University Press of Kansas, 1987. Examines the ideas underlying the U.S. Constitution.

STORING, HERBERT. *What the Anti-Federalists Were For.* Chicago: University of Chicago Press, 1981. Examines the case against the Constitution, as made by its opponents.

chapter 3

The Constitution In Action: Federalism, Nationalism, and Democracy

E ach year in January or February the president travels to Capitol Hill to address a joint session of Congress on the State of the Union. This annual event offers an interesting picture of how American constitutional government has evolved over the past two centuries. The address itself is clearly required by the Constitution; the president must, "from time to time," give Congress information on the state of the nation. Moreover, because the Constitution created two houses of Congress, both must be in attendance. Other participants in this event attend as a result of legislative actions: for example, the heads of executive departments, which were created by laws passed after the Constitution was written. But custom and tradition also play a role in shaping it—the fact that it is an annual occasion and that it requires a personal appearance by the president.

The State of the Union message is but one element of our complex political system. Like all other aspects of American politics, its roots lie in the Constitution. In Chapter 2, we saw how the framers constructed the nation's charter to embody grand ideals and practical compromises, providing the United States with a foundation for government that would be given life by men and women engaged in the practice of politics. Because the document itself is part of the process for promoting the goals it espouses, the handiwork of the framers has given our nation one of the most constitution-centered political systems in the world. If we want to make sense of how the United States evolved from the convention in Philadelphia in 1787 to the complex politics of Washington in the late twentieth century, we should look at how our national charter has been put into practice. We should observe the Constitution in action.

The Constitution was designed to be our fundamental law, providing a framework for public politics in the United States. To put the nation's charter into action, three operating principles have guided constitutional practice in America: constitutional supremacy, constitutional interpretability, and constitutional adaptability.

Principles: Fundamental Law in America

Constitutional Supremacy

Article V of the Constitution specifically establishes the document as the "Supreme Law of the Land," and both the national and state governments are bound by it. In Great Britain, the constitution is in reality a collection of traditions that have ancient origins but can be changed by a simple act of Parliament; there is no fixed foundation for government that is unchangeable by ordinary legislation. The U.S. Constitution is not ordinary law, but a set of rules that take precedence over the preferences and policies of government officials or public opinion. For example, there are many times when police and prosecutors would find it easier to punish criminals if they could coerce confessions from suspects, but the Constitution specifically guarantees that no one may be forced to testify against him- or herself. The substance of our fundamental law can be changed, but only through the means of amendment as outlined in Article V.

manifest constitution
Aspects of the Constitution that spell out government structure and process in fairly definite terms not requiring interpretation.

constitution of open texture Those aspects of the U.S. Constitution that involve matters implied but not specified and general phrases that must be defined. These aspects require interpretation.

On the other hand, this supremacy does not mean that the Constitution is an operating manual for government. The framers believed that the Constitution should be supreme, but not too detailed. At the Constitutional Convention of 1787, Edmund Randolph of Virginia communicated to his colleagues what he saw as the features of a constitution: essential principles, adaptability to future circumstances, and generality. The purpose of such a document is to create a political system and provide it with fundamental principles, not to attempt to set down government policy for all time.

Some state constitutions have taken the route of detail and rigidity; the Constitution of Texas (1876) contains literally hundreds of amendments, because the original text was specific even to the description of governmental policies on welfare and education. The United States Constitution is, instead, the framework for a working political system. As you can see in Appendix B, the document is relatively brief and runs to only a few printed pages.

As constitutional scholar Alexander Bickel pointed out, there are, in effect, two constitutions: a manifest constitution and a constitution of open texture.[1] The **manifest constitution** is the "constitution of structure and process . . . the constitution of the mechanics of institutional arrangements and of the political process."[2] This is the document that establishes a single president as chief executive, sets definite terms of office, provides a specific process for passing laws, and lays out other rather definite rules. **Constitution of open texture** means that the charter is marked by matters implied but not specified, blanks unfilled, and general phrases that must be defined. For example, Article I lists many powers of Congress, including the authority to regulate commerce

The U.S. Constitution is not merely an historical artifact. It continues to shape American politics—and political controversies—on a daily basis.

"among the several States," but does not define what commercial activity that phrase includes. As we shall see, the idea of what is considered interstate commerce has expanded dramatically over the course of our history.

Constitutional Interpretability

This open texture makes *constitutional interpretability* necessary and possible because the terse and often general language of the document must be interpreted in the day-to-day running of the political system. Since the Constitution provides the fundamental framework for government, much of the charter shows this face: the clause in Article I, Section 8 that grants Congress the power to make all laws "Necessary and Proper" to fulfill the responsibilities it has been given, the generally undefined extent of the president's role as commander in chief, the Contract Clause, the Interstate Commerce Clause, and so many other aspects of the document. Some of the most important controversies in American history—such as slavery and states' rights, federal regulation of business, civil rights, and abortion—have grown out of this open texture. As we shall see, this need to specify the meaning of the fundamental law has led to a large body of constitutional law in the form of court cases, a set of traditions and customs for carrying out different provisions of the document, and a series of political battles over the course of American history about how best to interpret the language of the framers.

Constitutional Adaptability

The Constitution's interpretability, plus the possibility of altering it through amendment, has led to a third operating principle for American government. *Constitutional adaptability* refers to the fact that constitutional government in America is not static, because the nation's charter can be changed and at times reinterpreted. As Justice Louis Brandeis once put it:

> Our Constitution is not a strait-jacket. It is a living organism. As such it is capable of growth—of expansion and of adaptation to new conditions. Growth implies changes, political, economic and social. Growth which is significant manifests itself rather in intellectual and moral conceptions than in material things. Because our Constitution possesses the capacity of adaptation, it has endured as the fundamental law of an ever-developing people.[3]

As we shall see, this adaptability has been a powerful force shaping the development of the American regime over the decades of national history. In three key areas, government under the Constitution has evolved in ways that were not necessarily anticipated by those who wrote the document in 1787: (1) the meaning of what is required for democratic government; (2) the relative power of the national and state governments; and (3) the distribution of power within the national government itself. We now examine how constitutional practice in these areas has shaped the political system we have today.

Process: The Means for Practicing Constitutional Government

Putting constitutional government into practice is a complex enterprise. On one level, it means obeying the mandates of the manifest constitution: holding elections as required, having officials assume or leave office on the basis of those elections, following the law-making process spelled out in Article I of the Constitution, and obeying other mandates of the national charter. Practicing constitutional government also means working with the interpretable and adaptable Constitution to deal with new events and circumstances that arise over time: deciding tough cases that call for clarification of the general phrases of the document, devising policies for issues such as space travel and other matters unheard of in 1787, and even altering the Constitution as the nation sees fit to do so. These tasks have been accomplished through amendments, through interpretation, and through the development of an "unwritten constitution" for the United States.

Amendments

The very existence of an amendment clause indicates that the framers expected constitutional changes to be made over time, but the difficulty of making and passing amendments means that they did not expect changes to be frequent or undertaken lightly. The mechanics of the amending process offer four possible routes to constitutional change, although in practice one of these has been used almost exclusively.

As we see in Figure 3.1, the Constitution provides two avenues for proposing amendments and two methods for ratifying such proposals. An amendment to the Constitution can be proposed either by two-thirds of each house of Congress or by a constitutional convention called by Congress upon request by two-thirds of the states. Once formally proposed, any potential amendment must be ratified by three-fourths of the states, either by state legislatures acting directly or by elected conventions called in each state.

The most common route to adopting amendments has been proposal by Congress followed by ratification by state legislatures. Congress has never called a convention, although state ratifying conventions were used once (for the Twenty-first Amendment, which repealed the prohibition on alcohol established in the Eighteenth). Not surprisingly, only 27 alterations to the text have survived the difficult method of amendment. Moreover, because the process is so difficult and because the Constitution's role is to serve as fundamental law for the nation, the changes that have been enacted generally have been rather fundamental ones demonstrating a broad national consensus about the need for reform.

The First Ten Amendments. The first ten amendments are known as the **Bill of Rights.** This set of changes was enacted in response to the debate over the ratification of the Constitution and offered to the states as part of the bargain to win support for the new national charter. (These amendments will be considered in more depth in Chapter 4, which explores citizen rights and liberties.)

Bill of Rights The first ten amendments to the U.S. Constitution; a statement of citizen liberties.

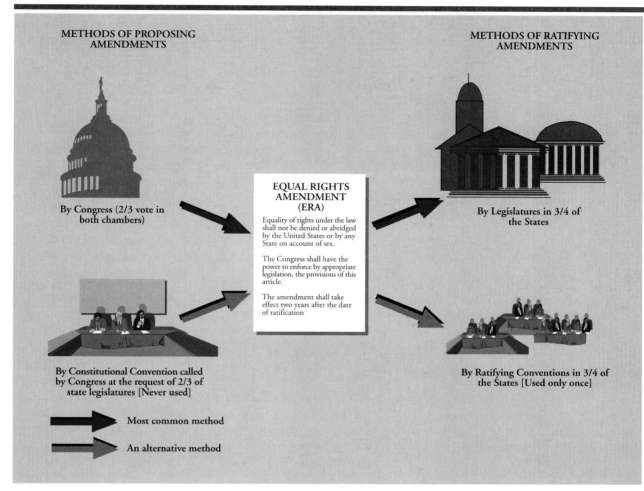

METHODS OF PROPOSING AMENDMENTS

By Congress (2/3 vote in both chambers)

By Constitutional Convention called by Congress at the request of 2/3 of state legislatures [Never used]

EQUAL RIGHTS AMENDMENT (ERA)

Equality of rights under the law shall not be denied or abridged by the United States or by any State on account of sex.

The Congress shall have the power to enforce by appropriate legislation, the provisions of this article.

The amendment shall take effect two years after the date of ratification

METHODS OF RATIFYING AMENDMENTS

By Legislatures in 3/4 of the States

By Ratifying Conventions in 3/4 of the States [Used only once]

➡ Most common method

➡ An alternative method

FIGURE 3.1 Methods of Amending the U.S. Constitution

Other amendments also tended to come in groups, reflecting periods in national history when the political environment was ripe for change.

The Civil War Amendments. After the war, it was necessary to alter the fundamental law to deal with the political consequences of that conflict. Slavery was abolished by the Thirteenth Amendment (1865). The Fourteenth Amendment (1868) made ex-slaves citizens, applied the Bill of Rights to states, and denied federal office to former rebels. The Fifteenth Amendment (1870) forbade using race as grounds for restricting the right to vote (although several states found ways to do so until well into the twentieth century).

The Progressive Era Amendments. Early in the twentieth century, reformers of the Progressive movement pushed for ways to make government more honest and more democratic. The Sixteenth Amendment (1913) authorizes the federal government to collect income taxes, while the Seventeenth Amendment (1913) provides for direct election of senators by voters in the states rather than state legislatures. Finally, women were guaranteed the right to vote by the Nineteenth Amendment (1920).

The Amendments of the 1960s and 1970s. A final burst of amendments was inspired by the change-minded 1960s. The Twenty-third Amendment (1961) gave voting rights in presidential elections to residents of the District of Columbia. The Twenty-fourth Amendment (1964) outlawed poll taxes, which were taxes on voting used to discourage political activity by minority citizens. The Twenty-sixth Amendment (1971) lowered the voting age to 18.

Other amendments have been ratified over the years. With the exception of technical ones such as the Twelfth Amendment (1804), which corrected a flaw in the Electoral College system for electing the president, these changes have played an infrequent but important role in American constitutional government. Because of amendments, the president is limited to two terms in office; both houses of Congress are directly elected; citizens' rights are the subject of considerable legal protection; and the right to vote has been greatly expanded from the days of the founding.

Who Interprets the Constitution?

The Constitution was not quite to Edmund Randolph's liking—he refused to sign it—still, it does follow the general guidelines he laid out. It consists of essential principles and is general in nature; therefore, it requires interpretation. But who is to do the interpreting?

The American political system has never developed a single final answer to that question. In one important respect, constitutional interpretation is almost a national pastime. When a member of Congress takes to the floor to denounce the latest presidential action as unconstitutional, interpretation occurs. It also occurs when a journalist criticizes restrictions on press coverage of military operations. It happens when opposing groups of protestors outside an abortion clinic shout back and forth about whether that procedure should be protected or declared illegal. It also happens when citizens privately discuss their views on whether capital punishment is so cruel as to be unconstitutional.

Public officials must engage in interpretation as they perform their duties. When Congress undertakes some action not specifically outlined in Article I— creating a space program, passing a civil rights law, raising the minimum wage—it engages in interpretation. Presidential actions that read meaning into the executive power or the role of commander in chief—signing executive agreements with other nations, sending American troops into combat abroad— also constitute interpretation. State and local officials also interpret their constitutional powers—by limiting gun ownership, for example.

Each of these acts has force, but one mode of interpretation has the greatest power of final authority in the American regime. This is **judicial review**—the power of the courts, ultimately the Supreme Court, to engage in constitutional review of the actions of other branches of government and all levels of government.[4] Judicial review itself grows out of interpretation; the document states that it shall serve as the supreme law of the United States but never specifies who has authority to interpret that fundamental law. Traditionally, it has been the province of the courts to interpret law, thus leading to the conclusion that courts should judge the constitutionality of government actions.[5]

Judicial review usually refers to the work of the Supreme Court, because it has the last word for the third branch of government. The Court renders decisions in individual cases, the cumulative effect of which is to develop a body of constitutional law that serves as a kind of appendix to the document itself. The first exercise of this power came in **Marbury v. Madison** (1803). In this case, the Court ruled unconstitutional a portion of the Judiciary Act of 1789—a provision that would have given to the courts the power to issue certain kinds of orders not authorized in the document itself. Writing for his colleagues, Chief Justice John Marshall declared that "It is, emphatically, the province and duty of the judicial department, to say what the law is. . . . If then, the courts are to regard the constitution, and the constitution is superior to any ordinary act of the legislature, the constitution, and not such ordinary act, must govern the case to which they both apply."[6]

The other branches now rely on judicial review. For example, in 1985 President Reagan signed the Balanced Budget Act (the Gramm-Rudman-Hollings law), which set up a complicated process for mandating an elimination of the federal deficit over a period of years. The president complained that he believed certain portions of the law to be unconstitutional. But rather than veto it for that reason, he said he would sign the law and let the courts sort out what was invalid in the act.

The "Unwritten Constitution"

As we saw earlier, the general and fundamental nature of the Constitution means that it does not cover all specifics for operating the regime. In consequence, over the course of national history a body of practices has developed to help the framers' system work. Some, like the annual State of the Union Address, are customary in nature. Others are extraconstitutional structures that shape the daily operations of the government. Collectively, these practices make up what political scientist Don K. Price calls the **unwritten constitution:**

> . . . the fixed political customs that have developed without formal Constitutional amendment, but that have been authorized by statute or frozen, at least temporarily, in tradition. The party conventions and the primary system, congressional committees and their staffs, the statutory structure of the executive departments, the Executive Office of the President, the press conference and television coverage, and freedom of information—none of these was established by the Constitution or foreseen by its framers, and all could be abolished without formal amendment.[7]

During his long tenure as Chief Justice of the United States, John Marshall authored many decisions in which the Supreme Court molded constitutional interpretation through judicial review.

judicial review The power of the courts—ultimately the Supreme Court—to review actions of government to assess whether those actions are consistent with the Constitution.

Marbury v. Madison 1803 case in which the Supreme Court first exercised the power of judicial review under the Constitution. In that case, it held that a portion of the Judiciary Act of 1789 was contrary to the charter and therefore null and void.

unwritten constitution The body of customs, precedents, structures, and arrangements that have grown up over the course of American history that shape the way governance is actually conducted in this regime.

The unwritten constitution shapes American government in a host of ways, but three major aspects merit consideration.

Internal Organization of the Three Branches of Government. Each branch has evolved along somewhat different lines. The judiciary is tightly organized by law, with a complex hierarchy of courts all subject to final review by the Supreme Court. Indeed, the number of justices on the high court (nine) is determined by Congress. It has been changed several times in American history, but not since the presidency of Ulysses Grant. The number nine has achieved such force that attempts to alter it have been met with great resistance. In 1936, President Franklin Roosevelt proposed enlarging the Court so he could appoint more justices favorable to his New Deal policies, many of which the High Court had struck down. FDR's "Court-packing" plan drew fire even from many of his staunchest supporters, because it proposed to alter the traditional size of the institution for political reasons. In the 1980s, Chief Justice Warren Burger tried to win support for an additional justice to help relieve the Court's caseload burden, but his idea was ignored by Congress.

The structure of the executive branch is quite different. Although it is composed of scores of agencies and administrative units (see Appendix E for an organizational chart of the U.S. government, including a lengthy list of executive agencies), only a few have the special status of departments of government. These departments are not necessarily any bigger than other units—for years, the largest single executive branch entity was the Veterans Administration, which became a department only in 1988. Nevertheless, they occupy a position of greater prestige than do other agencies and play a larger role in presidential policy making. While nominally under the president's direction, by law and politics these departments and agencies also serve Congress, since that body provides their authorization and funding.

The Executive Office of the President, which is the division of the executive branch that directly serves the chief executive, occupies a different role in the unwritten constitution. Created in 1939, it contains a large staff working aggressively to advance the political interests of the person who is president as much as (if not more than) the institution of the presidency. It allows the occupant of the Oval Office to play a large role in shaping national policy.

The internal organization of Congress is a central element of the unwritten constitution. As a result of tradition and the internal rules of each chamber, the House and Senate are divided along party lines (majority and minority), with power dispersed to committees and subcommittees. Reflecting that dispersal, the Congress as a whole, each committee, and individual members all have staffs of their own. Further complicating matters, a seniority system awards greater deference and influence to members with longest service. While the Constitution's law-making process is observed (as befits the manifest constitution), it is only the tip of a large iceberg of congressional organization and politics.

Political Parties and Candidate Selection. The Constitution provides for elections, but it leaves much unstated. Since the early days of the Republic, a two-party system has evolved that offers voters a choice of one party or the other in most elections. Nominees for state and congressional elections are chosen largely through party primaries, which are nearly universal but by no means required by the Constitution. Presidential nominations, once determined largely by state and local party "bosses" at national conventions, have for two decades been decided by voters in individual state primaries before the conventions meet.

Customs and Traditions. Over the decades, a number of customary practices have evolved as part of the unwritten constitution. Some of these practices do not appear to be important at first glance, but they do subtly affect the behavior of public officials. For example, were a president to skip a State of the Union Address, there would be no constitutional crisis, but certainly a political one: Washington would be abuzz with speculation about why the chief executive was avoiding this event. Other customs are also subtle but more obviously political:

> *Prerequisites for certain offices:* While the Constitution sets no career qualifications for federal judges, only attorneys are chosen for the job. Some observers have suggested that the Supreme Court might profit from the perspective of an economist or historian, yet no one but a lawyer would be considered qualified. Likewise, the Constitution specifies that the House of Representatives shall choose a Speaker but leaves the qualifications for that job undefined. In the early years of Congress, the job went to Henry Clay of Kentucky, elected Speaker in his first year in the House. Over time the position came to be offered only to a senior member of the majority party. In 1995, however, the extraordinary circumstances of the 1994 Republican election victories made possible a break in this long-standing custom when Newt Gingrich, a relatively junior member (less than 20 years in the Congress), was selected Speaker of the House.

> *How vice-presidential candidates are chosen:* Although technically the choice of the party convention, in practice the second spot on a party's national ticket is the choice solely of the presidential nominee. This is such a truism of American politics that the selection of a running mate is sometimes described as the first important decision of a newly nominated contender for the Oval Office. This custom was broken only once in modern times; in 1956, Governor Adlai Stevenson of Illinois asked the Democratic convention to choose his running mate.

> *The president's cabinet:* Perhaps the most powerful tradition in American politics not set down in the Constitution is one that most citizens do not even realize is customary in nature: the existence of the president's cabinet. Since the time of George Washington, chief executives have called upon the heads of the executive departments to give them advice on national affairs. This custom became such a fixture of the office that these department heads became known informally as cabinet secretaries, and one room in the White House is designated the Cabinet Room. Yet few

presidents in modern times have consulted this body as a group, although individual secretaries may be influential presidential advisers. Most presidents also rely for counsel on their personal staffs or an informal "kitchen cabinet" of private citizens.

The cabinet does not exist in law, executive order, or any other formal way. And presidents need not take the advice they are given by cabinet secretaries. In one story, Abraham Lincoln is said to have put a proposition to his cabinet. The vote was one "Aye" and the rest "No." "The Ayes have it," Lincoln declared, regarding his own vote as the only one that counted.

The power of custom is nevertheless strong. In the Twenty-fifth Amendment (1967), the cabinet is given a sort of quasi-constitutional status. That change establishes a means for declaring the president disabled so the vice-president can serve as acting president in the event of severe illness or injury restricting the chief executive's performance of office. The power to declare the president disabled is given to the vice-president and "the principal officers of the executive departments," that is, the cabinet. But the cabinet is not recognized as a body, only as a collection of department heads. Nevertheless, it is the force of custom that led the authors of this amendment to turn to these officials for a determination of disability, rather than Congress or the courts.

Constitutional Politics in America

The complete story of the practice of constitutional government in the United States is the record of national political history over the past two centuries. But certain themes outline how the fundamental law has evolved: a tendency toward greater democracy in the political system, the rise of the national government and a simultaneous change in federalism, and the growing complexity of the "Washington community." These themes help to explain how our political system has gone from a small national government that did little more than defend the borders, deliver the mail, and provide a common currency to a continental democracy in which the federal government is the nation's largest employer, nearly every adult has the right to vote, and an array of interests and citizen activists compete with parties and officials for influence over policy.

The Democratic Tendency in American Government

The American political system was created as a democratic republic, joining majority rule with various limits—such as the president's veto, judicial review, and constitutionally protected rights—on the power of majorities to work their will. Inevitably, there has been tension between the democratic and republican elements in our system. This is apparent any time a popular law, such as one against flag burning, is ruled unconstitutional because it violates some provision in the nation's charter. Nevertheless, the story of the American political system has prominently featured the expansion of its democratic elements. This tendency has been manifest in both the written and unwritten constitutions.

The Expansion of Voting Rights. The Constitution left control over **suffrage**—the right to vote—to the states, although it gave Congress certain powers in that area. At the time of the founding, state control over voting generally meant that only those men who paid taxes or held a certain amount of property were regarded as having a sufficient "stake" in the community to earn the right to participate in its decisions. Women, slaves, and younger adults were usually excluded. (In the period shortly before and after the writing of the Constitution, New Jersey permitted women who owned property to vote, but this practice was later abandoned.) As we shall see, this situation has changed dramatically, so that today nearly every citizen 18 years old and over can vote.

Pressure for greater democracy soon began to take hold. In the early nineteenth century, the *franchise* (right to vote) was extended to all free males (or white males in some places), setting the stage for the rise of mass political parties. In 1828, the election of Andrew Jackson transformed the presidency into a more democratic office than the framers had conceived it to be. The chief executive was nominated by a convention of citizen delegates and won in an election conducted under broad manhood suffrage. The president was now linked directly to citizens.

After the Civil War, voting rights were extended to African Americans, although southern states (and some northern ones as well) erected barriers to minority participation. During Reconstruction, black officials were elected in many states, but the removal of federal troops from former Confederate states soon meant that practices such as restrictive literacy tests for voting, poll taxes, and whites-only party primaries effectively shut the former slaves and their descendants out of the political process.

By the early twentieth century, renewed pressure for democratization ushered in further changes. In 1920 women were guaranteed the right to vote by constitutional amendment, although Wyoming had been the first state in modern times to provide for women's suffrage. Later in the century, radio and television become instruments for communication between politicians and citizens, and the invention of public opinion polling in the 1930s enabled officials to more systematically gauge popular opinion on a wide range of issues. Much of politics in the post–World War II period was shaped by a growing reliance by candidates and officeholders on mass communications for reaching voters and polls for learning about what citizens wanted (a development that is explored in greater depth in Chapter 5).

By the late 1950s, pressure for expanded voting rights was growing again. The civil rights movement was pressing for change, especially in the segregated South. By 1961, the Twenty-third Amendment extended the right to vote in presidential elections to citizens of the black-majority District of Columbia. In 1964, the Twenty-fourth Amendment abolished poll taxes, and the 1965 Voting Rights Act allowed federal intervention in states with a history of discrimination against minorities in order to register voters. By the time the Twenty-sixth Amendment (1970) gave those 18 years old and older voting rights, any adult citizen who was not mentally incompetent or a convicted felon was able to vote.

suffrage The right to vote.

The Constitution originally gave control over voting to the states, but later amendments guaranteed more groups (women, African Americans, those 18 years old and older) the right to vote.

Voter registration has also been made easier. Although by no means uniform, registration procedures across the country have become more convenient. Many states, such as Ohio and Texas, that had once made signing up to vote difficult now allow registration by postcard (usually widely available—voter registration cards can be found in many convenience stores in Texas). In 1993, Congress mandated that states must register to vote those applying for or renewing their driver's license (a move labelled "motor voter").

Democratization of Elections. Along with a broader right to vote, other changes gave citizens more opportunities to use that right. Beginning early in this century, Wisconsin initiated the use of primary elections to choose party candidates for office in order to break the hold of political "machines" and party "bosses." Other states would eventually follow suit. Greater use of primaries at all levels of government reshaped the process of choosing party candidates for office, just as television changed the methods of campaigning. The introduction of initiative and referendum methods for passing laws in California and other states meant that citizen activists could even bypass state legislatures to make policy. Term limits for legislators, tax reductions, the requirement that English be the official language of a state, and other policy decisions have all been made by voters in states using initiative and referendum elections. Since the Seventeenth Amendment (1913), senators have been popularly elected. This change means that only the president is indirectly elected, but the existence of political parties has reduced the Electoral College in most cases to a rubber stamp of the popular election. In effect, all elected federal officials depend on the people for office.

The courts have also contributed to this democratic trend, especially in the matter of defining the electoral bases of representation. In the case of *Baker v. Carr* (1962), the Supreme Court ruled that the issue of how legislative districts are apportioned is a matter subject to judicial review under the Fourteenth Amendment.[8] This decision ushered in an era of legal challenges to the drawing of district lines, because who is included in or excluded from a legislative district will affect who can be elected to represent that area. In *Wesberry v. Sanders* (1964), the Court maintained that the Constitution implied that each citizen's vote should have about as much weight as another's, thus establishing the principle that election districts and procedures must adhere to the doctrine of "one person, one vote."[9] And in *Reynolds v. Sims* (1964),[10] the High Court ruled that both houses in a state legislature must be chosen from districts that reflect population distribution. This decision ended an old practice whereby rural areas were given special protection in state senates by providing for an equal number of representatives from each county in the state (regardless of the county's population).

In 1992, another change to democratize the system even further was made. After public outrage over several scandals involving Congress (for example, mismanagement of a bank for members in the House of Representatives and unpopular congressional pay raises), the Twenty-seventh Amendment was adopted. It was actually one of the original 12 amendments proposed for inclusion in the Bill of Rights, but in 1791 only 10 were ratified. It provides that any pay raise Congress votes for itself will take effect only after a congressional election. (See Appendix B for a text of the Twenty-seventh Amendment.) While it is a relatively minor change, this rule is a sign of a public desire to retain at least a symbolic hold over representatives.

The Changing Meaning of Federalism

As we saw in Chapter 2, the Constitution weaves considerable tension into the American regime by creating two levels of government: national and state. Just as the charter does with the checks-and-balances system within the national government, the document divides some powers between Washington and the states while requiring the two levels to share other powers.

The Division of Power in the Federal System. As Figure 3.2 illustrates, the Constitution recognizes three types of governmental power in the federal system. First, **delegated powers** are those powers granted to the national government alone by the document. They include the conduct of diplomacy, national

delegated powers
Powers granted exclusively to the national government, such as the power to declare war and to regulate immigration and bankruptcy.

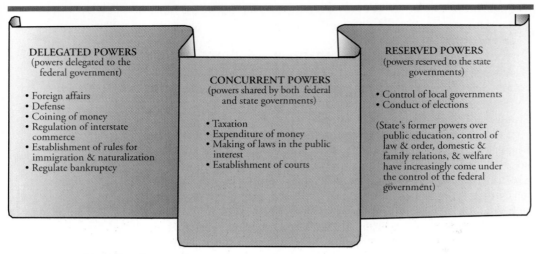

DELEGATED POWERS
(powers delegated to the federal government)

- Foreign affairs
- Defense
- Coining of money
- Regulation of interstate commerce
- Establishment of rules for immigration & naturalization
- Regulate bankruptcy

CONCURRENT POWERS
(powers shared by both federal and state governments)

- Taxation
- Expenditure of money
- Making of laws in the public interest
- Establishment of courts

RESERVED POWERS
(powers reserved to the state governments)

- Control of local governments
- Conduct of elections

(State's former powers over public education, control of law & order, domestic & family relations, & welfare have increasingly come under the control of the federal government)

FIGURE 3.2 The Federal System

concurrent powers
Powers shared by the national government and the states, such as the power to tax, spend money, make laws, and establish courts.

reserved powers Powers kept by the states after the creation of the national government, such as the power to create local governments and conduct elections.

nation-centered federalism The view that the Constitution created a union of *people,* as opposed to a union of *states.* The political consequence of the Civil War was to make this view the conventional understanding of the American regime.

defense, control over interstate commerce and bankruptcy, and rules for immigration and naturalization. Second, **concurrent powers** are those shared by the national government and the states, such as the powers to tax, to spend money, to make laws for the public interest, and to establish courts. Finally, **reserved powers** are those kept by the states after the creation of the national government. These include the powers to create local governments and to conduct elections. Many areas once considered to be the exclusive province of the states—public education, control over law and order, domestic and family relations (divorce, child custody, spousal and child abuse), and welfare—have come under greater and greater national government control in recent decades. This development has led some observers to question the fate of federalism in the face of an expansive national government.

The Evolving Face of Federalism. At the time of the founding the states were powerful, virtually autonomous entities, and the new national government was a small and limited operation. Indeed, during the Washington administration there were more people working on the president's personal estate at Mount Vernon than employed in the entire United States government. During the early decades of the constitutional regime, states would be dominant in the lives of citizens. The national government had its greatest role in foreign policy and defense, but it also financed certain "internal improvements," such as roads and canals. States enjoyed broad autonomy in self-government, education, and most internal affairs.

From the time of the adoption of the Constitution, a debate raged over federalism and national supremacy. On one side were those who took the view of **nation-centered federalism,** which held that the American Union was one of people. This was the position of Alexander Hamilton, John Marshall, and

Daniel Webster. They respected federalism but believed that the national government was the only hope for holding together the troubled young nation.

This view was triumphant in passage of Alexander Hamilton's financial program during the Washington administration, which included a Bank of the United States (1791–1811, revived in 1816). The bank represented a victory because the Constitution does not explicitly authorize Congress to establish a bank, although it gives the national government certain responsibilities over money and commerce. Hamilton was able to convince Congress that it had the authority to create a bank because Article I, Section 8 of the Constitution does permit the national government to do what is "necessary and proper" to fulfill the powers described in the document.

Chief Justice John Marshall defended this broad interpretation of the power of Congress in **McCulloch v. Maryland** (1819). Maryland had tried to attack the Bank of the United States, which operated in Baltimore, by imposing a tax on its operations. The Maryland legislature took the position that Congress could do only what was explicitly authorized in the Constitution. Writing for the Court, Marshall advanced the nation-centered view, thus voiding Maryland's attempt to limit the bank's activity.[11]

Marshall also advanced this nation-centered view in **Gibbons v. Ogden** (1824). Here, the issue was whether Congress's power to regulate interstate commerce extended to commercial activity within a single state. The case involved a New Jersey steamboat owner operating under a federal license who was sued by the holder of the New York State monopoly on the steamboat trade. The Court broadly interpreted Congress's power to regulate interstate commerce, even when a state had its own rules governing internal commerce.[12]

Arrayed against this view was **state-centered federalism**—the belief that the American Union is one of states rather than people. It was based on the idea of *states' rights*—the idea that the states have rights that precede any in the central government, which should be considered a creation of the states. This was the position of John Randolph of Virginia and of Robert Y. Hayne and John Calhoun of South Carolina. Supporters of this view saw the need for a central government for defense and foreign affairs, but not one that would interfere with the self-government of the states. Indeed, Calhoun became the leading theorist of states' rights. He advanced the concept of *nullification,* the idea that states possessed the power to declare acts of the national government "null and void" within their own territory. States' rights became a cardinal principle of the Constitution of the Confederate States of America.

Ultimately, the Civil War resolved the conflict in favor of nation-centered federalism, although questions about the power and role of the national government remained. To address these issues, the idea of **dual federalism** was developed. It held that the Constitution created two spheres of governmental power—national and state—and each was separate and distinct. While some matters were easily assigned to one or the other—foreign policy to the national government, internal police power to the states—other issues were more confusing. For example, how exactly can we separate commerce between the states (*inter*state) from commerce within one state (*intra*state)? In a series of cases,

McCulloch v. Maryland 1819 case in which the Supreme Court broadly interpreted the power of Congress to make such laws as are "necessary and proper" to fulfill its responsibilities.

Gibbons v. Ogden 1824 case in which the Supreme Court broadly interpreted the power of Congress to regulate commerce.

state-centered federalism The view that the Constitution created a union of sovereign states, which could overrule the national government when there was disagreement between the two levels. The Civil War effectively ended this interpretation.

dual federalism A theory intended to explain how powers are divided between the national governments and the states. It sought to distinguish national matters from exclusively state matters but was ultimately abandoned by the Supreme Court with the rise of a national economy and the growth of federal government power in the twentieth century.

the Supreme Court wrestled with these sorts of questions, striking down federal regulations on commerce in the name of state power. By the 1930s, however, it was becoming increasingly difficult to make these distinctions in the face of an integrated national economy.

The policies of President Franklin Roosevelt's New Deal ushered in an era of rising national government power. In response to the Great Depression, the national government moved into new areas once considered the reserve of the states or private institutions—employment, welfare, public works, stock and bond trading, labor unions, Social Security, unemployment insurance. The national government grew significantly and became a part of the everyday lives of citizens. The Supreme Court now accepted the new national government role. In *United States v. Darby Lumber Co.* (1941)[13] and other cases involving questions about the extent of Congress's power, the Court abandoned dual federalism and upheld congressional regulation of wages and other aspects of trade once regarded as state matters. By the time World War II brought total war to the "homefront," including a full-scale military draft, rationing of goods, and wage and price controls, a large national government had become a permanent fixture of American life. The federal government gave substantial sums of money to states to encourage them to promote national aims (for example, in education, highway construction, and provision of housing for low-income families).

Judicial review assisted in the expansion of national government authority. In *Heart of Atlanta Motel v. United States* (1964),[14] the Court interpreted Congress's power over interstate commerce to include nearly all economic activity in the country. In this case, a motel owner asserted the right to discriminate against African Americans because his business was small and did not affect trade between the states. Supporters of this interpretation saw the growth of the national government as necessary for bringing the full promise of democracy, civil rights, and opportunity to America, while opponents argued that citizens' freedoms were being eroded along with the declining independence of the states.

As the national government expanded its powers and responsibilities, the states came to depend on it for a larger share of their income. This trend was intensified under President Lyndon Johnson's Great Society, which accelerated national government involvement in education, civil rights, health insurance (Medicare and Medicaid), urban aid, and programs for nearly every national purpose. In the 1960s and 1970s, more federal grants to states and cities were established, offering money for such purposes as providing public housing, giving health benefits to the poor, cleaning up the environment, promoting education, undertaking urban renewal, building and repairing highways, as well as a wide variety of other activities. This practice of advancing national purposes through allocations of money to states became known as *fiscal federalism,* a term meant to imply that states now served as financial agents of the U.S. government. The states, eager to obtain revenue in order to pay for expanding government services, assumed responsibility for implementing many of the programs passed by Congress.

The Contemporary Era: From Fiscal Federalism to Unfunded Mandates.
Federal aid to states comes in four forms. First, it is given through *categorical grants*—money for specific purposes such as school lunches, highway construction, flood control projects, Medicaid, and Aid to Families with Dependent Children. The national government matches state funds with these grants.

A second type of aid is available through *project grants*. These are grants allocated to state and local governments, or even private organizations, on the basis of competitive applications. The best examples are federal research grants received by many colleges and universities around the country for studies in medicine, engineering, computer science, biotechnology, and other areas.

The third type of federal aid comes to states through *block grants*—grants of money for broad governmental purposes, such as education, health care, and social services. Unlike categorical grants, which are given for fairly specific programs or construction projects, block grants give states and local governments discretion about how money is spent within a general area.

Finally, federal aid is given through general *revenue sharing*—allocations of money to state and local governments to be used as the officials receiving this aid see fit (although there are some restrictions). Revenue sharing was first dispensed in 1972 and terminated in 1987, although in recent years there has been renewed interest in reviving the program as a means to enhance the autonomy of states and local governments.

Federal aid has been a vehicle for increasing national government power. By the end of the 1970s, money from Washington constituted about one-quarter of all funds spent by states and cities. Under the Reagan administration, many grants-in-aid were cut or reduced, although the national government continued to provide funds for highways and such programs as Aid to Families With Dependent Children (AFDC). By 1990, federal money constituted about 18 percent of state and local spending.

The decline in financial support did not necessarily mean an end to federal involvement in the states. With broadened powers acquired over the years and through the grants programs still in force, the national government continued to issue **mandates** (orders for government action) to the states. For example, Congress has mandated a national speed limit—55 mph in urban areas, 65 mph on rural highways—although traffic regulations have long been considered part of state police power. The vehicle for this action is a condition on federal highway funds, as it was in the 1993 passage of the Motor Voter Act requiring states to register voters at the time of driver's license application or renewal.

In the 1990s, states and local governments became increasingly vocal in criticizing Congress's practice of including in legislation unfunded federal mandates—orders that states take certain actions without providing the money necessary for compliance with these orders. Governors and mayors complained that meeting the obligations imposed by these mandates made it difficult or impossible for them to meet more pressing local needs, such as those in law enforcement. One study by the U.S. Conference of Mayors estimated that unfunded federal mandates consume almost 12 percent of locally raised revenues and will cost cities $54 million during the next five years.[15]

mandate A binding order; specifically, an order for state action imposed by Congress, such as setting a national speed limit to which all states must adhere.

The States on the Offensive

As we have seen in this chapter, the relationship between the states and the national government has changed dramatically over the course of American history. In the twentieth century, Washington became the dominant power in the nation, with a corresponding decline in the power of the states. This development led some observers to ask whether there is any point in having states anymore.

One argument for keeping the states and protecting their autonomy is that they serve as the "laboratories of democracy." In other words, states provide a place to test new policies or ideas about government that, if they prove useful, can then be adopted at the national level. In recent years states have experimented with welfare reform (Wisconsin), public education reform (several, including Texas and Arkansas), term limits for legislators (about half of the states), state health care systems (Oregon, Hawaii, and others), and other proposals.

Recently, states have adopted a new tactic aimed at protecting their autonomy: becoming aggressive adversaries of the federal government. This approach began in the late 1980s with the push among legislatures in several states to ratify the Twenty-seventh Amendment (the one affecting pay raises for Congress); the

amendment was promoted as a means to send Congress a message that it had lost touch with the American people. Around the same time, another anti-Congress campaign emerged in the states: the drive to amend state constitutions to limit the number of terms members of Congress could serve (in other words, a state-imposed term limit on representatives in Washington). This measure has been challenged in court and may not survive a constitutional test, but it represents a revival of interest in using state power against the national government.

In the 1990s, several states decided to take the national government to court over policies that impose costs on state governments. Florida and California sued the U.S. government over enforcement of immigration laws, claiming that the entry of illegal immigrants reflects a failure of Washington to meet its constitutional responsibility to police the national borders. Other states contended that unfunded federal mandates violate the Constitution. The Republican-dominated Congress proposed legislation to prevent imposition of further unfunded mandates. The next few years are likely to feature more conflicts between Washington and the states over national policies, as the laboratories of democracy become the battlegrounds of federalism.

These mandates are usually the results of laws that many Americans, including the governors and mayors just mentioned, could otherwise support, including laws to provide for Medicaid and Medicare, environmental protection, and the Americans With Disabilities Act. What states and localities object to is Washington's imposition of large expenses on them, depriving state and local officials of the ability to make decisions for their own communities. In 1991, Missouri Governor John Ashcroft complained that "The federal Congress and courts now effectively tell us how we must spend 35 percent of our total budget and 80 percent of our new general revenue."[16] Officials in other states have made similar charges. In California and Florida, the governors have sued the federal government for the cost of providing educational and medical services to undocumented aliens who entered the United States illegally but whom the federal government has required states to serve. The Current Issues box explores some of these conflicts.

The American regime has always included tension between the goals of national supremacy and state power. Evidence of that tension can be seen in the actions of President Clinton. While campaigning for office in 1992, he complained that as governor of Arkansas he had been burdened by too many unfunded federal mandates. Therefore, one of his first actions as president was to lift certain restrictions on state use of federal money in health and welfare programs. But he also signed the Motor Voter Act, imposing another mandate on the states. Likewise, in 1994 he signed legislation that required all states to pay for abortions for Medicaid patients in cases of rape or incest. Louisiana and four other states were required to amend their state abortion statutes to comply with that mandate.

The 1994 Republican "Contract with America" called for an end to unfunded mandates. Soon after taking power, congressional Republicans began working on legislation to make good on that promise, although legislators had different ideas about how best to do this. By mid-1995, it was clear that some kind of limit would be imposed on mandates, but details remained sketchy.

Copyright © 1995 by Herblock in *The Washington Post*.

Is Federalism a Thing of the Past? The growing power of the national government, the presence of unfunded mandates, and the financial reliance of the states on the national government have led some observers to question whether there is anything left to the idea of federalism. While at times it may seem that the national government is all that we have in the United States, clearly states and local government still matter very much in the lives of citizens. Most of the laws that shape our daily lives—laws about contracts, marriage and divorce, inheritance, property, corporations, education and care of children, traffic, and crime—are made at the state and local levels. There are some similarities in the laws among states, but there are differences: incorporation is much easier in Delaware than New York, which is why many large corporations are chartered in one of the nation's smallest states instead of one of its largest; divorce and child custody laws are not the same across the country, which is why decisions about alimony, child support, and which parent takes the children in a divorce will vary from one place to another. One state (such as Florida) may sentence murderers to death; another state (such as Wisconsin) may punish killers with life in prison.

Federalism does not only mean that laws will vary from one place to another, but that decisions made by one state may affect others in unexpected ways. For example, California's passage in 1994 of Proposition 187—a measure that cut off nonemergency state services to illegal immigrants—put pressure on the national government to tighten control of the U.S. border with Mexico, while at the same time increasing the chances that other aliens entering the country unlawfully would head for states such as Arizona, Texas, and New Mexico. Another example is differing state laws on intimate relationships between two people of the same sex. In 1994, Hawaii's Supreme Court indicated that it might find such unions to be protected under the state constitution, which raises the prospect that other states might have to recognize same-sex marriages contracted in the island state. The Full Faith and Credit Clause of the Constitution (Article IV, Section 1) requires each state to respect the judicial decisions of other states; this could enable Hawaii to reshape the marriage laws of other states. The states are not just geographic divisions of the country with interesting histories and unusual state birds, but governmental entities whose laws and policies have political consequences.

More and More Participants in the "Washington Community"

The political system established by the Constitution was designed to operate according to James Madison's dictum that "Ambition must be made to counteract ambition." With a tripartite government in place, this implied a kind of triangular politics in the "Washington community." Over the course of American history, relations in that community have not been static nor have they been merely triangular.

The central relationship in the regime is that between Congress and the presidency. Its ups and downs have shaped much of American political history. At times, assertive presidents have dominated the political landscape: Andrew Jackson in his day, Lincoln during the Civil War, Theodore Roosevelt advancing American power, Woodrow Wilson shaping legislation and the post–World War I world, Franklin Roosevelt in the New Deal and World War II, Lyndon Johnson's Great Society, Ronald Reagan's Reaganomics and anticommunism. In other periods, Congress has held the upper hand: in the days of national stalemate before the Civil War, in the "Gilded Age" of the late nineteenth century, in the mid-1970s after Watergate and the Vietnam War weakened the White House. Neither branch has become a permanent leader of the nation, for each possesses the instruments for challenging the other.

Not surprisingly, the power of all three branches has grown since the adoption of the Constitution. By its own assertions and with the approval of the courts, Congress now enjoys broad power to legislate on a wide array of subjects. Areas once regarded as the preserve of states are now open to congressional action. For example, in *Garcia v. San Antonio Metropolitan Transit Authority* (1985), the Supreme Court held that Congress could apply federal wage and working condition laws to state and local employees.[17] Where it does not possess direct authority, the legislature can use federal money to encourage states, local governments, and private entities to promote its aims. For example, private colleges that receive assistance from Washington are required to abide by the antidiscrimination provisions of federal law, while contractors on federally funded building projects must use affirmative action to increase hiring of minorities.

Congress has been able to exercise the full range of its broadened powers because of two facts of modern legislative life. First, it possesses large staffs to assist in drawing up legislation. Nearly forty thousand people work on Capitol Hill, making it possible for the national legislature to engage actively in policy making in all areas of public life. There has been a boom in laws on everything from carjacking to environmental pollution. (We explore the role of staffs further in Chapter 12.) Second, all this legislation is possible because Congress can assign more functions to the executive branch to carry out its policies. It passes many general laws that empower administrative agencies and regulatory commissions to fill in details. At the same time, Congress may write laws that advance ambiguous, competing, or even contradictory goals and assign to agencies the task of reconciling those ends in specific cases. For example, the law governing interstate highways makes the Department of Transportation responsible for finding the best routes that will do the least damage to park land,

One of the ways the federal government expands its power is by giving grants of money. Private colleges that accept federal funds must abide by anti-discrimination laws.

neighborhood communities, and jobs.[18] Congress acts because of the help it gets in framing and implementing legislation.

The power of the presidency has also expanded considerably. Once a modest office whose occupant was not expected to act as national leader, the president is now the single most important player in the Washington community. The demands of war and America's international role help to account for this change, as do laws giving the president greater responsibility for domestic affairs. For example, the Employment Act of 1946 assigns the president responsibility for promoting full employment and economic prosperity in the nation and authorizes emergency powers to implement wage and price controls if necessary. Court decisions were also important to the executive, especially in the area of foreign affairs. In *United States v. Curtiss-Wright Export Corporation* (1934), the Court ruled that the president enjoys broad authority to conduct foreign policy because every nation has the right to control its relations with other countries and because it is the executive's role to be in charge of foreign relations.[19] This decision set the stage for presidential dominance over national security affairs in the period following World War II.

Executive power means more than that the White House and other agencies of the government have enlarged their role. With Congress delegating to the bureaucracy authority to settle many of the details and applications of its general laws, agencies have gained considerable law-making ability. Each year executive branch units issue thousands of regulations that have the force of law. While Congress and the president do have some influence over the substance of these rules, usually they are able to alter or stop only the most controversial ones.

Be an Active Citizen

While constitutional practice usually involves government officials, citizens are not merely bystanders. Many contribute to the running of America's constitutional system. Here are some things that any citizen can do:

1. Keep abreast of developments in the evolving political system. You need not become a constitutional lawyer, but to be an active citizen you ought to have a good general idea of the state of constitutional government. Is the Supreme Court hearing cases on church-state issues or presidential war powers? Is Congress legislating in the area of environmental policy, education, or foreign aid? Is the president asserting independence from Congress or trying to work with Capitol Hill? Is your state government shaping policy—on schools, highways, or crime—that affects your life?

2. Communicate with political leaders. Citizens can express their views on the latest tax proposal or military operation abroad, as well as on the state of the political system. Representatives in national, state, and local government do influence the state of federalism, or the success or failure of proposed constitutional amendments. Active citizenship can and ought to range widely.

3. Participate in the political process. Citizens can and should make themselves heard, but politicians listen especially to the voters who can put them in or take them out of office.

Beyond the regular administrative units are independent regulatory commissions. These bodies are established by law to be independent of the president and Congress and to regulate areas of public policy free from political pressures. The Federal Reserve Board, the Federal Communications Commission, the Securities and Exchange Commission, and other such regulatory commissions play a large role in shaping rules by which much of American life and commercial activity are governed. Interest rates in the United States are controlled most directly by the Federal Reserve, which operates on its own. Since the 1970s the Federal Trade Commission has possessed the power to issue Trade Regulation Rules that govern industry trade practices, a power it has used extensively.

The judiciary has also expanded its power. Judicial review made the courts co-equal with the political branches of government, but judges have become policy makers in the decades since World War II. Under Chief Justice Earl Warren in the 1950s and 1960s, the Supreme Court adopted a mode of "judicial activism," by which it used its power as constitutional interpreter to prescribe policies in cases brought before it. This practice was highly controversial, especially because the policies favored by the Court had a decidedly liberal bent. As political scientist Martin Shapiro summarized the Court's influence: "It had initiated at least five major policies: school desegregation, reapportionment, reform of the criminal justice system, an emasculation of federal and state obscenity laws, and the opening of birth control and abortion services to millions of working-class women and girls."[20] In the decades that followed, this activism continued, even if it took a more conservative direction under chief justices Warren Burger and William Rehnquist. Such activism continues to be controversial, but no one is surprised when the courts are described as policy-making institutions.

This policy-making role of courts has also been enhanced by Congress's practice of delegation. Since new laws delegate extensive power to administrative agencies and are at the same time ambiguous, the courts are frequently called upon to determine whether regulations adopted by administrators match the laws they are implementing. As Martin Shapiro puts it: "The justices of the Supreme Court, but even more the judges of the federal district courts and circuit courts of appeal, have become important law makers in environmental, safety, health, and a half dozen other major areas of public policy."[21]

The upshot of these changes is that contemporary national government involves an increasingly complex association of the president, Congress, Supreme Court, bureaucracy, and regulatory commissions. Moreover, the presence of media organizations, interest groups, and large staffs at the White House and on Capitol Hill makes life "inside the Beltway" (the highway loop surrounding the Washington metropolitan area) much like that in an anthill. National policy is not made just by a tug of war between the two ends of Pennsylvania Avenue, but through an intricate and sometimes confusing interaction of these different governmental bodies. Certainly, the triangle set forth in the Constitution remains the most important part of the regime, but understanding American politics requires looking beyond these institutions to the other players in the Washington community.

open questions

How Are We to Interpret the Constitution?

Government by a written constitution is an ongoing enterprise. So long as the United States keeps the constitutional regime, it will be engaged in abiding by the manifest constitution and working out the meaning of the charter's open texture. Accordingly, there are always as many questions as there are answers in the practice of constitutional government: What are the extent and limits of presidential power, or of national government power? What is the proper role for courts? How much autonomy should bureaucratic agencies exercise? What are the limits on the rights and liberties of citizens?

All of these issues deserve attention and will receive it in other chapters. But perhaps the most important question that confronts Americans and their government is also one of the most fundamental: How are we to interpret the Constitution? Is there a correct way to do so or does everyone interpret it in his or her own way?

A variety of answers have been developed in response to these questions, but the main lines of argument can be summarized into three major positions on how best to interpret America's fundamental law: judicial activism, judicial restraint, and attempts to chart a compromise course between them. Each one has consequences for the practice of constitutional government.

Judicial activism refers to policy making by the courts, based on the idea that the proper role of judges is to protect rights and promote justice as they see it. It has been practiced by the Supreme Court for several decades now. This practice may require judges to "find" rights buried in the Constitution, such as a right to privacy, or to reinterpret constitutional text in light of the judges' own views of what is just. Former Justice William Brennan stated the position of many who adhere to this view: "We current Justices read the Constitution in the only way that we can: as Twentieth Century Americans . . . the ultimate question must be, What do the words of the text mean in our time? . . . Our Constitution was not intended to preserve a preexisting society but to make a new one, to put in place new principles that the prior political community had not sufficiently recognized."[22]

Judicial restraint holds that judges must *not* read their own views of right and justice into their decisions. Rather, as federal appeals court judge J. Clifford Wallace has put it, in resolving constitutional questions judges "should rely on the express provisions of the Constitution or upon those norms that are clearly implicit in its text . . . the original intention of the framers is the controlling guide for constitutional interpretation."[23] Much of the argument for judicial restraint rests on the concern that judges are not elected and therefore ought to defer as much as possible to those officials who are. Moreover, it is based on the concept of "original intent," that is, that the only proper way to understand the Constitution is to discern what its authors meant when they wrote it (or its amendments).

Another approach to restraint is to employ "strict construction" in reading the Constitution, that is, taking a narrow interpretation of the meaning of the text. For example, those employing a strict reading of the Constitution proclaim that there is no right to privacy because the document never mentions one.

The debate over activism versus restraint is often portrayed as a fight between liberals and conservatives. But this depiction, while often accurate, distorts the issue. As the experience of the Warren and Rehnquist Courts has shown (as well as that of earlier Supreme Courts), conservatives as well as liberals can be judicial activists. In the same way, there have been liberal judges and legal scholars who agree with the case for restraint, such as Supreme Court Justice Ruth Bader Ginsburg.

Are activism and restraint the only choices? Not necessarily. Some constitutionalists have attempted to chart a course between them. For example, constitutional scholar Alexander Bickel tried to articulate a kind of middle way. He agreed with those supporting judicial activism that the Constitution must be maintained as a "living organism" and applied to the problems of the day, but he also shared the caution of those favoring restraint about the difficulties of having unelected judges make policy. To resolve this dilemma, Bickel argued for a "computing principle" in judicial review. By this principle he meant that courts must carefully weigh the need for justice with the need for order in a democratic political system:

judicial activism
Active policy making by judges, based on the idea that the proper role of the courts is to protect rights and promote justice as judges see them.

judicial restraint
Refusal to engage in active policy making by judges, based on the idea that judges must not read their own views of rights and justice into their decisions.

82   Part 1/Constitutional Foundations

The judges, themselves abstracted from, removed from political institutions by several orders of magnitude, ought never to impose an answer on the society merely because it seems prudent and wise to them personally, or because they believe that an answer—always provisional—arrived at by the political institutions is foolish. The Court's first obligation is to move cautiously, straining for decisions in small compass, more hesitant to deny principles held by some segments of the society than ready to affirm comprehensive ones for all, mindful of the dominant role the political institutions are allowed, and always anxious first to invent compromises and accommodations before declaring firm and unambiguous principles.[24]

The difficulty in Bickel's "computing principle" is that, like many compromises, it fails to satisfy those on either side. It neither accepts judge-made policy completely nor offers a fixed point of reference (such as searching for the original intent of the framers of the Constitution).

The debate over constitutional interpretation rages on. Although politicians such as presidents and candidates for that office usually take firm positions one way or another, the controversy is not likely to be resolved by elections or the action of elected officials. For just as constitutional interpretation is a sort of national pastime and therefore a kind of intellectual struggle, so is the battle over the means for conducting it. So long as we have a written constitution, we will have disagreements over how to interpret it.

Principles. Three operating principles explain how the Constitution serves as the fundamental law of the United States: (1) constitutional supremacy—this includes understanding that there are two aspects to the document, a manifest constitution (specific rules and structures) and a constitution of open texture (the interpretable language); (2) constitutional interpretability; and (3) constitutional adaptability.

| Summary

Process. The Constitution is put into practice in several ways. Amendments have been used to change the document on a limited number of occasions. These changes tend to come in groups, including the Bill of Rights (first 10 amendments), the Civil War amendments (13 to 15), the Progressive Era amendments (16 to 19), and the amendments of the 1960s and 1970s (23 to 26). Other amendments have also been added. Constitutional interpretation is a necessary part of running the government and it occurs when officials perform their duties or commentators remark upon the propriety of government actions. One of the most important forms of interpretation is judicial review, which occurs when a court rules on the constitutionality of a government action. Judicial review has come to be accepted as very close to the last word on the meaning of the Constitution. An "unwritten constitution" also shapes how the government works, especially in three areas: (1) the internal organization of the three branches of government (such as the congressional committee system); (2) political parties and candidate selection (such as the two-party system); and (3) customs and traditions, such as the State of the Union Address or the president's cabinet, that influence the behavior of officials.

Politics. Certain themes illuminate the ways in which America's fundamental law has evolved. (1) The democratic tendency in American government: Over the course of American history, the trend has been for laws, executive actions, and court decisions to be directed toward making the political system more democratic (such as by expanding voting rights). (2) The rise of the national government and the fate of federalism: The constitutional system recognizes three types of governmental power—those delegated to the national government alone, those concurrent powers held by the national and state governments, and those reserved to the states. Over the course of American history, the relation between the two levels of government has changed. In the early years of the Republic, when the states were strong and the national government was small, there was competition between nation-centered federalism and state-centered federalism. As a result of the Civil War, the nation-centered view won out and dual federalism was advanced as a model of national-state relations. It died in the New Deal's expansion of the national government. Today, states are dependent on the central government for money and subject to various mandates from Washington. These orders, especially unfunded federal mandates, are the source of controversy.

Open Questions. An important unresolved issue in constitutional practice concerns the best way to interpret the national charter. Judicial review is the view that judges should apply their own ideas of what is good policy to shape constitutional decisions; this has been practiced by the federal courts in recent decades. Judicial restraint is the view that judges should defer to elected officials and not rule on the basis of their own views. Various attempts have been made to chart a third way through this debate, but no one has been able to devise a method of constitutional interpretation that will win a broad consensus.

Suggested Readings

BERNSTEIN, RICHARD B., with JEROME AGEL. *Amending America: If We Love the Constitution So Much, Why Do We Keep Trying to Change It?* New York: Times Books, 1992. The history of amendments, both successful and unsuccessful.

ELY, JOHN HART. *Democracy and Distrust.* Cambridge, Mass.: Harvard University Press, 1980. Proposes a theory of constitutional interpretation that is neither activist nor originalist.

FISHER, LOUIS. *Constitutional Conflicts Between Congress and the President,* 3rd ed. Princeton: Princeton University Press, 1992. Examines major constitutional battles between the branches.

GARRATY, JOHN A., ED. *Quarrels That Have Shaped the Constitution,* rev. New York: Harper & Row, 1987. Essays on 20 Supreme Court decisions that have shaped constitutional development.

GRAHAM, GEORGE J., JR., AND SCARLETT G. GRAHAM. *Founding Principles of American Government.* Chatham, N.J.: Chatham House, 1984. Despite its title, this book is as much about the practice of constitutional government as about the ideas underlying the regime.

IRONS, PETER. *The Courage of Their Convictions: Sixteen Americans Who Fought Their Way to the Supreme Court.* New York: Penguin Books, 1990. Stories of citizens whose cases were heard before the Supreme Court. A look at how constitutional interpretation affects people.

WOLFE, CHRISTOPHER. *The Rise of Modern Judicial Review.* New York: Basic Books, 1986. An outstanding history of judicial review in the American regime.

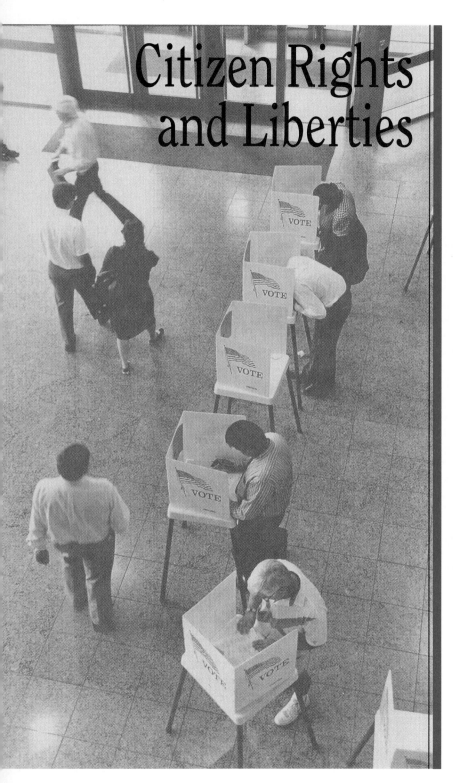

Citizen Rights and Liberties

writ of habeus corpus Order from a judge that requires the government to bring an arrested person before the court and formally charge that person with a crime. A legacy of English common law, the *writ of habeus corpus* is intended to prevent the indefinite imprisonment of criminal suspects.

ex post facto law Law that makes illegal something that happened before it was passed. Prohibited by the U.S. Constitution.

bill of attainder Legislative action that declares a person guilty of a crime without trial and orders a punishment. Prohibited by U.S. Constitution.

Writing a letter to the editor of a newspaper, burning the American flag, praying at a graduation ceremony, attending a racially integrated school, taking a breath-alcohol test when stopped by the highway patrol, prosecuting O.J. Simpson for murder. What do these things have in common? Although they may seem unrelated, each involves basic rights and liberties that the American system of government seeks to guarantee to citizens.

Each also bears on a challenge facing our political system: how to reconcile the competing claims of three levels in society—the individual; the groups within the society, such as Native Americans or people without children; and the community as a whole. The claims of each—the individual to a variety of freedoms, the groups to the same opportunities enjoyed by others, and the community to maintenance of order and the public interest—have merit and must be balanced against claims made by the others.

The American system was founded with an appreciation that reconciling liberty and the public interest would not be simple. On one hand, the original Constitution included some limitations on government and corresponding citizens' rights. For example, it prohibited imposing religious qualifications for office in order to promote greater religious freedom. It also guaranteed that the **writ of habeus corpus,** which is a court order allowing a judge to review an arrest, could not be suspended except in emergencies; this provision maintained an ancient device in English and American law for protecting against improper arrests. It prohibited the passage of an **ex post facto law,** a retroactive law that punishes actions that were not illegal when they were committed. The document also banned the passage of a **bill of attainder,** a legislative act that convicts and sentences a person without trial, in order to ensure that all persons accused of a crime receive a fair trial. (Table 4.1 itemizes protections for citizens contained in the original Constitution and those added later.)

On the other hand, the framers looked to the checks-and-balances system to protect liberty. As we saw in Chapter 2, the Constitutional Convention rejected George Mason's proposal for a bill of rights to be added to the new charter. Most delegates believed that the limited government created by the Constitution—one in which the three branches would act to restrain each other—would be more effective in stopping tyranny than any restrictions written on paper.

The Bill of Rights

The Antifederalists were able to cast doubt on the idea that checks and balances alone could protect rights. During the debate over ratifying the Constitution, they made a compelling case for an explicit bill of rights. After the First Congress assembled in 1789, it quickly passed and sent to the states a proposal for a bill of rights. By 1791, the Bill of Rights was ratified and added to the Constitution (see Table 4.1).

TABLE 4.1 Rights and Liberties in the U.S. Constitution and Its Amendments

The Original Text	The Bill of Rights	Amendments Added, 1865–1992
Article I **Section 9:** Guarantees *writ of habeus corpus* (except in emergencies); no bills of attainder; no *ex post facto* laws **Section 10:** No state may pass bills of attainder or *ex post facto* laws **Article III** **Section 2:** Jury trials required in all criminal cases **Section 3:** Restricted definition of treason; conviction of treason requires two witnesses to the same act or confession in open court **Article IV** **Section 2:** Citizens of each state are entitled to the "privileges and immunities" of citizens of the several states **Article VI** No religious "tests"—qualifications—for public office	**Fundamental Freedoms of Citizens** **Amendment 1:** No establishment of religion, free exercise of religion; freedom of speech and the press; right of the people to peaceably assemble and to petition government for a redress of grievances **Protections of Individual Security Against Government Power** **Amendment 2:** Right to keep and bear arms **Amendment 3:** No quartering of troops in homes during peacetime without consent of owner; in war only by law **Protections of Citizens Against Oppressive Police and Courts** **Amendment 4:** Right of people to be protected against unreasonable searches and seizures **Amendment 5:** Grand jury indictment required for serious crimes; no double jeopardy; no one may be compelled to testify against themself; no one may be deprived of life, liberty, or property without due process of law; no private property can be taken for public use without just compensation **Amendment 6:** Right to a speedy and public trial; right to examine witnesses in one's defense; right to counsel **Amendment 7:** Right to trial by jury **Amendment 8:** No excessive bail or "cruel and unusual" punishment **Limits on the National Government** **Amendment 9:** Rights of the people are not limited to those enumerated in the Constitution **Amendment 10:** Powers not delegated to the United States nor forbidden to the states are reserved to the states or to the people	**Amendment 13:** Prohibits slavery **Amendment 14:** States may not abridge "privileges and immunities" of citizens of the United States; states may not deny any person life, liberty, or property without due process of law; states may not deny any person equal protection of the laws **Amendment 15:** No citizen may be denied the right to vote on grounds of race **Amendment 19:** No citizen may be denied the right to vote on grounds of sex **Amendment 23:** Residents of the District of Columbia guaranteed the right to vote in presidential elections **Amendment 24:** Outlaws poll taxes (taxes on voting) in all elections **Amendment 26:** No citizen who is 18 years old or older may be denied the right to vote on grounds of age **Amendment 27:** Prohibits changing the salaries of congress persons during any given term of office

What Does the Bill of Rights Protect?

The Bill of Rights comprises the first ten amendments to the Constitution. The First Amendment provides for religious freedom, as well as freedom of speech, press, assembly, and the right to petition government. The Second Amendment guarantees citizens a "right to bear arms." The Third Amendment prohibits quartering of soldiers in private homes during peacetime—a response to one of the practices of the British colonial government in America before independence.

The next five amendments (Amendments Four to Eight) outline broad principles designed to ensure **due process of law,** that is, that citizens will be protected from arbitrary actions of the government by the requirement that government authorities follow specific legal procedures. Thus, the Fourth Amendment provides that Americans' homes and effects shall be secure against "unreasonable searches and seizures," which means that police cannot invade or confiscate citizens' property without following proper legal procedures. The Fifth Amendment is intended to protect citizens against abuses of the court system by guaranteeing that no one may be tried twice for the same crime; that individuals may not be compelled to testify against themselves; and that citizens may not be deprived of their life, liberty, or property without due process of law. The Sixth Amendment guarantees that a criminal trial shall be speedy (so that an innocent person's life is not ruined), public, and held before a jury, and that the person accused of a crime shall be assisted by an attorney and has the right to examine witnesses. The Seventh Amendment guarantees the right to a jury trial in most cases, while the Eighth Amendment prohibits "cruel and unusual" punishment.

The last two amendments seek to limit the power of the national government. The Ninth Amendment hints at rights beyond those enumerated in the original text and the first eight amendments, but it does not specify what those additional rights may be. The Tenth Amendment promises that the states and the people hold powers not delegated to the national government or prohibited to the states, although we shall see how this provision has been the weakest part of the Bill of Rights.

To Whom Does the Bill of Rights Apply?

due process of law
Constitutional guarantee
that each citizen is entitled to justice and the
proper functioning of
the legal system before
being denied life, lib-
erty, or property.

The Bill of Rights was originally written as a set of limits on the national government, not the states. In 1833 (in *Barron v. Baltimore*), the Supreme Court emphasized this point when it ruled that the first ten constitutional amendments did not apply to the states.[1] This decision meant that each state could take actions such as abridging freedom of the press prohibited to the national government. Many states possessed their own bills of rights, but still they could do things that Congress could not do. For example, in several states specific churches were given official status and supported by taxpayers. Eventually, the practice of established (that is, official) churches declined, but states were not considered bound by the national Bill of Rights until the twentieth century. After the Civil War, the Fourteenth Amendment attempted to deal with the legal status of former slaves by providing that no state may abridge the "privileges and immunities" of any American, nor deprive anyone of "life, liberty, or property, without due process of law." Nevertheless, black Americans were frequently denied constitutional rights, especially in southern states.

This situation changed in the twentieth century. In the case of *Gitlow v. New York* (1925), the Supreme Court accepted a different interpretation of the relationship between the Bill of Rights and state governments.[2] The Court now endorses the **doctrine of incorporation**—the idea that the Bill of Rights applies to the states as well as the national government because the Fourteenth Amendment guarantees that each state shall respect the rights that all Americans enjoy. In other words, the protections found in the first ten amendments, which are given to all Americans, must be respected by state governments as well. The doctrine of incorporation is not a blanket decree, however; it means that the Bill of Rights applies to the states, but not in all cases at all times. As we see in Table 4.2, the Supreme Court has used *selective incorporation* as its guiding principle; that is, specific portions of the first ten amendments are selectively applied to the states. Selective incorporation thus opened a door for challenges of state laws and policies that affected rights and liberties.

doctrine of incorporation Principle that the Bill of Rights applies to states as well as to the federal government because of the Fourteenth Amendment. Selective incorporation was accepted by the Supreme Court as a principle of constitutional interpretation in *Gitlow v. New York* (1925).

TABLE 4.2 Fourteenth Amendment Incorporation of the Bill of Rights to the States

1890	No taking of property without just compensation (*Chicago, Milwaukee and St. Paul Railroad v. Minnesota,* 134 US 418, 1890)
1925	Freedom of speech (*Gitlow v. New York*)
1931	Freedom of press (*Near v. Minnesota*)
1932	Fair trial (*Powell v. Alabama*)
1934	Free exercise of religion (*Hamilton v. Regents of California,* confirmed in 1940 by Cantwell v. Connecticut)
1937	Freedom of assembly (*De Jonge v. Oregon*)
1942	Right to counsel in capital cases (*Betts v. Brady*)
1947	Separation of church and state; establishment of religion (*Everson v. Board of Education*)
1948	Right to a public trial (*In re Oliver*)
1949	Right against unreasonable searches and seizure (*Wolf v. Colorado*)
1958	Freedom of association (*NAACP v. Alabama*)
1961	Exclusionary rule (*Mapp v. Ohio*)
1962	Right against cruel and unusual punishments (*Robinson v. California*)
1963	Right to counsel in felony cases (*Gideon v. Wainwright*)
1964	Right against self-incrimination (*Mallory v. Hogan*)
1965	Right to confront witnesses (*Pointer v. Texas*)
1965	Right of privacy (*Griswold v. Connecticut*)
1966	Right to an impartial jury (*Parker v. Gladden*)
1967	Right to a speedy trial (*Klopfer v. North Carolina*)
1967	Right to compulsory process for obtaining witnesses (*Washington v. Texas*)
1968	Right to a jury trial for all serious crimes (*Duncan v. Louisiana*)
1969	Right against double jeopardy (*Benton v. Maryland*)
1972	Right to counsel for all crimes involving a jail term (*Argersinger v. Hamlin*)

Principles: American Ideals of Liberty and Justice

As we saw in Chapter 1, ideas about freedom and the public interest can be traced to the ancient world, the Greek philosophers, the Judeo-Christian concept of human dignity and free will, and European history. The founders of the American Republic were well aware of legal protections set forth in the Magna Carta (1215) and the English Bill of Rights (1689), as well as the heritage of their colonial experience. Certainly, they agreed with John Locke and other thinkers who believed in the idea of **natural rights**—God-given rights—that individuals enjoyed by virtue of their humanity. The Declaration of Independence proclaims such rights, and the Constitution's Preamble declares liberty as one of its goals. Of course, that does not mean that the founders saw rights as absolute or in as expansive a way as we do today. We know that although some of the framers opposed slavery, others failed to see the ownership of humans as inconsistent with liberty for freeborn individuals. Moreover, very few believed that women ought to enjoy the same political rights as men.

Part of the reason for this apparent inconsistency between the language of rights and its practice was that founding-era Americans saw the actual definition of liberty in society as tightly bound up with law and tradition. Many of the "rights" articulated in the Constitution were products of English common law, itself the result of centuries of evolution. If the men of this period did not generally see political rights as extending to women and slaves, it was not because they were hypocrites. As hard as it may be for contemporary Americans to understand, the men of the founding era considered free males to be the political community, with women, children, and slaves under their protection. The founders believed passionately in liberty, but the tradition of which they were a part held that restricting the rights of certain groups—most notably, the slaves—was consistent with the overall notion of freedom. Nevertheless, commitment to individual rights and liberties became part of the American sense of "givenness," even if citizens often disagree about what limits (if any) ought to be placed on them.

As we saw in Chapter 2 and shall discuss later in this chapter, the privileged place of rights in our system shapes the way government and political debate have evolved in this country. The complex body of law and policy has developed from attempts to define the extent of rights in the United States and generally includes two broad categories of protections for citizens: civil liberties and civil rights.

natural rights The idea that humans possess certain rights given to them by God and to which they are entitled by virtue of their humanity; a key principle in the Declaration of Independence.

civil liberties Legal limits on the power of the state and the majority over the individual, such as legal protections of freedom of religion, of speech, and of the press, or the right to due process of law in criminal proceedings.

Civil Liberties

The concept of **civil liberties** encompasses the notion that there are legal limits on the powers of the state and the majority over the individual. Civil liberties that are protected by law include the freedom to practice the religion of one's choice, freedom of speech, freedom of the press, the right to assemble and to petition government, and the right to receive due process of law in criminal justice proceedings. These are the issues covered in the first ten amendments to the Constitution, which might be more accurately called the "Bill of Liberties." And the claim of any individual or group to any of these liberties must be bal-

90

anced with the claims for similar protection asserted by other individuals, groups in society, and the community.

Civil Rights

The idea of civil rights is the companion to that of civil liberties. In American politics, it can be traced to the period of Reconstruction after the Civil War, as lawmakers attempted to protect the legal and political status of the newly freed slaves. **Civil rights** involve the claims of individuals and groups in society to enjoy the same liberties and opportunities as everyone else, to be treated equally without regard to race, gender, ethnicity, or other specific conditions, such as age, pregnancy, or national origin. The major issues in this area include voting rights, equal representation in government, equal protection of the laws, and equality of opportunity in public and private endeavors. In recent years, some civil rights advocates have tried to expand this idea to include equality of outcomes. For example, they have argued that groups in society are entitled to have elected representatives in proportion to their share of the overall population.

While we can make a distinction between civil liberties on the one hand—freedom from oppressive government—and civil rights on the other—guarantees of equal citizenship, in practice the two are tightly interwoven. Both address the place of citizens, whether as individuals or as members of groups in society, in relation to the government and to each other. Because of this fact, we will examine citizen rights and liberties together. For an overview of the history of citizen rights and liberties in the United States, see Table 4.3.

civil rights Claims of individuals and groups in society to enjoy the same liberties and opportunities as everyone else—to be treated equally.

During the 1960s, African Americans conducted demonstrations and other political actions to press for civil rights. Here, students stage a sit-in to protest a lunch counter's policy of serving whites only.

TABLE 4.3 Major Events Affecting Citizen Rights and Liberties in America Since 1789

Year	Legislative Action	Court Ruling	Executive Action	Other Events
1789				Government under U.S. Constitution begins
1791	Bill of Rights ratified			
1830	Law requires moving Indians west of Mississippi River			
1833		*Barron v. Baltimore:* Supreme Court rules Bill of Rights does not apply to states		
1857		*Dred Scott v. Sanford:* Supreme Court rules African Americans are not citizens		
1861				Civil War begins
1863			Emancipation Proclamation	
1865	Thirteenth Amendment (outlawed slavery)			End of Civil War
1866	Reconstruction begins		Federal military occupation of southern states, 1866-77	
1868	Fourteenth Amendment (black citizenship)			
1870	Fifteenth Amendment (black suffrage)			
1875	Civil Rights Act of 1875			
1877	Reconstruction ends			
1883		*Civil Rights Cases:* Supreme Court invalidates 1875 Civil Rights Act; opens way for Jim Crow laws		
1896		*Plessy v. Ferguson:* Supreme Court rules racial segregation is constitutional		
1909				National Association for the Advancement of Colored People formed
1920	Nineteenth Amendment ratified (women's suffrage)			

Year	Legislative Action	Court Ruling	Executive Action	Other Events
1925		*Gitlow v. New York:* Supreme Court accepts selective incorporation of Bill of Rights (*overturns Barron v. Baltimore*)		
1944		*Korematsu v. U.S.:* Supreme Court rules federal internment of Japanese-Americans is constitutional		
1948			President Truman orders desegregation of U.S. armed forces	
1954		*Brown v. Board of Education:* Supreme Court finds segregated schools unconstitutional		
1955				Rosa Parks refuses to give up seat on bus in Montgomery, Alabama; bus boycott follows
1957	Civil Rights Act of 1957		President Eisenhower uses U.S. troops to enforce *Brown* decision in Little Rock, Arkansas	
1963		*Gideon v. Wainwright:* Supreme Court rules on right to counsel	President Kennedy calls for new civil rights law	Major civil rights march on Washington, D.C.— Martin Luther King's "I Have a Dream" speech
1964	Civil Rights Act of 1964 Twenty-fourth Amendment (ends poll taxes)	*New York Times v. Sullivan:* Supreme Court imposes "actual malice" test on liberal public figures		
1965	Voting Rights Act	*Griswold v. Connecticut:* Supreme Court finds right to privacy in U.S. Constitution	President Johnson inaugurates affirmative action in federal employment and contracts	
1966		*Miranda v. Arizona:* Criminal suspects must be informed of their constitutional rights		National Organization for Women founded

continued

TABLE 4.3 Major Events Affecting Citizen Rights and Liberties in America Since 1789 *(continued)*

Year	Legislative Action	Court Ruling	Executive Action	Other Events
1969			President Nixon calls for affirmative action "goals and timetables"	
1971	Twenty-sixth Amendment (18-year-old vote)			
1972	Equal Rights Amendment sent to states by Congress	*Furman v. Georgia:* Supreme Court rules death penalty unconstitutional		
1973		*Roe v. Wade:* Supreme Court legalizes abortion		Two decades of pro-life and pro-choice protests begin
1976				Phyllis Schlafly's Eagle Forum organizes drive to stop the Equal Rights Amendment
1978		*Gregg v. Georgia:* Supreme Court finds new Georgia death penalty law constitutional		
		Regents of University of California v. Bakke: Supreme Court accepts affirmative action		
1982	Equal Rights Amendment fails (too few states ratified)			
1989		*City of Richmond v. Croson:* Supreme Court puts limits on affirmative action programs		
		Webster v. Reproductive Health Services: Supreme Court allows limits on abortions		
1990	Americans with Disabilities Act		President Bush vetoes civil rights bill	
1991	Civil Rights Act of 1991 passes after Congress and President Bush compromise in wake of 1990 Bush veto	*Board of Oklahoma City Public Schools v. Dowell:* Supreme Court limits court control of school districts in segregation cases		

TABLE 4.3 Major Events Affecting Citizen Rights and Liberties in America Since 1789

Year	Legislative Action	Court Ruling	Executive Action	Other Events
1992		*Planned Parenthood v. Casey:* Supreme Court allows further limits on abortion		
1993		*Bray v. Alexandria Women's Health Center:* Supreme Court disallows use of 1871 law to stop protests at abortion clinics	President Clinton orders end to ban on homosexuals in U.S. military; controversy erupts, compromise reached	
1994		*Madsden v. Women's Health Center:* Supreme Court allows buffer zones around abortion clinics		

Placing guarantees of rights and liberties in the Constitution was just the beginning of a complex process for protecting them. The crucial sections of the Constitution involving rights and liberties require interpretation, so the actions of government play an important role in defining these freedoms on a daily basis. Moreover, the divided structure of the American political system means that protection and oversight of these issues are dispersed throughout the political system. The courts, Congress, the White House, the states, and citizen groups are all involved in the process for protecting civil rights and liberties.

Process: The Means for Protecting Citizen Rights and Liberities

Shaping Rights and Liberties by Judicial Review

Probably the most important method of shaping the actual meaning of rights and liberties in American society has been through the process of judicial review. Much of our understanding of citizen rights and liberties and of the rules for applying them has been the result of court rulings. For example, the extent and limits on freedom of speech have been defined almost exclusively by the courts. But do not expect complete consistency. The courts have handled thousands of cases over several decades, and the composition of the Supreme Court has changed over time, so inconsistencies and differing interpretations have crept into the body of case law that governs citizen rights and liberties. As we shall see in regard to capital punishment, rights of the accused, and affirmative action programs, the changing membership of the Supreme Court has led to differing interpretations of the extent and limits of constitutional rights and liberties.

In the 1950s and 1960s the Court, led by the liberal Republican Chief Justice Earl Warren, took an expansive view of rights and liberties. The Court set strict limits on how police and prosecutors could handle suspects and gather

Students at a high
school on Long
Island, New York,
wanted to use school
property after hours
for a meeting of their
religious organization.
School officials
objected, so the stu-
dents sued for their
right to free exercise
of religion. In 1994
the Supreme Court
ordered that the reli-
gious club be granted
the same access as
the various civic and
recreational groups
that the school district
permitted to use its
facilities.

Establishment Clause
Section of the First
Amendment that pro-
hibits Congress (and by
extension any other
governmental body)
from establishing an
official religion. Often
characterized as "the
separation of church
and state."

Free Exercise Clause
That part of the First
Amendment that pro-
hibits the government
from interfering with the
practice of religion.

evidence; it ordered desegregation of schools and other public facilities; and it
articulated a new right to privacy not found directly in the Constitution. The
Court under Republican Chief Justice Warren Burger (1969–1986) was somewhat
more conservative. For example, it allowed prosecutors greater freedom in
obtaining evidence for criminal trials. But the Burger Court disappointed many
conservatives because of its liberal decisions on abortion and capital punishment. Under Chief Justice William Rehnquist (1986–present), a more reliably
conservative Republican, the Court has been more restrictive in its interpretations of the Bill of Rights. The justices are more likely to accept programs
designed to increase opportunities for minority groups in hiring and education
in 1980 than they have been in the past few years. These differences do not
arise merely from changes in personnel, but from the conflicts over constitutional interpretation that we saw in Chapter 3. The openness of the Constitution
to continuing interpretation often makes it difficult to resolve such issues.

Freedom of Religion. The Constitution makes two specific prescriptions
regarding religion, and the courts have long been involved in sketching their
meaning. First, there can be no "establishment of religion" (the First Amendment). Certainly this means that no "Church of the United States" could be created and funded by taxpayers, as the Church of England is an officially supported institution in that country. The Supreme Court has held that the so-called
Establishment Clause (the part of the First Amendment that forbids establishment of an official religion) prohibits prayer in public schools,[3] as well as invocations and benedictions at graduation ceremonies.[4] But the Court has also
ruled that government may provide parochial school students with such aid as
bus transportation and textbooks, because while this assistance benefits the
children's education, it does nothing to establish a religion.[5] In 1994, the Court
defined a limit on how far government can go to benefit religion when it ruled
in *Board of Education of Kiryas Joel v. Grumet* that New York could not create a
school district in order to serve only the children of a village of Hasidic Jews.[6]

The **Free Exercise Clause** of the First Amendment prohibits government
from interfering with the practice of religion. Certainly this means that a state
cannot prohibit Buddhist or any other religious services. But it also means that
government and society must tolerate some behavior that, because it is motivated by religious principles, deviates from the norm. For example, the
Supreme Court held that a woman dismissed from a job because her religion
prohibited working on Sundays was entitled to unemployment benefits.[7] It also
ruled that a member of Jehovah's Witnesses cannot be compelled to salute the
American flag if this act violates his faith.[8]

But "free exercise" does not mean that religion protects any and every
activity. Federal courts have authorized public officials to secure medical treatment for children whose parents regard all medical science as blasphemous.[9]
The courts have also allowed states to outlaw ingestion of hallucinogenic drugs,
even if some Native Americans use them for religious purposes.[10] And the
Supreme Court upheld an Air Force regulation that prohibited an Orthodox
Jewish officer from wearing a yarmulke (a cap that male Orthodox Jews are

required by religious law to wear) while in uniform.[11] Congress later overturned this decision, resolving a conflict between faith and military service.

Adjudication has played a central role in outlining the limits of religious freedom, setting very broad limits in most cases but allowing state and federal authorities to restrict some religious practices. Americans often hear about a "separation of church and state," but in practice the law takes account of religion and its role in citizens' lives.

Freedom of Speech and Press. Two important rules have given individual speech and the news media special status in American politics. First, the courts have long held to a doctrine from English common law that prohibits **prior restraint** of the press, that is, preventing something from being published before it appears in print. For example, in *New York Times Co. v. United States* (1971),[12] the Supreme Court struck down an attempt by the Nixon administration to prevent the *Times* from publishing the so-called Pentagon Papers, an embarrassing internal government report on Vietnam War decision making. The case erupted when Daniel Ellsberg, a Defense Department official opposed to the war, turned the report over to the newspaper. The Court affirmed that freedom of the press has its limits, but that those limits do not include preventing a book or article from being published.

A second rule protecting freedom of speech and the press is that they enjoy a **preferred position** in law—these freedoms deserve special ("preferred") protection.[13] Indeed, the courts have undertaken a careful balancing act in weighing the preferred position of speech and the press against other considerations. They have extended protection to "symbolic speech" or nonverbal expression, such as forms of dress or specific acts, but they have also held that reasonable regulation of behavior can limit what might otherwise be construed as "political statements." For example, a school district cannot prohibit students from wearing armbands as an antiwar protest, and government cannot outlaw flag burning as a means of political expression, but the government can punish someone who interferes with government administration by burning a draft card. In the same way, "subversive" speech—speech that specifically attacks government policy—is protected so long as it does not incite "imminent lawless action."[14] So-called "hate speech," speech that vilifies others on racial, ethnic, or religious grounds, also receives constitutional protection so long as it does not include "fighting words" that incite violence.[15] For example, the Court has upheld the right of neo-Nazis to display the swastika symbol and of the Ku Klux Klan to use a burning cross as its symbol, but these groups are not free to engage in verbal assaults on African Americans or other minority groups.

The Constitution does not protect **libel,** which is the reporting of falsehoods that ruin a person's reputation. Libel is not a crime. Rather, it is an injury for which the offended party can seek relief under civil law, which is that part of the law dealing with disputes between individuals. However, the courts do not treat all libel cases equally. A "public figure" will find it more difficult to establish harm than someone who is not a celebrity. The reason for this distinction is that celebrities, especially those involved in politics or public office, have

prior restraint Action to prevent publication of material before it occurs. The Supreme Court has held that it is unconstitutional.

preferred position Legal doctrine that freedom of speech and of the press enjoy special consideration against other claims in society. While these freedoms are not absolute, they are to be given preference over other values and limited only when necessary.

libel Reporting falsehoods about someone that ruin that person's reputation; not protected by the First Amendment's guarantee of freedom of the press.

greater access to the media than private citizens in order to defend themselves against false charges. In *New York Times v. Sullivan* (1964)[16] and other cases, the Supreme Court has required that public officials and other public figures in libel suits must demonstrate "actual malice." This means that they must show that those reporting falsehoods about them knew the statements were untrue or had a "reckless disregard" for whether or not the information was true.

Due Process of Law. The various protections accorded to those suspected or accused of crimes have received intensive scrutiny, particularly in the decades since World War II. Together, these guarantees are referred to as **due process of law,** a term that appears in the Fifth and Fourteenth Amendments and has been interpreted to cover the behavior of police, prosecutors, and courts in all areas of the criminal justice system. For example, the Fourth Amendment covers the area of **search and seizure**—police actions to find and obtain evidence. The Supreme Court has insisted that these actions must be based on "probable cause" that the search or seizure will produce evidence of crime.[17]

This matter was in question in the actions of Los Angeles police investigating the 1994 O.J. Simpson case that involved the murders of Mr. Simpson's ex-wife and one of her friends. Shortly after police learned of the murders, investigators suspected Mr. Simpson of the crime and went to his suburban Los Angeles home in search of evidence. Detectives climbed over the wall of Mr. Simpson's mansion and began collecting evidence before a judge issued a search warrant. While certain circumstances may allow police to make a search or seizure without a court warrant, such as the "hot pursuit" of a lawbreaker, the existence of evidence in plain view, and emergencies, in most situations a warrant issued by a judge is required. The clear thrust of rulings in this area is to prevent unnecessary invasions on an individual's "reasonable expectation of privacy."[18] Weighing that expectation against the community's interest in order and safety has fueled a large body of case law, as courts have been called upon to determine whether the police acted appropriately in thousands of individual cases.

The processes of *arrest and obtaining of evidence* have also come under careful judicial scrutiny. The courts have held that local and state police must be held to the same standards in handling arrests as are federal officers.[19] Officers may use force in making arrests, even "deadly force," but only if they can show that such actions are reasonable and necessary to apprehend a criminal.[20] The issue of force fueled the controversy over Rodney King's arrest in Los Angeles in 1992. Mr. King had been chased and subdued by police using a considerable amount of physical force, which in turn touched off rioting in South Central Los Angeles. The officers involved were subjected to criminal trials for their actions.

An important part of the law governing arrest and evidence regulates the interrogation of suspects and the obtaining of confessions of guilt. Ever since the Supreme Court's ruling in *Miranda v. Arizona* (1966),[21] police have been required to inform all suspects of their legal rights at the time of arrest, especially the rights to remain silent and to obtain legal counsel. All law enforcement officers carry cards with these "Miranda warnings" printed on them. If a

due process of law
Constitutional guarantee that each citizen is entitled to justice and the proper functioning of the legal system before being denied life, liberty, or property.

search and seizure
Aspect of constitutional law dealing with the obtaining of evidence in criminal cases.

exclusionary rule
Rule of evidence established by the Supreme Court that excludes from use in a trial evidence that has been obtained in violation of principles of the due process of law, such as evidence obtained without informing defendants of their rights.

Gideon v. Wainwright
1963 case in which the Supreme Court held that states must provide counsel to defendants who cannot afford to hire attorneys.

98

confession or evidence has not been obtained in a manner the courts consider legal, then an **exclusionary rule,** a rule excluding from court consideration evidence obtained illegally, articulated in *Mapp v. Ohio* (1961), precludes use of that "tainted evidence" by the prosecution.[22] Despite some exceptions and qualifications of these requirements, in general police procedure since the 1960s has been altered to exhibit greater caution in the conduct of arrests and investigations.

Once a person is accused of a crime, other constitutional protections apply. One of the Supreme Court's most important guidelines for trial and punishment evolved out of the case of ***Gideon v. Wainwright*** (1963). Until that time, the courts had generally interpreted the Sixth Amendment's guarantee of a *right to counsel,* the right to be represented in court by an attorney, as meaning only that an accused person could hire a lawyer. But in *Gideon* the Court overturned precedent and held that states must provide counsel to defendants who cannot afford to hire attorneys on their own. The ruling explained that "in our adversary system of criminal justice, any person hauled into court, who is too poor to hire a lawyer, cannot be assured a fair trial unless counsel is provided for him."[23] This ruling not only affected the treatment of defendants, but led states and local governments to establish public defender systems.

One of the Constitution's most open-textured statements is its prohibition of "cruel and unusual" punishments. The death penalty has been a common means of punishment throughout history. The framers did not regard the Eighth Amendment's language as prohibiting a death sentence, only cruelties such as torture. But over time the issue of capital punishment has become highly controversial, and opposition to any executions has risen. In 1972, the Supreme Court voided a state death penalty statute in the case of *Furman v. Georgia.*[24] Some justices asserted in a concurring opinion that "evolving standards of decency" had made any use of capital punishment unacceptable. Four years later, however, the Court upheld a new Georgia death penalty statute in *Gregg v. Georgia* (1976) because the death sentence had been handed down according to strict guidelines laid out in the new state law.[25] In subsequent decisions, the Court has accepted use of capital punishment only when state law establishes clear rules for how it is to be applied and only in cases of first-degree murder. It has forced states to carefully rewrite their criminal justice statutes.

Desegregation and Equal Opportunity. Judicial review has played a catalytic role in the shaping of civil rights in American history. Before the Civil War, African Americans had been owned as slaves or given few rights as free citizens. After the adoption of the Civil War amendments to the Constitution (the Thirteenth, Fourteenth, and Fifteenth), Congress passed a number of laws to eliminate racial discrimination. For example, the Civil Rights Act of 1875 outlawed discrimination in places of "public accommodation" and "public conveyances." This law was aimed at ending the southern practice of separating blacks and whites in hotels, restaurants, trains, and schools. In the *Civil Rights Cases* (1883), the Supreme Court struck down the key provisions of that law on the basis of a narrow reading of the Fourteenth Amendment, holding that Congress could regulate only governmental and not private behavior.[26] This opened the way for states to enact a variety of so-called **Jim Crow laws** requiring segregation between the races in nearly all aspects of life.

Segregation had largely been a matter of custom and economic differences in the decades after the Civil War, but now states were institutionalizing it in law. When such laws were tested in court, the Supreme Court set the stage for decades of legal segregation in *Plessy v. Ferguson* (1896) by advancing the doctrine of **separate-but-equal** accommodations for blacks and whites—the idea that blacks and whites could be legally separated as long as they were given equal facilities.[27] In the years to come, states would require that everything from restrooms and buses to public schools and theatres be segregated, although the facilities provided for African Americans were almost never equal.

After World War II, the Supreme Court under Chief Justice Earl Warren became the catalyst for the undoing of segregation. In ***Brown v. Board of Education*** (1954) it overturned the precedent in *Plessy* and ruled that separate always meant unequal: "In the field of public education, the doctrine of 'separate but equal' has no place. Separate educational facilities are inherently unequal."[28] In a later case the Court ordered the end of segregated schools "with all deliberate speed." Eventually, the *Brown* decision came to serve as the landmark for a series of rulings in which the Court struck down *de jure* (sanctioned by law) and *de facto* (actual) segregation in nearly all areas of life. By 1969 the justices would declare that "all deliberate speed" was not fast enough and that educational segregation must be ended "at once."[29]

This sense of urgency has been moderated in recent years as desegregation has progressed, and the new justices have taken the view that federal courts should not be in the business of permanently overseeing public schools. In *Board of Education of Oklahoma City Public Schools v. Dowell* (1991),[30] the Court under Chief Justice William Rehnquist held that courts should not govern local schools "in perpetuity." The Court ruled that once a school district has complied with a desegregation order (from a federal court) for a "reasonable period of time," then the court order must be removed. In a subsequent decision, *Freeman v. Pitts* (1992), the Court held that courts should not maintain control over every facet of a school system that has complied with desegregation in some areas but not in others.[31] In other words, the Court ruled that lower federal courts should maintain supervision only over those aspects of schools in which segregation persists. While the Rehnquist Court has tried to put limits on the extent of judicial control over desegregation of schools, it has nevertheless held that school districts can be required to pay for desegregation against their will (*Missouri v. Jenkins,* 1990).[32]

Affirmative Action. By the late 1970s substantial progress toward desegregation had been achieved in public education and other key areas, which turned attention to new issues related to equality of opportunities. Much of the public controversy over civil rights now focused on federally mandated programs that give preferential treatment to members of minority groups in hiring, promotion, admission, or other selection decisions. Beginning in the 1960s, the federal government had

Jim Crow laws Laws adopted in southern states after Reconstruction that mandated racial segregation and prohibited or discouraged black political participation.

separate-but-equal Legal doctrine articulated by the Supreme Court in *Plessy v. Ferguson* (1896) that allowed segregation of blacks and whites in southern states. Abolished by the Supreme Court in *Brown v. Board of Education* (1954).

Brown v. Board of Education 1954 case in which the Supreme Court ruled that segregation of black and white students in public schools is inherently unequal and unconstitutional.

begun requiring that states, local governments, and even private organizations (employers, colleges) do more than merely end discrimination on the basis of race. These new programs required, for example, that medical and other professional schools make special efforts ("affirmative action") to admit minorities in order to make up for past exclusion of African Americans and other groups.

While the point of such **affirmative action** programs is to enhance opportunities for minorities and compensate for past discrimination, they have met resistance from those who regard them as a form of "reverse discrimination" instituted to punish innocent people for someone else's offense. Other critics attack these programs as violating the principle of equal opportunity because they favor some groups over others. Of course, such disputes have gone to court.

In *Regents of the University of California v. Bakke* (1978), the Supreme Court accepted the use of race as one of several criteria for promoting diversity in higher-education admissions, but it struck down a formal quota system that "set aside" a specific number of seats in a medical school class for members of particular minority groups.[33] In other decisions the Court has accepted affirmative action programs but imposed limitations on them. In *Fullilove v. Klutznick* (1980), the Court permitted a set-aside requirement in a federal public works program,[34] although a differently constituted Supreme Court struck down a similar municipal set-aside program nearly a decade later in *City of Richmond v. J.A. Croson Company* (1989).[35] Here is a clear case where the Court has not yet developed a consistent set of rulings to guide constitutional interpretation. The Court has accepted the idea of affirmative action programs but has not clearly defined what are and are not acceptable practices. Part of the reason for this confusion is the changing makeup of the Supreme Court between the *Bakke* and *Croson* cases.

affirmative action
Action by a governmental or private organization that gives preferential treatment to members of minority groups in hiring, promotion, admission, or other selection decisions. The intent of such actions or policies is to make up for past discrimination.

Angered that his medical school application was rejected to make room for minority students, Alan Bakke sued the university that turned him down. The Supreme Court ruled that race could be considered to enhance diversity in university admissions, but that a formal quota system for minority candidates was unconstitutional.

Clearly, we have yet to establish a precise and consistent set of guidelines for determining what is and is not constitutional in the creation and operation of affirmative action programs. Is that an indication that there is something inherently wrong with affirmative action? Or does it mean that we as a nation have not yet decided how to put an end to the legacy of segregation? Is this an issue that we should expect our courts to resolve? Is it an issue that we can resolve in any other way?

Law Making as a Method for Determining Rights and Liberties

The position of the Constitution as supreme law makes it a powerful device for defining citizen rights and liberties, which was precisely what led the Antifederalists to call for a Bill of Rights during the ratification debate in the eighteenth century. The power of the Constitution also explains why other amendments affecting rights and liberties have been added since that time (see Table 4.1).

Because a few constitutional amendments—especially the First, Fifth, and Fourteenth Amendments—have played such a large role in shaping civil liberties and civil rights in the United States, advocates for particular interpretations of rights have often sought to use fundamental law to settle some of the controversies that arise from the document's open texture. Most attempts of this sort never receive any formal attention from government officials, but a few have been acted on by Congress or state governments (Table 4.4). The proposed

TABLE 4.4 Proposed Constitutional Amendments That Would Affect Citizen Rights and Liberties

Proposal	Formal Government Action
Equal Rights Amendment (ERA)	Passed Congress 1972 35 states ratified (38 needed) Expired 1982
Human Life Amendment (bans abortions)	Nineteen states have petitioned Congress to call a constitutional convention to propose an amendment.
Reapportionment Amendment (would allow states to apportion seats in one house of state legislature on some basis other than population)	Twenty-seven state legislatures have petitioned Congress to call a constitutional convention to propose an amendment; one legislative house in six other states has also endorsed.
Flag Burning Amendment (would authorize Congress and states to outlaw and punish desecration of the American flag)	President Bush strongly endorsed Voted on in each house of Congress, but lacked the two-thirds majority needed to send amendment to states. Congress subsequently passed a flag burning law, but in 1990 the Supreme Court declared it unconstitutional.

amendment that came nearest to passage was the Equal Rights Amendment (ERA) of the 1970s, which after winning approval of both houses of Congress, failed to achieve ratification by the required number of states. (We discuss the ERA in more detail when we consider citizen participation as a method of pursuing citizen rights and liberties.)

Since the beginning of the American Republic, legislation has also been used to shape rights and liberties within the bounds of fundamental law. In 1798 Congress passed the Alien and Sedition Acts, which levied penalties for "any false, scandalous and malicious" writing against the government.[36] Thomas Jefferson and his followers bitterly attacked these laws as unconstitutional, violating the rights of free speech and press guaranteed in the First Amendment, and the legislation was so unpopular that it was allowed to lapse in 1801.

Other laws restricting speech and the press have not always been regarded as so offensive. For example, in 1989 Congress passed the Flag Protection Act as an alternative to President Bush's proposed constitutional amendment. The flag law, which prohibited flag burning as an act of protest, was voided by the Supreme Court in 1990,[37] but it had enjoyed broad public support as an appropriate restriction on an activity that many citizens considered objectionable. Another restriction on First Amendment rights that is widely accepted by the public is the limitation placed by most states and local governments on pornographic materials. Although restrictions on flag burning and pornography raise serious questions about First Amendment freedoms, they touch on deeply held convictions of many citizens that prevail over doubts about the constitutionality of such legislation.

A small business owner in Oregon wanted to expand his business by building a new store, but a local government regulation would have required him to set aside certain portions of the property for public access. Arguing that this requirement was a violation of the Fifth Amendment's provision that private property shall not be taken for public use without just compensation, the entrepreneur sued the city. In 1994, the Supreme Court ruled in *Dolan v. City of Tigard* that the city's regulation was an unconstitutional "taking" without compensation.

Certain key laws illustrate how legislation can help to shape rights and liberties. The first is the *Civil Rights Act of 1964,* which outlined broad protections for minorities in several areas:

- It outlawed discrimination on the basis of race, religion, or national origin in places of public accommodation.
- It made it more difficult for states to keep African Americans from voting.
- It authorized the attorney general to bring suit to force public school desegregation.
- It outlawed employment discrimination.
- It outlawed discrimination in any activity financed all or in part by federal funds.

Congress then passed the *Voting Rights Act of 1965,* which enables the attorney general to suspend tests for voting and to employ federal voting registrars and poll watchers in any state or local government area in which fewer than 50 percent of the voting-age population are registered to vote. This law had important consequences for increasing minority registration and voting, especially in the South.

Laws have also been used to define and protect the rights of women. The 1964 Civil Rights Act banned employment discrimination based on gender. A 1978 amendment to this law prohibited job discrimination against pregnant women; in 1993 the Supreme Court ruled that the 1964 law protects women against an "abusive working environment." In *Harris v. Forklift Systems, Inc.,* the Court set a standard of reasonableness for determining whether a woman had been the victim of sexual harassment in employment.[38]

In 1990 the *Americans With Disabilities Act* became law, barring discrimination against the disabled in employment, public accommodations, and transportation. This act led to subsequent regulations and court decisions expanding opportunities for citizens with physical and mental disabilities. Other legislation has been proposed that would establish or expand rights for a variety of groups in society, not only ethnic minorities but also gay men and lesbians, children, unmarried couples, and the homeless.

The Role of Executive Authorities in Shaping Rights and Liberties

Governmental interest in rights and liberties is not limited to the courts and legislative bodies. Officials in the executive branch have also been involved. Presidents have been instrumental in proposing, lobbying for, and enforcing a variety of laws that affect rights and liberties. For example, Lyndon Johnson pushed for the 1964 Civil Rights Act, and George Bush supported the Americans With Disabilities Act. The Justice Department includes a Civil Rights Division that brings suit against civil rights violators, such as those responsible for segregated school systems, and monitors voting and representation systems used by states and local governments.

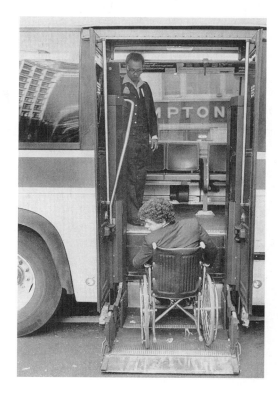

The 1990 Americans With Disabilities Act sought to guarantee equal rights to physically and/or mentally handicapped citizens.

Two independent executive agencies also monitor civil rights in the United States. The Commission on Civil Rights, established in 1957, collects and studies information on instances of discrimination or denials of equal protection of the laws, as well as on actual practices in voter registration and participation, education, employment, and housing. The commission has no enforcement authority but is a fact-finding body that makes recommendations to the president and Congress. Many of these proposals have found their way into policy as executive orders or legislation. The Equal Employment Opportunity Commission, on the other hand, does have enforcement authority. It receives and investigates complaints in the area of employment opportunity, using everything from conciliation and persuasion to lawsuits in order to alleviate discrimination.

Unilateral executive action has been important as well. One of the most significant developments in civil rights for African Americans, the Emancipation Proclamation of 1863, was issued by Abraham Lincoln on his authority as commander in chief of the Union Army (it affected only those states in rebellion). Many years later Harry Truman used the same authority to order desegregation of all U.S. military forces. Other presidents have used executive orders to establish affirmative action programs in federal endeavors.

In 1957 President Dwight Eisenhower faced a test of the *Brown* decision—the Supreme Court's ruling that segregated schools are unconstitutional—

when Governor Orville Faubus of Arkansas tried to block nine black students from entering the then all-white Little Rock Central High School, even calling out the state militia to assist him. Although Eisenhower had many reservations about the wisdom of the Court's ruling in *Brown,* he believed it to be his responsibility to enforce the ruling. He employed the 101st Airborne Division and took over control of the Arkansas militia to overrule the governor and escort the African American children into Central High.

In 1993 President Bill Clinton aroused monumental opposition to his plan to end the U.S. military's ban on gays and lesbians in the service, a change he had pledged to make during his campaign for office. His plan to issue such an order, based on his power as commander in chief, met resistance at the Pentagon and on Capitol Hill. The president saw the issue as one involving the rights of gays and lesbians to perform military service; his opponents defined the question as that of the claims of one group versus a larger public interest. Ultimately, a temporary compromise was reached. The Pentagon was ordered to adopt a policy of "don't ask, don't tell," which meant that service members would not be asked about their sexual orientation and should not discuss it. But some gay-rights activists suggested they would continue to press for the right to serve openly as gays and lesbians in the armed forces, while opponents of the new policy vowed to push for a return to the earlier ban.

Citizen Participation and Citizen Rights and Liberties

Another method used in the process of shaping rights and liberties is citizen participation that puts pressure on public officials. It is probably African Americans who have used this approach most successfully. Their civil rights movement gained momentum in the 1950s and 1960s, although it had roots early in the twentieth century. Civil rights advocates used a two-pronged strategy to advance their cause: legal action and an organized political campaign. The National Association for the Advancement of Colored People (NAACP) brought suits in federal court attacking segregated schools. At the same time, leaders like Dr. Martin Luther King Jr. organized the 1955–1956 boycott of the segregated bus system of Montgomery, Alabama, and nonviolent sit-ins and demonstrations seeking to desegregate restaurants and other public institutions. In 1963 King led a massive March on Washington to draw attention to the plight of African Americans. The civil rights movement included white religious and political leaders who assisted in voting registration drives in the South, participated in marches, and helped put pressure on Congress. Ultimately, the combined efforts of the two strategies led to enactment of major civil rights legislation—the Civil Rights Act of 1964, the Voting Rights Act of 1965, and other laws—and favorable court decisions. Although the movement lost momentum in the wake of these successes and the 1968 assassination of Dr. King, it had stimulated major changes in American law and society.

The record of the women's movement is more mixed, although it began even earlier than civil rights activism. As early as 1848, a convention was held at Seneca Falls, New York, to press for women's rights, especially *suffrage* (the right to vote) and the ability to hold public office. Early in the twentieth century the movement gained support, and in 1920 it won passage of the Nineteenth Amendment, which prohibits interference with any citizen's right to vote regardless of gender. Three years later the women's movement proposed a broader Equal Rights Amendment (ERA) that provided that "equality of rights under the law shall not be denied or abridged by the United States or any state on account of sex." For years Congress took no action on the amendment.

In the 1960s, with citizen activism on the rise in the civil rights and anti–Vietnam War protest movements, women started organizing to push for equality in employment, pay, education, and all other areas of life. The National Organization for Women (NOW), formed in 1966, fought for approval of the ERA. In 1972 the proposed amendment was approved by the House of Representatives and the Senate. It was then sent to the states for ratification (amendments can be added to the Constitution only upon ratification by three-fourths of the states). As NOW and other women's groups pushed for ratification, a counter movement led by conservative activist Phyllis Schlafly organized to oppose the amendment. Schlafly's successful lobbying in several states played a major role in ERA's failure to achieve ratification by the minimum number of

Although Americans revere their national flag, the Supreme Court has ruled that citizens have the right to burn it as an act of political protest.

states required. By the time the deadline for ratification was reached in 1982, only 35 of the 38 required states had approved the amendment.

Activists continue to push for adoption of the ERA, but it must now start all over again to win congressional approval and then state ratification. Nevertheless, the women's movement has had a considerable impact on American society. Women now hold many jobs formerly occupied exclusively by men, and equality for women has become a part of American "givenness" for many citizens. Women's rights advocates continue to press for further gains, arguing that women are still underpaid in comparison to their male counterparts, that women in the workforce occupy a disproportionate share of low-status and low-paying jobs (such as secretarial positions), and that too few businesses and other large institutions have women in the highest-level executive positions.

The method of citizen participation is used by many other groups in society to press for rights and liberties as they see them: women, African Americans, Hispanic Americans, the disabled, Native Americans, gays and lesbians, pro-life and pro-choice advocates, the elderly, and others. Their efforts continue to be a part of our national political life and play a role in shaping rights and liberties in the United States.

The Politics of Rights and Liberties

The combination of constitutional protection and a separation of powers system makes the politics of rights and liberties complex and difficult. The Constitution not only lays out a set of citizen rights and liberties, but it also charges the institutions of government with protecting liberty and the public interest. Yet it is the three branches of government, which are often in conflict with one another, that must carry out this mandate to reconcile rights of individuals, the interests of groups in society, and the larger public interest. The resulting situation is something of a hybrid—part constitutional law and part public policy. For lack of a better term, we can characterize what results as a kind of *constitutional politics*. It warrants a closer look.

The Complexities of America's Constitutional Politics

To begin with, American constitutional politics is quite different from the politics that affect similar issues in other countries. The politics that shapes rights and liberties in the United States involves a complex interaction of the different branches of government with each other and with the society, and between the federal government and state and local governments. For example, consider the rights of suspects in criminal cases. The great majority of criminal cases in the United States are handled in state courts, which must operate according to state law as well as the national Constitution. Congress and the presidency become involved through passage of federal anticrime legislation. So does the Supreme Court, which can review actions of state authorities on constitutional grounds. In the end, law and order in America are not some simple, clear-cut set of actions by one set of officials.

The American situation is quite different from what occurs in other countries. In many parliamentary systems, citizen rights are shaped and defined by action of unified political structures and thus are more likely to reflect the wishes of the majority or of the state. In Great Britain press freedom has a long heritage, but it is essentially what Parliament says it is. If it is in the interest of the British government to regulate the press, the courts are in no position to stop that action. In recent years, British political circles have called for an American-style bill of rights that can be enforced in the courts. And in some countries, politicians are eager to turn over to voters the power to decide divisive questions of citizen rights, such as abortion or capital punishment, through use of a national referendum. In this way, public officials can avoid taking a stand that may create bitter enemies no matter how the government chooses to decide the issue.

The absence of a national referendum device and the fact that no one part of the political system definitely has the last word on questions of rights and liberties makes constitutional politics in this country more complex and open ended than elsewhere. A good example of this fact is the issue of abortion. Before 1973 a woman's ability to obtain an abortion was under state control. Many states banned abortion outright. Some permitted it under certain circumstances, such as in the case of rape or if the woman's health was endangered. Still others permitted abortion under most circumstances. But the Supreme Court changed all that by its ruling in *Roe v. Wade* (1973), in which it struck down a restrictive Texas abortion statute and all similar laws.[39] The Court's ruling was built on an earlier decision, *Griswold v. Connecticut* (1965),[40] in which the justices had ruled that married couples enjoyed a **right to privacy**—a constitutional guarantee of privacy in personal matters, including matters of such an intimate nature as contraception. In *Roe,* the Court broadened the right to privacy to include unmarried individuals and abortion. The ruling held that government had to show a "compelling interest" to justify regulating abortion, and that "reasonable" regulations would be allowed, but not in the first trimester of pregnancy. The upshot of the Court's decision in *Roe* was to touch off a protracted political battle between those who opposed abortion (pro-life) and those who favored allowing it (pro-choice). As the box "The Issue of Abortion" demonstrates, both sides in this battle have used a variety of means to press for their position.

There is no evidence that the battle over abortion is likely to end soon. If the Supreme Court overturns *Roe v. Wade,* as some Court watchers believe that it may, regulation of abortion will return to the states, not end the political debate over the issue. If Congress were to pass the Freedom of Choice Act, pro-life forces would certainly test it in court, intensify their abortion clinic protests, and push harder for the Human Life Amendment. The twists and turns of our constitutional politics have resulted in a situation in which abortion enjoys constitutional protection under the right to privacy, but states, Congress, and the White House can impose—or remove—various restrictions on a woman's ability to seek an abortion. The Current Issues box explores these facets of abortion rights.

right to privacy Legal doctrine articulated by the Supreme Court in *Griswold v. Connecticut* (1965) that holds that individuals enjoy constitutional protection of their privacy from government intrusion unless a compelling reason warrants violation of personal privacy.

Abortion and Constitutional Politics

In order to advance their positions in the wake of *Roe v. Wade,* pro-life and pro-choice forces have advanced specific positions: Pro-life forces recommend a Human Life Amendment, while pro-choice advocates want a guarantee of abortion rights. Each side has also taken more direct steps to shape government policy.

LEGISLATION

Pro-life advocates have enacted the Hyde Amendment (prohibiting use of federal funds for abortions) and various state laws restricting or regulating abortion (for example, requiring waiting periods or mandatory counseling). In response, pro-choice forces have enacted state statutes protecting abortion and have proposed the Freedom of Choice Act that would effectively write the *Roe* decision into law.

EXECUTIVE ORDERS

Presidents Reagan and Bush used executive power to impose a "gag rule" against abortion counseling at federally funded clinics, to ban research using fetal tissue from abortions, to prohibit abortions at military hospitals, and to halt funding for overseas population-control programs employing abortion. One of President Clinton's first acts upon assuming office was to sign Executive Orders overturning these anti-abortion decrees, commenting as he did so that "We must free science and medicine from the grasp of politics."

LAWSUITS

Both sides have been engaged in almost continual litigation since 1973, trying to limit or to secure abortion rights. While the Supreme Court has not overturned *Roe,* it has moved away from the broad implications of that decision in several rulings. In *Webster v. Reproductive Health Services* (1989), it sustained a Missouri law that placed various restrictions on abortion. Both sides were disappointed by the decision: Pro-life groups were unhappy that the Court did not overturn *Roe;* pro-choice forces were angry that the Court allowed Missouri to prohibit state employees from performing abortions, assisting in them, or counseling women to seek abortions.

In *Planned Parenthood v. Casey* (1992), the Supreme Court further displeased both sides in the abortion debate in its ruling on a Pennsylvania abortion statute. Pro-life advocates were dismayed that the Court upheld the idea of a constitutional right to privacy that included the right to seek an abortion. Pro-choice advocates were alarmed that the Court allowed a state to require that a woman notify her spouse before obtaining an abortion, that minors get parental consent to obtain an abortion, and that a 24-hour waiting period elapse between a woman's request for an abortion and its performance.

CITIZEN PARTICIPATION

Abortion has become an issue in presidential politics, in congressional elections, and in every state as well. Political organizations such as the National Right-to-Life Committee and the National Abortion Rights Action League (NARAL) are deeply involved in supporting candidates and state referenda, lobbying officials in Washington and statehouses, using the media to spread their messages, helping to draft party platforms (NARAL for the Democrats, Right-to-Life for the Republicans), initiating lawsuits, and conducting marches and demonstrations.

One pro-life group, Operation Rescue, attempts to blockade abortion clinics. While the group has been accused of advocating violence against abortion clinics and doctors who perform abortions—there have been shootings at abortion clinics in Florida and Massachusetts—the organization's leaders maintain that they oppose the use of violence. But Operation Rescue's high-pressure tactics have stimulated lawsuits and even federal legislation to protect clinics and their staffs from the protests of pro-life forces. In *Bray v. Alexandria Women's Health Clinic* (1993), the Supreme Court overturned an attempt by abortion clinics to use an 1871 civil rights law to stop blockades by Operation Rescue (highlighting an interesting conflict between abortion rights and free speech rights). But the following year, in *Madsen v. Women's Health Center,* it upheld the power of judges to establish buffer zones around abortion clinics and the homes of their staffs in order to protect these institutions, their personnel, and their clients from protestors.

A Large Role for Courts in Our Constitutional Politics

It should not be surprising that a second distinguishing feature of constitutional politics in the United States is that the courts play a larger role in this area of politics than in any other. Political controversies involving flag burning, capital punishment, limits on speech, school busing to achieve racial desegregation, and other issues have been stimulated by judicial involvement. Unlike debates over the federal budget, health care, or foreign policy, the controversies of constitutional politics are very likely to end up in court. One important consequence of this situation is that elected officials who disagree with such court rulings may nevertheless defer to the courts rather than anger whichever group of citizens supports the relevant court decision(s). It is easier to abide by a court decision than to go on record one way or another to legislate on a politically sensitive subject. For example, when courts began ordering the busing of students in the 1960s to end segregation in the schools, many public officials denounced such decrees as unwise judicial activism. But in the 1970s several attempts in Congress to limit busing were quietly withdrawn because many members did not want to have to go on record either way for fear of angering antibusing parents or appearing to be racists (for opposing desegregation). Politicians in other countries may seek recourse to referenda to settle controversial questions, as Italian politicians did on the issue of abortion, but in the United States elected officials find protection from the wrath of angry citizens by accepting the decisions of unelected judges.

The Prevalence of "Rights Talk"

A third feature of American constitutional politics has been the proliferation of what political scientist Mary Ann Glendon calls "rights talk"—the use of claims of rights as a way of advancing the interests of a particular group or cause.[41] Glendon notes that Americans have become particularly adept at discussing and claiming rights but ignorant of or inattentive to corresponding responsibilities (such as respecting the rights of others), limits on rights, and the complex social-political environment in which rights are exercised.

Glendon asserts that U.S. citizens increasingly use rights talk to press claims for things that may be only partially about rights and liberties. One example can be found in the debate over health care reform, with some advocates for change asserting a "right" to adequate health care for all citizens. Even European nations that offer comprehensive government-provided health care programs to their citizens, such as Sweden and Britain, define this issue as a matter of policy rather than of rights. Calling health care a right transforms the debate from what is good policy (which elected officials decide) to what is the extent of the right (which tends to be a judicial matter). If something is a right, then the government's ability to regulate it is restricted. Rights have a kind of absolute quality that takes precedence over government policy and can be enforced in court.

Americans are devoted to the rights and liberties that distinguish our political system. Indeed, we are continually engaged in discussions about the

Stand Up for Your Rights

participate!

If you feel your civil rights or liberties or those of someone else have been violated, there are steps you can take to express your views and to protect your rights.

1. Know your rights and respect those of others. There is more to liberty than merely asserting one's own rights. Americans have become very adept at making claims of rights, but they often intrude on the freedom of others. For example, college campuses are often the scene of attempts by protestors to shout down speakers with whom they disagree. This tactic has not been limited to one group or another. In the 1980s, Reagan administration officials were victims of "shouting down," while in the 1990s anti-handgun activist Sarah Brady has also been subjected to attempts to keep her from speaking on campuses.

2. Do your homework. Guarding your own rights and liberties and knowing the difference between rights and policy are not always obvious or simple. A considerable amount of information is available about citizen rights and liberties. Begin at the library. At the end of the chapter there is a list of books with which to start. Another useful reference is a series of handbooks published by the American Civil Liberties Union, including *The Rights of Defendants and Prisoners, The Rights of Government Employees, The Rights of Veterans, The Rights of Employers and Employees,* and *The Rights of Minorities.*

3. Speak up. Laws and policies shaping rights and liberties are made by legislative bodies and executive officials. Citizens have a right to make their views known to these officials.

Members of Congress. To find out who your representatives are and how to address them, call your local chapter of the League of Women Voters or ask at the public library. The telephone number for the Capitol switchboard is (202) 224-3121. (For additional information, see Chapter 8.)

The President. You can write a letter to the president (The White House, Washington, DC 20500) or you can try to call him at (202) 456-1414. It's unlikely that you'll actually reach the president, but you will be able to speak with a staff member who can direct you to someone who can respond to your inquiry. (For further information on contacting the president, see Chapter 9.)

Other Executive Officials. The chief legal officer in the White House is the Counsel to the President (c/o The White House/ Washington, DC 20500). The Justice Department is in charge of all government legal affairs; its head is the attorney general (Justice Dept./ 10th St. and Constitution Ave., N.W./ Washington, DC 20530). If the matter pertains to civil rights, the relevant official is the assistant attorney general for civil rights.

State Officials. Contact your state representatives or your state's attorney general. Their names are available in the library or from the League of Women Voters.

Local Officials. Contact the officials in your municipality or other local government. These are often the easiest to reach, but contact them only on local matters.

4. Seek help when necessary. If you have a serious problem with infringements on your rights or liberties, there are several places to turn for help.

Civil Liberties Issues. Only a lawyer can provide legal help when that is what is needed. Many law schools have legal clinics that offer free legal advice and/or assistance where appropriate. The American Civil Liberties Union provides assistance when it believes that a citizen's liberties have been violated (32 W. 43rd St./ New York, NY 10036/ (212) 244-9800, plus chapters across the country), as do specific issue organizations such as the National Right-to Life Committee, National Women's Law Center, and so on. In many cases, a private attorney may be needed. Many universities offer free or inexpensive legal assistance to students—consult your student government association.

Civil Rights Issues. You can obtain legal assistance from private attorneys or groups such as the NAACP (which has chapters in most major cities). In addition, federal agencies are charged with receiving and investigating complaints of civil rights violations:

U.S. Commission on Civil Rights: The commission has no enforcement power but can refer complaints to the Justice Department. Contact Complaints Referral/ 1121 Vermont Ave., N.W./ Washington, DC 20425/ (800) 552-6843.

Equal Employment Opportunity Commission: (800) USA-EEOC.

Our tendency to define political issues in terms of rights has led to divisive battles over the various kinds of "rights." Here, smokers proclaim their right to smoke, in opposition to claims by others of a right to be free from smoke.

extent and limits of our rights. It seems that each day we hear of newly defined "rights" in our society: "animal rights," "children's rights," "parents' rights," "grandparents' rights," "men's rights," "the rights of the poor," "crime victims' rights," "smokers' rights," "nonsmokers' rights," and even a "right to telephone service."[42] Advocates for these rights see them as logical extensions of the traditional freedoms Americans enjoy; critics see them as an attempt to take questions of policy, such as what is a fair way to balance the interests of smokers and nonsmokers, and turn them into rigid and legalistic debates over rights.

Debates over the extent and limits of rights should not surprise us. Our political system was founded on an understanding of the tension between majority rule and citizen rights. As we saw earlier, putting representative democracy, checks and balances, and constitutionally defined liberties together in a single regime is bound to lead to a complex kind of constitutional politics. It is an almost uniquely American approach to government.

open questions

Should We Revise Our List of Rights?

Because the politics of rights and liberties is so open ended, many questions in this area remain unsettled. If you are interested in playing an active role in American politics, it is worth examining some of these issues in detail.

1. Specific rights may compete or conflict with one another. There is no guarantee that all rights will enhance one another. How are disputes between rights to be resolved? When a celebrated case goes to court, the accused party has significant due process rights to a fair trial, but the press has a constitutionally protected right to report on the case. If press coverage can make a fair judgment in the case difficult or even impossible (such as in the O.J. Simpson case), which rights should take precedence—the defendant's right to a fair trial, the media's right to press freedom, society's right to see justice done? Is there a middle ground? In addition, how should we balance the competing rights in criminal justice between society's need for protection and the individual's right to due process of law?

2. The boundaries of individual liberties and rights are often unclear. Defining the extent and limits of particular rights and liberties often poses a problem. The courts have held that people have a right to privacy, but that this right is not absolute. The Supreme Court has allowed limits on abortion, has accepted a Georgia statute outlawing sodomy, and has upheld a New York law requiring that official records be kept of prescriptions containing drugs (such as narcotics) for which there is a substantial illegal market. Where should we draw the line between privacy and the interests of the community?

Does a right to privacy include a right to commit suicide? Dr. Jack Kevorkian and others have advocated that we explicitly acknowledge a right to die, because it is a recognition of individual autonomy and can save the terminally ill from the pain and indignity of disease. Opponents of this view charge that allowing suicide will expose the sick and elderly to pressure to end their lives from those who must care for them or who stand to gain from their death. These critics also maintain that a right to die is but one step away from euthanasia—the killing of the elderly, disabled, and others who place a "burden" on society. Should we recognize a right to die?

When should privacy give way to interests of national security or the rights of others? This issue has arisen in the matter of drug testing by employers of their workers. In recent years there has been increasing use of drug tests on pilots, railroad engineers, ship crews, police officers, and others whose performance of duty affects public safety. While these tests have been challenged as violating personal privacy, what is even more controversial is the use of drug tests in jobs that have little or nothing to do with safety. For example, the company that owns the ABC television network ordered that all its employees take a drug test.

3. Do our rights and liberties need updating? Many critics of gun violence in the United States have argued that the Second Amendment's "right of the people to keep and bear arms" is outdated. They maintain that it was written for a more primitive age when marksmanship was a matter of life and death. These critics call for greater government control over crime and violence in America through the reduction in the number of guns that are distributed throughout the population. Of course, they are opposed by proponents of gun ownership, who maintain that the right to bear arms is a necessary bulwark against tyranny, because armed citizens have the power to revolt against an oppressive government. Other gun owners argue that nations that restrict gun ownership still have crime problems, so gun control only punishes hunters and other law-abiding citizens. Does this right need revision?

4. Should we have economic as well as political rights? President Franklin Roosevelt once challenged Congress to explore means for creating a "second bill of rights" that would ensure economic and social security for all Americans. Former Senator George McGovern and legal scholar Paul Savoy have taken up this cause, arguing that citizens ought to be guaranteed "a decent home and a decent job, nutrition, education, public safety and public transportation, medical care and preservation of the earth's resources."[43] They believe that these rights would make for a society that is fair economically as well as politically.

An economic bill of rights means something more than the provision of the government services that already exist in the United States. Social Security, welfare programs, and plans for national health insurance are matters of policy. They are created by elected officials who then define the extent and limits of these programs, who qualifies, what the benefits are, and how they will be funded. In contrast, creating a right to the things on the list made by McGovern and Savoy means that education, housing, employment, and other desirable benefits would enjoy the same status as the constitutional protections of speech, religion, press, and a fair trial.

Opponents of the idea of economic rights resist such calls because this second bill of rights would be prohibitively expensive to implement and would open the courts to a flood of lawsuits to probe the extent and limits of these guarantees. Moreover, critics charge that incessant suits and legal activity engendered by economic rights would make courts more powerful than ever, would increase state control over citizens, and would intensify the trend toward rights talk. They invoke Justice Oliver Wendell Holmes, who warned that "all rights tend to declare themselves absolute to their logical extreme,"[44] because a second bill of rights could lead to a situation in which the courts would make nearly all policy decisions in order to protect economic rights of citizens.

Should we add to our list of constitutional rights? Would a second bill of rights contribute to justice and liberty in our society or create serious grave new problems for the political system?

Summary

Protection of citizen rights and liberties is an essential component of the American political system. The main body of the Constitution included a number of limits on the power of government over citizens—protection of *habeus corpus,* no religious qualifications for office, and no bills of attainder—but the Bill of Rights was added to provide a larger list of citizen rights and liberties. Under the doctrine of incorporation, the Supreme Court interprets the Fourteenth Amendment as applying the Bill of Rights to the states.

Principles. The American regime is based on ideals of liberty and justice. The idea of citizen rights comes from a long tradition in Western civilization that recognizes human dignity and free will, but a major influence on the American founders were thinkers such as John Locke who advanced the idea of natural rights held by individuals. Our system recognizes civil liberties (limits on the power of government over individuals) and civil rights (claims of individuals and groups within society to enjoy the same liberties and opportunities as everyone else).

Process. There are four major methods by which citizen rights and liberties are protected in the United States:

1. *Judicial Review.* Judicial review has been important in defining the extent and limits of rights and liberties. Because there are divergent theories of constitutional interpretation, over time the Supreme Court has changed how it rules in particular cases involving freedom of religion, freedom of speech and press, due process of law, desegregation and equal opportunity, and affirmative action.

2. *Lawmaking.* Constitutional amendments have been used to shape citizen rights and liberties, as has legislation, including civil rights laws, voting rights laws, and laws prohibiting discrimination against Americans with disabilities.

3. *Executive Authority.* Presidents have used their power to desegregate the armed forces and public housing programs, to enforce Supreme Court decisions requiring the desegregation of schools, and to end a ban on gays and lesbians in the military. The U.S. Commission on Civil Rights advises Congress and the president on the state of civil rights in America, while the Equal Employment Opportunity Commission investigates charges of employment discrimination and can take action (negotiation, lawsuits, and so on) against offenders.

4. *Citizen Participation.* The actions of citizens can pressure public officials in the area of rights and liberties. The most successful use of participation was by the civil rights movement of the 1950s and 1960s. The women's movement employed similar methods but failed to win passage of the Equal Rights Amendment because a concerted anti-ERA citizens' movement blocked the change.

Politics. A political system dedicated to ideals of liberty and justice, operating through the methods described earlier, produces a kind of constitutional politics surrounding issues of citizen rights and liberties. We can identify three elements of this constitutional politics: (1) The various methods for shaping rights and liberties—judicial review, law making, executive power, and citizen participation—can all be seen at work in the controversy over abortion; (2) the courts play a larger role in this area of politics than in any other; and (3) there has been a proliferation of rights talk in American politics—a tendency to frame more and more political questions in terms of rights or claims of rights.

Open Questions. We can identify important unresolved issues in four areas: (1) How do we resolve conflicts or competition between different rights? (2) How do we define the specific boundaries of various rights? (3) Do our rights and liberties need updating? (4) Should we have economic as well as political rights?

ABRAHAM, HENRY J. *Freedom and the Court: Civil Rights and Liberties in the United States,* 5th ed. New York: Oxford University Press, 1988. Excellent survey by a leading scholar.

ALDERMAN, ELLEN, AND CAROLINE KENNEDY. *In Our Defense: The Bill of Rights in Action.* New York: William Morrow & Co., 1991. Stories of cases involving each amendment of the Bill of Rights. Engaging reading.

BERNS, WALTER. *The First Amendment and the Future of American Democracy.* New York: Basic Books, 1976. Examines the extent and limits of First Amendment freedoms.

GLENDON, MARY ANN. *Rights Talk.* New York: Free Press, 1991. Articulates Glendon's thesis that Americans have stretched the notion of rights too far, risking the very rights we want to protect.

LEWIS, ANTHONY. *Gideon's Trumpet.* New York: Random House, 1964. Fascinating account of the story behind the case of *Gideon v. Wainwright.*

MANSBRIDGE, JANE J. *Why We Lost the ERA.* Chicago: University of Chicago Press, 1986. Interesting analysis of the issues and politics surrounding the defeat of the ERA in the 1970s.

NIEMAN, DONALD G. *Promises to Keep: African-Americans and the Constitutional Order, 1776 to the Present.* New York: Oxford University Press, 1990. Useful discussion of the political and constitutional status of black Americans over the course of national history.

Suggested Readings

chapter 5

The Public's Role in American Politics

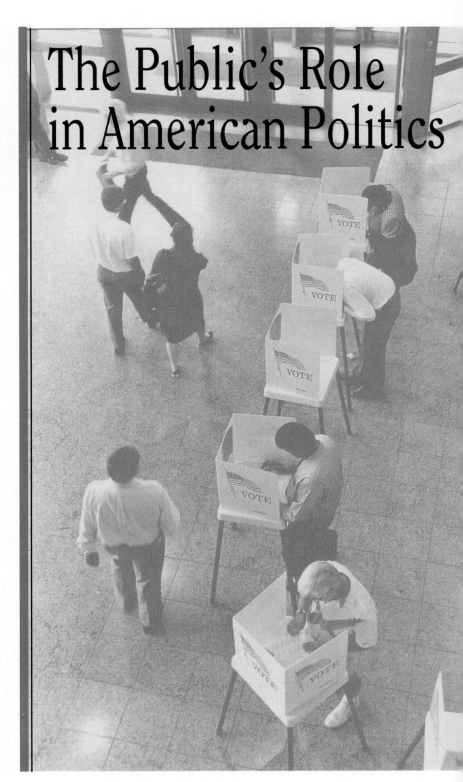

In 1994 the state of America's health care system became the subject of a national debate. As we saw in Chapter 1, President Bill Clinton proposed providing health insurance for all citizens of the United States, and Congress was considering a list of health care reforms. But the subject was not just getting attention from government officials; it was a focus of concern for the entire nation. The debate centered on what role government ought to play in directing the delivery of health care services and payment for those service.

The public did not serve merely as bystanders in this discussion, but participated in it. Citizens responded to the questions of a seemingly endless number of opinion polls. Interest groups lobbied Capitol Hill and produced television, radio, and newspaper ads to sway the public. Radio talk shows were inundated with callers voicing their opinions, and newspapers, congressional offices, and the White House received thousands of calls on the subject. Administration officials and members of Congress discussed health care with anyone who would listen. In order to build public support for his program, the president held numerous "town meetings" at which he was questioned by citizens with varying opinions on the issue. Americans discussed health care at work and with friends and family. Everyone had his or her own idea of what ought to be done or just believed that "something must be done" about health care in America.

The question of health care policy is a good example of how politics in Washington is bound up with public opinion. The major actors in the debate—

Americans have many opportunities to attempt to influence public officials. Few of these activities are as direct as this town meeting at which citizens speak to the president face to face.

the president, interest groups, members of Congress—all tried to sway Americans' views on health care, because they knew that in our political system the public passes judgment on government policies and the officials who create them. Citizens are part of the political system in more than an abstract sense. They are elements in a larger whole and affect the way it operates. We can distinguish between what goes on in the seat of government and politics in homes and on streets, but they are not isolated from one another.

Much of the attention given to politics in this or any other regime focuses on the structures of government—legislatures, executives, parties—but there is another part of the story that warrants our attention. In democratic regimes, citizens are the fundamental units of politics, whether as individuals, as part of a great mass, or as part of various organized and unorganized interests in society.

The public's role in American politics takes many forms, some obvious (such as voting) and others rather subtle (such as providing consent to the constitutional system). In this chapter, we look at how citizens fit into the regime, both as individuals and as members of the political community. Then we see some of the various means for the exercise of citizen politics and, ultimately, how they shape the operations of our system.

Principles: Citizenship and Political Community

In one sense our nation began its life with an appeal to public opinion. The Declaration of Independence proclaimed that part of its reason for being is that "a decent respect for the opinions of mankind" required that the 13 colonies (now independent states) explain their reasons for separating from Great Britain. The Constitution, too, proclaims the importance of the public; its opening words establish a regime in the name of "We the People." The public constitutes the basis of governmental power and the political community. Nevertheless, the American political system is characterized by an ambivalence about the public's role in politics.

Power to the People—But Not Too Much

Although public support has always been central to the legitimacy of the political system of the United States, as we saw in Chapter 2, the Constitution establishes a system of representative rather than direct democracy. These two facts are not contradictory but are further evidence that the American regime is built on a complex web of competing ideas and values. Three issues illustrate the ambivalent place of citizens in our politics.

Government of the People, But Not Always by the People. The framers of the Constitution understood that there is a tension between the public's capacity for self-government and the inherent imperfections of humanity. On one hand, the framers were committed to liberty and democratic government by a body of free citizens. In *The Federalist,* No. 51, Madison spoke of "a dependence on the people" as a key element of a successful regime and identified political legitimacy with a government based on public support. Likewise, in No. 57 he praised the "vigilant and manly [sic] spirit which actuates the people of America," qualities necessary for republicanism. The Constitution ensures citizens' opportunities to influence government affairs through elections and the First Amendment's guarantee of "the right of the people peaceably to assemble, and to petition the Government for a redress of grievances."

On the other hand, there is no doubt that Madison and most of his colleagues also held what we can describe best as a sober view of popular government. They were concerned about the influence of factions and their ability to undermine or sway the government in key areas (*The Federalist,* No. 10). In No. 51 Madison observes the political consequences of humanity's limitations:

> But what is government itself but the greatest of all reflections on human nature? If men were angels, no government would be necessary. If angels were to govern men, neither external nor internal controls on government would be necessary. In framing a government which is to be administered by men over men, the great difficulty lies in this: you must first enable the government to control the governed; and in the next place oblige it to control itself.

With fallible human beings at work in politics, whether as citizens or as officials, the public interest must be protected by what Madison calls "auxiliary precautions" (No. 51). As we saw in Chapter 1, Madison argued that the Constitution must include various provisions—representative institutions, checks and balances, the rule of law—to reduce the chances that human self-interest will prevail over the public interest. Moreover, the Constitution consistently employs representative democracy to arrive at governmental decisions. Most of the framers believed that deliberation was a value that needed to be promoted by the political system. The public was thus confined to selecting representatives and then trying to influence their judgments. The people were seen as an essential but imperfect element of the political system.

Government Should Be Responsive—But Not Oppressive. The ambivalence of the framers is still present today, as in the matter of how responsive government should be to the wishes of citizens. On one hand, the old expression *vox populi, vox dei* ("the voice of the people is the voice of God") is implicit in many discussions of public attitudes and opinions about politics. This sentiment points to the inevitable conclusion that public officials ought to do what the people want them to do. This is evident whenever a public opinion poll is invoked to back up a particular position on a policy question, as is common in debates about whether abortion ought to be restricted. On the other hand, we value deliberation, suggesting that *vox populi* might not always be right. For example, in 1991 several members of Congress were forced to spend considerable time and effort telling their constituents that a vote against authorizing the president to launch a war against Iraq was the right one, even if it was the minority view. These ideas are not just debater's points; they reflect competing values Americans hold.

Active Citizenship Recommended But Not Required. Americans are ambivalent about citizen participation in politics. On one hand, we hold up as virtuous active citizenship—voting, communicating with our representatives, and so on—and many avenues are available for those who wish to participate in the system. Yet there is also a competing assumption in our system that it is up to each individual to take the initiative to participate in politics. For example, the United States is the only major democracy in the world in which the burden for registering to vote falls entirely upon the citizen. In many other societies government officials make up lists of residents and automatically register them to vote. Australia and several other nations even require citizens to vote. But the tradition of our country was reflected in remarks that President Clinton made in 1993, when he was asked by a reporter to respond to the suggestion that the United States require its citizens to vote. He characterized the idea as "un-American."

The Ideal of a United Political Community

Just as there is an American ambivalence regarding the role of citizens in politics, so is there tension in the United States between individuals, groups in society, and the larger political community. The motto of the Republic is *E pluribus unum* (Latin for "From many, one"). That phrase presents a good summary of our ideal of political community: trying to reconcile a large, diverse society with the idea of a common good.

Our country gives individuals a large measure of personal liberty; the American regime is dedicated to promoting the general public interest; and American society is marked by **cultural pluralism**—diversity in race, religion, ethnic heritage, and a variety of other cultural factors. These three facts are not easily reconciled and make the American national identity distinctive from that of most other societies in the world. As the social commentator John O'Sullivan—an immigrant from Great Britain—has pointed out, our sense of national identity "remains more cultural than ethnic. . . . It is possible to *become* an American . . . in a way it is not possible to become a Slovak or a Pole."[1]

As a nation of immigrants, Americans have always been aware of their diverse origins. But the idea that one could *become* an American meant that differences of origin were unimportant in the "melting pot" of the United States, where everyone could merge into a common political culture. In recent years, however, a number of commentators have given increasing attention to **multiculturalism,** which indicates that the various groups that constitute American society have not melted into a single common culture. In contrast, they have pointed to the continuing importance of ethnic and racial differences in a society that is more like a mosaic than a melting pot. Does multiculturalism constitute a challenge to the ideal of an American political community? We shall return to this issue in the Open Questions section at the end of this chapter.

Political Community Through a Common Political Culture. Is there a binding force that holds together this diverse political community? The traditional answer has been that the nation is united by a common **political culture**—a

cultural pluralism Diversity in race, religion, ethnic heritage, and other cultural factors. A characteristic of American society.

multiculturalism The view that there is no single common American culture, but that the nation's society consists of distinct racial, ethnic, and religious groups that coexist with one another.

political culture A shared value system that influences ideas about how politics and governance ought to be conducted.

shared value system that influences ideas about how politics and government ought to be conducted.[2] Different societies have distinctive political cultures that are sometimes linked with the "character" of that group, and some diverse political systems may be made up of peoples with different political cultures. For example, the reunited country of Germany contains at least two political cultures: in the west, a democratic culture exhibits certain attitudes about governmental power (limited), democracy (expected), and capitalism (positive); in the east, the political culture is more accepting of government intervention in society and less tolerant of the inequalities created by a capitalist economy.

Americans have had their own political culture since colonial times. Although most residents of the 13 colonies regarded themselves as subjects of the British monarchy, they also considered themselves different from their cousins in the British Isles. Moreover, the population of the colonies included immigrants from other nations as well, as the French immigrant Hector St. John Crevecouer observed during the Revolution. He described his contemporaries as "a mixture of English, Scotch, Irish, French, Dutch, Germans, and Swedes" and found them a "strange mixture of blood" unlike that anywhere else on earth.[3]

Alexis de Tocqueville and the Values of American Political Culture. The United States is a country with considerable diversity from region to region, and this influences public attitudes about good government from one part of the country to another. Nevertheless, we can still discern a broad national political culture that makes American politics distinctive from that of other nations. One of the most astute observers of this culture was Alexis de Tocqueville, a French aristocrat and political philosopher who visited the young Republic in 1831 and 1832. Tocqueville's reflections on that visit were published in two volumes (1835 and 1840) as *Democracy in America*, a work that is recognized today as a classic meditation on the political society of the United States. He discerned a number of traits in the American character—an intense love of wealth, the rapidity with which styles and fashions change, and a tendency to overstatement—that continue to mark our society.[4] But Tocqueville's analysis is more significant for his ability to discern the political culture of the United States.

Alexis de Tocqueville, caricatured here, was one of the first observers to take note of Americans' tendency to form associations to deal with common problems.

Tocqueville's description of American culture is not easily reduced to a few points on a checklist, but we shall see how observations he made over a century ago continue to apply today. American political culture continues to be a focus of attention for political scientists and is marked by four major values: liberty and individualism, political equality, democracy, and citizen responsibility.[5]

Liberty and individualism make Americans more suspicious of governmental power than people in most democracies. Tocqueville observed that "democratic communities have a natural taste for freedom."[6] Americans value personal liberty in politics, including freedom of speech, a free press, and the ability to make their own decisions about voting and participation in politics. They value the right to own and use private property and support a market economy. They expect religious freedom. Finally, Americans value individual autonomy in most social behavior. Unlike Japanese political culture, where the emphasis is on the group, the culture of the United States is focused on the individual as citizen, as consumer, and as autonomous actor.

Political equality is both tied to liberty and in competition with it. Again, Tocqueville's observations are relevant. He concluded that while people in democracies love freedom, "their passion [for equality] is ardent, insatiable, incessant, invincible. . . . They will endure poverty, servitude, barbarism; but they will not endure aristocracy."[7]

Americans like to think that everyone ought to have roughly the same influence over politics as anyone else, even if they acknowledge that this ideal is rarely achieved. Many idealized portraits of the United States, such as the paintings of Norman Rockwell, depict a nation in which the opinions of the humble worker are respected (as in Rockwell's *Freedom of Speech*). This attitude contributes to American interest in the opinions of the "person on the street," a common feature of news programs and publications. It also feeds a dislike for the influence of "special interests." Indeed, much of the appeal of candidate Ross Perot in the 1992 presidential election was his message about restoring political equality by undercutting the political influence of lobbyists and interest groups.

Americans also value *popular government;* that is, they expect that those in power will be responsive to citizens. Citizens also believe that officials will assume responsibility for their own behavior. This attitude helps to shape a political environment in which there is intensive media scrutiny of public officials and frequent investigations (both official and by journalists) of alleged improprieties by politicians. The background and personal lives of candidates are routinely explored during a campaign, as are the private affairs of prominent officials. For example, the president's tax returns are made public each year, and journalists report on the First Family's income, assets, and even their charitable contributions. In addition, because of this emphasis on popular government, state and local regimes provide for the election of an amazing array of government officers, including coroners, clerks of court, auditors, and many other essentially technical officials.

Finally, American political culture places emphasis on *citizen responsibility.* This value affects a wide range of political attitudes, from the assumption that everyone ought to obey the laws to an expectation that all citizens should vote. Many Americans do not vote. Only slightly more than 50 percent of eligible voters participate in presidential elections, and fewer vote in local elections. But few people will publicly admit to not participating on election day. Many who do not vote admit guilt feelings because they believe it is their responsibility to vote, even if they see no candidate they wish to support. At the same time, even though not everyone is honest in filling out annual income tax returns, the collection of federal taxes is still based on what is essentially an honor system. To a great extent, the U.S. Internal Revenue Service (IRS) relies on voluntary compliance, borne of citizens' sense of responsibility, to keep returns generally accurate. The IRS lacks the capacity to enforce compliance on a national scale.

One feature of citizen responsibility that is particularly characteristic c Americans is our propensity to form associations through which groups of cit zens can promote a common cause. As Tocqueville observed, "Americans of a ages, all conditions, and all dispositions, constantly form associations. . . Wherever, at the head of some new undertaking, you see the government i France, or a man of rank in England, in the United States you will be sure t find an association."[8] As we shall see, these associations may be groups of cit zens working together to solve a common problem, such as setting up a neigh borhood watch group to deal with crime, or forming an interest group to advance a political cause.

The values that define American political culture exist in tension with one another. For example, liberty and civic responsibility compete in the area of voting. Citizens are expected to participate in elections, but they also want the freedom to decide for themselves whether they will do so. Moreover, citizens do not necessarily agree on which of these values deserve top priority or how best to promote them. Some Americans would place individualism first, others political equality. Political culture refers only to a broad set of values that are widely shared, not a program for detailed public policies.

In a regime that is based on the idea of the "consent of the governed," citizen politics can take several forms. It may be as subtle as providing legitimacy for the regime or as obvious as voting in the most recent election. We can identify four major means by which citizens become involved in the political system: through political socialization, through various expressions of public opinion, through political participation, and through interest groups. The first three will be explored here. The fourth—interest groups—deserves special attention and will be the focus of Chapter 6.

Political Socialization

Perhaps the most fundamental way in which citizens are linked to their regime is by the shared values of the political culture and by attitudes about politics. Political culture helps shape individual views of what government is for and how it ought to operate. We have also seen that political culture in the United States is marked by a sense of givenness about political values and institutions. But how is this idea of givenness transmitted from one generation to the next, or even to newly arrived citizens? How do they develop their fundamental political values?

Political socialization is the process by which citizens absorb these values and the political culture. Socialization is not a well-organized or tightly integrated mechanism in the United States; rather, it is a somewhat nebulous and disjointed combination of experiences that Americans undergo over the course of their lives. The family has the greatest influence in shaping citizen attitudes toward politics, although often in subtle ways. Parents usually do not give their

Process: How Citizens Are Linked to the Political System

political socialization Process by which citizens absorb politically relevant values and political culture.

children explicit lessons in citizenship, party preferences, or policy choices, but that does not mean that such values are unknown to the younger generation. Children see and hear many aspects of their parents' political attitudes and behavior. Families inculcate political values in two ways. First, children tend to model the political attitudes and actions of parents and other adult family members. If family members participate in politics by voting, flying the flag, displaying campaign materials such as bumper stickers, yard signs, political buttons, or even discussing politics, the children in that family receive lessons about the importance of citizen participation. If adults in the family do not participate in politics, this nonparticipation also sends a message to children. Second, political views tend to be handed down from one generation to the next. Evidence from political research indicates that the best predictor of an individual's preference for one political party over another—or independence from party loyalty—is the party preference of that person's parents. Yes, parents who are Democrats raise children who may become Republicans, but most Americans show loyalty to the same party as their parents.

Religion is also a means of political socialization. A family's religion may transmit politically relevant values: Jewish children tend to develop more liberal attitudes toward many issues, while those raised in evangelical Christian families tend to be more conservative, and Catholics tend to be more liberal on economic issues but conservative on social questions such as abortion. As individuals mature, their religious views play a powerful role in shaping their political attitudes. Religious faith teaches values—about life and death, war and peace, or the obligations individuals owe to one another—that are relevant to the political world. Churches need not make political statements to their congregations to influence their politics, nor will all members of the same church share the same positions.

School is another key agent of socialization. Many aspects of the curriculum and daily routine are directed toward transmitting a model of citizenship: a daily Pledge of Allegiance, celebration of national holidays, study of national history and customs, as well as curriculum projects to promote civic awareness (mock elections, writing letters to the president). Most schools today also include material in their curricula on the environment and recycling, which, while nonpartisan, has a political content nonetheless.

School also demonstrates the tension between unity and diversity in the United States. In recent years, most school curricula have maintained the symbols of unity—the flag, the Constitution, pictures of presidents—while incorporating materials on Black History Month, women's history, and other groups in society. Schools with large populations of students who do not speak English offer bilingual programs, and institutions with large concentrations of particular ethnic groups may organize their schedules around cultural events. For example, school districts in south Louisiana do not hold class on Mardi Gras in recognition of a traditional Cajun holiday.

One's surroundings—neighborhood, social group, ethnicity, geographic region, and other elements of the social environment—can also send messages about citizenship and political values. Those who grow up in New Hampshire,

Indiana, southwest Ohio, and many western states are more likely to be Republicans because that is the prevailing partisan preference in those areas. Likewise, individuals who are raised in New York City, Boston, Chicago, and many midwestern states are likely to see themselves as Democrats. When the political values of the family are reinforced by those of other groups in one's surroundings, a person is more likely to share those values.

Even events occurring during one's life can play a role in shaping political attitudes. For example, the generation that came of age during the Great Depression of the 1930s and World War II tended to take one view of politics, stressing individual responsibility and personal stability. The children of that generation, the so-called Baby Boomers, came of age during a period of prosperity, social change, and political upheaval brought on by the Vietnam War and the civil rights movement. The Baby Boomers tend to place greater emphasis than their parents on personal autonomy. The children of the Boomers, known to social critics as Generation X, are maturing in an environment of difficult economic times, a changing international scene, and concern about crime, drugs, and the natural environment. Some commentators have characterized the members of Generation X as being more interested in practical short-term results in politics than their Boomer parents, who are attracted to a politics of symbolism and idealistic goals.

The government also engages in socialization efforts, although in a democracy these activities are far less aggressive than what occurs in totalitarian systems. The federal government and states set aside certain days to commemorate patriotic events or heroes and often sponsor celebrations of these days. Certain national ceremonies, such as a presidential inauguration, commemorations of the fiftieth anniversary of D-Day and the twenty-fifth anniversary of the first moon landing, and the establishment and maintenance of memorials to soldiers, presidents, and other leaders, contribute to the inculcation of patriotic values. Government officials will also act to educate younger citizens. In the early days of his tenure, President Clinton participated in a question-and-answer session with children with television's "Mr. Rogers" as the host, while First Lady Hillary Rodham Clinton appeared on public television's *Sesame Street.*

Most socialization efforts of government are directed at children, although the process continues throughout the life span. Various advertising campaigns may be conducted around election time to encourage citizens to register and vote, and singing the National Anthem before a sporting event is part of society's effort to reinforce a sense of citizenship. At meetings of civic organizations (Kiwanis, Rotary, the P.T.A.) and governmental bodies such as school boards, reciting the Pledge of Allegiance usually precedes the business of the gathering.

Socialization helps to shape citizen politics in the United States, but it is not the means by which the people influence government. It is directed *at* citizens. But the public does not just receive attitudes; it also develops opinions and interests that are expressed to government in various ways. One of the most basic ways in which citizen views are transmitted to officials is through public opinion.

Measuring Public Opinion

Given the importance of the public in American politics, how do the attitudes of the public come to be translated into political action? Assessing **public opinion**—the views of citizens on contemporary issues—is a key element of the process of citizen politics. When the founders invoked "the people," they were essentially referring to elements of public opinion and attitudes. Elected officials have always been interested in the views of their constituents, even if they choose to vote against those views out of practical necessity. But how are we to know what the public's opinion is? The three basic ways to measure it are discernment, straw polls, and scientific polling.

Discernment. The oldest and most impressionistic way to gauge the public's views is to engage in **discernment**—to draw conclusions about what the public thinks from observation, conversations, correspondence, and other anecdotal information. Politicians have long relied on their ability to talk to people and draw conclusions based on a keen knowledge of their constituents' interests. A skillful politician in our time may not have hard evidence of the public's view on every issue but can often gain a fairly sophisticated idea of what people think about some public question by talking to constituents, other politicians, and interest group representatives. In addition, a politician knows from experience what constituents thought about similar issues. It is not uncommon for members of Congress to speak about what they have discerned from their constituents—from conversations, mail, and phone messages—before voting on a controversial matter.

Examples of discernment can be found throughout political life. Ronald Reagan, Bill Clinton, and Hillary Rodham Clinton are all famous for speeches in which they have told stories about people they met or spoke to about government waste (Reagan), about health care (Mrs. Clinton), or about the need for a stronger economy (President Clinton). Indeed, listen to the election-night remarks of almost any candidate for public office in the United States. Whether that person is claiming victory or conceding defeat, the candidate will talk about people he or she met on the campaign trail. The candidate—whether it is Pat Buchanan conceding defeat in the 1992 Republican presidential nominating contest, Christine Todd Whitman proclaiming victory as the next governor of New Jersey in 1993, or Mike DeWine winning the race for a U.S. Senate seat from Ohio in 1994—will almost inevitably refer to the election campaign as an opportunity to learn about the problems and concerns of constituents and conclude that this experience will make the officeholder a more effective public servant.

A more elaborate technique for discerning public opinion is the **focus group**—a gathering of a small number of individuals (no more than can actually talk to each other around a table, say five to ten). Borrowed from the market research methods of advertising executives, this device has become more common in recent years. A focus group is assembled by political consultants

public opinion Views of citizens on contemporary issues.

discernment The most impressionistic measurement of public opinion. It involves drawing conclusions about what the public thinks from observation, conversations, correspondence, and other anecdotal information. Still widely used by practicing politicians.

focus group A gathering of a small number of individuals to discuss issues, or their attitudes about a politician, or their reactions to a candidate's commercials or speeches. Borrowed from business marketing, this technique is widely used in political campaigns to test candidates, campaign themes, and advertising.

who bring together a number of citizens to watch campaign commercials, listen to a candidate's speech, or just discuss their views on the performance of an officeholder and the political problems they want to see addressed. In contemporary campaigns for Congress or the White House, consultants will "test market" campaign themes by having a focus group react to a candidate's draft speech. In 1992, the Clinton campaign relied on this technique to test its candidate's proposed theme of personal responsibility. When focus groups reacted coolly to the idea, Bill Clinton altered his message to one that his straw poll indicated would have greater appeal—a middle-class tax cut. During his years in the White House, President Clinton continued to use this technique for gathering information on the public's reaction to his performance in office.

The process of discernment depends heavily on the political skills of the individuals practicing it, so for decades journalists and social scientists have used more systematic means to measure public opinion. They have not abandoned discernment, only supplemented it with other techniques.

"And just who the hell are you to tell me I'm entitled to my opinion?"

Drawing by Mort Gerberg. ©1994 The New Yorker Magazine.

Straw Polls. Although **straw poll** is a systematic questioning of people on a specific question or set of questions, it is not a scientific measurement of opinion. For example, many radio and television stations have a "question of the day" about which listeners or viewers are asked to call in and comment. The station then tallies the result and reports it as evidence of what "people are thinking" about this question. Since the only people who respond are those who choose to do so, this self-selection may or may not reflect actual public opinion. Straw polls are systematic, but their value depends on how good a sample of the public is obtained by the methods employed. As we shall see later, an opinion survey must meet specific criteria on who is questioned in order to be a scientific and reliable poll.

The most famous straw poll in American history was the one conducted by the *Literary Digest* in 1936.[9] Beginning in 1920, the magazine used its subscription list to mail ballots on the presidential election as a means to test public opinion on the race for the White House. Over the course of several presidential elections, the *Digest* developed a reputation for being able to predict the winner from the responses of its subscribers. In 1936, the magazine sent surveys on that year's presidential election to all its subscribers, asking for whom they would vote in November. With over 2 million returned ballots, the *Digest* confidently predicted a Republican defeat of incumbent Franklin Roosevelt. But Roosevelt was reelected in a landslide, to the surprise of the editors. The fiasco of the *Digest's* poll is not surprising when one considers that the survey was merely a straw poll that was limited by the magazine's mailing list (which contained people who were much more affluent and conservative than the public at large) and by its dependence on who returned ballots (giving an advantage to those who made the effort to respond). Because of problems such as these, politicians, market researchers, scholars, and others worked to perfect methods that are less impressionistic than discernment or straw polls. Their efforts produced yet a third means to measure public opinion.

straw poll Systematic questioning of people on a specific question; not based on scientific sampling of the population.

The Art of Scientific Polling

scientific polling The use of statistical sampling and prediction techniques to gain information about what the public thinks. This method allows researchers to interview relatively small numbers of people (only a few thousand) in order to draw conclusions about general public opinion.

population In scientific polling, the total number of people about whom researchers want to know something.

sample In scientific polling, a small portion of the total population that reflects the overall makeup and diversity of the larger group. Also called a representative sample.

sampling error In scientific polling, an estimate of how likely a poll is to be wrong in representing a larger population. Sampling error gets smaller as the size of the sample increases.

probability sampling In scientific polling, a technique designed to give each individual in a population a roughly equal chance of being selected for the sample.

random sampling In scientific polling, selecting individuals to be interviewed without any discretion by the interviewer about who will be interviewed. Usually done through geographic sampling or random-digit phone dialing.

Scientific polling refers to the use of statistical sampling and prediction techniques to gain information on what the public thinks. Scientific polling was first developed in the 1930s by statisticians such as George Gallup and Elmo Roper. These pioneers invented methods that allowed them to interview relatively small numbers of people (only a few thousand) in order to draw conclusions about general public opinion. Gallup and Roper essentially invented a new profession in politics, that of the pollster.

The Sample, the Key to Scientific Polling. How does opinion polling work? It is based on the idea that it is necessary to test only a portion of a large group in order to learn something about the whole group. Consider a group, such as the residents of a particular area, the members of a particular profession, or the citizens of a community (city, state, country). This group is a **population**—the total number of people about whom we want to know something. Scientific polling works by taking a representative **sample**—a small portion of the total population, but one that reflects its overall makeup and diversity—in order to examine it in a way that would be impossible if one had to study the whole group. In a country the size of the United States, with 260 million people, the cost of obtaining information about everyone would be prohibitive. Even the U.S. Census Bureau, which theoretically counts all citizens and obtains information about them, does not actually contact everyone; it relies on one person in each household to fill out a form that reports on the residents of that place.

Pollsters are particularly concerned about **sampling error,** which is an estimate of how likely a poll is to be wrong in representing the population or universe. Sampling error is estimated by the principles of probability, and a larger sample decreases the amount of likely error. For example, a poll might ask one thousand people whether they approve of the job the president is doing. Let's say that 52 percent of those questioned approve of the chief executive's performance. A sample of this size has a sampling error of plus-or-minus 3 percent, which means that the actual percentage in the larger population may be anywhere from 49 percent (minus 3 percent) to 55 percent (plus 3 percent). Knowing about sampling error can be important in interpreting the results of a poll. For example, Table 5.1 shows sampling errors for different sized samples used in opinion polling. Major opinion polls—such as the Gallup, Roper, and Harris polls—usually have a sampling error of plus-or-minus 3 percent.

To make a sample representative of the larger population, pollsters usually employ **probability sampling,** a technique designed to give each individual in the population a roughly equal chance of being selected for the sample. This is accomplished by the use of **random sampling**—selecting individuals to be interviewed at random, without any discretion by the interviewer about who will be interviewed. Two common ways to achieve a random sample are through geographic sampling and random-digit dialing.[10]

Geographic sampling is used in personal interviewing. In this method, people are divided according to where they live. Smaller and smaller divisions are made, until some small unit such as a city block is chosen as the basis for the sample. Then interviewers are assigned to poll a specific number of people in each block, selecting every third or fourth or nth household to interview. In this way, a sample is obtained that has a geographic distribution, and everyone in each unit/block has a roughly equal chance of being selected.

Random-digit dialing is used in telephone interviewing. Pollsters obtain from the telephone company a list of all working phone numbers within a particular exchange (indicated by the three-digit prefix in a phone number). Then researchers decide how many numbers from each exchange will be contacted, depending on how many numbers there are in that group. Then a computer creates a list of numbers to be called at random, thus giving each phone number a roughly equal chance of being selected.

Polling the Sample. There are various methods for polling the sample. *Mail ballots* can be sent to the individuals identified for the sample. This method has the advantage of being a relatively inexpensive way of obtaining information and is useful when the survey includes complex questions or a long list of questions. The difficulty with this method is that the percentage of ballots actually completed and returned to researchers can be quite low, perhaps even too low to be useful. Another method of polling is the *personal interview,* in which interviewers actually go out and question subjects in person. This method has the advantage of a much better response rate, but it can be expensive to conduct on a large scale. One use of this method that has gained considerable attention in the past few years has been in *exit polls,* in which voters exiting a polling place on election day are asked who they voted for and why. Exit polls conducted at selected voting places have enabled news organizations to predict the outcome of presidential elections with a high degree of accuracy, although the results are available only a few hours before the official results. This method was used in the 1994 congressional elections to predict the Republican sweep of both houses before official results were available. A third method for polling the sample is the *telephone interview,* which has become the standard technique for large-scale polls today. With telephone service covering approximately 97 percent of American citizens, this method offers an effective means for reaching the vast majority of Americans at a cost much lower than that for personal interviews.

For all the money and effort spent to determine public opinion, the act of measuring it is still as much an art as it is a science. Successful pollsters must deal with several potential problems. First, to be useful a survey must be well designed. It must employ a representative sample, and questions must be written to actually tap public views. Extensive research indicates that the phrasing of questions, even the order in which questions are asked, can affect the results of a poll. A second problem is intensity. Most polls do not measure how strongly respondents feel about an issue or candidate, so they cannot always indicate how much people will care if one particular policy outcome is chosen over another. A third problem is that respondents to a poll may not have an opinion on some issues in a campaign or policy survey (e.g., about nuclear pro-

TABLE 5.1 How Sampling Error Varies

Approximate Size of Sample	Approximate Sampling Error
200	+/− 7%
300	+/− 6
400	+/− 5
600	+/− 4
1,000	+/− 3
2,500	+/− 2
10,000	+/− 1

Sampling error decreases as the size of a polling sample increases. The figures shown here are the approximate sampling errors that, according to statisticians, determine the reliability of polls in estimating the opinions of the larger populations from which samples are taken. For example, if in a poll of 1,000 people, 782 (78%) said they supported family leave for men and women, that figure would be considered accurate within 3 percentage points: It might actually be as low as 75%, but it might also be as high as 81% if the entire population were polled. However, if the sample polled was much smaller—say, 200 people, 156 of whom said they supported family leave, the sampling error would be far greater: this time the percent of the population that actually favored family leave might be as high as 85% or as low as 71%.

An exit poll questions voters as they leave the voting place. Because such polls give a fairly accurate picture of the outcome of an election, they are used by television networks to predict voting results in their election-night coverage.

liferation) until they are interviewed. Even if these individuals give an answer other than "Don't know," it is not clear that the results will be useful for indicating what people want. Finally, because of the increasing use of polling in our society, many people are refusing to talk to pollsters. Although well-designed polls can deal with a certain percentage of nonrespondents, public disinterest or antagonism toward being surveyed affects the accuracy of poll results.

Citizen Participation in the Political Process

Expressing opinions is a relatively passive means of involvement in citizen politics. It depends on someone asking a person's views. But individuals and groups often want to take a more active approach to influencing public affairs, so they engage in various activities to try to influence government. These activities are collectively known as **political participation.**

political participation
Various activities directed at influencing government decisions or public policy, including voting and other conventional and unconventional activities.

Voting. *Voting* is the most common and most obvious form of participation. Some observers regard it as the key method of participation, because voting directly influences who governs as well as substantive questions such as those about taxes. In *Yick Wo v. Hopkins* (1886), the Supreme Court held that voting is "a fundamental political right" because it is "preservative of other rights."[11] At the same time, federal and state governments retain the power to regulate the time, place, and manner of elections. States can require citizens to register to

132

vote, can set a minimum age for voting (no higher than age 18), and can establish registration procedures and rules for participation in elections. Although discrimination in voting rights is not allowed, a neutral limit such as the requirement of registering to vote is certainly acceptable. Therefore, the law recognizes voting as an essential, but not an unrestricted, part of citizenship.

As we saw in Chapter 3, suffrage (the right to vote) has expanded considerably over the course of American history. Constitutional amendments, laws, and court decisions have opened voting essentially to all adult American citizens who are not felons or mentally incompetent. Nevertheless, not all citizens choose to vote (see Figure 5.1 and Current Issues box). There is still considerable variation among the states regarding registration to vote. All states except North Dakota require citizens to register; Maine, Minnesota, Oregon, and Wisconsin allow registration on election day. There is considerable evidence that ease of registration affects voter turnout. States with election-day registration or no registration have the highest turnout rates. While the national average for turnout in the 1992 presidential election was 55 percent, Maine, Minnesota, and Wisconsin all had turnouts over 67 percent. Some states allow registration by postcard; others require prospective voters to sign up in the presence of an official. In 1993 Congress passed the Motor-Voter Act to make voter registration

FIGURE 5.1
Voter Turnout in Presidential Elections
Source: U.S. Bureau of the Census, *Statistical Abstract of the United States, 1993.*

Is Nonvoting A Problem?

Despite what is essentially universal adult suffrage, many Americans do not vote. This fact concerns some observers, who regard it as a sign of ill health in the American political system. Others see nonvoting as less of a problem or even a sign of strength, arguing that nonvoting is a sign of satisfaction. Much of the concern about voting arises from its central place in the theory of democracy; the vote is the tool that citizens can use to control government. One commentator went so far as to call it a "civic sacrament," indicating its importance to the proper functioning of the regime.

Is nonvoting a problem? The answer depends on what information one uses to calculate **turnout,** the measure of how many people actually vote compared to how many could vote. Traditionally, turnout in American elections has been expressed as the percentage of the voting-age population who actually vote. Measured this way, the United States ranks near the bottom of 24 major democratic nations, ahead of only Switzerland (see table). Moreover, there has

For Americans, voting is both a right and a duty.

been a general decline in voting turnout over the course of American history. In the early decades of the Republic, it was around 70 percent. It declined after the Civil War, falling to a low of 45 percent in 1924. It then rose again, reaching a high of 63 percent in 1940, but then fell and rose again. In 1960, turn-out was about 60 percent. Since that time, it has hovered in the 50+ percent range. It was about 55 percent in the 1992 presidential election. Turnout in nonpresidential lections is even lower: In the 1994 election that turned both houses of Congress over to Republican majorities, turnout averaged just under 39 percent across the nation.

One study suggests that a different standard of measuring turnout might change our perspective on the issue. David Glass, Peverill Squire, and Raymond Wolfinger found that if turnout is measured as a percentage of those registered to vote (the standard used in most countries), then turnout is over 80 percent in presidential elections. This result puts the United States in the middle of the group of 24 nations, and there is not a large gap between

available with driver's license renewal. Consistent with the idea that personal initiative ought to motivate voting, the law requires citizens to request registration rather than making it automatic.

The United States holds far more elections than any other democracy. There are national elections only every other year, but state and local elections may occur several times a year. Citizens are called upon to select governors (frequently in a year when presidential elections do not occur), state legislatures, county officials, municipal officers, school boards, and coroners. Their approval is required for local taxes, state constitutional amendments, referenda, and bond issues. Primary elections add another layer of voting. In November 1994, voters across the nation chose governors, state legislatures, and a new Republican majority in Congress. They also passed or defeated tax levies, imposed term limits on their legislators, and restricted the services available to illegal immigrants.

turnout The measure of how many people actually vote compared to how many could vote in an election.

the countries with highest turnout and American voting habits (see table below). Defining turnout as a fraction of registered voters who participate yields a more impressive figure than the traditional measure. Nonvoting may be less of a problem than many reports claim it to be.

Should we be concerned about nonvoting? How much weight should officials give to the views of those who vote over those who do not? The problem of identifying the elusive public does not lend itself to simple or obvious answers.

Ranking of Countries by Voter Turnout if United States Measured Turnout as Other Countries Do

Country	Turnout—Percentage of Registered Voters	Country	Turnout—Percentage of Registered Voters
1. Belgium	94.6	14. Denmark	83.2
2. Australia	94.5	15. Norway	82.0
3. Austria	91.6	16. Greece	78.6
4. Sweden	90.7	17. Israel	78.5
5. Italy	90.4	18. United	
6. Iceland	89.3	Kingdom	76.
7. New Zealand	89.0	19. Japan	74.5
8. Luxembourg	88.9	20. Canada	69.3
9. Germany	88.6	21. Spain	68.1
10. Netherlands	87.0	22. Finland	64.3
11. **United States**	86.8	23. Ireland	62.2
12. France	85.9	24. Switzerland	48.3
13. Portugal	84.2		

Note: The traditional measure of turnout for the U.S. is percentage of the voting-age population who actually votes. For other countries, the measure of turnout is percentage of registered voters who vote.
Source: David Glass, Peverill Squire, and Raymond Wolfinger, "Voter Turnout: An International Comparison," *Public Opinion* (December/January 1984): 49–55. Reprinted with the permission of the American Policy Institute for Public Policy Research, Washington, D.C.

Contacting Government Officials. Beyond voting, there are several avenues of political participation available to those who wish to take advantage of them. Many citizens *contact government officials* to express their views on political issues, whether by writing letters, making phone calls, or even making personal contact at town hall meetings. Writing one's representatives in Congress or state government has long been an activity undertaken by many citizens, with phoning and faxing officials becoming more common. Radio talk shows around the country often encourage their listeners to contact their representatives and the Capitol Hill switchboard routinely records a dramatic increase in calls when talk show hosts urge such action.

Working for Campaigns and Political Organizations. Many citizens *work in political campaigns,* whether on behalf of particular candidates, parties, or even nonpartisan causes. College-age and senior citizens usually provide the

Bob and Christine
were busy with their
family, a small farm in
southern Ohio, full-
time employment, and
church activities.
When in 1991 the
local school district
attempted to deny
their children bus
transportation to
school (on the
grounds that the cou-
ple lived too far out in
the country), they
filed an appeal with
state education
authorities. In more
than one meeting with
school officials, the
couple showed that
they had done their
homework and under-
stood Ohio school
law. Their resistance
forced school officials
to back down. They
also organized other
parents into an effec-
tive lobbying force to
push for a change in
the school district's
overall busing policy.
Bob later served as
manager of one
school board candi-
date's campaign. Both
Bob and Christine
refused opportunities
to run for office them-
selves, preferring to
be active but private
citizens.

largest number of volunteers for election campaigns or petition drives to influence public policy, because these groups have the greatest flexibility in their schedules. Some people *contribute to political campaigns or causes,* and not all of them are "fat cats." Thousands of individuals give contributions of $100 or less to candidates they support. Such money will not fund most campaigns, but it can provide politicians with important information about their base of support. Citizens also *work for or belong to political organizations,* such as labor unions, professional associations, or various issue-oriented groups (for example, the Sierra Club, the National Rifle Association, the NAACP). Simply belonging to these groups can be a form of participation if large membership lists give their leaders the ability to claim to represent an important block of voters.

A related kind of participation is *taking part in lawful marches, protests, and political rallies* to influence public officials. The right to assemble and petition government ensures that citizens have these opportunities, although the courts have held that the government may set reasonable restrictions on such activities to protect the peace and public order. During the Vietnam War, protests became a common practice on many college campuses, and in 1991, rallies were held in support of the Persian Gulf War.

Even activities that citizens might not consider overt political acts may be forms of participation. For example, *working with others to solve common problems* in one's community (for example, the need for scenic improvement or crime prevention) is a kind of participation. It does not matter that government is not involved, because such community-oriented activities are part of a larger concept of citizenship. *Discussing politics* with others, especially if you try to persuade someone else to adopt a particular position or support a candidate, is also a form of participation.

Confrontation as Participation. Then there are extraordinary forms of participation. **Civil disobedience,** which involves deliberately violating a law in order to draw attention to the unfairness or injustice of that law, has been used to advance a number of political causes. The civil rights movement frequently broke segregation laws in southern states by staging "sit-ins" at lunch counters or other whites-only facilities in order to bring pressure for change. Another approach to political action by unusual means is *litigation* (lawsuits). For several decades the NAACP and other groups have used lawsuits to advance their causes. In 1952 the *Brown v. Board of Education* decision represented one of the greatest successes of participation through this strategy. In 1993 conservative groups used the same approach to force President Clinton's health care task force to hold public meetings.

Protest and Political Assembly. Another strategy is to conduct a *publicity campaign* in an attempt to influence politics. It is not uncommon to find advertisements in major newspapers such as the *New York Times* or *Washington Post* that protest American policy in some foreign nation or that call upon the president and Congress to "do something" about some problem. In the fall of 1993, a spate of ads for and against the North American Free Trade Agreement (NAFTA) between the United States, Canada, and Mexico appeared in major newspapers and magazines and on television. While pro-NAFTA forces made their case, Ross Perot conducted a major campaign against the agreement. The climax of these two campaigns for public support was a debate on NAFTA between Perot and Vice-President Al Gore on CNN's *Larry King Live*. In 1994, health care became a hot issue and a war of ads erupted in order to sway public opinion. In Chapter 6, we shall see how that war was conducted.

The right of citizens to assemble for political purposes, such as for a march or rally, is protected under the First Amendment. This is true even if the views expressed are extreme and insulting to other citizens. In *National Socialist Party v. Skokie* (1977), the Court struck down an ordinance intended to prevent the American Nazi Party from staging a march in the predominantly Jewish community of Skokie, Illinois.[12] But communities may regulate political activity in public forums such as streets, parks, and other places designated for "expressive activity" if those rules are reasonable and can be justified as serving an important public purpose. The Supreme Court has ruled that communities may limit noise levels, confine political assemblies to particular places, and "prevent people from blocking sidewalks, obstructing traffic, littering streets, committing assaults, or engaging in countless other forms of antisocial conduct."[13]

Running for Office. One unusual but potentially effective form of participation is to *run for political office* strictly for the purpose of making a political statement. In 1965 conservative author William F. Buckley entered the race for mayor of New York City to focus attention on issues he claimed were not being addressed by the other candidates. Asked what he would do if he won, Buckley responded "I would demand a recount." A pro-life activist in Indiana ran for the House of Representatives in 1992 and 1993 in order to take advantage of lenient rules regarding campaign advertising. This strategy allowed him to show graphic anti-abortion commercials on television that he might not have been able to air otherwise. In 1992 Ross Perot ran for president with the declared purpose of forcing attention to the federal deficit. Although he later became caught up in the campaign itself, Perot maintained that his motivation was to promote issues rather than win office.

Involvement in political campaigns is a protected but not an unrestricted right. On one hand, individuals who seek public office can spend as much of their own money as they wish, on the grounds that such activity is a form of First Amendment speech. Likewise, if an individual or group spends money independently of any campaign or candidate—for example, to try to defeat an incumbent—no limits can be imposed. On the other hand, the same individuals or groups can be limited in their contributions to candidates or parties. (See Chapter 7 for more on campaign finance rules.) The federal government also has the power to prohibit civil servants from actively participating in political campaigns. The Court has upheld this reduction in First Amendment rights on the grounds that it is essential to limit the political influence of government workers in order to maintain the integrity of a civil service system based on merit.

THE CITIZEN AS LOCAL OFFICIAL

Michael Mignery is a high school teacher and football coach with an interest in his local community in rural Hanover Township, Ohio. He encourages his students to be active citizens, and one day he decided to take his own advice. Using a small amount of his own money, he ran for and won a seat on the township board of trustees. That three-person body is the local government for his community. He performs his official duties—including overseeing the township's budget, road maintenance program, and fire department— and still has time for his regular job, family, and other activities.

civil disobedience An act of deliberately violating a law to draw attention to the unfairness of that law.

Participation can be individual, cooperative, and even highly organized. When people with common views or interests band together to promote their objectives, they become an interest group. Chapter 6 will examine the role of organized interest groups in American politics.

The Politics of Citizenship and Community

We have seen that Americans tend to be ambivalent about their role in politics—believing it is important, but insisting that it be voluntary; wanting a responsive government, but one that also deliberates on the common good; and wanting majorities to rule, but not invade individual rights. Even the practice of citizen politics highlights this ambivalence. For example, voter turnout in the United States is not as strong as in some other democracies. Yet people in this country are more likely than their democratic cousins to engage in nonvoting forms of participation. Our politicians and journalists pay careful attention to public opinion, and most identify with some interest group; yet an individual such as Ross Perot could gain popularity by claiming to be unconcerned with polls or "special interests." Nearly everyone can point to the incredible diversity of the American people, yet talk of a common interest remains a central topic in our political rhetoric.

For all this complexity, what sense can we make of the public's role in American politics? Three general points stand out: one about what is meant by "the people," one about citizen participation, and one about the state of the American political community.

"We the People"—Elusive Creatures

The American regime was created in the name of "we the people," and almost everyone involved in national affairs invokes "the people" at some time or another. But it is often difficult to say just who "the people" are and what they want or need from government. Indeed, political commentator Walter Lippmann—a veteran of decades of observing Washington politics—once referred to the American people as the "phantom public." There are two major reasons why the public is so elusive.

The Public Plays a Variety of Political Roles. Politicians do not gaze upon the nation and see the American public with just one face. The public appears as *voters* in elections, but voters are not precisely the same as citizens. Voters are those (not everyone) who participate in an election (in which the choices are quite specific and limited) on a particular day (which is not every day). Voters are very important because they decide who will hold office and how many public questions will be resolved, but they are not precisely the same as "the people." Next, government officials have *constituents,* who are the people they represent. Officials know that constituents are not the same as voters, because many constituents did not vote, and many of those who did vote wanted someone else for the office. Moreover, the constituents of one officeholder—say, a member of Congress from Manhattan—will be different from the constituents of another—say, a member from central Iowa. The public also shows up as *participants in political action*—protestors, letter writers, callers to radio talk shows, campaign volunteers—but these individuals are activists with a greater than average interest in politics. Likewise, *citizens are part of various interests in society,* whether or not they support organized interest groups. How much weight should officials give to the views of activists and interest groups versus some idea of the "general public"?

These various guises for "the people" help to explain why politicians have come to rely so much on opinion polls for information about what the public wants. But even polls reveal the difficulty in identifying just what it is that the "phantom public" wants.

Opinion Polls Provide Only Partial Instructions for Policy Makers. There is no doubt that opinion polls have played an important role in American politics in recent decades. Politicians have been particularly interested in obtaining polling information, whether to assess their own popularity or to learn of public views on issues and policies. As a presidential candidate, John F. Kennedy employed Louis Harris (now head of a major opinion research firm) as his personal pollster. Since that time, other contenders for office have done likewise or hired pollsters as consultants to their campaigns. In each administration since the time of Jimmy Carter, the White House staff has included a presidential pollster (usually paid for by the president's party rather than the government). Even state and local candidates employ the services of pollsters. Once elected, these officials continue to use polls as a means to check their performance and

The public plays many political roles—as voters, constituents, representatives of various interests, and participants in political action. Here Rhode Island students stage a protest to demand more money for schools.

potential opposition and to measure their standing with the voters. At a conference on public opinion polling in 1993, presidential assistant Stan Greenberg revealed that the White House had used information obtained from polls to shape the Clinton administration's health care reform proposal.

News organizations have increased the importance of polling. All the major television networks and national newspapers conduct polling on elections, policy questions, and other current issues. Because of the expense of conducting national opinion polls, major news organizations have joined forces to conduct polls and disseminate their results: CBS with *The New York Times,* ABC with *The Washington Post,* NBC with *The Wall Street Journal,* and CNN and *USA Today.* Their reporting of poll results during campaigns and at other times has provided news about public opinion as well as information for politicians.

Despite all this attention to polls, their utility is limited. Polls do not ask questions about all issues. In each session of Congress, members are called upon to vote on bills such as banking regulation, international trade, and copyright law reform about which the public has not been asked and would probably not have an informed opinion anyway. Even when the public does have an opinion, it may be based on little or misleading information. For example, in 1987 an overwhelming majority of respondents told pollsters that they were opposed to members of Congress receiving a pay raise planned for that year. But researchers also found that 80 percent of the people with that view did not know how much their representatives were paid. Likewise, polls on the issue of abortion reveal that while 60 percent of Americans agree with the Supreme Court's decision in *Roe v. Wade* (1973), only 10 percent of the public has any real understanding of what the Court's ruling mandated.[14] How obligated should policy makers feel to obey the views of the public, even if officeholders know that the public is uninformed?

Public opinion may also seem contradictory. Various polls on health care reform proposals indicated in 1994 that 75 percent of those surveyed favored universal coverage for Americans, although there was much less support for requiring employers to provide coverage to workers and general opposition to higher taxes to pay for universal care. How are officials to make policy that will be responsive to contradictory public demands?

Sometimes public opinion may not be contradictory, but just ambiguous. For example, consider public views on abortion. Despite the tremendous amount of attention the subject has received in the past two decades, there is still a vast middle ground of opinion that scholar James Davison Hunter described as ambivalent. Hunter examined the available polling data and noted that "The figures will vary from poll to poll, but the general distribution of opinion is about the same: hardened opinion at each end of the debate and a larger, softer middle (of roughly 60 percent)."[15] He concluded that "The only way to find a majority on this issue is to fabricate one."[16] Nevertheless, both pro-choice and pro-life activists cite public opinion data to suggest that their position is the more popular one. To what extent can public officials use opinion polls as a guide when the results are unclear?

Learn to Make a Difference

Citizens get involved in politics for a wide variety of reasons—to support an interest, to protect something or someone they care about, to promote a cause they believe in, to make a difference in public decisions. Active citizens fit their participation into otherwise busy lives; they do not find it necessary to give up their regular pursuits in order to write letters, assist in organizations they support, or do other activities. Active citizenship is flexible. It is possible to do much or little, depending on your interests or abilities. Here are some things that you can do to be an active citizen:

1. **Stay Informed and Participate:** At least be prepared to participate if necessary. The philosopher Albert Camus once observed that not choosing is a kind of choosing. If you do not make choices, someone else will. Many means are available, from voting to more involved efforts at political action. Participation can have a local, state, or national focus.

2. **Learn How to Make a Difference:** You can improve your chances of making your efforts count if you learn some steps for effective citizen action:

- *Focus:* Identify a problem that needs to be addressed or find an issue that interests you.

- *Do your homework:* Do research to find out more about the issue or problem. Find out what government agencies are involved and what decision makers have authority.

- *Seek allies:* You do not have to start from scratch or work alone. You may find a group that is already working on your issue that you can join, or you may need to organize others in support of your goal. Policy makers are more likely to listen to many people than one or two.

- *Set reasonable goals:* You may be tempted to settle for nothing less than total victory, but remember that in politics compromise is often necessary. Decide which goals are essential and which can be tempered in the face of reality.

- *Develop strategies for success:* Determine what are the most effective means for getting what you want—negotiation, education, lobbying, litigation, or whatever.

- *Monitor results:* If you get results, follow through to make sure that decisions are implemented. If you fail, consider why, and see if you can improve your efforts and try again. Continue to monitor the issue for potential action in the future.

participate!

Like many other issues, abortion raises the problem of majority opinion versus other values in a democratic republic. Activists on both sides of the abortion issue may cite polls, but they will abandon opinion surveys if necessary to justify their views. They will argue that abortion is an issue of rights, of liberty, of morality, of life, or whatever, not a question that should be decided by majority preference. Likewise, gun control and the right to die are not merely questions to be decided by the majority, but are seen as rights that take precedence over what the public wants.

Even if rights are not at issue, the American regime was designed to promote deliberation, not just majority rule. All of the "auxiliary precautions" of the Constitution—checks and balances, an independent judiciary, staggered elections—were included precisely to make it difficult for temporary majorities to have their way. At what point should public officials do what they believe will promote the common good, even if it is not supported by public opinion? Should officials always feel bound by what polls tell them the people want?

The "general public" captured in polls is not the only face of the American people that officials see. Opinion polls tell leaders what the public thinks, but they include those who do not otherwise participate in politics along with people who do. Officeholders know that they must contend especially with active citizens.

The Many Opportunities for Active Citizenship

Americans have many opportunities to participate in politics, from voting to contacting officials and even more nontraditional forms of political action. Those who engage in active citizenship can increase their influence in politics, because they can multiply the number of political guises through which they present themselves to officials. Some methods of participation, such as voting, are easy; others require effort. And citizens should be aware that where they choose to participate can make a difference.

In Chapter 3, we saw how a large amount of governmental power has shifted to Washington from states and local communities. Despite this shift, states and localities continue to be where decisions that affect everyday life are made, and they are fertile ground for citizen participation. In these localities, the number of political participants involved, the size of government, the number of issues are smaller, and citizen proximity to decision makers is greater. Moreover, the costs associated with political activity are usually much lower in states and localities. For example, smaller numbers may be required for a group to be effective. Personal contact with city council members, county officers, even state officials may be easier to arrange and cheaper to undertake. Publicity campaigns, lobbying, even campaign contributions can all be effective at a much lower price than on a national level.

Citizen politics, whether individual participation or group activity, often begins on the local level. An example from my own experience will illustrate this point. In 1991 I was one of several parents in our school district who was upset by proposed changes in the school bus system. School district officials had inaugurated an economy plan that saved money by doubling and tripling the amount of time our children spent on buses going to and from school, sometimes as much as several hours. Concerned about the welfare of our children, we parents (many of whom had never been politically active before) organized into an effective lobbying group and pressed for change before the local school board. Faced with this citizen action, the board reversed its proposed change, and district officials even negotiated a compromise plan with the parents' group to accommodate their concerns. One woman in the group, a self-described "full-time mother," was stimulated to run for office and won a seat on the school board in the next election. Many in the parents' group became volunteers or contributors to her campaign.

Active citizenship is possible at any level of American politics but is particularly easy closer to home. The many opportunities for participation help to explain why Americans are more likely than people in other democracies to engage in nonvoting forms of participation, from contacting their representatives to joining politically active organizations. The political system offers many means for pursuing political goals, and the range of citizen politics in the United States reflects the great diversity of our society.

The Political Community: The "Pluribus" and the "Unum"

The philosopher John Courtney Murray once characterized a political system as a people "locked in argument,"[17] and it would be difficult to find a better phrase to describe the American political community. With such a high degree of social pluralism, the United States is a country in which political conflict is often tied to cultural differences. Americans are "locked in argument" by a common political system and a political culture that commits them to certain shared values, but within that framework there is considerable room for different political agendas, priorities, and visions of the common good.

One good example of how different agendas and visions shape our politics lies in what some observers have come to call America's "culture wars"—political clashes that have their basis in cultural differences. A number of commentators have noted an increase in political disputes over cultural issues, ranging from abortion to homosexuality to language to the arts to ethnic customs. Although they are complex, these disputes tend to center on a few core issues in contemporary society:

- *What are the limits of personal autonomy?*—Several issues revolve around fundamental questions of the extent and limits of personal autonomy, such as abortion, euthanasia and the "right to die," and condom distribution among minors; these issues are about who, if anyone, can set limits on each individual's autonomy in society.

- *How much power does the community have with which to protect common values?*—A number of issues involve questions of the extent to which society may regulate behavior in order to protect certain values, including regulation of pornography, prayer in the schools, restrictions on "vulgar" or obscene art and music, limits on "hate speech," and even zoning laws that attempt to regulate aesthetic values by prohibiting architecture, paint colors, or other external features of a home that some consider to be in bad taste.

- *To what extent should ethnic differences be recognized and protected by public policy?*—Several conflicts have arisen over claims by ethnic groups that certain aspects of their culture deserve special protection. For example, some African American leaders have pushed for the creation of schools employing an "Afrocentric" curriculum to offset what they regard as the pernicious effects of the dominant "Eurocentric" culture. The trend toward multicultural education in elementary and high schools has stimulated debate about how far government should go to recognize and even promote cultural differences. In other controversies, Mexican Americans have fought proposals in California and elsewhere to ban events involving horse-tripping in Mexican-style rodeos. They argue that a ban on this custom, in which horses are quite literally tripped and made to fall on their sides, would prevent them from preserving their cultural heritage. On several college campuses, groups of students have requested housing segregated by ethnicity. And for several years there has been a controversy over the extent to which governments must accommodate those individuals who do not speak English in voting, in government offices, in employment, and elsewhere.

As this sampling of issues suggests, culture wars often involve subjects about which people form passionately held positions. Because of these passions, cultural issues do not always open themselves to resolution by compromise, the traditional safety valve of American politics. On the contrary, they often become polarized between two sides separated by a great divide, each claiming not just the superior position but the only correct position. James Davison Hunter sees such division as the basis for the popular phrase **political correctness,** a term that refers to

> a position so "obviously superior," so "obviously correct," and its opposite "so out of bounds," that they are beyond serious discussion and debate. Indeed, to hold the "wrong" opinion, one must be either mentally imbalanced (phobic—as in *homophobic*—irrational, codependent, or similarly afflicted) or, more likely, evil. Needless to say, in a culture war, one finds different and opposing understandings of the politically correct view of the world.[18]

Political correctness has become the source of much humor in recent years, because of the extremes to which it has been taken. One face of political correctness is the creation of new terminology about personal and social differences that is intended to be inoffensive or positive, such as referring to short people as "vertically challenged," those who are overweight as "persons of size," and those who are clumsy as "alternatively skilled" (I use these examples because I fit all of these categories). Other politically correct language is designed to recast how people think about certain issues. Some animal-rights activists call cats "feline Americans" and dogs "canine Americans" and attack the eating of meat as consumption of "scorched animal carcasses." But the use of absolutist terminology in much contemporary political debate is a sign that the political community is not a homogeneous one. Moreover, it may be further evidence of the spread of rights talk in a different form; some positions in culture wars are stated in terms of absolute rights—such as the "right to die"—while others are articulated as the correct ones with which any reasonable person "must" agree.

political correctness
The alteration of language to reflect political positions that are assumed to be the "correct" ones. Terminology about personal and social differences must be inoffensive or positive.

In an ironic way, political correctness seems to be a peculiarly American way of dealing with social pluralism. It seeks to enforce a uniformity of language in order to recognize the differences in society. That attempt strikes many people, liberal and conservative alike, as the wrong way to encourage an appreciation of differences, but the tension between "pluribus" and "unum" is certainly nothing new in American politics.

open questions

Is Multiculturalism a Threat or a Promise?

As we have seen, the public plays a central yet ambiguous role in American politics. Citizens are the source of political power and legitimacy, yet they cannot be forced to participate; citizens are constantly polled for their views, yet politicians are criticized for paying too much attention to opinion polls. Because of this situation, a number of important questions remain unsettled on the kinds of fundamental issues that face the United States as it attempts to maintain a functioning democratic republic.

In the United States social pluralism has always existed in tension with the ideal of national unity. The idea of this country as a "melting pot" stands side-by-side with the idea that cultural and ethnic differences are to be not simply tolerated, but valued. African Americans, Asian Americans, Italian Americans, Jewish Americans, Irish Americans, Hispanic Americans, and other such groups have all retained elements of their ethnic roots, although many members of these communities do not choose to identify themselves primarily with any particular ethnic group.

The traditional American response was to emphasize national unity, accepting that ethnic differences were real but reminding everyone that "after all, we are all Americans." Historian Arthur Schlesinger Jr. has pointed out that the majority of Americans refuse to identify themselves with any particular ethnic group. In recent years, however, many critics of this approach have argued that this emphasis on unity has tended to portray the history of some Americans—the descendants of WASP (White Anglo-Saxon Protestant) settlers of New England and the other original colonies—as the history of all citizens, thus ignoring or downplaying the experiences and contributions of Africans, Asians, southern and eastern Europeans, Native Americans, and others.

The traditional emphasis on national unity was not always as one-sided as these critics suggest, but acknowledgment of America's multicultural society has become quite commonplace in recent years. For example, political socialization in schools now routinely portrays the United States as a country where not everyone is descended from the Pilgrims at Plymouth Rock, but as a society to which people came from all over the world, an approach often identified as *cultural pluralism*. One summary of current elementary and high school textbooks concludes that schoolchildren learn that

> the unique feature of the United States is that its common culture has been formed by immigrants, American Indians, Africans (slave and free) and by their descendants. American music, art, literature, language, food, clothing, sports, holidays, and customs all show the effects of the commingling of diverse cultures in one

nation. Paradoxical though it may seem, the United States has a common culture that is multicultural.[19]

This approach to multiculturalism—stressing integration of various cultures in a larger American whole—has been challenged by advocates for a different view. Former U.S. Assistant Secretary of Education Diane Ravitch calls this alternative view a *particularist* approach to multiculturalism,[20] because it rejects cultural pluralism and favors a view of society that regards different ethnic groups as having such enormous differences between them that individuals can understand the world only through the culture of their particular group. As Ravitch characterizes particularist multiculturalism, it proposes for schools "an ethnocentric curriculum to raise the self-esteem and academic achievement of children from racial and ethnic minority backgrounds."[21] Furthermore, it "teaches children that their identity is determined by their 'cultural genes.'"[22]

According to particularist analysis, the United States has five cultures: African American, Asian American, European American, Latino/Hispanic, and Native American.[23] Based on this approach, public school districts in Atlanta, Detroit, and Washington, D.C., have developed Afrocentric curricula. An Afrocentric curriculum teaches that "black Africa is the birthplace of science, philosophy, religion, medicine, technology, of the great achievements that have been wrongly ascribed to Western civilization."[24] Curricula centered on other cultures have also been developed, including one that teaches Mexican American children to appreciate science and mathematics by studying Mayan mathematics, the Mayan calendar, and Mayan astronomy, while botany "is learned by study of the agricultural techniques of the Aztecs" and "ethnobotanical" classifications for plant species instead of the standard Linnean system used by scientists.[25]

Are developments such as these healthy or dangerous? Whichever way the question is decided, the results will have important consequences for the American political community. As we saw earlier, schools are important agents of political socialization and what they teach one generation becomes part of what is passed on to the next. That is why the content of the school curriculum has become an issue in America's culture wars.

The case for a particularist kind of multiculturalism rests on the idea that it is a better description of American reality. As one advocate of this position has put it: "There is a common American society, which is quite different from a common culture. . . . To believe in multicultural education is to assume that there are many cultures."[26] The point of this recasting of education, then, is to break the grip of the Eurocentric bias in education, which conveys the message to minority students that WASP culture is superior.

The response to particularist multiculturalism comes from those who regard it as dangerous to the American political community. Those who stress assimilation argue that ethnocentric curricula teach students a false version of history. For example, one historian contends that ethnocentric history makes a weapon of history, because it seeks to raise the self-esteem of minorities by making false claims about their ancestors.[27]

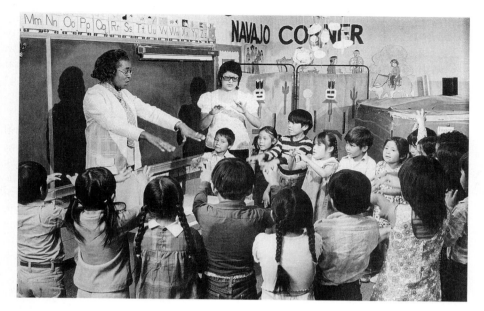

Courses based on Native American culture are designed to overcome what many see as a Eurocentric bias in education. Critics of these and other curricula that focus on minority cultures argue that this approach will contribute to social fragmentation and ethnic conflict.

Another objection to particularist multiculturalism holds that it threatens the ideal of a united political community. According to this argument, emphasizing ethnic differences over common values will serve to fragment the national community. Since our concept of national identity has allowed anyone who wanted to do so to *become* American, placing particular groups first will lead to division and ethnic strife rather than tolerance and peaceful diversity.

Multiculturalism has vocal adherents and articulate critics. Both sides agree that the issue is an important one, because of what it means to citizens' identity, the concept of national community, political socialization, and practical questions about what we should teach in our schools. Does multiculturalism promise a better, more tolerant future or one of separation and interethnic discord?

Summary

Principles. Our basic ideas and values regard "the people" as an indispensable but imperfect element of a successful political system. The American regime assumes that consent of the governed is the source of political legitimacy, but it channels citizens' power through representative institutions. Public opinion is important, but so are deliberation and individual rights. Citizens are expected to participate in politics, but we assume that the initiative to do so will come from the individuals involved and not the government.

Citizens do not just act individually; they are members of a political community marked by a distinctive political culture. American political culture has four central values: liberty and individualism, political equality, democracy, and citizen responsibility. While these values are widely shared by the public, we must be aware that the United States is a large, diverse society composed of a variety of peoples. Therefore, there has always been tension between *pluribus* (the many) and *unum* (unity) in the American political community. This tradition can be seen today in the positions on the issue of multiculturalism.

Process. The public's role in American politics operates through several mechanisms: (1) *political socialization*—citizens are exposed to political values through their families, religions, schools, communities, and other influences; (2) *measurement of public opinion*—through discernment (impressionistic judgments of opinion), straw polls (systematic but unscientific surveys of opinion), and scientific polling (identifying opinions of a large population through analysis of a representative sample); and (3) *citizen participation*—including voting, contacting public officials, joining politically active organizations, demonstrating, running for office, and even using civil disobedience, violence, and other extraordinary techniques.

Politics. The public's role in American politics belies the ambivalence with which we and the framers viewed that role. Although Americans tend to vote at lower rates than do citizens in other democracies, we are more likely than others to engage in nonvoting forms of participation.

Public opinion is carefully monitored and influences the actions of officeholders but is limited in its potential to offer a guide for officials. The public presents itself to officials in many roles—voters, constituents, respondents to polls, members of interest groups, and others—so officials do not receive just one message about what the public wants. Opinion polls cannot guide public decisions, because many important subjects are not covered in polls or because public opinion on important issues can be ambiguous or contradictory.

There are many opportunities for active citizenship. States and localities offer fertile ground for active citizenship. Opportunities to participate in politics, to contact government officials, and to make a difference are greater on the local level than on the national level.

The idea of a pluralistic political community has been at the center of a number of "culture wars" in recent years over issues of (1) the extent of personal autonomy, (2) the power of the community to protect certain values, and (3) the question of to what extent public policy should attempt to protect the heritage of ethnic groups in society.

Open Questions. There are many unsettled questions about the public's role in American politics, but we can focus on one that involves our understanding of the political community—does multiculturalism offer a better way to conceive of American society and culture, or is it a threat to the unity of the nation? This subject deserves careful consideration.

ASHER, HERBERT. *Polling and the Public: What Every Citizen Should Know.* Washington: CQ Press, 1988. Useful introduction to the problems and uses of polling.

BERMAN, PAUL, ED. *Debating P.C.* New York: Bantam, 1992. Primarily focused on how debates over multiculturalism and political correctness have affected college campuses in the United States; provides an excellent survey of the subject by presenting a wide range of views.

CONWAY, MARGARET. *Political Participation in the United States,* 2nd ed. Washington: CQ Press, 1990. Useful introduction to the topic.

DALTON, RUSSELL J. *Citizen Politics in Western Democracies.* Chatham, N.J.: Chatham House, 1988. Useful reading for comparing citizen politics in America to that in other democracies.

HUNTER, JAMES DAVISON. *Before the Shooting Begins.* New York: Free Press, 1994. Uses abortion as a prism through which to understand "culture wars" in American politics.

PAGE, BENJAMIN I., AND ROBERT Y. SHAPIRO. *The Rational Public.* Chicago: University of Chicago Press, 1992. Argues that public opinion has been sensible in its positions on issues over the past 50 years.

SCHLESINGER, ARTHUR M., Jr. *The Disuniting of America.* New York: W.W. Norton, 1993. A critical examination of multiculturalism.

Suggested Readings

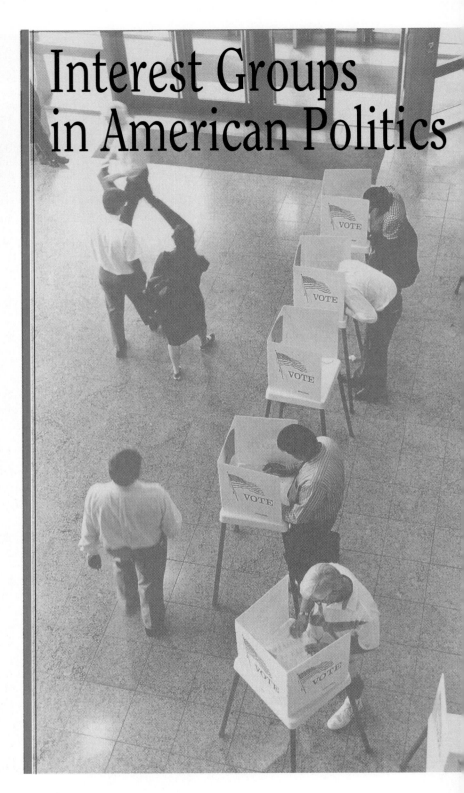

chapter

6

Interest Groups in American Politics

W ashington, D.C., is not only the seat of our national government; it is also home to a vast array of organizations that want to influence what that government does. A quick check of the metropolitan Washington phone book under the section beginning "American" or "National" gives a sense of the large number of groups that send representatives to the nation's capital.[1] Organizations such as Citizens Against Government Waste, the National Rifle Association, the American Nurses Association, the National Association of Realtors, the Fertilizer Institute, and the American League of Lobbyists are all found in the nation's capital.

This tour of the phone book presents a useful picture of how **interest groups**—organized bodies of individuals who share some common goals and who try to influence public policy[2]—fit into American politics. They occupy a central role in trying to shape public policy in the United States, whether by influencing decision makers or by attempting to win public support. Even when they represent controversial positions that others denounce as "special interests," interest groups often see themselves as defending the public interest. As we shall see, this central place for interest groups is neither new nor alien to American politics, although the character and form of interest-group politics has changed in recent decades.

Organization is what separates *interest groups* in politics from *interests*. For example, farmers and factory workers constitute interests in society, but the American Farm Bureau Federation, the National Milk Producers Association, and the AFL-CIO (the nation's largest labor organization) are interest groups. Politicians consider how different interests will be affected by public policy, but they deal more commonly with organized groups whose representatives communicate with officials.

Who or What Are the Interests?

There are many ways to classify interest groups and to explain why people support them. But a useful scheme for distinguishing the different types of groups divides them into three categories: traditional economic interests, new economic interests, and various idea-based groups (Table 6.1). As we shall see, these groups seek to influence the government from outside. Government itself is also a kind of interest, although of a different sort.

Traditional Economic Interests. Organizations that bring together individuals and/or institutions (such as corporations or unions) that share common material interests are the traditional economic interests. Business interests, agricultural interests, labor unions, professional associations form organizations in order to engage in political activity to protect the economic interests of their members. They include such organizations as the AFL-CIO, the National Association of Manufacturers, the U.S. Chamber of Commerce, the American Medical Association, and the National Education Association. While these interests are important and often effective, they face stiff competition for influence over government officials from two other kinds of groups.

interest group Organized body of individuals who share some common goals and who try to influence public policy.

TABLE 6.1 Who or What Are Some of the Interests?

Traditional Economic Interests

American Farm Bureau Federation
Food Marketing Institute
Motion Picture Association of America
National Association of Broadcasters
Alliance of American Insurers
National Association of Realtors
National Federation of Independent
    Business
American Paper Institute
Electronic Industries Association
Association of American Railroads
AFL-CIO
Association of Federal, State,
    County and Municipal Employees
International Association of Machinists

American Soybean Association
Tobacco Institute
U.S. Telephone Association
American Petroleum Institute
Independent Bankers Association
U.S. Chamber of Commerce
American Medical Association
American Hospital Association
Chemical Manufacturers Association
Semiconductor Industry Association
National. Automobile Dealers
    Association
Air Line Pilots Association
International Brotherhood of
    Electrical Workers
National Education Association

New Economic Interests

American Association of Retired Persons
American Association of State Colleges and
    Universities
American Public Welfare Association
National School Boards Association
United Way of America
American Library Association

American Association of Museums
National Association of Counties
American Institute of Physics
National Governors Association
National. League of Cities
U.S. Conference of Mayors
Planned Parenthood

Idea-Based Groups

American Israel Public Affairs
    Committee
Conservative Caucus
Consumer Federation of America
National Rifle Association
NAACP
People for the American Way
National Abortion Rights Action League
American Enterprise Institute
Heritage Foundation
Urban Institute
Joint Center for Political and Economic
    Studies

Children's Defense Fund
Common Cause
Greenpeace
Handgun Control, Inc.
National Organization for Women
League of Women Voters
Public Citizen
National. Right-to-Life Committee
Brookings Institution
Progressive Policy Institute
Carnegie Endowment for
    International Peace
Worldwatch Institute

Source: National Journal, January 23, 1993, pp. 179–88.

New Economic Interests. The expansion of federal government services and activities in the 1960s created a class of interests that includes private and public organizations that depend on government spending for their livelihood. Such new economic interests include health care providers who treat recipients of Medicaid and Medicare, state and local government agencies that receive federal funds and administer federal programs (food stamps, Head Start, and highways), defense-related industries, public radio and television stations, cultural institutions (museums, opera companies, orchestras), colleges and universities (which depend on federal grants and contracts), a variety of social service organizations (Planned Parenthood, United Way), and even associations of recipients of government benefits (veterans, Social Security recipients). Government workers—many of whom are members of the Association of Federal, State, County, and Municipal Employees (AFSCME)—are also part of this group. They constitute the fastest growing segment of organized labor in the United States.

One of these new economic interests, the American Association of Retired Persons (AARP), is the second largest nongovernmental organization in the United States (only the Roman Catholic Church is larger). It is twice the size of the AFL-CIO, with almost 30 million members. The AARP has a large headquarters in Washington with its own zip code, a staff of over one hundred, and well over a dozen registered lobbyists. It focuses its attention on issues of concern to America's elderly, especially protection of Social Security and health care. In 1990, the AARP was responsible for almost single-handedly pressuring Congress to repeal an increase in premiums for affluent Medicare recipients that was to pay for coverage of catastrophic illnesses.[3] In 1994, the AARP was an important player in the health care reform debate, as it sought to guarantee that coverage of long-term care for senior citizens would be included in any bill that passed Congress.

Thousands of American university faculty are also part of these new economic interests. They teach in educational institutions that depend on government subsidies (to the institution itself or in the form of student financial aid) for their existence. They perform research that is often funded by government (through the National Science Foundation, the National Endowments for the Arts and the Humanities, and the U.S. departments of Defense, Agriculture, Energy, and Commerce). And many work as consultants to government agencies or companies that do business with the government.

How can we distinguish between traditional and new economic interests? It is not always easy to do so. Take the example of a corporation such as General Electric (GE). GE is a huge company with divisions that clearly fall into the category of traditional economic interests: those that manufacture lightbulbs, radios, televisions, and other electronic products for the mass consumer market. But GE also has a jet engine division that depends primarily on sales of military aircraft to the U.S. government or foreign governments. This division constitutes a new economic interest. Likewise, GE has a division that builds submarines, not a typical consumer product. It, too, represents a new economic interest.

Idea-Based Groups. Organizations that are idea-based engage in political activities in pursuit of philosophical or ideological goals, rather than economic interests of members. Such groups are not entirely new in the United States. In the nineteenth century there were abolitionist groups opposing slavery and temperance organizations campaigning for the prohibition of alcohol. Their number and variety, however, have grown considerably since the 1960s. There are now a wide array of these organizations, although they tend to fall into three major types.

Some idea-based organizations are so-called **public-interest groups** that represent a vision of the common good defined by the groups themselves. One organization's view of the public interest may not correspond with another group's. Some groups arrive at their idea of the public interest through member participation (such as the Sierra Club), while in others a small circle of leaders determines the agenda and positions of the organization (such as Ralph Nader's Public Citizen).

Other idea-based groups are focused on narrow issues (for example, National Organization for the Reform of Marijuana Laws, Zero Population Growth). Many are arrayed against one another over such questions as abortion (the National Abortion Rights Action League versus the National Right-to-Life Committee) or gun control (the National Rifle Association versus Handgun Control, Inc.). Some of these groups represent people who support the organization's agenda; others are created and maintained by a small number of leaders who represent only themselves and the ideas that drive the group.

Since the 1960s, a third type of idea group has grown in importance, the **think tank.** A think tank is an organization that attempts to influence public affairs by research, conferences, and publishing rather than direct lobbying. Indeed, think tanks are distinguished from other interest groups in law as well as in approach. They are given a tax-exempt status by the government (because they are dedicated to the cultivation of knowledge), which in turn means that they are legally prohibited from engaging in lobbying. They try to influence public policy through their ideas and analyses of public issues.

Think tanks have been around for decades, but in recent years their number has mushroomed, and their opportunities for influencing public debate have expanded. Some are well-established institutions: the Brookings Institution, which is generally but not exclusively associated with the Democratic Party, has a large Washington headquarters and is staffed by politicians and scholars who move in and out of government; the American Enterprise Institute is a Republican-oriented counterpart to Brookings. Other think tanks make more explicit attempts to influence politics: in 1981, the conservative Heritage Foundation published *Mandate for Leadership,* a collection of policy studies that influenced the domestic policy proposals of the newly inaugurated Reagan administration; in 1993, the Progressive Policy Institute published a collection entitled *Mandate for Change,* hoping to play the same role in the incoming Clinton administration.

Government as an Interest. The three types of interests found in American politics are outside of government, although they may be intimately involved in the work of government. But government organizations themselves can also be a type of interest in American politics. For example, state and local governments have an interest in federal government policy, so they work to influence the decisions that will affect them. The nation's governors meet regularly, adopt positions on issues of common concern, and lobby the president and Congress to agree with their views. Mayors, especially those from large cities, frequently do likewise.

public-interest group Organization that represents a vision of the common good as defined by the group itself. Some public-interest groups arrive at their idea of the public interest through member participation; in others a small circle of leaders determines the agenda and positions of the organization.

think tank A nonprofit organization whose members engage in research that is often directed at influencing policy makers and their decisions through education rather than lobbying.

154

Idea-based groups, such as the National Organization for the Reform of Marijuana Laws (NORML), are focused on narrow issues. Some represent members who support the organization's agenda; others are created by leaders who represent only themselves and their ideas.

In the national government, the various departments and agencies do not all share a common purpose and interests. They work to defend their own interests against other government components with competing interests. For years, the Department of the Navy was divided over the issue of the nuclear submarine program. The navy's senior officers and civilian officials tried to cut appropriations for that program, while Admiral Hyman Rickover—the commander of the nuclear submarine program—worked effectively to ensure that Congress continued to fund his research. At least since the 1980s, all departments in the federal government have engaged in lobbying campaigns to protect their budgets from being cut. Scholars have coined the term "bureaucratic politics" to capture this idea that agencies are not neutral in their behavior, but can and do behave like interest groups to promote their own goals and defend their own interests.

Like many of the ideas underlying the constitutional system, the notion of special interests exists as a counterpoint to the principle of the public interest. Both the acceptance of interests and attempts to regulate them are as old as the American Republic.

Constitutional Principles:
Reconciling Factions and the Public Interest

The framers of the U.S. Constitution understood that in a political society all people would not have the same views on issues or the same interests. For example, the American colonies had been settled by immigrants belonging to a variety of churches, from the Congregationalists in New England to the Catholics of Maryland, the Quakers of Pennsylvania, and other Protestant and Jewish groups throughout the new nation. These different congregations existed precisely because of their differing views on important religious questions. Moreover, the diversity of geography, agriculture, and commerce in the young Republic made it clear to the founders that not all Americans would have the same stake in the policies of government. Slaveholding planters in South Carolina certainly had different views on trade from the merchants of Massachusetts, while small farmers in Georgia had different interests from the commercial fishers of New England.

Indeed, James Madison saw this diversity of opinions and interests as the source of both trouble and opportunity for constructing the American regime. In *The Federalist,* No. 10, Madison wrote:

> A landed interest, a manufacturing interest, a mercantile interest, a moneyed interest, with many lesser interests, grow up of necessity in civilized nations, and divide them into different classes, actuated by different sentiments and views. The regulation of these various and interfering interests forms the principal task of modern legislation and involves the spirit of party and faction in the necessary and ordinary operations of government.

When Madison characterized the "spirit of party and faction" as an intruder in government, he was addressing the ancient problem that we identified in Chapter 1: how to promote the public interest in the face of other interests in society. Madison's terms "party and faction" come close to our modern term "interest group," because he was concerned about those groups in society—which he called *factions*—that promote their own self-interest at the expense of the public interest. When we speak of interest groups, however, we do not assume that they want to undermine the public interest, only that they have some view or interest to promote.

As Madison understood, differences in society are both inevitable and in certain ways valuable. Any society that is larger and more complex than a primitive tribal arrangement will have different groups—those who farm, those who manufacture, those who trade, and so on—and they will often disagree about the best course for public policy. Indeed, this diversity of views also indicates the presence of liberty; free people can come to different conclusions about the issues presented to them. In one of his most memorable statements, Madison asserted that "Liberty is to faction what air is to fire" (*The Federalist,* No. 10). To suppress liberty in order to give everyone the same interests and opinions is worse than learning to live with the differences. Any attempt to eliminate factions is at least "folly" and more likely will lead to tyranny.

Madison considered the problem of factions to be the central challenge facing the American founders. How were they to deal with them while still preserving liberty? His answer was that the political system should be constructed so as to control the effects of factions rather than trying to root out their causes. But how was this to be done? Madison's answer was to create a big, diverse republic.

Rather than trying to ignore or go around the problem of factions, in *The Federalist,* No. 10, Madison proposes turning the reality of factions to the advantage of the American regime. This was to be done by appreciating the various circumstances under which factions could have greater or lesser influence in society, which are conditioned largely by the size and complexity of the political community in question. On one hand, small societies tend to be more homogeneous than large ones. They may be dominated by agriculture or by trade, but it is more likely that a small political community—a small town or even a small country—will have a majority faction that wants to promote its interests over the public interest or the rights of other citizens. For example, farmers in a small rural community might want to tax only property that is not used for farming, thus displacing the tax burden of the community to the

Pro-life and pro-choice demonstrators clash in front of an abortion clinic. James Madison believed that the political system created by the U.S. Constitution offered the best means for reconciling the public interest with the many concerns of different societal groups.

minority who do not farm. In such a situation, democracy is no defense against the tyranny of the farmers; they can have their way through majority rule.

Madison proposed building a large, diverse republic in which there would be many minority factions, each competing with the others. Rather than having several small republics—the states loosely connected through the Articles of Confederation—the Constitution would join together the merchant and fishing interests of New England with the southern planters, the small farmers of the mid-Atlantic states with the coastal traders. In such an environment, he contended, it is far more likely that the public interest and the rights of citizens can be protected. Moreover, with representative democracy in place, politics in this large republic will be marked not only by clashing interests but deliberation by those elected to public office. The overall result will be that it will be far more difficult in such a regime for a majority faction—such as the farmers in the previous example—to seize control of the national government. Once again, the Constitution makes a virtue (a large, complex, deliberative and free republic) out of necessity (the problem of factions).

Ross Perot's 1992 presidential candidacy was based on the idea of taking back the government from the special interests. In practice, however, citizens disagree strongly about who are the "special interests" and what is the common good.

The conflict between the public interest and special interests is also tied to other features of the Constitution: separation of powers, checks and balances, and federalism. Madison concluded that the complex political system created by the Constitution for governing a sprawling federal republic offered the best opportunity to reconcile the public interest with the other interests in society competing for influence over government policy.

My Interests, Special Interests, and the Public Interest

There is a national ambivalence that marks the involvement of interest groups in American public life. Everyone is against "special interests," but one person's definition of who they are differs from another's. Business, labor unions, ethnic groups, doctors, lawyers, welfare recipients, and a host of others have all been called special interests at one time or another, and there is no more damning charge in our political debate than to accuse someone of serving these interests. Ross Perot's 1992 presidential campaign was largely based on a promise to serve the people rather than special interests, while Bill and Hillary Clinton pressed for health care reform to undercut the power of special interests to control Americans' medical care.

Americans often identify their interests with the common good, but one of the most difficult problems is to identify just what it is that will benefit the common good. In the 1950s, this view was summarized by the president of the General Motors (GM) corporation, who coined the expression, "What's good for GM is good for the U.S.A." In the 1990s, the interests of the middle class were identified as the interests of the whole nation. Presidential candidate Bill Clinton proposed to reshape public policy in order to protect the "forgotten" middle class, offering that group a tax cut, health insurance reform, and economic prosperity. Since most Americans consider themselves to be part of the middle class, this message was seen as promoting the common good rather than advancing the desires of special interests.

Interest groups in our society do not ask for specific policies because they want to protect special interests; they ask for trade laws, exemptions from anti-monopoly laws, health and safety regulations, and other policies because they believe that these actions will promote the general good by protecting the interests of an important part of the economy or the community. A good example can be seen in the debate over health care reform in 1994. That debate has been characterized as involving the greatest—and perhaps the most expensive—clash of interest groups in modern American political history (see Current Issues box). The range of interests involved was enormous: doctors (divided by such things as specialties, outlook, geography), hospitals, insurance companies, big and small businesses, tobacco and alcoholic beverage producers, employee groups, retired people, the disabled, veterans, to name a few. Each group presented its position as being in the public interest: for example, calling for employer mandates to pay for universal health insurance; favoring or opposing "sin" taxes; being for or against abortion coverage; being for or against using health maintenance organizations (HMOs). Some observers might consider such appeals to be cynical, and certainly there were cases in which that was true; but in most cases the various groups pressing to include or exclude some provision from the health reform bills in Congress identified their work with the common good. While all of this activity was underway, journalists, politicians, and citizen activists frequently decried the influence of special interests in the debate over health care.

The conflict between the public interest and other interests is the same one that James Madison wrestled with in *The Federalist,* No. 10. The society that he helped to create through the Constitution can be characterized as the "interest-group society."[4] Ours is a society permeated by a vast array of interests, most of which seem to have an office in Washington and a mailing list with your name on it. We want our interests to be protected; we want the public interest to be promoted; but we certainly resent the influence of special interests. The result of our ambivalence is a political process in which interest groups play a central but never a completely comfortable role.

Process: The Place of Interest Groups in the Political System

Interest groups constitute a particularly sophisticated aspect of citizen politics. As Madison made clear, when citizens band together to promote common views or interests, they have a much better chance of achieving their objectives. Therefore, interest groups constitute a more aggressive form of citizen politics than any other kind of citizen participation. In order to understand the place of these groups in our politics, we must examine how groups are organized, how they operate, and how they are regulated by government.

Interest Group Organization

Interest groups vary considerably in their size, financial security, and purposes, but they share certain organizational characteristics. All interest groups must establish and maintain a base of support. For some groups, such as the AARP, their representation of a sizeable membership is their means of influence. Others may not even be membership organizations but may exert their influence as small lobbying groups that raise funds and consist only of a small staff.

Membership groups such as the AARP often offer services or benefits that encourage people who might not otherwise become involved in an interest group to join. For example, the National Rifle Association (NRA) offers a magazine, stickers, patches, and clothing with the organization's emblem; gun insurance; discounts on ammunition; sharpshooting lessons; and other nonpolitical benefits to encourage membership. These services help keep the NRA larger than it would be if it engaged only in lobbying, which in turn can make the group more influential because it represents more people. The AARP offers its members discounted health insurance programs, a discount prescription drug program, a magazine, tours, and other services; this enables it to be more influential than if it just depended on politically minded members. Membership groups can draw on fees and dues to provide a base of financial support, while nonmembership groups must solicit funds from sympathetic individuals or organizations.

Interest Groups Clash Over Health Care Reform

current issues

In their attempts to shape the outcome of the national debate over health care reform, interest groups have resorted to a range of strategies intended to sway policy makers and public opinion. Each group is determined to make sure that its interest is protected or that its point of view is considered as America ponders the question of what—if any—changes should be made in health care policy.

WHAT INTERESTS ARE INVOLVED?

By its very nature, the health care reform issue involves every type of interest in the country. *Traditional economic interests* include the insurance industry; the medical, dental, and other health professions who staff the health system; for-profit hospitals; pharmaceutical companies; medical supply businesses; and investors in health-related stocks and bonds. Because so much of health care in the United States is delivered through government agencies, a wide variety of *new economic interests* are also involved: the American Association of Retired Persons (AARP), for example; as well as medical schools (concerned about funding for research); public employees in government health programs and institutions; and not-for-profit health insurers and providers (such as Blue Cross/Blue Shield and Catholic hospitals) whose livelihood is affected by government policy. *Idea-based groups* have also been active participants in the debate. Some think tanks, including the Heritage Foundation, constructed their own reform plans as models for decision makers. Advocacy groups, especially Ralph Nader's Public Citizen group and several conservative organizations, have lobbied for or against cost controls on hospitals,

During the 1994 debate over health care reform, all sides tried to influence public opinion. For example, one insurance industry association produced a series of television commercials featuring "Harry and Louise," a fictitious couple nervous about the effects of the Clinton administration proposals on their lives.

inclusion of mental health coverage in a national health insurance scheme, or coverage of abortion services. *Government* itself has been an interest, whether because of states' role in programs such as Medicaid and funding public hospitals, or in public universities' role in training doctors and other health workers and conducting research. For example, the National Governors Association has been active in trying to protect states from carrying a bigger responsibility for funding health care than they already do.

WHAT STRATEGIES AND TACTICS HAVE INTERESTS USED?

The wide array of interests at work in the health care reform debate have used almost every conceivable technique for advancing their cause:

- *Lobbying:* Each time Congress has considered any legislation affecting health care, Capitol Hill has been overrun with representatives from the many interests with a position on the issue. For example, Senator John Breaux (D.-La.) reported that he had been approached by "everyone from A to Z"[1] who had something to say on health care. In 1994, he received visits from insurers, hospitals, and doctors, but also from music therapists, witch doctors, and wart removers, all of whom wanted their specialties covered by a reform bill.[2] Interest-group representatives met individually with members of Congress, testified before committees, and stalked the halls of the Capitol speaking to staff.

(continued)

- *Contributing to Campaigns:* One time-honored way that interest groups have used to try to influence legislation in Washington has been to contribute to political campaigns. In the first half of 1994 alone, health-related interest groups gave substantial sums of money to campaigns—the American Medical Association gave $977,704; the American Dental Association PAC gave $630,553; the National Association of Life Underwriters gave $612,301; the American Nurses Association gave $444,446; and the Independent Insurance Agents of America gave $371,260. Overall, between January 1993 and March 1994, health-related political action committees contributed a total of $26.4 million to congressional candidates.[3]

- *Advertising:* Television and radio have been important media for communicating the messages of many interests in the health care debate. For the year 1994 alone, estimates put the total spent on television advertising alone at about $60 million—more than the $50 million spent on television advertising during the 1992 presidential campaign.[4] One of the most famous efforts to sway the public through television was a series of commercials sponsored by the insurance industry that featured a ficticious couple—"Harry" and "Louise"—who discussed the adverse effects of changes in health care. The commercials spawned replies by advocates for major reform and even a parody of the couple starring Bill and Hillary Clinton as Harry and Louise.

- *Grass-Roots Organizing:* During 1994, the Clinton administration sponsored the Health Security Express, a cross-country bus tour designed to stimulate support for the president's health care reform plan. The effort encountered opposition from counter demonstrations put on by organizations, such as Taxed Enough Already, that wanted to stop the administration plan from becoming law.

- *Campaign-Style Politicking:* President Clinton, First Lady Hillary Rodham Clinton, and other advocates for the administration plan travelled extensively in order to rouse public support for health care reform. Others, including former presidential candidate Ross Perot, conservative activists, and various interest-group representatives, employed similar tactics.

- *Using the Media:* During the congressional debate on health care in 1994, television and radio talk shows continually featured discussions of the issue and representatives from the many interests involved. Sunday morning news programs featured members of Congress, administration representatives, and prominent speakers on behalf of interest groups.

---

[1]Quoted in *New York Times,* August 16, 1994, p. A10.
[2]Ibid.
[3]Ibid., p. A1.
[4]Ibid., p. A10.

All interest groups must have some kind of structure. Small groups may have a single office with a simple organization and a tiny staff. Large groups such as the AARP, the American Legion, and the Sierra Club may have local chapters, state organizations, and a complex hierarchy of officials. The group may use its own members or staff to communicate with government officials, or it may hire professional representatives to act on its behalf. Some interest groups do both: they hire experts to help them plan activities such as designing a publicity campaign or identifying which members of Congress are most likely to be sympathetic to the group's message; then they deploy their members (who portray themselves as "citizen activists" rather than political professionals) to carry the group's message.

Mal Enterprises, Inc.

AIDS activists have used advertising, public demonstrations, and even aggressive political action to force public officials to make AIDS research a government priority.

Interest Group Functions

Interest groups operate politically by performing at least one of four basic functions.[5] First, they offer citizens an opportunity to *participate* in the political process. Membership organizations offer individuals a chance to support the work of the group and promote their own interests or cause. Even nonmembership organizations offer people a chance to participate in politics, because those individuals have an institutional base from which to try to influence public affairs.

Second, interest groups *educate* the public and political leaders about political issues. Groups may employ publicity campaigns or send their representatives to public forums—congressional committee hearings, television and radio shows, town meeting gatherings, debates, and other assemblies—in order to provide citizens and officials with information about subjects of concern to the group. In 1988, the AARP was effective in drawing attention to the issue of long-term care for the elderly, which had the effect of obtaining a pledge to support such care from all major Democratic presidential contenders that year.

In 1994, an array of groups used television, radio, and print advertisements to inform the public about different aspects of health care reform proposals, a tactic that drew fire from media critics and politicians charging that the ads were inaccurate. This charge highlights an important issue in interest-group functioning, namely that groups exist to educate people to see an issue as the group sees it, which may not be the way other groups see it. That is why even public-interest groups cannot always be relied upon to present an issue objectively. This is not to suggest that no one tells the truth in politics; on the con-

Thomas Hale Boggs Jr. is the consummate Washington lobbyist. He is the son of two former members of Congress (Representatives Hale and Lindy Boggs, both Democrats from Louisiana) and the brother of a top Capitol Hill journalist (radio and television reporter Cokie Roberts). His firm, Patton, Boggs, and Blow, represents some of the biggest clients in the country—Chrysler, General Motors, Emily's List, and others. Boggs does his lobbying in the time-honored way: he relies on extensive personal contacts gained over a lifetime in Washington; he knows the players and the process well; and he is ever eager to do a favor that might be returned later. He assists congressional candidates in raising money for their campaigns and is an active presence at the many fund-raising receptions that dot the Washington social scene.

trary, the point is that the truth is often complex and not easily discernible in a 30-second commercial.

Third, interest groups engage in *agenda building;* that is, they seek to draw attention to issues that will not otherwise receive public or governmental attention. The goal of such agenda building is to pressure public officials to respond to the issue in question. In the 1980s, AIDS activists used advertising, public demonstrations, and other highly visible techniques to make AIDS research a government priority. Likewise, the group Mothers Against Drunk Drivers (MADD) pressed for policy reform to deal with that problem, while Handgun Control sought to make gun violence an important issue. When an interest group is successful in bringing public attention to an issue and getting a candidate or official to pledge to "do something" about it, then the group has gone a long way toward achieving its policy goal.

Finally, interest groups engage in *monitoring* of public policy and policy proposals. They track government involvement with the issue of their concern, whether through talking to lawmakers and their staffs, watching proposed regulations from bureaucratic agencies, listening to candidates, or observing the actions of executives. Members of groups such as the NRA or the AARP frequently receive a "Legislative Alert" informing them of bills in Congress that may affect the group's interests.

Government Regulation of Interest Groups

Interest groups occupy a position in law that is similar to the place of the media (see Chapter 12), although such groups do not have the prestige or rights that journalists enjoy. Interest groups are covered by certain constitutional provisions that protect their existence and activities, but officials can regulate their behavior.

The First Amendment protects interest groups' right to peaceably assemble and their right to petition government. These rights combine to effectively guarantee citizens a right to associate with others of similar views or interests and to communicate with government officers in order to advance their positions. Under the First Amendment, individuals or groups have the right to make their case to officials about how they want public policy to be shaped. Activities directed toward trying to influence the decisions of public officials are known as **lobbying.** Even those who are not U.S. citizens, such as members of foreign governments or corporations, can participate in lobbying.

Lobbying is not an unrestricted right, however. Officials can require professional **lobbyists**—those who engage in lobbying on behalf of their own organizations (for example, the Washington representative of a trade association) or for paying clients (for example, a lawyer who represents many interest groups)—to register with congressional officials, state governments, or the Federal Elections Commission. This registration usually involves filing a form indicating the group that the lobbyist represents and the issues of interest to that group. The point of registration is to reveal which interests are trying to influence government and on what issues, in order to make government more open and accountable.

The basic law that governs lobbying in the national government is the 1946 Federal Registration of Lobbying Act, which requires groups and individuals seeking to influence legislation to register with Congress and to submit quarterly financial reports. But because officials often work in close contact with lobbyists, and many of the most successful lobbyists are former government officials, there has been little effort to enforce the law. Lobbyists register and submit financial reports, but few resources are devoted to ensuring that all register or that reports are accurate. In consequence, the apparent goals of openness and accountability are often difficult to achieve, because it is difficult to determine just how many lobbyists are unregistered and how much money lobbyists have spent trying to influence policy.

The most carefully enforced laws regarding interest groups are tax laws. Contributions made to think tanks are tax deductible because these are research and educational institutions, but in exchange, these organizations are forbidden to engage in direct lobbying. The Internal Revenue Service monitors think tanks to ensure that they do not engage in prohibited activity, although in practice it is sometimes difficult to distinguish educational activities of a think tank from standard lobbying tactics. For example, a representative of the Progressive Policy Institute can be asked to appear before a congressional committee to testify for or against a bill as an expert witness, but the group cannot request (as other interest groups can) the right to appear before the committee.

As the preceding discussion suggests, interest groups can influence Congress directly by appearing before particular committees. Groups can also talk to legislators in their offices, engage in public advertising, organize letter-writing campaigns to get citizens to communicate with their representatives, or even contribute to political campaigns. Interest groups can make use of a number of strategies and tactics as they try to shape public policy.

What Do Interest Groups Do to Influence Public Affairs?

Interest groups employ two general strategies to influence public affairs, usually at the same time. One is to *work outside government*. Groups seek to influence public opinion by advertising in major publications or on radio and television; they send representatives to appear on news programs such as *The MacNeil/Lehrer News Hour* or in public forums; and they distribute everything from political buttons ("ERA Yes," "Pro-Choice," "Choose Life") to bumper stickers (the National Education Association has one stating "If you can read this, thank a teacher"). They use direct mail as a way to contact members, recruit new members, and raise money. Some groups, such as the National Rifle Association, People for the American Way, the American Legion, and the AARP, rely on direct mail to finance their activities and stimulate members to political action (such as writing their representatives).

One of the most important activities that groups undertake is participation in campaign politics to influence who wins public office. An organization may

Interest Groups in Contemporary American Politics

lobbying Activities directed toward influencing the decisions of public officials, especially face-to-face appeals.

lobbyist Individual who works on behalf of his or her own organization or for paying clients. The term implies one who does this for a living, as opposed to a citizen activist.

advertise for or against a candidate or provide volunteers to staff a campaign. Most significantly, interest groups contribute money to campaigns. Contributions may come from individuals or they may be made by **political action committees (PACs).**

PACs are fund-raising and contributing organizations. They contribute to candidates in congressional, presidential, state, and local campaigns. Many PACs are outgrowths of existing interest groups, although some are independent. Most are small, giving less than $20,000 in total contributions during a two-year congressional election cycle. But some PACs are big-time contributors (see Table 6.2). In 1992 the largest donor to House and Senate campaigns was Emily's List, which supports women running for office; it raised $6.2 million through 63,000 contributions and distributed the money to 55 women running for Congress who supported abortion rights. Emily's List uses a technique known as "bundling" (coordinating the giving of technically separate contributions) to get around campaign laws and funnel more money to candidates it supports.[6] Recipients of its contributions, including Governor Ann Richards of Texas, credited the PAC's help for their electoral success.

PACs created by the American Medical Association, the American Realtors Association, and other interest groups are important to the funding of campaigns. In the 1994 congressional elections, money from interest groups concerned with medical and other related fields constituted a major element of PAC

political action committee (PAC) Fundraising organization that contributes to candidates for public office. Their activities are controlled by the Federal Election Campaign Act and other laws.

TABLE 6.2 Top PAC Contributors to Federal Candidates, 1992

	(millions)
Realtors Political Action Committee	$2.9
American Medical Association Political Action Committee	2.9
Democratic Republican Independent Voter Education Committee	2.4
Association of Trial Lawyers of America Political Action Committee	2.3
National Education Association Political Action Committee	2.3
United Auto Workers Voluntary Community Action Program (UAW-V-CAP)	2.2
American Federation of State, County, and Municipal Employees (AFSCME)	1.9

Source: Federal Election Commission.

giving to candidates. PAC contributions account for over one-third of all money collected by House candidates and nearly a quarter of the funds raised by Senate candidates. There are over four thousand PACs registered with the Federal Elections Commission, the government agency responsible for overseeing campaign finance. Federal election law sets limits on PAC organization, fund raising, and contributions. (These matters will be addressed in Chapter 7.)

Interest groups also *communicate directly with government* to influence officials. First, they establish a presence in Washington or a state capital to do two things: listen (in order to learn about what officials are doing or contemplating) and lobby. While it may seem that all lobbyists do is talk to legislators and their staffs, just as important to their efforts is listening, because it can alert a group to policy proposals under consideration and the activities of other groups. Political scientist Robert Salisbury has pointed out that the tremendous increase in lobbying activity that has occurred in the past quarter-century can be explained by interest groups' need for information about what government officials are doing or planning to do, as much as it can be attributed to a desire by groups to influence policy.[7]

A group may establish its presence by locating its headquarters in the capital, by sending one or more representatives to the seat of government, or by hiring an agent to serve the group's interests. Prominent in Washington are full-time lobbyists who act as "hired guns" for organizations that pay for their services. One of the most prominent lobbying firms in national politics is Patton, Boggs, and Blow, a highly successful enterprise that represents Emily's List, corporations, foreign governments, and others who want ears and a voice in Washington. Indeed, successful lobbying firms like this one may even be hired by clients with conflicting positions on the same issue.

Beyond just having a presence in the capital, interest groups participate in the process of "petitioning government," which is guaranteed in the Constitution. They make contacts with government officials, whether by visiting legislators and executive officials in their offices or meeting them at parties that are part of the Washington social scene. Lobbyists give testimony on proposed legislation at committee hearings, attempting to persuade committee members that their groups' interests must be considered and protected in the legislative process. Interest groups will draft laws to give to sympathetic legislators, who may submit them as bills in Congress. Interest groups, especially public interest groups, may also submit **amicus curiae** briefs—documents filed by those who are not parties to a case but who are acting as "friends of the court" to try to influence the decision. For example, in each abortion-related case before the Supreme Court in recent years, there have been more than a dozen briefs filed by groups that were not parties in the case but wanted to shape the Court's ruling: the National Abortion Rights Action League, the American Civil Liberties Union, the National Right-to-Life Committee, and others. Groups may employ **grass-roots politics**—organizing citizens to become politically active in support of a common goal—to help persuade officials to go along with them. They call on members to write or phone representatives or organize teams of constituents to visit the officials. Interest groups often work together when they are promoting shared goals.

amicus curiae Latin for "friend of the court." A brief filed by a person or group not party to a case that is intended to influence the decision of the court.

grass-roots politics Organizing citizens to become politically active in support of a common goal.

Take Ten Steps to Effective Lobbying

Get organized: One reason there has been a proliferation of interest group activity in American politics is that organized political action is generally more effective than the collective effect of individual actions. Organized groups—from True Blue Patriots to the American Medical Association and the Sierra Club—have a much better chance of being heard and exerting some influence. One may find an existing group to join or may need to start from scratch. Students enjoy excellent opportunities to work for causes they support, while later in life demands on their time will be harder to juggle.

Learn the steps to successful lobbying: Lobbyists and those who study them conclude that there are certain rules you must follow to be more effective at lobbying. These rules do not guarantee that you will get your way, but failure to follow them almost ensures that you will not. Before you begin, decide what issue concerns you: Do you want to see health care reform succeed? Do you want a balanced budget amendment? Do you favor or oppose school prayer? Pick your issue and then follow the ten steps listed here:

- *Define your objective:* Public officials are busy and have limited time; focus on one issue and one clear message you want to communicate.
- *Know the process:* What are the rules for decision making? Is it a legislative body, a regulatory agency, or whatever? Decision makers work within a very specific set of rules and procedures; you must work with them.
- *Know the key players:* Find out who has influence over your issue; find out about them—their record on this issue, their likely position, the influences on them.

- *Understand the timing:* Policy makers focus on immediate issues and deadlines; is it too early to bring up the issue (because they aren't thinking about it yet) or too late (because a decision has been made)?
- *Anticipate opposition:* What are the objections to your position? Can you answer them? Can you help the officials you want to influence to answer them?
- *Provide useful information:* Give officials information they can use—statistics, stories about the consequences of not doing what you want, and so on—that can help them justify their decisions.
- *Always tell the truth:* Policy makers don't want to be deceived, and they don't want to be embarrassed.
- *Prepare materials to present to officials:* These should be made in light of points 1-7.
- *Support your friends:* Can you help others with similar goals? If so, they may be able to help you.
- *Be courteous:* Even if you are unsuccessful, keep channels open for the future.

Check out the political activities of the groups to which you belong: Many of the organizations to which citizens belong—business, labor and professional associations, issue groups, and so on—engage in political activity. If you belong to a union or professional association, find out what that group's political activities are. Do you know what political agenda the group is promoting? Who makes those decisions? Do you agree with them? Can you change them? You may find that the organization is promoting your ideas or interests, or you may be shocked that it stands for things you oppose.

The Evolution of Interest Group Politics

Interest group politics in the United States has changed in the second half of the twentieth century. Following World War II, Washington was a political community in which public opinion was still discerned more than it was measured, in which voting and letter writing to representatives were the chief means of individual participation with officials, and in which interest-group politics was relatively stable. Most of the groups with a presence in the nation's capital were traditional economic interests, and their attention was focused on the material concerns of their members.[8]

Indeed, in this relatively stable environment, certain cozy relationships developed between interest groups, the congressional committees that made policy relevant to interested groups, and the administrative agencies that carried out those policies. Political scientists called these three-way relationships **iron triangles** or *subgovernments* and explored how they shaped policy in various areas. In agriculture policy, farming interests allied themselves with congressional agriculture committees, which in turn had jurisdiction over the Department of Agriculture in the executive branch. On veterans policy, the American Legion and other veterans' groups maintained close contact with the veterans' affairs committees in each chamber and with the Veterans Administration. In the matter of regulating interstate trucking, large fleet trucking firms cultivated close ties with the Interstate Commerce Commission (which regulates trucking) and the relevant committees on Capitol Hill. Interest groups contributed to the campaigns of members of Congress, testified at hearings and helped provide information or draft legislation needed to make policy, and served as the source of many political appointees to run the administrative agencies. Committees wrote the legislation governing each area and provided the funds for programs and administration. Administrative agencies implemented the laws and programs.

Stable relationships of this sort began to give way, however, in the changing political environment of the 1960s and 1970s. The civil rights and antiwar movements opened a new era of participation through demonstration and litigation. For example, women's groups used protests to draw attention to their cause but also filed lawsuits intended to end discrimination in the work-

iron triangle Three-way relationship between a bureaucratic agency, an interest group, and a congressional committee. Also known as a *subgovernment*. In recent years, looser "issue networks" have replaced iron triangles in the making of policy.

Iron triangles feature tight connections between interest groups, bureaucratic agencies, and congressional committees. For example, interstate trucking companies cultivated close ties with the Interstate Commerce Commission and related committees on Capitol Hill. Today, iron triangles have given way to looser issue networks that include a wider array of organizations and interests.

TABLE 6.3
Some Facts About Interest Groups

In the United States there are:

250,000 religious congregations

2,000 trade associations

3,000 organizations with offices in Washington, D.C., one-quarter of them founded since 1970

More than 4,000 political action committees (PACs)

In Washington, D.C., there are:

29 percent of all national nonprofit associations

Representatives of more than 4,000 individual corporations

More than 37,000 lawyers

issue network Combinations of self-interested, issue-oriented, and ideologically based interest groups who interact with government officials and institutions to shape public policy in a specific area.

place, education, bank lending policies, and other areas. At the same time, the use of polling became more common and widespread, which in turn encouraged interest groups to try to sway public opinion and then employ public support as a weapon to pressure officials to support their positions. New government programs stimulated new economic interests; the creation of Medicare helped fuel the rise of the AARP as an organization dedicated to protecting the government benefits received by the elderly. Changes in society also sparked the rise of well-organized idea-based groups, such as consumer groups, new environmental organizations, gay-rights groups, and others. Finally, the expansion of television meant more publicity for all elements of the political system. By the late twentieth century, a "New Washington" had arisen, marked by a proliferation and fragmentation of interest groups, as well as an explosion in the number of lobbyists and group representatives working in the nation's capital (Table 6.3). In a political system that guarantees interest groups an opportunity to participate and relative freedom to do so, interests that wanted to play a part in the changing political scene were able to organize and try to influence policy.

Interest-group politics today is more open than it was in the "old Washington." Now that television is essentially universal and media such as talk radio are prominent, many means exist for transmitting political messages. Women, the disabled, gays and lesbians, and others have found that political action can be effective in promoting an interest group's political agenda. Turnout in elections has generally declined, but nonvoting participation is up. In recent years citizen contacts with representatives have increased dramatically, often at the behest of interest groups using grass-roots politics, presidents seeking to pressure Congress, or talk radio hosts advising people to "speak up." As we noted in our discussion of citizen rights and liberties, there has also been a growing tendency of groups to frame their demands in terms of rights. Interest-group activity feeds the trend toward "rights talk" that we discussed in Chapter 4.

In this open environment, there has been a tremendous fragmentation of interest groups. In the area of health policy, the once-dominant American Medical Association now competes with hospital associations, other doctors' groups, insurance interests, medical and dental schools, corporate medical research interests, pharmaceutical interests, veterans' interests, and others for influence over legislation. There has also been growth in the number and sophistication of idea-based groups, which compete with economic interests in their attempts to influence policy. Conservative and liberal advocacy groups, issue groups, and think tanks are now all part of loose arrays of interests that revolve around an issue. Iron triangles have passed from the political scene, because so many new groups have broken up the old subgovernments. Where there was once an iron triangle, there is now an **issue network**—a loosely connected web of government units, interest groups, experts, and activists who are concerned about a common issue.[9] Where once there were cozy and relatively predictable relations within a subgovernment, today an amazing vari-

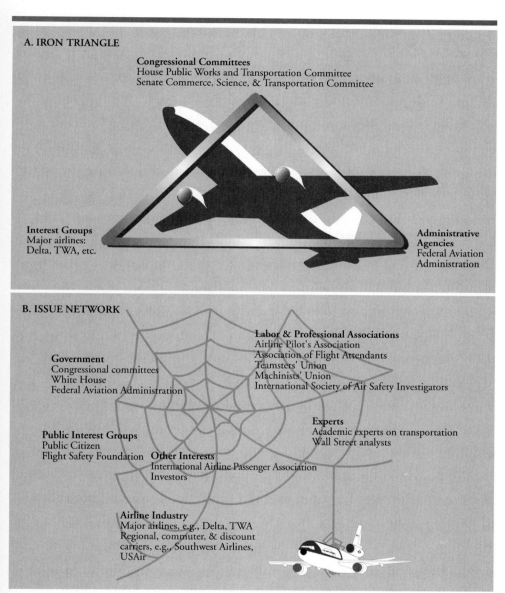

A. IRON TRIANGLE

Congressional Committees
House Public Works and Transportation Committee
Senate Commerce, Science, & Transportation Committee

Interest Groups
Major airlines:
Delta, TWA, etc.

Administrative Agencies
Federal Aviation Administration

B. ISSUE NETWORK

Government
Congressional committees
White House
Federal Aviation Administration

Labor & Professional Associations
Airline Pilot's Association
Association of Flight Attendants
Teamsters' Union
Machinists' Union
International Society of Air Safety Investigators

Public Interest Groups
Public Citizen
Flight Safety Foundation

Other Interests
International Airline Passenger Association
Investors

Experts
Academic experts on transportation
Wall Street analysts

Airline Industry
Major airlines, e.g., Delta, TWA
Regional, commuter, & discount
carriers, e.g., Southwest Airlines,
USAir

FIGURE 6.1 The Iron Triangle versus The Issue Network: Airline Transportation Policy

ety of self-interested, issue-oriented, and ideologically based groups and individuals are loosely connected in "shifting, almost kaleidoscopic configurations"[10] to shape public policy. The result is that while there are more interests and more group activity than ever before, interests have less clout in this wide open system than the few material interests did in the days of the "old Washington." In Figure 6.1, we can see in the example of airline transportation how an issue network is a larger and more unwieldy array of interests than an iron triangle.

Our Interest Group Society

Alexis de Tocqueville noted the American tendency to join organizations—evidence of a vigorous kind of citizen politics, but also the basis of interest-group activity. Therefore, interest group politics has always been a part of American politics, although it has expanded and fragmented in the "new Washington." In the past, government was smaller and political parties were stronger. Many interests in society had less need to organize and try to influence policy. As we shall see in the next chapter, however, electoral politics has become more individualistic and fragmented in the past quarter century. We also know that government does far more today than it did in the past. Government agencies also act more like interest groups, whether it is the National Governors Association pressing Washington for policy changes or the Clinton White House organizing the "Health Security Express" to pressure Congress to adopt the president's health care reform proposals.

With the rise of activist government, more interests in the American political community have felt the need to seek representation in Washington. In the process, our society of interests has become the interest-group society.

open questions

Is Interest-Group Politics Too Open?

There is broad agreement in the United States that our politics is marked by the presence and activity of a remarkable number of interest groups. Where there is disagreement, however, is in the question of what that presence and activity ultimately mean for the conduct of government. Does the political system perform as James Madison and his colleagues hoped it would, reconciling the demands of competing interests to promote the public interest? Or is the government a captive of special interests?

The answers to these questions lie in the notion of representation. On one hand, the proliferation of interest groups in recent decades has had a beneficial effect by making politics more representative than ever before. There are lots of new groups in American politics looking out for interests that traditionally were unorganized. Most occupation-based groups have long been well organized, but many other interests have not. African Americans, Hispanics, and women have mobilized since the 1950s and 1960s, and even animals and the unborn are well represented.[11] There is also a wide array of public-interest groups operating in contemporary politics. The explosion of interest groups has opened up the political process and transformed policy making. Where once iron triangles kept policy making in certain areas confined to a tightly knit subgovernment—as in agriculture policy—today only loose issue networks remain. These networks do not exercise the same kind of control over policy that their predecessor subgovernments did.

On the other hand, the increase in representation has not necessarily meant better policies or greater attention to the public interest. The proliferation of groups makes politics more complex and may place too many demands on decision makers, thus making it difficult for officials to work effectively. The content of groups' demands is often unclear, and it is hard to set priorities when hundreds of organizations are all clamoring for attention at once. Finally, elected leaders may find it almost impossible to build the kinds of political coalitions necessary to govern effectively.[12]

The upshot of greater participation by more groups is that the American political system could be vulnerable to the influence of minority factions. Some critics of contemporary interest-group politics have argued that this is exactly what is going on, that the public interest is lost in the realm of fragmented, aggressive, interest organizations promoting their own agendas.

These developments raise some important and difficult questions for American politics. In making politics more representative of the diversity of the nation, have we made the country too unwieldy to be governed effectively? Have interest groups protected their own interests at the expense of the larger public interest? Should we value representation over effectiveness, or should we favor decisive government even if not every interest is represented?

| Summary

Accepted as part of the political system, interest groups play a central role in the policy-making process. There are three major types of interest groups in American politics: (1) traditional economic interests—many business, labor, and professional groups seeking tangible benefits from government; (2) new economic interests—those groups representing interests in society that depend on "big government"; and (3) idea-based groups—those groups motivated by ideas, whether focused on a narrow issue or driven by a broad ideology, including think tanks that perform research and educational tasks. Government is also a kind of interest.

Principles. The American founders assumed that there would be different interests in society that would form organizations to promote their common goals. Government must deal with these groups and at the same time promote the public interest. In *The Federalist,* No. 10, James Madison presented an analysis of the problem of factions in society and how to deal with them. Factions are those groups that seek to promote their own interest at the expense of the public interest or the rights of others. Madison explained the inevitability of different interests and interest groups, but he argued that their effects could be controlled. To do this requires a big, diverse community so that there will be many minority factions in competition with one another. This will help promote the public interest.

Americans' thinking about interest groups in politics reflects some of Madison's ideas. Citizens and interests in society often see their own objectives as consistent with the public interest but are suspicious of the influence of special interests (whomever citizens believe them to be).

Process. Interest groups vary considerably in size and structure but share certain characteristics; all need a base of support and an organizational structure. All groups perform four key functions: they enable individuals to *participate* in politics; they *educate* the public and officials about issues (from each group's own perspective); they work on *agenda building* to draw attention to the issues that concern them; and they engage in the *monitoring* of policy and proposals for those who support them.

Governmental regulation of interest groups is minimal. The Constitution guarantees citizens the right to assemble peacefully and to petition government about concerns. A 1946 Federal Registration of Lobbying Act requires groups to register and submit financial statements, but enforcement has not been very aggressive.

Politics. Interest groups use two general approaches to shape policy: (1) they *work outside government* by employing publicity and other techniques to influence public opinion, and they contribute money to campaigns, hoping to help elect sympathetic officials to public office (through *political action committees*); and (2) they *communicate directly with government officials,* seeking to persuade those officers to shape policy as the group wants it to be shaped. This is known as *lobbying.*

Interest-group politics has changed in the past few decades. In the old Washington of the 1950s and 1960s, there were only a small number of interest groups represented, and policy making was often dominated by "subgovernments" or "iron triangles" that consisted of a congressional committee, a bureaucratic agency, and related interest groups. As government grew and took on more responsibilities and society changed, more interests in society began to organize. In today's Washington, a huge array of interest groups and lobbyists is at work, and policy making occurs amidst big and loosely drawn "issue networks" that link a wide range of public and private organizations, experts, and citizen activists.

Open Questions. Has the creation of a "new Washington" politics been for better or worse? On one hand, politics is now more open, and a greater variety of interests in American society have representation in policy making. On the other hand, the greater complexity and openness of government has not necessarily led to better policies, more effective government, or greater attention to the public interest.

BERRY, JEFFREY M. *The Interest Group Society,* 2nd ed. New York: HarperCollins, 1989. Capable discussion of interest-group politics within the context of Madison's ideas as discussed in *The Federalist,* No. 10.

BIRNBAUM, JEFFREY H., AND ALAN S. MURRAY. *Showdown at Gucci Gulch.* New York: Random House, 1987. Fascinating account of how interest groups did and did not influence the Tax Reform Act of 1986.

CIGLER, ALLAN A., AND BURDETTE A. LOOMIS. *Interest Group Politics,* 3rd ed. Washington: CQ Press, 1991. Good introduction to and overview of the subject.

MUNDO, PHILIP A. *Interest Groups: Cases and Characteristics.* Chicago: Nelson Hall, 1992. Interesting examination of six interest groups (business, labor, and citizens groups) in their organization and behavior.

WOLPE, BRUCE C. *Lobbying Congress: How the System Works.* Washington: CQ Press, 1990. A good primer on lobbying, with case studies of lobbyists at work and in competition with one another.

Suggested Readings

chapter 7

Elections, Parties, and Campaign Politics

Novermber 8, 1994, was a distinctive day in American history. Voters chose to turn control of both houses of Congress over to the Republican Party for the first time in over 40 years. That day marked an end, an event, and a beginning. It was the end of months of campaigning by candidates, their supporters, and an array of groups interested in the outcome of the vote. The event was the election itself: the central device for awarding political office and deciding many public issues in a democrary. It was the beginning of a new era for the nation's two major political parties—the Democrats becoming the minority in the House of Representatives for the first time in over two generations, the Republicans charged with selecting a Speaker and committee chairs for the House. It was also the beginning of the 1996 presidential campaign.

The results of that election day dominated the news for several weeks because of the changes a single day's voting had brought; however, each election is part of a larger swirl of activities. In this chapter we focus our attention on the key elements of electoral politics in the United States: the elections that lie at the heart of democratic government, the political parties that contend for votes, and the campaigns that are waged by candidates for office. As we shall see, the United States has a distinctive form of electoral politics.

What Are Elections and Who Is Involved in Them?

Elections are the events by which citizens cast votes to make public decisions. The United States has far more elections for a wider variety of offices and issues than any other nation. Not only are there elections for federal, state, and local officials, but citizens are called upon to decide a wide array of political issues—tax levies, proposed state constitutional amendments or ordinances, and bond issues. Add to these electoral decisions the extensive use of primary elections to select candidates to run for office, and the result is no surprise to most Americans: an almost continuous frenzy of campaigns and elections.

Types of Elections

The regular use of free and competitive elections is what distinguishes democratic regimes from nondemocratic ones. Three broad types of elections occur in the United States.

General Elections. In a **general election,** voters cast ballots to choose public officers. American elections choose officials for fixed terms of office. This feature has two fundamental consequences: (1) it places all elected offices in a highly predictable cycle of election and reelection; (2) it insulates public officials from short-term ebbs and flows of public opinion or political reputation.

Unlike a parliamentary system, in which the government might fall because of public displeasure, scandal, or a political setback, the American regime features elected leaders who may be weakened but are able to

general election Election held to fill a governmental office or offices.

weather difficult situations and govern until the next election. Recall as well that the Constitution staggers terms of office for the House, Senate, and presidency, so the leaders of the United States are not all chosen at the same time. This further emphasizes the relationship between officials and their individual constituents.

All of these elections take place in territorially defined districts. Some of these territories have fixed boundaries, such as states (for the U.S. Senate, governors, and other state officers), counties (sheriffs, county councils, and so on), and some local government entities (school districts, municipalities). But legislative districts are subject to change in order to maintain equality of representation in accordance with the principle of "one person, one vote." State legislatures control the **apportionment** (distribution) of citizens into districts for the U.S. House of Representatives and state legislatures. After each census (taken at the beginning of each decade), these lines must be redrawn to accommodate population shifts.

Referenda. A *referendum,* you will recall from Chapter 1, is an election in which voters are asked to decide on a question or issue of public importance, usually stated in a yes-or-no format: for example, should property taxes be increased by three mills to finance schools? A referendum is a form of direct democracy because it asks voters to make substantive decisions rather than choose leaders or candidates to make decisions for them. The most widespread referenda in the United States are tax and bond levies, which most local governments must use to win authority to raise new revenue. Also important are referenda on state constitutional amendments. Some states allow referenda on proposed laws. All states use referenda for making some governmental decisions, although the federal government does not.

Primary Elections. Primary elections are voting events used to choose candidates for public office. Party primaries are the means by which the Democrats and Republicans select candidates for Congress and most state offices. In presidential primaries, voters express their preference for specific candidates and/or select delegates to the presidential nominating convention.

A primary election may be one of several different types. It may be a **closed primary,** which means that only those who identify themselves as members of the party holding the primary may participate (how this identification is established is usually set by law). Or it may be an **open primary,** which allows any voter who so desires to participate. Another system is the **blanket primary,** used frequently in Louisiana, which pits all candidates against one another regardless of party. If one candidate receives a majority of votes, no general election is needed. Otherwise, the top two vote-getters face each other in the general election.

To further complicate the varieties of primary elections, the force of their results may be different. Primaries used to select candidates for congressional or

apportionment The determination of legislative district lines.

primary election Voting event used to choose candidates for public office.

closed primary A primary election in which only voters registered as members of the political party holding the primary may participate.

open primary Primary election in which any voter may participate, regardless of party affiliation or nonaffiliation.

blanket primary Primary election in which all candidates for an office, regardless of party, compete against each other. If one wins a majority, that person is elected. Otherwise, the top two vote-getters compete in the general election.

state offices are *binding,* which means that the winner in a primary race is the nominee of that party for that office. In the presidential nominating system, some states make primary results binding on the delegates selected to represent the state at the party's national convention, but in other states the presidential primary may be *nonbinding,* which means that the outcome does not necessarily obligate national convention delegates to vote a certain way. These events are considered "beauty contests" among candidates.

political party Voluntary organization of citizens who band together to nominate candidates and to influence the direction of public policy.

Political Parties

Political parties are voluntary associations of citizens who band together to nominate candidates for office and to influence the direction of public policy. Parties seem much like interest groups, but the fact that they select candidates and provide links between officials makes them distinctive. Although never mentioned in the Constitution, parties have been participants in American politics for so long that they are considered part of the unwritten constitution we discussed in Chapter 3. They are some of the most important informal structures of our political system.

National and statewide elections are generally dominated by candidates of the two major parties—the Democrats and the Republicans. Many local elections today are officially nonpartisan (candidates may not declare party affilia-

These signs from the 1994 New York governor's race are typical of contemporary American political campaigns.

Allen Hertzke is a professor of political science at the University of Oklahoma. In December 1993, he decided to run for the school board in his hometown of Norman, Oklahoma. Over the course of the next three months, he saw campaign politics from the inside. What Hertzke learned was that running for office requires planning, commitment, and a thick skin. Although he came in third in a multicandidate race, he regards the experience as an excellent learning opportunity that gave him a better understanding of his community, local politics, and American elections.

campaign All efforts undertaken by a candidate, party, or anyone else to influence the outcome of an election.

tion on the ballot), but most successful politicians in the United States are associated with one of the major parties. That is why we speak of our politics as a *two-party system.*

The elections of 1994 present a good illustration of the differences and similarities between America's two major parties. The Democrats favor an activist government, providing health care to all citizens, aggressive support for affirmative action, environmental protection programs, recognition of legal rights for gays and lesbians, gun control, and less money for defense spending. The Republicans call for lower taxes, smaller government that engages in less regulation of business and citizens, skepticism or outright opposition to gay rights, resistance to gun control, and more money for defense. Both parties support American involvement in world affairs, freer trade among nations, and federal action against crime and drug abuse.

Candidates and Their Campaigns for Office

Those who seek office through elections are called *candidates.* Candidates for office must meet the qualifications for the office they seek—usually a minimum age and certain residence requirements—but there are few formal criteria that determine who may seek a public office. In order to prevent frivolous candidates, states usually require that candidates for office submit a petition containing the signatures of some number of registered voters requesting that the candidate's name appear on official election ballots.

Candidates must be citizens of the United States. As citizens, they retain their constitutional rights while seeking office. For example, the Supreme Court has ruled that candidates may spend as much of their own money as they wish in order to support their own candidacy, on the grounds that such spending is much like political speech and therefore protected by the First Amendment. Candidates may be associated with a political party or independent; they are free to choose to associate with others or not.

All efforts undertaken by candidates, their supporters, and others to influence the outcome of elections are called **campaigns.** Campaigning can involve nearly any kind of activity directed toward shaping the results of an election, but it generally means such things as advertising, position taking, speech making, public appearances, contacting potential supporters, fund raising, and all manners of publicity. Campaigns are a flurry of activity aimed at the specific goal of achieving some electoral result.

Each of these components of American electoral politics—elections, candidates, parties, and campaigns—is connected to the others, leaving citizens who want to better understand campaigns and elections with a sort of chicken-egg problem: What comes first? It can all be made more comprehensible if we examine their foundations in the Constitution and certain values Americans hold. Then we can see how certain electoral structures—election districts, nomination and election systems, and parties—have developed. Then we can turn to the dynamics of campaign politics in the United States.

Elections are the means for making representative democracy work. As we saw in Chapter 5, a commitment to democracy is one of the central elements of American political culture. Democracy is not always easy or obvious to achieve, however. Just as Americans are ambivalent about participation in politics, they are uncertain about just how they want electoral politics to be conducted.

Representative democracy implies *equal representation,* or "one person, one vote." Several clauses of the Constitution and its amendments point toward this goal, but in 1964 the Supreme Court asserted that equality requires that one person's vote be worth about as much as another's. It is hard to find anyone who would disagree with this principle, but in practice there has been considerable controversy over just how far the government should go to achieve that goal. Moreover, the very definition of equality is difficult to obtain. This has been particularly apparent in the matter of drawing lines for legislative districts, as we see in the Current Issues box. Because "one person, one vote" is difficult to implement in practice, it opens for constitutional scrutiny the structure of elections, electoral districts, and nearly all other dimensions of representation through citizen voting.

In the matter of selecting candidates and leaders, election processes in the United States show a preference for *decisive outcomes* in elections. The prevailing principle in most American elections is "winner take all." This value is apparent in the use of plurality elections. A **plurality** victory means that the highest vote-getter in an election wins, even if that candidate did not receive a **majority** (more than half the votes). This rule is used for nearly all congressional seats, for deciding how a state's Electoral College votes will be cast for president, and for filling most state and local offices. Some states or localities insist that officials be elected by a majority of votes cast, but even this rule is meant to establish a decisive outcome.

What is less common in this country is **proportional representation,** which is a system for allocating votes in elections according to the percentage of total votes a candidate or party receives. Proportional representation is used in several European countries as a means of ensuring the representation of various minor parties in the legislature (for example, a party that wins 20 percent of the total national vote receives a proportionate number of seats in the parliament). Its most significant use in this country is in the Democratic Party's presidential primaries, in which candidates for the nomination receive a state's delegates in proportion to their share of all votes in the primary (even this rule is recent in origin, however).

The operative principle for financing American political campaigns is *self-help.* Candidates are expected to find their own sources of funds to pay campaign expenses. This means that fund raising becomes a major preoccupation of candidates for public office, as they seek money from individual citizens, party organizations, interest groups, other politicians, and even themselves. The ability to raise sufficient funds has long been a requirement for candidates; they either had to provide their own money or get it from various "fat cats" (wealthy contributors). Reform legislation has sought to reduce candidate dependence on large contributors, but it has not eliminated the need for money. Today, some wealthy candi-

Principles: Elections as the Heart of Democratic Politics

plurality Having the most votes (but less than a majority) in an election in which votes are divided between three or more choices.

majority More than half of a voting group.

proportional representation A system for allocating votes in elections according to the percentage of total votes a candidate or party receives.

Representation and/or Equality

Before the 1960s, district lines in many states (especially in the South) were drawn to favor rural voters over urbanites and whites over blacks. The Supreme Court ultimately ruled such practices discriminatory and therefore unconstitutional. As times changed, so did the beneficiaries of gerrymandering. After the 1990 census, several new districts were created in southern states to increase the chances of African Americans and Hispanics being elected to Congress. The 1992 election brought 13 new black and 6 new Hispanic representatives to Congress, plus court challenges protesting that the districts that sent them to Washington were created by racially motivated exercises in gerrymandering. During 1993 and 1994, federal courts ruled against six of these new districts. In *Shaw v. Reno* (1993), the Supreme Court held that racial gerrymandering could be challenged as a violation of the principle of "one person, one vote."

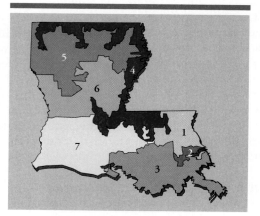

Source: U.S. Congressional Directory, 1993–1994.

The odd shapes of some of these districts made it difficult for their proponents to defend them. For example, consider Louisiana's Fourth Congressional District, shown by the shaded area in the map. The Fourth District was created after the 1990 census as one of several "majority-minority" districts designed to enhance minority representation by "packing" African Americans into a single district in which they would be the majority. Critics called the Fourth District the "mark of Zorro," while one of its designers described it as a "Z with drips." A federal court declared the Fourth District unconstitutional but allowed it to remain until a new apportionment map could be drawn.

Gerrymandering is not always overruled by the courts, because there is no constitutional guarantee that electoral districts be divided in some nonpolitical way. Democrats and Republicans are certainly free to try to protect their political interests, but the courts can and do step in when a legally relevant issue such as minority representation is in question. In the decades since the Supreme Court's "one person, one vote" principle was articulated, scores of reapportionment plans have ended up in court. While the Court has held that the racial and even partisan distribution of citizens can be taken into account in drawing district lines, it has not allowed just any system to be used. In some cases, legislators have been ordered to redraw lines. In others, such as several cases in Texas in the 1970s and 1980s, federal judges have ended up drawing legislative lines to produce representation schemes they considered acceptable.

The drawing of district lines illustrates a fundamental problem in achieving equal representation—defining the meaning of equality. Is the goal of equality better served by creating districts where minorities are the majority, or by distributing minority groups throughout other districts? Practical political concerns also become important—the majority-minority districts created after the 1990 census ensured a greater number of African Americans elected to Congress, but by concentrating black votes they also made it easier for Republicans to win the seats they needed to gain a majority in the House of Representatives in the 1994 elections.

dates bypass the need for fund raising by paying their own way: Senator Herb Kohl (D.-Wisc.), paid for his own campaign, and independent candidate Ross Perot spent $69 million of his own money to run for the White House in 1992.

Americans want elections that feature equal representation, but not at the expense of their own interests. We favor decisive outcomes, although at times we temper decisiveness with proportional representation. We want candidates to help themselves, perhaps with some assistance from the government. We are unequivocal in our commitment to democratic government, but ambivalent about what exactly that means. As we shall see, the result is a complex sort of "Politics, American Style."

Elections are the means for making key decisions in a democracy. They are not natural phenomena but are created by people to perform certain political functions, such as choosing representatives for a particular district, choosing presidential candidates, or selecting members of Congress and state and local officials. In the United States, elections are creatures of federal and state rules, as well as of the political parties that serve as informal institutions for organizing our politics.

Process: Electoral Structures in America

Who Controls Elections?

Elections are controlled by a complex mix of national and state rules. Congress has the power to regulate its own elections, but states can make important decisions regarding congressional primaries and even the size of the majority needed for winning a seat (Georgia requires an absolute majority, other states only a plurality). Presidential elections are the products of interactions between state and national laws, party rules, and even local traditions. (New Hampshire's "first in the nation" presidential primary is such a tradition—the state constitution requires that it be held before any other state's primary.)

While government authority to regulate elections is broad, it is not absolute. The Supreme Court has held that political parties are private associations and thus enjoy considerable autonomy in making important rules for selecting candidates. In *Cousins v. Wigoda* (1975)[1] and *Democratic Party v. LaFollette* (1981),[2] the Court held that parties and not states had ultimate control over election rules, nominees, and other essential decisions. But the actual structure of party nominations (primaries, delegate selection, and so on) have been the products of party rules and state laws. Since state laws are written by legislators associated with political parties, it is difficult in practice to sort out whether internal party decisions or state laws are the source of many elements of electoral processes in the United States.

Election Districts

Nearly all general elections in the nation fall into the category of **single-member district/winner-take-all (SMD/WTA)** elections. This term means that the election is designed to choose one officeholder for a single political office. That

single-member district/winner-take-all (SMD/WTA) Method of representation in which one representative is chosen from a particular area. It is the most common type of representation in the United States, as in the House of Representatives and the Electoral College.

office might be an executive position (president, governor, mayor, sheriff), a specific seat in a legislature (U.S. Senate or House, state senate or assembly, city council), a judgeship, or some kind of special governmental district or regulatory commission (for example, school board, state public service commission). In each case, a single official is chosen and only one winner is possible.

Less common, but not unknown, is the **multi-member district**—for example, a school board or city council for which the three highest vote-getters win election to fill three vacancies on the collective body. Multimember systems are most commonly found in local government. (For a comparison, see Figure 7.1.)

Of course the drawing of electoral district lines is not merely a mechanical exercise. The distribution of voters has important political consequences: it affects which party is stronger in one place or another; which social, religious, economic, and ethnic groups dominate a district; and ultimately who can be elected. Therefore, it is not surprising that apportionment and reapportionment (redrawing lines after a census) are highly politicized activities. The practice of drawing lines to give special advantage to one group over another, especially if the district created in the process is oddly shaped, is known as **gerrymandering.**

The practice of gerrymandering is an old one in politics. Indeed, the very term comes from the period of the early Republic, when Massachusetts Governor Elbridge Gerry saw to it that one legislative district was shaped so as to benefit his party. The resulting district was attacked by his opponents as resembling a salamander and so was dubbed a "gerrymander." Since that time, politicians have often worked to draw district lines to favor themselves and their colleagues and disadvantage their opponents. As we saw in the Current Issues box, the drawing of district lines—and questions about who does and who should benefit from them—has taken a new twist in recent years.

Electoral districts matter because they define the group of citizens who will cast votes. As we shall see, Americans vote in a variety of elections to select different kinds of officials. Each level of government has its own election structures.

Choosing Presidential Candidates

For most of American history, a presidential nominee was selected by political "insiders." Today, the nominee of each party is chosen through a complex process based in primary elections.

The Evolution of the Nominating System. The earliest nominating system consisted of a meeting of all of a party's members in Congress—this was how Presidents John Adams and Thomas Jefferson were chosen as candidates by their parties. But advocates of universal suffrage and a more open politics regarded "King Caucus" as elitist and introduced the *nominating convention.* First used by the Anti-Mason or "Know-Nothing" Party in 1831, it was soon adopted by the Democrats and ultimately the Republicans.

multi-member district
Legislative district from which more than one representative is chosen, such as many city councils and school boards.

gerrymandering
Term applied to the practice of drawing legislative district lines that give an advantage to one group or party over another.

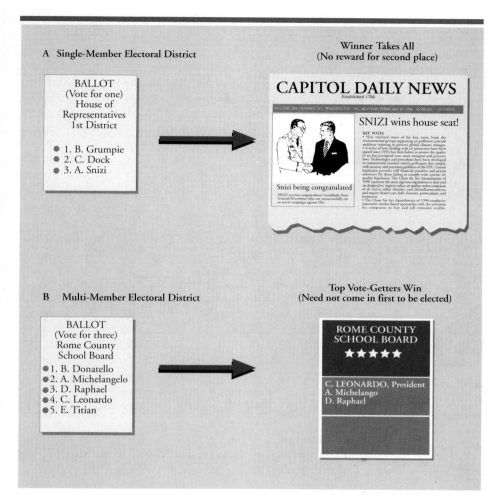

FIGURE 7.1
Single-Member Versus Multi-Member Electoral Districts. In a single-member district there can be only one winner; in a multi-member district, several top vote-getters win, so there is a reward for coming in second or third (up to the number of offices available).

The nominating convention was made up of delegates representing the party's various state and local organizations, usually under the control of the governor or some other powerful state political figure. Until 1972, the Democrats even required that all state delegate votes be cast for the same candidate (*unit rule*), which gave state delegation chairs great leverage in negotiating with potential presidential nominees for political benefits for themselves and/or their states. This system dominated presidential nominations for the rest of the nineteenth century.

Early in the twentieth century, the nominating process was modified by the introduction of *presidential primaries* in some states. This change created a kind of mixed system in which presidential candidates courted popular support in primary states (for example, West Virginia, Oregon, Minnesota) and insider support everywhere else. Primary victories were not essential to winning the nomination but were used by candidates to establish that they could win votes. For example, Senator John Kennedy entered only three primaries in 1960; the most important was in West Virginia, where the Catholic Kennedy proved that he could win large numbers of Protestant votes. Because the party's nominee was not usually chosen on the first ballot of the convention, considerable bargaining in "smoke-filled rooms" still influenced the ultimate choice of a nominee for the general election. The mixed system was last used in the election of 1968, in which Vice-President Hubert Humphrey won his party's nomination without having entered a single primary.

Humphrey's nomination came at a cost. His supporters had to agree to changes in the Democratic Party's nominating system that would make the choice of a presidential candidate more democratic. That deal set into motion a series of reforms that have not yet ended, in which the Republicans have, to some extent, been dragged along in their opponents' wake. Presidential nominees today are products of this new system.

The Current Nominating System. The contemporary nominating system is centered on a series of events held in the states to select delegates to each party's national convention and to express voter preferences for particular candidates. Most states hold presidential primary elections in which candidates for a party's nomination compete for a share of the vote. Delegates are awarded according to party rules: Republicans give most delegates to the highest vote-getter in a primary; Democrats award delegates according to the proportion of the vote each candidate receives. Some states hold **caucuses**—events in which voters gather in face-to-face meetings to discuss candidates and express their preferences.

The nominating process begins in February of each presidential election year, when Iowa holds caucuses and New Hampshire holds the nation's first primary. Soon after, in early and mid-March Junior Tuesday and Super Tuesday occur—days on which several states hold primaries simultaneously and almost one-half of all delegates are selected. Then other primaries are conducted over the remainder of the spring, until the primary season comes to a close in early June.

Each party holds its national convention to select its presidential and vice-presidential candidates in the summer of the election year. By mutual agreement, one party's convention is in July, the other in August. Because of the long primary and caucus process, the winner of the presidential nomination for each party is usually known before the convention begins. The party's presidential nominee selects a vice-presidential running mate at this time, and by Labor Day, the general election process begins.

The Presidential Election

In American presidential elections, the real contest will be between the two major-party candidates, although there are always minor candidates on the ballot (for example, the Libertarian Party candidate). Other than George Washington,

caucus Meeting held within a party to select candidates. In the early Republic, congressional caucuses within each party were used to select presidential candidates. Today, caucuses are held in a few states (such as Iowa). Citizens meet in local voting precincts to vote on candidates to nominate for office.

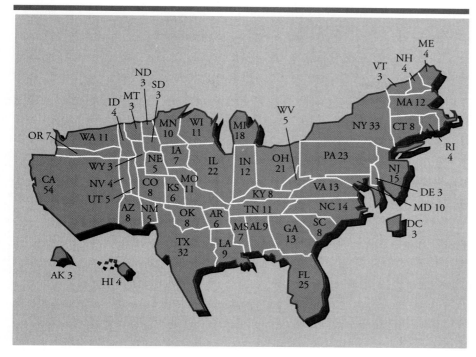

FIGURE 7.2
How States Would Look If Their Size Reflected Their Electoral Votes
Source: Holly Idelson, "Count Adds Seats in Eight States," *Congressional Weekly Report,* 48 (December 1990), p. 4240.

the United States has never selected a president who was not affiliated with a major party.

American presidents are chosen through the Electoral College system, which assigns each state electoral votes according to its representation in Congress (Figure 7.2). All states but two give all their electoral votes to the winner of the state's popular vote; Maine and Nebraska give electoral votes to the highest popular vote-getter in each congressional district. This system makes it difficult for anyone other than a major-party candidate to win electoral votes, because even a candidate who garners 20 percent of a state's vote (as Ross Perot did in 1992) receives no reward for a second- or third-place finish in the general election. The Electoral College is a winner-take-all system.

There have been third candidates who presented a more serious challenge to the Democrats and Republicans. The most successful were the ones who broke away from one of the major parties and/or used one defining issue to attack the two leaders: Theodore Roosevelt in 1912 (Progressive or "Bull Moose" Party); Senator Strom Thurmond in 1948 (States Rights or "Dixiecrat" Party); Alabama Governor George Wallace in 1968 (American Independent Party); and Ross Perot in 1992. While Perot lacked a base in either of the major parties, he had plenty of money to spend, a talent for using the media, and the issue of the deficit to attract about one-fifth of all voters that year.

participate!

Get Involved in the Electoral Process

1. Register and vote: The most direct way to influence what happens in your community, state, or nation is through the vote. There are other means of political participation, but only this one has such a binding effect on politics. A few votes often decide the outcome of local elections.

2. Participate in primaries and/or caucuses: Primaries involve some of the most important decisions made in state and congressional elections. Depending on your state, a primary or caucus is your best chance to influence who is nominated for president. (If you live in a late primary state, this is an opportunity to send a message—positive or negative—about a party's likely nominee.) Voting only in general elections cuts your voting power in half.

3. Volunteer to do campaign work: If you care about the outcome of a referendum or candidate race, help out a campaign on one side or another. This can increase your political muscle and expose you to the realities of politics. Campaigns always need help.

4. Contribute to campaigns. It does not take much money to contribute. The United States has the most broadly based campaign finance system in the world, and no one is against small citizen contributions. This is another way of sending a message about who or what is important to you.

5. Participate in political organizations: Local political groups such as the League of Women Voters, party organizations, and other institutions are good places for citizens to get information and political experience. Membership is usually open to anyone who supports the goals of the group and one can do as little or as much as one wants.

Congressional Nominations and Elections

These elections also have two distinct phases, but the congressional primary process is much less complex than the choosing of presidential nominees. For each congressional seat there is only one primary in each party (or a blanket primary), so a single vote determines the nominees. This shortens the length of active congressional campaigning, although in Chapter 8 we shall see how members of Congress engage in a "constant campaign" in attempts to ensure their reelection. The use of primaries puts control over the choice of a party's nominee in the hands of voters. This means that parties have little control over who will represent them in the general election and can thus exercise little discipline over party members in Congress.

Democrats and Republicans easily dominate the field in the general election. Independents are rarely elected to Congress. Moreover, most congressional elections involve an incumbent member of Congress seeking reelection, in which cases challengers are unlikely to unseat the person already in office. In the 1980s incumbent members of the House of Representatives were reelected over 98 percent of the time. In a dramatic contrast to this trend, many incumbents were unseated in the 1994 congressional elections.

With primaries used to select nominees and self-help governing campaigns, congressional elections are intensely candidate-centered. Parties seek influence over their own nominees by providing money to candidates, but campaign finance laws and competition from other contributors make it difficult for party organizations to serve as the major source of campaign funds. Successful con-

Nominating conventions reflect the state-based system of choosing our presidents through the electoral college.

gressional candidates enjoy a considerable amount of political independence and are generally concerned with the needs and interests of their constituents.

State and Local Elections

Certain broad similarities in state and local elections frequently mask considerable variations across the nation. Because state senates are subject to reapportionment of their district lines in the same way as are lower legislative houses, there is considerable controversy over line drawing. While legislatures generally look alike, some feature intense competition between Democrats and Republicans (California, New York, Ohio), while others are dominated by one party or the other. Legislative elections may encourage political amateurs in states with part-time legislatures (New Hampshire, Texas) or "old pros" in states with well-paid professional lawmakers (California, Minnesota). Nebraska's system is unique, because it has a nonpartisan, unicameral (single-chamber) legislature.

Local elections may be partisan or nonpartisan, depending on local and state law. Rural areas and smaller urban areas usually hold elections featuring an abundance of amateur politicians, because of the part-time nature of much of local government. In larger cities, however, elections often involve career politicians who want influence over local affairs or who are building a base from which to seek higher office. Some states provide public funds for campaigns; most do not. Referenda are common issues in many state and local elections.

By design, many of these subnational elections are held at a time other than when presidents and members of Congress are chosen. This alternation of elections contributes to the sense of endlessness in campaign politics and has been blamed for low turnout in local elections. Tax levies held in April or August of an odd-numbered year may see turnout figures in single digits (of registered voters), thus creating situations in which small numbers of voters decide major issues.

The Party System

Political parties are not mentioned in the Constitution, but few politicians can imagine how our electoral system or government could function without them. Parties are a key element of the unwritten constitution that shapes the operations of the government.

The Development of American Political Parties. Parties have been a part of American politics since the early days of the constitutional system. America's first political parties were the Federalists and the Republicans. The Federalists, led by Alexander Hamilton, favored active central government, a national bank, and support of Britain in its wars with France. The Republicans, led by Thomas Jefferson, favored states over the central government, distrusted a national bank, and wanted to support the revolutionary government of France against Britain. At first, the Federalists dominated national politics. After 1800, the Republicans gained the presidency and majorities in both houses of Congress. For nearly two decades, the nation had no functioning party system.

In the 1820s, a second party system arose. The Jeffersonian party became the Democratic-Republicans and later the Democrats. A new opposition party, the Whigs, formed to challenge it. Under the leadership of Andrew Jackson, the Democrats favored limited national government dominated by the executive and leaving most of government to the states. The Whigs favored legislative power in the national government and a program of federally funded internal improvements (roads, canals, and other projects).

The parties continued to evolve as the nation grew and new issues arose. Territorial expansion of the United States was a central concern, and the question of slavery was growing in importance. By 1860 the Whigs had been replaced by the Republican Party, which favored admitting new states as free states. The Democrats, with a stronger base in the South, looked for ways to protect the interests of slaveholders. The conflict erupted into the Civil War.

After the war, the Republicans dominated national politics, although the Democratic Party maintained firm control in what became known as the Solid South. Republican dominance lasted—with occasional interruptions—until the Great Depression of the early 1930s. In 1932, Franklin Roosevelt led the Democratic Party to victory through a grand coalition of labor union members, ethnic voters (Italians, Jews, African Americans, and others), and small farmers in the South. The party stood for an active federal government to promote civil rights, aid education, and support welfare programs. The Republican Party resisted the enlargement of the federal government and opposed the activist policies of the Democrats. Both parties agreed, however, on a foreign policy aimed at containing the influence of communism around the world. Republicans found success in presidential elections beginning in the 1950s, while Democrats held majorities in Congress almost continuously from 1932 until 1994.

By the 1980s, the Democratic grand coalition had begun to fall apart, in part because it had achieved many of its goals and in part because new issues (such as the federal budget deficit) often divided groups in the coalition rather than reinforcing their unity. This change gave the Republicans opportunities to attract younger voters and groups not included in the Democratic alignment (such as Christian conservatives). Republicans also found support in the South, a region that had changed considerably since World War II because of racial integration, industrialization, and education.

In 1994, the Republicans won majorities in both houses of Congress for the first time in half a century. But the White House was still in the hands of Bill Clinton and the Democrats. Divided government (when the White House and Congress are controlled by different parties) continues to be a feature of national politics, although the parties controlling each branch have changed. Republicans speculated on the possibility of a new era in which they could again dominate American politics. Democrats predicted that the Republican triumph would be short-lived.

Party Functions. Much of the importance of parties in our system stems from the functions that they perform in it. Their *electoral functions* include mobilizing individuals and groups of voters to support candidates. In a competitive party system, the need for votes often leads parties to include in their coalitions groups (for example, religious and ethnic minorities) that might otherwise not participate in politics. Parties also provide information to citizens about candidates and issues, packaging it in such a way as to improve the image of the party and undermine the opposition. Party platforms, campaign literature, and slogans are all devices for spreading the party's message. Parties also help to conduct elections by providing representatives who can ensure that voting occurs according to law. But perhaps the most important function of parties is that they help to simplify the complex world of politics by narrowing choices for voters: reducing the number of candidates for office, focusing on key issues, and giving voters party labels with which they can identify.

Between elections, parties perform several *governmental functions* of importance. They provide linkages between officials in different positions and between officials and the people they represent. Even if they are weak, these linkages can be especially important when they reach across the divisions created by the system of separation of powers and federalism. For example, the president uses party connections and mutual interest to appeal to other partisans in Congress, in the states, and in local communities. Parties also provide connections that are important for executive officials who must fill appointive positions: presidents looking for cabinet, sub-cabinet, and judicial appointees; governors looking for state officers; local officials who need road commissioners, health officers, and other appointees. In Congress and the states, parties also provide the basis for organizing legislative committees and conducting deliberations.

Party Organization and Characteristics. American political parties are somewhat distinctive in their structures and defining characteristics. In sharp contrast to the hierarchical and tightly organized political parties of parliamentary systems, American parties are *decentralized and complex institutions*. There are at least six major elements in the structure of the Democratic and Republican parties:

> *The National Convention:* This is the official rule-making body of the party, and it meets only in presidential election years. Because its delegates are chosen as part of the presidential nominating process, under the new system each convention becomes the creature of the nominee chosen that year.
>
> *The National Committee:* In charge of party affairs between conventions, the committee is usually weak. The party's national chair, who heads the committee, serves as representative of the party and may have influence over party matters if the White House is in the hands of the opposition.
>
> *The Congressional Party:* Consists of all members of the party in Congress, although members in the House and the Senate may operate quite autonomously of one another. Usually united on core organizational issues (for example, the election of the Speaker of the House), they may divide into several factions over policy and behave quite independently of other party units, especially the White House.
>
> *State and Local Parties:* Autonomous operations; may be strong or weak depending on party's history and strength in the area. Often pursue their own agendas independently of national party leaders.
>
> *Presidential Parties:* The president's coalition usually is not restricted to the party itself. Consists of groups supporting the president, political appointees, and various voters who may or may not support the party's other candidates.
>
> *Partisans in the Electorate:* A disparate group of people. Most are voters who identify themselves as members of the party or as independents "leaning" toward the party; a minority are committee activists who participate in primaries and caucuses, do volunteer work for the party's candidates, and strongly identify with the party. About 35 percent of American voters identify themselves as Republicans, while about 30 percent call themselves Democrats.

There can be overlap between these units, but each has its own identity and organization. No one element has central control over party affairs.

Another characteristic of American political parties is that the two major ones are *nonideological* in nature. Because they are composed of large and diverse coalitions of voters and groups, the Democrats and Republicans try to

Cartoon by Kirk Anderson, *The Capital Times*, Madison, Wisconsin.

represent the broad middle in American politics. They are generally more interested in winning elections than in taking the "right" position on issues. This tendency has led critics to claim that "there's not a dime's worth of difference" between them, but the parties continue to compete for votes in a winner-take-all system that rewards broad coalitions and punishes narrower groups.

Ideological parties do exist in American politics, but they seem to be relegated to the sidelines by their uncompromising views. Groups such as the Communist Party, the Libertarian Party, the Natural Law Party, and other minor parties enjoy strong support from those citizens who agree with their clear positions on issues, but they find it difficult to attract more than a small percentage of votes in most elections. Moreover, they usually lack the resources to compete on an equal basis with the two dominant parties. It is not surprising that all minor parties are thus lumped together as "third parties."

Finally, parties are *semi-autonomous* organizations. On one hand, the Supreme Court has held that they have the right to control their internal organizations, processes, and choices and cannot be controlled as arms of the state or federal government. On the other hand, however, state and federal law can significantly influence how parties operate in practice. Government can dictate the use, form, and timing of primary elections, as well as campaign finance rules that spell out how much support parties may give to their candidates.

America's Two-Party System. American elections exhibit a preference for two-party politics. Nevertheless, voters express dissatisfaction with the Democrats and Republicans, with large numbers declaring themselves "independents."

Ross Perot attracted millions of voters to his candidacy with attacks on the "gridlock" of "politics as usual." Moreover, many local elections are now by law nonpartisan in nature. In general, however, there is no sign that the two dominant parties are in danger of being driven from the scene (see Table 7.1). The vast majority of voters do not support independent candidates for Congress (only one independent currently serves in the House) or the presidency, and there is evidence that many so-called independents really tend to favor Democrats or Republicans in their voting behavior.

TABLE 7.1 Party Preferences of the U.S. Electorate

	Republican	Democrat	Independent
Sex			
Male	42%	45%	13%
Female	34	54	11
Race			
White	42%	46%	12%
Black	8	79	13
Hispanic	27	61	11
Age			
18-24	36%	46%	17%
25-34	40	46	14
35-44	38	51	11
45-54	40	50	11
55-64	36	54	10
65+	39	53	8
Income			
Less than $10,000	28%	56%	16%
$10,000-$19,999	30	59	11
$20,000-$29,999	30	56	14
$30,000-$39,999	42	48	10
$40,000-$59,999	45	47	8
$60,000+	54	37	10
Religion			
Jewish	9%	86%	5%
Catholic	33	55	11
Protestant	44	45	11
Ideology			
Liberal	14%	77%	9%
Moderate/Don't Know	31	53	16
Conservative	65	28	7
Region			
Northeast	32%	55%	13%
Midwest	43	45	12
South	34	53	13
West	44	49	8
Total	38	50	12

Source: The American National Election studies, conducted by the Center for Political Studies at the University of Michigan.
Note: Independents who lean toward a party were counted with that party.

For decades observers have predicted that the two major parties would soon pass from the scene, but the Democrats and Republicans continue to dominate national and state politics. Of course, their representatives in government enjoy considerable autonomy, but these self-selecting, independently acting politicians continue to cling to their party labels. It is not clear exactly what holds the two-party system together. A sense of givenness about a two-party system is part of the explanation; except for rare periods, two parties have dominated American politics since the early days of the Republic. Americans are generally socialized to see the two-party system as normal and essential to a free and stable political system.

Another reason is that the single-member district/winner-take-all structure of elections encourages two parties. When there is no reward for second (or third or fourth. . .) place in an election, there is strong incentive for large coalitions to form to increase a party's chances of winning. Any group that would break off and form a new party—the Bull Moose Progressives in 1912, the Dixiecrats in 1948, George Wallace's anti-integration southerners in 1968—gains little unless it can win elections. Minor parties in the United States (like the Libertarians) are pushed to the sidelines or they dissolve.

A final reason for two-party persistence is that the Democrats and Republicans have made it difficult for their hold on politics to be broken. State laws governing access to election ballots for candidates usually make it difficult for independents or minor-party challengers to get into the race, just as the federal program that gives money to presidential candidates (explained later) favors groups that have received a large percentage of votes in a previous election. It is easier for most politicians to work within the party system than outside of it. In this respect, Ross Perot in 1992 represents a new twist: a well-financed, media-savvy politician who can build his own organization to mount a race for president. While Perot has the potential to continue as a force in presidential politics, few others are similarly situated.

The term "campaign" derives from military use, and the analogy to war is not unrealistic, for a political campaign is a complex array of efforts directed toward the single goal of victory. Campaigns are where the action occurs; they are a frenzy of political activity. Seemingly endless rounds of campaigning and politicking are punctuated—indeed, shaped and defined—by the elections that occur with such regularity. In our time, American political campaigns display certain key tendencies: they are candidate-centered; they exhibit common organizational patterns; they employ similar strategies and tactics; they are long; and they are expensive.

Candidates and Campaign Politics in Our Times

Candidate-Centered Campaigns

At one time parties dominated electoral politics in the United States: candidates were chosen by party organizations; parties arranged the financing and advertising of campaigns; and public officials were tied together by various party link-

Contemporary campaigns are centered around candidates, who tend to be defined by personality rather than issues.

ages. Contemporary campaigns and elections revolve around candidates who may run under party banners but who enjoy considerable autonomy as political entrepreneurs. The use of primary elections has taken from parties one of their most important powers—the selection of candidates—and given it to whoever votes in those events. Campaign finance laws make party organizations one of several funding sources. The rise of television and the decline of political machines have focused attention on the individuals who run for office rather than the organizations (parties) that nominate them. Voters pride themselves on supporting "the candidate, not the party," thus further encouraging those seeking office to run as free agents loosely associated with the broad party organization.

The consequences for government are clear. American politics has been somewhat atomized in the past quarter century. Presidential candidates are chosen in a system that separates them from the rest of the party and encourages them to develop broad, nonpartisan coalitions of voters. Congressional candidates focus on their constituents and give priority to the needs of their individual districts and states. State and local party organizations work in their own spheres. Local officials, many of whom run in nonpartisan elections, build their own constituencies. All of this contributes to officeholders increasing their responsiveness to their own voters but makes it difficult for these officials to work cooperatively toward broader public goals.

Campaign Organization

Most campaigns are organized according to a common pattern, although the organization will be larger and more complex the higher the office sought and the larger the area that must be covered. At the core of the campaign is the candidate and a nucleus of senior staff. In local or U.S. House races, all staff are likely to be volunteers, but for statewide, Senate, and presidential races paid professionals ("hired guns") usually occupy the top campaign jobs. Whether or not they are paid, these senior campaign aides will work on strategy, scheduling, fund raising, advertising, position taking, research, coordinating volunteers, and other tasks necessary for success. Some duties, such as producing television ads or opinion polls, may be performed by consultants who work for several candidates because their services are too expensive for any one office seeker to acquire full time.

Most of the people working for the campaign will be citizen volunteers. They include members of interest groups that support the candidate, activists who agree with the candidate's position, family members and friends (especially in local politics), and others who want to become involved in politics. College students and senior citizens generally provide many volunteers for campaigns. Other voluntary help may come from celebrities who support the candidate: prominent political figures, such as congressional leaders or statewide officers, and even members of the entertainment industry. Popular musicians and movie stars are actively cultivated by many presidential and Senate candidates who want the money these celebrities can contribute and the glamor they might be able to transfer to those politicians they support. Barbra Streisand campaigned for Bill Clinton in 1992, and Arnold Schwarzenegger spoke for George Bush.

The party may provide assistance as well. One way that the two parties have attempted to increase loyalty from their candidates has been by offering campaign services to those running for office. For example, because incumbents are usually difficult to defeat, party organizations may recruit challengers to run against them by offering to help them raise money, build a staff, obtain advice on campaign strategy, and even arrange for endorsements from popular party figures such as the governor or a Senate leader.

Campaign Strategy and Tactics

Candidates develop campaign strategies on the basis of their political circumstances. Incumbents, especially popular ones, play to their strengths: name recognition (which research shows to be important), a record of achievement, experience, identification with constituent interests, and a promise of more to come in the future. Challengers must attempt to turn the tables; they stress the need for change, the shortcomings of the incumbent, and the promise of a better tomorrow. Playing on Americans' general ambivalence about the compromises inherent in government, nearly all candidates promise to end "politics as usual."

Citizens in Action

A COUPLE OF CAMPAIGNERS

Mary Matalin and James Carville are the odd couple of American electoral politics. She was the political director for George Bush's reelection campaign in 1992; he had the same job in Bill Clinton's campaign. Matalin and Carville were also engaged at the time and married shortly after the election. Matalin came up through the ranks of Republican Party politics, while Carville made his reputation masterminding state and local campaigns across the country. Their ability to separate their private and professional lives is not so surprising, however; they typify the generally nonideological style of American electoral politics. Their political differences, like those dividing the Democratic and Republican parties, are disagreements "within the family," obscuring many areas of commonly held values.

Campaigns in the United States are an interesting mix of cold political calculation and tribal ritual. Candidates direct their efforts toward assembling all the resources necessary to win voter support—raising money, building an organization, developing a coalition, developing positions on an array of issues, planning strategy—and then employing those assets toward the goal of victory. But they must also participate in activities that are demanded as much by tradition as anything else. For example, candidates make lots of personal appearances to appeal for votes, often at the cost of exhaustion, although they could reach all potential supporters through television and other forms of mass communication. Likewise, although most voters obtain most of their political information from television, campaigns produce mountains of literature: bumper stickers, yard signs, and buttons extolling the candidate's credentials and stands on issues. Why? According to one study, "basically, campaigns produce literature because campaigns have always produced literature."[3] In the same way, fewer and fewer voters watch the presidential nominating conventions of the two major parties each election year; yet these events continue to operate largely according to formats established in the nineteenth century. Part of the reason for this mix of tradition and calculation is that no one is precisely sure what works and what does not when it comes to attracting votes. An old proverb in American politics holds that "half the money spent on campaigns is wasted. The trouble is, we don't know which half."[4]

No one is really certain whether bumper stickers, yard signs, or other campaign paraphernalia win votes, but nearly all candidates use them.

America's Long Campaigns

Because candidates must build coalitions of interests and voters in order to win nomination and then election, they must begin campaigning early. British parliamentary campaigns are usually only a few weeks long; in the United States, campaigns are measured in months. This is particularly true in nomination races, where party identification is irrelevant. If all the candidates are of the same party, voters need some other basis on which to cast their ballots.

Presidential nominations offer a good illustration of long campaigns.[5] Indeed, over the past two decades, these campaigns have grown longer and longer. A presidential nomination campaign is an elaborate affair that unfolds in five distinct stages:

1. *The Exhibition Season* begins anytime before formal nomination contests occur. The official season of primaries and caucuses begins in February of a presidential election year and ends in June, but most challengers declare their candidacy by the fall of the previous year (some long-shot candidates even declare two years before the presidential election). It is not uncommon for five to eight candidates to vie for the nomination. During this time candidates must raise large sums of money and begin building a base of support in early primary and caucus states.

2. *The Winnowing Stage* occurs during February and early March, when early contests in Iowa and New Hampshire serve to "weed out" weak candidates. After these events, which are about two weeks apart, two or three leaders emerge from the pack. Everyone else is struggling to stay in the race. By this point in the 1992 race, the Democratic field had been narrowed to Bill Clinton and Paul Tsongas, with former California Governor Jerry Brown a distant third.

3. *The Breakaway Stage* takes place during Junior Tuesday and Super Tuesday, days in mid-March when several primaries are held at the same time. This highly compressed array of events around the country tests which candidates have broad appeal, lots of money, organization in several states, good media skills, and the momentum to put together a winning coalition. By the end of Super Tuesday (the third Tuesday in March), the field has been reduced to one front-runner, one or two remaining challengers (whose hopes are growing dim), and the memory of those who have withdrawn. In 1992 this stage made Bill Clinton the victor.

4. *The Mop-Up Stage* occurs over the course of the spring, as the front-runner secures a hold on the lead. This means that the leader's momentum carries that candidate to victory in enough states to obtain the delegates needed to secure the nomination. The primary season ends in early June. At this point, the likely nominee begins to consider strategy for the general election campaign.

Michael Huffington was a wealthy newcomer to politics. In 1994 he spent $28 million of his own money to mount a nearly-successful campaign for a U.S. Senate seat from California.

5. *The Convention* in mid-summer serves as an opportunity for the presumed nominee to put a personal stamp on the party. That task is accomplished by picking a vice-presidential running mate, overseeing the writing of a party platform—a statement of party principles and positions on issues—consistent with the candidate's stated positions, and putting on a good show. The convention serves as the informal kick-off of the fall campaign and reintroduces the nominee to the general public.

If a party has no president in the White House, each of these steps is followed in full; if the party has an incumbent president seeking reelection, the whole process is much simpler. The president is renominated, with or without resistance from dissident elements in the party. But the process takes almost as long as for those out of power, because primaries and caucuses must still follow the schedule the states have laid down. All of this makes for a protracted campaign. By the time of the election in early November, the new president (especially if that person has not been in office already) has been campaigning for at least a year.

Financing Campaigns

Campaigns require money. In contemporary elections, a large proportion of campaign expenditures goes to mass media advertising. In congressional campaigns, media expenses consume about half of an average candidate's budget. Those seeking the White House also advertise heavily, although they receive lots of free coverage by the media to increase their visibility.

In the general election of 1992, nearly $1 billion was spent to elect candidates for the White House ($400 million), U.S. House and Senate ($500 million), and state and local offices. Money is necessary to build a campaign organization, pay the rent and the bills, cover travel expenses, and spread a candidate's message. Indeed, one important reason why campaigns cost so much is that television time is expensive. Candidates seek all the free media time they can get but still spend large sums on commercials.

Campaigns for federal office require big "war chests" (see Figure 7.3). The average winning candidate for the U.S. House spends around $400 thousand, while the average winning Senate candidate spends almost $3 million. When Ross Perot announced that he would spend "whatever it takes" to run for president in 1992, he mentioned a figure as high as $100 million. While many observers found this number impressive, in reality it was not. In 1988 Michael Dukakis and George Bush each spent about that much; in 1992, the major-party candidates spent over 50 percent more (Clinton: $155 million; Bush: $179 million). In the end, Perot spent about $69 million. His original estimate was more routine than extravagant.

Campaign Finance Rules. The basic structure of campaign finance was set down by the **Federal Election Campaign Act (FECA)** of 1971. That law was subsequently amended by Congress in 1974 and 1976 and modified by the

Federal Election Campaign Act (FECA) 1971 law that sets the basic structure of campaign finance law in the United States. Subsequently amended and modified by *Buckley v. Valeo.*

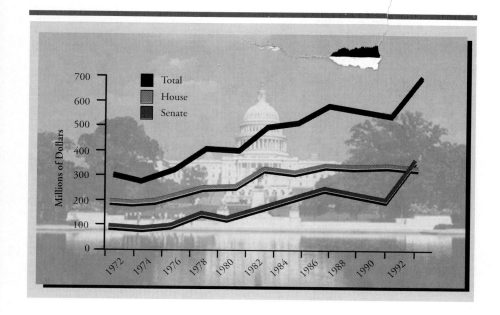

FIGURE 7.3
Two Decades of Rising Campaign Costs

Supreme Court. In the case of *Buckley v. Valeo* (1976),[6] the Supreme Court ruled that the government could not limit how much of their own money candidates spend in seeking office, because spending money in that way is an exercise of a citizen's right to free speech. Subject to this modification, FECA governs contributions and expenditures of presidential and congressional candidates. States set their own rules for state races, with variation among them, although state laws must conform to constitutional doctrine as outlined in the Court's ruling.

The FECA established the *Federal Election Commission (FEC)* to oversee implementation and administration of the law. Headed by a bipartisan group of commissioners, that agency serves primarily as an information clearinghouse on election finance. It lacks both the staff and the budget to be much of a watchdog agency; instead, it collects candidates' campaign finance reports and makes them available for public inspection. This is not to say that the FEC has no power, but it has little. Congress has always kept the agency on "a short leash and even shorter budgetary rations,"[7] thus limiting the FEC's effectiveness. To that extent, the FEC relies on the power of public information to help enforce the law.

Financing Congressional Campaigns. The law recognizes four sources of funds and sets different limits on how much each may contribute to candidates or political organizations: individuals, political action committees, party committees, and the candidates themselves. Individuals and PACs are treated the same, unless the PAC is what the law considers a "multicandidate PAC"—one that

TABLE 7.2 Campaign Finance Rules for Federal Elections

Donor of Funds	Recipient	Amount	Time Period
An individual contributor* may give to. . .	An individual candidate	$2,000 maximum	Per election ($1,000 for primary, $1,000 for general election)
	A PAC	$5,000 maximum	Per calendar year
	A party	$20,000 maximum	Per calendar year
A political action committee, or PAC, may give to. . ."	The same recipients as the individual contributor unless it is a multicandidate PAC" (see next panel)		
A multicandidate PAC may give to. . .	An individual candidate	$10,000	Per election ($5,000 for primary, $5,000 for general)
	Another PAC	$5,000	Per calendar year
	A party	$15,000	Per calendar year
A party committee may give to. . .	A House candidate	$30,000 plus "coordinated expenses"**	Per general election
	A Senate candidate	$27,500 plus "coordinated expenses"**	Per general election

*An individual contributor is limited to a maximum total campaign contribution of $25,000 within one calendar year.
**Party-paid general election expenses made in consultation with candidate and determined according to formula.
Note: Disclosure Rules require that all contributions over $100 be disclosed, including the name, address, and occupation of the contributor. No cash contributions in excess of $100 are permitted.

receives money from at least 50 contributors and gives money to at least 5 candidates. Party committees have higher limits on contributions—clearly the law is intended to encourage party giving. Individual contributions constitute about half of all money for congressional candidates, while PACs give about one-third, party committees about 1 percent, and candidates themselves about 8 percent. These proportions have been relatively stable over time.[8] While there are limits on contributions to candidates and parties (Table 7.2), there are no restrictions on how much candidates may spend in their pursuit of a seat in Congress.

matching funds
Money given by the government to candidates for their campaigns. The amount of money given matches the amount a candidate has raised according to certain rules.

Financing Presidential Campaigns. In campaigns for president, the law adds a fifth source of money to the four already mentioned: public funds. Private contributions are limited as they are for congressional campaigns. During the nomination phase of presidential elections, a candidate can receive **matching funds**—an amount paid to a candidate by the government equal to the amount raised by the candidate—by raising at least $5,000 in individual contributions of no larger than $250 in at least 20 states. Candidates who meet such requirements receive a dollar-for-dollar match of funds from the Presidential Election

Campaign Fund (paid for by the $1.00 check-off on income-tax returns), up to a maximum of $5 million in 1974 dollars ($16.5 million in 1992) for the nomination campaign. Candidates who accept federal funds must agree to abide by spending limits both nationally and for each state.

For the general election, the federal government provides money for the parties to hold their conventions ($11 million in 1992) and funds for each nominee's campaign (a grand total of $55.24 million in 1992). Again, spending limits must be observed, but candidates can circumvent them by raising and spending so-called **soft money.** This is money that is outside the restrictions of federal law but is nevertheless useful for financing a campaign (for example, money given to a party campaign committee to build the party organization in some state and enhance the candidate's chances for winning). While Bill Clinton and George Bush each received $55.2 million from the federal government for the 1992 presidential campaign, the grand total of all expenditures made by or "on behalf of" these candidates (by groups not formally affiliated with the candidates) was $155.9 million for Clinton and $179.5 million for Bush. Candidates who do not take federal money—John Connally in 1980; Ross Perot in 1992—are free to spend as much as they can afford.

Where Do Contributions Come From? The conventional wisdom is that the money for campaigns comes from a few special interests. But research has shown that the number of people who contribute to American political campaigns is indeed impressive. As one study put it, "we can confidently project between 13 and 15 million contributors at the least. No other system of campaign funding anywhere in the world enjoys so broad a base of support. None even approaches it."[9] Most individuals apparently contribute sums between $50 and $100, although others give considerably more. Their support makes up about half of the money raised for congressional campaigns. Other money comes from party committees, interest, borrowing, the government (for presidential candidates), and PACs.

PACs are important sources of campaign funds, but they do not dominate campaign finance or "buy elections" as many people seem to think. To the contrary, the evidence suggests that PAC money flows to likely winners, rather than a situation in which PACs pick their favorite candidates and buy an election. More often than not—except in an unusual year such as 1994—incumbents are the likely winners in elections. PACs are the source of about one-third of the funds spent in congressional races, but PAC contributions go to congressional incumbents far more than to challengers. What incumbents have on their side is not money, but "the expectation early in the election cycle that they can and will win reelection."[10]

Ever since FECA was passed, there has been pressure for even more sweeping reforms, such as the creation of a totally public financing system for elections or spending limits for congressional campaigns. Despite several proposals offered in Congress and interest in reform from President Clinton and others, the structure of campaign finance has remained relatively stable since the early 1970s.

soft money Money raised by candidates in political campaigns that is outside the restrictions of campaign finance law but is nevertheless useful for financing a campaign.

open questions

Does Money Play Too Big a Role in American Politics?

There are a variety of controversies surrounding American electoral politics: about the importance of elections, about voter turnout, about whether and how parties should be strengthened or changed, about PAC influence and regulation, and any number of other issues. One fundamental question has to do with the role of money in American elections.

No matter who pays the bills or for whatever reason, campaigns are expensive. But are they too expensive? Some critics of the system contend that they are, because of the influence of "special interests" (that is, PACs) and candidates' endless search for money. A senator who spends $3.5 to $4 million for a reelection campaign will have to raise an average of $12,000 a week for six years. House members need an average of $4,000 each week for two years to run for reelection. Members of Congress face what journalist Hedrick Smith calls "the drudgery of raising money."[11] In one month in the summer of 1985—one year before he was up for reelection—Senator Alfonse D'Amato (R.-N.Y.) held 20 fund-raising events in four states.[12] Former Senator Thomas Eagleton (D.-Mo.) estimates that incumbent senators facing reelection spend 70 to 80 percent of their personal time and effort raising money during the last two years of a six-year term.[13]

Some observers charge that the nation has ended up with a kind of "pay-to-play" politics in which only the rich can hold public office. As one reformer put it, "In the end, money may trample democracy as we are left with a Congress filled with millionaires and heirheads."[14] Most reformers call for public funding of congressional elections on a matching-funds basis, caps on PAC contributions, regulation of money spent "on behalf of" candidates, and other changes aimed at reducing the role of money in our politics. Some reformers go further and call for full public funding of election campaigns in order to make money essentially irrelevant to who wins office. They want the cost of elections to be held down and all candidates to have an equal chance.

In response, several analysts argue that the cost of campaigns has been overstated. By the standards of other democracies, American elections are relatively inexpensive. When measured in terms of cost per voter, elections in the United States ($3.25) cost more than those in Britain ($.50) or Canada ($1.43), but about the same as those in Germany ($3.20) and less than those in Ireland ($3.93), Israel ($4.34), and Venezuela ($26.35).[15] Moreover, campaigns must spend money to compete with a "literal blizzard of other information and noise—50 or more cable TV channels, newspaper and radio advertising, computer information systems, direct mail, and so on—that all makes it difficult to get any messages across."[16]

Some critics of reform are more concerned about the risks inherent in campaign finance reform than about problems in the current system. They contend that reformers will lead the nation to "dead ends" because their plans are based on a "primitive, unrealistic, and even undesirable view of representative government."[17] As one antireform critic put it, "One person's special interest is another's crusade. The function of politics is not only to govern in the general interest and to reconcile differences among specific interests; it is also to provide outlets for political and social tensions."[18] Critics charge that limits on campaign expenses will only benefit incumbents, because extra spending is one way that challengers actually have the opportunity to overcome the advantages that officeholders possess (such as name recognition). Moreover, public financing could have the effect of making challenges of incumbents so attractive that members of Congress "would seek to win the loyalty of groups that might finance independent election efforts on their behalf. This suggests new levels of sham, exertion, and influence brokering."[19]

Does money play too big a role in our electoral politics? If so, what can we do about it? Or is the role of money an imaginary "problem" concocted by those who really do not like the messy world of politics? These issues are important but controversial.

American politics is distinguished by the number of elections held to choose public officials (general elections), nominate candidates (primaries), or make policy decisions (referenda). Two major parties (Democrats and Republicans) dominate our elections.

|| Summary

Principles. Elections lie at the heart of democratic politics. Americans expect their elections to deliver decisive outcomes, favoring "winner-take-all" elections, although proportional representation is used occasionally. While some public funding of presidential campaigns is available, self-help by candidates is the order of the day.

Process. American elections generally take the form of a single-member district/winner-take-all system (SMD/WTA). Presidential elections are complex. The nomination system involves a series of primaries and caucuses held between February and June of the presidential election year. The general election is governed by the Electoral College system required by the Constitution; this supports a two-party system. Congressional elections are simpler, with a single primary selecting each party's nominee and a general election to fill a seat in the House or Senate. State and local elections vary considerably from one place to another. Often, local elections are by law nonpartisan in nature.

Political parties are important elements of the electoral process. They perform a variety of electoral functions (such as mobilizing voters and simplifying choices) and governmental functions (such as providing linkages between officeholders). American political parties are complex and decentralized institutions, composed of at least six major (and generally autonomous) elements—the national convention, the national committee, the congressional party, state and local parties, presidential parties, and partisans in the electorate. American political parties are generally nonideological in nature (although there are minor parties that have an ideological base) and are semi-autonomous in the conduct of their own affairs. Two-party politics dominates our electoral system (the Democrats and Republicans have dominated since 1860).

Politics. Political campaigns in the United States are candidate-centered, rather than party-centered. A campaign is a complex organization of professionals and volunteers. Candidates employ strategies depending on their own ideas of what will work and customs that have developed over time (such as yard signs). American political campaigns are long. Presidential nomination campaigns have five distinct stages: an exhibition season, a winnowing stage, a breakaway stage, a mop-up stage, and the convention. The Federal Election Campaign Act (1971) structures the rules of campaign finance. Political action committees (PACs) play a large role in funding campaigns, especially for Congress and the presidency.

Open Questions. Are American electoral campaigns too expensive? Some observers claim that they are, leading to a kind of "pay-to-play" politics in which only the rich can hold office and only those with money can have influence. Many observers favor campaign finance reform. Opponents argue that the cost of our elections is overstated and that campaigns in this country are less expensive per capita than in many other advanced industrial nations. These critics contend that proposed campaign finance reforms would bring more harm than good to the political system. The role of money in American elections is not easily resolved.

Suggested Readings

JACOBSON, GARY. *The Politics of Congressional Elections,* 3rd ed. (New York: HarperCollins, 1992). Concise survey of all aspects of this topic by a leading expert.

KAYDEN, XANDRA. *Campaign Organization.* Lexington, Mass.: D.C. Heath, 1978. The ins-and-outs of campaign organization in American politics.

————, AND EDDIE MAHE. *The Party Goes On.* New York: Basic Books, 1985. Examines how the Democrats and Republicans responded to changes in the political system since the 1970s.

MATALIN, MARY, AND JAMES CARVILLE, WITH PETER KNOBLER. *All's Fair: Love, War, and Running for President.* New York: Random House and Simon & Schuster, 1994. An inside look at the 1992 presidential race by the political directors of the Bush and Clinton campaigns, who happen to be married to each other.

NELSON, MICHAEL, ED. *The Elections of 1992.* Washington: CQ Press, 1993. Useful survey of the presidential and congressional elections of 1992, with attention to the importance of the election to long-term trends in American politics.

SORAUF, FRANK. *Inside Campaign Finance.* New Haven, Conn.: Yale University Press, 1992. Highly readable discussion of the myths and realities of campaign finance in the United States.

————, AND PAUL ALLEN BECK. *Party Politics in America,* 6th ed. Glenview, Ill.: Scott, Foresman, 1988. Good survey of all aspects of political parties in contemporary American politics.

The United States Congress

chapter 8

T he American regime is distinctive in that it includes an independent and powerful legislature—the United States Congress. In parliamentary democracies, the legislature debates the proposals of the executive and sometimes challenges them, but members of the majority party usually accept those policies in the name of party unity. Few policy initiatives come from the legislature. In contrast, Congress possesses an impressive array of specific powers that enables it to play an active role in the governing of the United States.

Congress: The First Branch of Government

Congress is the first branch of government mentioned in the Constitution. This status is not accidental. The national legislature was established to be the central institution for representation and law making in the American regime.

The Powers of Congress

Article I outlines broad powers for Congress: to make laws; to impose taxes and control appropriations (known as the power of the purse); to make rules on bankruptcy, immigration, patents, and copyrights; to regulate interstate and foreign commerce; to impeach (charge with an offense) government officials and remove them from office; to consent to nominations (for executive appointments and federal judges) and treaties; and to do whatever is "necessary and proper" to carry out the specific powers assigned to it in the Constitution. These powers, which are summarized in Table 8.1, make the legislature a formidable force in American government.

While charging Congress with these powers and responsibilities, the Constitution leaves control over its internal organization and operations to Congress. In consequence, Congress has developed a sophisticated network of structures for conducting its business—a complex committee system, party organizations, informal caucuses, and a large support staff. It carries on its decision making through a deliberative process that is governed by an elaborate set of parliamentary rules. As we shall see in the process section, these structures and rules shape the way Congress operates and what laws and policies emerge from it.

Bicameralism: Congress Means House and Senate

Perhaps the most important feature of Congress is its divided structure. **Bicameralism**—the division of Congress into two chambers, the House of Representatives and the Senate—means that the actions of the national legislature require agreement between the two halves of Congress, which are different in several ways.

Woodrow Wilson once observed that "House and Senate are naturally unalike." Members of the House are elected for short terms of office (two years), from districts roughly equal in population. Members of the House tend to be specialists. They work with less national visibility, less reliance on staffs, and less individualism than senators. House members are usually not well known by the public, but they know a lot about the policy areas on which they concentrate.

bicameralism The division of a legislative body into two chambers, as in the U.S. Congress.

TABLE 8.1 Congressional Powers

Exclusive Powers of the House of Representatives	Powers Held in Common
Originate money bills Vote impeachment Judge results of House elections Choose Speaker Make procedural rules Punish members Expel a member (by 2/3 vote)	Pass bills and resolutions to present to president for signature (becomes law) or veto Override presidential veto (by 2/3 vote) Hold hearings, issue subpoenas, conduct investigations Levy taxes Regulate interstate and foreign commerce Borrow money Establish rules for immigration and bankruptcy Coin money and punish counterfeiting Fix standards for weights and measures Establish postal service Regulate patents and copyrights Establish court system Regulate maritime law and international law Declare war Establish and support military forces Provide for militia Establish and regulate territory for seat of government (Washington, D.C.) Punish treason Regulate appeals to Supreme Court Admit new states Regulate territories of the United States Propose constitutional amendments (by 2/3 vote in each chamber)
Exclusive Powers of the Senate	
Approve treaties Confirm nominations to executive and judicial offices Try impeachments Judge results of Senate elections Make procedural rules Punish senators Expel a senator (by 2/3 vote)	

Each state has two senators, who are elected for six-year terms (until the Seventeenth Amendment, state legislatures selected senators). Senators work in an environment of greater prestige and media attention and more informal procedures, and they experience greater demands on their time. Senators are more visible than their counterparts in the House, more likely to be considered presidential or vice-presidential candidates, and more likely to be political generalists.

Despite these differences, the two chambers of Congress must work together for the legislature to do its job. Most of the powers assigned in Article I are shared equally by the House and Senate; this requires the two to act in unison on most legislative matters. As we shall see, acting in unison usually requires action on legislative proposals by a joint committee with members from both chambers. This action is required to produce a common version of any law or resolution to be passed by the two bodies. Some powers of the

TABLE 8.2 Key Differences Between the House and Senate

Factor	House	Senate
Membership		
Size	435	100
Minimum age	25	30
Electoral Base		
Term	2-year	6-year (overlapping)
Constituency	District (about 570,000)	State (ranges from Rhode Island to California)
Structure		
Presiding officer	Speaker (elected by House, powerful)	Vice-president of the United States (elected separately, largely ceremonial)
Distribution of power	Hierarchical	Dispersed
Rules and norms	Promote law making	Promote representation
Committee system	22 committees 138 subcommittees (Very important)	16 committees 86 subcommittees (Less important)
Complexity	More complex (4 calendars)	Less complex (2 calendars)
Staff support	Smaller, less reliance by members	Larger, more reliance by members
Floor debate	Limited	Unlimited
Nongermane amendments (riders)	Not allowed	Allowed
Policy Making		
Unique contribution	Originate money bills	Confirm nominations Approve treaties
Main policy role	Draft bills and pass laws	Set agenda and develop policy
Individual members	More specialists	More generalists
Speed of action	Faster	Slower
Political Character		
Partisanship	More partisan	Less partisan
Collegiality	Less collegial	More collegial
Visibility in media	Low	High

House and Senate are held by each chamber alone—only the House can initiate proposals to tax or spend, only the Senate can approve treaties and presidential nominations—but most legislative business requires cooperation between the chambers. Table 8.2 summarizes factors that distinguish the two bodies.

All of these realities, whether of power or behavior, have been shaped by the values and choices that underlie the nation's legislature. These principles, embodied in the Constitution and the operations of the House and Senate, have made Congress a force to be reckoned with in American government.

The two houses of Congress meet together only on special occasions. Here, both the House and Senate gather for the president's annual State of the Union address.

The framers' views on legislatures were somewhat paradoxical. On one hand, they regarded the existence of a representative assembly as part of the very definition of a republic. As Madison noted in *The Federalist,* No. 51, "In republican government the legislative authority necessarily predominates." On the other hand, they were intent on restraining the excesses of legislative government. What was the problem? Under the Articles of Confederation, the legislatures of the 13 states ran roughshod over governors and courts, voided contracts, and issued worthless paper money. As we saw in Chapter 2, these state legislatures were out of control. As Madison put it, "The legislative department is everywhere extending the sphere of its activity and drawing all power into its impetuous vortex."[1] Even Thomas Jefferson had been disillusioned by his experience with the Virginia legislature. He concluded that "One hundred and seventy-three despots would surely be as oppressive as one."[2]

To combat these problems, the framers embedded Congress in the checks-and-balances system, under which the legislature could act only in conjunction with the executive and under constitutional review by the judiciary. The Constitution makes Congress the effective centerpiece of national political institutions. It is the legislative body and the central representative organ of government. As we shall see, these two principles compete with one another, and in doing so shape Congress and its operations.

The Dual Constitutional Nature of Congress

In 1774 the English statesman and philospher Edmund Burke explained to his constituents that a legislative body could be one of two things. First, it could be "a Congress of ambassadors from different and hostile interests, which interests each must maintain, as an agent and advocate, against other agents and advocates."[3] Such a body is the General Assembly of the United Nations, whose members are representatives sent to protect the interests of their own countries. In contrast, a legislature could also be "a deliberative assembly of one nation, with one interest, that of the whole—not local purposes, not local prejudices, ought to guide, but the general good, resulting from the general reason of the whole."[4] Burke argued that Parliament was—or at least ought to be—this sort of assembly. It became clear at the convention that delegates wanted the American national legislature to both promote the public interest and protect local interests.

Congress as a Legislature for the Public Interest. Congress possesses broad powers to make laws, declare war, impeach officials, levy taxes, appropriate money, and approve or reject nominations and treaties. It has almost exclusive control over its internal organization. It possesses not only the ability to review the proposals of the executive—an old saying holds that "The president proposes and Congress disposes"—but the power to initiate actions as well. Unlike a parliament, which acts almost exclusively on executive proposals, each year Congress originates much of the important legislation that it passes. The Gramm-Rudman-Hollings Balanced Budget Act of 1985, the War Powers Resolution of 1973, the Tax Reform Act of 1986, the Budget and Impoundment Act of 1974, and other key laws originated on Capitol Hill. While most legislation is conceived in the executive branch, members of Congress author important bills. It is no coincidence that the key phrase in the First Amendment protecting personal freedom is stated as "Congress shall make no law . . ."

Congress as a Representative Body. The Great Compromise at the Constitutional Convention—two Senate seats for each state and House seats based on population—not only made possible the ultimate writing of the national charter, it also ensured that representation in Congress would not be a simple matter. On a superficial level, the House and Senate have obvious bases of representation: House members represent the people as people (in districts of roughly equal population) and senators represent the people as residents of states (this base was even more apparent before the Seventeenth Amendment, when senators were still elected by state legislatures).

But representation is not that simple. Members of Congress are also charged with representing the nation, and many also see themselves as advocates for interests or groups not necessarily confined to their districts or states. For example, women, African Americans, Latinos, and others may see themselves as advocates not only for their particular districts but for interests that bridge districts (but see Current Issues box). Those from rural areas and from cities and those who have interests in the arts, health care, AIDS, arms control, or whatever often regard themselves as having responsibility for particular issues or interests in American society. In recent years there has been a proliferation of groups in Congress that provide an organizational base for members who share common commitments to representing these various interests.

The Changing Face of Congress

Congress is often derided as a club for affluent white males. For much of American history, it has been occupied mostly by white men, although that group has not always been as uniform as it may appear on the surface. A wide array of ethnic groups—Irish Americans, Italian Americans, Jewish Americans, even Basque Americans—have sent representatives to Washington. Nevertheless, women, African Americans, and other minority groups have been rarities as elected officials on Capitol Hill until recent years.

The first woman elected to Congress was Representative Jeannette Rankin (R.-Mont.) in 1916. She became famous in American history as the only member of Congress to vote against U.S. entry into both world wars (Rankin was by religious conviction a pacifist). For most of the twentieth century, only a few women served in Congress. Some were famous—Representative Clare Booth Luce (R.-N.Y.), Senator Margaret Chase Smith (R.-Maine)—while many others were as little known outside of their own districts as most members of Congress. Some women were standing in for husbands who had died or gone on to other political offices. In the 1980s, the number of women in Congress began to rise. By 1988, there were 25 women in the House and 2 in the Senate. The 1994 election sent 46 women to the House (16 are Republican) and 8 to the Senate (3 are Republican). Women now have reached sufficient seniority to chair committees and subcommittees: Senator Nancy Kassebaum (R.-Kan.) chairs the Senate Labor and Human Resources Committee.

African Americans got an earlier start than women in Congress but were shut out of Capitol Hill for many years. The first black member of Congress was Senator Hiram Revels (R.-Miss.), who served from 1870 to 1871. When Jim Crow laws (see Chapter 4) gained hold in the South, blacks were unable to win elections. African Americans returned to Congress after World War II and their numbers have been rising. Senator Edward Brooke (D.-Mass.), who served from 1967 to 1979, was the only African American to hold a seat in the U.S. Senate in this century. Most African Americans hold seats in the House and most are Democrats. As a result of the 1994 elections, there are now 38 black members of Congress, including 2 Republicans.

The makeup of the 104th Congress (1995–1997) is shown in the table.

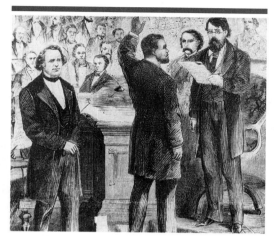

The first African American to serve in Congress was Senator Hiram Revels, a Republican who represented Mississippi from 1870 to 1871.

The 104th Congress, 1995–1997

	Senate	House of Representatives
Party		
Republicans	53	231
Democrats	47	203
Independents	0	1
Sex		
Men	92	387
Women	8	48
Race		
African American	1	38
Asian Pacific	2	4
Latino	0	18
Native American	1	0
White	96	374
Average Age	58	51

Your wishes are under thoughtful consideration!

James Larrick in the *Columbus Dispatch*.

What interests ought to guide members as they mold legislation and cast votes? One view holds that legislators should be a **trustee**—that is, they should be guided by the dictates of their own conscience. Others disagree with this kind of representation; they believe that a legislator should be a **delegate**—one bound by the views of constituents. How do members of Congress see themselves in this debate? They pay attention to their constituents' views and interests, especially on issues important to their states or districts. But on questions about which constituents have only marginal interest, members feel greater freedom to vote according to their own idea of the public interest or in response to party leaders, the White House, interest groups, or others. Most members of Congress try to split the difference in this way.

Operational Principles: The Unwritten Rules

Congress has developed along lines that have been shaped by its internal politics and the values of those in the institution. Several operational principles make the national legislature a distinctive body. First, like other legislative assemblies, it is a *procedurally oriented* organization. Each house of Congress, and the relations between them, is governed by an elaborate set of rules that control the internal distribution of power, the way business is conducted, and what can and cannot be done. Anyone who has ever participated in a meeting that uses parliamentary procedure has a superficial sense of the importance of procedure in Congress (Robert's Rules of Order were adapted from procedures of the early twentieth-century House of Representatives).

Second, Congress is a *partisan* body. Committee assignments, the division of time for debate, leadership posts, relations with the White House, control over staff, and even certain privileges for key members are influenced (if not controlled) by party divisions. But congressional parties are not tightly disciplined units as are those in parliamentary governments. Chosen by a candidate-centered election system, members enjoy considerable latitude in deciding whether or not to go along with their party's positions on most issues.

Third, Congress is a *decentralized* institution. Not only is Congress bicameral, but each house distributes power to committees, subcommittees, and even individual members. Such a situation is not inevitable. In the late nineteenth and early twentieth centuries, the House was a centralized body with extensive power vested in a strong Speaker; in the 1950s Majority Leader Lyndon Johnson centralized Senate power in himself. But the contemporary Congress is a body in which power is fragmented: delegated to committees and subcommittees, grabbed by influential members, shared by informal groups of members, taken over by aggressive staffers, and pursued by leaders seeking to keep the House and Senate effective.

Finally, Congress is an institution *reliant on informal rules and norms*. In addition to the formal procedures that organize life on Capitol Hill, a variety of customs and folkways shape the character of the institution. Members are expected to be faithful in performing the work of the committees to which they are assigned, and House members are expected to specialize in certain areas of

trustee Term applied to a legislator who seeks to make decisions on the basis of conscience and the public interest rather than constituent views and interests.

delegate Term applied to a legislative representative who votes according to constituent wishes.

policy. All members are expected to be collegial in their dealings with one another: friendly, courteous, and true to their word. In debates, members often refer to each other as "my distinguished colleague." On one occasion, the worst insult that one representative could bring himself to hurl against an opponent was that he held his adversary "in minimum high regard." Collegiality not only makes the general atmosphere among members more pleasant, but is a political necessity; without strong parties to assemble majorities, members know that today's enemy may be tomorrow's ally on a different issue.

Seniority is important: in the House, the most senior member of the majority party on a committee usually becomes the committee chair; in the Senate, party rules ensure that this always happens. Also important are the personal and political wishes of individuals. The Senate seldom holds votes after 7:00 P.M. on Tuesdays and Wednesdays to accommodate senators who have children at home. Any one senator can put a "hold" on a presidential nomination that is generally observed (but not indefinitely) by the leaders, allowing an individual to delay or even block important appointments. In the 1980s Senator Jesse Helms (R.-N.C.) used this device to put pressure on the Reagan and Bush administrations to alter foreign policy more to his liking. And an unwritten rule of **senatorial courtesy** allows a senator of the president's party to effectively veto any executive appointments (for example, federal judgeships) in that senator's home state.

Congressional norms are not fixed in stone. Some that were important in an earlier period—such as the idea that junior members should serve an "apprenticeship" until they had considerable seniority—have faded away. An old prohibition against seeking publicity has also died in the age of television. But unwritten rules still play a role in the way Congress works.

senatorial courtesy
Custom in the U.S. Senate of not approving nominations of judges or other presidentially appointed officials if the senator from the affected state objects to the person nominated.

standing committee
Congressional committee that has permanent existence, jurisdiction over an area of public policy, and membership determined by party leaders.

At times the United States Congress seems as if it is a world unto itself. It has its own methods of operations, its own rules, a bicameral structure, a complex committee system, and partisan organization. The structures and processes of Congress are not just decoration. They shape the life and operations of our national legislature.

Process: The Machinery of Representation and Deliberation

The Committee System

Committees have long been known as the "workshops of Congress." They are the places where the bulk of legislative work is done, from research and information gathering to bill drafting to negotiation and coalition building.

Three Types of Committees. Congressional committees are divided into three categories. **Standing committees** are permanent bodies that specialize in particular policy areas (armed services, labor, public welfare). Majority-party members always outnumber their minority counterparts. Standing committees are in turn broken down into subcommittees. Some standing committees with special assignments—the Intelligence and Budget Committees in each house—

have rotating memberships, (members serve on standing committees indefinitely). **Select (or special) committees** are created for specific assignments—such as the 1987 investigation of the Iran-Contra affair—and expire when no longer needed. **Joint committees** are special standing committees that have members from both houses (for example, the Joint Economic Committee).

Committees and subcommittees distribute power in each house of Congress by allocating influence over policy to many subunits. In the House, there are 22 standing committees and 138 subcommittees. The average member is assigned to two committees, with one being the member's main focus of attention. Half of the majority-party members of the House hold a committee or subcommittee chair. In the Senate, there are 16 standing committees and 86 subcommittees. Senators are usually assigned to 3 committees and often find themselves pulled among them. Nearly 9 out of 10 majority-party senators chair a committee or subcommittee. One veteran Democrat in the House remarked that if he could not remember the name of some junior representative in his party, he would just address that member as "Mr. Chairman," because there was a good chance that the title would be appropriate.

Committee Work. Much of members' time in Washington is taken up with committee responsibilities. Committees hold hearings in which information relevant to a proposal can be gathered, as well as support or opposition from particular groups identified. They are the highly visible activities in which cabinet officers, celebrities, interest-group representatives, experts, and ordinary citizens testify in order to inform or persuade Congress to adopt a particular policy. Some hearings, such as those involving Anita Hill on the nomination of Clarence Thomas to the Supreme Court, have drawn intense public interest and large television audiences, particularly among C-Span watchers. Most often, hearings feature an executive branch official, some lobbyists, or citizen members of interest groups (see Chapter 6). These garner less interest but are just as significant to law making. Even less visible are markup sessions in which committees draft bills to report to their respective floor leaders, but it is in these meetings that the main elements of most legislation are constructed. The greatest opportunity for senators and representatives to shape public policy (through legislation or influence on the executive) comes from their committee service, particularly as committee and subcommittee chairs.

Party Organizations and Leaders

It is rare for members of Congress not to be Democrats or Republicans, for reasons explored in Chapter 7. Occasionally independents or third-party candidates do win seats. Members are not required to belong to the party organizations that exist in each chamber, but there are powerful incentives for them to do so. For example, consider the fate of Senator James Buckley, elected in 1970 as the nominee of both New York's Conservative Party and its Republicans (New York

select (or special) committee Congressional committee whose members are appointed by the Speaker in the House and the president pro tempore in the Senate. Usually deal with sensitive issues such as intelligence.

joint committee Congressional committee made up of members from both the House of Representatives and the Senate.

has four major parties—Democrats, Republicans, Liberals, and Conservatives). At the same time the Senate included Harry Bird of Virginia, a former Democrat turned independent because of factional conflicts in his home state. Buckley half-jokingly suggested to Bird that they form their own party organization in the Senate; elect themselves its leaders; and reap the limousines, office space, and other benefits given to party leaders. When Senate Republicans heard Buckley's idea, they warned him that he had better get in line with the party or he would get no committee assignments. Buckley soon fell into line.[5] In 1990, Vermont elected Bernard Sanders, a Socialist, as its only representative in the House. Not wanting to be shut out of much of congressional life—especially committee assignments—Sanders allied himself with the Democrats.

Each party has its own organization in each chamber and, while the Senate and House groups of each party communicate with one another, each operates on its own. These structures are intimately tied to the leadership in each house; congressional leaders are party leaders, not nonpartisan figures.

Congressional hearings sometimes feature high-profile witnesses who can draw media attention to an issue. Here, film director Stephen Spielberg testifies on proposals to ban the colorizing of old black-and-white movies.

House Party Organization. The House is organized into the majority and the minority. Whichever party has the greatest number of members forms the majority and takes charge of overseeing House committees and operations. The minority is the smaller party. In the 104th Congress, elected in 1994, Republicans gained a majority after four decades of Democratic control of the House.

The **Speaker**—the presiding officer elected by the whole House—is de facto leader of the majority chosen from among its senior members. The Speaker is assisted by several party leaders. The *majority leader* helps control floor debate and the House agenda. The *whip* organization consists of the *majority whip* and over 90 deputy whips, at-large whips, and assistant whips, who distribute information to party members, determine how members are likely to vote, and perform much of the legwork of coalition building for the leaders.

The minority has a parallel set of leaders. It elects a *minority leader* (who is nominated for Speaker, but always loses), a *minority whip* and a *chief deputy whip*. These leaders are consulted by the majority on matters involving scheduling and House administration, but the minority has no real power to control the operations or agenda of the House.

In addition to majority and minority officers, each party has its own internal party groups. The Republican Conference includes all party members in the House. It is led by a conference chairman, vice-chair, and secretary. A Republican Policy Committee helps develop party positions on issues. The Republican organization makes committee assignments for its members, develops legislative proposals, and conducts information gathering and dissemination activities. The foundation of the Democrats' organization is the Democratic Caucus, which consists of all Democrats in the House. It elects party leaders, reviews committee assignments, and recommends changes in House procedures. The Democratic Steering and Policy Committee is similar to the Republican Policy Committee.

Speaker Presiding officer of the U.S. House of Representatives, elected by the House at the beginning of each Congress.

Senate Party Organization. Party organization in the upper house, as the Senate is sometimes called, is also divided along majority-minority lines, but it is not as hierarchically structured as that of the House. Smaller and more informal, it lacks the powerful figure of the Speaker. The vice-president is president of the Senate, but not part of the party organization in the Senate (as Lyndon Johnson learned when he moved from being majority leader to vice-president in 1961; Senate Democrats rejected his attempt to retain a leadership role). The position of *president pro tempore*—a senator who presides in the vice-president's absence—is largely ceremonial and always given to the most senior member of the majority party. The majority selects a *majority leader* and a *majority whip,* while the minority chooses a *minority leader* and a *minority whip.* These officers are similar to their counterparts in the House.

As a result of the 1994 elections, the Republicans gained majority status. All Republican senators belong to the Republican Conference, which elects the party leaders. The Republican organization also includes the Committee on Committees to make assignments to Senate panels, and the Policy Committee to develop positions on bills. All Democrats belong to the Democratic Conference, which elects party leaders. The Democratic Steering Committee makes committee assignments and the Democratic Policy Committee develops positions on issues.

Leadership Resources. In parliamentary legislatures, party leaders often have powerful weapons with which to command the loyalty of members; they control campaign funds, party nominations, even government ministries (if in the majority). Congressional leaders have much less potent resources. The Speaker and House majority leadership can use control over scheduling and procedure (through the Rules Committee), perform services for members (assigning office space, performing favors), and even influence committee assignments in order to win support from party members. In the Senate, where operations are less partisan and more collegial, majority and minority leaders use information and trading favors to induce support from party members. In both houses, leaders rely on persuasion-based strategies to hold their parties together. They cannot really command party members to vote a certain way, but leaders can offer their members such inducements as assistance with other legislation, better office space, desirable committee assignments, and influence over the party's agenda, in order to get party members to go along with the leaders. Congressional party organizations give their members considerable freedom and leeway. They are associations rather than armies.

Caucuses

Senators and representatives can join any of over one hundred informal *caucuses*—associations of members of Congress outside of the normal committee and party structures—that bring together representatives and senators with similar interests. African American members may join the Congressional Black Caucus; those interested in defense issues may participate in the Military Reform

Caucus; those from states with relevant industries may join the Mushroom Caucus, Steel Caucus, or the Congressional Jewelry Manufacturing Coalition.

Caucuses exhibit considerable variety in size and purpose: some are found in one house, some in both; many are bipartisan, some are partisan; some have broad policy agendas, others have a more limited focus. Political scientist Susan Webb Hammond identified six different types, according to why senators and representatives join them: (1) partisan caucuses (not to be confused with official party organs); (2) personal interest caucuses; (3) national constituency caucuses; (4) regional constituency caucuses; (5) state/district concern caucuses; and (6) industry concern caucuses.[6] Table 8.3 gives examples of each of these types.

Caucuses are a relatively new phenomenon on Capitol Hill. Before 1969, there were only three; by 1980, fifty-seven had been formed, and during the 1980s, the number climbed above one hundred. There are three times as many caucuses in the House as in the Senate[7], and members often belong to several. They join these associations in order to obtain information, coordinate activities, influence the agenda, develop legislation, build coalitions, monitor areas of policy, and provide tangible evidence of their efforts to promote the interests of their constituents.[8] While caucuses increase coordination among members, they function outside the normal committee and party structures, so their net effect is to further decentralize power in Congress.

Support Staff

Members of Congress have long been assisted by secretaries, parliamentarians, pages, and clerks. In the past quarter-century, however, there has been an explosion of staff in the national legislature. This proliferation of staff aides in Congress—part of a larger trend in American government that is explored in Chapter 12—led one observer to characterize Capitol Hill as an "anthill of activity." The metaphor is apt: over thirty-one thousand people work for Congress, providing professional policy assistance as well as performing more routine tasks. There are three general types of staffs on Capitol Hill: Congressional agencies, committee staffs, and personal staffs.

Congressional Agencies. Four **congressional agencies**—staff organizations that serve Congress as a whole—assist the legislature in key areas. Together, these agencies make up about 10 percent of the total Capitol Hill workforce. The *General Accounting Office* (GAO) conducts audits of government agencies and programs as well as undertaking studies on program efficiency and effectiveness. The *Congressional Research Service* (CRS) is a research arm of the Library of Congress. Its staff of experts responds to over 400,000 requests for information from members each year. The *Office of Technology Assessment* (OTA) provides technical information to congressional committees on topics ranging from alternative energy sources to genetic engineering. The *Congressional Budget Office* (CBO) provides budget information and economic forecasts, tracks congressional spending, and reports on budget policy options

congressional agencies Staff organizations that serve Congress as a whole and make up about ten percent of the congressional workforce. Included are the General Accounting Office (GAO), the Congressional Research Service (CRS), the Office of Technology Assessment (OTA), and the Congressional Budget Office (CBO).

TABLE 8.3 Congressional Caucuses

Type	Examples
Partisan concerns	Conservative Democratic Forum Conservative Opportunity Society Democratic Study Group Populist Caucus Republican Study Committee Wednesday Groups
Personal interest	Arms Control and Foreign Policy Caucus Arts caucuses Crime Caucus Environmental and Energy Study Conference Senate Caucus on the Family Human rights caucuses Military Reform Caucus Ad Hoc Monitoring Group on South Africa
National constituency	Congressional Black Caucus Congressional Hispanic Caucus Congressional Caucus for Women's Issues Vietnam Veterans' Caucus
Regional constituency	Border caucuses Conference of Great Lakes Congressmen Northeast-Midwest Coalition Congressional Sunbelt Council Tennessee Valley Authority Caucus Western State Coalition
State/district concerns	Export task forces Family farm task forces Irish caucuses Rural Caucus Suburban Caucus
Industry concerns	Automotive Caucus Coal caucuses Copper caucuses Mushroom Caucus Senate Wine Caucus Senate Footwear Caucus

Source: Adapted from Susan Webb Hammond, "Congressional Caucuses and the Policy Process," in *Congress Reconsidered,* 4th ed., ed. Lawrence C. Dodd and Bruce I. Oppenheimer (Washington: CQ Press, 1989), p. 353.

available to Congress. While useful to members and the legislative process as a whole, these agencies do not play a central role in shaping public policy.

Committee Staffs. These range in size from around 10 to over 200, but average about 50 staffers per committee. Committee staffs are involved in research, drafting legislation, arranging hearings (and writing many of the questions members ask), assembling coalitions, and dealing with lobbyists, the White House, and the bureaucracy. Most committee staffs are hired on a partisan basis; the committee chair hires most of the staff, but certain positions are controlled by the ranking minority member. Because they are "where the action is," committee staff jobs are some of the most sought-after staff positions on Capitol Hill.

Personal Staffs. These staffs also participate in policy making, but their responsibilities include more than that. Members rely on their staffs for assistance in the three dimensions of their lives. First, members of Congress are busy VIPs and need assistance in coping with their crowded political lives; staff answer phones, open the mail, schedule appointments, deal with the media, carry luggage, drive the boss to the airport, and so on. Second, members of Congress are legislators and want help in performing that aspect of their job; staff prepare speeches and press releases, draft bills and amendments, help digest the information each member receives, and deal with lobbyists, committees, the party, and the White House. Finally, members are constituent servants, and their aides provide help in this area as well; staff assist constituents who have problems with the bureaucracy or want to attend a military academy or visit Washington, respond to letters, faxes, and phone messages about legislative proposals, and help maintain good political relations with individuals and groups back home.

House members' personal staffs average about 15 people; those of senators average closer to 30. Each representative and senator also maintains one or more offices in the home district or state. Members enjoy tremendous latitude in controlling their staffs. While personal staff budgets are controlled by House and Senate rules, members determine how much they will pay their aides and what duties are assigned them.

How a Bill Becomes Law

The chief activity of Congress is the making of laws. While the Constitution requires only that proposed laws be passed in the same form by each house and presented to the president, the legislative process has grown into an elaborate system for deliberating on proposed laws. Each potential law begins as a **bill**—a formal proposal in the form of a law that is offered for consideration in the House or Senate by one or more members. A bill may be drafted to raise or lower taxes, to increase or decrease spending, to create a new government program or agency, to make a new law on crime or some other policy area, to alter an existing law, or even to repeal (wipe out) a law. The process by which a bill becomes a law, which is summarized in Figure 8.1, has five main steps: introduction, committee action, floor action, conference, and presidential action.

Introduction. To be considered, a bill must be introduced. House bills are dropped in a wooden "hopper" on the rostrum; Senate bills may be handed to a clerk or introduced from the floor. The bill must then be referred to a committee. In the Senate, committee referral is somewhat automatic. On the other

bill Proposed law under consideration by a legislative body.

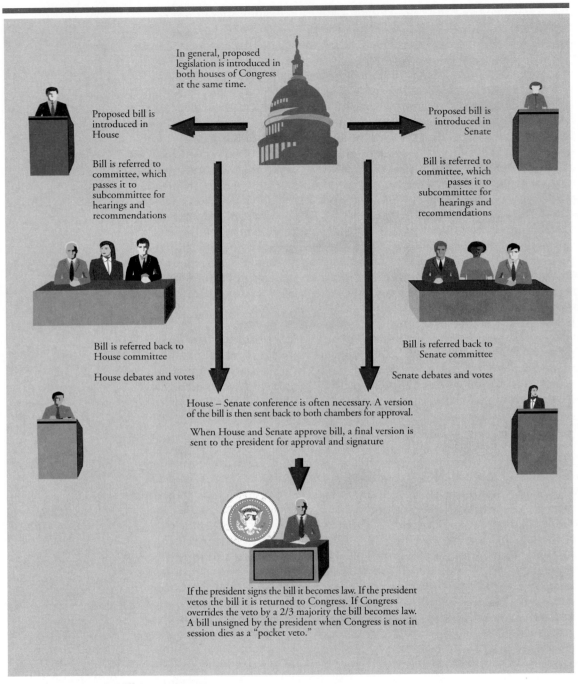

In general, proposed legislation is introduced in both houses of Congress at the same time.

Proposed bill is introduced in House

Proposed bill is introduced in Senate

Bill is referred to committee, which passes it to subcommittee for hearings and recommendations

Bill is referred to committee, which passes it to subcommittee for hearings and recommendations

Bill is referred back to House committee

House debates and votes

Bill is referred back to Senate committee

Senate debates and votes

House – Senate conference is often necessary. A version of the bill is then sent back to both chambers for approval.

When House and Senate approve bill, a final version is sent to the president for approval and signature

If the president signs the bill it becomes law. If the president vetos the bill it is returned to Congress. If Congress overrides the veto by a 2/3 majority the bill becomes law. A bill unsigned by the president when Congress is not in session dies as a "pocket veto."

FIGURE 8.1 How a Bill Becomes a Law

hand, the Speaker of the House has some discretion over the committee(s) to which a bill is referred.

Committee Action. A bill is assigned to at least one committee. In recent years, the development of complex legislation in areas such as energy and health care has meant that some bills must be considered by several committees. The 1990 clean air bill was sent to seven House committees. Each committee in turn will refer the bill to one or more subcommittees.

Most bills die at this point. That is, they are never given serious attention by the relevant committee or subcommittee. Congress has only so much time to consider a bill, which means only a fraction of those introduced can be seriously considered. Moreover, just because one or a few members introduce a bill does not mean that the proposal will receive high priority from party leaders and committee chairs. The bills that receive attention are those that have the support of powerful forces, such as a committee chair, the majority party leadership, the White House, or a very large number of members.

If action is to be taken, the subcommittee and its staff study the bill, hold hearings at which witnesses for and against the proposal can testify, and then make a recommendation to the full committee. The full committee may decide not to act on the bill, or it may hold hearings of its own before acting. Once the committee is ready to act, it will meet for a **markup session**—a working session of the committee during which the bill is reviewed line-by-line and a final draft is prepared to be sent to the floor. The "marked-up" version of the bill may take into account problems raised during hearings, political compromises made, or changes the committee wants to impose.

In the House there is an additional step; many bills must be sent to the Rules Committee, which is an agent of the majority leadership. It crafts for each bill a **rule**—an order that specifies the time allowed for debate on the bill and whether and how the bill may be amended. The rule may be one of three general types: an *open rule,* which allows germane (relevant) amendments to the committee bill (used for most bills); a *closed rule,* which prohibits amendments except those offered by the sponsoring committee; or a *restrictive rule,* which can limit which portions of a bill can be amended and by whom. The substance of each bill's rule can have a powerful effect on the fate of the proposal.

Floor Action. Many bills compete for a place on the crowded schedules of the House and Senate. Each chamber has its own method for deciding when and how to bring issues to the floor.

The House has an elaborate system for placing bills on its agenda. It has four **calendars** governing its business: (1) the *Union Calendar,* for revenue and appropriations bills, plus other public bills that directly or indirectly appropriate money or property; (2) the *House Calendar,* for public bills that do not raise revenue or appropriate money; (3) the *Private Calendar,* for bills that affect only those named in the bill; and, (4) the *Consent Calendar,* for noncontroversial bills that can be expedited. Given the amount of business competing for the time and attention of the House, it is clear that the calendars present a bottleneck through

markup session Meeting of a congressional committee during which a bill is drafted (or marked up) in the form in which it is to be sent to the House or Senate for consideration.

rule In the U.S. House of Representatives, an order that specifies the amount of time allowed for debate on a bill, any limits on the number or kinds of amendments that can be attached to the bill, and other restrictions affecting debate and potential passage of the proposed law.

calendar Schedule of business in the U.S. Congress. The House of Representatives uses four calendars to control its business; the Senate uses two.

which some bills do not pass. Moreover, no bill can come to the floor from the *Union* or *House* calendars without a rule from the Rules Committee.

The Senate's procedures are simpler but give the majority leaders less control over the structure of debate than majority leaders in the House have. Much of Senate business is conducted by the practice of **unanimous consent** motions, which means that a procedural motion is adopted so long as no one objects to it. Since its creation, the Senate has adhered to the principle of *unlimited debate,* that is, the right of any senator to speak indefinitely unless all have agreed to restrict the time for debate. The result of this system is that there are no committee-made "rules" governing floor action on bills. Senate rules place no limits on amendments to bills nor even require that they be germane. Unrelated amendments known as **riders** are often added to bills to increase support for the main bill or to help secure passage of a less popular idea by attaching it to a popular main bill.

The Senate also makes it possible for a minority (even of one) to halt a bill by trying to keep debate going until the bill's proponents compromise or surrender. This attempt to "talk a bill to death" is known as the **filibuster.** In 1993 Senate Republicans mounted a successful filibuster against President Clinton's economic stimulus package, forcing the White House and Democrats to withdraw the plan without a vote. A filibuster can be stopped only by wearing down those attempting it (essentially impossible if a group does it) or by voting **cloture** (closure), a motion that requires support from three-fifths of senators and then imposes a time limit on debate. Even the threat of a filibuster can be a powerful tool for encouraging the majority to compromise on a controversial bill.

The Senate uses only two calendars to control its agenda. The *Calendar of Business* contains all legislation and the *Executive Calendar* all presidential nominations and treaties. Because broad consent is needed, both majority and minority leaders participate in the scheduling of floor action. To expedite business, the Senate uses different "tracks" of debate whereby as many as five bills may be considered at one time; the House allows only one at a time.

Floor debate is lively and may be quite emotional. Time for debate is divided between those favoring the bill and those opposing it, with a *floor manager* appointed for each side (usually the majority appoints the manager in favor and the minority chooses the manager against the bill). The amount of time any member is allowed to speak is carefully monitored by the presiding officer. Unless the bill being debated is very controversial or of interest to most members, it is likely that few members will attend the floor debate beyond those with a direct interest in the bill. This fact of a poorly attended debate often surprises citizens who watch congressional debates, but most members do not rely on the floor debate to help them decide how to vote. Rather, they vote on the basis of many factors: party considerations, the report of the committee(s) that considered the bill, what the White House says, constituent interests, what lobbyists and citizen groups say, and their own convictions. Summoned by a system of bells and lights, members arrive at the chamber whenever a vote is to be taken.

unanimous consent Method of conducting business in the U.S. Senate by which most procedural motions are adopted as long as no senator dissents.

rider Amendment added to a bill that is not germane to the substance of the bill. Allowed in the U.S. Senate but forbidden by the House of Representatives.

filibuster Attempt to "talk a bill to death" in the U.S. Senate by taking advantage of the principle of unlimited debate. One or more senators holds the floor and refuses to allow business to proceed until the bill is withdrawn, a compromise is reached, cloture is invoked, or the senator(s) undertaking the filibuster gives up.

cloture Decision to end a filibuster by imposing a limit on debate in the U.S. Senate. Three-fifths of all senators must vote in favor of cloture for it to be imposed.

The Senate tradition of unlimited debate allows senators to filibuster, or talk a bill to death. In the classic film Mr. Smith Goes to Washington, *actor Jimmy Stewart portrayed an idealistic young senator who conducted a lonely filibuster against political corruption.*

Floor debate is usually the end of a long political process that has transpired in committees and backroom dealings. Seldom is it the most important phase of a bill's life, but there are important exceptions. In 1991 Congress considered a motion to authorize President Bush to employ American forces against Iraq; the floor debate in each house, carried live on television, constituted the most significant part of the deliberations on that proposal.

House-Senate Conferences. If the Senate and House drafts of a bill differ, a common version must be produced. This is the job of a House-Senate **conference committee**—a meeting of members of the two chambers to reconcile differences between the versions of the bill passed by each chamber. The conference committee is usually composed of members from the committee(s) in each chamber responsible for the bill. But conferees, as the members of these joint bodies are called, are not engaged merely in a technical task of reconciling two bills. Their job is eminently a political one.

Conference committees not only work to forge compromises that can win support in each house and at the White House, but they have the opportunity to redraft legislation in fairly significant ways. For example, the conference on a 1988 appropriations bill added 47 provisions to the final law that were not in either the House or Senate bills. This kind of influence has led some members to refer to conferences as the "third house of Congress."

conference committee Committee formed of members of the U.S. House of Representatives and the Senate who are charged to resolve differences in the different versions of a bill passed by the two houses of Congress. Such committees have sometimes been called the "third house" of Congress.

veto The power to say
no. Specifically, the
president's power to
reject bills passed by
Congress unless that
rejection is overridden
by a two-thirds vote in
each house of the legis-
lature.

pocket veto Veto
accomplished not by the
president actually rejecting a bill presented for
signature, but by Con-
gress adjourning while
the bill awaits the president's signature. Inac-
tion allows the presi-
dent to kill a bill
without vetoing directly.

TABLE 8.4 **Bills, Bills, Bills**

	Bills Introduced	**Bills Passed**	**Ratio of Bills Passed to Bills Introduced**
House			
1983–1984	7,105	978	0.137
1985–1986	6,499	973	0.150
1987–1988	6,263	1,061	0.169
1989–1990	6,683	968	0.145
1991–1992	7,771	932	0.120
Senate			
1983–1984	3,454	936	0.271
1985–1986	3,386	940	0.278
1987–1988	3,325	1,002	0.301
1989–1990	3,669	980	0.267
1991–1992	4,245	947	0.223

Source: Adapted from Norman J. Ornstein, Thomas E. Mann, and Michael J. Malbin, *Vital Statistics on Congress, 1993–1994* (Congressional Quarterly, Inc., 1994).

Presidential Action. If the House and Senate pass the conference version of the bill, it is sent to the president for final disposition. The president has three choices: sign the bill into law, use the **veto** (a presidential action that says "no" to the bill), or do nothing. If the bill is signed, the process ends. If the president vetoes the bill, then Congress can override that action by a vote of two-thirds of each house. If the president does nothing, the fate of the bill depends on timing: if Congress is still in session, the bill becomes law after 10 days (the 1989 Flag Protection Act passed this way); if Congress has adjourned, then the president's inaction constitutes a **pocket veto** that Congress is unable to reverse.

The legislative process is full of what political scientists call "veto points" (opportunities to kill a bill). To pass, the bill must survive each step along the way. It should not be surprising that while over ten thousand bills are intro-duced every year, only a few hundred become law. Table 8.4 shows the differ-ence between the number of bills introduced and those measures that have passed in recent years.

Congressional Politics

Edmund Burke conceived of the British Parliament as a body with only one goal in mind: to serve the public interest. For the United States Congress, such a situation might seem a luxury. Congress was established to promote both the common good and constituent interests, which creates a tension between the two goals of the institution that affects nearly everything about it and its mem-bers.

Members at Work

Members of Congress feel the tension inherent in their jobs quite keenly. As we shall see, it affects the way they perceive their jobs, how they balance demands on their time and effort, and how they vote. That fact, plus a constant campaign for reelection, keeps most senators and representatives moving at an almost frantic pace.

The Member's Juggling Act. Members divide their time, energy, and attention between their legislative responsibilities and the obligations they accept as constituent servants and candidates for reelection. They move back and forth between Washington and the home district/state, maintaining political connections while attending to legislative duties. Even in Washington, their time is allocated to committee work, meetings with lobbyists and constituents, party activities, fund raising, floor debate, and work with staff. As we see in the Citizens in Action box, their families often bear the brunt of these competing responsibilities.

To help balance their legislative and constituent obligations, senators and representatives tend to gravitate toward those issues and committee assignments that allow them to shape national policy while protecting their constituents. Senators Tom Harkin (D.-Ia.) and Jesse Helms (R.-N.C.) both give considerable time to their senior positions on the Agriculture Committee, whose jurisdiction is important to their home states. Likewise, Senator Sam Nunn (D.-Ga.) can use his influence as a member of the Armed Service Committee to shape defense policy and look after the large number of military installations in his state (Georgians have long been prominent on that committee).

Members may even be willing to trade away their votes on issues of peripheral importance to their districts in exchange for other members' support of bills important to their constituents. For example, a representative from a rural district may agree to support urban development aid in exchange for a city legislator's vote on agricultural programs. This practice is known as **logrolling.**

The Continual Campaign for Reelection. Most members of today's Congress plan to make their careers on Capitol Hill (unless a vacancy opens up at the White House), so they give high priority to getting reelected—and it generally works. In the past half-century, more than 90 percent of House members have won reelection.[9] Only rarely does a situation like that in 1994—when many incumbents were defeated—occur.

Members of Congress engage in three general activities to enhance their chances of reelection.[10] First, they use *advertising* to establish their importance in the national media, name recognition back home, or both. They provide information to reporters, even becoming standard sources for particular topics. As the *Washington Monthly* put it: "All reporters have a staple list. . . . Need the line on enterprise zones from a progressive Republican? You can always count on Jim Leach. From a man of the people? Al D'Amato. From a Washington

logrolling Practice of trading votes among members of Congress.

CITIZENS IN ACTION

CONGRESSIONAL FAMILIES

For members of Congress, buying a house can be a political decision. Those who move their spouses and children to the Washington, D.C., area can spend more time with their families but are open to charges of forgetting about the district. Floor debates and other meetings are often scheduled in the late afternoon and evening, making it hard for members to spend evenings at home. Those who leave their families back in the district see them less and spend more time commuting. To save money, some of these members have taken to sleeping in their offices during the week and flying home for weekends. While the Republican majority in the House has pledged to make Congress more "family-friendly," it is likely that families still bear much of the burden of congressional life.

insider? Vic Fazio."[11] Members send newsletters to constituents to trumpet their accomplishments and make frequent appearances in the district/state.

Second, members engage in *credit claiming* in hopes that constituents will reward them for their achievements. Senator Arlen Specter (R.-Penn.) ran for reelection in 1992 proclaiming his role in increasing federal funding for breast cancer research, despite the fact that "Senate insiders say Specter served mostly as spectator."[12] Senator Phil Gramm (R.-Tex.) claimed credit for a $1.5 million hazardous waste research grant to Lamar University in 1989, "despite being one of only eight senators to vote against that funding."[13] By custom, executive agencies awarding grants or contracts in local communities allow the relevant members to announce those awards. When in 1977 the Carter administration sought to win presidential support by making such announcements from the White House, a storm of protest arose on Capitol Hill.

Finally, members engage in *position taking* on a range of issues. This can be done by introducing legislation (even if it has no chance of passage), by making speeches on the floor (whether or not anyone is listening), through comments to journalists and letters to constituents, by voting on legislative proposals, or by joining as a co-sponsor of popular legislation. In recent years membership in the various caucuses on Capitol Hill has also served in this capacity, providing concrete evidence of commitment to constituent interests.

Taking Advantage of Incumbency. To help improve their chances of reelection to Congress, senators and representatives use several means to take advantage of their incumbency.[14] First, *video feeds* allow members in Washington to provide short messages on current affairs for local news in the district or state (serves as advertising and position-taking).

Second, *high-tech computerized mail* exploits members' **franking privilege** (right to send official mail without postage). Congress sends out nearly 4 million pieces of free mail every day it is in session, with the volume much heavier in election than nonelection years. But volume alone is not important; the key to successful use of mail is sophisticated mailing lists. A good example is Tim Wirth, who served in the House and Senate from 1974 to 1992. At its height, his mailing list included over 150,000 names in 1,000 categories, including people interested in environmental issues, women's issues (with even a subcategory for women in mining), the deficit, the nuclear freeze, and 18,000 people Wirth had met personally.[15]

Third, members perform *casework*. This refers to dealing with individual "cases" of constituents seeking the help of their legislators in an array of areas: straightening out problems with Social Security, veterans' benefits, unemployment compensation, or the military services; obtaining appointments to military academies; learning about legislative issues or government jobs; or obtaining flags that have flown over the U.S. Capitol. While all members of Congress are quick to point out that casework is nonpolitical and part of their job regardless of electoral considerations, they also see an electoral value in these services. House members carry an estimated caseload of about 10,000 cases a year, while

Members of Congress return to their home states or districts to maintain their connection with voters and stay in the public eye. Here, Senator Harris Wofford (D.-Penn.) addresses a rally; despite such efforts, Wofford was defeated in the 1994 election.

senators' annual caseload varies from 1,000 to 2,000 in small states to 30,000 to 50,000 in New York and California.[16]

Fourth, *presence back home* provides a way of showing constituents that members have their interests at heart. Some members belong to a group known informally as the "Tuesday-Thursday Club," because they spend those days in Washington and the rest of the week back home. One representative uses a refurbished R.V. as a kind of roving office to travel his district. Senator Bill Bradley (D.-N.J.) has walked the beach and stood in bus terminals to reach constituents.

Finally, members seek *political money*. As we saw in Chapter 7, they engage in almost continuous fund-raising activities, both to finance their upcoming reelection campaigns and to scare off potential challengers. Most senators and representatives find this part of incumbency essential but wearing.

Members of Congress do not make every move with reelection in mind, but being returned to office is a prominent goal for most senators and representatives. Are all these reelection-oriented efforts effective? The answer is generally yes, although there are important exceptions. In 1994, a number of prominent members of Congress were defeated in their bids for reelection. Perhaps the most visible was House Speaker Tom Foley (D.-Wash.), a 30-year veteran of Capitol Hill who was defeated by a political newcomer. Likewise Representative Mike Synar (D.-Ok.), a well-respected lawmaker with ties to the Clinton administration, failed to even win his party's nomination for his own seat; he was defeated by another newcomer who proclaimed his own independence and ties

franking privilege
The right of members of Congress to send official correspondence through the mail without paying postage; the expense is covered by annual payment to the U.S. Postal Service.

to the people of the district. Similarly, Senator James Sasser, chair of the Senate Budget Committee and a contender for the position of leader of the Senate Democrats, was beaten by an opponent who accused the incumbent of forgetting about his constituents' interests.

Congressional Policy Making

The dual nature of Congress means that the first branch tends to favor certain kinds of policies: those that allow it to protect constituent interests while promoting national goals. A good example of this reality is the Tax Reform Act of 1986, which created the most sweeping change in the federal tax code since World War II. Three provisions of the law highlight the tension between representation and the public interest:

1. Six million working poor were removed from the rolls of those liable to pay taxes.
2. Tax breaks for the oil and gas industry were maintained despite the sweeping elimination of other deductions and exemptions that littered the tax code.
3. Large contributors to the Louisiana State University and the University of Texas football programs were exempted from an IRS ruling that would prevent them from deducting the value of their tickets from their taxes as a business expense.[17]

The first of these actions was directed at promoting the broad public interest, while the second promoted one sector of the economy (either to protect that sector or its place in the overall economy), and the third benefited a small number of people with very narrow interests.

Another way in which Congress seeks to balance national and constituent interests is its frequent spending on "pork barrel" legislation, generally known in Washington as **pork**—tangible (usually monetary) benefits for specific districts or states. Each year the legislature appropriates millions of dollars for building projects (roads, bridges, post offices, dams, a national "weed center" in North Dakota, a nutrition research center in Louisiana), commercial subsidies (for sugar and tobacco production, to "promote the merits of eating fish," to protect honey producers), and other programs (such as a memorial to Lawrence Welk). As the *Wall Street Journal* has pointed out, "pork" comes in many forms: "Dams, roads and bridges . . . are old hat."[18] These days, there is also "academic pork" in the form of research grants to colleges, "defense pork" in the form of geographically specific military expenditures, and lately "high-tech pork," such as money for supercomputers. In one sense this sort of spending contributes to national objectives (transportation, research, commerce), but it is allocated according to the needs and wants of local communities and the influence of individual members. States and districts represented on House and Senate appropriations committees tend to receive the most money.

pork Term applied to government spending that provides tangible benefits for specific districts or states. Also known as porkbarrel spending.

230

Contact Your Representative

1. **Participate in the process of selecting members of Congress:** Generally, each citizen has two opportunities to help select senators and representatives—in the primary and in the general election. Citizens can also participate in campaigns or contribute to them. Incumbency is powerful, but there are enough cases of senior incumbents being unseated that reelection is not a foregone conclusion. Consider the results of the 1994 election: a turnover in control of both chambers, a sitting Speaker of the House defeated by a narrow margin, and many well-established incumbents denied reelection.

2. **Contact your senator or representative back home:** All members have one or more district/state offices that constituents can visit or call. Many members will hold office hours in the district to see constituents or provide other opportunities for citizens to reach them in the local community (town meetings, information sessions on military academy appointments, and so on). A local phone book or public library will have information on each area's representative and the state's two senators.

3. **Contact your senator or representative in Washington:** Most citizens who visit Washington will pay a call at the office of their representative, even if only to obtain passes to the House or Senate Visitor's Galleries. But citizens also go to Capitol Hill to lobby members.

   All members of Congress can be phoned through the Capitol Switchboard: (202) 224-3121. Legislative information can be obtained at (202) 225-1772. Information about Congress is also available on the Internet.

   To write to a member of Congress, use the following addresses:

   Sen. Martha Washington
   U.S. Senate
   Washington, D.C.
   20510

   Rep. James Madison
   U.S. House of
   Representatives
   Washington, D.C.
   20515

4. **When contacting a member of Congress, do it right:** Anyone can sign his or her name to a pre-printed postcard issued by some interest group or append his or her name to a petition; it is not surprising that most representatives give these kinds of correspondence little attention. Phone calls have immediacy and do communicate your views, but the most effective way to tell a representative your opinion is to write a personal letter. It can be typed or handwritten, so long as it is readable. Some rules for writing an effective letter to a member of Congress follow:

   1. *Keep it short and put it in your own words:* The letter should be one page or less. Take the time to write your own letter if you feel strongly about an issue—form letters mean little.

   2. *Be specific:* Refer to a bill by its name or number or both. This may require some research, but it can make the letter harder to ignore.

   3. *Make your case clearly:* State exactly what you want your representative to do. Explain why your position is the right one. Don't repeat slogans from organized campaigns for or against some bill. Provide examples or other useful information.

   4. *Know your representative's record:* Show your awareness of the legislator's past actions, especially on related issues. See Appendix F for information sources.

   5. *Be polite:* Don't threaten to vote against your representative if you cannot have your way. This makes you look hotheaded or childish. The letter will be taken more seriously if it makes an argument rather than a threat.

   6. *Ask for an answer:* Ask the member to respond and to tell you what he or she intends to do.

   7. *Follow up:* When you receive a reply, write another letter that restates your position and responds to what your representative has said.

participate!

Congress and the Executive

Although Congress possesses broad powers to shape and direct national policy, its bicameralism and internal distributions of power make it difficult for the first branch to predominate. Since the members of the party groups in Congress have a great deal of autonomy to vote as they see fit, congressional leaders are generally unable to impose central direction on the bills and resolutions passed each year. Each party may develop its own plans for policy, but at the end of a session the laws passed will not reflect any comprehensive "Democratic agenda" or "Republican program" such as are passed in parliamentary legislatures.

This fact invites, indeed requires, presidential leadership of Congress if the chief executive has legislative goals. When the president does not offer legislative leadership, as was the case with George Bush, members complain that the president is not leading. On a few occasions in modern times presidents have succeeded in winning passage of major legislative changes: Franklin Roosevelt's New Deal, Lyndon Johnson's Great Society, Ronald Reagan's tax cuts and defense spending increases. In general, presidents win less comprehensive successes, usually one bill at a time. Regardless of who initiates a proposal, a bill is far more likely to pass if it is supported by the White House.

Even without an ambitious presidential agenda, most laws passed by Congress are conceived in the executive branch. They may be initiatives from the president or, more commonly, proposals made by the bureaucratic agencies that administer laws and programs. One common estimate suggests that four out of five laws enacted on Capitol Hill began as some kind of executive initiative. Of course, that does not mean that important laws do not originate in Congress. As we saw, several major laws were conceived by members.

Once passed, laws and programs must be implemented. This task falls to executive departments and agencies. Because Congress writes the laws that create these agencies, assigns them powers and responsibilities, and appropriates the money they need to operate, it maintains close relations with the bureaucracy. Legislative activities to supervise the spending and operations of agencies are known as **oversight** and are carried out by committees and subcommittees. But oversight is an enormous task: the federal bureaucracy is large and complex; Congress is busy; and most members see this responsibility as tedious. So legislators tend to use two general approaches to oversight. They rely on the GAO to perform many of the more detailed aspects of supervision (for example, auditing agency records) and concentrate oversight efforts on problems brought to the attention of Congress by constituents, interest groups, or the media.

Americans' Love-Hate Relationship with Congress

oversight The power and responsibility of Congress to insure that administrative agencies act according to law and in the public interest.

Some of the most common political jokes in the United States involve Congress. An old one held that if the opposite of pro is con, then the opposite of progress is Congress. The national legislature's location has been called "Capitol Hell" and "Congressworld, a fortress of unreality."[19] As an institution, Congress usually gets low approval ratings in public opinion polls, and political commentators frequently attack the body as the source of many of the nation's problems. Congress is charged with being too parochial, too concerned with trivial matters and unwilling to tackle real problems, too slow and cumbersome. Yet members continue to be reelected at high rates, and most citizens express confidence in their own representatives.

Why this bifurcated attitude? The answer lies in the dual nature of the institution. Citizens tend to be satisfied with what their representatives are doing for their district, but unhappy with what Congress as a whole does. The very policies that allow members to balance national and local interests invite ridicule: "One person's pork is another's steak." Districts and states see the importance of their projects, but not those given to others.

open questions

Will Term Limits Improve Congress?

Because so many people—including members of Congress—are critical of the national legislature, calls for reform of the institution have been heard for years. Indeed, a centerpiece of the Republican Party's "Contract With America" during the 1994 election was a pledge to reform Congress and the way it does business. Reformers see the need for changes in the distribution of power in each house, in the conduct of floor debate, in the committee system, in the staff, in the procedures, and even in the legislature's fondness for commemorative resolutions that proclaim "National Dairy Goat Awareness Week," "National Drinking Water Week," "American Gospel Arts Week," and other memorials.

Is Congress in need of reform? If so, what kind of reform? These are legitimate questions that citizens may ask. But changing the internal operations of the national legislature—if change is indeed needed—is a task almost as complex as the institution itself. Are there not more focused kinds of reforms that can improve Congress?

Some observers argue that imposing term limits on members would go a long way toward improving Congress. As we saw in Chapter 1, in 1992 several states attempted to impose limits on how long their representatives in Washington could serve in the House or Senate. The move for congressional term limits became part of the Republican "Contract With America." Term-limit advocates maintain that no member should serve in Congress for more than a dozen years.[20] They see the high rates of reelection for incumbents as a major national problem, because chronic incumbency undermines the power of citizens' votes and takes members' minds off the constant campaign for reelection.

Reformers argue that term limits would lead to more frequent turnovers in congressional leadership—party leaders and committee chairs—thus infusing "new blood" into a body currently hobbled by excessive attention to seniority.

Advocates see term limits strengthening party organizations and encouraging members to focus more on the larger public interest. They regard the loss of experienced legislators as an acceptable price to pay for the benefits that would accrue from term limits.

In opposition, critics see term limits as more dangerous than the idea's advocates will admit. Opponents of term limits argue that these restrictions will ultimately limit the expertise and experience of those facing the problems of government.[21] Furthermore, critics contend that the loss of experienced members will mean that political power will be transferred to bureaucrats and lobbyists around long before and long after the brief tenure of legislators.[22] These critics charge that term limits will attract lower-quality candidates to Congress, provide incentives for members to think only of the here and now, and fill the House and Senate each session with many **lame ducks** (those on the way out) who could act irresponsibly because voters could not punish their misbehavior. Finally, critics maintain that we already have term limits: elections. They point to the dramatic results of the 1994 election as evidence that voters can remove incumbents when they believe that other officeholders would do a better job.

In 1995 the Supreme Court ruled that term limits on Congress could be imposed only by a constitutional amendment. This decision set back efforts to impose term limits by state action, but it has not ended the debate over whether term limits are a good idea.

Summary ▐

The United States Congress is the first branch of government. It is given broad powers and the ability to play an active role in American government. Congress is bicameral—divided into two chambers, the House of Representatives and the Senate.

Principles. Congress has a dual constitutional nature. On one hand, it is a *legislature for the public interest,* charged with advancing the good of the whole country. At the same time, it is a *representative body* whose members are expected to look out for the interests of their constituents and other groups in society. In addition, Congress was designed as a *bicameral* institution that is restrained by the checks-and-balances system.

Over time, Congress developed a set of operational principles for running itself: (1) It is *procedurally oriented;* (2) It is a *partisan* body; (3) It is a *decentralized* institution; and (4) It relies on *informal rules and norms* to regulate the behavior of its members. These principles shape the way the national legislature operates.

Process. The structures and processes of Congress are distinctive and make the legislature almost a world unto itself. It has an elaborate committee and sub-committee structure for considering legislation.

Each chamber of Congress has a complex set of party organizations and leaders that play a central role in organizing the agenda, deciding on commit-

lame duck: an office-holder who has been defeated for reelection or is ineligible for reelection.

tee assignments, and controlling floor debate. Although nearly all members of Congress belong to the Democratic or Republican Party, party leaders in the national legislature tend to lead through persuasion rather than command. They lack many of the resources that party leaders possess in a parliamentary system.

Members of Congress have different means for going outside the normal committee and party organizations to play a role in policy making. Most join *caucuses* concerned with issues of importance to them or their constituents, giving them a voice on these issues. All members have large staffs that assist them in their work, thus enabling representatives and senators to be less reliant on party leaders for information. In addition to *personal staffs,* there are also *committee staffs* and *congressional agencies* that make Congress an "anthill of activity."

The process by which a bill becomes a law has five steps: (1) introduction; (2) committee action; (3) floor action (tightly regulated in the House, much looser in the Senate); (4) House-Senate conferences to resolve differences; and (5) presidential action. This complex process provides many opportunities to kill a bill.

Politics. Members of Congress feel tension between their obligations to serve the public interest and to represent constituents. As members do their work, they juggle their time, energy, and attention between legislative responsibilities and work as constituent servants and as candidates for reelection. Members must also balance the interests of their constituents and the larger public interest. Members often use vote trading—*logrolling*—to help in this juggling act.

Members of Congress are constantly running for reelection. To do this, they engage in three general activities: *advertising, credit claiming,* and *position taking.* They use five techniques to take advantage of their incumbency and secure reelection: *video feeds, high-tech computerized mail, casework, presence back home,* and *political money.*

Policy making on Capitol Hill reflects the tension between Congress-as-legislator and Congress-as-representative body. Members look for ways to protect local interests while advancing the national interest. Congress also favors the use of *pork*—tangible benefits to districts or states—as another way to serve constituents. But Congress is not well equipped to dominate national policy making, which encourages presidential leadership in order to pass a legislative program.

Open Questions. Should term limits be imposed on members of Congress? Those who say yes argue that such limits will infuse "new blood" into the legislature, strengthen party organizations, and focus members' attention on the public interest. Opponents contend that term limits will lower the quality of candidates for Congress and make the legislature irresponsible.

Suggested Readings

DAVIDSON, ROGER, AND WALTER OLESZEK. *Congress and Its Members,* 3rd ed. Washington: CQ Press, 1990. Comprehensive survey of the congressional politics and operations.

FENNO, RICHARD F., JR. *Home Style: U.S. House Members in Their Districts.* Boston: Little, Brown, 1978. Classic study of how representatives relate to their constituents.

FIORINA, MORRIS. *Congress: Keystone of the Washington Establishment.* New Haven, Conn.: Yale University Press, 1977. Argues that Congress has established the bureaucracy so citizens will need help to deal with the government, ensuring members' reelection as a reward for constituent service.

FRANKLIN, DANIEL P. *Making Ends Meet: Congressional Budgeting in the Age of Deficits.* Washington: CQ Press, 1993. Provides an interesting snapshot of Congress as policy maker, telling the story of the making of the federal budget for fiscal year 1992.

MAASS, ARTHUR. *Congress and the Common Good.* New York: Basic Books, 1983. Argues—with lots of examples—that Congress serves the public interest.

MARTIN, JANET. *Lessons from the Hill.* New York: St. Martin's Press, 1993. Readable story of the author's experience as a Senate staffer working on an education bill.

OLESZEK, WALTER J. *Congressional Procedures and the Policy Process,* 3rd ed. Washington: CQ Press, 1988. Explains congressional procedures and their significance to how Congress operates.

The American Presidency

chapter 9

The last few weeks of 1992 were expected to be relatively uneventful ones for President George Bush. Defeated in his bid for reelection by Arkansas Governor Bill Clinton, Bush was headed for retirement. At a time when most observers thought he would be packing for a move to Texas and bidding farewell to the personnel of his administration, the president was actively employing the powers of his office. In early December he ordered American military forces to Somalia for a famine-relief mission that had been approved by the United Nations at his behest. Shortly before Christmas he pardoned six former Reagan administration officials indicted in connection with the 1987 Iran-Contra scandal. And at the beginning of the new year, he concluded a major nuclear-arms reduction treaty with the states of the former Soviet Union and launched bomber and missile attacks on Iraq.

Mr. Bush's postelection behavior presents a useful snapshot of the American presidency. His actions were those of an executive whose office is somewhat unique among the regimes of the world. Where most democratic executive leaders remain in office only with the support of a majority in a parliament, the president of the United States is an officer of government who wields power derived from the Constitution and from the voters for a fixed term. The chief executive is neither the servant of the legislature nor its master. The president is one of the most powerful figures in world politics, yet at home needs the agreement of Congress to enact most policy initiatives. All executive power is vested in this one individual, yet presidents are incapable of performing their duties without an extensive staff. The president is commander in chief of one of the deadliest fighting forces in history but can be removed from office without a shot being fired.

The President's Many Roles

American chief executives play particular roles in our political system. Many of these roles grow out of the constitutional powers and duties of the office and are sometimes portrayed as a selection of "hats" that the president wears. Others have been added over time because of the president's special status in American politics. While it is useful to think of the job of president as a collection of hats, we must always keep in mind that all the hats belong to the same officeholder, and that the chief executive frequently wears several (if not all) the hats at once.[1] (For sources of these roles, see Table 9.1 on pages 240–241.)

Chief of State

The president is the chief ceremonial officer of the government and a living symbol of the nation. That is why the president is accorded the respect of a special form of address (always "Mr. President"), the presidential seal, the White House, "Hail to the Chief," and pictures in American classrooms, government offices, and American embassies around the world. The president performs several duties, such as proclaiming special holidays, pinning medals on military and civilian heroes, supporting good causes (the Red Cross, United Way, the Boy Scouts and Girl Scouts), lighting the National Christmas Tree, receiving the recent Super Bowl and World Series champions, and hosting state dinners for the diplomatic corps.

Chief Executive

Not only does Article II of the Constitution vest "the executive power" in the president, but it also charges that officer to "take care that the laws be faithfully executed." In this capacity, the president performs several important functions. One of the most important is to direct the work of the executive branch, which includes the 14 cabinet departments and a wide array of independent agencies, boards, and commissions. The chief executive does this primarily by appointing and removing the officials who head these units (except, in certain cases such as regulatory commissions, when officials have fixed terms of service), who in turn carry out the president's policy initiatives.

Appointments. The operations of the executive branch reflect presidential influence but not White House command. The officers appointed by the president constitute only a small fraction of the most senior positions in the executive branch; 99 percent of executive positions are filled by the civil service system or through professional selection, such as scientists at NASA or medical researchers at the Centers for Disease Control. Moreover, executive agencies are charged by law with certain responsibilities, such as administering a welfare program or enforcing tax laws, that supercede any presidential priorities. And all units of the executive branch depend on Congress for funds, so they are attentive to the concerns of legislators on Capitol Hill.

Through appointees, the president can influence how aggressively civil rights laws will be enforced, how the military will plan and train for future missions, how carefully and honestly the vast amount of federal dollars will be spent, or what administrative regulations will be written to carry out the laws passed by Congress.

The Budget. The president carries out other functions as chief executive. For example, the president is charged with submitting to Congress a budget proposal each year. The White House uses this responsibility to put the chief executive's stamp on the priorities of the federal government. By requesting more or less money for defense, welfare, highways, foreign aid, environmental protection, and the myriad other federal initiatives, the chief executive influences and shapes national policy (with the agreement of Congress). Presidents certainly do not get all they want from budget votes in Congress, but they are able to use the budget as a means for affecting the work of the executive branch.

Administrative Clearance. The president can also shape the process of administrative rule making. Because Congress passes general laws that require further definition in order to be implemented and enforced, administrative agencies are empowered to draft rules that will provide the necessary details for carrying legislation into effect. The White House uses the Office of Management

Citizens in Action

THE PRESIDENT'S PARTNER

One of Washington's most difficult jobs is unofficial and unpaid: being the president's spouse. Because only men have been president, the customary title for this person is First Lady. The First Lady is hostess for social functions at the White House, advocate of good causes, confidante of the president, protector of the family, and guardian of what little privacy a president has. Edith Wilson played such a central role in assisting President Woodrow Wilson after his 1919 stroke that some historians have called her a "surrogate president." Eleanor Roosevelt, wife of Franklin Roosevelt, gave policy advice to the president, played an independent role in Democratic Party politics, and wrote a daily newspaper column. Hillary Rodham Clinton represents the beginning of an era in which the First Lady does what many presidents' wives have done in the past, but in a more public way.

TABLE 9.1 Presidential Roles

Roles Established by the Constitution

Function	Constitutional Source	Other Precedents
Chief of State Ceremonial head of U.S.A. Supports good causes Honors American heroes Hosts state ceremonies, dinners, etc.	Vesting Clause (Art. II, Sect. 1) "The executive Power shall be vested in a President of the United States of America"	First Congress voted large salary for president, commissioned a grand house for executive residence
Chief Executive Oversees work of Executive Branch Appoints executive officials and federal judges Oversees law enforcement Draws up annual budget proposal Oversees administrative rulemaking	Vesting Clause (Art. II, Sect. 2) gives president power to appoint executive and other officials, to require written opinions of executive officials, to appoint "inferior Officers." Take Care Clause (Art. II, Sect. 3) says president "shall Take Care that the Laws be faithfully executed"	First executive departments and agencies were created in 1789 Executive Office of the President was created in 1939
Commander in Chief Commands U.S. military and state militias (when called into federal service) Directs U.S. military policy at home and abroad Dispatches U.S. forces into foreign conflicts and peace-keeping activities	Art. II, Sect. 2: President made commander in chief of the army and navy and of state militias when they are called into service of the United States	Presidential military actions—e.g., interventions in Tripoli, Haiti, Nicaragua, Korea, Vietnam
Chief Diplomat Negotiates with other countries Concludes treaties and executive agreements Receives ambassadors Recognizes foreign governments	Art. II, Sect. 2: President given power to make treaties (with advice and consent of Senate), to appoint and receive ambassadors	*U.S. v. Curtiss-Wright Export Corp.* (1937) and *U.S. v. Belmont* (1937)—accepted broad executive powers in foreign affairs
Chief Legislator Proposes legislation for congressional consideration Signs or vetoes laws passed by Congress	Art. I, Sect. 7: President given qualified veto over bills passed Art. II, Sect. 3: President to advise Congress on State of the Union, to recommend "Measures," and to call special sessions of Congress	Truman began practice of submitting an annual legislative program to Congress—all presidents since then have followed this precedent

and Budget (OMB), a division of the Executive Office of the President (EOP), as an instrument for reviewing proposed rules and comparing them to the president's goals and priorities. Subject to limits imposed by law, the OMB engages in a process known as *administrative clearance* to approve, alter, or even reject

TABLE 9.1 Presidential Roles *(continued)*

Roles Established by Precedent or Law

Function	*Source*
Party Leader	
President can appoint chair of party national committee	Attached to presidency since nineteenth century—president is party's highest elected offical
President is symbolic leader of his or her party	
Protector of the Peace	
President ensures maintenance of law and order, up to and including use of military force	Lincoln's handling of Civil War established president as ultimate protector of domestic order
Manager of Prosperity	
President proposes policies to promote economic prosperity, low inflation, and low levels of unemployment	FDR's handling of Great Depression set precedent, confirmed in Employment Act of 1946
President may try to mediate labor-management disputes	Taft-Hartley Act (1947) enabled president to intervene in labor-management disputes
President negotiates with foreign governments to promote U.S. industry	
President has emergency power to impose wage and price controls	
Leader of Public Opinion	
President attempts to shape public opinion through use of radio, TV, and personal appearances	Radio and TV give president direct communication with most citizens
President submits to questioning by journalists in interviews and news conferences	News conferences became routine under FDR
World Leader	
President is leader of world's most powerful nation	American leadership in World Wars I and II and in opposing Soviet Union during cold war gave president this role
President takes lead in forging international coalitions to promote values important to U.S., such as opposition to communism or promotion of democracy	U.S. military arsenal (conventional and nuclear) gives president power base from which to play this role
President informal leader of the heads of the world's industrial democracies (such as Britain, Japan, Germany, etc.)	U.S. has world's largest economy

regulations it reviews. For example, the 1990 Wetlands Protection Act, which was intended to preserve areas such as the Florida Everglades and the Atchafalaya Basin in Louisiana, required the Environmental Protection Agency (EPA) to create rules that actually defined a wetland and specified procedures for making a reality of the law. In 1991, OMB rejected a broad definition of wetland that would have included substantial areas not originally intended by Congress to be covered by the law. The agency attempted to replace it with a much narrower definition, which environmental groups, EPA scientists, and several members of Congress regarded as too stringent. In the end, a compromise rule was adopted, illustrating both the limits and potential of presidential influence through administrative clearance.

Commander in Chief

This position empowers the president to command all the armed forces of the United States, as well as the militia (National Guard) of each state when it is called into federal service. Over the course of American history, this role has grown considerably. When George Washington was president, he interpreted it to mean that he was the supreme general of the army (commander in chief had been his title as leader of the Continental Army). When the Whiskey Rebellion broke out in 1794, Washington mounted his horse and led a force against the rebels. Later presidents would expand the role to include power to direct military policy at home (as in the Civil War) and abroad (as in Vietnam), whether or not Congress had authorized the use of military force. In 1973, Congress attempted to limit this power by passage of the War Powers Resolution (over President Nixon's veto). This law, which each president has contested as unconstitutional, sets restrictions on the use of the military abroad without congressional approval. In practice, however, it has not prevented several commanders in chief from dispatching American forces to Grenada, Panama, the Persian Gulf, or elsewhere. Nor did it stop Bill Clinton from threatening to invade Haiti in 1994, nor from sending American troops to that country to serve as a peace-keeping force.

Chief Diplomat

This role means that the president is the voice of the United States for communicating with foreign governments. American negotiations and relations with other nations, international organizations, or other international actors must be conducted through or with the consent of the president. Treaties and executive agreements are concluded through the president as well. While the Senate plays a constitutional role in the approval of treaties and ambassadors, the chief diplomat clearly has dominant power in the matter of foreign relations. In the years since World War II, this role has been important to the enlargement of presidential power. Through it, American presidents have committed the nation to several military alliances (such as the North Atlantic Treaty Organization) and participation in international organizations (such as the United Nations), shaped relations with the former Soviet Union and the People's Republic of China, concluded arms-control and trade agreements, and undertaken commitments to support and protect countries such as Israel and Japan.

Presidents have also acted as intermediaries to help resolve international conflicts. In 1905, Theodore Roosevelt intervened in the Russo-Japanese War, hoping to avoid a defeat for Japan that he believed would be against U.S. interests. He arranged a peace conference in Portsmouth, New Hampshire, that brought a peaceful resolution to the conflict and the ensuing Peace of Portsmouth earned him a Nobel Peace Prize. Later presidents would also attempt to settle foreign conflicts they regarded as inimical to American interests. For two decades, U.S. diplomats attempted to advance the cause of peace in the Arab-Israeli conflict. In 1978, Jimmy Carter negotiated peace between

"If George Washington never told a lie, how did he get to be president?"

©Edgar Argo. Reprinted from *Funny Times*.

Israel and Egypt at Camp David, Maryland, and in 1994, the Clinton administration helped arrange a peace accord between Israel and the Palestine Liberation Organization.

Chief Legislator

The Constitution gives the president a role in the legislative process. Article II authorizes the First Citizen to recommend legislative proposals to Congress and requires that all bills be presented to the president for signature or veto. If the president signs a bill, it becomes law. If the bill is vetoed, Congress can attempt to override that objection by a two-thirds majority in each chamber. On occasion, the president may choose to do neither—then the bill becomes law without the president's participation (unless Congress is not in session—then the bill dies without the president's signature). These simple elements enable the White House to become intimately involved in the law-making process. The Current Issues box discusses the line-item veto, which may become another tool of the president.

The relationship between the White House and Capitol Hill is often a contentious one, but Congress does tend to rely on the president to provide leadership on legislation. Since the time of President Franklin D. Roosevelt, the president has been expected to propose a legislative program, even if Congress is not inclined to act on it. Some presidents, such as Franklin Roosevelt, Lyndon Johnson, and Ronald Reagan, have had ambitious programs that they were able to see enacted, while executives such as Eisenhower and Bush had far more modest legislative agendas. Because of the legislature's broad power over domestic affairs, there is little that the president can do without Congress's endorsement. Bill Clinton wanted to create a system to provide Americans with universal health insurance, but he could not do it without legislation. Over a year after he went to Capitol Hill to issue his call for such a program, Congress had debated the idea but had not taken action on the president's plan.

Likewise, because of the decentralized politics of Capitol Hill, the president cannot count on Congress to pass executive initiatives without active White House involvement. Every president since Eisenhower has had a group of aides assigned exclusively to the job of "selling" the administration's legislative proposals to Congress. This staff—the White House Office of Congressional Relations—works with the congressional leaders of the president's party to try to coordinate efforts to advance the president's proposals.

Extra-Constitutional Roles

Over time, several additional roles have been added to the president's job description. For example, the nation's premier elected official has long been identified as *party leader.* In practice, however, because American political parties are diverse and decentralized bodies, America's top politician is often a figurehead rather than a boss. Another role is that of *leader of public opinion,* a function born of the president's national constituency and ability to reach the

The Line-Item Veto

The president's veto power applies to entire bills presented by Congress. For years, American chief executives have asserted that they could be more effective in holding down federal spending and imposing discipline on the executive branch if they possessed the *item veto*. An item veto, or line-item veto as it is often called, is a power held by about two-thirds of the nation's governors. It allows a chief executive to veto individual items in an appropriations bill—such as a specific program or construction project—and sign the remainder of the bill. The legislature may override these item vetoes but must do so by voting separately on each item vetoed by the executive. As with a regular veto, a two-thirds vote in each house of Congress would be needed to override an item veto.

President Clinton is the latest American chief executive to call for this power. He made it an issue in his campaign for the White House in 1992, although he backed down from that call after Democrats in Congress proved unwilling to consider the idea. Clinton, like many other advocates of the item veto, argued that this enhanced veto power would enable him to strike various pork-barrel projects and other forms of wasteful spending from the federal budget. Ronald Reagan and George Bush, like several other past presidents, had also made similar claims. The House Republicans' "Contract With America" included the item veto as one of its promises during the 1994 election.

The primary argument in favor of the item veto is that it strengthens the chief executive's hand in dealing with the legislature on spending. Those political leaders who want to see cuts in federal spending argue that the item veto will allow the president to eliminate projects that even members of Congress regard as unnecessary but find politically difficult to reject.

In response, critics of the item veto maintain that this change will be either ineffective or too effective. Some critics claim that the item veto will be ineffective, because the president will use the threat to veto pork-barrel projects in the districts of individual members of Congress as a weapon to win support for what the White House wants. In that case, the amount of wasteful spending in the budget could actually increase. On the other hand, some critics maintain that the item veto will make the president too powerful, because a determined chief executive could use it to slash even popular programs and gain the upper hand against Congress. In this case, spending for needed items might be eliminated.

Can the item veto make a difference? The experience of states is difficult to compare with that of the federal government in this matter, since state governments work with budgets far smaller than the federal one and with different tax bases and spending commitments. Only time and experience will tell whether the proponents or the critics are right.

public through the technology of mass communication. In times of domestic upheavals, such as riots and natural disasters, the president is looked to as *protector of the peace*. In all times, the president is considered *manager of prosperity,* although the ability of the White House to shape the American economy is greatly exceeded by public expectations of what the president can deliver. Finally, since World War II, the president of the United States has been a *world leader*. During the cold war, the president was the leader of the anticommunist regimes around the globe, and in the post–cold war era, the American chief executive remains one of the most influential actors in international politics and economics.

The powers and duties of the nation's chief executive, as reflected in these many roles, have been shaped by the values and choices that underlie the

The Constitution requires that every bill passed by both houses of Congress must be submitted to the president for his signature or veto. Here, President Clinton signs a handgun control law known as the "Brady bill," named for James Brady, former press secretary to President Reagan, who was severely wounded when Reagan was shot in 1981.

office of president. The principles embedded in the Constitution and in the operations of the executive have led to the rise of the powerful figure known to Americans and to the world as the president of the United States.

When the Constitutional Convention decided to form a new charter for government in 1787, the framers of the Constitution disagreed about many aspects of the new regime they were creating, but they shared a common view that an executive branch of government be included. This man or woman—the framers did not exclude the possibility of a woman president, although they did not anticipate one—was needed as a counterweight to the power of the legislature. The Articles of Confederation made no provisions for an executive branch, although committees of the Continental Congress employed secretaries to help them conduct their business. But the experience of the United States under the Articles, as well as problems that had arisen in several states with weak governors, led to growing consensus that the national government ought to have an executive independent of Congress. Not that they wanted a king, for they still chafed from the memory of royal government of the American colonies. They wanted a restrained executive who would not become a dictator.[2]

> The framers could not agree on the precise description of their new executive. Some, such as Alexander Hamilton, wanted a powerful "Governour" who would serve essentially for life ("during good behaviour" read Hamilton's proposal), a kind of elected monarch. Others, such as George Mason of Virginia, feared executive tyranny so intensely that they were loathe to give the executive much independence or power. James Wilson of Pennsylvania wanted a popularly elected executive who could rule in the name of the people. Many

Principles: Blueprints for the Presidency

delegates were reluctant to establish a single officer with a popular electoral base, for they feared that such an executive might be able to run roughshod over the deliberations of the legislature.[3]

Ultimately, what the Convention decided to do was to create a vaguely defined executive and count on the first president to give it shape through example and the power of precedent. The delegates assumed that George Washington, the hero of the Revolution and presiding officer of the Convention, would be the first president. No one else had his reputation for leadership or his national and international acclaim. In the end, they constructed an executive article for the Constitution (Article II) that was far more specific on the matter of electing a president than on the issue of what that officer would do once inaugurated. Article II outlines an executive who possesses certain limited powers and may fill a variety of undefined roles. It does not suggest the world leader of the twentieth century. Yet George Mason read into that outline the potential for enormous power. He described the presidency of Article II as the "foetus of monarchy."

Constitutional Principles

However vague the Constitution may be about the presidency, it still provides the ultimate foundation for that office. Article II reflects four basic values that the framers wanted in a chief executive. First, the president is an *independent executive*. Consistent with their belief that a separation of governmental powers was an important feature of a good regime and a bulwark of liberty, the framers wanted an executive who would not be beholden to the legislature. Too often had state governors of the period been subservient to their respective assemblies.

The president was to be chosen by a special body, the Electoral College (discussed in Chapter 7), in which members of Congress could not serve. Once elected, the chief executive would serve a term of four years, with unlimited eligibility for reelection (modified by the two-term limit of the Twenty-second Amendment). The term of office was considered a long one for an executive at that time (the powerful governor of New York served a three-year term), but the authors of *The Federalist* justified it as substantial enough to attract individuals of the highest talent. Unlimited potential for reelection was justified for a similar reason. The possibility of reelection could serve as an incentive for the president "to act his part well,"[4] just as it would allow the people to maintain in office an incumbent who did so. In this way, the presidency would be an independent position of substance by its selection and tenure.

The executive would also be independent by virtue of the president's ability to veto acts of Congress (subject to an override of the veto by two-thirds of each house). This negative power would enable the president to protect the executive branch of government by halting legislative actions designed to undo the separation of powers.

Second, the president is a *unitary executive*. The chief executive shares that power with no one. Article II begins with the statement that "the executive power shall be vested in a President of the United States." There was some discussion at the Constitutional Convention about sharing certain executive functions among a number of officers or between the president and a Council of State, but those who pressed for a single executive won out. They convinced the delegates that a unitary executive would be far more likely to produce the sort of energetic executive needed to administer the laws successfully. As Alexander Hamilton put the argument in *The Federalist,* No. 70, "That unity is conducive to energy will not be disputed. Decision, activity, secrecy, and dispatch will generally characterize the proceedings of one man [sic]."[5]

Third, the president is a *competent executive,* one who possesses sufficient power to do more than be a figurehead. In *The Federalist,* No. 70, Alexander Hamilton contended that "Energy in the executive is a leading character in the definition of good government." Although Article II is vague in many respects, it does grant to the president certain specific powers of importance: the veto, the position of commander in chief, the ability to make recommendations to Congress, the ability to make appointments (with consent of the Senate), the power to conclude treaties (with Senate consent), the ability to receive ambassadors and recognize foreign governments, the power to require reports from the heads of executive departments, and the power to pardon in all cases except those of impeachment. As we shall see, these powers did not necessarily make the president the dominant force in the government for a good part of American history, but they did mean that the chief executive would possess more than ceremonial responsibilities.[6]

Indeed, the vagueness of Article II is also a source of competence in presidential powers. Not only does the undefined nature of such roles as commander in chief allow for expansive interpretations of the force of the president, but the blanket assignment of "the executive power" opens considerable potential for action. For example, although the Constitution requires Senate participation in the making of treaties, presidents have been able to conclude executive agreements with other nations under this broad assertion of executive power. Similarly, the president issues executive orders, which have the force of law, to subordinates in the executive branch of government.

Finally, the president is a *republican executive.* Elected for a term of office, the chief executive is no hereditary monarch or lifelong dictator. Because the United States possesses no royal figurehead, the president (under "the executive power") also serves as chief of state. This role makes the chief executive the First Citizen of the United States, a living symbol of the nation and its chief ceremonial officer. The First Congress voted President Washington a salary of $25,000, the largest ever received by a public official at that time, in order to reflect the symbolic importance and dignity of his office. Since then, the president has continued to occupy a special place in national life: the chief politician who is also called upon to be leader of all citizens.

The framers conceived of the president's republicanism in another sense as well. They gave the executive a veto with which to frustrate a majority attempting to pass legislation. In this way, the Constitution encourages the legislature to deliberate on the public interest. Each time the president employs the

George Washington's presidency set many precedents for future chief executives, including the title of "Mr. President," the delivering of an Inaugural Address, and the formation of the Cabinet.

veto, one member of Congress is certain to accuse the chief executive of thwarting the will of the majority, and that is true. But that is also what the office was designed to do.

Operational Principles

Article II has been described as the most loosely drawn provision of the Constitution. Because of that fact, the presidency did not spring to life in its final form in 1789. Nor is it in its final form today. Rather, the functions of the chief executive have taken shape over the past two centuries, built on the foundation of the constitutional values outlined earlier and molded by three operational principles: malleability, precedent, and responsibility.

Given the vagueness of the constitutional presidency, the office has been a *malleable* one. One president may view the mandate of "the executive power" broadly, seeking to aggressively shape national policy at home and abroad; another may take a more minimal view of the job, choosing to allow Congress or the flow of events to shape the politics of an era. It has not been unusual in the course of American history for such divergent views of the office to be held by two presidents in succession: the energetic Jefferson followed by the more restrained Madison, the activist Truman followed by the passive Eisenhower, or the change-oriented Reagan succeeded by Bush's acceptance of the status quo.

Growing out of the malleable nature of the presidency is a second operational principle: the *importance of precedent* in defining executive powers. From the beginning of the Republic, the actions of one chief executive have played a crucial role in shaping and justifying the behavior of successive leaders. Indeed, before entering office, George Washington noted in his diary that nearly everything he would do as president would be used as a precedent by those who would follow him. And that is exactly what has happened in the history of the office.

Precedent has shaped the growth of the presidency in a multitude of ways. For example, Washington refused a request by the House of Representatives to permit them to examine the written instructions the president had given to his envoy John Jay for negotiations with Great Britain in 1795. His denial set a precedent for **executive privilege**—the idea that certain information held by the president need not be revealed to Congress. Over time this idea was expanded to include not only instructions to ambassadors, but the idea that the papers of the president and White House staff can be withheld from Congress, and that neither the chief executive nor presidential assistants can be summoned to appear before congressional committees except under special circumstances.

Another body of precedent has developed in the area of presidential war powers. Despite the Constitution's assignment to Congress of the power to *declare war,* chief executives had long asserted their authority to engage in military actions abroad in order to protect American interests. Adams conducted an undeclared naval war with France (1798–1800), Jefferson employed the Navy

executive privilege
Right of the president to withhold certain information from Congress.

against the Barbary Pirates (1801–1805), Polk launched a war with Mexico (1846), Truman waged war in Korea (1950–1952), presidents from Eisenhower through Ford carried on a conflict in Vietnam, Ronald Reagan invaded Grenada (1983), and George Bush invaded Panama (1989) and dispatched troops to Somalia. In each case, the president drew upon the conduct of one or more predecessors to justify the action of the moment.

These military activities stemmed from interpretations of the role of commander in chief, but they were also based on a third operational principle of the presidency. Because of the blanket nature of the executive power and the inability of other branches of government to respond to emergencies, the president has always been seen as possessing ultimate *responsibility* for the national interest. Indeed, our political system charges the chief executive with a *unique responsibility*: to deal with tough, unexpected situations for which there are no prearranged means of solution.[7] In other words, it falls to the president to be the "chief troubleshooter" of the political system, the one responsible for dealing with new and difficult problems facing the nation.

Each response to these problems sets a precedent for the future. For example, in 1803 Thomas Jefferson was presented the opportunity to buy the enormous Louisiana Territory from France, because Napoleon wanted to cut his losses in the New World and concentrate on becoming the master of Europe. The president truly believed that this vast land would be a boon to the growing United States, but he was stymied by the fact that the Constitution makes no provision for the acquisition of new territory (although it establishes a process, initiated by Congress, for admitting new states). He solved his problem and gained Louisiana by inventing a means for acquiring territory: a treaty with France for the purchase. Because treaties enjoy a special status under the Constitution (as part of the law of the land), the president was able to meet the challenge and establish a method for all future annexing of territory into the United States.

This unique presidential responsibility has helped to enlarge the office over the course of American history. When the Civil War threatened the Union, Abraham Lincoln undertook emergency measures to save it. Accused of violating the Constitution because he spent money, imprisoned suspected spies, and increased the army without congressional authorization, Lincoln replied that he had to save the entire constitutional system and not just individual articles of the document. His actions demonstrated a tremendous potential of presidential power and set an important precedent for future chief executives dealing with domestic emergencies. His actions, like those of Jefferson and others, expanded presidential power and helped fill in the outline of Article II.

Process: From Blueprints to Structure

The chief executive has been one of the most dynamic features of the American regime. From its rather austere beginnings in the administration of George Washington, when each decision about policy and protocol added a brick on top of the foundation laid by Article II, the presidency has evolved into an elaborate institution at the center of national affairs. Understanding its place in contemporary politics requires a sense of how the office has evolved and the contemporary structure of the presidency.

The Evolution of the Presidency

The history of the American presidency is often told as a series of biographies, focusing on the heroic presidents (Washington, Jackson, Lincoln, FDR, etc.) and passing over the unknown chiefs whose memory challenges experts in historical trivia (Millard Filmore, Benjamin Harrison, etc.). But the story is best told thematically, because individual histories obscure several trends that have marked the evolution of the office over the course of national history.[8] The key themes shaping the presidency have been a broadening of presidential responsibilities, a change in expectations about presidential behavior, and an expansion of the powers and structural resources for the president.

The Traditional Presidency. For much of American history, the chief executive was not expected to be the driving force in the government. Until well into the twentieth century, presidential activism was the exception rather than the rule. This first period can be characterized as the *traditional presidency*—an executive who, though energetic, did not attempt to dominate government in his time. Except in foreign affairs, where the Constitution gave greater power to the executive, the leading role in defining national policy was generally left to Congress, the first branch of government. Presidents contributed their suggestions and took some interest in legislation, but there was nothing like the presidential legislative program that is common today.

Nor did presidents enjoy much in the way of staff support. Administration of government affairs was left largely to the cabinet departments, which by law served Congress as well as the chief executive. The president did not even have a true office until Theodore Roosevelt added the West Wing of the White House early in the twentieth century, so the nation's chief worked out of a study or living room. A secretary might help with correspondence, but presidents frequently relied on family members or the executive departments for assistance.

Assertive use of presidential power was something reserved for extraordinary situations. Certainly, several chief executives acted forcefully. Some, such as Andrew Jackson or Teddy Roosevelt, did so because they believed that it was up to them to help shape national policy. Jackson eliminated the Bank of the United States and used the veto aggressively to stop legislation with which he disagreed. Roosevelt enlarged the American presence in world affairs and supported laws governing food purity, control over business monopolies, and other reforms. Others, such as Jefferson in the Louisiana Purchase or Lincoln in the Civil War, responded to what they saw as national necessity. But the actions of these incumbents were not seen by the nation as conventional presidential behavior. Indeed, the traditional presidency was guided by what can be called the "rule of restraint." According to this rule, unless there was some great public necessity that demanded assertive action by the president, the nation's first citizen was obliged to be restrained in behavior as was appropriate for a republican chief of state. In other words, the powers of the president were to be held in reserve for special circumstances.

When the times demanded actions, a "rule of necessity" took over. This rule meant that the chief executive was obliged to act in whatever fashion was necessary to protect the national interest. In the period of the traditional presidency, such occasions were rare.

These rules helped to define a place for the traditional presidency in the political system. The result of their observance was that many traditional presidents were minor figures in the politics of their time and in U.S. history. Such men as Millard Filmore, Warren Harding, and Chester Arthur are remembered humorously, or hardly at all. They appear more frequently in trivia games than in the pages of American history books.

Of course, not all traditional presidents have faded from memory. Most of America's great presidential heroes held office during this period: Washington, Jefferson, and Lincoln, for example, to name only the three to whom large memorials have been built in the nation's capital. Forceful actions taken by some traditional presidents set important precedents for the future, from Washington's Neutrality Proclamation to the Louisiana Purchase to the Civil War to Theodore Roosevelt's actions to enforce laws against business monopolies.

The Modern Presidency. The twentieth century brought with it an expanding role for the United States in world politics. As the American role in the world grew, so did the role of the president as the country's foreign-policy leader. Theodore Roosevelt was an international figure in his time, waving America's "big stick" in the Caribbean and arbitrating a peace in the Russo-Japanese War (1905). Woodrow Wilson not only sent American forces into World War I, but with the leaders of France and Britain shaped the Treaty of Versailles (1918) that ended that conflict. By the end of World War II, the United States had become a "superpower" and its president a world leader. The cold war with the Soviet Union would put the American chief executive in the position of "leader of the Free World," and as one who controlled atomic weapons, one of the two most powerful figures on the planet.

In addition to the increasing influence of the president in foreign affairs, presidential assertiveness in domestic affairs grew as well. Theodore Roosevelt pushed for several legislative proposals in Congress, including tariff reform, standards for food processing and sale, and enhanced federal regulation of interstate commerce. Wilson came to office in 1913 with a package of legislative proposals known as "New Freedom," which included reform of the national banking and currency system, further antitrust action, and the creation of the Federal Trade Commission to prevent unfair business competition. Franklin Roosevelt's "New Deal" offered the most sweeping policy agenda yet, including bank insurance, the Social Security system, public works programs, and a wide array of government services to respond to the Great Depression. By the end of FDR's presidency, every chief executive would be expected to offer a set of leg-

Woodrow Wilson (far right) demonstrated the extent and limits of presidential power. He was a major force shaping twentieth century Europe at the 1919 Versailles conference to draft a treaty settling World War I. At home, however, he was unable to convince the U.S. Senate to approve the treaty.

islative initiatives to Congress. Because of these changes, the presidency moved to the center of the government, replacing Congress as the focus of policy making and representation.

By the middle of the twentieth century, the traditional shape of the executive had given way to what was now being called the *modern presidency*—a powerful executive leading the nation with proposals for new legislation and an activist approach to government. Where presidential assertiveness had once been unusual, it was now considered normal. Instead of being the chief executive of an emerging (but nevertheless minor) international player, the president was now a world leader. Where presidents had once had little staff support, they now presided over an Executive Office of the President (EOP) that included an ever-growing array of assistants who worked exclusively for the chief executive. The president also became a more significant public figure, appearing frequently in the news and communicating directly with the people through radio and television.

In the second half of the twentieth century, the modern presidency became the dominant player in the American regime. The political system depended on presidential initiative for action, leadership, and energy. The office acquired broad powers, a large public role, and substantial resources for influencing national policy.

A Postmodern Presidency? Nothing remains static in politics, however. In the 1970s and 1980s, the United States and the world began to change. At home, Congress reasserted its role as policy maker. Responding to a war in Vietnam maintained by the presidency and the Watergate scandal, the legislature undertook internal reforms—such as an increase in congressional staff, the creation of committees on budget and intelligence issues, and a new process for drawing up the annual federal budget—that enabled it to challenge the White House for control over policy making. The cold war that had dominated world affairs came to an end in the late 1980s, leaving in its aftermath a complex and uncertain international order with several competing centers of power.

Some observers would characterize the result of these changes as the beginning of a new phase in the evolution of the office, the coming of a *postmodern presidency*[9]—an office that has changed on both domestic and foreign fronts, facing greater competition in both realms. The postmodern president is faced with competition from an assertive Congress, a large bureaucracy, and courts and regulatory agencies that are active policy makers. In response, presidents have come increasingly to rely on unilateral executive powers (such as control over regulation making in the executive branch) and public politics (such as direct communication through television) to influence events. Looking abroad, presidents see a world in which the United States remains a dominant military force, but faces stiffer economic competition than it did during the period in which the modern presidency arose. As a result, the president is an important but nevertheless somewhat diminished player in world politics. While it is still too early to tell whether a postmodern presidency is indeed underway, there have been changes in the office and these serve as a reminder of the malleable nature of the chief executive.

The Cabinet

The first structure that presidents built to assist them in their duties was the cabinet. As we saw in Chapter 3, it is a body that exists in custom rather than law. The **cabinet** consists of the heads of the executive departments and certain other senior officials and aides to whom the president awards "cabinet rank" (Table 9.2). In the nineteenth century, when presidents had little in the way of staff resources, the cabinet often served as an advisory body to the chief executive. In our time, with so many more assistants and informal advisers available to the president, the cabinet as a body serves more as an assembly that meets occasionally to reinforce the loyalty that department heads feel toward the occupant of the Oval Office. Individual secretaries may be important advisers to the president, but the cabinet has given way to other groups, often ad hoc groups of advisers formed for a specific issue or decision, as a body for assisting the chief executive in decision making.

cabinet Traditional advisory body to the president. It consists of the heads of executive departments plus other aides and executive officials designated by the president.

TABLE 9.2 The President's Cabinet (Presidency of Bill Clinton)

The Vice-President

Department Heads	Selected Officials from Executive Branch
Secretary of State	Administrator, Environmental Protection Agency
Secretary of Treasury	U.S. Ambassador to the United Nations
Secretary of Defense	
Attorney General	
Secretary of Interior	
Secretary of Agriculture	Senior Personnel from Executive Office of the President
Secretary of Commerce	Chief of Staff to the President
Secretary of Labor	Director, Office of Management and Budget
Secretary of Health and Human Services	U.S. Trade Representative
Secretary of Housing and Urban Development	Counselor to the President
Secretary of Transportation	
Secretary of Energy	
Secretary of Education	
Secretary of Veterans Affairs	

Note: Because the Cabinet is a creation of the president, each new chief executive decides who will be considered a member of this body. By custom, the vice-president and all heads of executive departments are members. By presidential order, others—top staff aides, heads of certain agencies, the U.S. Ambassador to the United Nations—also have what is known as "cabinet rank."

Executive Office of the President

Surrounding and assisting the chief executive is a presidential bureaucracy that consists of almost four thousand political appointees, career officials, and volunteers—the **Executive Office of the President (EOP).** The Executive Office has evolved from rather simple beginnings in the administration of Franklin Roosevelt. In 1939, Congress authorized greater staff assistance for the president, because the growing responsibilities of the modern presidency outstripped the limited resources of the White House in those days. FDR hired six assistants to the president and brought under his control the Bureau of the Budget, which until that time had been a division of the Treasury Department. Successive presidents added to that staff, creating new units in the EOP and delegating increasing power to aides who answered only to the chief executive.

The White House Office. The EOP today is composed of about a dozen divisions (Figure 9.1). Not all are of equal importance, however. Closest to the president and most powerful is the **White House Office,** which houses the most senior assistants. When the term "White House" is used in the news or reporters refer to the "president's aides," they usually mean officials in this division. The White House Office includes the president's top political and policy aides, speechwriters, and press secretaries, as well as those who assist in conducting ceremonial occasions and running the Executive Mansion (as the living quarters and public rooms of the building are called).

Presidents have come to rely heavily on their staffs for more than just coping with the demands of office. Chief executives also look to their aides for advice on political and policy questions that is not "tainted" by the interests of a

Executive Office of the President (EOP)
Official structure of the president's staff. It is composed of the White House Office, the Office of Management and Budget, the National Security Council, and other staff offices that assist the chief executive.

White House Office
Division of the Executive Office of the President composed of the president's most senior aides and politically oriented staff.

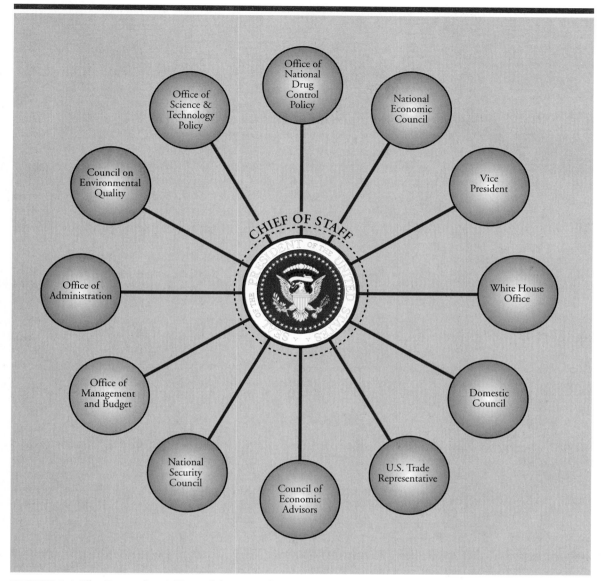

FIGURE 9.1 The Executive Office of the President

particular executive branch department. Presidents also rely on their aides to monitor the work of executive departments and agencies. Several former presidential assistants have commented that this task occupied most of their time while at the White House. They were generally busy seeing to it that the president's orders were being carried out. The president's staff also provides the chief executive with the resources necessary to propose legislation to Congress, to identify candidates for all the appointments presidents must make while in office, or to monitor the ever-changing flow of events that affect the Oval Office.

The National Security Council. One of the most important divisions of the EOP is the **National Security Council (NSC),** which is a committee established in 1947 to advise the president on all matters related to foreign and defense policy: diplomacy, the armed forces, intelligence, planning, and any related issues. While the council is composed of top government officials, including the president, vice-president, and secretaries of state and defense, it is the NSC staff that is really important. Since the 1960s, the NSC staff has played a key role in the shaping of American foreign policy. For example, during the Nixon administration it supervised the conduct of the Vietnam War and undertook secret negotiations with the Soviet Union and China. Headed by the president's assistant for national security affairs, the NSC staff has become a leading part of the "foreign policy government" of the United States.

The Office of Management and Budget. The most important EOP unit in the area of domestic policy is the **Office of Management and Budget (OMB),** a staff agency that assists in drawing up the president's budget proposal, monitoring regulations proposed by executive departments and agencies, and reviewing legislation for the president's endorsement or veto. OMB plays a central role in the contemporary White House. The director of OMB has become such a powerful player in national politics that since the 1970s Congress has required Senate confirmation for appointment to this office.

The White House Chief of Staff

How does the president control this complex operation that has grown up around the Oval Office? In recent administrations the answer has been to designate one senior aide as "chief of staff." That job remains the most poorly defined one in Washington, because it is totally dependent on the personality and working style of the president. As one former chief of staff put it, it is an office with a "constituency of one."

Despite the highly individual character of the relationship between a chief executive and the top White House aide, we can discern three broad types of presidential chiefs of staff: the gatekeeper, the coordinator, and the "first among equals" (Table 9.3). *Gatekeepers* are those staff chiefs who have been granted broad power to act in the president's name and who serve to control access to the Oval Office. The first White House chief of staff—Sherman Adams, former governor of New Hampshire—fit this description. He held the title of the "Assistant to the President," but was known to his colleagues as the "Abominable No-Man." H. R. Haldeman served Richard Nixon in a similar capacity, tightly controlling who could see and advise the president. He was the "Berlin Wall" who kept cabinet secretaries and others his boss did not want to see away from the president. Donald Regan, who served as Reagan's second staff chief, developed

National Security Council (NSC) Advisory body to the president created in 1947. A large staff, headed by the president's Assistant for National Security Affairs, enables the president to play an active role in the direction of foreign and military policy independent of the departments of State and Defense.

Office of Management and Budget (OMB) Agency in the Executive Office of the President responsible for assisting the president with preparation of executive budget requests, oversight of agency management, clearance of legislative proposals, and review of proposed regulations.

TABLE 9.3 White House Chiefs of Staff

President/Chiefs of Staff	Tenure	Role	Reason for Leaving
Eisenhower			
Sherman Adams	1953–1958	Gatekeeper	Scandal
Wilton Persons	1958–1961	Coordinator	End of administration
Kennedy—none			
Johnson—none			
Nixon			
H. R. Haldeman	1969–1973	Gatekeeper	Scandal (Watergate)
Alexander Haig	1974–1974	Coordinator	Stayed under Ford
Ford			
Alexander Haig	1973–1974	Coordinator	Reorganization
Donald Rumsfeld	1974–1975	First among Equals	Appointed Secretary of Defense
Dick Cheney	1975–1977	First among Equals	End of administration
Carter			
Hamilton Jordan	1978–1979	First among Equals	Moved to Carter reelection campaign
Jack Watson	1979–1981	First among Equals	End of administration
Reagan			
James Baker	1981–1985	First among Equals	Appointed Secretary of Treasury
Donald Regan	1985–1987	Gatekeeper	Forced to resign because of Iran-Contra affair
Howard Baker	1987–1989	First among Equals	End of administration
Bush			
John Sununu	1989–1991	Gatekeeper	Scandal
Samuel Skinner	1991–1992	Coordinator	Ineffective, given party post
James Baker	1992–1993	First among Equals	End of administration
Clinton			
"Mack" McLarty	1993–1994	Coordinator	Weak, reassigned
Leon Panetta	1994–	Coordinator	

a reputation for autocratic management that earned him the enmity of the president's wife, Nancy. John Sununu, who served as George Bush's first staff chief, conducted himself in such an abrasive manner that he alienated House Republicans during delicate budget negotiations in 1990; he eventually became a lightning rod for all dissatisfaction with Bush's presidency and had to resign. Each of these gatekeepers was performing as his boss desired, but the overbearing style that each developed tended to stimulate a backlash from other aides, cabinet secretaries, or members of Congress. In the end, each gatekeeper was done in by the perception that the chief of staff sees himself as "deputy president."

At the other extreme are those chiefs of staff who have served as more limited *coordinators* of the operations and details of White House management. The best example of this type was Thomas "Mack" McLarty, Bill Clinton's first chief of staff. A former Arkansas natural gas company executive, he had the double disadvantage of lacking any Washington experience and working for a president who did not want to delegate much authority to a chief of staff. McLarty presided over the routines of Clinton White House management for about a year and a half, until pressure to "shake up" the staff caused the president to assign him to a different job in the summer of 1994. McLarty was followed by Leon Panetta, former representative from California and director of the OMB. Panetta was promised broad authority to reorganize the staff and impose discipline in a White House notorious for disorganization. In September 1994, Panetta moved to replace several top Clinton aides and restrict the number of assistants reporting directly to the president, but he was overruled by the chief executive. As one example, when Panetta wanted to fire press secretary Dee Dee Myers, the president promoted her and gave her greater access to the Oval Office (although she was later replaced). Like gatekeepers, coordinators have as much authority as their bosses are willing to give them.

The most successful staff chiefs appear to have been those who acted as *first among equals,* or at least first among a small group of senior presidential aides: Donald Rumsfeld and Richard Cheney under Gerald Ford, Jack Watson under Jimmy Carter, and James Baker and Howard Baker under Ronald Reagan. Through a combination of personal political skills and delegated presidential authority, these chiefs of staff were able to assist the boss by making sure that the White House operated in an orderly fashion, that the president received all the information needed to make decisions, and that work was done on time.

No matter how great or how little power the chief of staff is given by the president, the job is a relatively thankless one. Dick Cheney once commented that when things go right in the White House, the president gets the credit; when things go wrong, the chief of staff gets the blame. Perhaps Jack Watson has described the job best: He maintains that the chief of staff must be the president's "quarterback, cheerleader, and javelin catcher."[10]

The Vice-President

Each president also has a vice-president, and the nation's second-highest office has changed considerably in recent decades. The vice-president was long a minor player in presidential affairs, except as a running mate in the election. Although technically America's Second Citizen, the V.P. was often ignored by the president or used only to give speeches and run political errands. When Lyndon Johnson was vice-president, he was seldom consulted by John Kennedy, despite Johnson's masterful knowledge of Congress. Indeed, early in 1963 Johnson privately discussed with friends the possibility of retiring from politics in 1964. He was so bored by the vice-presidency that he considered retiring to his ranch in Texas.

Times have certainly changed. Since the days of Walter Mondale under Jimmy Carter, vice-presidents have become more significant as senior advisers to the chief executive. One reason is the new presidential nominating system, which has brought to the office several presidents from outside Washington—Carter, Reagan, Clinton. Each of these chief executives chose as his vice-president someone with experience in the ways of the nation's capital—Walter Mondale (Carter), George Bush (Reagan), and Al Gore (Clinton). These "insider" V.P.s have been able to offer counsel on the ways of politics "inside the Belt-

Vice-president Al Gore enjoys increased influence as the nation's second in command. Here he signs a trade agreement with Russian prime minister Viktor Chernomyrdin.

way." Today, the V.P. has a large staff and an office down the hall from the Oval Office in the West Wing of the White House and is included in all important meetings.

Vice-President Al Gore's tenure provides a good example of how the office has changed. He has been closely involved with all major decisions of the Clinton administration, from cabinet appointments to strategy for winning passage of the president's budget in 1993. Gore took on Ross Perot in a TV debate over the North American Free Trade Agreement that same year and helped boost support for the proposal through his appearance. He chaired a highly publicized task force on reorganizing the federal government (see the Current Issues box, "Reorganizing the Bureaucracy," in Chapter 10), even appearing on David Letterman's television show to talk about government reform. He is regarded in Washington as part of the inner circle of the Clinton presidency.

The Presidency in American Politics

The American presidency is a unique political office. As we have seen, presidents possess tremendous actual and potential power, yet they are also hobbled by frustrating restraints. Some of our chief executives have been dominant figures in the politics of their time, while others are barely remembered and seem overrun by the forces of history. As we shall see, the very nature of the office and its operations make it the "splendid misery" that Thomas Jefferson called it a long time ago. To understand the presidency in American politics, we must turn our attention to three central political realities that presidents face: presidents govern in what is best described as a "separated system"; presidential power is complex and uneven; and the office is not exactly the same for all its occupants.

Governing in a Separated System

The American regime is sometimes described as a "presidential system," in the sense that we have an independent and powerful chief executive. But we cannot read too much meaning into the term "presidential system," because the political system does not revolve around the Oval Office, nor does it necessarily jump at the president's command. The United States has a political system marked by three kinds of separation. The president is an important actor in our "separated system."

Separated Powers. The Constitution establishes three branches of government. The president, while given a set of formal powers and a number of informal roles, cannot force Congress or the judiciary to conform to the wishes of the White House. In 1993, Bill Clinton made health care reform his chief domestic policy priority; by the fall of 1994, his party's leaders in Congress declared the topic dead until after the midterm congressional elections. The courts often uphold presidential power when it is contested; one study revealed that presidents have won far more cases than they have lost. The White House does lose, however, as Harry Truman did in 1950 when he attempted to seize control of American steel mills when a strike threatened to cut off production of weapons during the Korean War. The Supreme Court overruled Truman and he had to back down. The president may be our only nationally elected leader, but the chief executive is not our only government official.

Separate Levels of Government. Although the states have lost a considerable amount of autonomy in recent decades and the national government has expanded its power, states still exist, and they have direct power over the lives of citizens. As many presidents have learned, making domestic policy means dealing with the authority of state governments. Certainly, the national government has used grants and mandates to encourage and even force the states to comply with its goals, but nevertheless presidents cannot rule directly in areas of welfare, education, crime, and several other important matters. George Bush said he wanted to be the "Education President," but he found that he had to deal with several "Education Governors" who had different plans. Bill Clinton wanted to reform welfare and health care, but he found that state governments often opposed his reforms. After the 1994 election, the new majorities in Congress authored legislation to make it harder for the national government to impose unfunded mandates on the states. Although weakened since the time of the founding, federalism remains a fact of American political life.

Separated Parties. At least since the time of Woodrow Wilson, a number of reformers have looked to the political parties as the means for bridging the gaps created by the separation of powers system. These reformers have contended that strong, responsible parties could overcome the divisions between president and Congress—and even between Washington and the states—to enact sweeping policy programs that would better serve citizens. But American political parties have rarely been able to act in this way. As we know, there is no guarantee that the White House and Capitol Hill will be controlled by the same party. Moreover, even when they are, the members of the same party on each end of Pennsylvania Avenue may see things very differently. Jimmy Carter learned this lesson when he encountered resistance from congressional Democrats over his energy plan; George Bush found that the greatest opposition to his budget proposals in 1990 came from House Republicans; and Bill Clinton could not convince a Democratic Congress to act on his agenda. He relied on Republican votes to pass the North American Free Trade Agreement in 1993 and could not get a vote on health care reform in 1994.

The Practice of Presidential Power

The unique nature of the American presidency means that chief executives must employ a variety of methods and resources if they want to fulfill the many roles they are assigned. At base, the president relies on the constitutional authority outlined in Article II and additional powers assigned by law, but the exercise of presidential power is far more complex than that.

Command and Persuasion. Traditionally, analysts of the presidency looked to the chief executive's legal authority to understand the office. Presidents do indeed use those powers regularly, even if they do not call attention to the fact. When George Bush remained active until the end of his presidency, he was making use of the legal and constitutional basis of his office. This mode of action is usually classified under the heading "command." Because the chief executive is not a prime minister and therefore cannot draw upon the continuing support of a parliamentary majority, presidents must often use their executive and administrative powers of command to shape national policy.

Presidents are not dictators, however. Command alone is not enough to make the office work. Therefore the chief executive must persuade others in the government—members of Congress, senior officials in the bureaucracy, cabinet secretaries—to go along with presidential policies. Indeed, political scientist Richard Neustadt has gone so far as to say that "Presidential power *is* the power to persuade."[11] This statement reflects the president's need for the agreement, or at least the acquiescence, of other government officials in order to influence events. When President Bill Clinton wanted to remove restrictions on gays and lesbians serving in the American armed forces, he could as commander in chief have issued an order to that effect. But because of the controversial nature of that change, he had to gain the acceptance of senior members of Congress and the top echelons of the military in order to do so.

It is an overstatement to say that presidential power is only the power to persuade, however. Persuasion is important, but the job of president would be impossible if the chief executive had to develop a consensus on every proposed action. What presidents do is to employ a mix of persuasion and command, depending on their own goals and the likely reception their initiatives will receive. When Congress was deliberating on tax reform in 1986, President

Reagan used the threat of a veto to influence the kind of bill that was ultimately produced. He outlined his general goals for the law to legislative leaders and made clear what he would not accept. Then he and his staff lobbied Congress for a bill that reflected Reagan's preferences. This astute combination of command and persuasion resulted in the Tax Reform Act of 1986. In December 1990, President Bush made clear to Congress his determination to wage war against Iraq and drive its troops out of Kuwait. That message assisted him in winning legislative endorsement for his plan to use force.

Going Public. To aid their efforts at persuasion of other government officials, presidents in modern times have increasingly tended to "go public." As described by political scientist Samuel Kernell, **going public** refers to the use of direct communication with voters to gain support for the president.[12] The most obvious instrument of public politics is television, and presidents since John Kennedy have been familiar faces on television. President Reagan employed it to great effect, even choosing backgrounds for his speeches according to their TV value (such as a housing development in Fort Worth as a backdrop to an announcement on a rise in home building). But going public can take other forms, such as President Clinton's appearance on the *Arsenio Hall* and *Larry King Live* shows during the 1992 campaign, his use of bus tours and visits to shopping malls, and other activities to reach the public directly. Such efforts may be general actions to generate presidential popularity or they may be targeted to specific presidential initiatives. In 1981, President Reagan used a television address to encourage voter support for his budget proposal, then followed it with a lobbying effort on Capitol Hill. The intended effect was achieved; Congress perceived widespread public support for the president and passed his budget proposal. Going public is not always this effective, but it can provide assistance for presidential attempts at persuasion.

The Unevenness of Presidential Power. When it comes to wielding their influence, presidents are also conscious of an unevenness in their power. They have considerably more influence over the direction of foreign policy than they do over domestic affairs. Not only does the Constitution grant the chief executive broader powers in this area, but Congress and the American people are more likely to defer to White House leadership on foreign policy as well. In domestic matters Congress not only enjoys extensive power, but its members take a deep interest in issues that they see as having a direct effect on their constituents. This unevenness of power is often characterized as the *two presidencies*—one for matters at home and one for issues abroad.[13]

Because of this situation and the continual press of international affairs, presidents since World War II have tended to spend most of their time on foreign policy. For those inclined toward such issues, such as Richard Nixon and George Bush, this emphasis was welcome. For those more interested in domestic affairs, such as Lyndon Johnson and Bill Clinton, it has been frustrating. In September 1994, Clinton found that he could alter 30 years of American policy toward Cuba by ending the practice of granting asylum to Cuban refugees unilaterally, and

going public President's use of direct communication with the American people (such as a televised speech from the Oval Office) to gain support for policies or proposals.

Communicate Your Views to the President

1. **Participate in the presidential selection process:** Voting is still your most direct means for taking part in the choice of the president. Voters can also become campaigners—whether for or against someone. Every campaign can always use additional help and volunteers, usually students and seniors, can often set their own schedules.

2. **Communicate directly with the president:** Because of the increase in personal appearances, bus trips, call-in shows, town hall meetings, and other public events, citizens have greater opportunities to see and speak to the president. This takes effort, however. One critic has complained that an individual has more chance of winning the lottery than reaching the president on a call-in show. But, like the lottery, someone will get the opportunity.

3. **Communicate with the president through White House channels:** The general switchboard can be reached at (202) 456-1414 (along with nearly fifty thousand other calls).

Citizens with problems are referred to the Agency Liaison Office, which may contact the appropriate government agency, a member of Congress, or even deal directly with the matter. The Volunteer and Comment Office—(202) 456-7639—takes calls from those who want to share their opinions with the president. Mail and telegrams can be sent to The President/The White House/Washington, DC 20501. These are received and processed by the Correspondence Office. The White House can also be contacted through the Internet.

4. **Communicate with the president through others:** Interest groups often communicate with the White House Office of Public Liaison. Another route to the president is through your legislative representatives. Members of Congress not only handle constituent problems and views on their own (as explained in Chapter 8), but can bring issues and concerns to the White House if they believe that such matters are addressed better there.

could prepare to invade Haiti despite congressional and public opposition; on the other hand, he could not overcome resistance to his health care reform proposals.

Distinguishing the President from the Presidency

Although a body of precedents has grown up around the chief executive, the presidency is still a highly personalized office; it is not the same for all incumbents. Each may have a different agenda, possess different abilities, or face different circumstances. To understand how the presidency fits into American politics, we must acknowledge the fact that "the presidency" and "the president" are not the same. The presidency is an *institution* with an array of duties, powers, and potential for action; the president is an *individual* who holds that office for a number of years and must perform the duties and wield powers according to his or her own abilities.

Interpreting Presidential Power. The presidency is subject to divergent interpretations of its powers and role in government; indeed, it is one of the most significant aspects of the "constitution of open texture" (see Chapter 3). One of the best examples of this contrast is the dispute between Theodore Roosevelt and William Howard Taft, T.R.'s hand-picked successor. Roosevelt took an expansive view of presidential power, asserting his duty to "do anything that the needs of the Nation demanded, unless such action is forbidden by the Constitution or the laws."[14] In contrast, Taft saw the nation's "chief magistrate" (as he

President Theodore Roosevelt took an expansive view of presidential power; his successor and friend, William Howard Taft, interpreted executive power as more limited. The two clashed often during Taft's presidency, and Roosevelt opposed his hand-picked replacement in the election of 1912.

called the office) as far more limited. He held that the president "can exercise no power which cannot be fairly and reasonably traced to some specific grant of power or justly implied. . . . Such specific grant must be either in the Federal Constitution or in an act of Congress passed in pursuance thereof."[15] T.R. did all that he could to shape policy from the White House, using his office as a "bully pulpit" and brandishing a "big stick" in foreign affairs. On the other hand, Taft was more restrained in his exercise of power; he did not abandon presidential power but did not believe that it was as open ended as T.R. proclaimed it to be. Eventually, a frustrated Roosevelt felt compelled to run against Taft in 1912 as the candidate of the Progressive (Bull Moose) Party. The result was a split in the Republican Party that brought Democrat Woodrow Wilson to the presidency.

Another example of divergent interpretations lies in the area of the president's war powers. During the 1980s, Republicans tended to support unilateral presidential military actions—in Grenada, Panama, Kuwait, and elsewhere. Democrats frequently criticized the White House for ignoring the legitimate role of Congress in such decisions. Then, in 1994, with Bill Clinton threatening an invasion of Haiti, the tables were turned. Republican congressional leaders were lecturing the White House on the role of Congress, while Democratic speakers asserted the right and duty of unilateral presidential action. Each side could marshall evidence from the Constitution, the founders, and a variety of Supreme Court decisions to support their positions.

How Circumstances Affect Policy Making. The predominance of foreign affairs and the president's constrained power in domestic matters also mean that few modern presidents have been able to win support for major legislative programs. Only in rare political circumstances have chief executives been able to win passage of large-scale domestic policy changes. Indeed, scholars Erwin Hargrove and Michael Nelson have noted that a sort of rhythm marks the record of presidential domestic policy making.[16] They hold that major domestic legislative programs are won by a few *presidencies of achievement.* These include FDR and the New Deal, LBJ and the Great Society, and Ronald Reagan and Reaganomics. Each of these presidents was able to combine personal political skills, a sense of national urgency, support in Congress, and good timing to see their legislative proposals enacted into law.

Before such success, however, there may be one or more *presidencies of preparation,* during which the White House is used to promote certain issues, but the chief executive is unable to produce action on them. Presidents Kennedy and Carter fit this description. Many of the welfare and civil rights programs won by Lyndon Johnson had been introduced by JFK, while Carter's attempts to deal with energy, the environment, the budget, and government regulation anticipated many of the themes of domestic policy making during the Reagan administration (although Reagan's policy choices were different from Carter's). Is Bill Clinton in this category as well, drawing attention to new issues but unable to induce major policy changes?

Finally, after achievement there are *presidencies of consolidation,* during which the government and the nation have a chance to "digest" and implement the major programs passed by presidents of achievement. Dwight Eisenhower, Richard Nixon, and George Bush all served in this capacity. During periods of consolidation, much energy is directed toward rationalizing the large-scale changes recently enacted and dealing with issues such as government reorganization, because major policy changes often upset existing organizational arrangements.

Research indicates that the public tends to have very high expectations of what presidents can accomplish during their years in office, regardless of the factors that may assist or hinder presidential success. The American people expect their presidents to deliver economic prosperity, security and international prestige, and a sense of national pride. When the public gets these results, it tends to reward the incumbent president. Dwight Eisenhower and Ronald Reagan, for example, are remembered fondly for their years in office. When the desired results do not appear, the people place the responsibility on the White House. Jimmy Carter once complained that the public tends to give presidents far more credit than they deserve for prosperity and far too much blame for recession.

Since all presidents face high expectations, we should not be surprised that only a few are able to live up to them. As Hargrove and Nelson's rhythm of domestic policy making suggests, all presidents certainly will not be able to live up to the public's demand for prosperity, security, and confidence. All but one of the presidents of achievement in the twentieth century—Wilson, FDR, Johnson, and Reagan—were rewarded with reelection. Johnson was ruined by the Vietnam War and chose not to seek reelection. Presidents of consolidation can also be successful, especially if their handling of foreign policy instills public confidence (the case with Eisenhower and Nixon). But presidents of preparation tend to get only one term—perhaps the frustration of raising new issues without seeing them through makes presidents like Jimmy Carter (and Bill Clinton?) vulnerable to defeat.

open questions

Do Presidents Have Too Much Power Over Foreign Affairs and Too Little Over Domestic Affairs?

As this chapter makes clear, a number of unresolved issues surround the American presidency. Two particular ones stand out. The first is whether the president has too much power in the area of foreign affairs. Several critics point to the chief executive's broad power as commander in chief, which has been used to conduct "presidential wars" around the globe.[17] These uses of war powers essentially excluded Congress from the decision of whether the United States should be engaged in such conflicts, which critics regard as undemocratic and unconstitutional. Likewise, they point to the president's ability to conclude executive agreements with other governments, again excluding the legislature from important foreign-policy decisions. Many members of Congress objected to President Clinton's unilateral action in 1995 to provide $20 million in loan guarantees to Mexico. Finally, critics disapprove of secrecy as a tool of foreign policy, particularly the ability to withhold from Congress information that would be embarrassing or controversial. This is what the Reagan administration did when it concealed the arms-for-hostages deals it was making during the Iran-Contra affair. The upshot of these criticisms is a call for restrictions on the president's control over foreign policy, even to the point of constitutional changes to limit abuses.

In response, presidents and their defenders have argued that the nation needs a strong chief executive in foreign affairs who is capable of such unilateral and covert actions. While not excusing abuses, these defenders of the chief executive argue that so-called "excesses" of presidential wars have been able to occur only because Congress has allowed them.[18] For example, they point out that the legislature funded the Vietnam War over several years. Moreover, they argue that congressional attempts to micromanage (control the details of) foreign policy have not only intruded on the president's powers, but encouraged the executive to act in extraordinary ways that would circumvent congressional interference. Defenders of the presidency argue that each of the two branches has a proper role to play, and that for each to do so would be more beneficial than constitutional change.

The other side of the debate over presidential power is the question of whether it is too limited in the area of domestic policy. Since the president depends on Congress for the money and authority to achieve many executive goals, some observers maintain the need for enhanced domestic powers. As we saw in the Current Issues box, one proposal is to give the president a line-item veto over appropriations, which advocates argue would increase the executive's ability to impose priorities on spending. Another idea is to give the president's legislative proposals priority in Congress, so the executive could have more direct influence over the business of the House and Senate.

These proposals draw fire from those who argue that the line-item veto would give the president too much leverage with Congress. A determined chief executive could make the House and Senate yield on important policy questions rather than compromise as occurs now. In contrast, giving priority to the president's proposals does not guarantee that they will be passed. Nor do most presidents seem to have trouble getting Congress to pay attention to them.

In the end, the vaguely defined presidency of the Constitution has evolved into a central player in our politics. But, just as the framers could not resolve all issues to everyone's satisfaction, so the chief executive of our time remains the subject of debate and controversy. The presidency is one of the best examples of the open-ended nature of the American experiment.

‖ Summary

The American presidency is a unique office that combines specific constitutional powers with political characteristics and roles accrued over the decades.

Presidents play a variety of roles in the political system. There are five constitutional roles: *chief of state, chief executive, commander in chief, chief diplomat,* and *chief legislator.* In addition, presidents wear other "hats" beyond those assigned by the Constitution: *party leader, protector of the peace, leader of public opinion, manager of prosperity,* and *world leader.*

Principles. The framers of the Constitution wanted an executive that would be energetic but restrained. In the Constitution, the presidency is marked by four key characteristics: (1) an *independent executive,* (2) a *unitary executive,* (3) a *competent executive,* and (4) a *republican executive.* In addition, the history of the presidency has revealed three operational characteristics of the nation's highest office: *malleability, precedent,* and *responsibility.*

Process. The presidency has evolved through three stages. (1) The *traditional presidency* describes the office for most of its history, when the chief executive was not normally the dominant force in government; a "rule of restraint" regulated presidential behavior in normal times and was replaced by a "rule of necessity" in extraordinary times. (2) The *modern presidency* describes the presidency as it was transformed by Franklin Roosevelt, with a new "rule of responsibility" keeping the president at the center of American government. (3) The *postmodern presidency,* since Ronald Reagan, faces greater competition from other political actors at home and an external world of more diffuse power.

The structure of the presidency is complex. Presidents have long called together executive department heads and certain key aides as a *cabinet* to advise the chief executive, although in our time the cabinet has been overshadowed by ad hoc advisory groups and staff. The president's staff is housed in the *Executive Office of the President* (EOP), an organization of nearly 4,000 aides divided into about a dozen units. Some of the most important divisions of the EOP are the *White House Office, National Security Council,* and *Office of Management and Budget.* Recent presidents have relied on a White House chief of staff to help them manage this complex structure, although not all staff chiefs have had the same role or power in the White House. The vice-presidency, once insignificant, has come in the past 20 years to be an important advisory position.

Politics. Three general points help describe the presidency's place in American politics. (1) Presidents govern in a separated political system—it features separation of governmental powers; separate levels of government (federalism); and separated political parties (decentralized). (2) Presidential power is complex—it is a mixture of command and persuasion; it is uneven (greater in foreign policy than domestic affairs); and recent presidents have found that *going public* is a useful technique for communicating directly with voters. (3) One size does not fit all—presidents (and others) interpret presidential power differently; and circumstances affect presidential policy making (leading to a rhythm of presidencies of *preparation, achievement,* and *consolidation* in domestic policy). Regardless of circumstances, the public has high expectations of what presidents are able to achieve.

Open Questions. There are many unresolved issues surrounding the chief executive. One of the most important is whether the president has too much power in foreign affairs—some observers say yes, arguing that the chief executive has too much freedom to take the nation to war; others respond that such presidential power is necessary to deal with a complex and dangerous world. In domestic affairs, one important question is whether the president is too restrained. Some observers want the office to be strengthened through measures such as a line-item veto over appropriations, while others argue that the president is already powerful enough to do the job assigned by the Constitution and expected by the public.

Suggested Readings

BARILLEAUX, RYAN J. *The Post-Modern Presidency.* New York: Praeger, 1988. Analyzes the evolution of the presidency and argues that the office is changing.

BUCHANAN, BRUCE. *The Citizen's Presidency.* Washington: CQ Press, 1987. Looks at how citizens can and ought to evaluate presidents.

GREENSTEIN, FRED I., ED. *Leadership and the Modern Presidency.* Cambridge, Mass.: Harvard University Press, 1988. Includes studies of each chief executive from F.D.R. through Reagan.

McDONALD, FORREST. *The American Presidency: An Intellectual History.* Lawrence: University Press of Kansas, 1994. A history of the office that is particularly useful for understanding how the founders thought about executive power and how the office has developed in different areas of its power.

MILKIS, SIDNEY, AND MICHAEL NELSON. *The American Presidency: Origins and Development*. Washington: CQ Press, 1990. An excellent history of the office and its occupants.

NEUSTADT, RICHARD. *Presidential Power and the Modern Presidents*. New York: Free Press, 1990. The most influential study of the office ever published.

ROSSITER, CLINTON. *The American Presidency,* revised. New York: Mentor Books, 1960. An enduring study of the office and its role in American politics.

10

The Federal Bureaucracy

The term **bureaucracy** refers to a large, complex organization composed of appointed officials. Americans are in almost continual contact with bureaucratic organizations. Not only is there bureaucracy in government, but also in business and private associations: General Motors, IBM, Yale University, the American Red Cross, the Boy Scouts, the Girl Scouts, the Roman Catholic Church, United Way, and most large organizations in American society. The biggest and most complex bureaucracy in the United States is the federal government.

The federal bureaucracy touches nearly all aspects of citizens' lives. It collects income taxes and delivers the mail; it launches space shuttles and protects the president; it inspects meat and fish and regulates the sale of drugs and cosmetics; it enforces laws against counterfeiting, illicit drugs, pollution, and discrimination; it wages war and provides services to developing nations; it regulates the money supply, radio and television broadcasting, stock and bond trading, and commercial transportation.

A bureaucratic organization is marked by five distinctive features.[1]

- A bureaucracy is built on a **hierarchy,** a system for ranking roles and status in the organization. Figure 10.1 shows the hierarchical structure of the United States Department of the Interior from the Secretary of the Interior down to individual divisions and bureaus. Information flows up the hierarchy and control flows downward.

- *Specialization* is also a feature of bureaucracies, federal or otherwise. Bureaucracies have well-developed divisions of labor, with tasks assigned in increasingly narrow areas (from the national service to regional and specialized units to individual post offices and routes).

- Another feature of bureaucracy is its *formal rules and procedures,* which are developed to help the organization operate. Communication between components usually occurs through written forms, and extensive records are maintained. For example, a series of *Postal Service Manuals* issued by the United States Postal Service (USPS) outlines regulations covering domestic mail, international mail, postal operations, administrative support, employee relations, financial management, and postal contracting.

- *Merit and seniority* are important criteria for filling positions in the organization, although senior offices in government bureaucracies are usually assigned through political appointment. Competitive examinations are used to select many employees, although educational credentials and expertise feature in the hiring of finance officers, computer scientists, and other professionals.

- Finally, *size* is a feature of bureaucracy. There is no absolute minimum size that marks a bureaucracy, although one rule of thumb suggests that an organization becomes bureaucratic when its highest-ranking members know fewer than half of the other members.[2] For example, the USPS is a nationwide organization that employs more than 800,000 people.

What Are the Distinguishing Features of Bureaucracy?

bureaucracy Large, complex organization composed of appointed officials.

hierarchy System for ranking roles and status in an organization; a principle of bureaucracy.

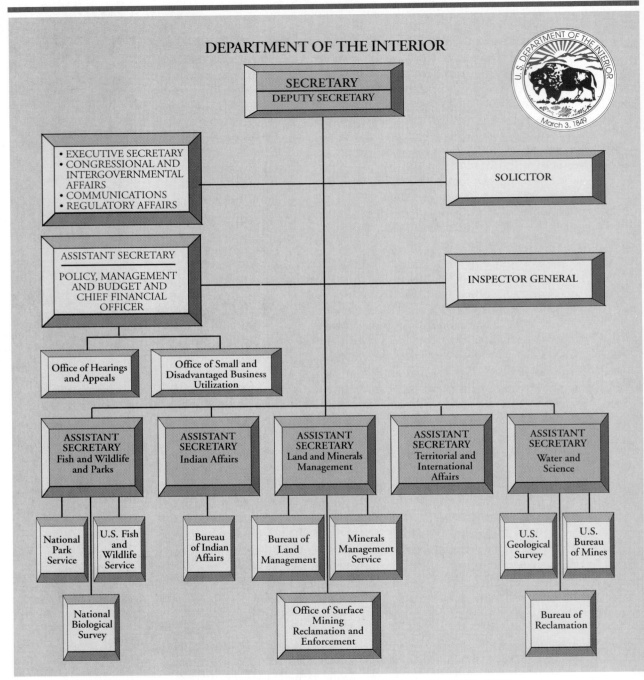

DEPARTMENT OF THE INTERIOR

SECRETARY
DEPUTY SECRETARY

- EXECUTIVE SECRETARY
- CONGRESSIONAL AND INTERGOVERNMENTAL AFFAIRS
- COMMUNICATIONS
- REGULATORY AFFAIRS

SOLICITOR

ASSISTANT SECRETARY
POLICY, MANAGEMENT AND BUDGET AND CHIEF FINANCIAL OFFICER

INSPECTOR GENERAL

Office of Hearings and Appeals

Office of Small and Disadvantaged Business Utilization

ASSISTANT SECRETARY Fish and Wildlife and Parks

ASSISTANT SECRETARY Indian Affairs

ASSISTANT SECRETARY Land and Minerals Management

ASSISTANT SECRETARY Territorial and International Affairs

ASSISTANT SECRETARY Water and Science

National Park Service

U.S. Fish and Wildlife Service

Bureau of Indian Affairs

Bureau of Land Management

Minerals Management Service

U.S. Geological Survey

U.S. Bureau of Mines

National Biological Survey

Office of Surface Mining Reclamation and Enforcement

Bureau of Reclamation

FIGURE 10.1 Bureaucratic Organization: The U.S. Department of the Interior, 1994–1995.

In addition to these characteristics, bureaucratic organizations also tend to be impersonal and routinized and have their own special language. Bureaucracy aims at eliminating "emotions, idiosyncrasies, and personal biases from the performance of individual bureaucrats."[3] Bureaucracies also tend to operate in ways that are standardized, such as through the development of forms for filing tax returns, procedures for purchasing items or disbursing money, and all sorts of everyday activities of an organization. They develop *standard operating procedures*—standard methods of handling routine matters—that frustrate those who want things done differently. Citizens who have dealt with the federal bureaucracy are well aware of its specialized language. It is replete with titles (for agencies, programs, officials, locations), jargon (the army calls a parachute an "aerodynamic personnel decelerator"), an alphabet soup of initials (FAA, FCC, FTC, FFB, FERC, FDA, FCA, FAS, FHA), and codes (Social Security numbers, the forms and schedules of income taxes, pay grades).

Interestingly, many bureaucratic entities develop a sense of *mission* that is widely shared by members of the organization. A mission gives an agency a sense of purpose and direction, boosts morale and employee commitment, and improves the prospects for success in achieving organizational goals. In the 1960s, the National Aeronautics and Space Administration (NASA) had a clear mission: land Americans safely on the moon. After that task was accomplished, the agency lacked a clear mission, and a number of managerial problems arose. In an era of tight budgets, NASA has found itself unable to maintain the high public and congressional support it had during the years of the Apollo program.

How Is the Federal Bureaucracy Organized?

Most Americans are familiar with some parts of the federal bureaucracy. They learn of cabinet departments in the news and encounter the work of other agencies—the Federal Deposit Insurance Corporation (FDIC), the Federal Housing Administration (FHA), or the Food and Drug Administration (FDA)—in daily life. But they are generally unaware of the range and complexity of its bureaucratic organizations. Table 10.1 lists the major types of government organizations.

Executive Departments

Law and custom give special prominence and status to the "departments" of government, whose heads (each bears the title of secretary, except the attorney general) have traditionally served as members of the president's cabinet. The cabinet is theoretically the senior advisory body to the chief executive on national policy, although the president is not bound to consult it or heed its suggestions.

Cabinet departments are generally large conglomerate organizations made up of various bureaus and offices. They are charged with enforcing laws, administering programs, and developing policy in the areas under their jurisdiction. Four departments that can trace their origins to the earliest days of the Constitution are responsible for broad national issues: the Departments of State (foreign affairs), Defense, Treasury, and Justice. The others were created in the nineteenth and twentieth centuries, usually at the behest of interest groups who

TABLE 10.1 Representative Agencies of the Federal Bureaucracy

Executive Departments (The Cabinet)

State
Treasury
Interior
Agriculture
Justice
Commerce
Labor

Defense
Health and Human Services
Housing and Urban Development
Transportation
Energy
Education
Veterans Affairs

Independent Agencies

ACTION
Central Intelligence Agency
Farm Credit Administration
General Services Administration
National Aeronautics and Space
   Administration

National Archives and Records
   Administration
Office of Personnel Management
Peace Corps
Small Business Administration

Independent Regulatory Commissions

Commodity Futures Trading Commission
Federal Communications Commission
Board of Governors of the Federal Reserve System
Federal Trade Commission
Nuclear Regulatory Commission
Securities and Exchange Commission

Government Corporations

Federal Deposit Insurance Corporation
United States Postal Service
Federal Savings and Loan Insurance Corporation
Amtrak (railroad company)
Tennessee Valley Authority

Government Foundations and Institutes

Inter-American Foundation
National Foundation on the Arts and the Humanities
National Science Foundation
Smithsonian Institution

Boards, Commissions, and Committees

American Battle Monuments Commission
Appalachian Regional Commission
Board of Foreign Scholarships
Citizens' Stamp Advisory Committee
Harry S Truman Scholarship Foundation
Japan–United States Friendship Commission
President's Foreign Intelligence Advisory Board
United States Holocaust Memorial Council

Note: Except in the case of the Cabinet, only some examples of each type of agency are given.

wanted representation at the cabinet table (Agriculture for farmers, Education for teachers). In some cases, existing government agencies were consolidated: the Department of Energy was created in 1977 from the Energy Research and Development Administration, the Federal Energy Administration, the Federal Power Commission, four regional power administrations, and portions of several departments and agencies. In other cases, independent agencies were elevated to cabinet status: in 1988 the Veterans Administration became the Department of Veterans Affairs. Some are created by separating out a division of another department: the Office of Education in the Department of Health, Education and Welfare (HEW) became a department in 1979, and HEW became Health and Human Services.

Not only are cabinet departments responsible for some of the most important functions of government, they also constitute a substantial portion of the bureaucracy. The Department of Defense has the largest civilian workforce in the federal government, around one million employees. The Department of Health and Human Services controls some of the federal government's largest medical and welfare programs.

Independent Agencies

These are administrative units that are under the political control of the president but independent of the departments. Some of the organizations that fall in this category are the Central Intelligence Agency (CIA), the Peace Corps, NASA, EPA, and the National Archives and Records Administration.

These agencies are independent in order to keep them free from domination by a large department, because of conflicts over which department should be responsible for them, or for other political reasons. For example, in 1994 the Social Security Administration was removed from the Department of Health and Human Services and made an independent agency. This move was motivated by the desire of decision makers in Washington to indicate that the Social Security program would be protected from deep cuts as the White House and Congress sought to deal with the federal budget deficit.

Independent Regulatory Commissions

These are bureaucratic agencies established to control specific areas of economic or governmental activity (see Table 10.1). Their structure is designed to insulate them from political control by the president. They are headed by boards or commissions rather than a single appointee; commission members serve for long, overlapping terms of office; and commissioners can be removed only for "cause" (that is, for specific reasons stated in law). A good example is the Federal Reserve Board (the "Fed"), which controls the money supply, interest rates, and certain aspects of the banking industry. Its board of governors consists of seven members, each serving a 14-year term (one vacancy occurs every two years). The board's chair serves a four-year term that does not coincide with a presidential term. This allows the Fed to regulate interest rates according to its own determination of good economic policy.

Regulatory commissions have been created to allow certain policy areas to be controlled by expert and technical considerations rather than political ones. For example, members of the Federal Election Commission (FEC), which administers campaign finance laws, are not only insulated from the president

**government corpora-
tion** Bureaucratic
organization structured
much like a business
enterprise, but owned
by the government
rather than private
shareholders.

but must also be divided between the major political parties. Of course, that does not mean that regulatory commissions are immune to politics. Presidents often appoint commissioners who reflect their views regarding the work of the agency, and a two-term president can fill a majority of seats on a commission. Ronald Reagan's appointees to the Federal Communications Commission were eventually able to adopt policy changes reflecting a more hands-off approach to regulating broadcasting. But overlapping terms mean that such a takeover is slow and that commissioners cannot be fired if their decisions are not to the president's liking.

Other Federal Institutions

Not all bureaucratic units fit into neat categories. **Government corporations** are organized much like private businesses but are owned by the nation rather than stockholders. The FDIC, USPS, Amtrak, the Tennessee Valley Authority (TVA), and other corporations provide goods or services for which their users must pay. Customers pay postage to send mail and premiums for bank deposit insurance; they buy tickets for travel on Amtrak trains and purchase electricity from the TVA. But government owns and often subsidizes these enterprises because Congress has decided that there is a compelling national interest in having their activities under public control.

The bureaucracy also includes a number of foundations and institutes (see Table 10.1). Some of them—the National Science Foundation, the National Foundation on the Arts and the Humanities, and the Inter-American Founda-

The Heye Center of the National Museum of the American Indian in New York City is one of the newest branches of the Smithsonian Institution, which itself is one of a number of federally supported foundations and institutes for science and the arts.

tion—were established to make grants to individuals and institutions in support of research, culture, and human development. Others are "quasi-official agencies" established by Congress but structured to provide special services and operate independently of political control. The most famous is the Smithsonian Institution, which serves as an umbrella organization for an array of museums and cultural institutions.

Beyond these units, the federal bureaucracy also includes a large number of boards, centers, commissions, councils, panels, study groups, and task forces (see Table 10.1). There are also a large number of federal advisory committees. The *U.S. Government Manual*, a directory of federal agencies published annually by the government, suggests the extent of the bureaucracy. The *Manual* does not even attempt to list the many advisory panels, and in each issue its section on "Boards, Committees, and Commissions" requests information on federal establishments that have been left out. In other words, even the federal government is not sure that it has a complete listing of its own bureaucracy.

Jane Alexander, head of the National Endowment for the Arts in the Clinton administration, testifies before Congress to try to protect the NEA's funding.

The federal government employs around 5 million people, 60 percent of whom are civilians and the rest military personnel. These employees can be divided into two major categories: political appointees and career officials.

Political Appointees

Approximately four thousand top jobs in the bureaucracy are filled by presidential appointment, including cabinet secretaries and assistant secretaries, agency directors, commissioners, ambassadors, U.S. attorneys, and other policy-making positions. This number also includes so-called **Schedule C** employees not subject to Senate confirmation but chosen by political appointment. Schedule C officials have policy-making responsibilities or work closely with their political superiors as executive or confidential assistants.

New presidents want to put their own people in charge of government, so with each new administration there is significant turnover in these posts. At the beginning of each presidential term, the best-selling book of the Government Printing Office is a document known universally but unofficially as the "Plum Book," which contains a listing of positions subject to presidential appointment (its name comes from the color once used on its cover, but now refers to the "plums" of government employment).

Career Officials

Ninety percent of federal civilian employees are chosen through some type of merit system. Several agencies maintain their own merit system, including the CIA, FBI, Postal Service (which has the only federal employees governed by collective bargaining), State Department (the Foreign Service), Public Health Service (physicians), and the Department of Veterans Affairs. Military personnel are recruited, promoted, and disciplined within the Defense Department.

Who Works in the Federal Bureaucracy?

Schedule C: A category of federal officials who have policy-making responsibilities or who work closely with political superiors as executive or confidential assistants. Appointed by the president but do not require Senate confirmation.

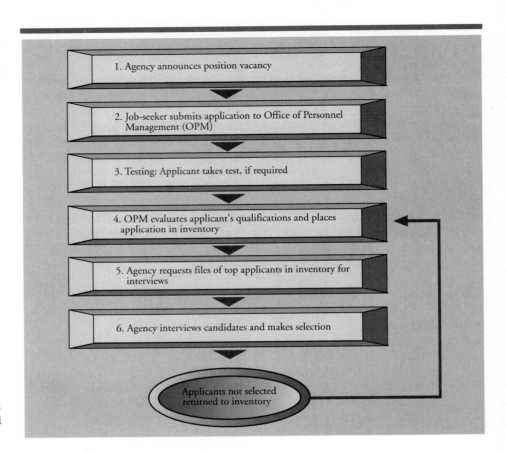

FIGURE 10.2 Steps in Hiring a Federal Civil Servant.

About 60 percent of federal civilian employees are part of the civil service. They are selected through a process based on qualifications for the position to be filled. The appointment of citizens to jobs in the civil service is a protracted process that often involves passing a competitive examination. Figure 10.2 provides an overview of this hiring system.

The merit system is administered by the Office of Personnel Management (OPM). OPM administers exams for civil servants. It also maintains a hiring system for professional personnel, such as government scientists and staff attorneys, who fill specialized posts that cannot be filled through the normal examination process. It also trains personnel and provides benefits to active and retired civil servants. Personnel practices, appeals of personnel actions (such as dismissals), and hearings on charges of employee wrongdoing are conducted by the Merit Systems Protection Board, which is responsible for protecting the integrity of the merit systems.

Civil servants work in an environment that is tightly structured by laws and agency procedures. For example, the pay and benefits of federal employees are not subject to the whims of supervisors or competition with private employers.

Each agency establishes a separate pay scale for its white-collar career employees, but ranks (called grades) and pay steps in the civil service correspond to a General Schedule established by Congress. Table 10.2 shows the pay standards for white-collar workers in the civil service in 1994. In addition, employees at federal offices around the country may also receive a salary supplement meant to adjust their pay to meet the cost of living in different parts of the nation.

The merit system is designed to insulate federal civil servants from the shifting winds of politics. The personnel procedures for the career service are voluminous and complex. Vice-President Al Gore attempted to make an issue of this situation in the early days of the Clinton administration. He would often display a photograph of a roomful of books and then comment, "The books you see in this picture contain the regulations you have to follow in order to hire, fire or promote a federal employee. . . . They weigh 1,088 pounds. The comparable volume of material at the Saturn [automobile] plant in my state is about 20 pages."[4]

The principle of merit is not absolute, however. Just as is true with any other organization, a number of nonmerit considerations have been added to bureaucratic hiring by law or by the practices of officials. As Washington-watcher Charles Peters points out,

> Veterans get five free points added to their civil service exam score; disabled veterans get an extra ten. For nonveterans the trick is to know someone inside the agency. People already in the system are the first to know about a job opening,

TABLE 10.2 **The 1994 General Schedule for Federal Career Employees**

GS Grade	Step									
	1	2	3	4	5	6	7	8	9	10
1	$11,903	$12,300	$12,695	$13,090	$13,487	$13,720	$14,109	$14,503	$14,521	$14,891
2	13,382	13,701	14,145	14,521	14,683	15,115	15,547	15,979	16,411	16,843
3	14,603	15,090	15,577	16,064	16,551	17,038	17,525	18,012	18,499	18,986
4	16,393	16,939	17,485	18,031	18,577	19,123	19,669	20,215	20,761	21,307
5	18,340	18,951	19,562	20,173	20,784	21,395	22,006	22,617	23,228	23,839
6	20,443	21,124	21,805	22,486	23,167	23,848	24,529	25,210	25,891	26,572
7	22,717	23,474	24,231	24,988	25,745	26,502	27,259	28,016	28,773	29,530
8	25,159	25,998	26,837	27,676	28,515	29,354	30,193	31,032	31,871	32,710
9	27,789	28,715	29,641	30,567	31,493	32,419	33,345	34,271	35,197	36,123
10	30,603	31,623	32,643	33,663	34,683	35,703	36,723	37,743	38,763	39,783
11	33,623	34,744	35,865	36,986	38,107	39,228	40,349	41,470	42,591	43,712
12	40,298	41,641	42,984	44,327	45,670	47,013	48,356	49,699	51,042	52,385
13	47,920	49,517	51,114	52,711	54,308	55,905	57,502	59,099	60,696	62,293
14	56,627	58,515	60,403	62,291	64,179	66,067	67,955	69,843	71,731	73,619
15	66,609	68,829	71,049	73,269	75,489	77,709	79,929	82,149	84,369	86,589

Source: Office of Personnel Management.

and knowing both the applicant and the job, they can tailor the job description to fit the person they want to hire. So the civil service is a patronage ring based not on politics but on friendship.[5]

This practice, used especially in filling professional positions, is known as the "buddy system."

One special class of career officials is the **Senior Executive Service (SES),** a corps of over eight thousand high-level bureaucrats. SES members can be transferred from one agency to another or to different positions within the same organization. They are also subject to a system of rewards and penalties designed to make them more responsive to their political superiors, although, in practice, sanctions (such as dismissal) have been more common than promised cash bonuses. Since its creation by Congress in 1978, the SES has increased bureaucratic responsiveness but has contributed to lower morale among civil servants.

The federal government is the nation's single largest employer and is a central component of American government. Contrary to popular wisdom, the federal bureaucracy has not grown wildly over recent years; as Figure 10.3 shows, the numbers of state and local government employees have risen at a much greater rate than the numbers of federal employees.

Principles: Administration for a Democratic Republic

The Constitution's framers wanted to overcome the inefficiencies of the Articles of Confederation, under which the Continental Congress handled its administrative business through committees. John Adams served on 90 different committees, including some that dealt with planning specific military operations. Although the Congress eventually appointed officers—of war, marine, finance, and foreign affairs—to assist it, its committee-based operations created an administrative nightmare.[6]

To remedy this chaos, the framers agreed that administration in the new regime should be carried out by executive departments under single department heads. But the delegates could not agree on how much control the president should have over those heads, so they left most of the administrative structure for Congress to decide after the Constitution was ratified. As a result, the federal government's bureaucracy has developed since the founding as an enterprise based on constitutional and statutory law, precedent, and the internal logic of administrative organizations.

Constitutional Principles

As the preceding discussion suggests, bureaucracy is one of the great "blanks" in the Constitution (see Chapter 3). But the document is nevertheless relevant to bureaucracy. The Constitution lays down basic principles on which an administrative apparatus has been built.

First, *bureaucracy must conform to the Constitution and law.* One of the most important issues here is that of appointment to administrative posts. Article

Senior Executive Service (SES) Corps of over 8,000 high-level federal bureaucrats who can be transferred from one agency to another or moved to different positions in the same organization. Members of SES are subject to a system of rewards and punishments intended to make them responsive to their politically appointed superiors.

II specifies that the president (with Senate consent) makes all appointments to office, but "Congress may by Law vest the Appointment of such inferior Officers, as they think proper, in the President alone, in the Courts of Law, or in the Heads of Departments."

While these guidelines are generally clear, they do leave some issues open to interpretation. Where should the line be drawn distinguishing "inferior" from major offices? Staff are certainly considered "inferior" enough to be left to the discretion of the president, legislators, or high officials, but what else? This question became important in the matter of the position of independent counsel, which was created to provide a means for investigating and prosecuting official misconduct in the executive branch. By law, an independent counsel is appointed by a panel of judges upon the request of the attorney general. The Reagan administration challenged this process as a violation of the president's appointment powers but was rebuffed by the Supreme Court's ruling that the independent counsel is an "inferior" official.

As this example makes clear, judicial review is important to ensuring that the structure of the bureaucracy conforms to the Constitution and law. Moreover, it is used to consider administrative authority, rule making, procedures, and some decisions. Administration may be a blank in the charter, but it does not take place beyond the document's reach.

As the language of Article II suggests, a second principle underlies the federal bureaucracy: *Political authority over the bureaucracy is divided between the president and Congress*. This provides a marked contrast to parliamentary systems, in which government ministers are drawn from members of the majority party or coalition that controls the parliament.

American bureaucracy serves two masters. As we saw in the previous chapter, agencies are part of the executive branch, and their top officials are appointed by the president. But agencies are created, given legal authority, and funded by Congress, which reserves to itself the power to oversee bureaucratic operations. Bureaucrats must therefore pay close attention to Capitol Hill as well as to the White House. That is why a common sight on the evening news is an administrator testifying before a congressional committee on the work of that official's agency or providing expert information for legislative investigations. This division of authority also explains why nearly all federal agencies have organized a legislative liaison unit.

A final constitutional principle relevant to bureaucracy is *federalism*. National government organizations operate in a political system in which they must share authority with related agencies in state or local government. For example, the U.S. Department of Education does most of its work through state education agencies, individual institutions of higher education, and local school boards. Likewise, many federal programs—including Aid to Families With Dependent Children, highway funding, Medicaid, and others—are conducted by giving grants to state and local governments (and even private organizations). By this means, subnational governments become agents of national policy and extensions of the federal bureaucracy. Even federal agencies that have direct authority over citizens,

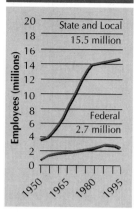

FIGURE 10.3 Employees of Federal, State, and Local Governments. From 1950 to 1995, the number of state and local government employees more than tripled. The number of federal employees grew slightly over the same period but a slight downward trend began in 1990.
Source: Statistical Abstract of the United States, 1995.

Under President Ronald Reagan, Oliver North (top) and John Poindexter (bottom) bypassed the federal bureaucracy and its rules and regulations, selling arms to Iran, channeling secret funds to rebel forces in Nicaragua, and engaging in other secret and illegal activities. Following congressional hearings, both Poindexter and North were convicted of felonies, but these convictions were later overturned, and North ran for political office in 1994. He was defeated.

such as the FBI or the Social Security Administration, devote considerable time and effort to coordinating their activities with related national bureaucracies.

Special Characteristics of the Federal Bureaucracy

All bureaucratic organizations are not identical, although they do share certain common characteristics. Large corporations may resemble government departments in some ways—hierarchical structure, division of labor, and other characteristics—but they are private entities that are not bound by the same rules as public agencies engaged in governing. The American federal bureaucracy is marked by two special characteristics.

While all bureaucratic organizations involve politics, *the federal bureaucracy formally mixes political and nonpolitical organization.* At the top of the Departments of Commerce and State, the Environmental Protection Agency, the National Aeronautics and Space Administration, and other departments and agencies are political appointees. Usually they have some career experience or substantive expertise that recommends them for presidential appointment, but in some cases these agency heads may have no further qualifications than loyalty to the chief executive or political experience. Lower-level jobs in the departments and agencies are filled through a variety of merit systems and are protected by a system of bureaucratic tenure that makes it exceedingly difficult to fire any career official. Between the top and bottom are an intermediate level of senior career officials whose job performance evaluations are based in part on how well they respond to the direction of their political superiors.

Another way in which the bureaucracy mixes the political and the nonpolitical can be seen in the use of boards and commissions to control many governmental functions. These organizations—which control broadcasting, the bureaucratic merit system, stock and bond trading, and other areas—are directed by panels of officials appointed by the president and confirmed by the Senate. Their appointments are for multiyear terms of office and are staggered. For example, the USPS is headed by nine governors appointed for overlapping nine-year terms. These governors select the postmaster general, who is the chief executive of the Postal Service. This structure is designed to ensure that the leadership of the organization will be changed slowly and be insulated from the shifting winds of politics.

The federal bureaucracy blurs the separation of powers. Although they are generally included in the executive branch, federal bureaucratic organizations are not strictly executive in nature. Nearly all engage in some form of *rule making,* which means that they have the power to issue administrative regulations that have the force of law. As political scientist Martin Shapiro has explained, many of the major laws enacted in the past quarter-century—on the environment, health, welfare, safety, nuclear power, education, and energy—have given extensive legislative power to bureaucracy:

> Congress often ended up delegating rule-making power to administrators and telling them to weigh a number of factors and arrive at a balanced judgment, but

frequently did not specify what weight or priority should be given to each factor. [Highway laws] could be read as telling the secretary of transportation to reach a routing decision by taking into account the importance of preserving parks, the value of preserving long-standing neighborhoods that provide their residents a sense of community, the need to preserve jobs that may be lost if highway construction causes the tearing down of a factory, and the need to get the most highway we can for our money.[7]

In addition to making rules and enforcing them, regulatory agencies often act as "quasi-judicial bodies" (a term used officially by several regulatory agencies). That means they adjudicate violations of laws and/or agency rules.

As we have seen, the federal bureaucracy is a special kind of bureaucracy. It shares the characteristics of all bureaucratic organizations, but it is distinguished from large corporations or other private groups by special features imposed on it by law and politics. The federal bureaucracy is big, hierarchical, and impersonal, but it also operates within the confines of the constitutional system and set of laws established by Congress.

In order to fill in the blank space left in the Constitution regarding administration, Congress has established a variety of structures, rules, and assignments. Over time, an elaborate complex of institutions, people, and laws has developed into what we call the federal bureaucracy.

Process: Operations of the Federal Bureaucracy

The Jobs of the Bureaucracy

Three general tasks are assigned to the bureaucracy. First, agencies are responsible for *enforcing the laws* passed by Congress. The FBI, Secret Service (for counterfeiting), Drug Enforcement Administration, Environmental Protection Agency, Internal Revenue Service, and other units are all obvious examples of such activities. But agencies also enforce their own regulations, such as the FDA requiring that drugs be subjected to certain tests before being cleared for public consumption.

Second, the bureaucracy provides for *implementation* of government policies. This may involve the administration of federal programs, whether on welfare, agriculture, highway construction, or foreign assistance. It may involve carrying out executive decisions on foreign policy, military operations, and intelligence. Much of implementation is routine administrative paperwork, but it also requires rule making to fill in the details of policy. Moreover, as Martin Shapiro's example of highway routing decisions makes clear, administrators often exercise considerable discretion in implementation. This means that they must make judgments about what is the best way to achieve program goals.

Third, some bureaucratic organizations are delegated authority to *regulate* certain areas of policy. Examples include the FCC's holding broadcasters to its rules on personal attacks, equal opportunities, and reasonable access (see Chapter 12) or the Interstate Commerce Commission's control of surface and waterborne commercial traffic.

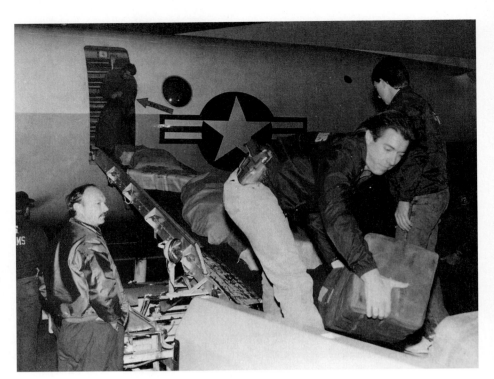

Agencies of the bureaucracy are often responsible for enforcing laws passed by Congress. Here, U.S. Customs agents seize more than two tons of cocaine flown into the country from Colombia.

No matter which job they are performing, bureaucratic agencies exercise considerable power in American society. Not everyone participates in politics, but all citizens are affected by the work of the bureaucracy.

Governing the Bureaucracy

Laws, court decisions, and procedures have been developed to control administrative activities that are intended to make agencies accountable and to prevent abuses of bureaucratic power.

Administrative Procedures Act (APA). This law serves as the most important set of ground rules for the operations of the federal bureaucracy. Originally passed in 1946 and amended since then, the APA was designed to promote fair administration and prevent arbitrary bureaucratic actions. It outlines procedures for rule making, records, hearings before administrative bodies, secrecy, and most other issues that could arise in the course of administration.

APA recognizes three types of rules that agencies can issue, although not all units have the power to employ all three kinds. First, there are *procedural rules,* which are guidelines that govern the internal operations of a bureaucratic unit. So long as one of these rules does not violate some constitutional provision (such as discriminating unfairly against a particular religious group), agen-

Administrative Procedures Act 1946 law that outlines procedures for rule making, records, hearings before administrative bodies, secrecy, and other aspects of federal bureaucratic operations.

cies have broad authority to make rules for their own operations. Second, some agencies have the power to issue *legislative rules,* which are substantive policy mandates that have the same force as a law passed by Congress and signed by the president. Regulatory commissions are established precisely to issue legislative rules for broadcasting (Federal Communications Commission), stock and bond trading (Securities and Exchange Commission), and other areas of policy, but many administrative agencies also make substantive rules of this sort. For example, the Federal Aviation Administration issued a rule that banned smoking on all domestic airline flights of less than two hours. So long as a legislative rule is not otherwise unconstitutional, it is enforceable as law. Finally, nearly all administrative agencies issue *interpretative rules* that interpret and implement the laws passed by Congress for which the agencies are responsible. Some interpretative rules are technical in nature; for example, to implement a requirement that employers demonstrate that each person hired after a certain date is a U.S. citizen or resident alien, the Immigration and Naturalization Service issued a rule specifying what evidence it would accept to prove eligibility for employment.

Other interpretative rules are more substantive. For example, Congress passed the Wetlands Protection Act to halt construction in sensitive areas that could further reduce the extent of the nation's marshes, estuaries, and other wetlands, but it was left to the Environmental Protection Agency to define "wetland" in order to determine what areas would be protected. The EPA drafted an interpretative rule that would have protected almost every piece of real estate in the country with standing water on it for more than a few days (including vacant lots in cities), but uproar over the proposed rule from Congress and interest groups forced the agency to back down. As this example shows, interpretative rules are the weakest kind of rules that agencies produce. Not only are they subject to change under pressure from Congress and the public, but judges have long believed themselves competent to interpret laws and to judge whether an agency's interpretation is valid.

In order to promote "administrative due process,"[8] APA imposes several rules on the bureaucracy: Agencies must make public their proposed rules (by publishing them in the *Federal Register,* an official government information source); they must allow those potentially affected by rules to comment on those proposals and then take public comments into account when drafting final rules; when agencies make decisions that affect citizens or organizations, they must allow affected parties to seek legal help in challenging decisions; and agency rules and decisions are subject to internal appeals and external review by courts. Figure 10.4 summarizes the administrative rule-making process required by this law.

Freedom of Information Act (FOIA). First passed in 1967 and revised in 1974, this act requires agencies to make public all records except those kept secret for legitimate reasons of national security, to protect privacy personnel records, or to ensure trade secrets of companies doing business with an agency. To ensure that agencies cannot easily circumvent the law, FOIA sets time limits

Freedom of Information Act (FOIA) 1967 law that requires federal agencies to make public all records except those kept secret for legitimate reasons of national security, to protect private personnel records, or to insure trade secrets of companies doing business with an agency.

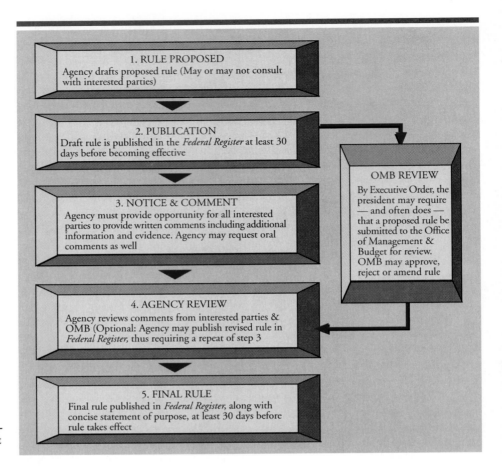

1. RULE PROPOSED
Agency drafts proposed rule (May or may not consult with interested parties)

2. PUBLICATION
Draft rule is published in the *Federal Register* at least 30 days before becoming effective

3. NOTICE & COMMENT
Agency must provide opportunity for all interested parties to provide written comments including additional information and evidence. Agency may request oral comments as well

4. AGENCY REVIEW
Agency reviews comments from interested parties & OMB (Optional: Agency may publish revised rule in *Federal Register,* thus requiring a repeat of step 3

5. FINAL RULE
Final rule published in *Federal Register,* along with concise statement of purpose, at least 30 days before rule takes effect

OMB REVIEW
By Executive Order, the president may require — and often does — that a proposed rule be submitted to the Office of Management & Budget for review. OMB may approve, reject or amend rule

FIGURE 10.4 Administrative Procedures Act Rule-Making Process.

on agency responses to requests for information, limits how much agencies can charge citizens for the expense of copying records, provides for court review if citizens challenge agency claims regarding the secrecy of materials, and even authorizes punishment of administrators who improperly withold information that should be released.[9]

FOIA has not unleashed a flood of information about administrative practices, but it has made it possible for determined citizens and researchers to obtain files on themselves or controversial actions. For example, some political activists have won the release of records that the FBI once collected on prominent dissidents and "subversive organizations." Historians and biographers have found FOIA a useful tool for learning more about the life of figures such as Martin Luther King Jr. or administrative actions regarding the record of nuclear safety.

In order to comply with FOIA, federal departments and agencies have established FOIA offices that citizens can call for more information on how to obtain government materials. (See *Participate!* box for advice on obtaining information under FOIA.) Despite improved access to information under FOIA, critics contend that agencies continue to resist requests for information and that patience and diligence are required to obtain desired information.

Other Laws Controlling the Bureaucracy. The Government in the Sunshine Act (1976) requires agencies to hold open, public meetings when important policy decisions are to be made. The Hatch Act (1939) seeks to prevent civil servants from being the subjects of undue political pressure by their appointed superiors. Other statutes, such as the 1972 Federal Advisory Committee Act or the Occupational Safety and Health Act, also regulate bureaucratic operations. For example, the advisory committee law requires that any federal committee that includes citizen members (people who are not federal employees) must hold open meetings, provide opportunities for public comment, and make all records public.

Beyond statutory law, administrative due process is maintained by subjecting bureaucratic actions to adjudication. In other words, rules and decisions can be appealed and reviewed by officials other than those who took the actions in the first place. Within agencies, this adjudication is carried out by those holding the office of **administrative law judge** (ALJ). These officials are employees of bureaucratic agencies who act in a judicial capacity to hear appeals of agency rules and decisions. The federal government employs over one thousand ALJs, about 70 percent of whom work for the Social Security Administration. They are appointed for life on the basis of experience and examination and given a certain measure of independence from their agencies by the APA, but they are also dependent on their employing agency for operating resources. Many are former staff attorneys for the agencies they now serve as ALJs. These circumstances have led to questions about whether ALJs are sufficiently objective,[10] since ALJs are employed by the agencies against whom they are being asked to rule. (Many other countries use administrative courts to overcome the ambiguities in the position of ALJs.)

Appeals of agency actions do not end within the bureaucratic unit itself. Federal courts are also involved in reviewing the rules and decisions reached by bureaucrats. In consequence, a substantial body of administrative law has developed in American courts, as judges have interpreted the Constitution, APA, FOIA, agency rules, and other relevant sources in pursuit of fair administration. For example, in *Bowen v. City of New York* (1986) the Supreme Court voided a Social Security Administration (SSA) rule that provided only 60 days for persons denied disability benefits to file an appeal. The Court found that SSA had never published the 60-day deadline and ruled that this "clandestine policy" violated the APA. It ordered the agency to reopen the cases of all persons denied benefits under the restriction.[11]

Law provides the basis for the structure and operations of the federal bureaucracy, but administration is not a mechanical exercise. Agencies are just as much a part of the political system as the presidency or Congress.

Get Help with Bureaucratic Problems

1. Seek information on the bureaucracy: Good information is easily available, especially from agencies themselves. Several key sources are available at public and college libraries:

- The *U.S. Government Manual* contains information on department and agency structure, mission, legal authority, senior personnel, employment, and ways to communicate with the relevant organization.
- The *Federal Register,* published each working day, contains all proposed and final drafts of administrative rules and regulations, as well as other official notices.
- The *World Almanac of U.S. Politics* (New York: Pharos Books, 1991) contains extensive information on how to contact agencies.

2. Request assistance with bureaucratic problems from your representatives in Congress: Do you have a problem getting veterans' benefits? Is some one in your family having trouble with Social Security? All congressional offices are geared to dealing with a wide range of casework, such as citizen problems with the bureaucracy. (Members cannot help people who have tax or legal troubles.)

- Include all information that may help to identify your case: name, address, and phone numbers for home and work.
- Describe your problem clearly, completely, and accurately.
- Explain what actions you have taken to resolve the problem already (if any).
- Contact only one member of Congress at a time—having several congressional offices work on your case can actually take longer and confuse things.
- Stick to the facts: Don't accuse someone of trying to hurt you and do not threaten to vote against your representative if the problem is not resolved to your satisfaction.
- Don't wait until the last minute to seek help: Casework often takes time.

3. Seek information on bureaucratic actions under the Freedom of Information Act: FOIA enables citizens to obtain information from agencies on a wide range

of issues, but invoking it effectively requires following the right procedures, understanding the law's exceptions (for information that does not have to be released), and being prepared to appeal denials of requests. Several guides currently exist to assist citizens who want to obtain bureaucratic records under FOIA (and under the Privacy Act, which gives citizens access to files on themselves). A good one available in public and college libraries is *Freedom of Information Guide* (Washington, D.C.: WANT Publishing Co., 1984). Those making a request should be patient; agencies have 10 days to respond to an initial request and 20 working days to reply to an appeal. Many government agencies also consistently fail to meet these deadlines.

The following list contains FOIA contact numbers for federal departments and selected agencies:

DEPARTMENTS

Agriculture	(202) 720-8164
Commerce	(202) 482-4115
Defense	(703) 697-1180
Education	(202) 708-9263
Energy	(202) 586-6025
Health and Human Services	(202) 690-7453
Housing and Urban Development	(202) 708-3054
Interior	(202) 208-5342
Justice	(202) 514-1938
Labor	(202) 219-8188
State	(202) 647-7740
Transportation	(202) 366-4542
Treasury	(202) 622-0930
Veterans Affairs	(202) 233-3616

SELECTED AGENCIES

Central Intelligence Agency	(703) 351-2770
Commission on Civil Rights	(202) 376-8351
Environmental Protection Agency	(202) 260-4048
National Archives and Records Administration	(301) 713-6730
Nuclear Regulatory Commission	(301) 492-8133
Selective Service System	(703) 235-2272

participate!

The federal bureaucracy is not a machine that translates policy into organizational routines with precision. Indeed, its political aspect has led some observers to call bureaucracy the "fourth branch of government." The political side of the bureaucracy can be seen most clearly in two areas: how the bureaucracy reflects the American system of separated powers and federalism, and how bureaucracy fits uneasily into our democratic republic.

Divided Authority and Federalism

Federal agencies operate in a political environment shaped by the sharing of powers inherent in the constitutional system. Several consequences develop as a result of this situation: relative independence for bureaucratic entities; an uneven distribution of power in the executive branch; a collaborative relationship between the national government and state and local agencies; and the growth of issue networks as links between bureaucratic agencies, interest groups, elected officials, and a variety of others interested in policy. We shall examine each of these in turn.

The Power of Bureaucracies to Act Independently. American government bureaucracies enjoy greater autonomy than their counterparts do in other democracies. As we have seen, they are given considerable discretion in implementing the goals established by political leaders. Moreover, the presidential-congressional division of authority means that bureaucrats not only serve two masters, but can often play one off against the other. Agencies can also put their own interests ahead of those of their political superiors.

Several examples of autonomy illustrate this point. One famous one was the navy's nuclear submarine program, which was headed for many years by Admiral Hyman Rickover. Despite repeated attempts by several secretaries of defense to cut funds for nuclear submarines in the name of economy, Rickover managed to protect and even increase his program's appropriations by cultivating support for it among powerful legislators on Capitol Hill. Another example from the military came when President Clinton proposed altering the policy on gays and lesbians serving in the armed forces. Although the commander in chief could order such a change, top military leaders used congressional resistance to the plan to force Clinton to adopt a "don't ask, don't tell" compromise.

Autonomy is not limited to the military, however. A common complaint from the White House about cabinet secretaries and other appointees is that they begin to put departmental interests or congressional concerns ahead of presidential priorities. Presidential aides often complain that appointees identify with the bureaucrats of their agency rather than with the White House (known in Washington as "going native") and are thus untrustworthy. Alexander Haig, who served as Ronald Reagan's first secretary of state, encountered this problem shortly after assuming office in 1981. After several encounters with presidential counselor Edwin Meese in which the secretary supported his department's resistance of White House direction, Haig was forced to resign.

Likewise, Reagan was frustrated with his first secretary of education, Terrell Bell, who became an advocate for his department's interests. The president eventually replaced him with a secretary more to his liking (conservative intellectual William Bennett).

Several commentators have argued that the existence of a large, powerful, and relatively autonomous bureaucracy has created an *administrative state*. This term suggests much the same idea as calling the bureaucracy the "fourth branch of government": the notion that bureaucracy shapes public policy, the work of government, and the lives of citizens as an independent force in the regime, not as a subordinate to political leaders.

Differences in Power Among Bureaucratic Departments. All cabinet secretaries may enjoy equal trappings of status—large offices, limousines, seats at the cabinet table in the White House—but they are not equal in their importance to the chief executive and their influence on presidential policy making. Indeed, political scientist Thomas Cronin divides departments into two distinct groups: an Inner Cabinet and an Outer Cabinet.[12] The **Inner Cabinet** consists of the departments of State, Defense, Justice, and Treasury; their heads are in regular and close contact with the chief executive and are usually major figures shaping presidential policy initiatives. The **Outer Cabinet** consists of all other departments; their heads may be important at times, depending on the president, current issues, and the personality of the secretary; but these agencies are not consistently significant to presidential policy making. The heads of these departments may find that the chief executive is something of a stranger. Walter Hickel, who served as Richard Nixon's first interior secretary, once complained that he could not get an appointment to meet privately with the president, and Samuel Pierce, who served as secretary of Housing and Urban Development in the Reagan administration, found that the president who appointed him did not recognize him at a public gathering. In consequence, Outer Cabinet departments devote considerable energy to cultivating support among the legislators who provide their funding and authority.

City, State, and Local Governments Act as Agents of the Federal Government. As we saw in Chapter 3, fiscal federalism and federal mandates to states and localities, along with other actions, have led to a situation in which states, cities, and other local governments act to carry out national government policies. Political scientist William Lunch calls state and local governments "franchise operations in a largely uniform national conglomerate" and sees this development as the best evidence of the "nationalization of American politics."[13]

This development has several serious consequences. First, it contributes to the decline of federalism in that states and cities are more beholden to the federal government and so are less autonomous. Subnational governments today are far more restricted than they once were. Second, this "franchise" system increases support for federal bureaucracies and the programs they administer, both among their subnational agents and the clients who receive the benefits of these pro-

Inner Cabinet Heads of the departments of State, Defense, Treasury, and Justice; they have frequent contact with the president and are more likely to affect presidential decisions than other cabinet members.

Outer Cabinet Majority of the heads of executive departments who are likely not to see the president frequently and who do not have continuing influence on presidential policy making.

Because of their financial ties to federal programs, state, city, and other local governments have increasingly become part of the federal bureaucracy. At the 1992 National Governors' Conference, governors from the 50 states met to discuss their problems in carrying out mandates of federal law.

grams. State and local governments now constitute a major lobbying group in Washington; they have a vested interest in the maintenance of the federal programs that underwrite their budgets. Finally, it means that intergovernmental coordination becomes an important factor determining the government's ability to achieve its goals. For example, since public education in America is carried out by local school districts under state authority, federal education policy can be successful only to the extent that officials in the U.S. Department of Education are able to work with and through state and local education agencies.

The Rise of Issue Networks. In Chapter 6 we saw how relationships developed between interest groups, congressional committees, and bureaucratic agencies. In the "old Washington," these iron triangles created subgovernments controlling areas of policy (agriculture, veterans benefits, and others). In the "new Washington" of more open politics, messier and more diffused issue networks have replaced the iron triangles of old. On the surface, this may make it seem that the powerful alliances among interest groups and various government officials are less important. On the contrary, it is precisely because of those divisions that complex issue networks have developed. Bureaucrats operate in an environment in which White House officials and members of Congress and their staffs must often compete with a bewildering array of interest group representatives to influence administrative rule making and decision making.

Some critics have charged that agencies are often "captured" by the interests they are supposed to govern. Famous examples include the Agriculture Department and farmers or the Interstate Commerce Commission and the trucking industry. These criticisms are often accurate, but they are incomplete. In many agencies competing interests vie for influence, winning battles on occasion but seldom gaining permanent dominance. For example, the Federal Communications Commission once seemed captured by the three major television networks, but today's communications industry is divided among these networks, their affiliates (who have different interests), new networks (Fox, public broadcasting), cable companies, independent broadcasters, consumer and ideological groups (Action for Children's Television, People for the American Way), various radio interests, and others. As we saw in Chapter 6, the politics of issue networks is not as simple as old-style triangular politics.

Checks and Balances on Bureaucratic Power

For many Americans, the very term "bureaucracy" is a negative one. One of the most popular promises political candidates can make is a pledge to reduce bureaucracy and end the waste, fraud, and abuse generally believed to accompany it. Voters who supported Ross Perot in the 1992 election indicated that the independent candidate's attacks on waste and bureaucracy were significant factors in their support for him and remained important to them as they evaluated the performance of President Clinton.[14] But public attitudes about bureaucracy are complex. Although the public dislikes "bureaucracy" and faceless "bureaucrats," surveys indicate that citizens generally report satisfaction from their actual encounters with government administrators. Moreover, while there is widespread support for cutting waste in government, both particular interests and the public at large do not want to see many programs cut.

Presidents and Bureaucratic Power. Public dislike for "bureaucracy" is echoed and amplified by political leaders. Every president since Richard Nixon has campaigned for office on a pledge to reduce the size and power of the federal bureaucracy. Once in office, these chief executives have tried to overcome their frustrations with administrators through a variety of methods. Every president tries to appoint executive officials who will serve White House interests, but as we have already seen, this outcome is difficult to ensure. Torn between the president, Congress, and departmental interests, many appointees work to protect the autonomy of their own agency. The efforts of several presidents to reform the bureaucracy are described in the Current Issues box.

Not satisfied with this situation, some presidents resort to using their aides to monitor bureaucratic behavior. One factor fueling the growth in the Executive Office of the President has been the desire of chief executives to oversee administrative operations. As we saw in Chapter 9, the Office of Management and Budget (OMB) has been central to overseeing domestic affairs. Since the time of Harry Truman, OMB has reviewed the suggestions that agencies make to Congress regarding legislation (usually based on agency experience with implementing and enforcing laws). Recent presidents have also charged OMB with responsibility for reviewing all proposed regulations drafted by executive agencies, a process known as *administrative clearance*. While administrative clearance has been controversial—critics charge it was used by the Reagan and Bush administrations to weaken environmental regulations—it was maintained by the Clinton White House as a device for monitoring bureaucratic policy making.

Reorganizing the Bureaucracy

One of the most enduring problems in American government has been managing the federal bureaucracy. Throughout the twentieth century, there have been a series of presidential commissions and task forces assigned the job of investigating the problems of the bureaucracy and recommending reforms. These groups (which are usually known by the names of their chairs) have always included prominent citizens and public officials among their members. Each has produced a report outlining proposed changes for the federal executive, but by no means have all or even most of these reforms been adopted.

One impetus for creating these commissions was to seek ways to make bureaucracy more efficient and businesslike. This was the goal of the Cleveland Commission (1912), the two commissions headed by ex-President Herbert Hoover (1947 and 1949), and the Grace Commission (1984). Another motivation for these bodies was to find ways to make bureaucracy more accountable to the American people and their elected representatives. The Brownlow Commission (1937) under President Franklin Roosevelt and similar ones under Presidents Johnson and Nixon made accountability their chief concern.

The latest effort at bureaucratic reform was produced under the direction of Vice-President Al Gore. This project, known as the National Performance Review, made "reinventing government" its motto, and its 1993 report advocated *Creating a Government That Works Better and Costs Less*. The general spirit of the Gore report was in line with earlier commissions favoring more businesslike practices in government. What distinguished this effort was that its vision of successful business owed more to McDonald's than to General Motors. In other words, the National Performance Review stressed "putting customers first" rather than corporate efficiency. It called for "empowering employees," by which it meant giving bureaucrats more flexibility to serve their customers (citizens) by reducing the number of rules and regulations (red tape) that limit the actions of civil servants. By the fall of 1994, one year after its report was released, the National Performance Review had yet to realize many of its major goals.

Reorganization and reform have not been completely unsuccessful. The Brownlow Commission's report provided the basis for creating the Executive Office of the President in 1939, and the Gore report helped push Congress to simplify government purchasing procedures. Other reforms, often of a technical nature, have also resulted from these groups.

Some presidents go even further, creating organizations in the Executive Office that allow them to bypass the rules and regulations of the bureaucracy. Deeply suspicious of the Foreign Service, Richard Nixon allowed his aide Henry Kissinger to construct a miniature State Department in the National Security Council staff. Kissinger and his staff conducted policy planning, arms control negotiations, and even directed aspects of the Vietnam War out of the White House. A more extreme example was the covert operation that John Poindexter and Oliver North operated under Ronald Reagan in the Iran-Contra affair. They conducted arms-for-hostages negotiations, sold arms to Iran, channelled secret funds to rebel forces in Nicaragua, and engaged in other secret (and illegal) activities outside of the normal military, diplomatic, and intelligence structures.

Congress and the Federal Bureaucracy. Congress has generally reacted to the bureaucracy in two ways. One is to use its powers of investigation, appropriation, and oversight to monitor agency actions. Several agencies labor under this kind of scrutiny: the Departments of Agriculture and Veterans Affairs, the

Social Security Administration, the Army Corps of Engineers (which maintains the nation's inland waterways and builds other large-scale projects at Congress's orders), and even the technically independent Federal Trade Commission. Members of Congress often criticize the Food and Drug Administration (FDA) for either rushing risky new drugs into pharmacies or withholding new drugs from those who would benefit from them.[15] For example, not long after the 1994 election, Representative Newt Gingrich (R.-Ga.), speaking on policies his party wanted to reform when he became Speaker of the House the following year, attacked the FDA for keeping out of the United States a device that could aid victims of heart attacks.

The other form of congressional response to the bureaucracy has been to perform casework, that is, to intervene with the bureaucracy on behalf of citizens experiencing problems with administrative agencies. Whether it is in helping to find a lost Social Security check, obtain a special leave for a sailor with family problems, expedite a veteran's home loan application, or question a ruling of the Immigration and Naturalization Service that adversely affects a constituent, members of Congress (through their staffs) are continuously involved in assisting citizens frustrated or harmed by the impersonal and seemingly arbitrary ways of bureaucracy. This kind of intervention is handled in many countries by a government officer known as an *ombudsman*. Proposals to create a similar official in the United States government have met with no success; casework allows Congress to reap constituent gratitude and at the same time monitor bureaucratic activity.

Elected officials have used other means to challenge or reduce bureaucratic power. One of these has been **privatization**—employing private businesses instead of public bureaucracies to perform governmental functions. Privatization has been tried for such diverse purposes as garbage collection, mail delivery, school administration, and even operating prisons. While only a few advocates of privatization see it as possessing the potential to replace most of bureaucracy, elected officials in Washington and elsewhere see it as a device for improving governmental efficiency by going outside standard bureaucratic channels. Critics have argued that privatized services may cost less but lack the accountability of public organizations.

open questions

Does the Federal Bureaucracy Undermine Democracy?

As the idea of an administrative state and matters of privatization and bureaucratic power suggest, one of the major issues raised by the large and powerful federal bureaucracy is that of accountability. Observers wonder whether bureaucracy and democracy can reach a harmonious accommodation.[16]

Some critics of the federal bureaucracy argue that its enormous size, power, and tenure have made it a "lethargic, self-protective monster."[17] They charge that the executive branch is a bloated corps of officials who are overpaid, underworked, and do not advance the public interest. They blame Congress for delegating too much power to the bureaucracy, which they maintain surrenders vast powers to independent federal agencies over which Congress and the president have little or no authority: "Bureaucrats in such agencies feel beyond public control. Even when Congress or the president gives them an order, they find ways to subvert it."[18] For example, despite the Government in the Sunshine Act, about 60 percent of federal agency meetings held each year are improperly closed to the public.[19] Finding this situation incompatible with democracy, these critics call for radical cuts in the size and power of the bureaucracy and the reintroduction of politics. They want as much as 50 percent of administrative posts to be filled by political appointment, because this change will make the bureaucracy responsive to political leaders who are, in turn, accountable to citizens.[20]

In contrast, there are those who defend the administrative state as compatible with the principles of the Constitution. Indeed, these defenders argue that the bureaucracy now upholds some of the key values favored by the framers better than the political branches of government. For example, bureaucracy offers the continuity, wisdom, and expertise that the framers expected the Senate to provide; while the Senate has become too politicized to do the job it was created to do.[21] Likewise, these defenders argue that the vast federal bureaucracy serves the goal of representation better than Congress or the president, because it offers "millions of its employees the opportunity to fulfill the aspirations of citizenship—to rule and be ruled."[22] Defenders of the federal bureaucracy conclude that it is not only compatible with democracy, but essential to its survival and success.

Is the administrative state a threat to the democratic republic or its salvation? Are reforms necessary to make bureaucracy more compatible with the constitutional system? There are no easy answers to these questions. But it is clear that a large and complex bureaucracy is here to stay.

▌Summary

Bureaucracy refers to a large, complex organization composed of appointed officials. Federal administration exhibits the key features of bureaucratic organization: *hierarchy, specialization, formalization, merit and seniority* in hiring and promotions, and *size* (large). It also exhibits the special characteristics of bureaucracy: *impersonality, routinized behavior,* and *specialized language.* *Standard operating procedures* are developed to handle routine matters. Many bureaucratic entities develop a sense of *mission* that drives the organization.

The federal bureaucracy is composed of four major types of organizations: (1) executive departments—14 in number; (2) independent agencies—an array of separate executive agencies; (3) independent regulatory commissions—to control certain areas of public policy according to expert and technical considerations; and (4) a variety of other institutions, including government corporations, foundations, institutes, boards, centers, commissions, councils, panels, study groups, and task forces. Even the national government has a difficult time keeping track of all these units.

There are two types of personnel in the bureaucracy. At the top of departments, agencies, and other administrative entities are political appointees, who are involved in policy making. Beneath these appointees are career officials, who make up 90 percent of federal civilian employees. Some agencies have their own merit systems for hiring and promotion, but about 60 percent of the federal civilian workforce is part of the civil service. The civil service is administered by the Office of Personnel Management and its integrity is safeguarded by the Merit Systems Protection Board. Merit is the chief characteristic of hiring and promotion in the career service, although other considerations, such as prior military service, may influence decisions. The highest-level career officials belong to the Senior Executive Service, a corps of officials who form a kind of administrative elite.

Principles. The bureaucracy is shaped by constitutional and operational principles. Three constitutional principles shape the federal bureaucracy: (1) Bureaucracy must conform to the Constitution and law—bureaucracy does not exist in a vacuum; (2) political authority over the bureaucracy is divided between the president and Congress—the bureaucracy is part of the executive branch, but Congress creates agencies, gives them authority, and appropriates their budgets; and (3) federalism affects bureaucratic structure in that national government agencies must share authority with related state and local agencies or work in coordination with these subnational agencies.

The federal bureaucracy is a mix of political and nonpolitical organizations, and it often blurs the separation of powers by exercising all three types of governmental power (rule making, administration and enforcement, and adjudication).

Process. The federal bureaucracy is charged with three general tasks: (1) enforcing the laws; (2) implementing government policies and programs; and (3) regulating certain areas of policy. A complex body of *administrative law* provides ground rules for the work of the federal bureaucracy. Especially important to shaping these rules are the Adminstrative Procedures Act and the Freedom of Information Act. Violations of administrative rules are adjudicated before administrative law judges who are employed by agencies, although their decisions can often be appealed to a federal court.

Politics. The bureaucracy is not completely insulated from politics. Divided authority over bureaucracy and federalism has led to several consequences for agencies and administrators: (1) bureaucratic autonomy (leading some observers to suggest the existence of an "administrative state"); (2) inequality among cabinet departments; (3) state and local governments acting as agents of the national government; and (4) the rise of "issue networks" that make up the political environment in which bureaucrats operate.

Bureaucracy plays a large role in American government and citizens are often uncomfortable with that fact. Attacks on bureaucracy by politicians are popular. Some presidents have resorted to various techniques—monitoring agencies, administrative clearance, and circumventing the bureaucracy by creating White House agencies—to gain control over the bureaucracy or limit its power. Members of Congress rely on casework and oversight to check up on the bureaucracy. Other techniques, including weakening bureaucratic tenure and privatizing government services, have been used to weaken the power of career officials.

Open Questions. Are bureaucracy and democracy compatible? Some observers have argued that they are not. They call for radical cuts in the size and power of agencies and a greater dose of politics in government administration. In contrast, defenders of bureaucracy argue that a large and powerful bureaucracy is consistent with the principles of the Constitution. Whether or not bureaucracy is compatible with democracy, it is likely to be around for a long time.

DOWNS, ANTHONY. *Inside Bureaucracy.* Boston: Little, Brown, 1967. An economist's analysis of bureaucratic organization, behavior, and problems.

NACHMIAS, DAVID, AND DAVID H. ROSENBLOOM. *Bureaucratic Government USA.* New York: St. Martin's Press, 1980. A well-written and widely cited examination of the role of bureaucracy in contemporary government.

ROURKE, FRANCIS E. *Bureaucracy, Politics, and Public Policy,* 3rd ed. Boston: Little, Brown, 1984. Good introduction to bureaucracy and its role in modern government.

ROURKE, FRANCIS E., ed. *Bureaucratic Power in National Policy Making,* 4th ed. Boston: Little, Brown, 1986. Essays on the growth, behavior, and power of the federal bureaucracy.

WARREN, KENNETH F. *Administrative Law in the Political System,* 2nd ed. St. Paul, Minn.: West Publishing Co., 1988. Excellent introduction to the legal aspects of bureaucracy.

WILSON, JAMES Q. *Bureaucracy.* New York: Basic Books, 1989. Survey of bureaucrats, organizations, and political leaders involved with bureaucracy.

Suggested Readings

chapter 11

The American Judiciary

In 1993 President Bill Clinton nominated Ruth Bader Ginsburg, a federal appeals court judge, for the post of associate justice of the U.S. Supreme Court. Considerable anticipation preceded the chief executive's announcement. The retirement of Justice Byron White meant that this was the first opportunity since the 1960s for a Democratic president to appoint a member of the High Court. Members of Congress, the media, and other "Court watchers" waited with great anticipation to see how Mr. Clinton might affect the balance between liberals and conservatives on the Supreme Court, whether he would select a woman or a minority candidate for the job, and whether the nominee would engender national controversy. Recent presidential choices for the Court—Robert Bork in 1987 and Clarence Thomas in 1991—had led to acrimonious battles between supporters and opponents of each candidate. Mr. Clinton undertook a torturous search for a nominee, considering and rejecting several possibilities before settling on Judge Ginsburg.

Once her selection was announced, Ginsburg became the focus of intense scrutiny. All of her speeches, judicial opinions, scholarly writings, and other legal work were combed for insights into her views on the Constitution, the courts, abortion, and other questions of law. Members of the Senate, as well as various interest groups, began lining up for or against her confirmation. The Senate Judiciary Committee conducted hearings on her nomination, and she was eventually confirmed.

The events that transpired from the retirement of Justice White to the seating of his replacement provide a look into the role of the judiciary in the contemporary American regime. As we have seen in Chapters 3 and 4, judicial decisions can affect the lives of Americans and the course of national politics. While courts may seem remote from most citizens, in reality they are as closely tied to everyday life as the cases and laws they must judge. And the federal judiciary, which will be the main focus of this chapter, plays a particularly important role in American life.

American Law

We American citizens are governed by laws that affect most aspects of our lives. Each year, we pay our income taxes. When we drive (an activity licensed and controlled by government), we must obey traffic regulations. Our commercial transactions are governed by law, as are the sales taxes that most of us pay when we buy something. So are other facets of our lives: the property we own, the schools we attend, the money we save or spend, and nearly anything else. Even the limits on the government's control over us—our freedoms of speech and religion and so on—are ultimately defined by law.

Law is so pervasive that we almost take it for granted. It is part of the fabric of our everyday lives. For example, consider a cheeseburger that you might buy for lunch. What does law have to do with it? Much more than you think. Every part of that burger is controlled in some way by a legislative act, a court decision, or an administrative regulation that has the force of law.[1] The content of the hamburger patty must be beef and cannot contain extra ingredients. Under the Federal Meat Inspection Act, the meat is checked as many as six times from the time the cow goes to the slaughterhouse until the wrapped package of ground beef is sold. The milk fat content of the cheese is regulated, as are the bun, the mayonnaise, and the lettuce and tomato placed on the sandwich. Even ketchup is regulated; to be considered Grade A Fancy ketchup, it must flow no more than 9 centimeters in 30 seconds at 69° Fahrenheit. If you want pickle slices, they are also controlled; they must be between ⅛ and ⅜ inches thick.

Not only is the production of your burger more of a legal matter than you thought, but it offers us a look at the nature of law in America. Law is a body of rules that has been created by government to control some aspect of life. It is created by several different authorities and affects our relations with each other as well as with the government.

The Sources of Law

As our cheeseburger example indicates, law is created by different governmental bodies. In the United States, there are four major sources of law: common law, statutory law, administrative law, and constitutional law.

Common Law. The bulk of legal rules governing matters of everyday life, from property and contracts to inheritance, is a product of court decisions that have accrued over centuries. Beginning in the twelfth century, judges in the royal courts of England issued decisions intended to establish a uniform body of legal rules for the entire kingdom. These decisions came to be known as the "common law," that is, law common throughout the king's dominions. **Common law** is thus a body of judge-made law that sets out principles and rules for deciding disputes between individuals over property, contracts, and injury. The chief principle of the common law is that of ***stare decisis,*** a Latin term meaning "let the decision stand." By this principle, past decisions serve as precedents for present and future cases.

When the British colonies in North America were established in the seventeenth and eighteenth centuries, they naturally employed English common law. After American independence, these newly sovereign states retained the common law, although over time they passed laws to modify it according to American ideas of justice. For example, the states enacted laws altering the common law rules of inheritance by which the eldest son in a family received the bulk of a family's estate. Today, all American states except Louisiana use the common law as the basis of their legal system. Because it deals with matters that are generally under the authority of the states, there is no common law in the federal government.

common law Body of judge-made law that sets out principles and rules for deciding disputes between individuals over property, contracts, and injury.

stare decisis Latin for "let the decision stand." This is the principle underlying the notion of precedent in court decisions.

Statutory Law. As valuable as the common law has been for establishing and maintaining principles of justice, it cannot be the sole source of law. Most of the common law deals with matters of property, and because it is centuries old it is often too rigid to deal with new legal matters that arise (such as automobiles and surrogate motherhood). Therefore, another major source of laws is needed:

the enactments of legislative bodies. These acts are called *statutes*. The acts of Congress, the acts of state legislatures, and the ordinances of city or county councils are all statutes.

Statutory law is much more flexible than the common law. It can make rules for subjects not covered in the centuries-old precedents. It can also modify or overturn the common law. As we noted earlier, Americans of the founding generation passed statutes to alter the common law rules of inheritance. Over the decades since independence, the American states have enacted many such changes.

Administrative Law. As we saw in Chapter 10, administrative agencies make rules and regulations that have the force of law. Administrative law is the fastest growing body of law in the United States; agencies issue thousands of regulations each year. Most administrative law rules can be overridden by statute; however, because these rules usually deal with fairly specific and detailed matters (such as rules implementing a federal program), Congress seldom passes statutes to overturn administrative regulations. Like all other forms of law, administrative law is subject to judicial review.

Constitutional Law. As we saw in Chapter 3, the U.S. Constitution is subject to interpretation. On one hand, the manifest constitution of rules and structures is usually uncontroversial: elections take place on schedule; presidents and members of Congress serve specified terms; and the underlying forms of government go on. On the other hand, because the constitution of open texture is so large, many aspects of the nation's charter require interpretation. In consequence, a large body of constitutional law has grown up in the United States, usually in the form of Supreme Court rulings. Because the Constitution is the supreme law of the land, constitutional law takes precedence over all other forms of law.

The Subject Matter of Law

The source of law is important, because not all sources are equal. The common law and administrative law can be overridden by statutes, but legislative acts must themselves conform to the Constitution. Just as important is the subject matter of law, which affects the parties involved, the rules governing court proceedings, and the penalties that may be incurred. The subject matter of law is generally divided into civil law and criminal law.

Criminal law deals with matters of public order, and the punishments for violating it are imposed by the government. Cases at criminal law are always brought by a governmental authority, and the penalties involved range from fines and community service to imprisonment and even execution.

Civil law deals with relations between individuals and defines their legal rights. Cases at civil law involve disputes between individuals and/or private organizations (such as corporations), such as one person seeking compensation for injury or damages inflicted by another person. Most civil law cases in

criminal law That area of the law that deals with matters of public order and the punishments imposed by government for violating it.

civil law That area of the law that deals with relations between individuals and defines their legal rights.

Most civil law cases involve disputes between individuals and/or private organizations in which one party seeks compensation for damages inflicted by another. Crashing a car into a store would doubtless engender a lawsuit by the store owner; such a suit would come under the jurisdiction of a state court, though the federal government can bring civil actions in certain cases.

America—those involving divorces, injuries, contracts, and inheritance—come under the authority of state courts.

Federal law allows the U.S. government to bring either civil law actions or criminal charges against individuals or corporations in certain cases. Civil law actions are easier to bring and to win than charges of criminality. Civil law can be used in cases involving violations of an individual's civil rights or in antitrust cases. For example, in order to end American Telephone and Telegraph Corporation's (ATT) monopoly on phone service, the U.S. government filed a civil lawsuit against the company. The case, which eventually became the biggest and most expensive in American history, resulted in the breakup of ATT into several regional phone companies (the so-called "Baby Bells").

Whatever the subject of the case or the source of law involved, the forum for resolving these disputes is a court of law. Because they are involved in everything from a traffic violation or a mischievous pet to great constitutional questions, the courts play an important role in the American political system.

America's Dual Court System

As we saw in Chapter 3, one consequence of federalism is that the lives of Americans are governed by two sets of laws—federal and state. Therefore, the United States has a *dual court system* for making legal judgments—a federal judiciary and the state court systems. As we shall see, the federal courts are established by the Constitution and national law, while each state has the power to create and staff its own judiciary.

The Federal Courts

Under the Constitution, there are two kinds of federal courts: **constitutional courts** include the Supreme Court, circuit courts of appeal, and district courts explicitly mentioned or implied in Article III. But there are also several different **legislative courts,** such as the Court of Military Appeals, the tax court, and territorial courts of American territories and possessions, that have been created by Congress under its authority to establish "inferior Courts" as it sees fit. Although Article III establishes the judicial branch, it has taken acts of Congress to actually organize and define the structure of the federal courts. The most fundamental of these laws was the Judiciary Act of 1789, which established the basic three-tier system of federal courts.[2] Figure 11.1 shows the structure of the federal courts and the way the state and other lower courts are related to that system.

District Courts. At the bottom of the judicial system are the U.S. *district courts,* 94 in all. There is at least one district court in each state. Each court may have several judges, depending on the caseload of the district, but usually only one judge hears an individual case. For certain extraordinary and controversial cases, such as a challenge to the constitutionality of the 1985 Balanced Budget Act, Congress has provided for special three-judge panels.

District courts are the primary trial courts of the federal judiciary and hear around 200,000 cases a year. Federal courts hear both civil and criminal cases. Criminal cases involve a charge that some person or persons violated a federal law, such as evading income taxes or counterfeiting money. Persons found guilty of such offenses are subject to fines or imprisonment. All cases involving alleged violations of federal laws are heard in federal courts. Civil cases in federal court must involve disputes over which the United States government has authority, such as charges that one person's civil rights have been violated by another. Under the Constitution, bankruptcy law is also the exclusive domain of the federal government, and federal courts hear about 300,000 bankruptcy cases each year.

Special Courts. In addition to district courts, Congress has established a number of *special courts.* These include the U.S. Tax Court, which hears appeals of decisions made by the Internal Revenue Service; the U.S. Court of Claims hears suits (other than tax cases) against the federal government; the U.S. Court of International Trade deals with tariff cases and appeals of decisions of the U.S. International Trade Commission. The U.S. Court of Military Appeals hears appeals of courts-martial convictions; it is distinctive because its decisions are final.

Circuit Courts of Appeal. Above the district and special courts are the 13 U.S. *circuit courts of appeal.* Eleven of these cover three or more states in a group (circuit); one hears appeals from the district court in the District of Columbia; and one is the Court of Appeals for the Federal Circuit (for hearing appeals

constitutional courts
The Supreme Court, circuit courts of appeal, and district courts explicitly mentioned or implied in Article III of the Constitution.

legislative courts
Courts established by Congress pursuant to its power to create judicial bodies, such as courts for tax cases and military appeals.

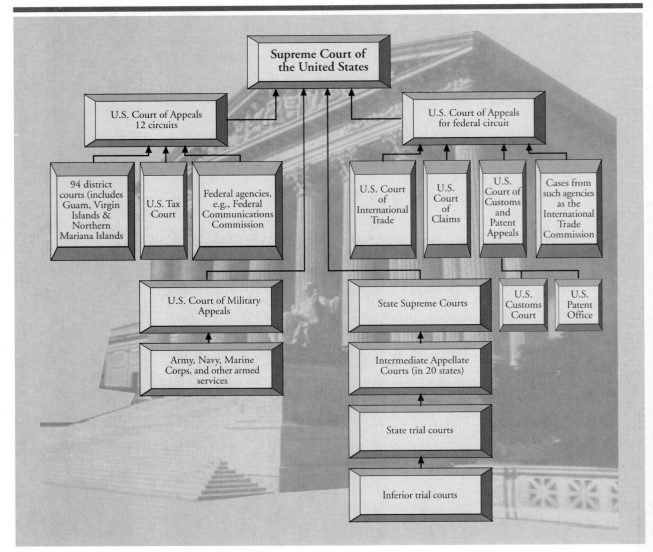

FIGURE 11.1 The United States Court System. Arrows indicate the route by which cases appealed at lower levels may reach the Supreme Court. Note that both the Federal Circuit Court of Appeals and the 12 district circuit courts of the U.S. Court of Appeals are represented on the map in Figure 11.2.

Source: Administrative Office of the U.S. Courts.

from special courts). These courts also receive appeals from decisions of regulatory commissions, with the Court of Appeals for the District of Columbia hearing most of these actions. Figure 11.2, shows how the nation is divided into circuits for the purpose of determining which court of appeal will review cases appealed from a lower court.

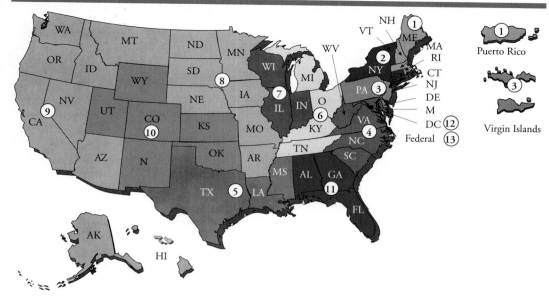

FIGURE 11.2 The Thirteen Federal Judicial Circuits.
Source: Administrative Office of the U.S. Courts.

The appellate courts consist of a number of judges assigned according to the caseload of the court—from 6 in the First Circuit (New England) to around 30 in the Ninth Circuit (which includes California). Appeals are heard by three-judge panels, chosen at random, and decisions are rendered by a majority of the judges assigned to the case. An appeal is different from a trial. Rather than listening to a case all over again, appellate courts review trial records, receive written briefs from both parties in an appeal, and listen to strictly limited periods of oral arguments. Appeals tend to focus on points of law or the Constitution rather than the testimony of witnesses or the presentation of evidence, as in a trial. The judgments of appellate courts are subject to review by the Supreme Court.

The Supreme Court. The pinnacle of the federal judicial system is the U.S. Supreme Court. Because its decisions have such significance in interpreting law and the Constitution, and because the Supreme Court has its own unique procedures for deciding cases, we shall examine the nation's highest court later.

The State Courts

State court systems are established by state constitutions and/or legislatures. These courts deal with the vast majority of American legal business: estates, contracts, family law, injuries, medical malpractice, criminal cases, and other matters. While the decisions of state courts are ultimately subject to review by the United States Supreme Court, federalism defines the power for states to establish and maintain their own legal systems.

While many state court systems are modeled on the federal system, others are quite different. Texas has parallel court systems for criminal and civil cases, culminating in a pair of courts of final appeal; Louisiana's state law is derived from the Napoleonic code of nineteenth-century France. Each state establishes its own system, although all state court decisions are potentially subject to review by the United States Supreme Court.

The Matter of Jurisdiction

The fact that we have a dual court system does not mean that Americans can just choose to pursue cases in federal or state court depending on convenience or whether they believe they are more likely to win in one or the other. Instead, a case must be heard by the court that has jurisdiction over it. *Jurisdiction* refers to the authority of a court to hear and rule in a particular case. Jurisdiction is determined by several factors: the level of government—federal or state—that has authority in the case; whether the case is in trial stage or under appeal; and the subject matter of the case.

Original Jurisdiction. Courts of **original jurisdiction** have the authority to hear cases that have not been previously heard in another court. In other words, these are trial courts in which cases such as the O.J. Simpson murder trial or a divorce suit are decided. This jurisdiction is original because cases enter the legal system through these courts.

State law determines which courts have original jurisdiction over cases involving different subject matter. Some state courts have broad jurisdiction, such as over all civil cases in a particular area. Others are more limited: family courts are established in many states to hear cases involving child custody and juvenile matters; traffic courts hear only cases involving traffic violations; and small claims courts offer quick and inexpensive resolution of civil suits involving small amounts of money (less than $1,500).

The original jurisdiction of the federal courts is limited to five kinds of cases: (1) those involving ambassadors and other diplomats; (2) those in which the United States is a party (including violations of federal law and the Constitution); (3) those involving disputes between states; (4) those involving citizens of different states (but Congress has provided that the case must involve more than $50,000 or be settled in state court); and (5) disputes between citizens of the same state over land grants from different states. The U.S. Supreme Court has original jurisdiction in only a few cases: those involving diplomats and those in which a state is a party.

Appellate Jurisdiction. Courts of **appellate jurisdiction** review decisions rendered by other courts. States establish their own systems for appeals. Federal cases can be appealed from a district or special court—such as the tax court—to a court of appeals. Many, but certainly not all, decisions of courts of

original jurisdiction
Authority of a court to hear cases that have not previously been heard in another court and appealed to the higher body. The U.S. Constitution limits the original jurisdiction of the Supreme Court to certain kinds of cases, but it is almost never exercised.

appellate jurisdiction
Power of a court to hear cases on appeal from a lower court.

appeals may be appealed to the U.S. Supreme Court. Decisions of a state's highest court may be appealed directly to the U.S. Supreme Court if federal law or the Constitution is at issue. The vast majority of cases heard by the High Court are appeals. Article III of the Constitution authorizes Congress to limit the appellate jurisdiction of the Supreme Court, but the national legislature seldom does so.

An understanding of the American judiciary begins with two simple facts: that many of the Constitution's framers were lawyers and that they feared legislative dominance. As lawyers, they were steeped in the ideals and values of English common law as it had developed in colonial America. Many of their assumptions about the principles of justice and legal process were derived from William Blackstone and other British legal commentators. Their grounding in law is perhaps one reason why the Constitution that they wrote works so well. The framers were also determined to establish courts that would be independent of the political branches of government, so they created a judiciary rooted in England that would be uniquely American.

Principles: American Ideals of Justice and Law

An Independent Judiciary

James Madison had written in *The Federalist,* No. 10 that "Justice is the end of government. It is the end of civil society." A court system established as a third branch of government was one of the most important means for achieving that end. But the Constitution goes further; in effect, it gives judges life tenure in office. Article III states that they will serve during "good behavior," which means for as long as they commit no crimes making them subject to impeachment. In *The Federalist,* No. 78, Alexander Hamilton asserted that life tenure/good behavior is "the best expedient which can be devised in any government to secure a steady, upright, and impartial administration of the laws."

Judicial Authority

The judiciary is the branch of government charged only with deciding disputes over law and the Constitution. As Hamilton further observed in No. 78, the executive controls the military, and the legislature controls the rules and funds of the state, but the judiciary "has no influence over either the sword or the purse; no direction either of the strength or wealth of the society, and can take no active resolution whatever. It may truly be said to have neither FORCE nor WILL but merely judgment; and must ultimately depend upon the aid of the executive even for the efficacy of its judgments." This weakness, he maintained, makes it the "least dangerous branch" of government. Courts not only decide guilt or innocence in criminal cases and which side deserves victory in a lawsuit, but even whether the laws themselves conform to the Constitution. In other words, judgment implies judicial review of laws passed by the legislature.

accusatorial procedure Cornerstone of Anglo-American jurisprudence, that an accused person is "innocent until proven guilty." The judge serves as a neutral party between prosecution and defense.

inquisitorial procedure Judicial method of countries operating outside of the Anglo-Saxon common-law tradition and based on the Napoleonic Code (a revision of Roman law). The accused is assumed guilty until proven innocent. In this method, the judge is an active participant in the questioning of the accused.

adversarial process Method of conducting legal trials, with two sides competing with one another to win the case.

The Importance of Precedent

Anglo-American law is based in individual cases, with decisions in current cases being guided by precedents set in prior cases covering the same issues of law and fact. The rule of *stare decisis* is not necessarily a straitjacket, but it does bind judges to follow long-standing legal principles or *landmark* (precedent-setting) decisions of an authoritative court such as the Supreme Court. A decision such as *Brown v. Board of Education* (1954) provides a landmark for lower federal courts and state courts to follow. But even though the Supreme Court adheres to *stare decisis,* it may overturn a previous decision and create a new precedent if it determines that the earlier case was decided incorrectly. In the *Brown* case, the Court under Chief Justice Earl Warren overturned the 1896 ruling in *Plessy v. Ferguson.*

Presuming Innocence

In criminal cases, the prevailing legal principle is that of "innocent until proven guilty." This means that courts must presume a person accused of a crime innocent until the prosecution has proven that the accused is guilty. Legal scholars characterize this **accusatorial procedure** as a "cornerstone" of Anglo-American justice,[3] and it is designed to protect innocent citizens from harassment by the government. Judges remain neutral during trials; they do not question witnesses unless they believe that they must do so in order to avert a serious injustice. This principle contrasts sharply with the **inquisitorial procedure** used in countries such as France and Mexico, which presumes that the accused is guilty until proven innocent. In such systems judges actively question witnesses in search of the truth.

These principles make the judiciary an important part of the American political system. They shape the processes by which courts decide cases and administer justice in the United States.

The Judicial Process: How the Court System Works

Courts have their own procedures for conducting their affairs, and judicial process is not the same in all societies. The basis of the American legal system is the **adversarial process,** in which two sides compete to win the case: the prosecution versus the defense in criminal cases; the plaintiff(s) (those who sue) versus defendant(s) or respondent(s) (those being sued) in civil cases. The idea behind the adversary system is that it will best protect rights and find a just solution. Federal courts follow a uniform standard of procedure. State courts follow similar procedures, although there is variation from one state to another.

Procedure in Civil Cases

Civil cases involve disputes in which individuals or groups bring actions in court against other individuals or groups by whom they charge that they have been wronged. Civil procedure involves four major steps.[4]

Take Part in the Judicial Process

The judiciary is that part of government in which the influence of individual citizens is the weakest, just as the framers designed it to be. Citizens' opportunities to participate in the judicial process are highly structured by law and circumstances.

1. **Don't avoid jury service:** One of the most common responses to a summons to jury service is to try to figure out how to get out of it. Yet the judicial system depends on citizens for juries to work. Alexis de Tocqueville noted that juries are as important for their members—who learn to think in terms of law and not just their own wishes—as they are for the values they bring to justice. Jury service is the average citizen's greatest chance to participate in the judicial process.

2. **Get a lawyer:** Other than small-claims court, where you must represent yourself, or a minor traffic violation, any appearance in court as a plaintiff or a defendant calls for a lawyer. The United States is brimming with attorneys, and even lower-income people can obtain legal assistance from court-appointed attorneys (in criminal cases) or the Legal Services Corporation (for civil cases). Lawyers are often criticized for needlessly complicating life. Such criticism is well deserved; nevertheless, lawyers are essential.

First, the case begins upon the *commencement of the action*. This is done by the **plaintiff**—the party bringing the suit—against the **defendant** or *respondent* (both terms are used). To bring a suit, a plaintiff must do three things: select the correct court in which to file the suit (the court that has jurisdiction); have the defendant or the defendant's possessions brought before the court; and present the charges—or *complaint*—and ask the court for the appropriate remedies. In order to assist with the task of bringing the defendant to court, the plaintiff asks the court to issue a *summons* or *subpoena* that will compel the defendant (or the defendant's attorney) to answer the complaint. If the defendant fails to comply with the summons or subpoena, the court will automatically rule in favor of the plaintiff or charge the defendant with contempt of court (which carries criminal penalties).

Next are the *pleadings,* in which the two sides exchange formal written statements intended to narrow the issues and facts of the case. The defense must provide a formal *answer* to the complaint that initiated the case. A pre-trial conference between the two parties and the judge may also occur in an effort to settle the case. In fact, it is at this stage that many civil suits are settled (what is popularly known as "settling out of court").

If the case cannot be settled, then the third step—the *trial*—occurs. The trial itself will be shaped by the nature of the issues in the case. If the case involves a dispute over law (that is, if the circumstances are not at issue, but the legal principle that should resolve them is), then the case is conducted through legal *argument* between attorneys for each side before the judge. No witnesses need be called, and no jury will be involved. If the case involves a dispute over facts, as many do, then witnesses may be called and a jury trial may be required (although a jury trial can be waived by mutual consent). A jury is required in all federal civil cases involving more than $20, which means essentially all cases.

plaintiff The party bringing a suit in a court of law.

defendant A person charged with a crime in a court of law.

Post-trial proceedings then begin.[5] A decision, or *verdict,* determines the winner and loser in the case. A *judgment* follows, issuing remedies as appropriate. The verdict must be enforced; the court may instruct law-enforcement officers to ensure that the decision is obeyed. Finally, the case may be appealed, which initiates new proceedings before a higher court that may drag on for months or years.

As this summary suggests, civil actions take time and can be expensive, so it is not surprising that over 90 percent of these cases are settled before trial.

Procedure in Criminal Cases

Because of the nature of the charges involved and the penalties that may be imposed, such as imprisonment or death, criminal cases are more elaborate and more formal than civil cases.[6] The government is always a party—the *prosecution* that initiates the case and brings it to court.

Early Stages. A criminal case begins with the *apprehension*—that is, the arresting of a criminal suspect. The suspect, who will become the *defendant* if charged with a crime, must be arrested while committing a crime, while fleeing, or as a result of an arrest warrant obtained in advance.

Once arrested, the defendant becomes part of the elaborate machinery of the criminal justice system. The arrested person is brought before a judge for the *preliminary examination,* in order for the judge to assess whether the defendant should be released or *held to answer.* The defendant may have an attorney present at this and all other proceedings. As a result of the Supreme Court's ruling in *Gideon v. Wainwright* (1963, see Chapter 4), the court must appoint an attorney if the defendant cannot afford one. The court then determines whether the defendant will be held in custody or released on bail until such time as the defendant is formally charged with a crime.

Formal *accusation* constitutes the third step of the criminal judicial procedure. This occurs in one of two ways. The simpler of the two is the process of *information,* wherein a prosecutor submits an affidavit of evidence to the appropriate court charging the defendant with the crime and providing evidence to support the charge. A preliminary hearing may be held to determine whether there is enough evidence for a trial, as occurred in the O.J. Simpson murder case in 1994.

The other procedure for accusation is for the prosecutor to seek an **indictment**—an action that formally charges a person with a crime and prompts a criminal trial. An indictment can be issued only by a **grand jury,** a body of citizens assembled by the court to review evidence in order to determine whether prosecutors have sufficient information on which to base a case. A grand jury is required in federal criminal cases by the Constitution but is used in only a minority of states. A federal grand jury consists of 23 citizens selected from registered voters; state grand juries are often smaller. A unanimous vote is

indictment: The procedure by which a person or group is formally charged with a serious crime.

grand jury Panel of citizens who evaluate evidence presented by a prosecutor in the matter of serious crimes. Charges can be brought against a person or group only if the grand jury approves an indictment.

not needed to indict a defendant; for federal grand juries 16 jurors are a quorum and 12 votes are needed to issue an indictment.

Going to Court. After indictment, the accused is brought before the judge in the fourth step, the *arraignment.* The formal charge against the defendant is read in court, and the defendant enters a *plea* of guilty or not guilty. If the process of information is used, the arraignment and plea occur before the preliminary hearing. It is at this point that the prosecution and the defense may try to reach an agreement in order to prevent a trial. For example, the defendant may agree to plead guilty to a lesser charge in order to avoid the penalty for a more serious charge, while the prosecution avoids the time, trouble, and risk (of losing) of a full-scale trial. Such an agreement is popularly known as *plea-bargaining.*

If the case goes to *trial,* the actual courtroom clash that is familiar to many Americans from television and movies may be preceded by a lengthy series of motions, hearings on evidence, changes in the charges or the plea, and other legal maneuverings. Citizens who followed the O.J. Simpson case got a sense of how elaborate a difficult case can become, although most defendants do not have the money or amount of legal expertise to draw out their cases in the way that defendant Simpson did. In our determination to adhere to the principle of "innocent until proven guilty," we have developed elaborate procedures for allowing defendants maximum opportunity to protect themselves from conviction. The role of juries is discussed in the Current Issues box.

The trial itself is conducted before a judge, with a jury present or not depending on the jurisdiction, the type of case, and the prevailing laws. Juries are required in all federal criminal trials. The **petit jury**—that is, the trial jury—traditionally consists of 12 citizens, although states often use smaller juries (for example, 6 jurors). Federal criminal juries must have 12 members, and a unanimous vote is required for conviction. The Supreme Court has accepted non-unanimous convictions from state juries in cases that do not involve the death penalty.

As with civil procedure, the battle in court is followed by a number of *post-trial proceedings.* There is a *verdict,* or decision, and then *judgment and sentencing.* These decisions are often followed by *appellate review,* which is automatically required in all cases when a defendant has been sentenced to death. The *execution of the sentence* will also occur in the event of a conviction.

Evolving Standards of Judicial Process

While grounded in ancient practices, federal judicial processes have undergone changes in recent decades. In the area of criminal law, the Supreme Court under Chief Justice Earl Warren (1953–1969) greatly expanded the rights of accused criminals. It stiffened the rules for search and seizure and the arrest and questioning of suspects, guaranteed legal counsel to all defendants, and elaborated on the requirements of "due process" (see Chapter 4). Since that time, the Court under

petit jury A trial jury.

The American Jury

current issues

One distinctive feature of the American judicial system is its extensive use of juries in both civil and criminal trials. Almost 2 million citizens annually serve on state and federal juries. Our Constitution requires the use of juries in all federal criminal trials and in essentially all federal civil trials (unless a jury is waived by agreement of both parties to the case). This requirement is one of the legacies of ancient English legal practices that Americans kept after independence, and the nation's founders regarded the jury as so important that they protected it in the Bill of Rights.

The trial jury in a criminal case is traditionally made up of twelve citizens, although in some states the number is as few as six.

Once common to nearly all West European legal systems, juries are still used in such countries as Austria, Denmark, Greece, Norway, and several Latin American states. The jury as a legal instrument has declined, however. France and its former colonies do not use juries, nor do many other nations. The use of juries has been curtailed in Great Britain, where grand juries were abolished in 1933 and trial juries are used in only about 5 percent of cases—less than 1 percent of civil cases and about 4 percent of criminal cases. Many American states have cut back on the use of juries—less than half of the states use grand juries.

Jury service is rewarding for those who participate, even if jurors don't always receive the respect they deserve. Americans serve as jurors despite a boring jury selection process, financial sacrifices (many employers do not pay for lost work time), personal inconvenience, and a good chance of being dismissed by one party to a case. In addition, events such as the O.J. Simpson murder trial, the Rodney King trial, and the trial of the Menendez brothers, illuminate the difficulties in selecting jurors for high-profile cases. The court questioned dozens of citizens before assembling a panel of 12 jurors and 12 alternates. Americans who actually serve on juries report a positive experience in which ordinary citizens have an opportunity to decide important questions of right and wrong, life and death, and who is at fault in cases involving large amounts of money. The jury is an institution that puts average citizens in control of a vital part of our legal system.

Chief Justices Warren Burger (1969–1986) and William Rehnquist (since 1986) has taken a more restrictive view of many of these rights. For example, where the Warren Court strictly limited the ability of police to obtain evidence and would not allow use of evidence obtained improperly, more recent decisions have allowed use of evidence obtained by authorities under "good faith" even if the police violated search and seizure rules. Supporters of these changes see them as necessary corrections of the Warren Court's excesses, while critics see them as retreats from a commitment to due process for all.

In the area of civil law, the judicial activism of the Warren Court ushered in an era in which litigation (lawsuits) could be used to advance political goals in the areas of abortion rights, desegregation, school prayer, church-state relations, and others. This political use of lawsuits, which we noted in Chapter 5, has been called the "new litigation"[7] and is best understood in contrast to the "old litigation." The old litigation was narrow in scope, based on specifics, covered events of the recent past, and involved courts as limited arbiters of disputes. It still exists and continues to characterize most civil suits in the United States. The new litigation is broad in scope and often occurs through **class action suits** filed on behalf of broad categories of plaintiffs (such as all members of a minority group), many of whom are unaware of the suit. It is often based on intangibles, such as loosely defined psychological harm to groups of people. And it may involve issues of the distant past or something anticipated in the future. This new-style civil litigation has increased the use of the courts as institutions for social change. Many of the lawsuits that are filed with respect to abortion fall into the category of new litigation.

If law is based on precedent, then how could such changes be made? The answer is that the Supreme Court has reinterpreted statutory and constitutional provisions to open new avenues for litigation and reverse older rulings, and these new interpretations serve as precedents for future decisions. The new litigation also opened the way for continued judicial activism by the Burger and Rehnquist Courts, although these Courts have tended to move in a more conservative direction than the liberal-minded Warren Court. Supporters of the new litigation see it as a valuable means to advance social change in the nation, when such change is otherwise blocked. They point to examples such as school desegregation in which class action suits were used to end decades of racial discrimination. Critics contend that the new litigation has led to politicization of the judiciary and a subversion of democratic processes.

The Supreme Court

At the top of the dual court system stands the U.S. Supreme Court. Although the High Court has both original and appellate jurisdiction, it rarely hears cases except those that come to it on appeal. Therefore, its main function is to exercise judicial review and to serve as the court of final appeal in American law.

The Structure of the Court

The Supreme Court consists of the chief justice and eight associate justices. The office of chief justice is separate from that of the associates and is appointed by the president. The chief is responsible for court administration as well as directing the work of the associates, although in deciding cases the chief justice's vote counts no more than that of any other justice. There have been only 16 chief justices over the course of American history (Table 11.1).

While its role in American life and law is large, the Court itself is a small institution. Its staff is barely more than three hundred people, and its total budget is only around $18 million. Justices are assisted in their work by an administrative, clerical, and legal staff. In addition, each justice hires three or four law clerks for periods of one or two years. The staff includes officers such as the clerk of the court (the administrative supervisor), the marshal (who oversees the Court building and security), and other officials. Justices' clerks are the most

class action suit Suit that seeks relief on behalf of a broad category of *plaintiffs* (such as all members of a minority group), many of whom may be unaware of the suit.

TABLE 11.1. Chief Justices of the United States

Chief Justice	Appointing President	Dates of Service
John Jay	Washington	1789–1795
John Rutledge	Washington	1795
Oliver Ellsworth	Washington	1796–1800
John Marshall	John Adams	1801–1835
Roger B. Taney	Jackson	1836–1864
Salmon P. Chase	Lincoln	1864–1873
Morrison R. Waite	Grant	1874–1888
Melville Fuller	Cleveland	1888–1910
Edward D. White	Taft	1910–1921
William. Howard Taft	Harding	1921–1930
Charles Evans Hughes	Hoover	1930–1941
Harlan Fiske Stone	F. Roosevelt	1941–1946
Frederick M. Vinson	Truman	1946–1953
Earl Warren	Eisenhower	1953–1969
Warren Burger	Nixon	1969–1986
William Rehnquist	Reagan	1986–

PLEADING HER OWN CASE

Despite the old saying that "To be one's own lawyer is to have a fool for a client," Silvia Ibanez represented herself before the U.S. Supreme Court. An accountant who also practiced law in Winter Haven, Florida, Ms. Ibanez was forbidden from advertising her professional services by a state law. She regarded that law as an unconstitutional infringement on her First Amendment right of free speech and sued the state. She was vindicated by the Supreme Court in its ruling in *Ibanez v. Florida* (1994). Ms. Ibanez won the right to advertise and demonstrated that her client wasn't so foolish after all.

important staffs for affecting the actual decisions of the Court, because they perform the research and often draft the opinions of their bosses. As we shall see in our discussion of "unelected representatives" in Chapter 12, the role of law clerks in writing opinions has stimulated considerable criticism.

The work of the Supreme Court is conducted during an annual session (*term*) that begins on the first Monday in October. The Court usually hears arguments on cases during two-week sessions separated by recesses of two weeks or longer to consider cases and deal with other business.[8] It continues working, with short breaks for holidays, until the last decision is announced in June or July.

Lawyers also play a large role in the workings of the Court. The Bar of the Supreme Court is an association of all attorneys qualified to practice before the High Court. Nearly two hundred thousand lawyers have been admitted to the organization, many for the professional prestige that membership brings. But membership in the Supreme Court bar, while relatively easy to obtain, is mandatory for any attorney who wishes to bring a case to completion before the Supreme Court.

The most important lawyer in the Court is the **solicitor general** of the United States, a high-ranking officer of the Justice Department who represents the federal government before the High Court. Although this officer serves the president, the solicitor general is expected to provide the Supreme Court with sound legal (as opposed to strictly political) advice in many cases. For that reason the solicitor general is sometimes called the "tenth justice."

The Court at Work

Appealing a case to the High Court is neither easy nor guaranteed. The justices enjoy almost complete discretion over which cases they will hear. Of the

solicitor general High-ranking Justice Department official who represents the United States government before the Supreme Court. Also controls appeals of cases in which the U.S. government is a party.

The U.S. Supreme Court, 1995. Seated in the center of the front row is Chief Justice William Rehnquist. With him in the front row are (from left to right) *Associate Justices Antonin Scalia, John Paul White, Sandra Day O'Connor, and Anthony Kennedy. In the rear are Associate Justices Ruth Bader Ginsburg, David Souter, Clarence Thomas, and Stephen Breyer.*

approximately four thousand cases appealed to the Court each year, only about 150 to 200 receive the full attention of the justices.[9] Those cases that make it to the "marble temple" are subjected to a lengthy process by which the Supreme Court agrees to hear a case and then decides on it.[10]

Bringing a Case to the Court. There are several methods by which cases reach the High Court from other tribunals. One is by *appeal,* in which the appellant files a statement explaining why the Court has jurisdiction and should hear the case. This method is rarely used. A second method is *certification,* in which a lower court asks the Supreme Court for a ruling on a question of law. This method is also rarely used.

By far the most common way to reach the High Court is by filing a petition for a **writ of certiorari**—a document that takes a case under review by

writ of certiorari
Order transferring a case to the Supreme Court from a lower court. Four justices must vote in favor for a writ to be issued in a case.

While conventional
lobbying of judges is
not allowed, an indi-
vidual or a group who
is not a party to a
case before the
Supreme Court can try
to sway the Court's
decision by filing an
amicus curiae ("friend
of the court") brief.
This brief outlines
arguments for one
side or the other in
the case. In recent
years, the filing of
amicus briefs has
become a popular
way to try to
influence the outcome
of controversial cases,
such as those involv-
ing abortion. In *Web-
ster v. Reproductive
Health Services* (1989),
an unprecedented 78
amicus curiae briefs
were filed. Over four
hundred organizations
co-sponsored these
briefs, with thousands
of individual citizens
signing them. It is
difficult to assess the
impact of these briefs
on the ultimate deci-
sion in the case, but
citations in the Court's
ruling indicate that the
justices did consider
the arguments pre-
sented by the friends
of the court.

the Supreme Court. For the Court to "grant cert" at least four justices must vote to hear the case. This is known as the **Rule of Four.** These votes are taken in private conferences in which only the members of the Court participate and only results are reported. The justices grant writs of certiorari to only 10 to 15 percent of the petitions that they receive.

The Court has a set of rules governing the form of these petitions, and it assesses fees from petitioners. But it does not require the U.S. government to pay fees and waives fees and simplifies filing procedures for those too poor to meet the normal requirements. Such petitioners may file *in forma pauperis* (as a pauper), and the Court has a special office devoted to handling such cases. Many come from prisoners seeking to correct the injustices they see at work in their convictions. Clarence Earl Gideon, the Florida prisoner whose petition led to the right-to-counsel decision in *Gideon v. Wainwright* (1963), submitted his petition in this way.

Written and Oral Arguments. Once placed on the *docket* (the Court's formal agenda), a case is scheduled for arguments. Written arguments, or *briefs,* are submitted by the parties to the case and often by others with an interest in the outcome of the case. As we saw in Chapter 5, an *amicus curiae* ("friend of the court") brief may be filed by individuals, interest groups, or governments who are not parties to the case. The solicitor general's office may submit an *amicus curiae* brief stating the Justice Department's position on the case. These briefs are studied by the Court and its clerks before oral arguments are held.

Oral arguments are held before the justices in public session in the Supreme Court's courtroom. Time is strictly limited; each side usually receives only a half-hour to make its case and be questioned by the justices. Some justices will interrupt attorneys frequently with questions or challenges, while others sit quietly listening to the discussion.

The Court Deliberates. A few days after oral arguments conclude, the Court holds a private meeting to discuss the case. This meeting is known as the *case conference.* At this conference, the justices take a preliminary vote on the case, which is crucial for shaping the remainder of the decision-making process.

After the vote is taken, a justice is assigned to draft the *majority opinion*— a statement of the official reasoning of the Court. Ordinarily the chief justice decides who will be assigned the case; but if the chief is not in agreement with the majority, the senior associate in the majority makes that assignment. Over the years there have been rumors that some chief justices have voted with the majority in some cases in order to reserve to themselves the power to write the Court's opinion and thus shape the ultimate impact of the decision.

Majority opinions often go through several drafts before they satisfy the various justices who vote with the majority. There may be one or more *minority opinions*—statements of alternative views on the case—written by those who disagree with the Court's decision. Likewise, those justices who have voted with the majority but disagree with the reasoning in the majority opinion may file separate *concurring opinions,* statements expressing agreement with the ruling of the Court but giving different reasons for that ruling than are contained in the majority opinion. As the Court nears a final resolution of the case, justices will *join*—add their names to—a majority, concurring, or dissenting opinion that best reflects their views of the issues. Opinions may be hotly debated as the drafter of a majority opinion seeks to hold together support for a controversial decision.

While the vote of any justice in a particular case may be influenced by the circumstances of the case, by the majority opinion, or even by interpersonal relations on the Court, individual members of the Court usually vote in identifiable ideological patterns on most issues. Justices may not be perfectly consistent, but experienced Court watchers are often able to predict how particular justices will vote on the basis of their previous record.

The Court's Decision. At the close of the process, the Court publicly announces its decision, and the justice who drafted the majority opinion gives a brief summary of the reasoning behind it. But it is the full published opinion that will be studied by politicians, the media, interest groups, lower-court judges, and legal scholars for an understanding of the Court's ruling. Published opinions form the chief means for the Court to shape constitutional interpretation.

The vote on a case can influence its impact. *Plurality decisions* are those in which there is not a majority of justices joining the ruling of the Court. Such opinions reflect sharp divisions on the Court and almost always invite further litigation to seek a clearer resolution. *Majority decisions* are most common; they are accompanied by one or more dissents. *Unanimous decisions* have the greatest force, for they reflect no disagreement among the justices about the resolution of the case.

"In a 5 to 4 decision today, the Supreme Court ruled the Constitution itself unconstitutional."

Baloo Enterprises.

The judiciary exists outside normal politics, but it is also a political institution. The federal judiciary is not subject to elections, but its members are nominated and confirmed by politicians. Its cases often have political content, and its decisions certainly influence government and political life. Possessing the power of both constitutional and statutory review, it can challenge the workings of the other branches of government. The principles and processes of the judiciary result in a kind of judicial politics that is uniquely American in character.

▌Politics and the Judiciary

The Politics of Judicial Selection

Because the courts can exercise such important political power, politicians and political activists are particularly concerned about those who become federal judges. All federal judges are appointed by the president with consent of the Senate and serve "during good behavior." These nominations have been closely watched and often hotly contested in recent years.

Rule of Four Supreme Court's requirement that at least four justices must vote to review a case before that case will be placed on the docket.

Although a vacancy on the Supreme Court occurs on the average every two or three years, other judgeships require a steady stream of nominees. There are 710 judgeships besides the Supreme Court, and the current pace of vacancies from retirements or resignations is about 10 each month.[11] When he became president, Bill Clinton had the opportunity—or the burden—of finding candidates for 115 judgeships left unfilled by George Bush.[12] Over the course of a single term in office, a president appoints hundreds of judges.

Because the Senate must approve nominees, presidents must calculate what legislators will accept in the way of candidates for the judiciary. In the matter of the Supreme Court, this determination is made by the White House and Justice Department, often with great secrecy. In the matter of other posts, particularly federal district judges, senators of the president's party play a role in identifying and suggesting possible nominees to the chief executive. Some senators have even established nominating committees to identify candidates whom they can then recommend to the White House. If a nominee meets opposition from a home state senator of the president's party, "senatorial courtesy" (explained in Chapter 8) obliges other legislators to vote against the president's choice. Fearing problems from the Senate and sometimes using nominations as bargaining chips to win a senator's support on other issues, the president usually pays careful attention to the possible choices sent from Capitol Hill.

Also involved in the process is the American Bar Association (ABA), which has a special committee for reviewing the legal education and experience of nominees for federal judgeships. The Association's assessment of a candidate, particularly if it is negative, can affect that person's chances of winning Senate approval. The Reagan administration criticized the ABA's panel as too liberal to give conservative Republican nominees a fair evaluation, but the association continues to play this professional screening role in the nomination process.

Judicial appointments represent a president's best opportunity to affect the course of constitutional interpretation and judicial review, and they have clearly tried to shape the Supreme Court and lower courts through their appointments. For example, Ronald Reagan used his appointments to place conservatives such as Antonin Scalia on the High Court and make William Rehnquist the chief justice.

In recent years, presidential attempts to shape the Supreme Court have been met with considerable resistance from those opposed to the views of nominees to the High Court. President Reagan was unable to win support for Judge Robert Bork, a controversial conservative legal scholar, after a heated battle pitted Bork against those who asserted that his constitutional views fell outside the mainstream of legal thought. When George Bush nominated Clarence Thomas to serve as an associate justice on the High Court, there was an even more intense battle over the Senate's decision. Thomas faced charges of sexual harassment from his former aide, Professor Anita Hill, in several days of televised hearings. Thomas was ultimately confirmed by the Senate, although the veracity of Professor Hill's charges was never substantiated or disproven.

In the wake of these battles, President Clinton moved carefully when presented with opportunities to nominate candidates for the High Court. He gave considerable thought to how his first Supreme Court appointment would affect

Appointments to the Supreme Court have become increasingly political. Clarence Thomas, nominated by President George Bush, faced an intense battle to gain Senate confirmation, including charges of sexual harassment made by his former aide, law professor Anita Hill, during several days of televised hearings.

the balance between liberals and conservatives among the Justices. He ultimately chose Judge Ruth Bader Ginsburg because she had a reputation as a consensus builder and agreed with the president's pro-choice position on abortion. When he had a second opportunity, Clinton chose Stephen Breyer—a federal judge and legal scholar—to replace retiring Justice Harry Blackmun. Breyer's reputation as a judicial moderate and his experience as an aide in the U.S. Senate made his confirmation for the post relatively easy.

Not all chief executives have been successful in finding nominees who suited their purposes. President Eisenhower once commented that his biggest mistake in office was nominating Earl Warren for chief justice, because he fiercely disagreed with Warren's judicial activism.

Political Consequences of Judicial Review

Although it is not explicitly authorized in the Constitution, the framers anticipated that the courts would exercise judicial review. The authors of *The Federalist,* No. 78 declared that constitutional government would not survive without "courts of justice, whose duty it must be to declare all acts contrary to the manifest tenor of the Constitution void." This means that the "constitution of open texture"—the many places where the document is vague, ambiguous, or even silent—leaves considerable room for the judiciary to decide whether the actions of government are consistent with the national charter. As we have seen throughout this text, court interpretations of the Constitution have been important to the development of the American regime. Cases such as *Marbury v. Madison, McCulloch v. Maryland, Brown v. Board of Education,* and *Gideon v. Wainwright* have profoundly shaped the operations of the political system, the rights of individuals, and relations between citizens and their government.

Judicial review is the means of constitutional interpretation that has the greatest air of final authority. Through it, courts in America have achieved a political power that is rarely equalled by the judiciary in other nations. This fact has several political consequences.

The Search for Judicial Remedies. In the United States, many issues are brought to court that would be resolved by political means in other societies. For example, disputes over the structure and power of government are constitutional questions that might be settled in cases such as *Marbury v. Madison* or *U.S. v. Nixon* (the case that tested whether the president had to turn over to a federal court secret tapes made in the Oval Office). As we saw in Chapter 3, elected officials have even come to rely on court rulings of constitutionality rather than take a stand on issues themselves. Ronald Reagan and many members of Congress found it politically expedient to support the Balanced Budget Amendment of 1985 despite serious constitutional questions, and "let the Supreme Court settle it."

The Importance of Statutory Judicial Review. Often overlooked in discussions of judicial power is the courts' power of *statutory judicial review.*[13]

Judges are frequently called upon to determine whether government agencies have acted in accordance with statutes (laws) passed by Congress. But statutory review is not always simple. Congress often passes general laws that may contain many potentially contradictory provisions. For example, laws governing interstate highways require the Department of Transportation and state highway officials to simultaneously protect parks, neighborhoods, jobs, the environment, and economic efficiency. Many laws passed in recent years have also created new "rights," whether to clean air, clean water, or public safety. Finally, Congress has delegated large amounts of rule-making power to executive agencies and regulatory commissions—to control broadcasting, pollution, stock and bond trading, consumer safety, and working conditions. All of these actions by the legislature have the result of giving administrators broad responsibilities and power for making substantive decisions that affect the lives and property of citizens and communities. Nearly any decision that administrators make to implement vaguely worded legislation, such as where to place a highway or whether to allow economic development in an environmentally sensitive area, can be challenged as violating the law. Almost inevitably, such disputes end up in court, and judges must interpret the laws in question. Courts thus become the arbiters of how well statutory mandates are being carried out.

Using Courts as Instruments of Political Change

Because federal courts are institutionally independent and possess at least the potential for political power, they have often been used to stimulate or prevent political change. When the courts respond affirmatively to these invitations—when they engage in *judicial activism*—they become policy makers. There have been two major periods in national history when individuals and groups have sought to use the courts as political instruments.

The Era of Substantive Due Process. The first period came during the last decades of the nineteenth century and the first half of the twentieth, in the wake of changes in the American economy brought on by the Industrial Revolution. In response to the development of large-scale corporations and manufacturing industries, states and the federal government began regulating business mergers, labor conditions and collective bargaining, wages, health standards, and other aspects of urban industrial society. Opponents of such regulations, usually in business, found support from an activist Supreme Court that used its power of judicial review to reject such developments as child labor laws, income taxes, maximum work-hour provisions, and labor unions.

These disputes came to a climax when key elements of President Franklin Roosevelt's New Deal were held unconstitutional by the Supreme Court under a legal concept developed to nullify most governmental regulation of business. That idea was known as "substantive due process," and it asserted that the government could not interfere with most private business decisions. Frustrated by several defeats in court, the president in 1937 proposed that the Supreme Court be expanded to allow the chief executive to appoint new justices to balance any of those over age 70. Although Roosevelt's "court-packing" scheme was roundly condemned even by his political allies, the Supreme Court got the message and acquiesced in future New Deal programs. This about-face became known as "the switch in time that saved nine." Substantive due process was abandoned.

Chief Justice Earl Warren's tenure was marked by judicial activism. In the 1950s and 1960s the Court was a source of political change in the areas of school desegregation, reform of the criminal justice system, and the availability of birth control and abortion services to working-class women.

The Modern Era of Judicial Activism. The second period began in the 1950s and 1960s, when Chief Justice Earl Warren led the High Court. With the rise of the new litigation, the Supreme Court became a permanent policy maker in the federal government. Judicial action was the primary source of political change in five major areas of policy: school desegregation, reapportionment of representative districts, reform of the criminal justice system, virtual elimination of federal and state obscenity laws, and opening birth control and abortion services to millions of working-class women and girls.[14]

When Chief Justice Warren retired in 1969, many opponents of judicial activism called for the Supreme Court to refrain from further policy making. Despite such hopes, judicial activism continued in the era of the more conservative Burger and Rehnquist Courts. Continuing to accept class action suits and other elements of the new litigation, the Supreme Court has only changed the direction and substance of its policy making. One careful observer characterizes the Court under these Republican chiefs as employing "a roving, ad hoc, balancing-doctrine activism."[15] In other words, the Supreme Court continues to engage in judicial activism, but of a different sort than that practiced in the years of the Warren Court. There is still a substantial amount of litigation that seeks judicial decisions as instruments of political change.

Responses to Judicial Activism. The controversial court decisions handed down in recent years have stimulated intense reactions. Court-ordered school busing, liberalization of abortion, and other decisions have been met with political action and even violence. For example, in 1957 Governor Orville Faubus of Arkansas attempted to stop desegregation of his state's public schools, a result of the *Brown* decision, by calling out the state militia. President Dwight Eisenhower, while personally disagreeing with the Supreme Court's decision, felt obliged to overrule the governor and used his authority to enforce the ruling. A popular bumper sticker in the Deep South during the 1960s read "Impeach Earl Warren," because of his activist rulings on desegregation, criminal justice, and other issues. In the 1970s, angry parents in South Boston opposed school busing of their children with demonstrations that turned violent. Supporters of judicial activism have argued that such developments are regrettable, but that the changes brought about in equal opportunity and other areas outweigh the negative costs involved. Opponents of activism warn that the courts risk social instability by ordering changes that the political system has not yet accepted.

Limits on Judicial Power

As the preceding discussion makes clear, the federal judiciary is certainly a powerful branch of government. Are there limits to its power? Yes—some are self-imposed and others are imposed by the elected branches of government.

Self-Imposed Limits on the Judiciary. By their nature, courts are passive institutions. In sharp contrast to the president—who can take actions such as making a speech, drafting a legislative proposal, dispatching emissaries abroad, or ordering American forces into battle—or to the Congress—which can pass laws and resolutions—the judiciary must await cases that come to it. It cannot initiate cases or make rulings on hypothetical questions, although at times the Supreme Court has indicated in its opinions that it is interested in seeing certain kinds of cases brought to it. Being limited to actual cases, the judiciary lacks the power of initiative that is essential to the workings of the other branches of government.

Even bringing a case to court does not guarantee that the judiciary will rule on it. A long-standing doctrine in American law is that some issues are beyond judicial resolution because they are **political questions**—matters that must be resolved in the give-and-take of the political process. Issues such as what should be the foreign policy of the United States, how high taxes ought to be, or how many years Congress will allow states to consider a proposed constitutional amendment before declaring it extinct have all been held as outside the province of the judiciary. One area in which the courts have been reluctant to tread has been foreign policy. In 1990 several members of Congress tried to prevent President Bush from launching a war against Iraq without congressional authorization by seeking help in federal court. But the judge refused to rule, on the grounds that nothing had yet happened, saying in effect that war is a political question.

External Limits on the Courts. The other two branches of government have formal and informal means by which they can potentially limit judicial power. Through nominations to the Supreme Court and lower courts, presidents attempt to shape judicial decisions by the individuals who sit on the bench. Congress also has the power to control the appellate jurisdiction of the Supreme Court, although that power is seldom used. As we saw in the example of President Franklin Roosevelt's court-packing plan, the size of the High Court is fixed by law, not the Constitution. Roosevelt's proposal to enlarge the Supreme Court, although controversial, put sufficient pressure on the justices to affect their decisions.

The White House also uses the solicitor general to try to influence the Supreme Court. If the federal government is a party to a case and loses in the court of appeals, the solicitor general (under presidential direction) decides whether the case will be appealed to the Supreme Court. In 1994, the U.S. Navy was ordered by a federal appeals court to reinstate to active duty a sailor who

political questions
Matters such as the appropriate rate of taxation that the courts consider beyond judicial resolution. Must be settled through the give-and-take of the political process.

had been discharged because he was gay. The Clinton administration, which favored allowing gays and lesbians to serve in the armed forces, chose not to appeal that decision. The effect of the solicitor general's refusal to appeal was to confirm the appeals court decision. The solicitor general, like interested citizens and interest groups, also attempts to influence Supreme Court rulings by filing *amicus curiae* briefs.

An Assessment of Judicial Power

The power of the judiciary is broad, but not unlimited. Perhaps that is why the Supreme Court has been most likely to render activist decisions in cases affecting citizen rights and liberties—in which the government has an interest, but not always a direct role—rather than take on the White House and Capitol Hill directly as it might if the Court attempted to rule on matters of foreign policy.

The influential role of courts in the American regime means that law, the Constitution, and rights remain central in discussions about and the conduct of national politics. As we saw in Chapters 3 and 4, the American political system has not developed only on the basis of the give-and-take of partisan politics, but with substantial involvement by the courts in defining citizen rights, refereeing disputes between the political branches, and insisting on at least the facade of constitutional justification for government acts. The result is that our politics is driven more by these kinds of issues than that of any other society. Whether that is for better or worse is a different question. No matter what judicial philosophy holds sway, or whether it is the old or new litigation at issue, the American judiciary remains an important and powerful element of the political system.

open questions

What Role Should Ideology Play in the Selection of Supreme Court Justices?

It is clear from the preceding discussion that a number of important issues surround the role of the judiciary in the American regime. In Chapter 3, we examined the issues of judicial activism, judicial restraint, and attempts to chart an alternative course. That subject remains significant. But another issue has arisen in recent years that strikes at the very structure of the judiciary and the method for selecting federal judges.

In the Bush and Reagan administrations, critics of the White House's choices for judicial nominees (at all levels) charged that these presidents were using individuals' views on specific issues to select candidates for various judgeships. This idea that potential nominees would be acceptable or unacceptable on the basis of their views on a single question has been termed a "litmus test" by commentators. The term suggests that nothing else matters—not a candidate's education, experience, or intellect—only a nominee's position on one issue the administration considers paramount. The most important such test had to do with abortion. Many Democrats and some Republicans maintained that Reagan and Bush preferred mediocre but pro-life judges to those of higher ability with the opposing view on abortion.

When Bill Clinton ran for the presidency in 1992, he said in effect that as president he would apply a reverse litmus test and nominate for judgeships only those with clear pro-choice sentiments to balance years of Republican appointments. Some of Clinton's Democratic colleagues praised his conviction; others condemned it as no better than the Reagan-Bush approach to the judiciary.

Should a president employ litmus tests when selecting judicial nominees? The issue could affect how the chief executive chooses candidates and what kinds of questions administration screeners will ask them. Two of Yale University's law faculty disagree on the subject. Stephen L. Carter argues that

> It is impossible to seek "balance" except by naming individuals whose votes are predictable. But appointing Justices who make up their minds before, not after, hearing arguments threatens judicial integrity and interferes with the Court's proper functioning. It was wrong for the Republicans to do it; it would be wrong if the Democrats do it.[16]

Carter further argues that treating judicial decisions as part of the spoils of electoral victory will diminish respect for the courts and for the Constitution.

In contrast, Paul Gewirtz maintains that "there is nothing improper about looking for nominees who hold certain general views about the Constitution or who embrace a constitutional right repeatedly recognized under settled law."[17] He argues that the judicial philosophy and legal views of a nominee are important because "they are relevant to how he or she will perform the job."[18] Moreover, Gewirtz sees the appointment process as one of the few "democratic controls" on an unelected and powerful judiciary. Given the infrequency of vacancies on the High Court, he concludes that even litmus tests are appropriate to selecting Supreme Court justices.

There will be more vacancies on the Supreme Court and more presidents who want to influence its decisions. Is it interference or democratic control if a president uses litmus tests in selecting nominees? The issue remains open for further consideration.

‖ Summary

The main role of courts in the United States is to enforce the rule of law. Law is important to the conduct of American political and social life. It comes from four main sources: *common law* (judge-made law based on precedents dating back as far as the Middle Ages), *statutory law* (made by legislative bodies), *administrative law,* and *constitutional law.* There are two main subject areas of law: *criminal law* and *civil law.*

The United States has a dual court system: state courts, established under the authority of each state's government, and a federal court system established by Congress. All courts in the United States are subject to review by the U.S. Supreme Court.

Principles. American courts are created to advance the principles of justice and rule of law. To do this, the United States has an *independent judiciary* that has authority under the Constitution to exercise judicial review. The courts rely on precedents when deciding cases. In criminal law, American courts presume the innocence of those accused of crimes.

Process. An elaborate body of procedures has been developed to guarantee justice and the rule of law in cases that come before courts. Civil and criminal cases each follow their own procedures. At the pinnacle of the court system is the Supreme Court, which has its own deliberative process for deciding which cases it will review and how it will rule in those cases.

Politics. While insulated from the elected branches of government, the judiciary is not immune to politics. Politics affects the selection of judges, and presidents often attempt to shape the judiciary through their court appointments. Judicial review, which the courts exercise as part of the checks and balances system, makes the judiciary a politically powerful part of the government. The courts' use of this power to shape policy is known as *judicial activism.* Judicial activism remains very controversial. There are also limits on judicial power, such as the self-imposed doctrine of *political questions* and the power of the other branches of government.

Open Questions. What role should ideology play in the selection of candidates for the federal judiciary? Some observers—including President Clinton—have maintained that it is legitimate for chief executives to inquire into potential judges' views on specific issues that may come before the courts (such as abortion) and in deciding who the president will nominate for a federal judgeship (especially a seat on the Supreme Court). Critics argue that this use of ideology improperly alters the relationship between the courts and the elected branches of government.

Suggested Readings

ABRAHAM, HENRY. *Justices and Presidents,* 2nd ed. New York: Oxford University Press, 1985. Fascinating stories of the appointments of Supreme Court justices by presidents.

———. *The Judicial Process,* 5th ed. New York: Oxford University Press, 1986. Excellent one-volume overview of judicial processes in the United States and other Western countries.

CONGRESSIONAL QUARTERLY. *The Supreme Court at Work.* Washington: Author, 1990. Clear and well-organized overview of the history, powers, organization, operations, and decisions of the Supreme Court.

IRONS, PETER, WITH STEPHANIE GUITTON. *May It Please the Court.* New York: New Press, 1993. Transcripts of the oral arguments in 23 of the most significant cases before the Supreme Court since 1955. Accompanied by audiotapes of the arguments.

O'BRIEN, DAVID. *Storm Center: The Supreme Court in American Politics.* New York: W.W. Norton, 1990. Readable history of the Supreme Court and its place in American life.

POSNER, RICHARD A. *The Federal Courts.* Cambridge, Mass.: Harvard University Press, 1985. Interesting and useful discussion of the operations of contemporary federal courts by a sitting federal judge and legal scholar.

WOODWARD, BOB, AND SCOTT ARMSTRONG. *The Brethren: Inside the Supreme Court.* New York: Simon & Schuster, 1979. Readable account of the inner workings of the Supreme Court 1969–1975.

Unelected Representatives

chapter 12

A mericans who are not in church or in bed on Sunday mornings find the television schedule full of political talk shows. One of the most popular is ABC's "This Week," which provides a snapshot of contemporary Washington in more ways than just the information exchanged. Its host is David Brinkley, a veteran journalist who began as a newspaper reporter and was one of the pioneers of television news ("The Huntley-Brinkley Report"). A regular questioner is George Will, an academic political scientist turned U.S. Senate aide and ultimately a journalist. But the guests are also part of the picture: a senator, the secretary of state, the White House chief of staff, or the president's national security adviser.

No matter the precise mix of people, the show gives its viewers a look at who is important in American politics today. The traditional actors are there—the elected officials and cabinet officers. But so are a group of powerful unelected players in the game of American politics, the news media and the staffs of government officials. In contemporary politics, those who assist high officials and those who report on them have become "movers and shakers" in Washington, too. Citizens should be aware that their government is now influenced by these "unelected representatives." One way to note their importance is to consider that both staffs and media have been called "the shadow government." Not only do they shape the environment in which presidents, members of Congress, and other political leaders operate, but they frequently interact with one another to make the news that citizens receive about American government.

Government Officials' Staffs

American government officials have always had assistants, but for most of our national history, they were few in number. George Washington employed one private secretary, and his successors generally had to make do with little more in the way of staff help. Indeed, it was not uncommon for chief executives to enlist family members to assist them in clerical and administrative aspects of their job. Congressional committees generally employed only part-time assistants through most of the nineteenth century. At the turn of the century, there were only slightly more than one hundred full-time assistants working for committees. Supreme Court justices did not begin hiring law clerks until 1882. All this changed in the twentieth century.

The twentieth century has been marked by **stafflation**—a swift and significant growth in the size of officials' staffs. Although it came at different times for each branch, stafflation marks the institutions of national government in modern times. But why did it occur? Senator Daniel Patrick Moynihan (D.-N.Y.) explains the phenomenon by what he calls the "Iron Law of Emulation." A former professor and a student of governing, Moynihan observed: "Whenever any branch of government acquires a new technique which enhances its power in relation to the other branches, that technique will soon be adopted by those other branches as well."[1] When the "swelling of the presidency" made possible aggressive presidential policy making in the 1930s and 1940s and then again in the 1960s and 1970s, Congress responded by enlarging its staff. For example, in the 1970s Congress found itself at a disadvantage in budget making because the

stafflation Rapid growth in the size, complexity, and power of the staffs of high government officials in recent decades.

Office of Management and Budget (OMB) within the executive branch possessed greater information and expertise than the legislature. So Capitol Hill responded by creating its own Congressional Budget Office. Each of the three branches, plus the officials at the top of the bureaucracy, possesses a large staff.

Presidential Staffs. The president's staff was the first to grow appreciably. As a result of the expansion of presidential power in the New Deal, Franklin Roosevelt found himself drowning in the work of his office and pleaded for help. In 1939 Congress authorized more staff and created the Executive Office of the President (EOP) to house it. FDR hired six assistants to the president and brought under his control the Bureau of the Budget (now known as the OMB), which until that time had been a division of the Treasury Department. Successive chief executives added to that staff.

It is difficult to gauge the exact size of the president's staff today.[2] Chief executives have jealously guarded information about the number of people working for them, their precise duties, and the organization of various EOP units. The vast majority of EOP employees are not subject to Senate confirmation and answer only to the president. Moreover, for decades the White House has "borrowed" personnel from various departments and agencies. This practice not only allows the chief executive to enlarge the EOP without spending more money, but also to shield the actual size and cost of the staff from Congress and the public. In addition, several subdivisions of the White House use volunteers to help with a variety of social and political activities. Most estimates put the total workforce of the EOP at around 1,700 people. But one estimate by a former staffer that includes volunteers, Secret Service agents, and military personnel puts the number at over 3,800.[3] Official figures put the budget for this staff near $100 million; one public interest group puts the estimate at over $180 million.[4]

Congressional Staffs. Congressional staffs began growing after World War II. Legislation passed in 1946 began to allow for larger personal and committee staffs. Then in 1970 the Legislative Reorganization Act paved the way for real stafflation. It increased the number of staff members each committee could hire, provided staff support for the minority party as well as the majority, authorized use of consultants, provided for larger personal staffs, and increased the size and number of congressional support agencies. By the 1990s, the number of committee staffers rose to over 3,300, personal staffs to a strength of over 11,000, and the grand total of all employees of Congress to around 31,000 people.[5] The budget for operating the legislative branch is now close to $2 billion. As part of the reforms promised by the Republican majority that assumed power on Capitol Hill in 1995, committee staffs were cut by about one-third. In the Current Issues box, "Has the Tide Turned for Stafflation?," we explore the question of whether these and other staff cuts herald a new trend in Washington.

Judicial Staffs. The judiciary cannot match the other branches in sheer numbers, but its reliance on staffs has likewise grown. Supreme Court justices each had a single law clerk beginning in the late nineteenth century; in 1947 each

Has the Tide Turned for Stafflation?

The size of officials' staffs has been a controversial issue for many years. In the 1970s, critics charged that a large White House staff contributed to the "imperial presidency" they saw under Presidents Johnson and Nixon. More recently, Republicans attacked large congressional staffs as part of the foundation of the "Imperial Congress" they overthrew in the 1994 election. Downsizing staffs has become a standard part of the reformer's creed, but does it mean an end to stafflation?

When President Carter was campaigning for office in 1976, he promised to substantially cut the size of the White House staff. Once elected, he did so only by redefining a large number of Executive Office administrative personnel as working outside the White House. He created a separate Office of Administration that was not a part of the White House Office, and he actually increased his own political staff. Likewise, in 1992 Bill Clinton promised a major cut in the president's staff. Early in his presidency he proclaimed a 25 percent cut in staff. On closer examination, however, the reduction was revealed to be much smaller than advertised. The 25 percent cut was calculated by excluding two of the largest Executive Office units: the Office of Management and Budget and the Office of Trade Representative. Most of the actual reductions in staff were achieved by firing nonpolitical employees such as drivers and mail clerks. The actual number of political aides declined only slightly, and some outside analysts estimate that the budget for Clinton's Executive Office actually increased in his first year in office.

The Republican majority that took control of Congress after the 1994 election promised to cut committee staffs by one-third. Cuts were achieved, and they were substantial; these cuts, however, affected only a small portion of congressional staffs. Even before the cuts, committee staffs constituted only about one-fifth of all House staffs and one-sixth of all Senate staffs. There are still over twelve thousand staffers working for individual members of Congress and congressional leaders, plus thousands more in units that serve the Congress as a whole (for example, in the Capitol Police and the General Accounting Office). The total congressional staff workforce is still well above twenty thousand people.

was given a second, then a third in 1970 and a fourth in 1978. Appellate court judges began hiring clerks in the 1930s and were given a second in 1970 and a third in 1980. District judges began hiring clerks in the 1940s, and in 1965 each was given a second. Since the 1970s the courts of appeal have also hired staff attorneys—clerks who work for the whole court rather than a single judge. Since 1960 the number of clerks employed by the courts has doubled for the Supreme Court and the district courts and quadrupled for the courts of appeal.[6] These aides perform research, analyze cases, and draft opinions for the judges under whom they work.

Other Staffs. The increase in staffs has occurred throughout the federal government. Each cabinet secretary has an Office of the Secretary or some other similarly named organization in the department's hierarchy that includes administrative assistants, speechwriters, schedule keepers, and other staffers. Likewise, agency directors have staffs to assist them. In fact, officials' dependence on staffs has become legendary in contemporary Washington. For example, when William Ruckelshaus, a senior official in several Republican administrations, returned to private industry after leaving government in the 1980s, he often called his old staff to brag about how he was actually able to travel from one city to another by airplane without assistants to tell him where to go. Not so

Washington officials have come to rely more and more on their staffs, which may include administrative assistants, research assistants, schedule keepers, and speechwriters. Here, a staff assistant briefs Senator Orin Hatch during a Judiciary Committee meeting.

fortunate was Charles Schulze, who had been director of the Office of Management and Budget in the Johnson administration. After leaving the government, he travelled to Philadelphia to give a speech at a conference; without his former staff to take care of him, Schulze found himself stranded in the city without a clue as to where the conference was being held or even whom he should call for information. Officials rely on their aides for a variety of services.

The News Media

Politicians and citizens have long recognized the importance of journalists to politics. Even in the days before radio and television, reporters were sometimes called the fourth branch of government. The news media not only reported the events of politics, but also commented on them and helped to focus public attention on political developments of the day. During the period of the American founding, newspapers served as vehicles for much of the debate over the Constitution; during the period before the Civil War, abolitionist papers helped to keep the issue of slavery before the eyes of the northern public. Later, newspapers brought stories of American involvement in the Spanish-American War and World War I.

The rise of mass communication—specifically radio and television—made the news media and journalists an even more immediate presence in the lives of Americans. Radio reporters Lowell Thompson and Edward R. Murrow became not only the reporters of events abroad, but celebrities themselves.

Murrow achieved fame broadcasting from war-torn London in the days of German bombing before the United States entered World War II; later, he would be a pioneer in television news. Walter Cronkite of CBS News, a protege of Murrow, became one of the most trusted men in the nation and was even mentioned as a possible presidential candidate. When he broadcast a documentary critical of the Johnson administration's conduct of the Vietnam War in 1967, he helped sway public opinion against that conflict.

Clearly, journalists are not just neutral intermediaries of political news. Rather, they serve as unelected representatives of the public who question public officials and investigate the actions of politicians and the government.

The Structure of the Media

The media can be divided into two major categories according to the means for their distribution of information: print media and electronic media. The *print media* are marked by tremendous diversity. There are thousands of newspapers around the country, many linked to major newspaper chains (Knight-Ridder, Gannett, Hearst), and some independent. At least three major newspapers are distributed nationally: the *New York Times, Wall Street Journal,* and *USA Today.* Most newspapers receive their national news from wire services (the Associated Press, the *New York Times* wire service, the chains). In addition, there are newsmagazines that are weekly variations on the daily papers; *Newsweek, Time,* and *Insight* are among the most common. There is not much diversity in the coverage of news here, because these publications rely on the same sources, and their national (that is, Washington and New York) reporters travel in the same "pack." Among policy makers and opinion leaders in Washington and New York, the *New York Times* and *Washington Post* are very influential, although the Republican majority that took control of Congress in 1994 favors the more conservative *Washington Times* and *Wall Street Journal.* Most of the differences in these publications are seen on their editorial pages.

Variety can be found in the more specialized publications available in the United States: newsmagazines for those who want intensive coverage of Washington politics and policy (*National Journal*) or of Congress (*Congressional Quarterly Weekly Report*); ethnic (*Ebony*), regional (*Texas Monthly, New York*), and special interest newspapers and magazines that appeal to more limited audiences. Then there are the journals of opinion, magazines that focus on analyzing politics and society from a particular perspective; they range from conservative (*National Review, The American Spectator*), to neoconservative (*Commentary, The Public Interest, The National Interest*), to moderately liberal (*The New Republic*), to more explicitly liberal (*The Nation, Atlantic Monthly, The Progressive*). Journals of opinion have more limited circulation than general-interest magazines but are influential because they are avidly read by opinion leaders around the nation and in Washington.

The *electronic media* are less diverse but reach more citizens. Despite the wide array of print media, Americans get most of their news from television (see Figure 12.1). Not only do nearly two-thirds of Americans rely on television as their primary source of information about politics, but research reveals that a majority of citizens regard television as the most reliable source of news.[7] Television news is reported by the "big three" commercial networks (CBS, NBC, ABC), which long dominated news broadcasting, plus three relative newcomers (Public Broadcasting Service/PBS, Cable News Network/CNN, and Cable-Satellite Public Access Network/C-SPAN). C-SPAN broadcasts political events with little or no editing; the other television news sources provide so-called "objective" reporting that puts a premium on summarizing major facts and providing "both sides" of most controversies.

There is somewhat greater variety on radio. With the advent of television, radio news moved toward the production of brief headline services, often on an hourly basis. In recent years, however, two new kinds of news radio have developed. One is public radio (National Public Radio/NPR, American Public Radio/APR), which features in-depth coverage akin to television's morning and evening news programs (NPR produces "Morning Edition" and "All Things Considered"; APR distributes "Monitor Radio," "Fresh Air," and other shows). The other is "talk radio," which usually features a host responding to callers and/or commenting on the events of the day. Most of these are limited to one station, although some, for example, the conservative "Rush Limbaugh Show," have a national audience.

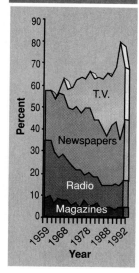

FIGURE 12.1 The Sources of Our News.

The Media's Roles in American Politics

The press plays several important roles in politics. Taken together, these roles give the news media a central role in the operations of American politics.

Information Gathering and Distribution. For a substantial part of human history, people knew only what occurred in their own small corner of the world. They might hear stories of wars and other great events that happened far away, but they knew little of politics in their country's capital or other important political developments away from home. The development of newspapers, and then radio and television, changed all that. The news is now within reach of everyone. The news media are the chief vehicle through which Americans learn about their government and politics.[8] The most basic function that journalists perform is to gather news and report it to the public. As we shall see when we discuss the media at work, the ways in which reporters obtain information affect what we receive as news.

Gatekeeper. Journalists do not report everything they learn. There is not enough time or space to do so, nor are all stories equally newsworthy. The constraints of journalism (the front page is only so big; there are only 22 minutes in which to tell the evening news) demand that journalists be selective; they act as gatekeepers deciding which stories will receive coverage and which will not. Because journalists on the major political "beats"—the White House, Capitol Hill, the Supreme Court—receive their information from the same sources and spend large amounts of time together, they tend to report on the same things.

Sandy Gilmore of NBC and other television news reporters who cover the White House are a primary source of information about politics and political events for the American public.

This results in what is known as "pack" journalism; news organizations tend to follow, and to miss, the same stories. The top two or three stories on the evening news on any given day are likely to be roughly the same.

Scorekeeper. News reports routinely follow stories of votes in Congress by the conclusions that "this represents a victory for the president" or a "setback for the administration." A new abortion decision from the Supreme Court is described as a "victory" or a "defeat" for pro-choice or pro-life forces. One of the most pervasive forms of scorekeeping comes during presidential elections, when reporters tend to concentrate on what are generally called the "horse race" aspects of the campaign: who is ahead in the polls, who is behind in the delegate count, who has more money, and so on. Much of the reporting on presidential primaries tends to focus on whether candidates performed "better than expected," "as expected," or "worse than expected." This kind of coverage is intended to simplify political developments for the audience, although it tends to inaccurately portray politics to be much like sports.

Watchdog. Tom Wicker of the *New York Times* once explained that journalists regard freedom of the press as imposing on them a "constitutional obligation to act as a check on government."[9] This means that reporters see it as their responsibility to seek out and expose corruption, abuses of power, and personal indiscretions by government agencies, officials, and the powerful in society. Watchdog journalism can be seen in investigations of everything from bureaucratic waste to influence peddling by officials to the private behavior of political candidates. In the 1988 presidential election, reporters from the *Miami Herald* engaged in surveillance of the Washington home of Senator Gary Hart

(D.-Colo.), then the leading candidate for the Democratic nomination. Their videotape of his entering and leaving the house with a woman who was not his wife, combined with other evidence of marital infidelity, led to Hart's withdrawal from the race. In 1992, reporters investigated charges of infidelity against Bill Clinton and also allegations that he had used influence and deception to avoid military service during the Vietnam War. Clinton put the infidelity charges to rest during an interview with his wife on CBS's "Sixty Minutes," but he was dogged by the draft-evasion charges for the rest of the campaign.

Government Regulation of the Media

The First Amendment offers protection to all journalists, although not in equal amounts. The print media are largely unregulated in the United States, because the possible number of outlets for publication is virtually unlimited. The Supreme Court has even protected publishers from government attempts to impose prior restraint (that is, injunctions against publishing a story) on information that is potentially damaging to national security.

In contrast, American law regards the electromagnetic spectrum (the "airwaves") as public property subject to government control "in the public interest." The controlling principle here is **spectrum scarcity,** the notion that only a finite number of electronic signals can fit in the spectrum without interfering with one another. Commercial radio and television share the airwaves with military communications, weather radar, police radio, citizens' band, and shortwave radio, each operating on a narrow segment of the airwaves.

Electronic broadcasting is regulated by the **Federal Communications Commission (FCC),** which is an independent regulatory commission created by Congress to license radio and television stations. Licenses are issued for a period of five years, and the FCC uses the threat of nonrenewal as its major sanction to ensure compliance with its rules. The FCC has licensed nearly ten thousand commercial radio and television stations to broadcast in the United States.

Rules Governing News Broadcasting. There is a substantial body of law governing the media generally and broadcasting specifically, but three FCC rules form the core of the regulatory environment in which broadcasters operate. The *personal attack rule* provides that if an attack is made on the integrity or other personal qualities of an individual during a report on controversial issues, the injured party must be provided an opportunity within a reasonable time to reply to the attack. Exceptions are made for foreign persons or groups, political candidates, and news coverage of political matters.[10] The *equal opportunities rule* provides that if a station allows use of its facilities (whether for free or for a fee) by a qualified candidate for public office, it must also provide equal opportunities to all other candidates for that office to do likewise (news coverage is excluded). The *reasonable access rule* provides that broadcasters must provide "reasonable access to . . . or permit purchase of reasonable amounts of time"[11] to qualified candidates for public office through sale of advertising time to

spectrum scarcity Fundamental assumption behind broadcast regulation that the amount of space on the airwaves is limited, and that the federal government must regulate broadcasters in the public interest.

Federal Communications Commission (FCC) Independent regulatory commission created by Congress to license and regulate radio and television stations.

candidates or by providing access for candidates by airing programs in which all candidates can participate on an equal basis.[12]

One additional rule is no longer in force, but it has shaped the way that television news covers many controversial issues. This rule was the *fairness doctrine,* which held that broadcasters had to devote a "reasonable percentage" of their air time to news and/or shows about public affairs and that they must "afford reasonable opportunity for the discussion of conflicting views on issues of public importance."[13] In practice, notes political scientist Austin Ranney, this rule led to a situation in which "broadcasters have satisfied the FCC by portraying political issues as conflicts between a pro side and an anti side and presenting the statements of at least one advocate for each side."[14] The FCC repealed the fairness doctrine in 1987 and Congress was unsuccessful in restoring it through legislation. The result has been that some broadcasters, especially non-network television stations or music-oriented radio stations, have dropped most of their news or public-affairs programming. But the ghost of the fairness doctrine continues to shape television reporting. As one scholar comments: "The view of political conflict that emerges from network news programs is that every issue has two, and only two, sides."[15]

The Special Case of War Reporting. One area in which government control affects both print and electronic media is wartime restrictions on reporting. During World War II, the 1983 invasion of Grenada, and the 1991 Persian Gulf War, the U.S. military imposed several limitations on journalists. One technique was the use of "pool reporting," in which military personnel escort a committee of reporters into combat areas and carefully control what information they and their colleagues receive about operations. Another technique was to require journalists to submit stories for clearance before they could be broadcast or published. Many journalists consider these practices censorship, but they have generally gone along with them because they fear total news blackouts of military operations.

When the United States is not at war, journalists chafe at any restrictions on their access to information. By and large, government officials provide information—either openly or in secret. All departments and agencies of the government have offices dedicated to dealing with the news media, and many practitioners of Washington politics have long experience in quietly releasing information to reporters.

Citizens in Action

CHAD PERGRAM GETS HIS BREAK IN WASHINGTON

Chad Pergram grew up in Jacksonville, the smallest incorporated city in Ohio. He always wanted to work in the radio business and had a clear, resonant voice suited to it. While in high school, he was an intern at a local radio station. Eventually, he became a part-time reporter. During and after college, he gained more experience, working in radio, television, and a local newspaper. In 1994, he went to Washington seeking a job in public affairs broadcasting and landed a position as a producer for C-SPAN, the public affairs cable service.

Principles: An Active Government Covered by a Free Press

Americans have long understood the tension between the need for a government that is effective and one that is accountable. In *The Federalist,* No. 51, Madison captured this problem nicely: "You must first enable the government to control the governed; and in the next place oblige it to control itself." He was discussing the matter of separation of powers, but his argument applies more broadly as well. The framers of the Constitution wanted a government that could be active in the life of the nation, but they expected a free press to be one of the means by which officials could be held accountable to citizens. To help advance these goals, two key principles have shaped government and the media over the course of American history—one gives autonomy to officials, the other to journalists.

Give Each Branch a Will of Its Own. As Madison indicated in *The Federalist,* No. 51, each branch of government needed "a will of its own." In other words, for Congress to be able to do its job well, it had to be able to make decisions as its members saw fit, not as they might be forced to do if the legislature were dependent on the executive. Likewise, the chief executive could not be effective if the president were a servant of Congress, nor could courts properly enforce the rule of law without a great degree of independence from elected officials.

This independence implied that each branch would have a fair amount of control over its internal affairs. Article I empowers each house of Congress to establish its own rules. As we saw in Chapter 8, the House of Representatives has tended to favor more restrictive rules, while the Senate has favored a looser set of rules. Congress has also established a large network of staffs to serve members and committees. Article II states that Congress may authorize the president, heads of departments, and courts to appoint "inferior Officers" without approval of the Senate; this provision allows executive officials and judges to hire staffs that can assist them in the performance of their duties. Thus were laid the foundations for the provision of staff to assist each of the branches of government. Staff support enables officials in each branch to act aggressively in the performance of their duties and even to take on greater responsibilities. Not surprisingly, officials' staffs have become part of the unwritten constitution.

A Free Press. While the nation's founders expected the checks-and-balances system to prevent runaway government, they believed that another way to promote government accountability was by guaranteeing freedom of the press. The First Amendment embodies this idea, making the United States the first political system to offer constitutional protection to the press. (In Britain press freedom is a venerable tradition, but easily modified—as it has been in the past—by an act of Parliament.) A free press has long been seen as one of the keys to preventing tyranny. In *Democracy in America,* Alexis de Tocqueville commented: "I approve of [press freedom] from a consideration more of the evils it prevents [that is, tyranny], than of the advantages it insures."[16] As columnist William Rusher put it, a free press makes it possible for "a free citizenry . . . to play an intelligent part in the political process."[17]

Of course, press freedom has not been interpreted as an absolute value. In Chapter 3, we saw how the media are restrained by legal prohibitions against libel and slander. Journalists cannot release information that they know is false or in "reckless disregard" of the truth. In addition, as we saw earlier in this chapter, the electronic media (radio and television) are subject to government regulation.

Because America has both a free press and branches of government that can hire and control their own staffs, Washington politics involves far more people than just the officeholders who occupy the central positions of the federal government. In our time, politics in the nation's capital usually involves the participation of staffs and an array of journalists who often work together to shape the news. Indeed, *New York Times* writer Michael Kelly sees officials' staffs and the Washington reporters who cover them as part of one big community that he calls the "Insiders."[18] Insiders participate in a political process that emphasizes image and has its own language for describing the events of politics and media coverage. According to Kelly, this is how Insiders would describe the passage of a day:

> The day is composed, not of hours or minutes, but of *news cycles.* In each cycle, *senior White House officials* speaking *on background* define *the line of the day.* The line is echoed and amplified *outside the Beltway* to *real people,* who live *out there....* During the *roll-out* of a new policy, the President, coached by his *handlers* and working from *talking points* and *briefing books* churned out by *war room* aides, may permit his own head to talk. There are various ways in which he might do this, ranging from the simplest *photo op* to a *one on one* with a media *big-foot,* to the more elaborately orchestrated *media hit* . . . to the full-fledged spectacle of a *town hall....* Reaction to the line is an important part of the cycle, and it comes primarily from Congressional leaders of both parties . . . whose staff-written utterances are often delivered directly to *media outlets* via *fax attacks.* The result of all this activity . . . is cut into tiny, easily digestible *sound bites* and fed to already overstuffed *pundits,* who deliver the ultimate product of the entire process, a new piece of the *conventional wisdom.*[19]

Kelly's description of the Insiders and their jargon gives us an exaggerated picture of Washington politics. All the terms and expressions used in the Insider's day come right out of the shoptalk of Washington, but few journalists or staffers see politics as a game in quite the way suggested by Kelly's description. Nevertheless, his exaggerated picture does tell a story about how the media work, how staffs operate in contemporary government, and how the two often work together.

Making Policy, Shaping News: Staffs at Work

In previous chapters on Congress, the presidency, and the courts, we looked at the structure of the staff in each branch of government. We noted that each branch has come to regard its staff as indispensable to survival in contemporary politics. Why is that so?

Staffs Extend the Reach of Officials. In the twentieth century, the presidency, Congress, and the courts all experienced a tremendous increase in their workloads. Faced with growing responsibilities and a finite amount of time, officials came to rely on staff to do the extra work. Large staffs provide officials with an *extended reach.* Members of Congress and presidents can follow more

Like most public officials, Bob Kerrey was constantly surrounded in his 1992 primary campaign by the media.

issues, undertake policy initiatives in more areas, deal with more people and groups, and generally wring more work per hour out of each day when they are assisted by staffers. Staffs do research and detail work for their bosses and provide technical expertise to supplement an official's generalist knowledge or lack of information. Nearly all elected officials must spend time working on the next election, so staffs help to make up for the time lost in that way.

Harry McPherson, a former aide to President Johnson, points out another function that staffs perform for their bosses: *They maintain communication with an array of sources of political and technical knowledge.* He raises the question of "How does [the president] find out what's going on in the country?" His answer is "That's why he has a staff . . . who have big ears and listen and meet with people all the time and will send him memoranda and will talk to him on the phone and tell him what they think is going on."[20] Although his comments are specific to the presidency, McPherson also helps to explain why members of Congress rely on their staffs. Large staffs multiply the number of eyes and ears that can be alert for useful information.

Influencing Policy. Staffs are not just neutral forces in government. They affect the decisions that officials make. Staffers often bring issues to the attention of their bosses; they provide information that decision makers will need; and they move the decision-making process along smoothly. For example, Paul Light was a senior member of the staff of the Senate Government Affairs Committee in 1987 and 1988, when Congress considered and ultimately passed a bill to elevate the Veterans Administration to the status of a cabinet department. Working for the committee's chair, Senator John Glenn (D.-Ohio), Light performed

13 different tasks just to ensure that the committee's hearings on the bill went smoothly and produced the result that Senator Glenn wanted. He compared his role in organizing the hearings to that of a director staging a Broadway play: He found a "cast" (witnesses for the hearing); drafted opening remarks for the chair; rehearsed many of the witnesses on their presentations; helped orchestrate press coverage; prepared questions for Senator Glenn (and follow-up questions for difficult answers); briefed other senators' staffs on the hearing; assembled a "script" containing all testimony, speeches, and other information; briefed the committee chair; rehearsed witnesses again; sat in on the hearing; reviewed press coverage; corrected transcripts of the hearing; and edited the final copy of the printed record of the hearing.[21] Certainly, Light was working at the direction of his boss, but his work just as surely shaped the legislative decision-making process.

How Staffs Influence the News. Staffers are common sources of reporters' stories. Much of the information they provide to journalists is given *on background,* which means that reporters can use it but not identify the source. The widespread use of terms such as "sources close to the president," "senior administration officials," "a ranking Republican on the committee," or just "sources say" indicates that the information was received in this manner. Often, indeed usually, such terms indicate that a staffer was the source of news.

One special kind of background information is the **leak,** which refers to information that is released that someone in power would rather keep secret. Often, leaks are used to test potential reaction to policy proposals. On other occasions, information is leaked to kill plans in the works or embarrass someone. Some staffers give out leaks to improve their reputations among journalists.

One of the most important functions that staffs perform with regard to the media is in the practice of **spin control,** that is, attempts to shape how stories will be reported. One common way to engage in spin control is to provide reporters with carefully crafted press releases that make the writing of the news story easier and more to an official's liking. Spin control is also one of the most common commodities on political talk shows. For example, after Republicans introduced a balanced-budget constitutional amendment for debate in the 104th Congress, the White House dispatched Chief of Staff Leon Panetta to an interview on public television's "MacNeil-Lehrer News Hour" to provide the president's view on the issue.

Spin control is a common practice during campaigns, especially after candidate debates. In 1992, two Clinton aides followed a Bush-Clinton-Perot debate by entering the press room from opposite doors and racing together to give a "high five" before the assembled press corps. Their clear intent was to influence journalists' perception of who won the debate. Spin control also goes on between elections and is one of the most important responsibilities of officials' press secretaries. On the morning of the opening of the 104th Congress in January 1995, Tony Blankley, official spokesman for House Speaker Newt Gingrich (R.-Ga.), gave reporters his boss's version of the events of the day and the

leak Information released to the news media that a government official (or officials) wanted to keep secret.

spin control Attempts made by government officials, political candidates, or staffs to influence the way stories are reported by the news media.

significance of the new Republican majority in Congress. Blankley characterized the new Congress as "The Dawn of a New Era" in American politics.[22]

How We Get the News: The Media at Work

When Americans turn on the evening news, open the daily paper, or partake of any other form of the news media, they see only the final product of journalism. What lies beneath this surface is a three-step process for finding the news, deciding what to report, and disseminating the news to the public.

Finding the News. Where and how do journalists get their information? More often than not, they get it from government officials or their staffs. This practice is known as *source journalism*. One media critic notes that "The first fact of American journalism is its overwhelming dependence on sources, mostly official, usually powerful."[23] A study of 2,850 news stories that appeared in the *New York Times* and *Washington Post* between 1949 and 1969 revealed that nearly four out of five of these stories involved official sources. Journalists covering the national government get their information largely from daily briefings and by talking to officials and staff, whether on the record, on background, or through leaks.

A twist on source journalism is what might be called "interactive news." The press conference is a traditional form of such interaction, but recent years have seen the rise of political talk shows such as "This Week," "Face the Nation," "Nightline," "Larry King Live," and others. On these programs, sources appear face-to-face with reporters or take calls from viewers, making "news" as they talk. The Monday morning headlines of major newspapers often reflect the news made on Sunday's shows. Indeed, a maxim of contemporary Washington holds that no political figure should appear on the Sunday morning political talk shows except to create a headline for the next day.

The other major way of obtaining information is through *investigative journalism*. As one media analyst put it, "when a reporter actually looks for news on his or her own it is given a special name. . . . It is investigative journalism that wins professional honors, that makes what little history the American press ever makes, and that . . . proves the rule: the American press, unbidden by powerful sources, seldom investigates anything."[24] This characterization is a bit overstated, but it does make a crucial point: Investigative journalism, while on the rise, is less common than source journalism.

Investigative journalism has become more popular among reporters since the 1970s, because of the role it played in the Watergate scandal. In 1973, two reporters from the *Washington Post* uncovered evidence that linked President Richard Nixon's reelection campaign organization to a break-in at the headquarters of the Democratic National Committee at the Watergate office building in Washington. The *Post*'s investigation helped to stimulate congressional hearings and a criminal investigation. In the end, the trail of the investigation led directly to the Nixon White House, because several top aides to the president had been

The reporting by Carl Bernstein (left) *and Bob Woodward* (right) *of the Watergate scandal that led to Richard Nixon's resignation as president won their newspaper,* The Washington Post, *a Pulitzer Prize.*

involved in attempts to cover up their knowledge of the break-in. The scandal ultimately led to the resignation of President Nixon in 1974.

While source journalism remains the primary means of journalistic information gathering, the investigation bug has bitten reporters everywhere. For example, one Cincinnati television station has an "I-Team" investigative unit that ferrets out stories of government corruption and other problems. In 1990, the station broadcast a week-long exposé on a city "pothole repair" crew that spent most of its time doing nothing or running personal errands. The ensuing uproar forced the resignation of the city manager.

Deciding What to Report. Who decides what stories will be reported and how? Those kinds of decisions are made by editors. Reporters go out to find the news or receive it from officials. Editors assign reporters to cover stories or "beats" (an area of coverage that requires a journalist's attention on a continuing basis, such as the White House, Congress, the Defense Department, or environmental news), decide what stories will be reported, and often shape how a story will be presented to the audience.

Some editorial decisions are easy. Major political developments, such as an election or a war, obviously require attention. Major presidential speeches or actions always receive coverage. Other decisions are not so easy, and editors must evaluate whether one story is important enough to crowd out others.

In making these decisions, the media influence what stories and issues get public attention. For example, by giving increasing attention to the private lives of public officials in recent years, journalists have made politicians' personal

WELCOME TO "INSIDE THE BELTWAY." TONIGHT— THE GERGEN APPOINTMENT

FIRST WE'LL TALK WITH THE NEW DEMOCRATIC ADVISER DAVID GERGEN

THEN WE'LL GET THE REPUBLICAN VIEWPOINT WITH... DAVID GERGEN

AND FINALLY, AN ANALYSIS FROM OUR COMMENTATOR... DAVID GERGEN

affairs into campaign issues. Bill Clinton's alleged infidelity, the circumstances of Newt Gingrich's divorce from his first wife, and other matters once considered private are now discussed publicly. An even more pronounced example of the media's influence over public attention was journalists' coverage of the 1979–1980 Iranian hostage crisis: CBS News ended every evening's news program with a count of the number of days since Americans had been taken hostage; ABC aired a nightly update on the event ("America Held Hostage," which became the long-running "Nightline" program); and reporters made this issue the top news story for months. The result of this coverage was to nearly paralyze the Carter administration's last year in office by keeping this story above all others.

Reporting the News. Once journalists have obtained information and decided what to report, they must decide the form and placement of the story. These decisions also affect how the public will perceive the story. A story that is told first on the evening news or that gets front-page coverage in the paper will be seen as far more important than one buried at the end of a broadcast or back with the classified ads. Moreover, the actual content of the story can make a difference. If the reporter describes a vote in Congress as a "major defeat for the president," the news will be taken as more significant than if the story tells of a "minor setback" in the White House's legislative program.

Television news, which is America's primary source of political news, shapes the information that citizens receive in several key ways. Research indicates that the format of television news gives priority to interesting pictures at the expense of what are probably more newsworthy stories. Perhaps the one who feels the effects of this need for pictures the most is the president. When Gerald Ford occupied the White House, the evening news often featured stories about the chief executive bumping his head when climbing out of an aircraft or slipping on stairs. Such stories were not only devoid of news content, but they gave a false impression of a man who was actually quite athletic by nature. Ford, who possessed a prestigious law degree and had served as House minority leader, quickly got a public reputation for being a bumbler. This priority given to images helps to explain some of the obsession with images that Michael Kelly pointed to in his description of the Insiders.

The Political Consequences of Our Unelected Representatives

As the preceding discussion makes clear, staffs and the media are not merely neutral forces in Washington. Rather, their prominence has several consequences for the conduct of American politics.

Journalism and Staff Work: Unconventional Political Participation

Working on officials' staffs or in the media provides a means of unconventional political participation for many citizens. Journalists, especially those who cover the institutions of national government, exercise political power by their gatekeeping, scorekeeping, and watchdog roles. A journalist who is able to focus public attention on an issue or expose a problem or scandal in the White House has political power. Many of the people who seek careers in journalism are drawn to it precisely by a desire to take part in the shaping of the news. Serving on the staffs of public officials is likewise a form of participation. It offers staffers an opportunity to play a part in the making of public policy without having to seek election or a high-level appointment.

These opportunities are particularly appealing to younger people who are frequently found on officials' staffs. Many of the professional staffs on Capitol Hill are recent graduates from college or law school. For many of them, working in Congress offers excitement, success, and influence beyond what they could otherwise achieve as junior lawyers or in business. Presidential staffs always include an element that several analysts refer to as "the kids": young people seeking political experience and influence. President Clinton's White House has been noted for its large number of young people (the youngest was 19 at the time of Clinton's inauguration). George Stephanopoulos, one of the president's top aides, was only 31 years old when he went to work at the White House. Judicial clerks are usually young people fresh out of law school who are intimately involved in researching and even drafting opinions of the Supreme Court and lower courts.

For some people, staff work may be a career. They come to Washington when they are young and work in one or more branches of government on

TABLE 12.1 Former Staffers Who Went on to Public Office

Officeholder	Office	Former Staff Position
John Breaux	U.S. senator (D.-La.)	Congressional aide
Stephen Breyer	Associate justice of the Supreme Court	Senate aide
Carol Browner	Administrator, Environmental Protection Agency	Senate aide
Dick Cheney	U.S. representative (R.-Wyo.), Secretary of defense	White House chief of staff
Bill Clinton	U.S. president	Senate aide
Daniel Patrick Moynihan	U.S. senator (D.-N.Y.)	White House aide
William Rehnquist	Chief justice of United States	Supreme Court clerk
Pat Roberts	U.S. representative (R.-Kan.)	Congressional aide
Paul Sarbanes	U.S. senator (D.-Md.)	White House economist
Antonin Scalia	Associate justice of the Supreme Court	White House aide
John Paul Stevens	Associate justice of the Supreme Court	Supreme Court clerk and congressional aide
Clarence Thomas	Associate justice of the Supreme Court	Senate aide
Fred Thompson	U.S. senator (D.-Tenn.)	Congressional aide

officials' staffs for the rest of their lives. A common pattern is for a new young congressional aide to begin in a member's office, gain experience, and then move to a committee staff or the staff of a congressional leader or work on executive branch staffs (in the White House or other executive offices). George Stephanopoulos followed this path; he had worked for Representative Richard Gephardt (D.-Mo.) in the House majority leader's office before joining the Clinton presidential campaign.

For others, staff work is one stage in a political career. Many staffers leave Congress or the executive branch to become lobbyists, as did Harry McPherson, Clark Clifford (Truman's counsel), Theodore Sorensen (JFK's counsel), and Stuart Eisenstadt (Carter's domestic policy adviser). Some congressional or executive staffers seek elected offices, and some former Supreme Court clerks end up as judges or justices. Table 12.1 shows how many prominent American political figures worked on officials' staffs earlier in their careers.

The Political Consequences of Stafflation

Stafflation also has consequences for the conduct of American politics. One is that legislators, presidents, and judges must all be managers of their staffs. The more officials come to rely on staffs, the more time and effort they must put into coordinating and supervising these aides. Legislators spend less time deliberating on laws, and judges have less time for adjudicating; even presidents find that more of their time is spent on management and less on leading the nation.

A second consequence of stafflation is that the pace of governing has increased, with a concomitant decrease in quality. Michael Malbin, who has

Be an Intern

A good way to learn more about staff or the media is from the inside, as an intern. Internships are also a good way to begin a career in journalism or public affairs. Most interns are college students or recent college graduates. Summer is prime time for internships, although there are interns in Washington all through the year. Some are paid; others volunteer their labor in exchange for the experience and inside view.

Capitol Hill internships are some of the most popular. To find out about opportunities, contact your representative and/or senators. They can tell you what internships their offices offer, whether or not they pay, when they are available, and how to apply. See Chapter 8 for information on how to contact your representatives in Congress.

For more information on internships, several good sources are available. Check with your college's placement office or career center.

Consult books such as *The Internship Series*, edited by Ronald W. Fry (Hawthorne, N.J.: Career Press), which includes volumes on newspaper and magazine internships, as well as radio and TV internships. Another useful source is *The Complete Guide to Washington Internships*, by Jeffrey Marc Parness (Halbrook, Mass.: Bob Adams, 1990). It provides step-by-step information on finding an internship, planning and budgeting for an internship (especially for one that does not pay), housing, and other important matters.

If you want to know how to make the most of your internship, the American Political Science Association (APSA) publishes *Storming Washington: An Intern's Guide to the National Government*. This booklet is often available from your college's Department of Political Science or can be obtained from APSA: 1527 New Hampshire Ave., N.W., Washington, D.C. 20036; or call (202) 483-2512.

worked as a Capitol Hill aide and as a think tank analyst, argues that large congressional staffs have meant a dramatic increase in the number of hearings held and amendments offered to legislation. Members have less time for reading and thinking about the business before them: "Instead of freeing the members to concentrate, the staffs contribute to the frenetic pace of congressional life that pulls members in different directions, reduces the time available for joint deliberation, and makes concentration all but impossible."[25]

The courts have also been affected by the proliferation of law clerks. Richard Posner, a federal judge and scholar of the judiciary, argues that clerk-drafted opinions are different from judge-written ones in several ways. The style of these opinions is "colorless and plethoric, and also heavily given to euphemism,"[26] and they are considerably longer than judge-written ones. Less research goes into clerk-drafted opinions, because clerks are busy writing and have less time for it (research was the original job of clerks). Finally, having clerks as authors makes judicial opinions less useful, because if everyone knows that clerks write opinions, they carry less weight than what the judges themselves write.[27]

Stafflation is thus more than just a situation of spending more money to get the same work done. The work of each branch of government is affected by the proliferation of staff, and so is the work of the media.

On political talk shows, the host, the reporter, and the political strategist are often hard to distinguish. David Gergen worked on White House staffs for four presidents—Nixon, Ford, Reagan, and Clinton. Between assignments he was a news commentator on Public Television's "McNeil-Lehrer News Hour."

Insider Culture: The Staff-Media Connection

Some individuals move back and forth from government to the media. As journalist Michael Kelly has put it, "Yesterday's reporter is today's White House spokesman is tomorrow's pundit. On the Sunday talk shows, the celebrity host and the celebrity reporter and the celebrity political strategist sit side by side, and the distinctions between them are not apparent to the naked eye."[28]

This back-and-forth movement is part of the reason why top staffers and influential journalists look like one big group of Insiders to some observers. Perhaps the best example of the Insider is David Gergen, who worked on the White House staff for Presidents Nixon, Ford, Reagan, and Clinton, as well as having been an editor at *U.S. News and World Report* and a commentator on Public Television's "MacNeil-Lehrer News Hour." When Gergen's appointment as a communications counselor to President Clinton was announced in 1993, he not only appeared on "MacNeil-Lehrer" for an interview as a new government official, but remained for the rest of the program to serve in his old capacity as a commentator on the news. As we see in Table 12.2, Gergen is not the only person who has worked on both sides of the Insider group.

As we noted earlier, this idea of Insiders does not give a complete picture of American politics. Working in Washington does not necessarily mean sub-

TABLE 12.2 The Media-Staff Revolving Door

Individual	Media Job	Staff Job
Ken Bode	TV news reporter	Press secretary
Patrick Buchanan	TV commentator	Speechwriter
David Gergen	Newsmagazine editor and TV commentator	White House aide and communications director
Chris Matthews	Newspaper columnist	Press secretary
John McLaughlin	TV commentator	Speechwriter
Bill Moyers	Newspaper editor and TV commentator	Press secretary
Peggy Noonan	Radio scriptwriter	Speechwriter
William Safire	Newspaper columnist	Speechwriter
Pierre Salinger	TV news reporter	Press secretary
Dianne Sawyer	TV news anchor	White House aide
Tony Snow	Newspaper columnist	Speechwriter
John Sununu	TV commentator	White House chief of staff
George Will	TV commentator and newspaper columnist	Senate aide

scribing to a cynical image-oriented view of politics, nor does work on staffs or in the media mean that the individuals involved have nothing to contribute to their country. Nevertheless, media and staffs do serve as unelected representatives who work in the rarified environment of the nation's capital, which may help to explain why politicians who argue for change—from Bill Clinton to Newt Gingrich—are often critical of the conventional wisdom that develops inside the Washington Beltway.

open questions

How Well Do Our Unelected Representatives Serve Us?

As the preceding discussion makes clear, media and large staffs affect the operation of American government and politics. Many issues flow from this, but one large question looms over all others: How well are we served by our unelected representatives?

In the case of the media, the question can be framed in this way: Is the press giving Americans the kind of information they need to be effective citizens? Take the example of political campaigns. Several critics have charged that the press has concentrated excessively on "sleaze journalism," that is, character issues and the private lives of candidates. At least one political scientist argues that overattention to such matters as Bill Clinton's alleged marital problems is "decivilizing politics."[29] During the 1992 presidential campaign, Ross Perot frequently attacked the press for failing to cover issues in order to focus on his personal character. Carl Bernstein, one of the reporters who investigated Watergate, argues that journalists' placing character and "sleaze" ahead of hard news is creating an "idiot culture" in which "the weird and the stupid and the coarse are becoming our cultural norm."[30]

In response, several journalists have defended their coverage of character issues in campaigns. Michael Gartner, president of NBC News and owner of a daily paper in Iowa, maintains that "Some gossip is true, and we're in the business of printing truth and airing truth. . . . So, sure, we put gossip on NBC, we put gossip in our newspapers—when it's true."[31] Other observers suggest that the primary-based method for choosing candidates means that voters need lots of information about candidates for high office: "The only hope of achieving informed choices is by means of publicly available information. Thus, it may be regrettable but it is understandable that journalists are leaning toward disclosure and away from the protection of candidates' private lives."[32]

In the matter of staff, the issue can be framed in this way: Has "salvation by staff" created a cure that is worse than the disease? Some observers charge that officials have become too dependent on their aides, which leads to government by staff. Many analysts blame the 1987 Iran-Contra affair on President Reagan's excessive reliance on his aides. Many observers of Congress maintain that large staffs lead to more work, even to the point of overloading the legislature's capacity to function effectively.[33] One critic goes so far as to say that "sometimes staffers steal the ball on policy, and members complain of being at the mercy of staffs, often forced to fight fires started by overly aggressive staff aides."[34] In the matter of law clerks, former Justice Department official Terry Eastland asks "was it really Justice Blackmun who wrote the decision on some point of constitutional law today, or was it a 26-year-old clerk never appointed by the President or confirmed by the Senate?"[35] He asserts that "relying on clerks is a cheat on democratic government."[36]

In response, some officials argue that staffs are unavoidable and that their power is overrated. Defenders of large staffs argue that aides have only as much power as their bosses allow, so any problems are to be blamed on officials and not the staffs that serve them. Moreover, former Senate Majority Leader Howard Baker states that lobbyists and journalists pay too much attention to staffs, calling claims of excessive staff influence "an illusion . . . when I met with most committee chairmen every Tuesday morning around the conference table in my office, I saw how it worked. They would really go at it hammer and tongs on particular items within their jurisdiction."[37] While Baker believes that there are too many staffers on Capitol Hill, he does not see them as too powerful. Nor does Judge Harry Edwards believe that judges' clerks wield too much power: "Careful judges will not allow an opinion to issue in their name until the words constituting the opinion precisely reflect their views on the proper disposition of the case."[38]

There are no easy answers to these questions. While a free press is a fundamental element of our political system, it is free for reasons beyond the interests of journalists. In the same way, staffs serve officials, but the officials serve citizens. Are Americans getting all that they should from their unelected representatives?

Summary

Two types of unelected representatives play important roles in contemporary American politics: officials' staffs and the media. The twentieth century has been a decade of *stafflation*—a rapid growth in the size and power of officials' staffs (in the presidency, Congress, the courts, and in the bureaucracy). The media have always been important but are even more so in an age of television. Print and electronic media compete for public attention.

The media play four key roles in national politics: information gatherer, gatekeeper, scorekeeper, and watchdog. While print media are largely unregulated, the Federal Communications Commission has broad authority to control electronic media. It establishes and enforces rules that affect television and radio news.

Principles. The Constitution establishes a government that can be active, with each branch having a will of its own. To help hold this government accountable to the public, a free press can report and comment on the news and government actions.

Process. Staffs are important to officials because they extend their bosses' reach and help them communicate with other parts of the political system. Staffs not only help shape policy, but also direct how government actions are reported. Staffs are often important sources of journalists' information. The media must find the news, decide what to report, and then tell the news to the public; as a result, staffs and the media are not neutral forces in government.

Politics. Work in journalism or on official staffs is an unconventional form of political participation for the people in these positions. It gives them political influence beyond that of other citizens. The growth in staff size and power affects the pace of government and decision makers' ability to govern effectively. The strong connections between staffs and the media mean that an "insider culture" helps to shape Washington politics.

Open Questions. How well are citizens served by their unelected representatives? Are journalists giving us the news coverage we need, or are they overly concerned with gossip and unimportant trivia? Are staffs too powerful? These questions are difficult to answer, but important to the conduct of American government.

BURKE, JOHN. *The Institutional Presidency*. Baltimore: Johns Hopkins University Press, 1993. Excellent study of the growth and development of the Executive Office of the President.

FOX, HARRISON W., JR., and SUSAN WEBB HAMMOND. *Congressional Staffs*. New York: Free Press, 1977. Systematic study of stafflation in Congress and its consequences.

GRABER, DORIS. *Mass Media and American Politics*, 4th ed. Washington: CQ Press, 1993. Surveys the topic in a comprehensive and readable manner.

HESS, STEPHEN. *Live from Capitol Hill!* Washington: Brookings Institution, 1991. Explores relations between members and the media that cover them.

MALBIN, MICHAEL. *Unelected Representatives: Congressional Staff and the Future of Representative Government*. New York: Basic Books, 1980. Informed and thoughtful look at the effect of large staffs on the operations of Congress.

MALTESE, JOHN A. *Spin Control: The White House Office of Communications and the Management of Presidential News*. Chapel Hill: University of North Carolina Press, 1992. Examines the work of the White House staff unit that coordinates relations between the media and the presidency.

PATTERSON, BRADLEY. *The Ring of Power: The White House Staff and Its Expanding Role in Government*. New York: Basic Books, 1988. A useful survey of the president's staff informed by an insider's perspective.

Suggested Readings

13

Chapter

Domestic Policy

Americans love pizza and hate big government deficits. The first half of that statement seems to have little to do with the second. But in 1987 it was used to justify an attempt to use the federal budget as a means to require special labeling on frozen pizzas sold in the United States. What do pizzas have to do with the budget? The answer is illuminating, for it reveals much about the making of public policy in contemporary America.[1]

Each year consumers purchase over 700 million frozen pizzas, unaware that most are made with artificial cheese. The substitute product, which is mostly vegetable oil and casein, was developed in the 1970s when milk prices began to skyrocket. Artificial cheese hurt sales of the real thing, so the National Milk Producers Federation turned to the U.S. government for help. First, it tried to win relief through regulation but met with mixed results because of divided bureaucratic responsibility for pizza control.[2] Frozen pizzas without meat are under the jurisdiction of the Food and Drug Administration (FDA), which responded by requiring that all pizzas using the cheese substitute be prominently labeled to indicate that fact. But at the Department of Agriculture (USDA), which controls pizzas with meat, a similar labeling rule was blocked by objections from the Committee for Fair Pizza Labeling—a lobbying group assembled by pizza manufacturers.

The milk producers then sought help from Congress. Senator Bob Kasten (R.-Wisc.) introduced the Truth in Frozen Pizza Labeling Act, which would impose a labeling rule on all such products using artificial cheese. But instead of employing the normal legislative process to win passage of the bill, its supporters attempted to expedite consideration by attaching it to the federal budget bill being written that summer. Their justification was that the labeling law would encourage the use of real cheese, which in turn would reduce the amount of surplus cheese the government would have to purchase (a separate program requires USDA to buy up surplus dairy products). The savings from buying less surplus cheese would shrink the budget of USDA, thus contributing to the goal of deficit reduction. Therefore, supporters claimed that pizza labeling was an attack on the deficit.

The labeling law ran into trouble when powerful legislators refused to allow it to pass through this budgetary shortcut. Instead, they insisted that the bill undergo the normal process of hearings, debate, and vote that is time consuming and difficult. A General Accounting Office (GAO) study was also ordered, further complicating matters. In the end the proposal died a quiet death, sharing the fate of most bills introduced in Congress. The dairy industry ultimately took recourse in voluntary labeling of all products containing "real" dairy ingredients.

The story of pizza labeling may be peculiar, but it provides an interesting snapshot of contemporary American government. In the national government, there are multiple avenues through which decisions are made that affect the lives of citizens and the livelihood of the nation. These decisions shape that product of government we call public policy.

What Is Public Policy?

Public policy refers to government activities, whether direct or indirect, that affect the lives of citizens. Policy may be in the form of a law, an executive order or decision, a court ruling, an administrative regulation, or some combination of them. Officials make policy under the authority of the political system, and it is backed by the rewards (such as licenses, grants of money, authority to act) and punishments (such as fines and imprisonment) that the government is able to impose.[3]

In our frozen pizza example, the existing government policy was to make no distinction between real and artificial cheese. The milk producers tried to have that policy changed by administrative regulation and failed; they then tried to change it through law but were also unsuccessful. Had the policy been changed, the government could have used its power to enforce the pizza labeling that dairy interests wanted.

Facets of Public Policy

Our definition of public policy is broad, but that is because policy covers a broad area. It involves the myriad choices that government officials make, putting those choices into action, and the ways those choices affect the lives of citizens.

Policy Choices. Making public policy involves making choices. Officials must make choices about what issues or problems they think government should tackle: to reduce the deficit, reform welfare, become involved in a foreign conflict, or support the arts. Officials must then make choices about what they will do to address these issues. If they choose to try to reduce the size of the federal budget deficit, will they do so through tax increases, spending cuts, a Balanced Budget Amendment to the Constitution, a combination of these, or even some other means? These choices will usually be recorded and formalized in some fashion: as a law, executive order, regulation, ruling, or other instrument.

Putting Choices into Action. If officials decide to do nothing, policy choices are self-executing. In our pizza example, officials decided to leave things alone—this decision took care of itself. But, if they had chosen to make a change, they would have had to execute their decision through action.

Policy choices are put into action through a variety of tools that government can use. A *law* can be enforced: the U.S. Treasury Department enforces the laws against counterfeiting money. A *service* can be provided to citizens: the National Park Service maintains natural scenic areas that citizens may visit as tourists; the U.S. Postal Service sells stamps and collects and delivers the mail. *Money* can be distributed to individuals (such as through Social Security checks), groups (such as a grant from the National Endowment for the Arts to a local symphony), or to other governments (such as federal highway grants to states). Government has other tools at its disposal as well. It can control *credit* (through loan guarantees), provide *insurance* (such as insuring bank deposits), and even employ *force* (as in war or other military actions) to carry out officials' choices. Finally, government often uses *persuasion* to try to bring others in line

public policy Government activities, whether direct or indirect, that affect the lives of citizens.

with what officials want. For example, since the 1960s, the federal government has worked to convince Americans to quit smoking cigarettes, and in 1995 the president tried to persuade major-league baseball players and team owners to end a lengthy strike.

The Effects of Policy. What impact does public policy actually have? The answer to that question may not always be the one that policy makers want. Therefore, as we study public policy, we must also distinguish the effects of policy from its intentions and government actions. For example, several years ago the city council of Beverly Hills, California, wanted to discourage smoking in public by banning it in restaurants. The council passed an ordinance to that end but exempted bars from the ban. In response, many restaurants in Beverly Hills remodeled their interiors so the bar area took up most of the restaurant. Customers who wanted to smoke could eat at tables that technically were in the bar. The effect of the policy was that the amount of public smoking decreased very little.

Public policy is made at all levels of government, but in this chapter, we focus on public policy making by the national government. Policies affect the lives of citizens here in the United States and also how the nation relates to the rest of the world. We call policies at home *domestic policy* and those that are directed abroad *foreign policy,* but there are issues that blur this distinction.

Formulating Domestic Policy

Domestic policy covers a wide range of issues: education, public safety, economic prosperity, public welfare, the environment, culture, health, and other matters.[4] We examine four types of domestic policy: distributive, protective regulatory, competitive regulatory, and redistributive policies.

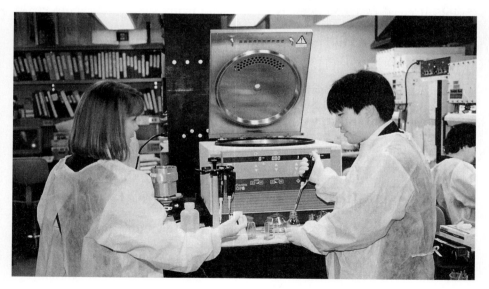

Distributive policies provide for the distribution of public money for such purposes as research on AIDS.

Early in 1994, the U.S. House of Representatives considered educational reform legislation that enjoyed bipartisan support. Buried in the bill was a provision to require that all states ensure that all teachers be certified in the field they were teaching. The measure elicited criticism on the grounds that it was one more attempt to control American life from Washington, but its greatest opposition came from thousands of parents nationwide who educate their children at home. Mobilized by a grass-roots network, tens of thousands of home-schooling parents and parents of children in private schools flooded Capitol Hill with phone calls, telegrams, faxes, and letters protesting the measure as a threat to their liberty. In response to the outcry, the House voted 422-1 to delete the certification requirement.

Distributive policy refers to policies and programs that provide subsidies to private activities that government wants to promote.[5] For example, the federal government wants to encourage certain types of scientific research, especially research that can benefit medical care. The U.S. government gives out large sums of money to AIDS research, thus encouraging prominent medical research institutions, pharmaceutical companies, hospitals, and universities to conduct studies of new drugs, treatments, and understanding of the cause of AIDS. The national government has also had a long-standing policy to develop an interstate highway system, so it has given substantial grants to states to build and maintain the nation's highways.

The area of distributive policy also includes agricultural assistance programs and grants for building airports, hospitals, and other facilities. The income-tax deduction for home mortgage interest rewards those who buy or build homes. All of these government activities are distributive because they distribute public money to projects that the U.S. government wants to promote. As we saw in Chapter 10, bureaucratic agencies are usually assigned the task of overseeing these policies.

Protective regulatory policy refers to government rules and actions that are intended to protect the public by setting the conditions under which various private activities can take place.[6] On one hand, the government prohibits activities that are considered harmful to the public, such as producing toxic waste or manufacturing unsafe foods and drugs. U.S. law also prohibits false advertising, using the mail to send dangerous objects or to defraud someone, and bribing public officials. The Federal Communications Commission prohibits television and radio stations from carrying ads for tobacco products.

An important area of protective regulatory policy in the past quarter-century has been civil rights policy. As we saw in Chapter 4, the federal government has enacted a series of civil rights laws designed to prohibit segregation based on racial or ethnic identity in housing, employment, education, credit, and public accommodations. To advance these policies, the government sets conditions on federal aid to states, local governments, and private institutions. In Chapter 3, we saw that private colleges that accept federal money cannot discriminate in their admissions. Similarly, the government punishes individuals or groups who violate the civil rights of others.

On the other hand, instead of prohibiting action, the government requires citizens to undertake activities that officials consider beneficial. For example, because officials believe that consumers need to know the terms and conditions of any loans or credit they receive, credit-card companies must inform card users of restrictions, charges, interest rates, and other pertinent information. Federal regulations also require individuals or companies who sell houses to disclose any known defects in the property being sold to protect potential buyers.

Competitive regulatory policy refers to rules and actions designed to limit the provision of specific goods and services by controlling who may deliver such services or products. For example, as we saw in Chapter 12, the federal government licenses radio and television broadcasting; only stations with a fed-

Through protective regulatory policy the government protects the public by prohibiting such things as the manufacture of unsafe foods, advertising tobacco products on radio or television, and the production of toxic waste.

eral license may broadcast on American airwaves. Another example is telephone service; federal rules allow local telephone companies to operate monopolies in specific geographic areas, although long-distance companies can compete with one another for each consumer's business. In fact, as part of being granted a monopoly in one city or area, a local phone company must offer consumers a choice of long-distance companies. In this way, government policy restricts who may offer one kind of phone service and guarantees competition among those who offer a different kind of service. The federal government also regulates airline routes.[7]

Competitive regulatory policy is often controlled by independent regulatory commissions. In Chapter 10, we saw how such agencies were established to regulate public policy in a way that is insulated from direct influence by the president or Congress.

Redistributive policy refers to government rules and actions designed to alter the distribution of wealth, property, rights, or other values in society. A wide array of government policies fall into this category, including progressive income taxation (taking more money from the wealthy to give to those with less), welfare programs (to aid the needy), affirmative action programs (to give opportunities to groups once denied certain jobs or admission to educational institutions), job training (to give employment opportunities to the poor), and legal services for the poor (so they can receive the same legal protections that others have).[8]

Redistributive policies are usually enacted through major laws passed by Congress at the urging of the president, as occurred during the period of Franklin Roosevelt's New Deal (1930s) and Lyndon Johnson's Great Society (1960s). Bureaucratic agencies and programs were created to carry out these policies, such as the Legal Services Corporation or the Aid to Families With Dependent Children (AFDC) program.

In one of the first "crossover ventures" between telephone and cable-TV companies, Time-Warner's cable company was poised in late 1994 to offer phone service in Rochester, New York. About the same time, New Jersey's Bell Atlantic phone company won the FCC's permission to build the first large-scale video network for Dover Township.

Public policy can affect nearly any aspect of national life. Policy is not confined to the borders of the United States, however, but also looks outward to American relations with the rest of the world. Foreign policy, which we discuss in Chapter 14, covers a broad array of government activities that include such undertakings as American negotiations with the Ukraine and Russia over the future of nuclear weapons and a diplomatic mission to the Middle East to promote peace between Israel and its Arab neighbors. However, once totally domestic issues such as business and trade have often taken on the characteristics of both domestic and foreign policy matters.

Redistributive policies alter the distribution of wealth, property, rights, or other values in society. Job training for inner-city youth and other disadvantaged people, legal aid services, affirmative action, and welfare are among the programs that reflect this area of public policy.

Intermestic Issues: The Interface of Domestic and Foreign Policy

In recent years there has been a blurring of issues once clearly domestic or international, as some have come to overlap different types of policy. As a result we have a new category of problems called *intermestic* issues—matters that have both *inter*national and do*mestic* content.

The best example of an intermestic issue is foreign trade. In 1993, the Clinton administration urged the U.S. Senate to accept the North American Free Trade Agreement (NAFTA), a plan to create a free-trade zone to include the United States, Mexico, and Canada. The debate over this agreement shows why intermestic issues blur traditional categories. Advocates of the pact saw it as a means to promote trade with America's neighbors and strengthen the nation's position in the world economy; opponents worried about the loss of jobs in the United States from the movement of industries to Mexico in search of lower paid workers. Each side emphasized a legitimate side of the issue; neither exclusively domestic nor foreign matters were in question.

Immigration is also an intermestic issue. In 1994 voters in California endorsed Proposition 187, a ballot issue that cut off non-emergency services for illegal immigrants. Proponents framed the issue as revolving around the domestic costs of illegal immigration. Opponents of the measure, including representatives of the Mexican American community, stressed the adverse effects on American relations with other nations.

What makes intermestic issues difficult is that some observers tend to define these questions as matters of foreign relations. Vice-President Al Gore and others have tended to treat the issue of environmental protection as an international one requiring international solutions. Others stress the domestic impact of intermestic issues. Former President George Bush often clashed with Gore, then a Senator, arguing that each nation must protect its own interests in dealing with environmental matters.

Principles: Policy Making in the Constitutional Republic

As we have seen throughout this text, the Constitution is chiefly concerned with the process of policy making, rather than the substance of policy. Most of our national charter focuses on the structures of government, the law-making process, and the allocation of powers. The Preamble does state general goals for the government but does not specify the policies that will advance those goals.

There are a few policy-specific provisions in the Constitution. The Contract Clause does give preference to a market-based economy by protecting free contracts from legislative disruption. Article I prohibits the granting of titles of nobility, the levying of export taxes, and the use of religious tests for public office. It also authorizes Congress "To promote the Progress of Science and useful Arts, by securing for limited Times to Authors and Inventors the exclusive Right to their respective Writings and Discoveries," which is the basis for patents and copyrights.

There has been one major attempt to enshrine a public policy in the Constitution. The Eighteenth Amendment (1919) prohibited the "manufacture, sale, or transportation of intoxicating liquors," but it was repealed a few years later by the Twenty-first Amendment (1921). Recently there have been proposals to incorporate other policy decisions—term limits or a balanced federal budget—in the Constitution.

Although it generally does not prescribe policy, the Constitution does have policy consequences. The most important of these is that the American political system is biased in favor of the status quo and incremental change. The checks-and-balances system was designed to encourage deliberation and make sweeping change difficult. The earlier chapters have shown how rapid change is unusual and difficult to achieve. The process of making policy in our constitutional republic is an elaborate and cautious one.

The Policy-Making Process

Making public policy in the United States involves many components of the political system: the limited constitution, separation of powers, federalism, interest groups, parties, elections, and the public, among others. The influence and power of each of these elements vary according to the type of policy or issue, the circumstances, time, personalities and interests involved, and even the urgency that policy makers feel with regard to the need to address a problem.

Certain common threads run through all areas of policy making. Regardless of whether the matter at hand is national defense, child welfare, or law and order, certain broad similarities characterize the process of public policy making. Political scientists have identified several general stages in the policy-making process: (1) agenda-setting, (2) making policy choices, (3) budgeting, (4) implementation, and (5) evaluation. Each of these merits closer consideration.[9]

Agenda Setting

The first step in making any public policy is to discern an issue or problem appropriate for public concern. This is the most amorphous stage of the policy process, because there is no one concrete list of public problems that is published in the newspapers or voted on by the people. Each of us can draw up a list of problems that we face as individuals or as a society, but we do not see all of them as matters for government intervention. One might be convinced that the quality of play in major league baseball is not what it was in the days of Ted Williams and Mickey Mantle but still not see this problem as one that can or ought to be solved by public officials. Our concern is with what political scientists call the **political agenda,** which includes issues that citizens believe are matters requiring public attention and that are within the legitimate scope of government authority.[10]

Who sets the political agenda? In a large sense, all elements of the political system are involved, although government officials play a large role in defining it. For example, during the first half of his presidency, Bill Clinton made health care an issue of national concern. By public statements and official actions, officials seek to identify the urgent issues of the day. Interest groups try to influence what issues are on this agenda, as the National Milk Producers Federation did when it pushed for pizza labeling. So do unelected representatives in the media and staffs. In 1987, talk radio hosts made a major issue of a proposed pay raise for federal officials; and in recent years news reports of famine in Africa and the "boat people" from Haiti put these issues on the agenda. Political parties and candidates use campaigns to raise issues for the political agenda. In 1984, Democratic presidential hopeful Gary Hart tried to make the troubles in Northern Ireland a matter for concern in American politics. The political agenda may even be influenced by events beyond the control of any of these actors; Hurricane Andrew in 1992, midwest flooding in 1993, and the Northridge earthquake in California in 1994 made disaster preparedness a national concern.

Political entrepreneurs are individuals or groups who use effective communication skills to focus national attention on an issue that has been otherwise of little or no interest. One of the most successful political entrepreneurs is Ralph Nader, whose widely publicized attacks on General Motors in the 1960s helped launch the consumer movement (Nader is profiled in the Citizens in Action Section in Chapter 5). Other successful political entrepreneurs include Howard Jarvis, who led a campaign to pass a property-tax rollback in California; Candy Lightner, who founded Mothers Against Drunk Drivers; and Sarah Brady, whose organization Handgun Control helped make handgun violence a national issue.

Even when issues find a place on the political agenda, that is no guarantee that the government will actually attempt to deal with them. Therefore, we must give attention to a smaller **governmental agenda** that consists of those issues explicitly up for active and serious consideration by public officials.[11] The governmental agenda is shaped by many of the same forces as the larger political agenda, although the relative influence of public officials is magnified.

In reality, there are several governmental agendas because there are different policy-making institutions in the government. But the president has the greatest influence over what problems will be addressed by national policy. Most of the business of Congress in any given year is consideration of presiden-

political agenda Issues that citizens believe are matters requiring public attention and that are within the legitimate scope of governmental authority.

political entrepreneur An individual or group who uses effective communication skills to focus national attention on an issue that has been otherwise of little or no interest.

governmental agenda Those issues explicitly up for active and serious consideration by government officials.

tial proposals on the budget, treaties, new legislation, and appointments. Many of the major policy initiatives of the past half-century originated at the White House: FDR's New Deal, Truman's foreign policy of containing Soviet influence, Eisenhower's interstate highway network, LBJ's Great Society, Nixon's opening to the People's Republic of China, Reagan's tax cuts and defense buildup, Bush's intervention in the Persian Gulf crisis, and Clinton's health care reform proposals. Presidential interest is certainly no guarantee that an issue will result in a national policy, but that interest certainly places an issue on the governmental agenda.

Other government institutions have their own agendas, and the issues on them may stimulate the development of new policies. Members of Congress have brought several issues into focus. In the 1970s, members made human rights an issue in foreign policy before President Carter took it as his own, and tax reform in 1986 began as a congressional initiative. In 1995 the new Republican leadership in Congress came to power armed with an agenda it called the "Contract With America," which opened a rare moment in American history. Not since the nineteenth century had Congress been the branch that provided the dominant set of issues for the national government.

The bureaucracy can also play a role, as the surgeon general's office has done with smoking and health since the 1960s. In the 1950s and 1960s, the Supreme Court put segregation on the governmental agenda when many elected officials were unable to do so.

Factors outside government (interest groups, entrepreneurs, events, and so on) will also shape the agendas of government institutions, but their ability to do so is dependent on those in office. For example, gay-rights groups had tried for years, albeit unsuccessfully, to alter the U.S. military's policy of excluding homosexuals. This situation changed when Bill Clinton became president. Even getting the attention of government officials is no guarantee of policy success, for there are more steps in the policy process.

Making Policy Choices

Public policy is developed by the institutions of government through a variety of means—bills and resolutions in Congress, executive orders and other presidential directives, regulations, court rulings, and even inaction (a policy of not doing something). We have seen this part of the policy-making process already at work. In earlier chapters, we saw the legislative process in Congress, the president at work, the administrative rule-making process, and the Supreme Court's deliberative process.

The choices involved may take years as a problem is addressed and solutions are tortuously considered, or officials may move decisively in a short time to deal with a crisis. Because of America's separation-of-powers system of government, the stage of making choices may take a long time. Indeed, policy may be developed over the course of many years, as small decisions are made over time or an issue is debated for a long period of time. At some point, whether

Help Shape Public Policy

1. *Pick an issue:* Citizens who want to be effective and to make a difference in public policy are best advised to focus their attention, at least at the outset, on a specific issue. Select one that interests you or that directly affects your life.

2. *Do research:* An informed citizen can be far more effective than an uninformed one. Here is what you need to know: what current policy is, who makes policy in this area, who can change the policy, who has been effective in the past trying to influence this issue, and why.

3. *Seek out allies:* There is strength in numbers, as we have seen in Chapter 5 and elsewhere.

4. *Make yourself heard:* Once you know where to direct your efforts, do so. Look back over the similar sections in previous chapters for advice on how to approach particular policy makers or to make the most of citizen action.

5. *Follow through:* As we noted in earlier chapters, effective citizens do not stop at the first success or failure. They continue to keep an eye on the policy issue on which they have devoted so much energy. You can certainly broaden your horizons to other issues as you gain experience.

because political circumstances have changed or officials have decided that the time has arrived to act, policy choices long put off may be made in a short time. Two examples can show policy choice at work.

One issue that took a long time to build was civil rights for African Americans. The issue had been around since the end of the Civil War, but it began to get national attention only after World War II. In 1948 the Democratic Party called for civil rights legislation in its party platform. In 1957 a Civil Rights Law was passed, although it was limited in scope. Pressure for change continued to mount, as did resistance to change. Then, in the wake of racial unrest in the South and the death of President Kennedy, a sense of national urgency on the issue quickly developed. In 1964, as President Johnson pressed Congress for action on a major civil rights law, Senate Republican leader Everett Dirksen (Ill.) summarized the case for action. He told the Senate, "Stronger than armies is the power of an idea whose time has come." The law passed quickly.

Another example of this slow-then-quick process of choice was the 1986 Tax Reform Act. Ideas for tax reform had been circulating through Washington for several years. Several prominent members of Congress had achieved considerable attention for their reform proposals—such as Representative Jack Kemp (R.-N.Y.) and Senator Bill Bradley (D.-N.J.)—but little congressional action had occurred. Then the Reagan administration took an interest in the issue, and events began to move. Soon, both houses of Congress were actively considering tax reform legislation, and before the year was over a new law had been passed.

Deciding on a policy does not make it a reality. It must be carried out, which may prove difficult. And most policies involve money, which means they must be subjected to the process of budgeting.

The U.S. budget is a key feature of the politics surrounding policy decisions. Here, Alice Rivlin, Director of the Office of Management and Budget, briefs reporters on Clinton administration budget proposals.

Budgeting

The federal government's $1.5 trillion budget constitutes almost one-fourth of America's *gross domestic product* (the sum of all goods and services produced in the domestic economy in one year). It serves not only as a device for tracking government income and expenses, but also shapes policy in several ways.

The Budget as an Instrument of Policy. Because the federal government cannot do everything it wants to do, *the budget sets government priorities.* For example, the shift of national resources to military spending and away from domestic programs in the Reagan years represented one set of priorities, whereas an opposite shift under Bill Clinton set different priorities. There are few government activities that are not affected by the amount of money available for them.

As we saw in our pizza labeling example, *the budget is often used to alter existing laws and programs.* In the past two decades, food stamps, Medicaid and Medicare, and other programs have all been reshaped by budget bills. On several occasions, such as in 1993, the budget was used to raise taxes and user fees. Substantive policy changes have also been included in the budget, such as in 1989 when the federal pension law was revised to give employees a bigger say in company-controlled pensions.

How are these changes made through the budget? The answer lies in a legal device called **reconciliation,** a technical part of the budget process

reconciliation An aspect of the federal budget process whereby the budget is used as a kind of super-law to alter other laws in order for budget goals to be accomplished.

364

through which laws that do not conform to this year's budget can be amended to fit current budget needs. In our pizza example, backers of pizza labeling assumed that labeling artificial cheese would increase the use of real cheese, thus decreasing the amount of money the federal government would have to spend to subsidize milk prices. Thus, the budget would amend existing federal law in order to require labeling so the government could save money.

The budget affects economic policy. The various provisions of the annual budget not only affect the state of the nation's economy, but are explicitly used to influence economic activity. By providing subsidies for certain kinds of activities, such as growing tobacco or building low-income housing, the budget encourages some economic endeavors. By appropriating money for welfare or public television, the budget makes certain services or programs available that affect the economy. By funding research and defense spending, the budget enlarges the high-tech sectors of the economy. A budget deficit requires the government to borrow money, which affects the amount of money available for other investments. Interest rates, unemployment, investment, economic growth, and even consumer confidence will be affected by the budget. The annual summary of goverment income and expenses has real economic consequences.

The Federal Budget Process. The federal government must produce a budget for each **fiscal year (FY),** an annual accounting cycle that runs from October to September. FY 2000 begins on October 1, 1999 and ends on September 30, 2000. The process for producing this plan begins several months before the fiscal year begins. The president compiles budget requests from the executive departments and agencies and prepares a budget that stresses the administration's priorities and plans for the coming year. This plan is sent to Congress, which takes most of a calendar year to move the budget through subcommittee

fiscal year (FY) An official accounting year for budgetary purposes. The federal fiscal year runs from October 1 to the following September 30 and is designated by the calendar year in which it ends.

Don Wright, The Palm Beach Post.

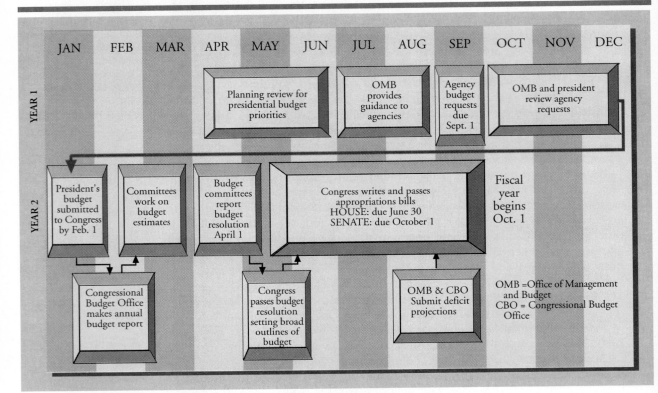

FIGURE 13.1 The Federal Budget Process. The budget process begins nineteen months before the fiscal year begins. *Year 1* is a planning period during which the Office of Management and Budget assists the president in preparing the president's budget proposal. *Year 2* is the period in which Congress studies and approves the budget in time for the start of the new fiscal year, October 1. The Congressional Budget Office assists the House and Senate committees in drawing up the budget.

and committee consideration, floor debate, conference committee, and final passage. Figure 13.1 summarizes this 19-month process.

There are two main components to the budget. **Revenues** are the various forms of government income: taxes, fees on government products or services, interest earned by government investments, even fines paid to the government. As Figure 13.2 illustrates, the primary source of federal revenue is individual income taxes (over one-third of revenues). Borrowing amounts to about one-sixth of revenues. **Expenditures** refer to the different ways in which government money is spent. Figure 13.2 shows that the largest single category of expenses is benefit payments to individuals. Interest payments on the federal debt now consume about one-sixth of federal spending.

Federal policy makers do not have complete freedom when they make up the budget for an upcoming fiscal year. Over 60 percent of the budget is composed of *nondiscretionary spending,* which means spending obligations budget

revenues Government income, such as from taxes, tariffs, and other sources.

expenditures Government spending.

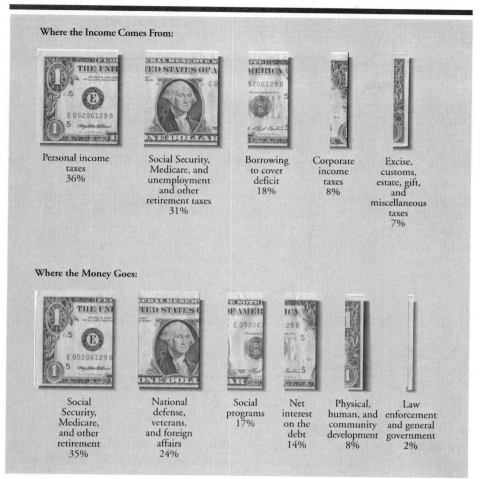

Where the Income Comes From:

Personal income taxes 36%	Social Security, Medicare, and unemployment and other retirement taxes 31%	Borrowing to cover deficit 18%	Corporate income taxes 8%	Excise, customs, estate, gift, and miscellaneous taxes 7%

Where the Money Goes:

Social Security, Medicare, and other retirement 35%	National defense, veterans, and foreign affairs 24%	Social programs 17%	Net interest on the debt 14%	Physical, human, and community development 8%	Law enforcement and general government 2%

FIGURE 13.2 The Federal Government Dollar. The figures shown here are estimates for fiscal year 1996.
Source: Budget of the United States, FY 1996, U.S. Office of Management and Budget.

makers must cover as they allocate funds (see Table 13.1). Interest payments are nondiscretionary because they must be made in order to maintain the credit of the federal government. So are forms of *mandatory spending,* spending on programs for which the federal government is legally bound to pay. Retirement pensions for federal employees, unemployment insurance, and bank deposit insurance are part of mandatory spending. So are **entitlement programs**— programs that give benefits to which qualified recipients have a legal right, such as Medicaid, Medicare, and Social Security. Entitlement programs account for over one-third of all federal spending. They can be changed only by altering the structure of the programs.

entitlement programs
Programs to which those who qualify are legally entitled, such as Social Security. Qualified recipients cannot be denied benefits because of lack of funds.

TABLE 13.1 Discretionary and Nondiscretionary Federal Spending (in Billions of Dollars)

	1993 Actual	Estimate					
		1994	*1995*	*1996*	*1997*	*1998*	*1999*
Discretionary:							
Defense discretionary	292.4	280.6	271.1	261.6	257.0	257.1	258.1
Nondefense discretionary	250.0	269.5	271.3	282.3	287.3	291.0	296.3
Discretionary health care reform	—	—	—	2.2	3.4	−3.7	−6.1
Subtotal, discretionary	542.5	550.1	542.4	546.1	547.8	544.4	548.3
Mandatory:							
Social Security benefits	302.0	317.7	334.5	353.7	369.5	389.6	410.8
Federal retirement benefits[a]	59.8	63.0	65.2	67.9	71.3	74.6	78.9
Medicare	127.8	140.8	153.3	173.1	192.9	202.2	215.0
Medicaid	75.8	87.2	96.4	104.6	109.7	105.9	100.9
Unemployment benefits	35.5	26.7	23.0	23.5	23.9	24.0	25.1
Means-tested entitlements benefits[b]	80.8	89.4	96.7	102.4	109.9	116.6	124.0
Deposit insurance	−28.0	−3.3	−11.1	−11.3	−6.1	−4.9	−3.3
Health care allowances[c]	—	—	3.0	16.4	39.9	83.3	101.8
Undistributed offsetting receipts	−37.4	−37.9	−42.5	−41.6	−39.4	−41.4	−40.5
Other	50.7	46.7	45.2	37.9	38.1	38.3	38.7
Subtotal, mandatory	666.9	730.3	763.7	826.6	909.7	988.3	1,051.3
Net interest	198.8	203.4	212.8	224.2	234.0	244.6	254.4
Total outlays	1,408.2	1,483.8	1,518.9	1,596.9	1,691.4	1,777.4	1,854.0

[a]Civil service and military retirement.
[b]Food stamps and food aid to Puerto Rico, family support payments, SSI, child nutrition, EITC, veterans pensions.
[c]Premium subsidies, long-term care, other mandatory health reform, and 1995 "pay-as-you-go" items. The impact of health reform on Medicare and Medicaid is included in the Medicare and Medicaid estimates shown above.
Source: Office of Management and Budget, *Budget of the United States, Fiscal Year 1995* (Washington, D.C.: Government Printing Office, 1994).

Discretionary spending accounts for only slightly more than one-third of the budget (see Table 13.1). This includes most defense spending and a range of domestic programs for agriculture, research, education, the arts, transportation, and other purposes. One reason why so much attention has been focused on proposals to cut defense spending in recent years is that it constitutes the largest category of discretionary spending.

Implementing Policy

Once made, most public policy choices must be carried out by someone in or out of government. The act of implementing a policy can determine the actual shape and content of that policy. Political scientist Robert Lineberry has identified at least four major elements to implementation:[12] (1) bureaucracy, (2) rules and routines, (3) coordination of resources, and (4) staffing and funding.

Generally, implementation is carried out by the bureaucracy. A new staff agency must be created and staffed to implement a new policy, or else an existing agency and its personnel must be assigned responsibility for implementing it.[13] New departments and agencies have been created over time as new government policies have been developed: NASA was established to carry on a space program; the Federal Communications Commission was created to regulate emerging radio and television technology; and the Green Berets were created to fight guerrilla wars. But often existing agencies are assigned new policies: The Secret Service, which had been created as an anticounterfeiting agency, was given the job of presidential protection; the Department of Defense was instructed to implement President Clinton's change in its policy on gays in the military. Of course, some policies may not be entrusted to the bureaucracy: President Nixon so feared bureaucratic resistance to his foreign policy goals (arms control with the Soviet Union, opening contacts with the People's Republic of China) that he used his national security adviser (Henry Kissinger) to implement his plans.[14]

Second, rules and organizational routines must be developed to implement a policy.[15] Administrative rules and regulations provide the details that will shape the policy as actually carried out by the bureaucracy. As we saw in Chapter 10, Congress has grown increasingly reliant on these regulations to determine the final content of policy on the environment, safety and health, transportation, and many other areas. All bureaucratic organizations develop standard operating procedures (SOPs) for handling their business. These routines can affect how policy is implemented. During the 1962 Cuban Missile Crisis, President Kennedy ordered a naval blockade of Cuba; the U.S. Navy's SOP for blockades almost provoked a confrontation between American and Soviet ships before Moscow could consider the risks of war; unchanged, the Navy's routine could have led to nuclear war.[16]

Third, agency resources and expenditures must be coordinated and an appropriate division of responsibility between the agency and related agencies must be developed.[17] In other words, responsibility and bureaucratic "turf" must be settled. The fate of one federal program intended to create jobs for minority workers in Oakland, California, is a good example.[18] In 1966 the U.S. Commerce Department's Economic Development Administration (EDA) announced a plan to stimulate employment in Oakland through grants and loans that included money for a new World Airways terminal. The program, which was predicted to create three thousand jobs, was received enthusiastically and with no organized opposition. Yet three years later little had been done and only about thirty jobs created. Why? One of the main reasons was that EDA and other organizations involved in the program approached its implementation with different priorities (some wanted to emphasize minority jobs; others wanted to promote the airline industry in Oakland), different levels of commitment and resources (EDA considered the project a priority, but other federal and state agencies involved did not), and conflicting views about who was responsible for what (there were serious disagreements about which government agency controlled various parts of the project). The lack of coordination among several federal, state, local, and private organizations meant that a popular policy ended in failure. In contrast, many policies have been successfully implemented through effective coordination of agency responsibilities and resources.

Finally, the policy must be adequately funded and staffed.[19] As we will see, even a well-designed and coordinated policy may not achieve its goals if it

THE VOTERS SPEAK

All elections are
important for deciding
who will occupy posi-
tions of power, but in
our separation-of-
powers system few
alter the direction of
national policy. Some
elections have been
crucial for shaping
government policy:
The 1932 election
brought on the New
Deal; 1964 brought on
Lyndon Johnson's
Great Society; 1980
brought redirected
budget priorities and
inaugurated the Rea-
gan defense buildup.
Republicans claimed
that the 1994 election
would mark the
beginning of a new
era in American poli-
tics. Time will tell
whether they were
right.

lacks sufficient resources. In the 1980s, Congress undertook a well-publicized effort to escalate the "war on drugs" by creating a cabinet-level Office of National Drug Control Policy. This organization was to coordinate all antidrug efforts by the U.S. government, but it was never given the funding commensurate with its responsibilities. Consequently, it has had only limited impact on the problem of drug abuse.

Implementation is often the downfall of many well-intentioned public policies. It is hard enough to design and win support for public policies and programs, but it is even more difficult to implement them in a way that pleases anyone at all, including the supposed beneficiaries or clients.[20]

Policy Evaluation and Change

After public policies have been proposed, adopted, and implemented, they are ultimately assessed by the officials who created them, the groups affected by them, independent analysts, journalists, and just about anyone who chooses to do so. Extensive (and expensive) efforts are made to evaluate policies in an objective and rigorous way. One of the most prominent tools for doing this is *cost-benefit analysis,* a method drawn from economics and management science to provide quantifiable evidence of the relative value of a policy or program. The basic idea of this technique is to list the positive features of a program and attach some monetary value to them, then do the same for the negative features.[21]

Cost-benefit analysis is often used by government agencies, outside consultants, and scholars to assess policies. It has been applied to government activities from the B-1 bomber to the food stamps and Head Start programs. In the federal government, the General Accounting Office (GAO) regularly performs analyses of programs (especially high-priced, high-tech weapons) using a type of cost-benefit methodology. GAO analyses can be influential. In the 1980s one GAO study suggested that President Reagan's "Star Wars" proposal (to put anti-missile defense systems in orbit) had enough merit to warrant further research; that conclusion helped save the program from being gutted by a skeptical Democratic majority in Congress.

Even if cost-benefit analysis is used, elected and appointed policy makers often rely on more politically based determinations of the value of policy. For example, Congress has ordered that expensive weapons systems be built despite poor cost-benefit results and over Defense Department objections, because members want industries and jobs in their states to benefit from the prosperity that such projects bring. Likewise, President Reagan's enthusiasm for the "Star Wars" program had less to do with a cost-benefit calculation than it did with Reagan's interest in a high-tech defense shield.

Evaluations of policy may lead to change. Implementing agencies will often recommend ways to improve programs, and individuals and groups affected by policies may react to the government's actions. But for change to occur, the cycle of policy making, and all its attendant complications, must begin again.

Public policy provides one of the best examples of American government in action. Here the lobbying of interest groups, the maneuverings of legislators, the speeches of presidents, and the activities of bureaucrats combine to produce results that affect the lives and fortunes of citizens on a daily basis. Taxes are raised or lowered; medical care is made available or denied to veterans or the poor; businesses are given the flexibility to produce products or told how their endeavors will be regulated; and farmers receive subsidies or find that they have been cut off.

Factors Affecting Policy Change

When we consider that the Constitution favors the status quo and that the policy-making process is long and difficult, we should not be surprised that most changes in policy are small and modest. Laws and programs are relatively stable, and the revenues and expenditures in the budget tend to remain largely the same from one year to the next. So rare are major shifts in policy that we tend to mark the unusual periods in our history when they have occurred, giving these changes such names as the Progressive Era, the New Deal, the Great Society, and Reaganomics.

In general, major changes in national policy occur only under certain conditions. One such condition is a *sense of national urgency or crisis.* The Great Depression—during which one-third of the labor force was out of work, the stock market crashed, and thousands of farms went bankrupt—created such a sense of crisis in the nation that Congress was willing to pass many of President Franklin Roosevelt's early legislative proposals with little or no debate. After World War II, the rise of a Soviet empire in Eastern Europe so alarmed American leaders that the U.S. Senate was willing to break a century-and-a-half tradition and bind the nation to a peacetime military alliance (the North Atlantic Treaty Organization, or NATO).

Another condition that allows for major policy change is the *alignment of political forces in the direction of change.* For example, Lyndon Johnson's War on Poverty became policy because the president could take advantage of big Democratic majorities in both houses of Congress achieved in the 1964 election, a large personal mandate in that election, general economic prosperity (to pay for programs), and national sorrow over the assassination of John F. Kennedy (whom Johnson repeatedly invoked).

In contrast, Jimmy Carter found that strong opposition to policy change made such change all but impossible. In 1977 he summoned the nation to undertake the "moral equivalent of war" to change energy policy, but he found that the alignment of political forces was not in his favor. He had few ties to Democrats in Congress; the legislature was in no mood to follow any president's lead in that period (following the Vietnam War and Watergate); public opinion did not respond to his "moral equivalent of war"; major interest groups opposed him; and a general sense of declining material wealth made any new program seem too expensive.

During the Great Depression jobs were so scarce that many were reduced to selling on the streets. This sense of national crisis helped President Franklin Roosevelt get many of his proposals for new public policies through Congress with little or no debate.

Bill Clinton also found that a misalignment of political forces can block the grand plans of policy advocates. Clinton made health care reform his central domestic-policy initiative in the first two years of his presidency, yet between problems in the administration's own plan and resistance to it, Clinton was unable to achieve even a small part of his proposed national health care system before the 1994 elections ushered Republican majorities into Congress.

These conditions affect innovation in large areas of policy. What about innovation in narrower policy areas? In general, small-scale innovations and large-scale change require similar conditions.[22] The differentiating characteristic is that it is far easier to meet the two conditions of crisis and political force for change in a narrow area than in a large one. Another factor that distinguishes small-scale innovations is who may enact them. Large-scale innovations require legislation and all the complicated procedures and compromises involved in passing laws. But narrower innovations can be accomplished outside the legislative process—in the courts (for example, desegregation), the White House (Nixon's renewal of American diplomatic contact with China), or the bureaucracy (in 1992 the Food and Drug Administration's new policy requiring detailed labeling of the ingredients of all packaged foods).

Welfare Reform

Almost since the early days of the "war on poverty" in the 1960s, there have been those who have called for reform of America's welfare system. Tales of welfare cheating have become part of our national folklore, although actual evidence of fraud is mixed at best.

"Welfare" is not a single program, but actually a term that applies to a range of government programs (run by the federal and state governments in different degrees) intended to help the poor and needy. It includes programs such as Aid to Families With Dependent Children (AFDC); food stamps; the Supplemental Security Income portion of Social Security; Medicaid; educational grants and loans; public housing; the Women, Infants, and Children assistance program (WIC); and other lesser programs. It is administered by several federal agencies, as well as state governments.

Plans to reform welfare date at least to the Nixon administration, which proposed a Family Assistance Plan that it maintained would overcome many of the problems of welfare and strengthen families. The plan was rejected by Congress as too expensive.

In recent years, President Bill Clinton campaigned for office promising to "end welfare as we know it," a phrase that different observers took to have different meanings. Many thought Clinton was calling for a radical plan to cut off all welfare benefits to recipients after a specified period. In fact, the Clinton administra-

tion's plan did not propose to cut off welfare benefits but instead to transfer welfare recipients, after two years, to a different form of welfare. The plan did not make clear, however, precisely how this new system would work. This plan suffered from two problems: it would have been more expensive than all current welfare programs, and it was abandoned by the administration as the president devoted his attention to trying to win passage of his health care reform plan.

In the 1994 election, the Republican Contract With America called for a two-year maximum for any individual to receive welfare benefits. This plan stimulated considerable debate about the merits of welfare and the ethics of cutting off recipients. Proponents of the limit maintained that forcing people off welfare would only require them to do what they should do already: find work or assistance from private charities. Opponents maintained that such a scheme would only create more homeless and hopeless people, with children bearing the biggest burden of the plan.

Whatever the results of the latest debate over welfare reform, it is likely that the issue will remain part of the political agenda for some time. There are no easy answers to the problems of welfare—people who need assistance, people who abuse assistance, a complex welfare bureaucracy, and frustrated taxpayers.

current issues

Even narrow policy changes must occur within the same political system as large-scale ones. Congress's policy-making power is broad. It can intervene to overturn or modify many innovations that it opposes. Although the Federal Trade Commission (FTC) tried for several years to ban all tobacco advertising, it was stopped by the legislature (under pressure from tobacco interests) from doing so. Consequently, the FTC has adopted smaller changes in this area, such as banning radio and television advertising of tobacco, and requiring warning labels on cigarettes and tobacco ads.

Political Patterns That Shape Policy

As we have seen, continuity is more common than change in national policy. We can also note some general patterns that shape specific areas of policy. The making of distributive policy, such as farm subsidies and grants for highway development, tends to be highly stable. It is also the policy area in which iron triangles (discussed in Chapter 6)—interest groups, congressional committees, and bureaucratic agencies—are most likely to be found. In contrast, protective regulatory policy is less stable, with shifting coalitions of legislators, executive officials, and interests shaping policy. Compromise over such issues as the regulation of pollution tends to mark this area. Control over much of competitive regulatory policy, such as for broadcasting or stock and bond trading, has been delegated to experts who run independent regulatory commissions. In these organizations, ideology (such as favoring or opposing government regulation) often shapes policy. Finally, redistributive policy involves a high degree of conflict, because these policies are intended to alter society and create "winners" and "losers." We can see such conflict in recent battles over welfare reform (see the box "Welfare Reform"). Both the White House and Congress play important roles in decisions over whether and how to redistribute wealth and opportunities in society.

In all areas of policy, with the possible exception of crisis policy, America's budget situation has become the starting point for most policy debates. From health care reform to the nation's role in a changing world, the choices and opportunities facing policy makers are to a greater or lesser degree conditioned by the budget. This situation has arisen because of large budget deficits each year since the early 1980s. In the 1990s, with a sense that deficits had gotten "out of control," policy makers were forced to consider nearly all issues—from defense to welfare reform to immigration—in terms of how they affect the deficit. Concern over the deficit also stimulated interest in a constitutional amendment to require a balanced federal budget each year.

open questions

What Should Our Policy Be Toward the Budget Deficit?

In one sense, nearly all questions related to public policy are open. There are few final answers to questions such as what policy should we adopt with regard to education? defense? poverty? The very question of which issues demand the most attention right now also is an open one. But some issues have come to dominate the political scene in recent years: in foreign affairs, America's role in the post–cold war world; in domestic policy, what to do about the budget.

Since the early 1980s, the federal government has been running deficits of more than $100 billion each year, usually more than $200 billion. Each year's deficit adds to the total federal debt, which is now approximately $5 trillion (about equal to one year's gross domestic product, or over $16,000 per person).

Citizens, commentators, and policy makers have expended considerable energy on the question of what to do about continuing budget deficits. Some observers have even asked whether we ought to be concerned about deficits at all. The debate over budget policy is an important one. Citizens must pay attention to it because any action—or no action at all—has consequences for the future of all Americans.

The fact that there has not been a balanced federal budget since 1969 has led many Americans, including congressional Republicans, to endorse the idea of a constitutional amendment to require a balanced budget each year, but a strenuous debate erupted over this proposal. Most states have such requirements in their constitutions, and supporters of a federal amendment argue that the time has come for the national government to have one, too. The case for a Balanced Budget Amendment is based on two assumptions: that the best economic policy proceeds from a balanced budget and that "politics as usual" prevents such a policy from being enacted.

Supporters of the amendment argue that interest groups block the kind of spending cuts, reductions in entitlements, new taxes, or other unpopular choices that are necessary to bring the federal budget into balance. They maintain that a constitutional requirement will impose necessary discipline on budget makers and force them to do what is in the national interest. Several versions of such a proposal exist, but the most common ones allow deficit spending only in the event of a declaration of war (most American wars have been financed through borrowing) or if a supermajority (such as three-fifths) of each house of Congress votes to spend more than revenues take in.

Opponents of the proposal make several arguments. Some question the wisdom of mandating balanced budgets at all. They maintain that deficits or surpluses should be used as tools of economic policy, so no fixed policy should be mandated. Others argue that big deficits are less significant than they seem to be, because the nation has been running them for years without obvious disaster. But most opponents share the position that a balanced budget requirement is a bad idea because it will not work. Most versions of the proposal do not provide an enforcement mechanism for punishing policy makers if they produce unbalanced budgets; budget assumptions can be manipulated to make a budget look balanced even if it is not; and expensive items can be put "off-budget," and not be included in deficit calculations.

Should a Balanced Budget Amendment be adopted? Is it necessary? Would it work? Are there other policy prescriptions that ought to be added to the Constitution? These questions deserve our attention and have no easy answers.

Summary

Public policy refers to direct or indirect government activities that affect the lives of citizens. It involves the choices that officials make, how those choices are put into action, and what effects those choices have on people. *Domestic* policy includes distributive policy, protective and competitive regulatory policies, and redistributive policy. *Intermestic* issues are policy matters that have aspects of both domestic and foreign policy.

Principles. The Constitution is more concerned with the institutions and process of policy making than with the substance of policy. It does have policy consequences, though, especially by favoring the status quo.

Process. Policy is made through a five-step process. *Agenda-setting* is the stage that identifies problems that government officials will attempt to solve. In the second stage, officials *make policy choices.* Then *budgeting* becomes important, because the federal budget can affect how policies are implemented and what government can afford to do. Policy is then *implemented*—put into effect. This stage can affect the actual shape of policy. Finally, policy is *evaluated and changed.*

Politics. The American political system is marked by continuity in policy, with major change coming only under certain conditions. Those conditions—a sense of urgency or crisis, an alignment of political forces in the direction of change—occur infrequently.

Open Questions. What should we do about our federal budget problems? Should we amend the Constitution to require a balanced budget? Proponents argue that such a change would impose the discipline policy makers need to make hard budget choices. Opponents argue that the change would be ineffective or lead to dishonesty in budget calculations. Would such a plan work? Even if it would work, is it a good idea?

Suggested Readings

JONES, CHARLES O. *An Introduction to the Study of Public Policy,* 3rd ed. Monterey, Calif.: Brooks/Cole, 1984. A highly readable survey by an authority in the field.

PETERS, B. GUY. *American Public Policy: Promise and Performance,* 3rd ed. Chatham, N.J.: Chatham House, 1993. A good survey of the policy process and several major policy issues.

RIPLEY, RANDALL B., and GRACE A. FRANKLIN. *Bureaucracy and Policy Implementation,* 2nd ed. Homewood, Ill.: Dorsey Press, 1986. Interesting study of how bureaucracy shapes policy as it carries it out.

———. *Congress, the Bureaucracy, and Public Policy,* 3rd ed. Homewood, Ill.: Dorsey Press, 1984. Excellent overview of policy making through legislation.

SAVAGE, JAMES D. *Balanced Budgets and American Politics.* Ithaca, N.Y.: Cornell University Press, 1988. An excellent introduction to the whole issue of budget deficits and public policy.

SHUMAN, HOWARD E. *Politics and the Budget,* 2nd ed. Englewood Cliffs, N.J.: Prentice Hall, 1988. Clear and readable survey of the politics and processes involved in federal budgeting.

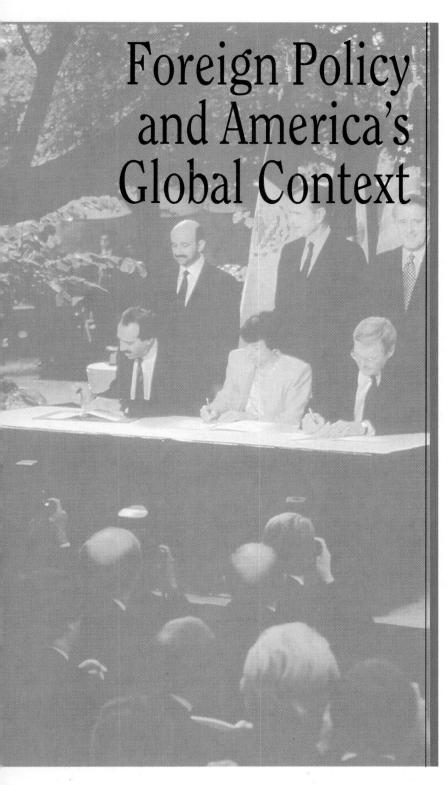

Foreign Policy and America's Global Context

Chapter 14

The evening news brings us not only the events of our local communities and the latest political developments in Washington but also stories of what is happening in the larger world beyond our borders. Americans watched as the Berlin Wall was torn down; we saw the war against Iraq from the top of a hotel in Baghdad; we saw U.S. Marines come ashore in Somalia in 1992; and we followed the cleanup in Kobe, Japan, after the 1995 earthquake. Even without these dramatic reminders of world affairs, we are aware that our nation is part of a larger international environment.

That environment is both strange and familiar to us. In the age of instantaneous communication, parts of it have become strikingly familiar. Americans know what Grozny, the capital of Chechnya in the former Soviet Union, looks like; we have seen air raids in Tel Aviv as Israel awaited the attack of Iraq's Scud missiles in 1991; and we have watched Great Britain's royal family live out the highs and lows of their lives—from marriages and state ceremonies to divorces and family scandals. Yet much of the international environment remains a mystery to American citizens: the complex racial and ethnic politics of South Africa, the isolated culture of North Korea, or the warring factions in Bosnia.

In this chapter, we examine how the United States relates to this larger world. There are many reasons why Americans ought to know about foreign policy and the world beyond our borders: our citizens do billions of dollars worth of business with other nations; Americans often live or travel abroad; many of our people have immigrated from other lands or are recent descendants of those who did; and our involvement in several wars has shown us that political developments in other lands can affect us here at home. We will see what policies our government has developed to guide its relations with other nations, how our political system compares with the many others with which the United States must deal, and what issues confront our nation in a changing world.

America and the World

The United States must carry on in the strange and yet familiar world that we see on the news, even if we would prefer to focus our attention at home. The American people have often tended to look inward rather than concern themselves with global affairs. For much of our history, we have prided ourselves on being removed from the "Old World" and its various problems. Some of the great themes of American history—such as building a new nation, settling a continent, and establishing a prosperous economy—have also fostered a sense of our country as different from others. It is only in the twentieth century that the United States has become a continuous player in world politics.

What is the nature of the international environment of which we are a part? How does the nation make its way through that vast external realm? The answers to these questions will help us to understand America's role in the world and the challenges facing our nation in the future.

What Is the Nature of World Politics?

World politics is a web of interactions among actors with different goals, resources, and cultures and with varying amounts of political and economic power.[1] The United States is a major actor in international affairs, but, as we will see, it is certainly not the only one. What we will also find is that world politics operates somewhat differently from the give-and-take of politics within the American political system.

International Anarchy. The most fundamental condition affecting world politics is *international anarchy,* the absence of a world government or any other institution with the authority to set and enforce rules that all must obey. Anarchy does not necessarily mean chaos, but it does mean that the various actors in world politics are regulated largely by force and the mutual interests among them. Thus armed conflict is a common device for settling disputes. There are "rules" in this anarchic environment—a body of international law, treaties, and other formal agreements; and customary practices of diplomatic protocol—but these are generally maintained because actors in world affairs have an interest in imposing some order on what could be a chaotic environment.[2] Among these actors are two broad types—states and nonstates.

States in World Politics. The most important actors in international affairs are states, which are also known as countries. They share certain characteristics. States are *territorial* in nature, controlling specific sections of land, water, and even sky. States possess *sovereignty;* this means that a country possesses absolute control over its internal affairs and its decisions involving other actors in the international system. Of course, in practice, many states are not completely free. Their behavior is influenced by the power of other states, by economic considerations, or by dependence on larger states for support. Modern states are also usually associated with the concept of the nation. **Nationalism** refers to a strong sense of group identity and emotional ties among a particular people. Nationalism is a powerful force that has stimulated a number of conflicts in contemporary world politics.

In modern times, the term "nation-state" has sometimes been used interchangeably with "state," indicating how closely the two have been related.[3] States and nations are different, however. States are political/legal units (such as the Federal Republic of Germany), whereas nations are social/cultural entities (such as the German people, who do not all live inside the Federal Republic). This does not mean that the term nation-state is wrong, only that it is limited; not all states are nation-states. Japan, France, and Germany are nation-states— their regimes are closely tied to specific groups of people with a common history and culture. In contrast, many states created from former colonies of the European imperial powers are not nation-states. For example, Nigeria—created from British imperial territory in western Africa in 1964—is a state with a

nationalism A strong sense of group identity and emotional ties among a particular people.

intergovernmental organization (IGO) An international body that links states in the international environment. Examples include the United Nations and military alliances.

population that consists of several different ethnic groups, some of whom were divided between Nigeria and its neighbors. India, the world's largest democracy, is also not a nation-state—it is made up of a collection of several different (and often conflictual) groups.

Nonstate Actors That Influence World Politics. Three types of nonstate actors participate in the international environment.[4] First, there are *nationalist groups* that want independence for their people from a larger state or control over what they regard as their native territory. The Palestine Liberation Organization (PLO) seeks a Palestinian state in contemporary Israel and Jordan; the Irish Republican Army wants an end to British rule of Northern Ireland. Second, there are *nongovernmental organizations* that are active in more than one country and have goals that are not related to territory. They are also mostly nonpolitical in nature. This group includes religious organizations (such as the Catholic Church), international charities (such as the International Red Cross), and multinational corporations (such as Gulf Oil and General Electric).

A third type of nonstate actor, the **intergovernmental organization** (IGO), links states in ways that are important to the conduct of world affairs and often affect the domestic politics of members. The largest IGO is the *United Nations (UN),* which provides a forum for intergovernmental coordination and communication. The UN has played a role in peacekeeping operations around

The United States is a major player in world affairs. It has been involved in a number of conflicts around the world, including the continuing troubles in Northern Ireland. Here, an American conference on foreign policy hears from Gerry Adams (center), head of Sinn Fein, the Irish Republican Army's political wing. With Adams are William J. Flynn (left) chair of the National Committee, and Ambassador Angier Biddle Duke, chair of the conference.

the world (for which it won the Nobel Peace Prize), as an institution for coordinating and facilitating military operations (in the Korean and Persian Gulf Wars), and as a means for peaceful resolution of some international conflicts (for example, the Suez crisis in 1956). Other types of IGOs are military alliances and economic alliances. For example, the United States belongs to the *North Atlantic Treaty Organization (NATO)*, a military alliance formed to provide protection for the democratic nations of Western Europe.

Power in World Politics. Only a few countries have the ability to play continuing and influential roles in world politics. They are known as *great powers.* Traditionally, great powers were defined by their military power: the British Empire of the nineteenth century, the Soviet Union, the United States in the twentieth century, and others. Economic power often (but not always) accompanied such military might. But in our time some states have considerable economic power but less military force; Japan and Germany are the most obvious examples. Each possesses a large and powerful economy but has a small military establishment. Japan's economy is one of the world's largest; the country manufactures a wide array of industrial and electronic machinery, but its national self-defense force has almost no significance in world military affairs. Most countries are small powers and have little influence over the general direction of world affairs. A few states are sometimes referred to as middle powers; countries such as Canada, South Korea, Australia, Brazil, and Egypt may be important in a particular region of the world or on certain kinds of issues, but they cannot seriously challenge the great powers for general influence.

In the decades after World War II, a new category of countries emerged: the *superpowers*—countries with such overwhelming military power that they were able to dominate world affairs. For most of the second half of the twentieth century, the United States and the Soviet Union were the only two states that possessed the military power necessary to be called superpowers. These two countries were divided by an ideological gulf between communism and democracy that led them to conduct a decades-long **cold war**—a state of tension in which actual war was avoided while both sides competed through military alliances, arms buildups, and diplomatic confrontations. Both countries also supported friendly forces in Asia (in Korea, Vietnam, and Laos), Africa (in Angola and elsewhere), and Latin America (such as in Cuba and Nicaragua). China seemed to possess the potential for superpower status, but the attention of its leaders was focused inward, and China has not emerged as a consistent force in the world arena.

The cold war ended in the late 1980s in the wake of the collapse of the Soviet Union and its East European empire. As the Soviet state disintegrated into Russia, the Ukraine, and other states, the United States remained as the only superpower. America faced growing economic competition from Japan, the European community, and other economic powers, but it continued to be the only "great power" in terms of both military and economic superiority.

cold war The forty-year standoff between the United States and the Soviet Union that began after World War II and ended when the Soviet Union and its domination of Eastern Europe collapsed in the late 1980s.

American Foreign Policy

America's official relations with the rest of the world are gathered under the term "foreign policy," which is part of the larger web of public policy that results from the choices officials make, how those choices are carried out, and the effects of those choices. American foreign policy is a specialized form of policy because it shapes our nation's role in world affairs, matters of war and peace, and even the economy. It includes our diplomatic relations with other countries and organizations in the international environment, uses of our military forces, international trade and economic behavior, and even how we exchange cultural and scientific information with others. Foreign policy has three main facets: structural, strategic, and crisis policy.

Structural Policy. The basic rules, structures, and resources for conducting American foreign policy are laid down by Congress and the president. These include the size, training, and equipping of our armed forces—how many soldiers the nation will have in uniform; what kinds of ships, planes, and tanks they will use, and where we will maintain military bases. Both Congress and the executive are intimately involved in this type of policy making. Because of its power to appropriate money and its authority to make laws that regulate the armed forces, Congress participates in such decisions as which weapons systems the government will acquire (such as the Stealth bomber or a battleship) and how military pay and benefits will be determined. Of course, the president and the Department of Defense play a large role in shaping these decisions, but most structural policies are the product of compromise between the branches. As Figure 14.1 shows, since the end of World War II (1945),

FIGURE 14.1 Defense Spending as a Percent of Gross Domestic Product, 1955–1993.
Source: Budget of the United States, FY 1995, Office of Management and Budget.

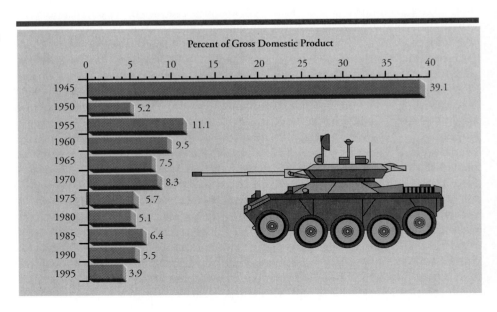

Percent of Gross Domestic Product

Year	Percent
1945	39.1
1950	5.2
1955	11.1
1960	9.5
1965	7.5
1970	8.3
1975	5.7
1980	5.1
1985	6.4
1990	5.5
1995	3.9

defense spending has shown a gradual decline. Turns upward in 1955, 1970, and 1985 reflected cold war spending, the costs of the Vietnam War, and increased spending by the Reagan administration to strengthen the nation's nuclear weaponry.

Local considerations and interest group activity often influence foreign policy outcomes. For example, the placement of military bases in the southeast United States is the result of political rather than military decisions. Indeed, despite efforts to reduce defense spending in a post–cold war era, Congress has found it difficult to injure local economies by closing military bases no longer needed by the Defense Department. In the past few years, Congress has turned to an independent citizens commission to decide on base closings, leaving elected officials the job of accepting or rejecting an entire list of obsolete facilities rather than having to choose which districts would suffer.

Also included in the category of structural policy are the ground rules for U.S. trade with other countries. American laws define tariffs (taxes) on imports and set conditions on trade with other countries. For example, current law forbids American trade with nations that the government believes support terrorism or violate human rights (unless the president can certify that there is a compelling national interest in conducting such trade).

Strategic Policy. This concerns political judgments about the outlook, goals, and strategy of American foreign policy. What will be the goals of our foreign policy? To enlarge the number of democratic nations in the world? To promote human rights? To protect American business abroad? To promote freedom even at the risk of war? What kinds of agreements will the nation enter to pursue its goals? Will it support one side or another in conflicts such as that in Bosnia, or will the United States remain neutral? These are the kinds of questions that decision makers must answer to establish how the nation and its representatives will act in world affairs.

As we saw in Chapter 9, the executive is usually dominant in this area. As commander in chief and chief diplomat, the president plays the leading role in shaping national strategy, and this aspect of the president's responsibilities has become increasingly important since the end of the cold war. Congress is not left out, however; many major policy decisions, such as the establishment of military alliances or acceptance of trade and arms-control agreements, usually require legislative involvement. But in most cases, Congress follows where the president leads.

Crisis Policy. Crisis policy is made almost exclusively by the president and a select group of executive advisers. This area involves developing responses to urgent situations in which policy makers believe that national interests are threatened unless they decide quickly what course they will follow.[5] Examples include such events as the invasion of South Korea in 1949, the Cuban Missile Crisis in 1962, the 1973 Arab-Israeli (October) war, and Iraq's invasion of Kuwait in 1990. Given the urgency of response and the stakes involved in such situations, presidents usually make decisions unilaterally and inform Congress of their choices only after the fact. Although this contact with Capitol Hill is referred to as "consultation," it is more accurately described as the executive prescribing policy and the legislature accepting it.

 ## The Instruments of Foreign Policy

Foreign policy is conducted through several means. Officials can employ *diplomacy*—persuasion, discussion, negotiation and bargaining—to advance the nation's goals. They can use military force or even *espionage*—spying and secret operations. They can use *economic tools* of influence: the United States gives almost $20 billion a year in foreign aid to other nations; in 1995 the Clinton administration offered loan guarantees to Mexico to help that country with an economic crisis; and the United States provides countries with assistance in developing their economies (such as a Peace Corps project to teach farmers in Guatemala more productive agricultural techniques). Officials may often employ a mix of several of these instruments at once. Table 14.1 shows how different instruments are employed in structural, strategic, and crisis policies adopted by the government. This table also helps us to see how foreign policy is more than just what actions the president may take to respond to the events of today.

American relations with Mexico form an important part of the nation's foreign policy. In 1995, newly elected Mexican President Ernesto Zedillo, shown here just after his victory, won U.S. support for his efforts to prevent the collapse of the Mexican economy.

PART 4/DOMESTIC AND GLOBAL POLICY

TABLE 14.1 Foreign Policy in Action

	Diplomacy	Force	Espionage	Economic Tools
Structural Policy	Logan Act, 1791, prohibits diplomacy by private citizens	Laws governing size of military, choice of weapons, location of military bases	Laws establishing CIA and other intelligence agencies	Trade laws Tariffs Foreign aid
Strategic Policy	Clinton administration policy of seeking "enlargement" of democratic governments in world	Military alliances (NATO and others)	Spying in Soviet Union and Eastern Europe during cold war	President conducts economic negotiations among major industrial nations
Crisis Policy	U.S. diplomatic activity to try to end Middle East war, 1974	U.S. invasion of Grenada, 1983 U.S. invasion of Panama, 1990	United States used aerial photography to detect and monitor Soviet missile buildup in Cuba, 1962	Clinton administration offers loan guarantees to Mexico to deal with Mexican economic crisis, 1995

America's response to the world has not been the same over the course of national history. From the earlier days of the nation, U.S. foreign policy moved through two major phases and, in the 1990s, began a third.[6]

Early Isolationism

For most of our history, **isolationism**—the idea that the United States should remain aloof from most controversies of world politics—was the prevailing philosophy governing our approach to international affairs. Beginning with a Neutrality Proclamation by President Washington that kept the young Republic out of Europe's conflicts, and following the advice in his Farewell Address to avoid "entangling alliances" abroad, the United States tried to avoid sustained involvement in world politics while it concentrated on domestic affairs. Of course, that did not mean that there was no foreign involvement. The nation took on the Barbary Pirates under Thomas Jefferson, declared in the Monroe Doctrine that it would protect the Western Hemisphere from European domination, and became involved in the War of 1812 against Britain. But the assumption behind foreign policy in the nineteenth century was that the United States should stay out of the affairs of Europe's great powers unless a compelling national interest was at stake.

Principles: What Ideas Direct American Foreign Policy?

isolationism The view that the United States should not play an active role in world affairs on a continuing basis.

In the twentieth century the nation began to play a larger role in world affairs. Theodore Roosevelt asserted the need to develop and occasionally employ U.S. power in the Americas and the Pacific. When Woodrow Wilson brought the nation into World War I, he was able to do so only by selling his policy as the necessary response to an extreme crisis: American involvement was crucial to success in the "war to end war." But Wilson was unable to win support for his plan to bring the United States into the League of Nations he had helped create (a forerunner of the UN), because of domestic reluctance to avoid "entangling alliances." After Wilson, the country elected Warren Harding in 1920 on a platform pledging a return to "normalcy," which in part meant a return to isolationism.

Internationalism: Shaping World Affairs

Not until World War II did the second phase of American foreign policy begin. The war against Nazi Germany and Japanese militarism left most American leaders—and the public—with the view that the country had to remain involved in world affairs even after peace was achieved. Foreign policy was now driven by the philosophy of **internationalism**—the idea that it is necessary and proper for America to play a role in shaping world events.

Within a few years after the end of the war, Harry Truman gave this general internationalism a particular shape by providing a specific goal for U.S. foreign policy: stopping the spread of communism and restraining the influence of the Soviet Union in Europe. **Containment**—the idea of limiting the spread of Soviet power and thus communism—became the overarching philosophy of foreign policy. At first, it was focused on responding to the Soviet empire in Eastern Europe. Eventually, the idea of containment was widened to include stopping communism around the world. In 1949, the United States, Canada, and several West European countries formed NATO, the first permanent "entangling alliance" for Americans. Over the next several years, similar regional arrangements were made with anticommunist regimes around the world.

The breadth of these commitments led some observers to describe containment as *globalism*, because the United States had taken upon itself the task of directing opposition to Soviet influence around the world. Under the policy of containment, the United States led UN forces in defense of South Korea against North Korea (1950–53), conducted a lengthy and divisive war in Vietnam from the late 1950s to 1975, opposed the government of Fidel Castro in Cuba, and supported anticommunist governments and forces around the globe.

Another aspect of containment was nuclear *deterrence*, by which the acquisition and improvement of a formidable nuclear arsenal was designed to inhibit Soviet threats to the United States. Because the Soviet Union also possessed a nuclear arsenal, the resulting standoff and cold war meant that much of the U.S.-Soviet rivalry took place through diplomatic maneuvering and involvement in conflicts around the globe. When world politics was divided between "the West" (the U.S. and European democracies) and the "communist bloc," most developing nations in Latin America, Africa, and Asia were considered part of a *Third World* of developing nations.

internationalism The view that the United States should play an active role in world affairs.

containment The guiding philosophy of American foreign policy during the cold war; its goal was to stop the spread of communism and restrain the influence of the Soviet Union.

Near the end of the Vietnam War, the focus of American containment policy shifted to lessening the threat of nuclear war through a series of summit meetings and arms-control agreements with the Soviet Union. Rivalry between the superpowers continued and each side worked on its nuclear arsenal, but actual conflict seemed to be less of a threat than it had been in the 1950s and early 1960s.

Future Trends

The world situation changed dramatically in the 1980s. Countries in Eastern Europe that had once been dominated by the Soviet Union moved quickly and peacefully to end their communist regimes. Germany, divided since the end of World War II, was reunified. By the end of 1991 the Soviet Union had ceased to exist, and the cold war was clearly over. The proclaimed success of containment greatly reduced fears of nuclear conflict and opened new possibilities for world politics, but it also had important implications for the United States.

The end of the cold war changed the shape of global politics, but Russia remains a formidable presence. In recent years the United States has been concerned about the stability of Russia's emerging democracy, led currently by President Boris Yeltsin.

With the end of the cold war, American foreign policy entered its third major phase. With containment obsolete as a policy, the nation had no general philosophy on how to respond to the world beyond American shores. President George Bush spoke of a "new world order" dawning; but by the time he left office early in 1993, he had not articulated a policy to guide the United States in that new situation. Bill Clinton campaigned for the White House in 1992 with little attention to foreign affairs, but once elected president he found himself confronted with problems in Somalia, Iraq, Bosnia, Russia, and elsewhere. He attempted to deal with each issue on its merits but also did not develop an overarching policy to define the goals of American foreign policy in a post–cold war world.

In the post-containment era, two general philosophies compete for direction of American policy. One is internationalism, advocated by those who argue that as the sole superpower the United States has a special role to play in promoting international peace and stability. The other is a revived form of isolationism, held by those who argue that the nation should concern itself primarily with internal matters and leave foreign problems to others. Whichever view prevails, or whatever hybrid is formed between them, is likely to shape foreign policy for a long time.

How will we decide which ideas ultimately guide our relations with the world? The answer lies in the process by which the United States makes foreign policy.

Foreign policy is made by the same constitutional system as any other kind of policy, but there is a distinct difference between the way policy is made for matters here at home and for those abroad. Officials have a greater amount of leeway in making foreign-policy decisions than they do domestic ones. Moreover, the relative influence of officials within the government is different for foreign affairs than it is for matters at home.

The Process of Making American Foreign Policy

The Primary Role of the President

CITIZENS IN ACTION

JOHN SCALI'S DIPLOMATIC CAREER

John Scali, a professional journalist, twice moved from reporting on American foreign policy to participating in making it. In 1962, when the United States and Soviet Union confronted one another over Soviet missiles in Cuba, Scali served as a secret communication channel to Moscow for the Kennedy White House. In 1971, he was appointed U.S. ambassador to the United Nations by President Nixon. After serving there for two years, he resumed his career in journalism.

In domestic policy making, Congress has a large constitutional role that legislators are eager to play. Members of Congress are deeply concerned with domestic issues, just as their constituents are, because they see these issues as having a direct effect on their families, jobs, incomes, and the overall quality of their lives. In contrast, Congress has fewer constitutional prerogatives in the area of foreign policy. Moreover, even though legislators regard foreign policy as important, they see it as less important than questions of taxes, crime, education, and employment. As a result, primary responsibility for American foreign policy is in the hands of the president.

Constitutional Authority. As we saw in Chapter 9, three constitutional roles of the president give the chief executive considerable authority to direct and shape American relations with the rest of the world: (1) as *chief diplomat,* the president has the power to send out ambassadors and other representatives of the United States, to control negotiations between our government and other international actors, and to receive representatives of other countries; (2) as *commander in chief,* the president can order American military forces anywhere in the world, use force to deal with crises that threaten U.S. security, and decide on whether and when to employ the nation's nuclear arsenal; (3) as *chief executive,* the president not only appoints and supervises the officials of the government who deal with diplomacy, defense, and espionage but also has a broad mandate to create a strategy for American foreign policy. For example, the president can decide to get involved in a foreign conflict, such as that in the Middle East, or to remain aloof from it. These three roles give the chief executive broad authority to initiate and implement most foreign-policy decisions.

Extra-Constitutional Power in Foreign Policy. The president's primacy in foreign policy is based on the Constitution, but it has been enhanced by other political developments. As we saw in Chapter 9, in the twentieth century the American chief executive has acquired the role of world leader. Because of the American role in resisting the influence of the Soviet Union and maintaining the policy of containment, the U.S. president was often called the "Leader of the Free World" during the cold war. This position gave presidents such as Truman, Eisenhower, Nixon, and Reagan extensive influence over the foreign policies of U.S. allies. Other nations, such as Great Britain and Germany, often followed America's lead in matters such as the Vietnam War, arms control, and relations with the Soviet Union.

This position as a world leader, combined with broad constitutional authority, has strengthened the president's ability to dominate the making of American foreign policy. Both Congress and the public tend to defer to presidential initiatives in foreign affairs, even when members of Congress have doubts about the wisdom of a president's policy. For example, during the 1980s, many members of Congress disagreed with the Reagan administration's policy of supporting the *Contra* rebels fighting the revolutionary government of

Nicaragua. Despite this general reluctance and the fact that the Democratic Party's majority leadership in each house opposed such support, Congress often voted to give money to the *Contras* (although at other times it cut off such funding). Another example was the Persian Gulf War in 1991; Democratic majority leaders in Congress opposed endorsing President Bush's plan to launch a war against Iraq to liberate Kuwait, but both the House and Senate went ahead and supported the president's plan. On several occasions, presidential action leads to public acceptance. After President Reagan sent American forces to Grenada in 1983 to overthrow its Marxist government, public opinion shifted toward support of the action; this also occurred after President Clinton sent troops to Haiti in 1994.

One of the most important foreign-policy officials in American government is the president's assistant for national security affairs. When Henry Kissinger was national security assistant to President Richard Nixon, his power in the job rivaled (and sometimes outshone) the influence of the secretary of state.

Organizing the Government to Conduct Foreign Policy

Within the executive branch, the president presides over a "foreign-policy government" that consists of three major components: the State Department, which handles day-to-day diplomacy and monitoring of international events; the Defense Department, which handles the development and implementation of the nation's military policies and programs; and the intelligence establishment, which is headed by the Central Intelligence Agency but also includes other units such as the National Security Agency, which handles electronic information gathering.

The foreign-policy government is big and diverse. For example, the State and Defense Departments often view foreign-policy problems quite differently. State often takes the position that international issues are best resolved by diplomacy, whereas Defense may argue for the use of force to deal with a problem (although these generalizations do not apply in all cases).

The National Security Council. To make sense of the competing and often conflicting perspectives provided by these institutions, in recent decades presidents have tended to rely on the staff of the National Security Council (NSC) for a coordination of information and a "presidential" perspective on foreign policy. The NSC was created in 1947 as an advisory committee to assist the chief executive in coordinating the different elements of the nation's foreign policy. It consists of the vice-president, the secretaries of state, defense, and treasury, and the attorney general. The director of Central Intelligence—who heads the Central Intelligence Agency but also serves as the coordinator of all American espionage and intelligence-gathering activities—is an official adviser to the NSC. The council has a staff—now almost one hundred strong—that is directed by the president's assistant for national security affairs.

The Assistant for National Security Affairs. The president's reliance on the NSC effectively means reliance on the assistant for national security affairs (also known as the national security adviser). This official is a senior member of the White House staff who often plays a large role in contemporary American government. Some security assistants—Richard Nixon's Henry Kissinger or Jimmy Carter's Zbigniew Brzezinski—have been aggressive in the job and have competed with the secretaries of State and Defense for the president's ear and for influence over foreign policy. Others—Dwight Eisenhower's Robert Cutler, George Bush's Brent Scowcroft, and Bill Clinton's Anthony Lake—have tended to act as an "honest broker" responsible for seeing that the chief executive has all the information necessary to be an effective decision maker.

Other Foreign-Policy Officials. As important as the National Security Council staff has become, it is still only part of the foreign-policy government. Most of the responsibility for carrying out the nation's relations with the world lies with the Departments of State and Defense. The heads of these departments are thus major advisers to the president on international affairs. Once the president's single most important adviser on foreign policy, the secretary of state must now often compete with the secretary of defense and the assistant for national security affairs for influence. In the past few decades, each president has arrived at a different relationship with these three officials. Some presidents, such as Truman, Eisenhower, Ford, and Bush, have given primacy to the secretary of state. In other administrations, such as those of Kennedy, Nixon, Carter, Reagan, and Clinton, the president has given a large measure of influence to the assistant for national security affairs. Under Lyndon Johnson, whose foreign policy was dominated by the Vietnam War, the secretary of state was third in influence behind his counterpart at defense and the president's national security assistant. It may seem to vary from one president to another but no law or organizational chart can dictate which official will advise or influence the chief executive. Each president decides how to use the officials who have a role in carrying out the nation's foreign policy.

Making Foreign Policy

The president does not shape foreign policy alone, nor does the executive branch have sole authority over it. Congress has constitutional powers to influence foreign policy. It appropriates money and sets regulations governing the armed forces. It establishes the institutions of the foreign-policy government (the departments and agencies) and passes laws that provide the ground rules for the conduct of foreign policy (such as trade laws). Also, the Senate must approve ambassadors and treaties.

Congress does not generally use these powers in a way that dominates foreign policy. Instead, as we saw earlier in this chapter, the legislature tends to use its powers primarily to influence structural policies in foreign affairs. Members of Congress tend to be most concerned about those elements of foreign policy that have the clearest link to life at home, such as the location of military bases inside the United States (important sources of jobs), which weapons systems are built (also important sources of jobs at defense-related factories), rules governing imports, and appropriations for foreign aid (often a target of budget cutters because no one at home will immediately suffer from cuts).

Presidents must validate their policies with Congress by seeking legislators' approval for treaties, appropriations, nominations, declarations of war, and other presidential initiatives, but the relationship between the two branches is generally one of executive initiative and congressional acquiescence. Although in some ways the Constitution is "an invitation to struggle" over foreign policy,[7] in general the situation is one of presidential preeminence in the conduct of American foreign relations. Indeed, Thomas Jefferson may have exaggerated, but he came close to the practical truth when he asserted that "the transaction of business with foreign nations is executive altogether."[8] Decades later Harry Truman echoed this sentiment when he told a group of visitors from abroad, "I make American foreign policy."

When Ronald Reagan became president in 1981, world politics was dominated by the cold war, as it had been since the 1940s; and no one really anticipated that any significant change in world affairs would occur in the twentieth century. Yet by the time George Bush left office in 1993, the situation had certainly changed. In the wake of the end of the cold war and the collapse of the Soviet Union, America's foreign policy makers had to respond to a different set of problems and issues than their predecessors faced only a few years earlier.

Politics and American Foreign Policy

Reprinted with special permission of King Features Syndicate.

Become Active in Foreign Policy Issues

participate!

1. Educate yourself about foreign policy issues: Where does the United States have international commitments? Should we offer assistance to nations, such as Mexico, experiencing economic trouble? There is plenty of information available on international issues and foreign policy. In addition to standard news sources, *The Christian Science Monitor* contains extensive international coverage; *The Wall Street Journal* covers international economic issues; *The Economist* (despite its name) covers a wide range of issues in world politics; and the journals *Foreign Affairs, The National Interest,* and *Foreign Policy* offer in-depth discussions of foreign-policy issues.

2. Join a citizens group: Many college campuses and cities have organizations that bring together people interested in foreign affairs.

These often go under the name of World Affairs Councils, International Club, or other such titles. They can provide speakers, information on issues, and ways to learn more.

3. Make yourself heard: In addition to contacting the president (see Chapter 9) and representatives in Congress (see Chapter 8), you can contact the secretaries of state and defense, relevant congressional committees, and other officials. Consult Appendix F for sources of information on whom to contact, as well as addresses and phone numbers.

4. Get personally involved: You can seek an internship (see Chapter 13) or even a career in foreign affairs. For a list of some possibilities, see the appendix in John T. Rourke, Ralph G. Carter, and Mark A. Boyer, *Making American Foreign Policy* (Guilford, Conn.: Dushkin Publishing Group, 1994).

The State of Democracy and Liberty in the World

A stable democratic government and a large measure of liberty may be political arrangements Americans take as given, but most of the world's people do not share such expectations. Indeed, today, most of the world's population lives under regimes that are either nondemocratic or have yet to establish fully functioning democratic governments. Many still live under governments that pay little respect to the citizen rights and liberties Americans take for granted.

Why is this fact significant? It matters because it means that the United States is among a minority of the world's states. Political scientist W. Phillips Shively has calculated that of the 122 states that were independent between 1963 and 1993, only 29 had uninterrupted democratic governments during that time.[9] As American policy makers look out on the larger world, they see a variety of regimes. Only a few share our commitment to democracy and liberty.

Nondemocratic Regimes. Nondemocratic regimes are often quite different from one another, except that their leaders are not chosen through free and fair elections. There are three major types of these governments. First, there are *traditional regimes*—those that are governed by rulers (usually crowned heads) who claim authority through inheritance. States such as Saudi Arabia, Oman, Nepal, Bhutan, and Tonga all have monarchs whose power is defined, legitimized, and limited only by tradition. (These are much like Aristotle's concept of monarchy that we discussed in Chapter 1.) Except for the Arab oil states, most of these countries are small states on the fringes of the international community, and their traditional cultures prevail.

Then there are *military regimes*—governments in which the armed forces have seized control of the state or support the dictatorial rule of a civilian chief executive. Approximately one-tenth of the world's countries are governed in this way.[10] Military governments have held power at some time in Panama, Paraguay, Nigeria, Liberia, Pakistan, Greece, and the Philippines.

Finally, there are *one-party regimes*—governments in which a single ruling party claims authority to direct the policies of the state. That ruling party may be the only one allowed to legally exist, as is the case in Saddam Hussein's Iraq, the People's Republic of China, and Cuba. Otherwise, the dominant party allows other parties but maintains control through corruption, the pattern in Mexico, Zaire, and a number of other states. In some one-party systems the government is *totalitarian*. The ruling party adheres to a comprehensive political philosophy that is aimed at nothing less than the transformation of all society according to images of a "master race," "New Soviet man," or some other utopian ideal. This kind of vision drove the Nazi and Soviet states and has largely passed from the world stage, although it is still used to justify the oppression of millions of people in China, Cuba, and North Korea.

Democratic Regimes. Democratic regimes share certain characteristics in our times: officials are selected through free and competitive elections; representative democracy may be used exclusively or mixed with elements of direct democracy; and some kind of fundamental law (whether written or unwritten) shapes the structures and operating rules of the regime.[11] There are differences among them. In some, central governmental power is unified in a *parliament* (as in Great Britain) or divided between a president and legislature (as in the United States). Democratic regimes may also differ over how representatives should be selected and whether state power should be retained by the central government or distributed to other levels of government. Some democracies retain essentially all political power in the national government; this arrangement is called a *unitary government*. It is found in France, Norway, Ireland, and Israel. Other democracies employ *federalism*, in which power is divided between the national government and other levels of government. This is the arrangement in Canada, Switzerland, Germany, Australia, and the United States.

America's Response. The variety of political systems around the world—especially the tenuous status of democratic government—is apparent when Americans venture out into the international environment. Foreign policy is our response to the larger world and its challenges. It must be framed for a world in which so many political systems are unlike our own.

How are American leaders to respond to this world? During the cold war, our nation often supported nondemocratic regimes that shared our interest in stopping the influence of the Soviet Union and China. In a post–cold war world, however, we no longer have the idea of containment to guide our foreign policy. Some analysts, including prominent members of the Clinton administration, have argued that the nation should adopt a foreign policy aimed at enlarging the number of democracies in the world. Other analysts suggest that support for democracy must be tempered by concern about other aspects of American national security, such as avoiding conflict, and that in many of the world's trouble spots democracy is only a dream. In places such as Bosnia, Rwanda, Haiti, and Chechnya, events are driven by issues of survival, control of territory, and nationalist and ethnic differences.

Whatever policy our leaders should choose to pursue in dealing with the world, they will be working in an international environment in which the United States is among the minority. Our nation may be the only superpower of the post–cold war world, but it looks out on an array of countries and nonstate actors. Some share our values and interests; many do not.

Issues Facing American Foreign Policy

After it became clear that the cold war was over in the late 1980s, President George Bush described the international situation as a "new world order." This new order is more complex and uncertain than the situation it replaced.[12] Certainly, world affairs have improved in important ways. For example, the prospects for nuclear conflict have been greatly reduced. In addition, the breakup of the Soviet empire means that millions of people have been released from totalitarian rule and have at least the potential for democratic government. With the end of U.S.-Soviet competition, America does not need

With the end of the cold war, nationalist differences began to fuel conflicts around the globe. In 1995 President Clinton made a personal appeal to Russian President Yeltsin to stop the fighting in Chechnya, where Russian troops fought Chechen soldiers for control of the small Russian republic.

The Challenge of Nationalism

In some countries—the United States, Japan—the nation and the state are roughly the same. But that is certainly not universally true. Yugoslavia, which was created after the collapse of the Austro-Hungarian Empire in World War II, itself collapsed into small states that did not correspond to national groupings. Now, states such as Serbia, Bosnia-Hertzegovena, Montenegro, and Macedonia have been wracked by protracted and bloody interethnic war. Likewise, Ireland is divided between the Republic of Ireland in the south and British-controlled Northern Ireland, where the Catholic minority considers itself Irish and the Protestant majority considers itself British.

Nationalist sentiments and differences are important forces fueling much contemporary international activity and conflict. German nationalism fueled reunification of the two German states created after World War II, and today it is the source of conflict between ethnic Germans and immigrants (from Turkey and Italy) to the German republic. Parts of the former Soviet Union have pressed for national independence: In the Ukraine and Georgia, Russia has been unable to halt their determination to be free from Moscow's control; in Chechnya, the Russian government has used violent force to keep a nationalist group under its control.

Nationalist conflict presents a challenge for America's foreign policy makers. How much are nationalist differences and conflicts strictly internal matters, and how much are they international problems that necessitate intervention by other states? The United States, the European countries, and the United Nations have wrestled with this problem regarding the war in Bosnia. Should there be international intervention—and by whom, and of what type—to lessen the suffering caused by "ethnic cleansing" and other atrocities in a messy and ancient conflict? What principles should guide American foreign policy in dealing with ethnic conflicts such as this one?

Problems presented by nationalism are not transitory. Across central Europe, it is apparent that over a half-century of Nazi and Soviet rule did little to erase nationalist loyalties and conflicts that existed before Hitler and Lenin and reemerged soon after the cold war ended. Senator Daniel Patrick Moynihan, a student of world affairs, has found a term to describe the impact of nationalist problems on the international political scene: "pandaemonium." In the face of such a situation, it is not clear how the United States should respond.

to devote as large a share of its resources to high-tech weapons development as it once did.

At the same time, the new world order brings with it new problems and the reemergence of many old ones. For example, the United States must define for itself a role in a world no longer divided between Washington and Moscow. Are we to be the guardian of stability and order, the promoter of democracy, or should we refrain from further involvement? Another new issue is international cooperation. Should the United Nations be the vehicle for such undertakings, or should other institutions perform this function?

Nationalism is another source of problems in contemporary world politics. As the evening news regularly shows, many conflicts around the globe—in Bosnia, Chechnya, Ireland, and India—arise from nationalist and ethnic differences. The Current Issues box examines the challenges that nationalism presents for American foreign policy.

Another set of important international post–cold war issues involves economics. Developing countries in Central Europe, Africa, Asia, and Latin America are experiencing long-term problems of poor finances, limited resources, unemployment, and pollution. But major industrial nations are also experiencing problems. The highly publicized difficulties of the United States—a sagging economy and large public debt—are not unique; the economic powerhouses of Japan and Germany are also facing difficult economic situations. These issues will continue to loom large in the foreseeable future.

So will other issues. In recent years considerable attention has been paid to environmental problems around the world: deforestation in South America, polluted land and water in Central Europe, acid rain in the United States and Canada, air pollution in places like Mexico City and Athens, nuclear waste, and other difficulties. There are also natural disasters—droughts, floods, earthquakes, volcanoes, and hurricanes—that have international implications. They create famines, homelessness, and devastation that often require international efforts to overcome. Diseases such as AIDS and a resurgence of smallpox present challenges for both developing countries and industrial states.

An old French saying has it that the more things change, the more they stay the same. To some extent, that is a good characterization of the international system. It is in the midst of dramatic changes stimulated by the end of the cold war, natural events, and industrialization, but it also operates under some of the same conditions—anarchy and self-interest, conflict and cooperation—that America's founders understood. The challenge for American policy makers is to chart the nation's course in this familiar and yet strange international environment.

open questions

Where Do We Go From Here?

What should be the guiding principles of American foreign policy in this new world order? Should the nation assume a role of leadership in shaping the course of international affairs, or should it refrain from interfering in the affairs of others? Can the nation afford to exhaust its resources abroad when there are so many problems at home? We have as yet developed no national consensus on these questions, and there are passionate and articulate voices on both sides.

If the United States does play a leading role in the world, what should be the goals of American policy? Should they be limited to promoting peace and stability in the international scene or to protecting "vital national interests" (however those are defined)? Or should our goals be more expansive, such as actively promoting democracy abroad? Promoting democracy is certainly consistent with American history and national purpose, but it opens the nation to charges of intrusion in the sovereignty of other states because we are trying to impose our ways on societies with histories very different from our own. Moreover, the cause of democracy might embroil the nation in conflicts between warring factions in some countries. Again, there are articulate voices on each side and no national consensus on the answers to these questions.

The nation is now poised at a rare moment in national history. At only a few other times in American politics has the country been without an overarching philosophy to guide its foreign policy: shortly after the founding, after World War II, and after the cold war. The situation that the country faces today is reminiscent of the Chinese ideographic character for the word "crisis," which combines the characters for "threat" and "opportunity." Such is the state of American foreign policy as we face this new world order.

America and the World. The United States is part of an international environment marked by anarchy—the absence of central government to keep order and resolve disputes. In this environment there are *states* (countries) and three kinds of *nonstate actors:* nationalist groups, nongovernmental organizations, and intergovernmental organizations. America develops structural, strategic, and crisis foreign policies to respond to world politics, employing a variety of instruments or tools to do so.

Principles. America has always had a tendency toward *isolationism*—remaining aloof from world politics. After World War II, our foreign policy shifted toward *internationalism*—the view that America should actively try to shape the direction of world affairs. With the end of the cold war, many analysts are calling for a return to some form of isolationism.

Process. Foreign policy is made primarily by the president, who relies on the staff of the National Security Council for assistance. The head of that staff, the president's assistant for national security affairs, has become a major foreign-policy adviser to the president. The secretaries of state and defense often compete with the security assistant to influence the president. Congress is most involved in issues directly related to constituent interests, but it generally defers to presidential leadership.

Politics. America faces a world that has been transformed by the end of the cold war. The United States is part of a minority of democratic regimes in the world. Most of the world's people live under nondemocratic governments. A range of difficult issues confront policy makers, including economic problems, conflicts arising from nationalism, and changes since the end of the cold war.

Open Questions. What principles should guide American foreign policy in a post–cold war world? Some argue for continued internationalism; others counsel a form of isolationism. The answers are neither easy nor obvious.

Summary

Suggested Readings

DRAGNICH, ALEX N., ET AL. *Politics and Government,* 2nd ed. Chatham, N.J.: Chatham House, 1987. A good survey of political systems in several countries, including the United States, Britain, France, Germany, Japan, and Mexico.

KEGLEY, CHARLES W., JR., AND EUGENE R. WITTKOPF. *The Future of American Foreign Policy.* New York: St. Martin's Press, 1992. Useful collection of essays representing a diverse array of views on the future of America's role in the world.

————. *World Politics: Trend and Transformation,* 4th ed. New York: St. Martin's Press, 1993. Excellent introduction to international relations and world politics.

RANNEY, AUSTIN. *Governing,* 7th ed. Englewood Cliffs, N.J.: Prentice Hall, 1996. Comprehensive survey of politics in the United States and abroad.

ROTHGEB, JOHN M., JR. *Defining Power: Influence and Force in the Contemporary International System.* New York: St. Martin's Press, 1993. Good introduction to the operations of international politics.

SHIVELY, W. PHILLIPS. *Power and Choice,* 3rd ed. New York: McGraw-Hill, 1993. Excellent brief survey of politics and political systems around the world.

Americans and Their Government

America is in many ways a land of contradictions. It possesses one of the most enduring and stable democratic regimes in the world, yet someone is always warning of grave crises in our political system. Americans hold Congress in low esteem, yet they regularly reelect incumbents. Citizens rail against government regulation and taxes but vigorously oppose attempts to cut public services. And while a large number of Americans exhibit indifference or even outright hostility to "politics," most tell pollsters that they understand that governing takes a different set of skills from business and other walks of life.[1]

There is really nothing wrong with these contradictions because they demonstrate that the relationship between Americans and their government is as it has always been. Citizens of the United States have always valued patriotism and felt a sense of givenness about the constitutional regime, yet they have also tended to adhere to a philosophy of individualism. They are not easily governed, in the sense that Americans want government but not too much of it.

What can we say then of the American political system? Is it performing as it should? Would something else be better? Would we be happier with some other set of political arrangements? Where do citizens fit in? All of these questions are appropriate to anyone who has surveyed the American regime and its operations. This final chapter will first offer some guidance for readers who need to make sense of the political system and their place in it, and then explore some open questions about the American political order.

Making Sense of American Politics

According to one story, Benjamin Franklin was once party to a conversation in which someone was denouncing a plan with which the old Patriot was familiar. "It's madness," Franklin's counterpart proclaimed. "Yes," agreed Franklin, but then he observed, "but there is a method to it."[2] If you are tempted to throw up your hands and declare that American politics—in all its vote-gathering, deal-making, slow-moving, convoluted glory—is madness, consider for a moment: there is a method to it. You may disagree with the method or want to improve upon it, but it is not reasonable to merely denounce the operations of the political system without first understanding it and then considering the advantages and disadvantages of the alternatives.

To help you get a better sense of how the American political system works, we turn our attention to three important issues that confront all citizens. First, we consider how politics is an inevitable phenomenon both of life and of government. Next we explore the ways in which citizens can engage in a kind of everyday political analysis that may help them make sense of political developments in the United States. Then we look at the realities of what citizens can do in this political system. Our examination of these issues will enable us to discuss a number of proposals that have been advanced to alter the American political system.

The Inevitability of Politics

As we saw in Chapter 1, politics is a phenomenon of human life. It exists outside of government as well as in it. Moreover, it can be a means of accomplishing positive things as well as negative ones. And as we saw in the last chapter, although democracy may seem the natural condition of Americans, it is a rare commodity in all but a few societies. If we are to make sense of national politics, we must move beyond sweeping generalizations about the evil nature of "politics."

Effective citizenship requires a sophisticated understanding of the American regime, both in principle and at work. This does not mean that you must accept without question what government does, but it does mean that you cannot expect to wave a magic wand and eliminate "politics." In recent years there has been support for the notion that government ought to be run like a business. Those who support this idea generally mean that public activities should be conducted with greater efficiency than at present—a suggestion that has virtue but does not ensure better government.

Greater efficiency would make better use of taxpayers' money and perhaps enhance trust in government. But efficiency is not the only (or even the most important) value in politics. Civil rights and liberties are inefficient, just as are deliberation and democracy itself. Those who want government to be run more like a business do not mean they want to dispense with rights and democracy; they want to stop "waste, fraud and abuse" (a popular term used by many political speakers, including Ross Perot and former President Ronald Reagan). Yet even business has its inefficiencies: companies can suffer from bloated bureaucracy (General Motors, Sears, Procter and Gamble, and IBM have all had this problem), fraud (the white-collar crime of stealing from one's company is epidemic), waste, and various abuses. Moreover, business organizations are full of politics—the boardroom politics of large corporations and the office politics of small businesses. Business enterprise is not conducted by automatons, but by men and women who have all the attributes of humanity. Human beings, as Aristotle taught centuries ago, are social and therefore political animals. Both government and business are run by human beings, and thus both are subject to human imperfections.

Everyday Political Analysis

Making sense of American politics means giving up utopian ideas about what government ought to be like. We can certainly want it to be better, or even different, but it cannot—because we cannot—be perfect. The framers of our Constitution were tremendously optimistic about the prospects for creating a better political system than the one that they were living under, but they were not unrealistic. They offered the best proposals they could achieve, given the limits of human nature and the political realities of America in 1787.

How do we move from the founding period to our own time? How do we discern why American politics turns out the way that it does? To answer these questions, we must go first to the roots of the regime and whatever aspect of it is in question. What principles underlie the policy-making process, the presidency, or the protection of rights and liberties? Next, we need to look at how those ideas and assumptions shape the processes that determine what the government does. Then, we must consider how politics is shaped by process. How have battles over school busing, abortion, taxes, affirmative action, policy toward the Middle East been affected by the "rules of the game"? Finally, we must consider whether the result—a policy that is adopted, a right that is guaranteed, a compromise that is achieved—is in the public interest. If it is not, we need to explore other ways of achieving our objective. And even if it is, we need to ask whether we might have reached our goal more efficiently.

These tasks are less difficult than they may seem at first glance. We've taken the first few steps in this text, or have at least suggested how you can take them. What is left for you to do on your own, or in consultation with others, is to make judgments about whether the public interest is being served. In a democratic republic, that job is not reserved to individuals in positions of official responsibility. Rather, it is the opportunity—and some believe it is the duty—of each citizen to make assessments in this area. Active citizenship means more than just going to the polls at each election. It also means being mentally engaged in observing, thinking about, and discussing public affairs with others.

The Citizen in the Political System

Of course, we must all undertake this responsibility within the constraints imposed by our lives. Few of us have the leisure time to cultivate citizenship as an art, as did the citizens of ancient Athens. Those affluent men had the time to gather on the hillside and debate public issues. We have less time and live in a political system too large for such assemblies, but we do have the capacity to make judgments about what is going on in American public life. Armed with an understanding of the regime and with the analytical tools suggested in this book, we can make sense of national politics.

Not everyone can meet the challenges of citizenship with equal facility. The demands of work, limitations on income, and numerous other factors make it possible for some individuals or groups to have greater influence than others, or to deal more readily with the obligations of participation in political argument, political opinions, and voting. But that does not mean that anyone who is not rich and well-connected is incapable of being an effective citizen. Just about every adult citizen in the United States can vote, and everyone can try to influence government through individual or group action. Indeed, sociologist David Walls has noted the universality of opportunities for citizen involvement:

> Becoming a citizen activist is as simple as picking up a pen, or sitting down at a word processor. Writing letters to legislators or the local newspapers is a useful place to begin. Notices of current key bills are available to anyone who joins a leg-

islative alert network. You can lobby legislators by telephone to their Washington or home offices, or make an appointment to visit when they are back in the district. Join or help organize a local group of a national organization. Learn how to raise money, put out a newsletter, take part in direct action. Have fun, and learn from experience.[3]

You may not want to go as far with activism as Walls suggests, but that is no reason to withdraw from politics entirely. As you have seen throughout this book, especially in the Citizens in Action and Participate! features, it is easy for citizens to become active. Opportunities for active citizenship are all around: all you have to do is take advantage of them.

One way in which all citizens can participate is to contribute to the public conversation about the regime, its components, and government policies. In each of the preceding chapters, some of the issues in that conversation—term limits, campaign finance, constitutional amendments, presidential power—have been surveyed. As we have seen, there have been many proposals for change in the American political system—some large and sweeping, others small and limited. As a citizen, you are often called upon to take positions on proposals for change, whether presented in the form of ballot issues, constitutional amendments proposed in Congress or state legislatures, or topics debated in a political campaign. As a citizen, you can use the information gained from this text to form conclusions about proposals that have gotten attention in recent years.

Should We Alter the American Regime?

Since the founding of the constitutional regime, would-be reformers have called for changes in the system they maintain would improve the state of government in America. Over the decades, some of these have been enacted into law: the direct election of senators, the extension of voting rights, the guarantees of equality. But should we consider further changes in our regime?

Complaints about the political system have prompted calls for change. Some observers say that the government is not responsive enough to the views of citizens; that is, they claim that government officials do not attend closely enough to what polls and other sources tell them the American public wants. Others complain that public officials do not and cannot adequately represent the many varying interests in American society. For example, although the fundamental premise of the composition of the House of Representatives is proportional representation, 435 representatives (in 1929 Congress set this number as the maximum) are hard put to represent 260 million people. Some critics hold that this relatively small group cannot reflect the diversity of the American people. And still others charge that our eighteenth-century Constitution needs to be reconsidered in an age of high technology and rapid change.

Several proposals advanced are thoughtful enough to warrant serious discussion here. Even if we reject them, the act of examining them is a useful one for exploring the nature and operations of our political system. There are five major categories of proposed reforms:

1. We should introduce elements of direct democracy into our national government.
2. We should alter the electoral bases of officials to promote greater harmony among them.
3. We should streamline the separation-of-powers system, moving more toward a parliamentary system of government.
4. We should abandon federalism and adopt a more unitary political system.
5. We should call another constitutional convention.

Direct Democracy and American Government

Nearly all Americans have experience with both representative and direct democracy. Although the Constitution provides for only the first to be used in the national government, states and local governments have long employed direct democracy methods to make many public decisions. Three basic devices that states use have been proposed for adoption at the national level: recall, initiative, and referendum.

By **recall,** a specified percentage of voters may petition for a special election to determine whether an elected official should be allowed to complete a term of office. If the majority says no, then the officeholder is removed and another special election must be held to complete the term. Several states use the recall, and advocates suggest that it could be used to keep members of Congress and the president responsive to the interests of the people. Opponents argue that the recall simply encourages leaders to do what is popular and to avoid tough decisions that might engender well-organized opposition.

The initiative and referendum are more aggressive forms of direct democracy. The **initiative** makes it possible to place constitutional amendments or legislative proposals on a general election ballot after a certain percentage of qualified voters (requirements vary according to state) sign a petition requesting such an action. Almost half of American states make provision for some kind of citizen ballot initiative. The initiative is followed by a **referendum,** in which the electorate renders judgment on the proposal by a yes or no vote.

A referendum may be held not only on a citizen-initiated proposal but on some question put to public vote by a legislative body. For example, a local school board may propose a rise in the property tax to increase funding for the school system, or a state legislature may propose a constitutional amendment and put it before the voters for approval. Again, about half of the states (but not exactly the same group that allows initiative) provide for this device.

Advocates of national initiative and referendum devices argue that these methods would allow important questions to be put to a popular vote. Several divisive issues have been suggested for public decision: the 1978 Panama Canal treaties, abortion, school busing, abolition of the Electoral College, a balanced-budget constitutional amendment, and congressional term limits.[4]

The case for a national initiative and referendum system is built on the idea that American democracy would be energized by offering citizens the

recall A direct-democracy device by which citizens unsatisfied with the performance of an elected official may petition to hold an election to determine whether or not that official should remain in office. If a majority vote for recall, then the official is removed.

initiative A device for direct democracy through which a petition with a sufficient number of signatures of registered voters may place a policy question on a ballot to be decided by popular vote in a referendum.

referendum An election in which voters are asked to make substantive governmental decisions rather than select officials, such as in deciding on tax levies, policy questions, or proposed constitutional amendments.

opportunity to play a direct role in shaping public decisions. Opponents maintain that they would actually weaken government by giving public officials an easy way out of tackling tough problems. Moreover, opponents assert that initiative and referendum will not really advance the general public interest. The pros and cons of a national system of initiative and referendum are summarized in Table 15.1.

The issue of initiative and referendum was revived indirectly in 1992 when presidential candidate Ross Perot called for using television to hold "national town meetings" in which citizens could discuss issues. Although Perot's proposal was never specific, at times he implied that these town meetings could be accompanied by referenda that allow citizens to vote on policy issues; at other times, he seemed to suggest that citizens could express their views through mail-in ballots or by phone. Whatever form the proposal took, it was an electronic variation on the old idea of national initiative and referendum. (For more on "electronic democracy," see "American Politics Goes Online.")

The fundamental question these proposals raise is whether the United States ought to introduce elements of direct democracy into our constitutional regime. If we did so, many questions would be ripe for resolution by initiative and referendum, such as federal funding of abortions, American intervention in foreign conflicts, illegal immigration, and federal support to public broadcasting

TABLE 15.1 Should We Incorporate Direct Democracy into Our National Government?

Pros	Cons
1. Direct democracy gives citizens a larger voice in government.	1. Direct democracy favors the passions of the mob over deliberation and compromise.
2. Citizen participation is more meaningful when public control of government is more direct.	2. Initiative and referendum would lead to simplistic solutions to the complex problems facing the nation.
3. Initiative and referendum could lead to greater citizen participation in public affairs.	3. National campaigns over issues would be dominated by television ads and other superficial treatments of public problems.
4. Direct democracy could help citizens overcome the influence of interest groups and PACs in politics.	4. Direct democracy does not provide a place for dealing with the concerns of minorities, only the opinions of the majority.
5. Initiative and referendum would force the media to pay more attention to issues and less to scandals.	5. Interest-group influence would not diminish but get worse as groups competed with one another for public attention and votes.
6. Direct democracy would remind federal officeholders of their constituencies.	6. Reliance on direct democracy undermines respect for representative government.
7. Highly controversial issues like abortion could be resolved by public vote.	

American Politics Goes Online

Ours is the age of electronic communication and information management. Some political observers believe that it may also be the dawn of an age of electronic democracy. An estimated 20 million Americans use electronic mail (E-mail), which allows them to communicate with one another through their personal computers and tap into an enormous network of information and opinion known as the Internet. A quick look at computer ads in the daily newspaper reveals what these millions already know—that America has gone *online*. In other words, citizens are traveling the information superhighway. It should not surprise us, then, that politics is part of this electronic revolution. Some candidates for public office use this new technology to develop an electronic dimension to their campaigns, and government agencies use online services to provide information to citizens.

In 1994 several candidates used E-mail to communicate with journalists and potential voters. Fob James, a former governor of Alabama who ran for that office once again, obtained an E-mail address so that politically interested and electronically sophisticated voters could contact his campaign headquarters. His electronic mailbox was usually full. In the state of Washington, Democrat Mike James held a "town meeting" on the Internet in September 1994 and invited voters to contact him with questions.

Interest groups have been the most adept at mastering the new technology, using E-mail, faxes, and information databases to organize, plan strategy, and lobby government officials. Groups from Amnesty International to the Rotary Foundation have online systems to reach supporters and mobilize them as a grassroots lobbying force. On Capitol Hill, members receive faxes from constituents every day, and House Speaker Newt Gingrich (R.-Ga.) is a big fan of the new communications technology.

Early in 1995, Gingrich even advocated tax breaks for poor citizens to enable them to buy laptop computers. Under Gingrich's direction, the Library of Congress has inaugurated an online congressional information service called THOMAS (after Thomas Jefferson), which provides excerpts from the *Congressional Record* and summaries of bills pending before Congress.

Republicans have generally stayed ahead of Democrats in adapting to the electronic revolution. Several analysts cite Republican skill in using computer networks and fax and video technology when explaining how the party upset the Democrats and took control of Congress in the 1994 election. But not all Democrats are content to allow Republicans this technological advantage. At the Clinton White House, Vice-President Al Gore and other administration officials have pushed for the new technology, and the White House has developed an online information service through which citizens can access information databases, obtain press releases, and communicate with officials. In 1993, middle-school students in Oxford, Ohio exchanged messages with the president via E-mail, and in January 1994, the vice-president held a conference on CompuServe (a major commercial computer network) in which over 900 CompuServe subscribers participated.

The enthusiasm of Clinton and Gore for high-tech information exchange has not spread throughout the government, however. One agency notorious for its resistance to the electronic revolution has been the Department of State. To the surprise of many Clinton administration appointees, America's first department of government has remained in the electronic dark ages, using computing systems that are badly out of date. One Clinton appointee summed up the situation in her shocked reaction on learning that she was younger than her computer.

and the arts. As citizens we should consider whether submitting such issues to a national vote would strengthen our political system or weaken it.

Terms of Office of Public Officials

Some observers find fault not in the American regime's lack of direct democracy but in terms of office. Two kinds of proposals have been made with regard to the electoral bases of public officials: the first concerns the office of president; the second concerns Congressional officeholders.

Since the nineteenth century there have been calls for changing the president's term of office. When the confederate states drafted their constitution in 1861, they maintained many of the features of the federal charter, but they gave their chief executive a single six-year term of office. Over the decades a number of Americans, including several former presidents, have endorsed such a change in the provisions of the U.S. Constitution.

The case for a single six-year term is based on a simple assumption: a president with that much time in office and no chance of reelection could concentrate exclusively on promoting the national interest. The president would be able to do more than consider short-term consequences of policies and would be free of reelection worries. The result would be better, less partisan, and more enlightened government.

Opponents of this plan challenge its basic assumption. They maintain that it is when presidents cannot look forward to reelection—in their second term under the present system—that they are weakest. A single six-year term, these observers insist, would make every president a "lame duck" (a political term for an official who is headed out of office and therefore weakened) so his or her best intentions would not matter. Moreover, opponents argue, cutting presidents off from reelection would encourage them to engage in risky schemes that no politician seeking future votes would attempt.

A different proposal has been suggested for Congress: altering the length of legislative terms. Over the years several presidents and political commentators have called for lengthening the term for members of the House of Representatives to four years and synchronizing this term with presidential elections. The intent here is to tie the electoral fate of House members more closely to that of the president, thus increasing the chances for cooperation between the White House and the lower house of Congress. Proponents also argue that doubling the term of House members would lessen the need for members to engage in almost continual fund raising in order to secure their seats. The ultimate benefit, advocates claim, would be to make the House more willing and able to work with the president to advance the public interest.

This proposal is sometimes accompanied by the suggestion that the Senate's electoral base be altered as well. One scheme would give senators an eight-year term, with half the Senate elected every four years.[5] Because this arrangement would give the president a four-year term, senators an eight-year term, and representatives a four-year term, this proposal has been dubbed the "4-8-4 plan." Because under this plan half the Senate would be elected every four years, it is assumed that the Senate and the president would be tied more closely in terms of political leanings, but senators would still retain their longer term.

Opponents of these plans make two arguments. First, lengthening the term of House members would make them too distant from the people. Indeed, at the time of the Constitutional Convention, Antifederalists were fond of repeating that "Where annual elections end, tyranny begins." Two years was considered long by many observers at the time of the founding, who feared that four years would enable House members to ignore their constituents. The second argument against altering congressional terms is that synchronizing legislative and executive terms would not guarantee greater cooperation between the branches of government and could inhibit the ability of Congress to act as a check on presidential power.

A related proposal, which we discussed in Chapter 8, is to call for term limits for members of Congress. Some advocates of lengthened congressional terms believe that term limits would keep representatives from serving too long on Capitol Hill. Advocates of longer terms suggest that the length of term and the number of terms members can serve are unrelated issues.

Clearly, the six-year presidential proposal is inconsistent with the altered terms for Congress. But any of these proposals would be a significant change in the way we choose officials and could have a substantial effect on the way officials behave. Any reform that limits an elected official's tenure in office affects the way that official views the duties of office. If a president has only one term or a member of Congress can serve only a limited number of years, these officials need not be concerned about pleasing the voters when making public decisions. On one hand, freed from fear of the voters, officials might decide to do what they think is in the public interest and make difficult choices that candidates for reelection cannot or will not make. On the other hand, freed from fear of the voters, officials might act irresponsibly because they know they cannot be punished in the next election. Deciding which of these scenarios is the more likely is clearly the central issue to be considered. How do you think we might go about making this determination? Or do you think we must simply try these new ideas and see how they work? Whatever your idea, you can discuss it with others and communicate your views to your representatives in Washington.

Streamlining Government

The constitutional system of separated powers has long been blamed for fostering needless conflict and stalemate in government. In recent years when the White House and Capitol Hill have been controlled by different parties, critics have argued that the system of checks and balances leads to gridlock. In other words, they charge that the very structures designed by the framers to protect liberty created a government unable to govern.

In the 1980s a group of scholars, prominent citizens, and current and former government officials assembled into what they called the Committee on the Constitutional System (CCS). The CCS issued a report calling for constitutional changes to end gridlock and to promote cooperation between the executive and legislative branches. The CCS discerned several problems in the operations of American government: divided government (different parties controlling different branches), lack of party cohesion, a loss of accountability, and frequent deadlock that leads to stagnation.[6] To remedy these problems, the group supports a number of constitutional changes. It endorses the 4-8-4 plan for official terms, but then goes beyond that idea to propose several additional reforms that would move the United States in the direction of a parliamentary system, because they would tie the operation of the national government more closely to disciplined party majorities in Congress.

Without calling for an end to the separation of powers, the CCS seeks to streamline the American regime by measures to improve interbranch collaboration, strengthen party cohesion and accountability, and reduce the likelihood of divided government.[7] The group wants members of Congress to be able to serve in the Cabinet in order to broaden the base of political support for the executive administration. It wants to reduce the required number of votes for treaty ratification from two-thirds to 60 percent, in order to strengthen the president's hand in winning approval of controversial treaties, but it also wants the president to appear before Congress to testify and answer questions. The CCS would like the U.S. system to take on more of the attributes of a parliamentary form of government. In the British system, for example, the parliament is divided in two: the government is run by the majority party, and the minority party is organized into a formal "opposition," presenting an alternative to the administration in office.

Finally, CCS wants to increase interbranch cooperation either through *team-ticket voting* (voters would cast one ballot for president, House member, and senator) or by having congressional elections fall shortly after the presidential choice when voters would know who is president. The result of these changes would be a hybrid of traditional American separation of powers and a pure parliamentary system. The changes would not give the United States a British-style parliamentary system, but they would make majority rule by unified political parties more likely.

The CCS proposals stimulated considerable debate over the merits of the American constitutional system. One of the most articulate opponents was political scientist James Q. Wilson.[8] Wilson argues that there is no need to alter the Constitution along quasi-parliamentary lines, because the problems claimed by critics such as CCS are overstated and the remedies suggested are unwise. First, Wilson maintains that the very real problems facing the United States are not the fault of the constitutional system. One example of such a major problem is the large federal deficits, which the CCS and others blame on gridlock between the branches. Wilson notes that if one calculates the national debt as a percentage of gross national product, the size of America's debt is less than that of many parliamentary regimes, including Canada, Sweden, Denmark, Belgium, and Spain, and not much higher than the national debts of Britain, Japan, and Germany.[9] Next, Wilson holds that supposed problems in foreign affairs will not be solved by the proposals of the CCS:

But it is unlikely that any of the most frequently discussed constitutional changes would materially improve the president's bargaining position [vis-à-vis the Senate in treaty matters]. Putting members of Congress in the cabinet . . . or having the president and House members run as a team would leave the president and Congress in essentially the same relationship they are now: rivals for control over the direction of foreign policy.[10]

Wilson argues that the real target of reform ought to be the "unwritten constitution." Most relevant in this regard is "the internal organization and procedures of Congress."[11] Wilson lays much of the blame for presidential problems with Congress on the extreme decentralization of that body that has come about in recent years. He argues that strengthening the power of the party leaders in Congress will go a long way toward restoring coherence and discipline to an institution in which each member is too free to stop legislation or demand a large role in shaping policy. Moreover, he states, changes of this sort would not require constitutional change.[12]

The issue of whether our government should be streamlined is an important one (see Table 15.2 for a summary of some of the proposals for changing government and arguments for and against them). Does the government need to be streamlined? Would constitutional change be the best way to accomplish it? Those who argue for greater efficiency in government assert that our separation of powers system only sets obstacles in the way of accomplishing the many tasks before the government, such as reducing the deficit, balancing the budget, reforming health care and the welfare system, and improving the educational system. In other words, the case for streamlining lies in the assumption that budget problems and other national issues could be resolved if only we were to remove the institutional barriers to quicker action. The case against streamlining, however, stresses the need for deliberation and suggests that even an efficient quasi-parliamentary system would not solve difficult national problems. The question of streamlining comes down to priorities: efficiency and action versus deliberation and caution.

Altering Federalism

As we saw in Chapter 3, the system of federalism creates a tension in the American regime between the national government and the states. Over the course of our national history, that tension has tended to be resolved in favor of Washington. But the states have their spheres of authority, although a number of observers find the balance of power between state capitals and the national capital unacceptable.

A number of commentators have argued that federalism itself ought to be abolished. They argue that it is a relic of the eighteenth century that has done little good, serving to protect first slavery and then segregation and other local prejudices. This has led some critics of federalism to call for an end to the protections for the states in the Constitution, reducing the fifty subdivisions of the country to provinces, geographic units, or at best administrative divisions of the

TABLE 15.2 Proposals for Streamlining American Government and Some Arguments For and Against

Proposal	Argument For	Argument Against
Proposals to Change the Nature of System		
Alter congressional terms to synchronize with the term of the president, such as 4 years for House and 8 years for president	Would reduce likelihood of divided government (president of one party facing at least ½ of Congress controlled by other party)	Would reduce House's ability to respond to changing voter attitudes (as occurred in 1994)
Allow members of Congress to be Cabinet secretaries	Increase cooperation between branches	No guarantee of cooperation Two jobs may be too much
Allow Cabinet secretaries who are not members of Congress to sit as non-voting senators	Increase cooperation between branches	No guarantee of cooperation
Mandate that voters must vote for a president and members of Congress from the same party	Strengthen parties Guarantee that one party controls both the White House and Congress	Restrict voters' choice too much No guarantee of cooperation
Proposals to Change the System's Operations		
Hold special presidential election if a majority of both houses of Congress vote "no confidence" in the president	Allow replacement of a failed president	Weakens presidency
President could call special congressional elections if deadlock occurred over important issue	Break deadlock between branches by offering voters chance to replace members of Congress	Special election could produce another deadlock
Give president power to make formal legislative proposals that Congress must act on within a specified time	Give president a chance to shape legislative agenda	Reduce Congress's ability to serve as a deliberative body
Reduce the number of senators required for treaty ratification from ⅔ to ⅗ of the Senate	Make it easier for president to direct foreign policy	A treaty represents a national commitment, and thus should require more than a simple majority

federal government. This move would lead to a system of government with true national uniformity in which all citizens would be treated alike and would be subject to the same laws.

Abolishing federalism would create a *unitary political system* such as exists in Great Britain and France. In such a system, all issues are national issues, to be decided by the national government. Advocates of unitary government maintain that the problems confronting the United States in our time are best understood as national ones and best resolved by that level of government in which all citizens are represented. For example, consider the issue of environmental protection. In addition to national laws governing the environment, each state sets its own standards. California has air-pollution standards that are much stricter than those of the federal government, so cars licensed in the Golden State must meet stringent standards not found elsewhere. Other states have chosen not to have such strict standards, especially those states (such as Texas) that are concerned about attracting industry to their territory. But advocates of uniformity argue that the environment does not stop at state boundaries or even national ones, so this system of environmental federalism ultimately damages the environment. They maintain that the abolition of federalism would protect the air and water more effectively than the artificial boundaries of the fifty states.

Some critics who bridge the anti and pro federalist arguments have been willing to maintain the protections accorded states but want to change the map of the states to make more homogeneous entities in which relatively similar interests can govern themselves. This state revision plan would carve the largest states into smaller units and merge little ones into larger ones. This idea sees the states having continuing importance, but regards the present alignment of state boundaries as essentially arbitrary.

Those who support federalism wholeheartedly believe that the autonomy of the states ought to be strengthened and protected from any further diminution of their power. They argue for decentralization of national government authority, giving back state control over many matters now directed from Washington: education, welfare, law and order, and other areas. Similarly, they want to end the practice of the federal government imposing unfunded mandates (discussed in Chapter 3) on the states. The Republican majority that took control of Congress after the 1994 election presented many such proposals in their Contract with America.

Advocates of the decentralist position maintain that the level of government closest to the people is the one best suited to make important decisions about citizens' lives. Therefore, these new federalists call for more power in the states, not less. For example, political scientist John Kincaid has proposed that the states be strengthened by amending the Constitution to require a three-fourths vote in the Supreme Court rather than a simple majority to overturn state laws.[13] Such a measure would give states much greater autonomy because the federal government would find it very difficult to alter or void a state statute.

What, if anything, should the United States do about federalism? Should we maintain the current balance of power between the central government and the states, alter it by enhancing the states, or diminish the autonomy of subnational government? Any of these choices has consequences for the state of the regime, for policy making, and for the conduct of politics. If we weaken or abolish the states, then all important issues would be decided in Washington. If we allow the states more power, many issues now debated on Capitol Hill—such as the future of public education—would be decided in statehouses around the nation. As a citizen of both a state and of the United States, each American has a stake in the resolution of this issue.

The Call for Another Constitutional Convention

One final idea that merits consideration is the proposal to call a second constitutional convention. Unlike the previous four proposed changes we have discussed here, holding another constitutional convention would be a means to an end, not an end in itself. However, because a constitutional convention would have the potential for proposing many major changes in the system, the idea of such a convention deserves its own discussion.

What are the stated motives for holding another constitutional convention? Some advocates want a convention in order to put before the states specific amendments that have not passed Congress: for example, a balanced budget amendment, a term limits amendment, a right-to-life amendment, a school prayer amendment, the Equal Rights Amendment, or a direct-democracy amendment. Other advocates want a convention to debate the very nature of the American regime: whether it ought to be reshaped into a parliamentary system, whether it should be restructured into a system of truly proportional representation, or whether it should include an economic bill of rights (discussed in Chapter 4) among its guarantees to citizens. After the Balanced Budget Amendment failed to pass the U.S. Senate in 1995, advocates urged state legislatures to petition Congress to call a convention to press for such an amendment.

Whatever the motive, the call for another constitutional convention is made possible by Article V in the U.S. Constitution, which provides that amendments may be recommended to the states by a two-thirds vote of each house of Congress *or by a convention* called upon petition of two-thirds of the states. This second option has never been employed (see also Figure 3.1). In recent years, 32 states have petitioned Congress to call such an assembly, usually for the purpose of drafting a Balanced Budget Amendment. However, questions have been raised about the legitimacy of these petitions because many have taken differing forms in different states; for example, some have stated very specific purposes, but others have been open ended, simply proposing a constitutional convention. But as we have said, the idea of another constitutional convention is larger than any single proposed amendment, because such a convention could potentially draft amendments on a much wider range of issues.

Advocates of such a convention argue that one is necessary because Congress has not acted on many important issues and because it would be a good idea to end the congressional monopoly on drafting amendments. The first point, like the case for the initiative and referendum, stems from the idea that elected

Become an Interactive Citizen

Connect to the Internet. The Internet is an electronic network of computer users and information sources that allows a user access to a great deal of information. There are two major ways to gain access to the Internet:

1. Nearly all American colleges and universities offer direct Internet connections. Subscribers can send and receive E-mail, as well as connect to *bulletin boards* (general files containing information and commentary that all subscribers can access and through which they can communicate with each other) and a wide variety of information services (such as the Library of Congress catalog, texts of presidential press releases, or the latest sports scores). Some colleges and universities provide students with E-mail accounts free of charge; check with your campus computer service for information on opening an account and for help in using it.
2. Commercial services enable just about any American with a personal computer, a phone line, and a *modem* (a device that allows computer users to communicate with others through phone lines) to gain entry to the Internet. These services also offer their own bulletin boards and specialized information services. Several commercial services are available in the United States: all involve the purchase of software, either directly from the service or from a local computer supply store (if you purchase a service's software you usually get a discount on the company's monthly fee). For more information on the most popular services, call:

CompuServe (800) 524-3388,
    Representative 449
America Online (800) 827-6364,
    extension 0568
Prodigy (800) 776-3449,
    extension 92

Get access to information. The problem with the information superhighway is not a lack of information but an overabundance of it. There are ways to wade through this ocean, however:

- Each of the commercial services offers its own features, from forums for exchanging opinions on politics, to transcripts of political speeches, to databases on government and politics. These features are selected from menus that enable a subscriber to quickly

officials are either unable or unwilling to tackle difficult problems and must be overridden by citizens directly or through representatives who have no reelection considerations to distract them. The second point holds that another convention would be in the spirit of 1787, when the framers of the Constitution took a bold step and suggested more than a mere revision of the Articles of Confederation. Griffin Bell, attorney general of the United States under President Carter, summarized the case for a convention by telling its critics to "stop the hand-wringing" because a convention could do nothing more than recommend amendments for consideration by the states.[14] No matter how many amendments such a convention might endorse, and no matter how sweeping those changes might be, no action of the convention would be final until state ratification, which is required for every proposed change in the U.S. Constitution.

In response, opponents of the constitutional convention worry that such an assembly could be a "runaway" that could propose wholesale and ill-considered changes in the Constitution. Melvin Laird, a former member of Congress and defense secretary under President Nixon, calls the idea a "radical" one that threatens to undo the delicate balance of principles and structures that make up sort through the available choices and find one of interest.

- The Internet features a wide array of bulletin boards and databases. One of the most important tools for finding information on the Internet is the Gopher, a program that acts as a search tool. Many colleges that are connected to the Internet can access Gopher by entering the command "GOPHER." If your college does not provide such easy access, there are other ways that are almost as simple. Consult your computer service for more specific information.

- What kind of information might you want to find on the Internet? Let's say you are interested in environmental issues. You can access bulletin boards for comments from across the nation or across the world. You can obtain news on environment-related legislation pending in Congress through THOMAS (available through World Wide Web, a part of the Internet). Or you can access the White House's electronic service to find out what the administration thinks about the issue.

Communicate with public officials electronically. For the time being, the easiest way to contact members of Congress directly is through a regular phone call, fax, or old-fashioned mail. Some commercial services transmit

E-mail messages to Capitol Hill, but the cost is high (as much as $2.50). This situation may change in the future. The White House is easier to reach online, but don't expect an answer. For now, the White House is set up to receive E-mail from citizens and provide information, but not to carry on interactive communications with computer users. (The school kids in Ohio that we mentioned in the Current Issues box got extraordinary treatment.) Commercial services have their own means to contact the White House. On the Internet, the address is: president@whitehouse. gov.

Find out more about how to become an interactive citizen. To get the most out of online communications, the following books provide good leads:

Adam Gaffin, *Everybody's Guide to the Internet* (Cambridge, Mass.: The MIT Press, 1994).
Paul Gilster, *Finding It on the Internet: The Essential Guide* (New York: John Wiley and Sons, 1994).
Lawrence J. Magid, *Cruising Online* (New York: Random House, 1994).

the American charter.[15] He even predicts a "constitutional crisis" if another convention were called, because it could "engender crippling domestic and international uncertainty"[16] about the state of the nation's fundamental law.

Another constitutional convention—"runaway" or not—would not be a trivial event. Our nation's charter has been amended only twenty-seven times in two hundred years. Each proposed amendment represents a change in the fundamental law of the United States, so a convention empowered to propose such changes needs very careful consideration.

▌Conclusion

The American regime is a well-established political system for a large and complex country. It has served for over two centuries to promote the values of liberty, order, justice, and stability, but neither its framers nor their successors regarded it as perfect. No political system is or can be. But it is, however, a system in which there is the capacity for change when necessary and in which citizens play an active part in deliberations about proposals for change. To take part in the political conversation of the nation requires information and understanding: understanding of the roots, structures, and operations of the system, and information on the issues of the day. I hope that this text has made it easier for you to become part of that conversation.

Summary

Making Sense of American Politics. Politics is an inevitable part of human life. Efficiency is not the only value that we ought to consider in evaluating public affairs; we must also consider the need for justice and deliberation. To make sense of politics, we can employ the principles/process/politics method explained in this text.

Should We Alter the American Regime? All citizens can take part in discussions about changing our political system. Many proposals for change have been advanced by those who see problems in American political life and believe that structural reforms will solve those difficulties.

Direct Democracy: One proposal is to institute mechanisms of direct democracy into our political system, specifically *recall, initiative,* and *referendum.* These devices are intended to give citizens a much more direct voice in government, although critics see them as dangerous innovations that will weaken government and place passion over deliberation.

Terms of Office: Other proposals alter the terms of elected officials, such as restricting the president to a single six-year term of office or altering congressional terms to four years for the House and eight years for the Senate. All of these proposals change the relationship between voters and their elected representatives. Longer congressional terms are intended to make representatives less concerned about reelection; a single presidential term is intended to remove reelection considerations from the chief executive's mind altogether. Proponents believe officials will be able to pay more attention to the public interest; opponents fear that self-interest will be more powerful.

Streamlining Government: Some observers want to make the American regime more like a parliamentary system in order to make government operate more smoothly and reduce the obstacles to majority rule. Proponents, including a group called the Committee on the Constitutional System, want reforms that increase cooperation between the president and Congress. Opponents argue that such changes are unnecessary and not likely to solve any national problems.

Altering Federalism: Federalism has changed greatly over the course of American history. Today, some observers want to abolish it entirely in order to promote national uniformity in matters such as environmental protection, education, and other issues. Others want the states to have greater autonomy because they believe that the level of government closest to the citizens is the one that should have greatest power.

Another Constitutional Convention: Several proposals call for a constitutional convention, whether to vote on specific amendments or to reconsider the entire nature of American democracy. Advocates see a second convention as a means to get around Congress, which has not endorsed amendments on a balanced budget, school prayer, and other issues. Opponents fear that a convention could far exceed its mandate and call for sweeping changes in the American political system.

CRONIN, THOMAS E. *Direct Democracy.* Cambridge, Mass.: Harvard University Press, 1986. Excellent survey of the subject, with good attention to the positive and negative aspects of such devices as initiative, referendum, and recall.

LUNCH, WILLIAM M. *The Nationalization of American Politics.* Berkeley, Calif.: University of California Press, 1987. Survey of changes in American politics during the 1960s and 1970s and the implications of those changes for the political system.

KING, ANTHONY, ED. *The New American Political System,* 2nd version. Washington: American Enterprise Institute, 1990. Articles discuss the major elements of the American political system in the late twentieth century.

SMITH, HEDRICK. *The Power Game.* New York: Random House, 1988. A fascinating albeit overly long journalistic account of the ins and outs of Washington politics.

SUNDQUIST, JAMES. *Constitutional Reform and Effective Government.* Washington: Brookings Institution, 1986. Excellent survey, by a member of the Committee for the Constitutional System of proposals for constitutional reform.

The Declaration of Independence

Appendix A

IN CONGRESS, JULY 4, 1776
(The unanimous Declaration of the Thirteen United States of America)

PREAMBLE
When, in the course of human events, it becomes necessary for one people to dissolve the political bands which have connected them with another, and to assume, among the powers of the earth, the separate and equal station to which the laws of nature and of nature's God entitle them, a decent respect to the opinions of mankind requires that they should declare the causes which impel them to the separation.

NEW PRINCIPLES OF GOVERNMENT

We hold these truths to be self-evident; that all men are created equal, that they are endowed by their Creator with certain unalienable rights, that among these are life, liberty, and the pursuit of happiness.

That, to secure these rights, governments are instituted among men, deriving their just powers from the consent of the governed.

That whenever any form of government becomes destructive of these ends, it is the right of the people to alter or to abolish it, and to institute new government, laying its foundation on such principles, and organizing its powers in such form, as to them shall seem most likely to effect their safety and happiness. Prudence, indeed will dictate that governments long established should not be changed for light and transient causes; and accordingly all experience hath shown that mankind are more disposed to suffer while evils are sufferable, than to right themselves by abolishing the forms to which they are accustomed. But when a long train of abuses and usurpations, pursuing invariably the same object, evinces a design to reduce them under absolute despotism, it is their right, it is their duty, to throw off such government, and to provide new guards for their future security.

REASONS FOR SEPARATION

Such has been the patient sufferance of these colonies; and such is now the necessity which constrains them to alter their former systems of government. The history of the present king of Great Britain is a history of repeated injuries and usurpations, all having in direct object the establishment of an absolute tyranny over these states. To prove this, let facts be submitted to a candid world.

He has refused his assent to laws, the most wholesome and necessary for the public good.

He has forbidden his governors to pass laws of immediate and pressing importance unless suspended in their operation till his assent should be obtained; and when so suspended, he has utterly neglected to attend to them.

He has refused to pass other laws for the accommodation of large districts of people, unless those people would relinquish the right of representation in the legislature, a right inestimable to them, and formidable to tyrants only.

He has called together legislative bodies at places unusual, uncomfortable, and distant for the depository of their public records, for the sole purpose of fatiguing them into compliance with his measures.

He has dissolved representative houses repeatedly, for opposing, with manly firmness, his invasions on the rights of people.

He has refused, for a long time after such dissolutions, to cause others to be elected; whereby the legislative powers incapable of annihilation, have returned to the people at large for their exercise; the state remaining, in the meantime, exposed to all the dangers of invasion from without and convulsions within.

He has endeavored to prevent the population of these states; for that purpose obstructing the laws of naturalization of foreigners, refusing to pass others to encourage their migration hither, and raising the conditions of new appropriations of lands.

He has obstructed the administration of justice, by refusing his assent to laws for establishing judiciary powers.

He has made judges dependent on his will alone for the tenure of their offices, and the amount and payment of their salaries.

He has erected a multitude of new offices, and sent hither swarms of officers to harass our people and eat out their substance.

He has kept among us, in times of peace, standing armies, without the consent of our legislature.

He has affected to render the military independent of, and superior to, the civil power.

He has combined with others to subject us to jurisdiction foreign to our constitution and unacknowledged by our laws, giving his assent to their acts of pretended legislation:

For quartering large bodies of armed troops among us;

For protecting them, by a mock trial, from punishment for any murders which they should commit on the inhabitants of these states;

For cutting off our trade with all parts of the world;

For imposing taxes on us without our consent;

For depriving us, in many cases, of the benefits of trial by jury;

For transporting us beyond seas, to be tried for pretended offenses;

For abolishing the free system of English laws in a neighboring province, establishing therein an arbitrary government, and enlarging its boundaries, so as to render it at once an example and fit instrument for introducing the same absolute rule into these colonies;

For taking away our charters, abolishing our most valuable laws, and altering, fundamentally, the forms of our governments;

For suspending our own legislatures, and declaring themselves invented with power to legislate for us in all cases whatsoever.

He has abdicated government here, by declaring us out of his protection and waging war against us.

He has plundered our seas, ravaged our coasts, burned our towns, and destroyed the lives of our people.

He is at this time transporting large armies of foreign mercenaries to complete the works of death, desolation, and tyranny already begun with circumstances of cruelty and perfidy scarcely paralleled in the most barbarous ages and totally unworthy of the head of a civilized nation.

He has constrained our fellow-citizens, taken captive on the high seas, to bear arms against their country, to become the executioners of their friends and brethren, or to fall themselves by their hands.

He has excited domestic insurrections among us, and has endeavored to bring on the inhabitants of our frontiers the merciless Indian savages, whose known rule of warfare is an undistinguished destruction of all ages, sexes, and conditions.

In every stage of these oppressions we have petitioned for redress in the most humble terms; our repeated petitions have been answered only by repeated injury. A prince whose character is thus marked by every act which may define a tyrant is unfit to be the ruler of a free people.

Nor have we been wanting in attention to our British brethren. We have warned them, from time to time, of attempts by their legislature to extend an unwarrantable jurisdiction over us. We have reminded them of the circumstances of our emigration and settlement here. We have appealed to their native justice and magnanimity; and we have conjured them, by the ties of our common kindred, to disavow these usurpations, which would inevitably interrupt our connections and correspondence. They, too, have been deaf to the voice of justice and of consanguinity. We must, therefore, acquiesce in the necessity which denounces our separation, and hold them, as we hold the rest of mankind, enemies in war, in peace, friends.

We, therefore, the representatives of the United States of America, in General Congress assembled, appealing to the Supreme Judge of the world for the rectitude of our intentions, do, in the name and by authority of the good people of these colonies, solemnly publish and declare, that these united colonies are, and of right ought to be, free and independent states; that they are absolved from all allegiance to the British crown, and that all political connection between them and the state of Great Britain is, and ought to be, totally dissolved; and that, as free and independent states, they have full power to levy war, conclude peace, contract alliances, establish commerce, and do all other acts and things which independent states may of a right do. And, for the support of this declaration, with a firm reliance on the protection of Divine Providence, we mutually pledge to each other our lives, our fortunes, and our sacred honor.

The Constitution of the United States of America

THE PREAMBLE

We the People of the United States, in Order to form a more perfect Union, establish Justice, insure domestic Tranquility, provide for the common defense, promote the general Welfare, and secure the Blessings of Liberty to ourselves and our posterity, do ordain and establish this Constitution for the United States of America.

ARTICLE I—THE LEGISLATIVE ARTICLE

Legislative Power

Section 1 All legislative Powers herein granted shall be vested in a Congress of the United States, which shall consist of a Senate and House of Representatives.

House of Representatives: Composition; Qualifications; Apportionment; Impeachment Power

Section 2 The House of Representatives shall be composed of Members chosen every second Year by the People of the several States, and the Electors in each State shall have the Qualifications requisite for Electors of the most numerous Branch of the State Legislature.

No Person shall be a Representative who shall not have attained to the Age of twenty-five Years, and been seven Years a Citizen of the United States, and who shall not, when elected, be an Inhabitant of that State in which he shall be chosen.

Representatives and direct Taxes[1] shall be apportioned among the several States which may be included within this Union, according to their respective Numbers, *which shall be determined by adding to the whole Number of free Persons, including those bound to Service for a Term of Years, and excluding Indians not taxed, three fifths of all other Persons.*[2] The actual Enumeration shall be made within three Years after the first Meeting of the Congress of the United States, and within every subsequent Term of ten Years, in such Manner as they shall by Law direct. The Number of Representatives shall not exceed one for every thirty Thousand, but each State shall have at least one Representative; and until such enumeration shall be made, the State of New Hampshire shall be entitled to choose three, Massachusetts eight, Rhode Island and Providence Plantations one, Connecticut five, New York six, New Jersey four, Pennsylvania eight, Delaware one, Maryland six, Virginia ten, North Carolina five, South Carolina five, and Georgia three.

When vacancies happen in the Representation from any State, the Executive Authority thereof shall issue Writs of Election to fill such Vacancies.

The House of Representatives shall choose their Speaker and other Officers; and shall have the sole Power of Impeachment.

Senate Composition: Qualifications, Impeachment Trials

Section 3 The Senate of the United States shall be composed of two Senators from each State, *chosen by the Legislature thereof,*[3] for six Years; and each Senator shall have one Vote.

Immediately after they shall be assembled in Consequence of the first Election, they shall be divided as equally as may be into three Classes. The Seats of the Senators of the first Class shall be vacated at the Expiration of the second Year, of the second Class at the Expiration of the fourth Year, and of the third Class at the Expiration of the sixth Year, so that one third may be chosen every second Year; *and if Vacancies happen by Resignation, or otherwise, during the Recess of the Legislature of any State, the Executive thereof may make temporary Appointments until the next Meet-*

---

[1]Modified by the 16th Amendment

[2]"Other Persons" refers to black slaves. Replaced by Section 2, 14th Amendment

[3]Repealed by the 17th Amendment

ing of the Legislature, which shall then fill such Vacancies.[4]

No person shall be a Senator who shall not have attained to the Age of thirty Years, and been nine Years a Citizen of the United States, and who shall not, when elected, be an inhabitant of that State for which he shall be chosen.

The Vice President of the United States shall be President of the Senate, but shall have no Vote, unless they be equally divided.

The Senate shall choose their other Officers, and also a President pro tempore, in the Absence of the Vice President, or when he shall exercise the Office of the President of the United States.

The Senate shall have the sole Power to try all Impeachments. When sitting for that Purpose, they shall be on Oath of Affirmation. When the President of the United States is tried, the Chief Justice shall preside: And no Person shall be convicted without the Concurrence of two thirds of the Members present.

Judgment in Cases of Impeachment shall not extend further than to removal from Office, and disqualification to hold and enjoy any Office of honor, Trust, or Profit under the United States; but the Party convicted shall nevertheless be liable and subject to Indictment, Trial, Judgment and Punishment, according to law.

Congressional Elections: Times, Places, Manner

Section 4 The Times, Places, and Manner of holding Elections for Senators and Representatives, shall be prescribed in each State by the Legislature thereof; but the Congress may at any time by Law make or alter such Regulations, except as to the Places of choosing Senators.

The Congress shall assemble at least once in every Year, *and such Meeting shall be on the first Monday in December, unless they shall by Law appoint a different Day.*[5]

Powers and Duties of the Houses

Section 5 Each House shall be the Judge of the Elections, Returns and Qualifications of its own Members, and a Majority of each shall constitute a Quorum to do Business; but a smaller Number may adjourn from day to day, and may be authorized to compel the Attendance of absent Members, in such Manner, and under such Penalties as each House may provide.

Each House may determine the Rules of its Proceedings, punish its Members for disorderly Behavior, and, with the Concurrence of two thirds, expel a Member.

Each House shall keep a Journal of its Proceedings, and from time to time publish the same, excepting such Parts as may in their Judgment require Secrecy; and the yeas and Nays of the Members of either House on any question shall, at the Desire of one fifth of those Present, be entered on the Journal.

Neither House, during the Session of Congress, shall, without the Consent of the other, adjourn for more than three days, nor to any other place than that in which the two Houses shall be sitting.

Rights of Members

Section 6 The Senators and Representatives shall receive a Compensation for their Services, to be ascertained by Law, and paid out of the Treasury of the United States. They shall in all Cases, except Treason, Felony, and Breach of the Peace, be privileged from Arrest during their Attendance at the Session of their respective Houses, and in going to and returning from the same; and for any Speech or Debate in either House, they shall not be questioned in any other Place.

No Senator or Representative, shall, during the time for which he was elected, be appointed to any civil Office under the authority of the United States, which shall have been created, or the Emoluments whereof shall have been increased, during such time; and no Person holding any Office under the United States shall be a Member of either House during his Continuance in Office.

Legislative Powers: Bills and Resolutions

Section 7 All Bills for raising Revenue shall originate in the House of Representatives; but the Senate may propose or concur with Amendments as on other Bills.

Every Bill which shall have passed the House of Representatives and the Senate, shall, before it becomes a Law, be presented to the President of the United States; if he approves he shall sign it, but if not he shall return it, with his Objections, to that House in which it shall have originated, who shall enter the Objections at large on their Journal, and proceed to reconsider it. If after such Reconsideration two-thirds of that House shall agree to pass the Bill, it shall be sent, together with the Objections, to the other House, by which it shall likewise be reconsidered, and if approved by two thirds of that House, it shall become a Law. But in all such Cases the Votes of both Houses shall be determined by yeas and Nays, and the Names of the Persons voting for and against the Bill shall be entered on the Journal of each House respectively. If any Bill shall not be returned by the President within ten Days (Sundays excepted) after it shall have been presented to him, the Same shall be a Law, in like

---

[4]Modified by the 17th Amendment

[5]Changed by the 20th Amendment

Manner as if he had signed it, unless the Congress by their Adjournment prevent its Return, in which Case it shall not be a Law.

Every Order, Resolution, or Vote to which the Concurrence of the Senate and the House of Representatives may be necessary (except on a question of Adjournment) shall be presented to the President of the United States; and before the Same shall take Effect, shall be approved by him, or being disapproved by him, shall be repassed by two-thirds of the Senate and House of Representatives, according to the Rules and Limitations prescribed in the Case of a Bill.

Powers of Congress

Section 8 The Congress shall have the Power To lay and collect Taxes, Duties, Imposts, Excises, to pay the Debts and provide for the common Defense and general Welfare of the United States; but all Duties, Imposts, and Excises shall be uniform throughout the United States;

To borrow Money on the Credit of the United States;

To regulate Commerce with foreign Nations, and among the several States, and with the Indian Tribes;

To establish a uniform Rule of Naturalization, and uniform Laws on the subject of Bankruptcies throughout the United States;

To coin Money, regulate the Value thereof, and of foreign Coin, and fix the Standard of Weights and Measures;

To provide for the Punishment of counterfeiting the Securities and current Coin of the United States;

To establish Post Offices and post Roads;

To promote the Progress of Science and useful Arts, by securing for limited Times to Authors and Inventors the exclusive Right to their respective Writings and Discoveries;

To constitute Tribunals inferior to the supreme Court;

To define and punish Piracies and Felonies committed on the high Seas, and Offenses against the Law of Nations;

To declare War, grant Letters of Marque and Reprisal, and make Rules concerning Captures on Land and Water;

To raise and support Armies, but no Appropriation of Money to that Use shall be for a longer Term than two Years;

To provide and maintain a Navy;

To make Rules for the Government and Regulation of the land and naval Forces;

To provide for calling forth the Militia to execute the Laws of the Union, suppress insurrection and repel Invasions;

To provide for organizing, arming, and disciplining, the Militia, and for governing such Part of them as may be employed in the Service of the United States, reserving to the States respectively, the Appointment of the Officers, and the Authority of training the Militia according to the discipline prescribed by Congress;

To exercise exclusive Legislation in all Cases whatsoever, over such District (not exceeding ten Miles square) as may, by Cession of particular States, and the Acceptance of Congress, become the Seat of the Government of the United States, and to exercise like Authority over all Places purchased by the Consent of the Legislature of the State in which the Same shall be, for the Erection of Forts, Magazines, Arsenals, dock-Yards, and other needful Buildings;—And

To make all Laws which shall be necessary and proper for carrying into Execution the foregoing Powers, and all other Powers vested by this Constitution in the Government of the United States, or in any Department or Officer thereof.

Powers Denied to Congress

Section 9 The Migration or Importation of such Persons as any of the States now existing shall think proper to admit, shall not be prohibited by the Congress prior to the Year one thousand eight hundred and eight, but a Tax or Duty may be imposed on such Importation, not exceeding ten dollars for each Person.

The privilege of the Writ of Habeas Corpus shall not be suspended, unless when in Cases of Rebellion or Invasion the public Safety may require it.

No Bill of Attainder or ex post facto Laws shall be passed.

No Capitation, or other direct, Tax shall be laid, unless in Proportion to the Census or Enumeration herein before directed to be taken.[6]

No Tax or Duty shall be laid on Articles exported from any State.

No Preference shall be given by any Regulation of Commerce or Revenue to the Ports of one State over those of another; nor shall Vessels bound to, or from, one State be obliged to enter, clear, or pay Duties in another.

No Money shall be drawn from the Treasury, but in Consequence of Appropriations made by Law; and a regular Statement and Account of the Receipts and Expenditures of all public Money shall be published from time to time.

No Title of Nobility shall be granted by the United States; and no Person holding any Office of Profit or Trust under them, shall, without the Consent of the Congress, accept of any present, Emolument,

---

[6]Modified by the 16th Amendment

Office, or Title, of any kind whatever, from any King, Prince, or foreign State.

Powers Denied to the States

Section 10   No state shall enter into any Treaty, Alliance, or Confederation; grant Letters of Marque and Reprisal; coin Money; emit Bills of Credit; make any Thing but gold and silver Coin a Tender in Payment of Debts; pass any Bill of Attainder, ex post facto Law, or Law impairing the Obligation of Contracts, or grant any Title of Nobility.

No State shall, without the Consent of the Congress, lay any Imposts or Duties on Imports or Exports, except what may be absolutely necessary for executing its inspection Laws: and the net Produce of all Duties and Imposts, laid by any State on Imports or Exports, shall be for the Use of the Treasury of the United States; and all such Laws shall be subject to the Revision and Control of the Congress.

No State shall, without the Consent of Congress, lay any Duty on Tonnage, keep Troops, or Ships of War in time of Peace, enter into any Agreement or Compact with another State, or with a foreign Power, or engage in war, unless actually invaded, or in such imminent Danger as will not admit of Delay.

ARTICLE II—THE EXECUTIVE ARTICLE

Nature and Scope of Presidential Power

Section 1   The executive Power shall be vested in a President of the United States of America. He shall hold his Office during the Term of four Years, and, together with the Vice President, chosen for the same Term, be elected as follows:

Each State shall appoint, in such Manner as the Legislature thereof may direct, a Number of Electors, equal to the whole Number of Senators and Representatives to which the State may be entitled in the Congress: but no Senator or Representative, or Person holding an Office of Trust or Profit under the United States, shall be appointed an Elector.

The Electors shall meet in their respective States, and vote by Ballot for two Persons, of whom one at least shall not be an Inhabitant of the same State with themselves. And they shall make a List of all the Persons voted for, and of the Number of Votes for each; which List they shall sign and certify, and transmit sealed to the Seat of the Government of the United States, directed to the President of the Senate. The President of the Senate shall, in the presence of the Senate and House of Representatives, open all the Certificates, and the Votes shall then be counted. The Person having the greatest Number of Votes shall be the President, if such Number be a Majority of the whole Number of Electors appointed; and if there be more than one who have such Majority and have an equal Number of Votes, then the House of Representatives shall immediately choose by Ballot one of them for President; and if no person have a Majority, then from the five highest on the List the said House shall in like Manner choose the President. But in choosing the President, the Votes shall be taken by States, the Representation from each State having one Vote; A quorum for this Purpose shall consist of a Member or Members from two thirds of the States, and a Majority of all the States shall be necessary to a Choice. In every Case, after the Choice of the President, the person having the greatest Number of Votes of the Electors shall be the Vice President. But if there should remain two or more who have equal Votes the Senate shall choose from them by Ballot the Vice President.[7]

The Congress may determine the Time of choosing the Electors, and the Day on which they shall give their Votes; which Day shall be the same throughout the United States.

No Person except a natural born Citizen, or a Citizen of the United States, at the time of the Adoption of this Constitution, shall be eligible to the Office of President; neither shall any Person be eligible to that Office who shall not have attained to the Age of thirty five Years, and been fourteen Years a Resident within the United States.

In Case of the Removal of the President from Office, or of his Death, Resignation, or Inability to discharge the Powers and Duties of the said Office, the same shall devolve on the Vice President, and the Congress may by Law provide for the Case of Removal, Death, Resignation, or Inability, both of the President and Vice President, declaring what Officer shall then act as President, and such Officer shall act accordingly, until the Disability be removed, or a President shall be elected.[8]

The President shall, at stated Times, receive for his Services, a Compensation, which shall neither be increased nor diminished during the Period for which he shall have been elected, and he shall not receive within that Period any other Emolument from the United States, or any of them.

Before he enter on the Execution of his Office, he shall take the following Oath or Affirmation:—"I do solemnly swear (or affirm) that I will faithfully execute the Office of President of the United States, and will to the best of my Ability, preserve, protect and defend the Constitution of the United States."

[7]Changed by the 12th and 20th Amendments
[8]Modified by the 25th Amendment

Powers and Duties of the President

Section 2   The President shall be the Commander in Chief of the Army and Navy of the United States, and of the Militia of the several States, when called into the actual Service of the United States, he may require the Opinion in writing, of the principal Officer in each of the executive Departments, upon any Subject relating to the Duties of their respective Offices, and he shall have Power to grant Reprieves and Pardons for Offenses against the United States, except in Cases of Impeachment.

He shall have Power, by and with the Advice and Consent of the Senate, to make Treaties, provided two thirds of the Senators present concur; and he shall nominate, and by and with the Advice and Consent of the Senate, shall appoint Ambassadors, other public Ministers and Consuls, Judges of the supreme Court, and all other Officers of the United States, whose Appointments are not herein otherwise provided for, and which shall be established by Law: but the Congress may by Law vest the Appointment of such inferior Officers, as they think proper, in the President alone, in the Courts of Law, or in the Heads of Departments.

The President shall have Power to fill up all Vacancies that may happen during the Recess of the Senate, by granting Commissions which shall expire at the End of their next Session.

Section 3   He shall from time to time give to the Congress Information of the State of the Union, and recommend to their Consideration such Measures as he shall judge necessary and expedient; he may, on extraordinary Occasions, convene both Houses, or either of them, and in Case of Disagreement between them, with Respect to the Time of Adjournment, he may adjourn them to such Time as he shall think proper; he shall receive Ambassadors and other public Ministers; he shall take Care that the Laws be faithfully executed, and shall Commission all the Officers of the United States.

Section 4   The President, Vice President, and all civil Officers of the United States, shall be removed from Office on Impeachment for, and Conviction of, Treason, Bribery, or other High Crimes and Misdemeanors.

ARTICLE III—THE JUDICIAL ARTICLE

Judicial Power, Courts, Judges

Section 1   The judicial Power of the United States shall be vested in one supreme Court, and in such inferior Courts as the Congress may from time to time ordain and establish. The Judges, both of the supreme and

inferior Courts, shall hold their Offices during good Behavior, and shall, at stated Times, receive for their Services, a Compensation, which shall not be diminished during their Continuance in Office.

Jurisdiction

Section 2   The judicial Power shall extend to all Cases, in Law and Equity, arising under this Constitution, the Laws of the United States, and Treaties made, or which shall be made, under their Authority;—to all Cases affecting Ambassadors, other public Ministers and Consuls;—to all Cases of admiralty and maritime Jurisdiction;—to Controversies to which the United States shall be a Party;—to Controversies between two or more States; *between a State and Citizens of another State;*[9]—between Citizens of different States;—between Citizens of the same State claiming Lands under Grants of different States, and between a State, or the Citizens thereof, and foreign States, Citizens, or Subjects.

In all Cases affecting Ambassadors, other public Ministers and Consuls, and those in which a State shall be Party, the supreme Court shall have original Jurisdiction. In all the other Cases before mentioned, the supreme Court shall have appellate Jurisdiction, both as to Law and Fact, with such Exceptions, and under such Regulations as Congress shall make.

The Trial of all Crimes, except in Cases of Impeachment, shall be by Jury; and such Trial shall be held in the State where the said Crimes shall have been committed; but when not committed within any State, the Trial shall be at such Place or Places as the Congress may by Law have directed.

Treason

Section 3   Treason against the United States shall consist only in levying War against them, or in adhering to their Enemies, giving them Aid and Comfort. No Person shall be convicted of Treason unless on the Testimony of two Witnesses to the same overt Act, or on Confession in open Court.

The Congress shall have Power to declare the Punishment of Treason, but no Attainder of Treason shall work Corruption of Blood, or Forfeiture except during the Life of the Person attainted.

ARTICLE IV—INTERSTATE RELATIONS

Full Faith and Credit Clause

Section 1   Full Faith and Credit shall be given in each State to the public Acts, Records, and judicial Proceedings of every other State. And the Congress may by

[9]Modified by the 11th Amendment

general Laws prescribe the Manner in which such Acts, Records and Proceedings shall be proved, and the Effect thereof.

Privileges and Immunities; Interstate Extradition

Section 2 The Citizens of each State shall be entitled to all Privileges and Immunities of Citizens in the several States.

A person charged in any State with Treason, Felony, or other Crime, who shall flee from Justice, and be found in another State, shall on Demand of the executive Authority of the State from which he fled, be delivered up to be removed to the State having jurisdiction of the Crime.

No person held to Service or Labor in one State, under the Laws thereof, escaping into another, shall, in Consequence of any Law or Regulation therein, be discharged from such Service or Labor, but shall be delivered up on Claim of the Party to whom such Service or Labor may be due.[10]

Admission of States

Section 3 New States may be admitted by the Congress into this Union; but no new State shall be formed or erected within the Jurisdiction of any other State; nor any State be formed by the Junction of two or more States, or Parts of States, without the Consent of the Legislatures of the States concerned as well as of the Congress.

The Congress shall have Power to dispose of and make all needful Rules and Regulations respecting the Territory or other Property belonging to the United States; and nothing in this Constitution shall be so construed as to Prejudice any Claims of the United States, or of any particular State.

Republican Form of Government

Section 4 The United States shall guarantee to every State in this Union a Republican Form of Government, and shall protect each of them against Invasion; and on Application of the Legislature, or of the Executive (when the Legislature cannot be convened) against domestic Violence.

ARTICLE V—THE AMENDING POWER

The Congress, whenever two thirds of both Houses shall deem it necessary, shall propose Amendments to this Constitution, or, on the Application of the Legisla-

tures of two thirds of several States, shall call a Convention for proposing Amendments, which in either Case, shall be valid to all Intents and Purposes, as Part of this Constitution, when ratified by the Legislatures of three fourths of the several States, or by Conventions in three fourths thereof, as the one or the other Mode of Ratification may be proposed by the Congress; Provided that no Amendment which may be made prior to the Year One thousand eight hundred and eight shall in any Manner affect the first and fourth Clauses in the Ninth Section of the first Article; and that no State, without its Consent, shall be deprived of its equal Suffrage in the Senate.

ARTICLE VI—THE SUPREMACY ACT

All Debts contracted and Engagements entered into, before the Adoption of this Constitution, shall be as valid against the United States under this Constitution, as under the Confederation.

This Constitution, and the Laws of the United States which shall be made in Pursuance thereof; and all Treaties made, or which shall be made, under the Authority of the United States, shall be the supreme Law of the Land; and the Judges in every State shall be bound thereby, any Thing in the Constitution or Laws of any State to the Contrary notwithstanding.

The Senators and Representatives before mentioned, and the Members of the several State Legislatures, and all executive and judicial Officers, both of the United States and of the several States, shall be bound by Oath or Affirmation to support this Constitution; but no religious Test shall ever be required as a Qualification to any Office or public Trust under the United States.

ARTICLE VII—RATIFICATION

The Ratification of the Conventions of nine States, shall be sufficient for the Establishment of this Constitution between the States so ratifying the Same.

Done in Convention by the Unanimous Consent of the States present on the Seventeenth Day of September in the Year of our Lord one thousand seven hundred and Eighty seven and of the Independence of the United States of America the Twelfth. *In Witness whereof We have hereunto subscribed our Names.*

THE BILL OF RIGHTS

[The first ten amendments were ratified on December 15, 1791, and form what is known as the "Bill of Rights"]

[10]Repealed by the 13th Amendment

AMENDMENT 1—RELIGION, SPEECH, ASSEMBLY, AND POLITICS

Congress shall make no law respecting an establishment of religion, or prohibiting the free exercise thereof; or abridging the freedom of speech, or of the press; or the right of the people peaceably to assemble, and to petition the Government for a redress of grievances.

AMENDMENT 2—MILITIA AND THE RIGHT TO BEAR ARMS

A well regulated Militia, being necessary to the security of a free State, the right of the people to keep and bear Arms, shall not be infringed.

AMENDMENT 3—QUARTERING OF SOLDIERS

No Soldier shall, in time of peace be quartered in any house, without the consent of the Owner, nor in time of war, but in a manner to be prescribed by law.

AMENDMENT 4—SEARCHES AND SEIZURES

The right of the people to be secure in their persons, houses, papers, and effects, against unreasonable searches and seizures, shall not be violated, and no Warrants shall issue, but upon probable cause, supported by Oath or affirmation, and particularly describing the place to be searched, and the persons or things to be seized.

AMENDMENT 5—GRAND JURIES, SELF-INCRIMINATION, DOUBLE JEOPARDY, DUE PROCESS, AND EMINENT DOMAIN

No person shall be held to answer for a capital, or otherwise infamous crime, unless on a presentment or indictment of a Grand jury, except in cases arising in the land or naval forces, or in the Militia, when in actual service in time of War or public danger; nor shall any person be subject for the same offense to be twice put in jeopardy of life or limb; nor shall be compelled in any criminal case to be a witness against himself, nor be deprived of life, liberty, or property, without due process of law; nor shall private property be taken for public use, without just compensation.

AMENDMENT 6—CRIMINAL COURT PROCEDURES

In all criminal prosecutions, the accused shall enjoy the right to a speedy and public trial, by an impartial jury of the State and district wherein the crime shall have been committed, which district shall have been previously ascertained by law, and to be informed of the nature and cause of the accusation; to be confronted with the witnesses against him; to have compulsory process for obtaining Witnesses in his favor, and to have the Assistance of Counsel for his defense.

AMENDMENT 7—TRIAL BY JURY IN COMMON LAW CASES

In Suits at common law, where the value in controversy shall exceed twenty dollars, the right of trial by jury shall be preserved, and no fact tried by a jury shall be otherwise re-examined in any Court of the United States, than according to the rules of the common law.

AMENDMENT 8—BAIL, CRUEL AND UNUSUAL PUNISHMENT

Excessive bail shall not be required, nor excessive fines imposed, nor cruel and unusual punishments inflicted.

AMENDMENT 9—RIGHTS RETAINED BY THE PEOPLE

The enumeration in the Constitution, of certain rights, shall not be construed to deny or disparage others retained by the people.

AMENDMENT 10—RESERVED POWERS OF THE STATES

The powers not delegated to the United States by the Constitution, nor prohibited by it to the States, are reserved to the States respectively, or to the people.

AMENDMENT 11—SUITS AGAINST THE STATES [Ratified February 7, 1795]

The Judicial power of the United States shall not be construed to extend to any suit in law or equity, commenced or prosecuted against one of the United States by Citizens of another State, or by Citizens or Subjects of any Foreign State.

AMENDMENT 12—ELECTION OF THE PRESIDENT [Ratified July 27, 1804]

The Electors shall meet in their respective states, and vote by ballot for President and Vice-President, one of whom, at least, shall not be an inhabitant of the same state with themselves; they shall name in their ballots the person voted for as President, and in distinct ballots the person voted for as Vice-President, and they shall make distinct lists of all persons voted for as President, and of all persons voted for as Vice-President, and of the number of votes for each, which lists they shall sign and certify, and transmit sealed to the seat of the government of the United States, directed to the President of the Senate;—The President of the Senate shall, in presence of the Senate and House of Representatives, open all the certificates and the votes shall then be counted;—The person having the greatest number of votes for President, shall be the President, if such number be a majority of the whole number of Electors appointed; and if no person have such majority, then from the persons having the highest numbers not exceeding three on the list of those voted for as President, the House of Representatives shall choose immediately, by ballot, the President. But in choosing the President, the votes shall be taken by states, the representation from each state having one vote; a quorum for this purpose shall consist of a member or members from two-thirds of the states, and a majority of all the states shall be necessary to a choice. And if the House of Representatives shall not choose a President whenever the right of choice shall devolve upon them, *before the fourth day of March next following,* then the Vice-President shall act as President, as in the case of the death or other constitutional disability of the President.[11] The person having the greatest number of votes as Vice-President shall be the Vice-President, if such a number be a majority of the whole number of Electors appointed, and if no person have a majority, then from the two highest numbers on the list, the Senate shall choose the Vice-President; a quorum for the purpose shall consist of two-thirds of the whole number of Senators, and a majority of the whole number shall be necessary to a choice. But no person constitutionally ineligible to the office of President shall be eligible to that of Vice-President of the United States.

AMENDMENT 13—PROHIBITION OF SLAVERY [Ratified December 6, 1865]

Section 1 Neither slavery nor involuntary servitude, except as a punishment for crime whereof the party shall have been duly convicted, shall exist within the United States, or any place subject to their jurisdiction.

Section 2 Congress shall have power to enforce this article by appropriate legislation.

AMENDMENT 14—CITIZENSHIP, DUE PROCESS, AND EQUAL PROTECTION OF THE LAWS [Ratified July 9, 1868]

Section 1 All persons born or naturalized in the United States, and subject to the jurisdiction thereof, are citizens of the United States and of the State wherein they reside. No State shall make or enforce any law which shall abridge the privileges or immunities of citizens of the United States; nor shall any State deprive any person of life, liberty, or property, without due process of law; nor deny to any person within its jurisdiction the equal protection of the laws.

Section 2 Representatives shall be apportioned among the several States according to their respective numbers, counting the whole number of persons in each State, excluding Indians not taxed. But when the right to vote at any election for the choice of electors for President and Vice President of the United States, Representatives in Congress, the Executive and Judicial officers of a State, or the members of the Legislature thereof, is denied to any of the male inhabitants of such State, being twenty-one[12] years of age, and citizens of the United States, or in any way abridged, except for participating in rebellion, or other crime, the basis of representation therein shall be reduced in the proportion which the number of such male citizens shall bear to the whole number of male citizens twenty-one years of age in such State.

Section 3 No person shall be a Senator or Representative in Congress, or elector of President and Vice President, or hold any office, civil or military, under the United States, or under any State, who, having previously taken an oath, as a member of Congress, or as an officer of the United States, or as a member of any State legislature, or as an executive or judicial officer of any State, to support the Constitution of the United States, shall have engaged in insurrection or rebellion against the same, or given aid or comfort to the ene-

[11]Changed by the 20th Amendment

[12]Changed by the 26th Amendment

mies thereof. But Congress may by a vote of two-thirds of each House, remove such disability.

Section 4 The validity of the public debt of the United States, authorized by law, including debts incurred for payment of pensions and bounties for services in suppressing insurrection or rebellion, shall not be questioned. But neither the United States nor any State shall assume or pay any debt or obligation incurred in aid of insurrection or rebellion against the United States, or any claim for the loss or emancipation of any slave; but all such debts, obligations, and claims shall be held illegal and void.

Section 5 The Congress shall have the power to enforce, by appropriate legislation, the provisions of this article.

AMENDMENT 15—THE RIGHT TO VOTE
[Ratified February 3, 1870]

Section 1 The right of citizens of the United States to vote shall not be denied or abridged by the United States or by any State on account of race, color, or previous condition of servitude.

Section 2 The Congress shall have power to enforce this article by appropriate legislation.

AMENDMENT 16—INCOME TAXES
[Ratified February 3, 1913]

The Congress shall have power to lay and collect taxes on incomes, from whatever source derived, without apportionment among the several States, and without regard to any census or enumeration.

AMENDMENT 17—DIRECT ELECTION OF SENATORS [Ratified April 8, 1913]

The Senate of the United States shall be composed of two Senators from each State, elected by the people thereof, for six years; and each Senator shall have one vote. The electors in each State shall have the qualifications requisite for electors of the most numerous branch of the State legislatures.

When vacancies happen in the representation of any State in the Senate, the executive authority of such State shall issue writs of election to fill such vacancies: *Provided,* That the Legislature of any State may empower the executive thereof to make temporary appointments until the people fill the vacancies by election as the legislature may direct.

This amendment shall not be so construed as to affect the election or term of any senator chosen before it becomes valid as part of the Constitution.

AMENDMENT 18—PROHIBITION
**[Ratified January 16, 1919;
Repealed December 5, 1933 by Amendment 21]**

Section 1 After one year from the ratification of this article, the manufacture, sale, or transportation of intoxicating liquors within, the importation thereof into, or the exportation thereof from the United States and all territory subject to the jurisdiction thereof for beverage purposes is thereby prohibited.

Section 2 The Congress and the several states shall have concurrent power to enforce this article by appropriate legislation.

Section 3 This article shall be inoperative unless it shall have been ratified as an amendment to the Constitution by the legislatures of the several states, as provided in the Constitution, within seven years from the date of the submission hereof to the States by the Congress.[13]

AMENDMENT 19—FOR WOMEN'S SUFFRAGE
[Ratified August 18, 1920]

The right of the citizens of the United States to vote shall not be denied or abridged by the United States or by any State on account of sex.

Congress shall have the power to enforce this article by appropriate legislation.

AMENDMENT 20—THE LAME DUCK AMENDMENT
[Ratified January 23, 1933]

Section 1 The terms of the President and Vice President shall end at noon on the 20th day of January, and the terms of Senators and Representatives at noon on the 3rd day of January, of the years in which such terms would have ended if this article had not been ratified; and the terms of their successors shall then begin.

Section 2 The Congress shall assemble at least once in every year, and such meeting shall begin at noon on

---

[13]Repealed by the 21st Amendment

the 3rd day of January, unless they shall by law appoint a different day.

Section 3 If, at the time fixed for the beginning of the term of the President, the President elect shall have died, the Vice President elect shall become President. If a President shall not have been chosen before the time fixed for the beginning of his term, or if the President elect shall have failed to qualify, then the Vice President elect shall act as President until a President shall have qualified; and the Congress may by law provide for the case wherein neither a President elect nor a Vice President elect shall have qualified, declaring who shall then act as President, or the manner in which one who is to act shall be selected, and such person shall act accordingly until a President or Vice President shall have qualified.

Section 4 The Congress may by law provide for the case of the death of any of the persons from whom the House of Representatives may choose a President whenever the right of choice shall have developed upon them, and for the case of the death of any of the persons from whom the Senate may choose a Vice President whenever the right of choice shall have devolved upon them.

Section 5 Sections 1 and 2 shall take effect on the 15th day of October following the ratification of this article.

Section 6 This article shall be inoperative unless it shall have been ratified as an amendment to the Constitution by the legislatures of three-fourths of the several States within seven years from the date of its submission.

AMENDMENT 21—REPEAL OF PROHIBITION [Ratified December 5, 1933]

Section 1 The eighteenth article of amendment to the Constitution of the United States is hereby repealed.

Section 2 The transportation or importation into any State, Territory, or Possession of the United States for delivery or use therein of intoxicating liquors, in violation of the laws thereof, is hereby prohibited.

Section 3 This article shall be inoperative unless it shall have been ratified as an amendment to the Constitution by conventions in the several States, as provided in the Constitution, within seven years from the date of the submission hereof to the States by the Congress.

AMENDMENT 22—NUMBER OF PRESIDENTIAL TERMS [Ratified February 27, 1951]

Section 1 No person shall be elected to the office of the President more than twice, and no person who has held the Office of President, or acted as President, for more than two years of a term to which some other person was elected President shall be elected to the Office of the President more than once. But this Article shall not apply to any person holding the office of President when this article was proposed by the Congress, and shall not prevent any person who may be holding the office of President, or acting as President, during the term within which this Article becomes operative from holding the office of President or acting as President during the remainder of such term.

Section 2 This Article shall be inoperative unless it shall have been ratified as an amendment to the Constitution by the legislatures of three-fourths of the several States within seven years from the date of its submission to the States by the Congress.

AMENDMENT 23—PRESIDENTIAL ELECTORS FOR THE DISTRICT OF COLUMBIA [Ratified March 29, 1961]

Section 1 The District constituting the seat of Government of the United States shall appoint in such manner as the Congress may direct:

A number of electors of President and Vice President equal to the whole number of Senators and Representatives in Congress to which the District would be entitled if it were a State, but in no event more than the least populous State; they shall be in addition to those appointed by the States, but they shall be considered, for the purposes of the election of President and Vice President, to be electors appointed by a State; and they shall meet in the District and perform such duties as provided by the twelfth article of amendment.

Section 2 The Congress shall have power to enforce this article by appropriate legislation.

AMENDMENT 24—THE ANTI-POLL TAX AMENDMENT [Ratified January 23, 1964]

Section 1 The right of citizens of the United States to vote in any primary or other election for President or Vice President, for electors for President or Vice President, or for Senator or Representative in Congress, shall not be denied or abridged by the United States or any State by reason of failure to pay any poll tax or other tax.

Section 2 The Congress shall have power to enforce this article by appropriate legislation.

AMENDMENT 25—PRESIDENTIAL DISABILITY, VICE PRESIDENTIAL VACANCIES
[Ratified February 10, 1967]

Section 1 In case of the removal of the President from office or of his death or resignation, the Vice President shall become President.

Section 2 Whenever there is a vacancy in the office of the Vice President, the President shall nominate a Vice President who shall take office upon confirmation by a majority vote of both houses of Congress.

Section 3 Whenever the President transmits to the President pro tempore of the Senate and the Speaker of the House of Representatives his written declaration that he is unable to discharge the powers and duties of his office, and until he transmits to them a written declaration to the contrary, such powers and duties shall be discharged by the Vice President as Acting President.

Section 4 Whenever the Vice-President and a majority of either the principal officers of the executive departments, or of such other body as Congress may by law provide, transmit to the President pro tempore of the Senate and the Speaker of the House of Representatives their written declaration that the President is unable to discharge the powers and duties of his office, the Vice President shall immediately assume the powers and duties of the office as Acting President.

Thereafter, when the President transmits to the President pro tempore of the Senate and the Speaker of the House of Representatives his written declaration that no inability exists, he shall resume the powers and duties of his office unless the Vice President and a majority of either the principal officers of the executive departments, or of such other body as Congress may by law provide, transmit within four days to the President pro tempore of the Senate and the Speaker of the House of Representatives their written declaration that the President is unable to discharge the powers and duties of his office. Thereupon Congress shall decide the issue, assembling within 48 hours for that purpose if not in session. If the Congress, within 21 days after receipt of the latter written declaration, or, if Congress is not in session, within 21 days after Congress is required to assemble, determines by two-thirds vote of both houses that the President is unable to discharge the powers and duties of his office, the Vice President shall continue to discharge the same as Acting President; otherwise, the President shall resume the powers and duties of his office.

AMENDMENT 26—EIGHTEEN-YEAR-OLD VOTE
[Ratified July 1, 1971]

Section 1 The right of citizens of the United States who are eighteen years of age, or older, to vote shall not be denied or abridged by the United States or by any State on account of age.

Section 2 The Congress shall have power to enforce this article by appropriate legislation.

AMENDMENT 27—CONGRESSIONAL SALARIES
[Ratified May 7, 1992]

No law, varying the compensation for the services of the Senators and Representatives, shall take effect, until an election of Representatives shall be intervened.

The Federalist, Essays No. 10, No. 51

THE FEDERALIST, NO. 10, BY JAMES MADISON

To the People of the State of New York: Among the numerous advantages promised by a well-constructed union, none deserves to be more accurately developed than its tendency to break and control the violence of faction. The friend of popular governments, never finds himself so much alarmed for their character and fate, as when he contemplates their propensity of this dangerous vice. He will not fail, therefore, to set a due value on any plan which, without violating the principles to which he is attached, provides a proper cure for it. The instability, injustice, and confusion introduced into the public councils, have, in truth, been the mortal diseases under which popular governments have everywhere perished; as they continue to be the favorite and fruitful topics from which the adversaries to liberty derive their most specious declamations. The valuable improvements made by the American constitutions on the popular models, both ancient and modern, cannot certainly be too much admired; but it would be an unwarrantable partiality, to contend that they have as effectually obviated the danger on this side, as was wished and expected. Complaints are everywhere heard from our most considerate and virtuous citizens, equally the friends of public and private faith, and of public and personal liberty, that our governments are too unstable; that the public good is disregarded in the conflicts of rival parties; and that measures are too often decided, not according to the rules of justice, and the rights of the minor party, but by the superior force of an interested and overbearing majority. However anxiously we may wish that these complaints had no foundation, the evidence of known facts will not permit us to deny that they are in some degree true. It will be found, indeed, on a candid review of our situation, that some of the distresses under which we labor have been erroneously charged on the operations of our governments; but it will be found, at the same time, that other causes will not alone account for many of our heaviest misfortunes; and, particularly, for that prevailing and increasing distrust of public engagements, and alarm for private rights, which are echoed from one end of the continent to the other. These must be chiefly, if not wholly, effects of the unsteadiness and injustice, with which a factious spirit has tainted our public administrations.

By a faction, I understand a number of citizens, whether amounting to a majority of the whole, who are united and actuated by some common impulse of passion, or of interest, adverse to the rights of other citizens, or to the permanent and aggregate interests of the community.

There are two methods of curing the mischiefs of faction: the one, by removing its causes; the other, by controlling its effects.

There are again two methods of removing the causes of faction: the one, by destroying the liberty which is essential to its existence; the other, by giving to every citizen the same opinions, the same passions, and the same interests.

It could never be more truly said, than of the first remedy, that it was worse than the disease. Liberty is to faction what air is to fire, an aliment without which it instantly expires. But it could not be a less folly to abolish liberty, which is essential to political life, because it nourishes faction, than it would be to wish the annihilation of air, which is essential to animal life, because it imparts to fire its destructive agency.

The second expedient is as impracticable, as the first would be unwise. As long as the reason of man continues fallible, and he is at liberty to exercise it, different opinions will be formed. As long as the connection subsists between his reason and his self-love, his opinions and his passions will have a reciprocal

431

influence on each other; and the former will be objects to which the latter will attach themselves. The diversity in the faculties of men, from which the rights of property originate, is not less an insuperable obstacle to an uniformity of interests. The protection of these faculties is the first object of government. From the protection of different and unequal faculties of acquiring property, the possession of different degrees and kinds of property immediately results; and from the influence of these on the sentiments and views of the respective proprietors, ensues a division of the society into different interests and parties.

The latent causes of faction are thus sown in the nature of man; and we see them everywhere brought into different degrees of activity, according to the different circumstances of civil society. A zeal for different opinions concerning religion, concerning government, and many other points, as well of speculation as of practice; an attachment to different leaders ambitiously contending for preeminence and power; or to persons of other descriptions whose fortunes have been interesting to the human passions, have, in turn, divided mankind into parties, inflamed them with mutual animosity, and rendered them much more disposed to vex and oppress each other, than to cooperate for their common good. So strong is this propensity of mankind, to fall into mutual animosities, that where no substantial occasion presents itself, the most frivolous and fanciful distinctions have been sufficient to kindle their unfriendly passions and excite their most violent conflicts. But the most common and durable source of factions, has been the various and unequal distribution of property. Those who hold, and those who are without property, have ever formed distinct interests in society. Those who are creditors, and those who are debtors, fall under a like discrimination. A landed interest, a manufacturing interest, a mercantile interest, a moneyed interest, with many lesser interests, grow up of necessity in civilized nations, and divide them into different classes, actuated by different sentiments and views. The regulation of these various and interfering interests forms the principal task of modern legislation, and involves the spirit of the party and faction in the necessary and ordinary operations of the government.

No man is allowed to be a judge in his own cause; because his interest will certainly bias his judgment, and, not improbably, corrupt his integrity. With equal, nay, with greater reason, a body of men are unfit to be both judges and parties at the same time; yet what are many of the most important acts of legislation, but so many judicial determinations, not indeed concerning the right of single persons, but concerning the rights of large bodies of citizens? And what are the different classes of legislators, but advocates and parties to the causes which they determine? Is a law proposed concerning private debts? It is a question to which the creditors are parties on one side, and the debtors on the other. Justice ought to hold the balance between them. Yet the parties are, and must be, themselves the judges; and the most numerous party, or, in other words, the most powerful faction, must be expected to prevail. Shall domestic manufacturers be encouraged, and in what degree, by restrictions on foreign manufacturers? Are questions which would be differently decided by the landed and the manufacturing classes; and probably by neither with a sole regard to justice and the public good. The apportionment of taxes, on the various descriptions of property, is an act which seems to require the most exact impartiality; yet there is, perhaps, no legislative act, in which greater opportunity and temptation are given to a predominant party to trample on the rules of justice. Every shilling, with which they overburden the inferior number, is a shilling saved to their own pockets.

It is in vain to say, that enlightened statesmen will be able to adjust these clashing interests, and render them all subservient to the public good. Enlightened statesmen will not always be at the helm, nor, in many cases, can such an adjustment be made at all, without taking into view indirect and remote considerations, which will rarely prevail over the immediate interest which one party may find in disregarding the rights of another, or the good of the whole.

The inference to which we are brought is, that the causes of faction cannot be removed; and that relief is only to be sought in the means of controlling its *effects*.

If a faction consists of less than a majority, relief is supplied by the republican principle, which enables the majority to defeat its sinister views, by regular vote. It may clog the administration, it may convulse the society; but it will be unable to execute and mask its violence under the forms of the Constitution. When a majority is included in a faction, the form of popular government, on the other hand, enables it to sacrifice to its ruling passion or interest, both the public good and the rights of other citizens. To secure the public good, and private rights, against the danger of such a faction, and at the same time to preserve the spirit and the form of popular government, is then the great object to which our inquiries are directed. Let me add, that it is the great desideratum, by which alone this form of government can be rescued from the opprobrium under which it has so long laboured, and be recommended to the esteem and adoption of mankind.

By what means is this object attainable? Evidently by one of two only. Either the existence of the same passion or interest in a majority, at the same time, must be prevented; or the majority, having such coexistent passion or interest, must be rendered, by their number and local situation, unable to concert and carry into effect schemes of oppression. If the impulse and the opportunity be suffered to coincide, we well know that neither moral nor religious motives can be relied on as an adequate control. They are not found to be such on the injustice and violence of individuals, and lose their efficacy in proportion to the number combined together; that is, in proportion as their efficacy becomes needful.

From this view of the subject, it may be concluded, that a pure democracy, by which I mean a society consisting of a small number of citizens, who assemble and administer the government in person, can admit of no cure for the mischiefs of faction. A common passion or interest will, in almost every case, be felt by a majority of the whole; a communication and concert, results from the form of government itself; and there is nothing to check the inducements to sacrifice the weaker party, or an obnoxious individual. Hence, it is, that such democracies have ever been spectacles of turbulence and contention; have ever been found incompatible with personal security, or the rights of property; and have in general been as short in their lives, as they have been violent in their deaths. Theoretic politicians, who have patronized this species of government, have erroneously supposed, that by reducing mankind to a perfect equality in their political rights, they would, at the same time be perfectly equalized and assimilated in their possessions, their opinions, and their passions.

A republic, by which I mean a government in which the scheme of representation takes place, opens a different prospect, and promises the cure for which we are seeking. Let us examine the points in which it varies from pure democracy, and we shall comprehend both the nature of the cure and the efficacy which it must derive from the union.

The two great points of difference, between a democracy and a republic, are, first, the delegation of the government, in the latter, to a small number of citizens, elected by the rest; secondly, the greater number of citizens, and greater sphere of country, over which the latter may be extended.

The effect of the first difference is, on the one hand, to refine and enlarge the public views, by passing them through the medium of a chosen body of citizens, whose wisdom may best discern the true interest of their country, and whose patriotism and love of justice, will be least likely to sacrifice it to temporary or partial considerations. Under such a regulation, it may well happen, that the public voice, pronounced by the representatives of the people, will be more consonant to the public good, than if pronounced by the people themselves, convened for the purpose. On the other hand the effect may be inverted. Men of factious tempers, of local prejudices, or of sinister designs, may by intrigue, by corruption, or by other means, first obtain the suffrages, and then betray the interest of the people. The question resulting is, whether small or extensive republics are most favourable to the election of proper guardians of the public weal; and it is clearly decided in favour of the latter by two obvious considerations.

In the first place, it is to be remarked that, however small the republic may be, the representatives must be raised to a certain number, in order to guard against the cabals of a few; and that however large it may be, they must be limited to a certain number, in order to guard against the confusion of a multitude. Hence, the number of representatives in the two cases not being in proportion to that of the constituents, and being proportionally greatest in the small republic, it follows, that if the proportion of fit characters be not less in the large than in the small republic, the former will present a greater option, and consequently a greater probability of a fit choice.

In the next place, as each representative will be chosen by a greater number of citizens in the large than in the small republic, it will be more difficult for unworthy candidates to practice with success the vicious arts, by which elections are too often carried; and the suffrages of the people being more free, will be more likely to centre in men who possess the most attractive merit, and the most diffusive and established characters.

It must be confessed, that in this, as in most other cases, there is a mean, on both sides of which inconveniences will be found to lie. By enlarging too much the number of electors, you render the representatives too little acquainted with all their local circumstances and lesser interests; as by reducing it too much, you render him unduly attached to these, and too little fit to comprehend and pursue great and national objects. The federal constitution forms a happy combination in this respect; the great and aggregate interests being referred to the national, the local and particular to the state legislatures.

The other point of difference is, the greater number of citizens, and extent of territory, which may be brought within the compass of republican, than of democratic government; and it is this circumstance principally which renders factious combinations less to be dreaded in the former, than in the latter. The smaller the society, the fewer probably will be the distinct parties and interests composing it; the fewer the distinct parties and interests, the more frequently will a majority be found of the same party; and the smaller the number of individuals composing a majority, and the smaller the compass within which they are placed, the more easily will they concert and execute their plans of oppression. Extend the sphere, and you take in a greater variety of parties and interests; you make it less probable that a majority of the whole will have a common motive to invade the rights of other citizens; or if such a common motive exists, it will be more difficult for all who feel it to discover their own strength, and to act in unison with each other. Besides other impediments, it may be remarked, that where there is a consciousness of unjust or dishonourable purposes, communication is always checked by distrust, in proportion to the number whose concurrence is necessary.

Hence, it clearly appears, that the same advantage, which a republic has over a democracy, in controlling the effects of faction, is enjoyed by a large over a small republic—is enjoyed by the union over the states composing it. Does this advantage consist in the substitution of representatives, whose enlightened views and virtuous sentiments render them superior to local prejudices, and to schemes of injustice? It will not be denied that the representation of the union will be most likely to possess these requisite endowments. Does it consist in the greater security afforded by a greater variety of parties, against the event of any one party being able to outnumber and oppress the rest? In an equal degree does the increased variety of parties, comprised within the union, increase the security? Does it, in fine, consist in the greater obstacles opposed to the concert and accomplishment of the secret wishes of an unjust and interested majority? Here, again, the extent of the union gives it the most palpable advantage.

The influence of factious leaders may kindle a flame within their particular states, but will be unable to spread a general conflagration through the other states; a religious sect may degenerate into a political faction in a part of the confederacy; but the variety of sects dispersed over the entire face of it, must secure the national councils against any danger from that source: a rage for paper money, for an abolition of debts, for an equal division of property, or for any other improper or wicked project, will be less apt to pervade the whole body of the union than a particular member of it; in the same proportion as such a malady is more likely to taint a particular county or district, than an entire state.

In the extent and proper structure of the union, therefore, we behold a republican remedy for the diseases most incident to republican government. And according to the degree of pleasure and pride we feel in being republicans, ought to be our zeal in cherishing the spirit, and supporting the character of federalists.

THE FEDERALIST, NO. 51, BY JAMES MADISON

To what expedient, then, shall we finally resort, for maintaining in practice the necessary partition of power among the several departments as laid down in the Constitution? The only answer that can be given is that as all these exterior provisions are found to be inadequate the defect must be supplied, by so contriving the interior structure of the government as that its several constituent parts may, by their mutual relations, be the means of keeping each other in their proper places. Without presuming to undertake a full development of this important idea I will hazard a few general observations which may perhaps place it in a clearer light, and enable us to form a more correct judgment of the principles and structure of the government planned by the convention.

In order to lay a due foundation for that separate and distinct exercise of the different powers of government, which to a certain extent is admitted on all hands to be essential to the preservation of liberty, it is evident that each department should have a will of its own; and consequently should be so constituted that the members of each should have as little agency as possible in the appointment of the members of the others. Were this principle rigorously adhered to, it would require that all the appointments for the supreme executive, legislative, and judiciary magistracies should be drawn from the same fountain of authority, the people, through channels having no communication whatever with one another. Perhaps such a plan of constructing the several departments would be less difficult in practice than it may in contemplation appear. Some difficulties, however, and some additional expense would attend the execution of it. Some deviations, therefore, from the principle must be admitted. In the constitution of the judiciary department in particular, it might be inexpedient to insist rigorously on the principle: first, because peculiar qualifications being essential in the members, the primary consideration ought to be to select that mode of choice which best secures these qualifications; second, because the permanent tenure by which the appointments are held in that department must soon destroy all sense of dependence on the authority conferring them.

It is equally evident that the members of each department should be as little dependent as possible on those of the others for the emoluments annexed to their offices. Were the executive magistrate, or the judges, not independent of the legislature in this particular, their independence in every other would be merely nominal.

But the great security against a gradual concentration of the several powers in the same department consists in giving to those who administer each department the necessary constitutional means and personal motives to resist encroachments of the others. The provision for defense must in this, as in all other cases, be made commensurate to the danger of attack. Ambition must be made to counteract ambition. The interest of the man must be connected with the constitutional rights of the place. It may be a reflection on human nature that such devices should be necessary to control the abuses of government. But what is government itself but the greatest of all reflections on human nature? If men were angels, no government would be necessary. If angels were to govern men, neither external nor internal controls on government would be necessary. In framing a government which is to be administered by men over men, the great difficulty lies in this: you must first enable the government to control the governed; and in the next place oblige it to control itself. A dependence on the people is, no doubt, the primary control on the government; but experience has taught mankind the necessity of auxiliary precautions.

This policy of supplying, by opposite and rival interests, the defect of better motives, might be traced through the whole system of human affairs, private as well as public. We see it particularly displayed in all the subordinate distributions of power, where the constant aim is to divide and arrange the several offices in such a manner as that each may be a check on the other—that the private interest of every individual may be a sentinel over the public rights. These inventions of prudence cannot be less requisite in the distribution of the supreme powers of the State.

But it is not possible to give to each department an equal power of self-defense. In republican government, the legislative authority necessarily predominates. The remedy for this inconveniency is to divide the legislature into different branches; and to render them, by modes of election and different principles of action, as little connected with each other as the nature of their common functions and their common dependence on the society will admit. It may even be necessary to guard against dangerous encroachments by still further precautions. As the weight of the legislative authority requires that it should be thus divided, the weakness of the executive may require, on the other hand, that it should be fortified. An absolute negative on the legislature appears, at first view, to be the natural defense with which the executive magistrate should be armed. But perhaps it would be neither altogether safe nor alone sufficient. On ordinary occasions it might not be exerted with the requisite firmness, and on extraordinary occasions it might be perfidiously abused. May not this defect of an absolute negative be supplied by some qualified connection between this weaker department and the weaker branch of the stronger department, by which the latter may be led to support the constitutional rights of the former, without being too much detached from the rights of its own department?

If the principles on which these observations are founded be just, as I persuade myself they are, and they be applied as a criterion to the several State constitutions, and to the federal Constitution, it will be found that if the latter does not perfectly correspond with them, the former are infinitely less able to bear such a test.

There are, moreover, two considerations particularly applicable to the federal system of America, which place that system in a very interesting point of view.

First. In a single republic, all the power surrendered by the people is submitted to the administration of a single government; and the usurpations are guarded against by a division of the government into distinct and separate departments. In the compound republic of America, the power surrendered by the people is first divided between two distinct governments, and then the portion allotted to each subdivided among distinct and separate departments. Hence a double security arises to the rights of the people. The different governments will control each other, at the same time that each will be controlled by itself.

Second. It is of great importance in a republic not only to guard the society against the oppression of its rulers, but to guard one part of the society against the injustice of the other part. Different interests necessarily exist in different classes of citizens. If a majority be united by a common interest, the rights of the minority will be insecure. There are but two methods of providing against this evil: the one by creating a will in the community independent of the majority—that is, of the society itself; the other, by comprehending in the society so many separate descriptions of citizens as will render an unjust combination of a majority of the whole very improbable, if not impracticable. The first method prevails in all governments possessing an hereditary or self-appointed authority. This, at best, is but a precarious security; because a power independent of the society may as well espouse the unjust views of the major as the rightful interests of the minor party, and may possibly be turned against both parties. The second method will be exemplified in the federal republic of the United States. Whilst all authority in it will be derived from and dependent on the society, the society itself will be broken into so many parts, interests and classes of citizens, that the rights of individuals, or of the minority, will be in little danger from interested combinations of the majority. In a free government the security for civil rights must be the same as that for religious rights. It consists in the one case in the multiplicity of interests, and in the other in the multiplicity of sects. The degree of security in both cases will depend on the number of interests and sects; and this may be presumed to depend on the extent of country and number of people comprehended under the same government. This view of the subject must particularly recommend a proper federal system to all the sincere and considerate friends of republican government, since it shows that in exact proportion as the territory of the Union may be formed into more circumscribed Confederacies, or States, oppressive combinations of a majority will be facilitated; the best security, under the republican forms, for the rights of every class of citizen, will be diminished; and consequently the stability and independence of some member of the government, the only other security, must be proportionally increased. Justice is the end of government. It is the end of civil society. It ever has been and ever will be pursued until it be obtained, or until liberty be lost in the pursuit. In a society under the forms of which the stronger faction can readily unite and oppress the weaker, anarchy may as truly be said to reign as in a state of nature, where the weaker individual is not secured against the violence of the stronger; and as, in the latter state, even the stronger individuals are prompted, by the uncertainty of their condition, to submit to a government which may protect the weak as well as themselves; so, in the former state, will the more powerful factions or parties be gradually induced, by a like motive, to wish for a government which will protect all parties, the weaker as well as the more powerful. It can be little doubted that if the State of Rhode Island was separated from the Confederacy and left to itself, the insecurity of rights under the popular form of government within such narrow limits would be displayed by such reiterated oppressions of factious majorities that some power altogether independent of the people would soon be called for by the voice of the very factions whose misrule had proved the necessity to it. In the extended republic of the United States, and among the great variety of interests, parties, and sects which it embraces, a coalition of a majority of the whole society could seldom take place on any other principles than those of justice and the general good; whilst there being thus less danger to a minor from the will of a major party, there must be less pretext, also, to provide for the security of the former, by introducing into the government a will not dependent on the latter, or, in other words, a will independent of the society itself. It is no less certain that it is important, notwithstanding the contrary opinions which have been entertained that the larger the society, provided it lie within a practicable sphere, the more duly capable it will be of self-government. And happily for the *republican cause,* the practicable sphere may be carried to a very great extent by a judicious modification and mixture of the *federal principle.*

Presidents and Vice-Presidents of the United States

President	Party	Vice-President
1. George Washington (1789–1797)	Federalist	John Adams (1789–1797)
2. John Adams (1797–1801)	Federalist	Thomas Jefferson (1797–1801)
3. Thomas Jefferson (1801–1809)	Democratic-Republican	Aaron Burr (1801–1805) George Clinton (1805–1809)
4. James Madison (1809–1817)	Democratic-Republican	George Clinton (1809–1812) Elbridge Gerry (1813–1814)
5. James Monroe (1817–1825)	Democratic-Republican	Daniel Thompkins (1817–1825)
6. John Quincy Adams (1825–1829)	Democratic-Republican	John C. Calhoun (1825–1829)
7. Andrew Jackson (1829–1837)	Democrat	John C. Calhoun (1829–1832) Martin Van Buren (1833–1837)
8. Martin Van Buren (1837–1841)	Democrat	Richard Johnson (1837–1841)
9. William H. Harrison (1841)	Whig	John Tyler (1841)
10. John Tyler (1841–1845)	Whig	
11. James K. Polk (1845–1849)	Democrat	George M. Dallas (1845–1849)
12. Zachary Taylor (1849–1850)	Whig	Millard Fillmore (1849–1850)
13. Millard Fillmore (1850–1853)	Whig	
14. Franklin Pierce (1853–1857)	Democrat	William R. King (1853)
15. James Buchanan (1857–1861)	Democrat	John Breckinridge (1857–1861)
16. Abraham Lincoln (1861–1865)	Republican	Hannibal Hamlin (1861–1865) Andrew Johnson (1865)
17. Andrew Johnson (1865–1869)	Union	
18. Ulysses S. Grant (1869–1877)	Republican	Schuyler Colfax (1869–1873) Henry Wilson (1873–1875)
19. Rutherford B. Hayes (1877–1881)	Republican	William A. Wheeler (1877–1881)
20. James A. Garfield (1881)	Republican	Chester A. Arthur (1881)
21. Chester A. Arthur (1881–1885)	Republican	
22. Grover Cleveland (1885–1889)	Democrat	T.A. Hendricks (1885)
23. Benjamin Harrison (1889–1893)	Republican	Levi P. Morgan (1889–1893)
24. Grover Cleveland (1893–1897)	Democrat	Adlai E. Stevenson (1893–1897)
25. William McKinley (1897–1901)	Republican	Garret A. Hobart (1897–1899) Theodore Roosevelt (1901)
26. Theodore Roosevelt (1901–1909)	Republican	Charles Fairbanks (1905–1909)
27. William H. Taft (1909–1913)	Republican	James S. Sherman (1909–1912)
28. Woodrow Wilson (1913–1921)	Democrat	Thomas R. Marshall (1913–1921)
29. Warren G. Harding (1921–1923)	Republican	Calvin Coolidge (1921–1923)

30. Calvin Coolidge (1923–1929)	Republican	Charles G. Dawes (1925–1929)
31. Herbert Hoover (1929–1933)	Republican	Charles Curtis (1929–1933)
32. Franklin D. Roosevelt (1933–1945)	Democrat	John Nance Garner (1933–1941)
		Henry Wallace (1941–1945)
		Harry Truman (1945)
33. Harry S. Truman (1945–1953)	Democrat	Alben W. Barkley (1949–1953)
34. Dwight Eisenhower (1953–1961)	Republican	Richard Nixon (1953–1961)
35. John F. Kennedy (1961–1963)	Democrat	Lyndon Johnson (1961–1963)
36. Lyndon Johnson (1963–1969)	Democrat	Hubert Humphrey (1965–1969)
37. Richard M. Nixon (1969–1974)	Republican	Spiro Agnew (1969–1973)
		Gerald Ford (1973–1974)
38. Gerald Ford (1974–1977)	Republican	Nelson Rockefeller (1974–1977)
39. Jimmy Carter (1977–1981)	Democrat	Walter Mondale (1977–1981)
40. Ronald Reagan (1981–1989)	Republican	George Bush (1981–1989)
41. George W. Bush (1989–1993)	Republican	Dan Quayle (1989–1993)
42. William Clinton (1993–)	Democrat	Albert Gore (1993–)

Appendix E: The Government of the United States

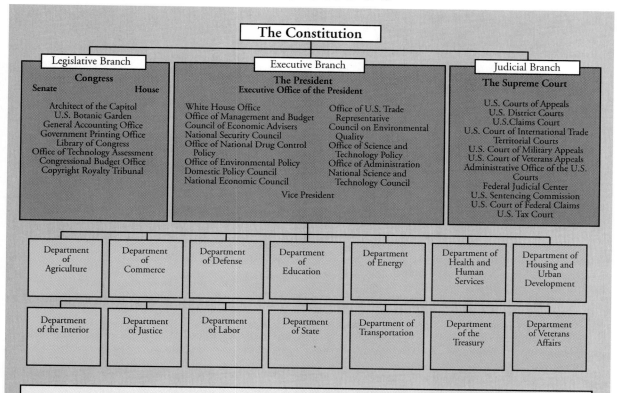

The Constitution

Legislative Branch

Congress
Senate   House

Architect of the Capitol
U.S. Botanic Garden
General Accounting Office
Government Printing Office
Library of Congress
Office of Technology Assessment
Congressional Budget Office
Copyright Royalty Tribunal

Executive Branch

The President
Executive Office of the President

White House Office
Office of Management and Budget
Council of Economic Advisers
National Security Council
Office of National Drug Control
 Policy
Office of Environmental Policy
Domestic Policy Council
National Economic Council

Office of U.S. Trade
 Representative
Council on Environmental
 Quality
Office of Science and
 Technology Policy
Office of Administration
National Science and
 Technology Council

Vice President

Judicial Branch

The Supreme Court

U.S. Courts of Appeals
U.S. District Courts
U.S. Claims Court
U.S. Court of International Trade
Territorial Courts
U.S. Court of Military Appeals
U.S. Court of Veterans Appeals
Administrative Office of the U.S.
 Courts
Federal Judicial Center
U.S. Sentencing Commission
U.S. Court of Federal Claims
U.S. Tax Court

Department of Agriculture	Department of Commerce	Department of Defense	Department of Education	Department of Energy	Department of Health and Human Services	Department of Housing and Urban Development
Department of the Interior	Department of Justice	Department of Labor	Department of State	Department of Transportation	Department of the Treasury	Department of Veterans Affairs

---

Independent Establishments and Government Corporations

Administrative Conference of the U.S.
African Development Foundation
Central Intelligence Agency
Commission on Civil Rights
Commodity Futures Trading Commission
Consumer Product Safety Commission
Corporation for National and Community Services
Defense Nuclear Facilities Safety Board
Environmental Protection Agency
Equal Opportunity Employment Commission
Export-Import Bank of the U.S.
Farm Credit Administration
Federal Communications Commission
Federal Deposit Insurance Corporation
Federal Election Commission
Federal Emergency Management Agency
Federal Housing Finance Board
Federal Labor Relations Authority
Federal Maritime Commission
Federal Mediation and Conciliation Service
Federal Mine Safety and Health
 Review Commission

Federal Reserve System
Federal Retirement Thrift Investment
 Board
Federal Trade Commission
General Services Administration
Inter-American Foundation
Interstate Commerce Commission
Merit Systems Protection Board
National Aeronautics and Space Administration
National Archives and Records Administration
National Capital Planning Commission
National Credit Union Association
National Foundation of the Arts
 and Humanities
National Labor Relations Board
National Mediation Board
National Railroad Passenger
 Corporation (Amtrak)
National Science Foundation
National Transportation Safety Board
Nuclear Regulatory Commission
Occupational Safety and Health
 Review Commission
Office of Government Ethics
Office of Personnel Management

Office of Special Counsel
Panama Canal Commission
Peace Corps
Pennsylvania Avenue Development
 Corporation
Pension Benefit Guaranty Corporation
Postal Rate Commission
Railroad Retirement Board
Resolution Trust Corporation
Securities and Exchange Commission
Selective Service System
Small Business Administration
Tennessee Valley Authority
Thrift Depositor Protection Oversight
 Board
Trade and Development Agency
U.S. Arms Control and
 Disarmament Agency
U.S. Information Agency
U.S. International Development
 Cooperation Agency
U.S. International Trade Commission
U.S. Postal Service

Selected Information Sources

GENERAL INFORMATION

The Almanac of American Politics (Washington: National Journal)—biennial editions. Sometimes called the "Bible of American politics," the *Almanac* contains a wealth of information on the members of Congress, their home states and districts, and voting records. It is one of the best sources available for understanding what is going on in Washington and how that is connected to what goes on "beyond the Beltway."

Federal Regulatory Directory (Washington: Congressional Quarterly)—biennial editions. Information on agencies and personnel and summaries of major laws underlying federal regulation.

Haas, Lawrence J. *The Washington Almanac* (New York: Henry Holt & Co., 1992). Where to go and whom to contact to get help in Washington.

Lesko, Matthew, *Information U.S.A.* (New York: Penguin Books)—several editions. Names, addresses, and phone numbers, plus good, practical advice on dealing with government institutions and officials.

U.S. Government Manual—annual editions. The official listing of government agencies, organizational charts, officials, and other information.

Washington Information Directory (Washington: Congressional Quarterly)—biennial editions. Vast array of information on Washington and the federal government—officials, organizations, media, pay scales for federal employees, etc.

World Almanac of U.S. Politics (New York: Pharos Books)—biennial editions. Useful collection of information on a wide array of topics.

INFORMATION ON FEDERAL GOVERNMENT INSTITUTIONS

Guide to Congress (Washington: Congressional Quarterly, 1993).

Guide to the Presidency (Washington: Congressional Quarterly, 1989).

Guide to the U.S. Supreme Court (Washington: Congressional Quarterly, 1990).

INFORMATION ON STATE AND LOCAL GOVERNMENTS

The Book of the States (Lexington, Ky.: Council of State Governments)—annually. Compendium of information on state governments, politics, and policy.

Inside the Legislature (Centerville, Mass.: State Legislative Leaders Foundation)—updated periodically. Guide to state governments and policy makers.

State Legislative Sourcebook (Topeka, Kans.: Government Research Service)—updated periodically. Information on procedures and activities of state legislatures.

League of Women Voters. In most communities, the league provides information on local, state, and national government institutions and officals.

DEFINITIONS, EXPLANATIONS, DATA

Robert's Rules of Order—many editions. The source of rules for conduct of meetings throughout the United States.

Shafritz, Jay M., *The HarperCollins Dictionary of American Government and Politics* (New York: HarperCollins, 1992). Excellent reference source for meanings of common political terms and concepts and for identification of important court cases.

Urofsky, Melvin I., ed., *Documents of American Constitutional and Legal History,* 2 vols. (New York: Knopf, 1989). Texts of important documents, such as the Constitution and important Supreme Court decisions.

Vital Statistics on American Politics (Washington: Congressional Quarterly)—editions about every other year. Convenient source of data on all aspects of American politics.

WHO'S IMPORTANT

The Capital Source (Washington: National Journal)—annually. Phone book, organized topically, containing information on federal offices and officials, corporations, professional associations, the media, think tanks, interest groups, and anyone else who is trying to have influence in Washington.

Washington Representatives (Washington: Columbia Books)—annually. The representatives of interest groups and foreign governments; the law firms and lobbyists at work in Washington and whom they represent.

THE CITIZEN AND THE GOVERNMENT

Dumouchel, J. Robert, ed., *Government Assistance Almanac* (Detroit: Omnigraphics)—biennial editions. Sourcebook for learning about what government assistance exists and how to get it.

Marwick, Christine M., *Your Right to Government Information* (New York: Bantam, 1985). Useful guide to obtaining government information through the FOIA.

You and the Law (Chicago: American Bar Association, 1991). Basic guide to law and legal questions for the general reader.

PAST AND CURRENT POLICY ISSUES BEFORE THE GOVERNMENT

Congressional Quarterly Weekly Report. Articles on all aspects of congressional politics and policy making, plus texts of important speeches and press conferences, votes taken in Congress, reports on the status of major bills, and updates on newly registered lobbyists.

Congressional Quarterly Almanac—annually. Compiles the information of the *Weekly Report* into an annual format.

National Journal—weekly. Articles on policy making in the federal government, with emphasis on the executive branch. Summaries of recent public opinion polls and analysis of current politics.

Glossary

accusatorial procedure: The "cornerstone" of Anglo-American jurisprudence, that an accused is "innocent until proven guilty." The judge serves as a neutral party between prosecution and defense.

administrative law judge: Officials of bureaucratic agencies who act in a judicial capacity to hear appeals of agency rules and decisions.

Administrative Procedures Act: 1946 law that outlines procedures for rule making, records, hearings before administrative bodies, secrecy, and other aspects of federal bureaucratic operations.

adversarial process: The method of conducting legal trials, with two sides competing with one another to win the case.

affirmative action: An action by a governmental or private organization that gives preferential treatment to members of minority groups in hiring, promotion, admission, or other selection decisions. The intent of such actions or policies is to make up for past discrimination.

amicus curiae: Latin for "friend of the court." A brief filed by a person or group not party to a case that is intended to influence the decision of the court.

Antifederalists: The name given to those who opposed ratification of the U.S. Constitution.

appellate jurisdiction: The power of a court to hear cases on appeal from a lower court.

apportionment: The determination of legislative district lines.

Articles of Confederation: America's first constitution, adopted in 1777. It created a weak association of states, each retaining absolute sovereignty. The Continental Congress had little real power.

authority: The legitimate possession and/or use of power.

bicameral, bicameralism: The division of a legislative body into two chambers, as in the U.S. Congress and many state legislatures.

bill: A proposed law under consideration by a legislative body.

bill of attainder: A legislative action that declares a person guilty of a crime without trial and orders a punishment. Prohibited by U.S. Constitution.

Bill of Rights: The first ten amendments to the U.S. Constitution; a statement of citizen liberties.

blanket primary: A primary election in which all candidates for an office, regardless of party, compete against each other. If one wins a majority, that person is elected. Otherwise, the top two vote-getters compete in the general election.

Brown v. Board of Education: 1954 case in which the Supreme Court ruled that segregation of black and white students in public schools is inherently unequal and unconstitutional.

bureaucracy: A large, complex organization composed of appointed officials.

Cabinet: The traditional advisory body to the president. It consists of the heads of executive departments plus other aides and executive officials designated by the president.

calendar: A schedule of business in the U.S. Congress. The House of Representatives uses four calendars to control its business; the Senate uses two.

campaign: All efforts undertaken by a candidate, party, or anyone else to influence the outcome of an election.

caucus: Meeting held within a party to select a candidate. In the early Republic, congressional caucuses within each party were used to select presidential candidates. Today caucuses are held in a few states (such as Iowa). Citizens meet in local voting precincts to vote on or nominate candidates.

certiorari, writ of: An order transferring a case to the Supreme Court from a lower court. Four justices must vote in favor for a writ to be issued in a case.

civil disobedience: An act of deliberately violating a law in order to draw attention to the unfairness of that law.

civil law: That area of the law that deals with relations between individuals and defines their legal rights.

civil liberties: Legal limits on the power of the state and the majority over the individual, such as legal protections of freedom of religion, of speech, and of the press, or the right to due process of law in criminal proceedings.

civil rights: The claims of individuals and groups in society to enjoy the same liberties and opportunities as everyone else—to be treated equally.

class action suit: A suit that seeks relief on behalf of a broad category of plaintiffs (such as all members of a minority group).

closed primary: A primary election in which only voters registered as members of the political party holding the primary may participate.

cloture: The decision to end a filibuster by imposing a limit on debate in the U.S. Senate. Three-fifths of all senators must vote in favor of cloture for it to be imposed.

cold war: The forty-year standoff between the United States and the Soviet Union that began after World War II and ended when the Soviet Union and its domination of Eastern Europe collapsed in the late 1980s.

common law: A body of judge-made law that sets out priniciples and rules for deciding disputes between individuals over property, contracts, and injury.

concurrent powers: Powers shared by the national government and the states, such as the power to tax, to spend money, to make laws, and to establish courts.

conference committee: A committee formed of members of the U.S. House of Representatives and the Senate who are charged to resolve differences in the different versions of a bill passed by the two houses of Congress. On occasion, such committees have been called the "third house" of Congress.

congressional agencies: Staff organizations that serve Congress as a whole and make up about ten percent of the congressional workforce. Included are the General Accounting Office (GAO), the Congressional Research Service (CRS), the Office of Technology Assessment (OTA), and the Congressional Budget Office (CBO).

constitution of open texture: Those aspects of the U.S. Constitution that involve matters implied but not specified, and general phrases that must be defined. These aspects require interpretation.

containment: The guiding philosophy of American foreign policy during the cold war; its goal was to stop the spread of communism and restrain the influence of the Soviet Union.

Contract Clause: Article I, Section 10 of the U.S. Constitution, which specifies that "No State shall . . . pass any . . . Law impairing the Obligation of Contracts."

criminal law: That area of the law that deals with matters of public order and the punishments imposed by government for violating it.

cultural pluralism: Diversity in race, religion, ethnic heritage, and other cultural factors. A characteristic of American society.

Declaration of Independence: The 1776 document in which the Continental Congress proclaimed and defended the decision of the American colonies to declare independence from Britain.

defendant: A person charged with a crime in a court of law.

delegate: Term applied to a legislative representative who votes according to constituent wishes.

delegated powers: Powers granted exclusively to the national government, such as the power to declare war and to regulate immigration and bankruptcy.

democracy: According to Aristotle, rule by the lower classes; in modern times, the doctrine of rule by the mass of people in a society.

democratic republic: The joining together of popular rule (democracy) with divided governmental power and other limits on majority rule (republicanism), as in the American regime.

direct democracy: Any system of government or device for direct majority control over public policy decisions, such as in *initiative* and *referendum.*

discernment: The most impressionistic means to measure public opinion, it involves drawing conclusions about what the public thinks from observation, conversations, correspondence, and other anecdotal information. Still widely used by practicing politicians.

dual federalism: A theory intended to explain how powers between the national government and the states are divided, it sought to distinguish national matters from exclusively state matters. Ultimately abandoned by the Supreme Court with the rise of a national economy and the growth of federal government power in the twentieth century.

due process of law: A constitutional guarantee that each citizen is entitled to justice and the proper functioning of the legal system before being denied life, liberty, or property.

Electoral College: The mechanism for electing the president. Voters in each state select electors, who in turn meet and cast votes for president and vice-president. Electoral votes are allocated to states according to their representation in Congress.

entitlement programs: Programs to which those who qualify are legally entitled, such as Social Security. Qualified recipients cannot be denied benefits because of lack of funds.

Establishment Clause: Section of the First Amendment that prohibits Congress (and by extension any other governmental body) from establishing an official religion. Often characterized as "the separation of church and state."

exclusionary rule: Rule of evidence established by the Supreme Court that excludes from use in a trial evidence that has been obtained in violation of principles of the due process of law, such as evidence obtained without informing defendants of their rights.

Executive Office of the President (EOP): The official structure of the president's staff, it is composed of the White House Office, the Office of Management and Budget, the National Security Council, and other staff offices that assist the chief executive.

executive privilege: The right of the president to withhold certain information from Congress.

expenditures: Government spending.

ex post facto law: A law that makes illegal something that happened before it was passed. Prohibited by the U.S. Constitution.

factions: According to Madison, groups in society "who are united and actuated by some common impulse of passion, or of interest, adverse to the permanent and aggregate interests of the community" (*The Federalist,* No. 10).

Federal Communications Commission: Independent regulatory commission created by Congress to license and regulate radio and television stations.

Federal Election Campaign Act (FECA): 1971 law that sets the basic structure of campaign finance law in the United States. Subsequently amended and modified by *Buckley v. Valeo.*

federalism: System of government in which there is a strong and permanent central authority (in the U.S., the federal government) and strong and permanent subnational authorities (in the U.S., states).

Federalists: Name adopted by those who favored ratification of the U.S. Constitution. Later adopted as the name of the political party that formed under the leadership of Alexander Hamilton.

filibuster: An attempt to "talk a bill to death" in the U.S. Senate by taking advantage of the principle of unlimited debate. One or more senators holds the floor and refuses to allow business to proceed until the bill

is withdrawn, a compromise is reached, cloture is invoked, or the senator(s) undertaking the filibuster gives up.

fiscal year (FY): An official accounting year for budgetary purposes. The federal fiscal year runs from October 1 to the following September 30 and is designated by the calendar year in which it ends.

focus group: A gathering of a small number of individuals to discuss issues or their attitudes about a politician, or to react to a candidate's commercials or speeches. Borrowed from business marketing, this technique is widely used in political campaigns for testing candidates, campaign themes, and advertising.

franking privilege: The right of members of Congress to send official correspondence through the mail without paying postage (although the expense of this privilege is covered by annual payment to the U.S. Postal Service).

Freedom of Information Act (FOIA): 1967 law that requires federal agencies to make public all records except those kept secret for legitimate reasons of national security, to protect private personnel records, or to insure trade secrets of companies doing business with an agency.

Free Exercise Clause: That part of the First Amendment which prohibits the government from interfering with the practice of religion.

general election: An election held to fill a governmental office or offices.

gerrymandering: Term applied to the practice of drawing legislative district lines in order to give an advantage to one group or party over another.

Gibbons v. Ogden: 1824 case in which the Supreme Court broadly interpreted the power of Congress to regulate commerce.

Gideon v. Wainwright: 1963 case in which the Supreme Court held that states must provide counsel to those defendants who cannot afford to hire attorneys on their own.

givenness: The belief that values in America are in some way automatically defined—"given" by the special nature of national history and geography. Articulated by historian Daniel Boorstin.

going public: A president's use of direct communication with the American people (such as a televised speech from the Oval Office) to gain support for policies or proposals.

government: The people who hold formal positions of responsibility within a regime and wield political power on behalf of the state.

government corporation: A bureaucratic organization structured much like a business enterprise, but owned by the government rather than private shareholders.

governmental agenda: Those issues explicitly up for active and serious consideration by government officials.

grand jury: A panel of citizens who are presented evidence by a prosecutor in the matter of serious crimes. Charges can be brought against a person or group only if the grand jury approves an indictment.

grass-roots politics: Organizing citizens to become politically active in support of a common goal.

Great Compromise: Agreement on representation in Congress that broke deadlock over that issue at Constitutional Convention. Called for a legislature in which one house is divided according to population (House of Representatives) and other divided equally among states (Senate).

habeus corpus, writ of: An order from a judge that requires the government to bring an arrested person before the court and formally charge that person with a crime. A legacy of English common law, the _writ of habeus corpus_ is intended to prevent the indefinite imprisonment of criminal suspects.

hierarchy: A system for ranking roles and status in an organization; a principle of bureaucracy.

incorporation, doctrine of: Principle that the Bill of Rights applies to states as well as the federal government, because of the Fourteenth Amendment. Selective incorporation was accepted by the Supreme Court as a principle of constitutional interpretation in _Gitlow v. New York_ (1925).

indictment: The device by which a person or group is formally charged with a serious crime. An indictment must be approved by a grand jury.

initiative: A device for direct democracy through which a petition with a sufficient number of signatures of registered voters may place a policy question on a ballot to be decided by popular vote in a referendum.

Inner Cabinet: The heads of the departments of State, Defense, Treasury, and Justice; they have more frequent contact with the president and are more likely to affect presidential decisions.

inquisatorial procedure: The judicial method of countries operating in the civil law tradition, that is, outside of the Anglo-Saxon common law tradition and based on the Napoleonic Code (a revision of Roman law). In this method, the judge is an active participant in the questioning of the accused, as part of a search for the truth. The accused is assumed guilty until proven innocent. Used, for example, in Mexico and France.

interest group: An organized body of individuals who share some common goals and who try to influence public policy.

intergovernmental organization (IGO): An international body that links states in the international environment. Examples include the United Nations and military alliances.

internationalism: The view that the United States should play an active role in world affairs.

iron triangle: Three-way relationship between a bureaucratic agency, an interest group, and a congressional committee. In recent years looser _issue networks_ have replaced iron triangles in the making of policy.

isolationism: The view that the United States should not play an active role in world affairs on a continuing basis.

issue network: Combinations of self-interested, issue-oriented, and ideologically-based interest groups who interact with government officials and institutions to shape public policy in a specific area.

Jim Crow laws: Laws adopted in Southern states after Reconstruction that mandated racial segregation and prohibited or discouraged black political participation.

joint committee: A congressional committee made up of members from both the House of Representatives and the Senate.

judicial activism: Active policy making by judges, based on the idea that the proper role of the courts is to protect rights and promote justice as judges see it.

judicial restraint: Refusal to engage in active policy making by judges, based on the idea that judges must not read their own views of rights and justice into their decisions.

judicial review: The power of the courts—ultimately the Supreme Court—to review actions of government in order to assess whether or not those actions are consistent with the Constitution.

lame duck: An officeholder who has been defeated for reelection or is ineligible for reelection.

leak: Information released to the news media that a government official (or officials) wanted to keep secret.

legislative court: A court established by Congress pursuant to its power to create judicial bodies, such as specialized courts for tax cases and military appeals.

libel: Reporting falsehoods about someone that ruin that person's reputation; not protected by the First Amendment's guarantee of freedom of the press.

liberty: The concept of a large measure of personal freedom in politics, economics, religion, and social behavior. The Declaration of Independence refers to it as one of humanity's natural rights, and the Preamble of the Constitution declares the protection of liberty as one of the charter's goals.

lobbying: Activities directed toward trying to influence the decisions of public officials, especially face-to-face appeals.

lobbyist: An individual who engages in lobbying on behalf of his or her own organization or for paying clients. The term implies one who does this for a living, as opposed to a citizen activist.

logrolling: The practice of trading votes among members of Congress.

majority: More than half of a voting group.

mandate: A binding order; specifically, an order for state action imposed by Congress, such as requiring a national speed limit to which all states must adhere.

manifest constitution: That aspect of the Constitution that spells out government structure and process in fairly definite terms not requiring interpretation.

Marbury v. Madison: 1803 case in which the Supreme Court first exercised the power of judicial review under the Constitution. In that case, it held that a portion of the Judiciary Act of 1789 was contrary to the charter and therefore null and void.

markup session: A meeting of a congressional committee during which a bill is drafted (or marked up) in the form in which it is to be sent to the House or Senate for consideration.

matching funds: Money given by the government to candidates for their campaigns. The amount of money given matches the amount a candidate has raised according to certain rules.

McCulloch v. Maryland: 1819 case in which the Supreme Court broadly interpreted the power of Congress to make such laws as are "necessary and proper" to fulfill its responsibilities.

multiculturalism: The view that there is no single common American culture, but that the nation's society consists of distinct racial, ethnic, and religious groups that coexist with one another.

multi-member district: A legislative district from which more than one representative is chosen, such as many city councils and school boards.

nationalism: A strong sense of group identity and emotional ties among a particular people.

National Security Council (NSC): An advisory body to the president created in 1947. Of greater importance to the chief executive is the staff of the NSC, headed by the president's Assistant for National Security Affairs, which enables the president to play an active role in the direction of foreign and military policy independent of the departments of State and Defense.

nation-centered federalism: The view that the Constitution created a union of people, as opposed to a union of states. The political consequence of the Civil War was to make this view the conventional understanding of the American regime.

natural rights: The idea that humans possess certain rights given to them by God and to which they are entitled by virtue of their humanity; a key principle in the Declaration of Independence.

New Jersey Plan: Proposal introduced at the Constitutional Convention as a challenge to the *Virginia Plan*; it called for revisions to the Articles of Confederation rather than a national government.

Office of Management and Budget (OMB): Agency in the Executive Office of the President that is responsible for assisting the president with preparation of executive budget requests, oversight of agency management, clearance of legislative proposals, and review of proposed regulations.

open primary: A primary election in which any voter may participate, regardless of party affiliation or non-affiliation.

original jurisdiction: The authority of a court to hear cases that have not previously been heard in another court and appealed to the higher body. The U.S. Constitution limits the original jurisdiction of the Supreme Court to certain kinds of cases and it is almost never exercised.

Outer Cabinet: The majority of the heads of the executive departments, who are likely not to see the president frequently and who do not have continuing influence on presidential policy making.

oversight: The power and responsibility of Congress to insure that administrative agencies act according to law and in the public interest.

petit jury: A trial jury. Compare *grand jury*.

plaintiff: The party bringing a suit in a court of law.

plurality: Having the most votes (but less than a majority) in an election in which votes are divided between three or more choices.

pocket veto: A veto that is accomplished not by the president actually rejecting a bill presented for signature, but by Congress adjourning while the bill awaits the president's signature. This inaction allows the president to kill a bill without vetoing it directly.

political action committee (PAC): A fundraising organization that contributes to candidates for public office. Their activities are controlled by the Federal Election Campaign Act and other laws.

political agenda: Issues that citizens believe are matters requiring public attention and that are within the legitimate scope of governmental authority.

political correctness: The alteration of language to reflect political positions that are assumed to be the "correct" ones. For example, terminology about personal and social differences must be inoffensive or positive.

political culture: A shared value system that influences ideas about how politics and governance ought to be conducted.

political entrepreneur: An individual or group that uses effective communication skills to focus national attention on an issue that has been otherwise of little or no interest.

political participation: Any of various activities directed at influencing government decisions or public policy, including voting and other conventional and unconventional activities.

political party: Voluntary organization of citizens who band together to nominate candidates and to influence the direction of public policy.

political questions: Matters—such as the appropriate rate of income taxation—that the courts consider beyond judicial resolution, which must be settled through the give-and-take of the political process.

political science: A field of knowledge in which those things termed "political" (defined very broadly) are studied in a systematic fashion.

political socialization: The process by which citizens absorb politically relevant values and political culture.

politics: The struggle over power and claims to authority in society.

popular sovereignty: The idea that all political power is derived from the people and that a legitimate regime is one that establishes "government by the consent of the governed."

population: In scientific polling, the total number of people about whom we want to know something.

pork: A term applied to government spending directed toward providing tangible benefits for specific districts or states. Also known as *porkbarrel spending*.

power: The ability to exert one's will, to command or prevent action, or to achieve desired outcomes.

preferred position: The legal doctrine that freedom of speech and of the press enjoy special consideration against other claims in society. In other words, while these freedoms are not absolute, they are to be given preference over other values and limited only when necessary.

primary election: A voting event used to choose candidates for public office.

prior restraint: Action to prevent publication of material before it appears. The Supreme Court has held that it is unconstitutional.

privacy, right to: Legal doctrine articulated by the Supreme Court in *Griswold v. Connecticut* (1965), which holds that individuals enjoy constitutional protection of their privacy from government intrusion unless a compelling reason warrants violation of personal privacy.

privatization: The practice of providing public services or functions by having the government contract with a private company to obtain the desired activities (for example, a city hiring a private company to collect garbage instead of maintaining a public fleet of garbage trucks and crews).

probability sampling: In scientific polling, a technique designed to give each individual in the population a roughly equal chance of being selected for the sample.

proportional representation: A system for allocating votes in elections according to the percentage of total votes a candidate or party receives.

public-interest group: An organization that represents a vision of the common good as defined by the group itself. Some public-interest groups arrive at their idea of the public interest through member participation; in others a small circle of leaders determine the agenda and positions of the organization.

public opinion: The views of citizens on contemporary issues.

public policy: Government activities, whether direct or indirect, that affect the lives of citizens.

random sampling: In scientific polling, selecting individuals to be interviewed at random, without any discretion by the interviewer about who will be interviewed. Usually done through geographic sampling or random-digit phone dialing.

recall: A direct-democracy device by which citizens unsatisfied with the performance of an elected official may petition to hold an election to determine whether or not that official should remain in office. If a majority vote for recall, then the official is removed.

reconciliation: An aspect of the federal budget process whereby the budget is used as a kind of super-law to alter other laws in order for budget goals to be accomplished.

referendum: An election in which voters, rather than their elected representatives, are asked to make substantive governmental decisions on tax levies, policy questions, or proposed constitutional amendments.

regime: A set of institutions and laws through which the dynamics of public politics in a society or group is organized and formalized.

representative democracy: A system of government in which voters choose officeholders to govern on their behalf.

republicanism: The idea of a system of government in which power is distributed among various officers and institutions in order to prevent tyranny.

reserved powers: Powers kept by the states after the creation of the national government, such as the power to create local governments and to conduct elections.

revenues: Government income, such as from taxes, tariffs, and other sources.

rider: An amendment added to a bill that is not germane to the substance of the bill. Allowed in the U.S. Senate but forbidden by the House of Representatives.

rule: In the U.S. House of Representatives, an order that specifies the amount of time allowed for debate on a bill, any limits on the number or kinds of amendments that can be attached to the bill, and other restrictions affecting debate and potential passage of the proposed law.

Rule of Four: The Supreme Court's requirement that at least four justices must vote to review a case before that case will be placed on the docket of the high court.

sample: In scientific polling, a small portion of the total population that reflects the overall makeup and diversity of the larger group. Also called a *representative sample*.

sampling error: In scientific polling, an estimate of how likely a poll is to be wrong in representing a larger population. Sampling error gets smaller as the size of the sample increases.

Schedule C: A category of federal officials who have policy-making responsibilities or who work closely with political superiors as executive or confidential assistants. The appointment of these officials is made by the president but does not require Senate confirmation.

scientific polling: The use of statistical sampling and prediction techniques to gain information on what the public thinks. This method allows researchers to interview relatively small numbers of people (only a few thousand) in order to draw conclusions about general public opinion.

search and seizure: An aspect of constitutional law dealing with the obtaining of evidence in criminal cases.

select committee: A type of congressional committee whose members are appointed by the Speaker in the House and the president pro tempore in the Senate. Usually deal with sensitive issues such as intelligence.

senatorial courtesy: The custom in the U.S. Senate of not approving the nominations of judges or other presidentially appointed officials if the senator(s) from the affected state objects to the person nominated.

Senior Executive Service (SES): A corps of over eight thousand high-level federal bureaucrats who can be transferred from one agency to another or moved to different positions in the same organization. Members of SES are subject to a system of rewards and punishments intended to make them responsive to their appointed political superiors.

separate-but-equal: Legal doctrine articulated by the Supreme Court in *Plessy v. Ferguson* (1896). It allowed segregation of blacks and whites in southern states. Abolished by the Supreme Court in *Brown v. Board of Education* (1954).

Shays's Rebellion: 1786 anti-tax uprising in Massachusetts that sent shock waves around the young United States, contributing to fears of impending anarchy if the Articles of Confederation were not revised. Helped build support for the Constitutional Convention of 1787.

single-member district/winner-take-all (SMD/WTA): A method of representation in which one representative is chosen from a particular area. The most common type of representation used in the United States, as in the House of Representatives and the Electoral College.

Slave Trade Clause: Constitutional provision that authorized Congress to outlaw the importation of slaves only after 1808.

soft money: Money raised by candidates in political campaigns that is outside the restrictions of campaign finance law but nevertheless useful for financing a campaign.

Solicitor General: The third-highest official in the Justice Department; represents the U.S. government before the Supreme Court. Also conducts appeals of cases in which the U.S. government is a party.

Speaker: The presiding officer of the U.S. House of Representatives, elected by the House at the beginning of each Congress.

spectrum scarcity: The fundamental assumption behind broadcast regulation; specifically, the idea that the amount of space on the airwaves is finite and that the federal government therefore can regulate broadcasters in the public interest.

spin control: Attempts made by government officials, political candidates, or staffs to influence the way stories are reported by the news media.

stafflation: Term applied to the rapid growth in the size, complexity, and power of the staffs of high government officials in recent decades.

standing committee: A congressional committee that has permanent existence, jurisdiction over an area of public policy, and membership determined by party leaders.

stare decisis: Latin for "let the decision stand"; the principle underlying the notion of precedent in court decisions.

state-centered federalism: The view that the Constitution created a union of sovereign states, which could overrule the national government when there was disagreement between the two levels. Effectively ended by the Civil War.

straw poll: A systematic questioning of people on a specific question that does not include a scientific sampling of the population.

suffrage: The right to vote.

think tank: A non-profit organization whose members engage in research that is often directed at influencing, through education rather than lobbying, policy makers and their decisions.

Three-fifths Clause: A provision of the U.S. Constitution that embodies a compromise made over slavery. Under it, only three-fifths the number of slaves in any state were counted toward the state's population for purposes of determining the apportionment of seats in Congress.

tripartite government: Term applied to the kind of republicanism adopted in the United States, in which governmental power is divided among three branches (legislative, executive, judicial).

trustee: Term applied to a legislator who seeks to make decisions on the basis of conscience and the public interest rather than constituent views and interests.

turnout: The measure of what percentage of possible voters actually votes in any given election; may be determined as a percentage of all potential voters or all registered voters.

unanimous consent: The normal method of conducting business in the U.S. Senate, by which most procedural motions are adopted so long as no senator dissents.

unwritten constitution: The body of customs, precedents, structures, and other arrangements that have grown up over the course of American history and which shape the way governance is actually conducted in this regime. None have been added to the written constitution, but all influence national politics.

veto: The power to say no; specifically, the president's power to reject bills passed by Congress unless that rejection is overridden by a two-thirds vote in each house of the legislature.

Virginia Plan: Scheme presented at the Constitutional Convention of 1787 that called for replacement of the Articles of Confederation by a national government with three branches.

White House Office: That division of the Executive Office of the President that houses the president's most senior aides and the most politically oriented staff.

Notes

Chapter 1

1. Adapted from David Edwards, professor of government at the University of Texas at Austin. Edwards articulated a somewhat different definition of politics in his American Government class, for which I was his teaching assistant in 1980 and 1981. I have altered the definition to fit my own needs, and he is not to be blamed for it.
2. Adapted from Forrest McDonald, *The American Presidency: An Intellectual History* (Lawrence: University Press of Kansas, 1994), p. 1.
3. See Stephen L. Wasby, *Political Science: The Discipline and Its Dimensions* (New York: Charles Scribner's Sons, 1970).
4. Ernest Barker, ed. *The Politics of Aristotle* (Oxford: Clarendon Press, 1950), p. 130.
5. Z. Anthony Kruszewski, a former colleague of mine and native of Poland, related this story to me.
6. Barker, *Politics of Aristotle,* p. 133.
7. Ibid, pp. 210–211.
8. *The Federalist,* No. 10. As part of the public record of the American founding, *The Federalist* is available in several editions. All references to those essays in this book will be by the number (the individual essays bear no titles).
9. "Groundlings" were those who could not afford seats in the theatres of Shakespeare's day and thus stood on the ground around the stage—in other words, the masses of common people.
10. Forrest McDonald, *Novus Ordo Seclorum: The Intellectual Origins of the Constitution* (Lawrence: University Press of Kansas, 1985), p. 60.
11. Daniel Boorstin, *The Genius of American Politics* (Chicago: University of Chicago Press, 1953), p. 9.
12. Ibid.
13. Ibid., p. 23.
14. Ibid., pp. 28–29.

Chapter 2

1. A. M. Rosenthal, "200 Years in the News," *New York Times,* September 11, 1987, p. A31.
2. For an interesting summary of the American colonial situation, in the context of the evolution of Western civilization, see Russell Kirk, *The Roots of American Order* (Malibu, Calif.: Pepperdine University Press, 1977). For a different interpretation of the sources of the American Revolution, see Bernard Bailyn, *The Ideological Origins of the American Revolution* (New York: Macmillan, 1967).
3. The classic interpretation of the Declaration is found in Carl Becker, *The Declaration of Independence* (New York: Random House, 1958).
4. Catherine Drinker Bowen, *Miracle at Philadelphia* (Boston: Little, Brown, 1966), p. 9.
5. See Forrest McDonald, *Novus Ordo Seclorum: The Intellectual Origins of the Constitution* (Lawrence: University Press of Kansas, 1987), pp. 173–179.
6. See ibid.
7. This paragraph is drawn from the discussion in Bowen, *Miracle in Philadelphia.*
8. Quoted in ibid., p. 42.
9. This paragraph is drawn from Herbert Storing, *What the Anti-Federalists Were For* (Chicago: University of Chicago Press, 1981).
10. Ibid.
11. *The Federalist,* No. 51.
12. See McDonald, *Novus Ordo Seclorum,* pp. 10–36.
13. Charles Beard, *An Economic Interpretation of the Constitution* (New York: Macmillan, 1913). See also Edward Greenberg, "Class Rule Under the Constitution," in *How Capitalistic Is the Constitution?,* ed. Robert Goldwin and William Schambra (Washington, D.C.: American Enterprise Institute, 1982), pp. 22–48.
14. Forrest McDonald, *We the People: The Economic Origins of the Constitution* (Chicago: University of Chicago Press, 1958).
15. This section draws heavily on the work of Forrest McDonald, particularly "The Constitution and Hamiltonian Capitalism," *How Capitalistic Is the Constitution?,* pp. 49–74. See also McDonald, *Novus Ordo Seclorum.*
16. McDonald, "The Constitution and Hamiltonian Capitalism," p. 55.
17. Ibid.
18. Quoted in ibid., p. 90.
19. As is true of *The Federalist,* several editions of Smith's work are available.
20. Richard Neustadt, *Presidential Power and the Modern Presidents* (New York: Free Press, 1990), p. 29.

21. Michael Parenti, "The Constitution as an Elitist Document," in *How Democratic Is the Constitution?*, pp. 39–58.
22. Joshua Cohen and Joel Rogers, *On Democracy* (New York: Penguin, 1983). This paragraph is a summary of their argument and the author's interpretation of it.

23. This paragraph is drawn from Walter Berns, "Does the Constitution Secure These Rights?," in *How Democratic Is the Constitution?*, pp. 59–78. It represents the author's own understanding of Professor Berns's arguments.
24. Ibid., p. 77.

Chapter 3

1. Alexander Bickel, *The Morality of Consent* (New Haven, Conn.: Yale University Press, 1975), p. 29.
2. Ibid.
3. Quoted in Alexander Bickel, *The Least Dangerous Branch* (New York: Bobbs-Merrill, 1962), p. 107.
4. Ibid., p. 1.
5. Ibid.
6. *Marbury v. Madison*, 1 Cranch 137 (1803).
7. Don K. Price, *America's Unwritten Constitution* (Baton Rouge: Louisiana State University Press, 1983), p. 9.
8. *Baker v. Carr*, 369 U.S. 186 (1962).
9. *Wesberry v. Sanders*, 376 U.S. 1 (1964).
10. *Reynolds v. Sims*, 377 U.S. 533 (1964).
11. *McCulloch v. Maryland*, 4 Wheat. 316 (1819).
12. *Gibbons v. Ogden*, 9 Wheat. 1 (1824).
13. *United States v. Darby Lumber Co.*, 312 U.S. 100 (1941).
14. *Heart of Atlanta Motel v. United States*, 379 U.S. 241 (1964).
15. Susan Eckerly, "No Money . . . No Mandate!" *Washington Times*, June 7, 1994, p. A14.

16. Quoted in G. Tracy Mehan III, "'The Buck's Passed Here: Unfunded Mandates for State and Local Government," *The Heritage Lectures*, No. 467 (Washington, D.C.: The Heritage Foundation, 1933), p. 1.
17. *Garcia v. San Antonio Metropolitan Transit Authority*, 469 U.S. 528 (1985).
18. Martin Shapiro, "The Supreme Court from Early Burger to Early Rehnquist," in *The New American Political System*, second version, ed. Anthony King (Washington, D.C.: AEI Press, 1990), p. 77.
19. *United States v. Curtiss-Wright Export Corporation*, 299 U.S. 304 (1936).
20. Shapiro, "Supreme Court," pp. 47–48.
21. Ibid., p. 78.
22. Quoted in William Lasser, *Perspectives on American Government* (New York: D.C. Heath, 1992), p. 558.
23. J. Clifford Wallace, "The Case for Judicial Restraint," *Judicature* 71 (August/September 1987): 82.
24. Beckel, *The Morality of Consent*, p. 26.

Chapter 4

1. *Barron v. Baltimore*, 7 Peters 243 (1833).
2. *Githlow v. New York*, 45 S.Ct. 625 (1925).
3. *Engle v. Vitale*, 370 U.S. 421 (1962).
4. *Lee v. Wiseman*, 112 S.Ct. 2649 (1992).
5. *Brown v. Board of Education*, 67 S.Ct. 504 (1947).
6. *New York Times*, July 8, 1994, p. B10.
7. *Sherbert v. Verner*, 83 S.Ct. 1790 (1963).
8. *West Virginia State Board of Education v. Barnette*, 63 S.Ct. 1178 (1943).
9. *In the Matter of Hamilton*, 657 S.W. 2d 425 (Tenn. App. 1983).
10. *Employment Division v. Smith*, 494 U.S. 872 (1990).
11. *Goldman v. Weinberger*, 106 S.Ct. 1310 (1986).
12. *New York Times Co. v. United States*, 91 S.Ct. 2140 (1971).
13. *Murdock v. Pennsylvania*, 63 S.Ct. 870 (1943).
14. *Brandenburg v. Ohio*, 89 S.Ct. 1827 (1969).
15. *R.A.V. v. St. Paul*, 112 S.Ct. 2538 (1992).
16. *New York Times v. Sullivan*, 84 S.Ct. 710 (1964).
17. *Brinegar v. United States*, 69 S.Ct. 1302 (1949).
18. *Katz v. United States*, 88 S.Ct. 507 (1967).
19. *Ker v. California*, 83 S.Ct. 1623 (1963).
20. *Tennessee v. Garner*, 105 S.Ct. 1694 (1985).
21. *Miranda v. Arizona*, 86 S.Ct. 1602 (1966).
22. *Mapp v. Ohio*, 81 S.Ct. 1684 (1961).
23. *Gideon v. Wainwright*, 83 S.Ct. 792 (1963).
24. *Furman v. Georgia*, 92 S.Ct. 2726 (1972).
25. *Gregg v. Georgia*, 96 S.Ct. 2909 (1976).
26. *Civil Rights Cases*, 3 S.Ct. 18 (1883).

27. *Plessy v. Ferguson*, 16 S.Ct. 1138 (1896).
28. *Brown v. Board of Education*, 74 S.Ct. 686 (1954).
29. *Alexander v. Holmes County*, 90 S.Ct. 29 (1969).
30. *Board of Education of Oklahoma City Public Schools v. Dowell*, 111 S.Ct. 630 (1991).
31. *Freeman v. Pitts*, 112 S.Ct. 1430 (1992).
32. *Missouri v. Jenkins*, 110 S.Ct. 1651 (1990).
33. *Regents of the University of California v. Bakke*, 438 U.S. 265 (1978).
34. *Fullilove v. Klutznick*, 448 U.S. 448 (1980).
35. *City of Richmond v. J.A. Croson Company*, 488 U.S. 469 (1989).
36. Otis H. Stephens Jr. and John M. Scheb II, *American Constitutional Law* (Minneapolis: West Publishing, 1993), p. 602.
37. *United States v. Eichman*, 496 U.S. 310 (1990).
38. *New York Times*, November 10, 1993, p. A14.
39. *Roe v. Wade*, 410 U.S. 113 (1973).
40. *Griswold v. Connecticut*, 381 U.S. 479 (1965).
41. Mary Ann Glendon, *Rights Talk: The Impoverishment of Political Discourse* (New York: Free Press, 1992). The following summary and conclusions drawn from it are my own. Any misinterpretation of Professor Glendon's argument is mine.
42. Fred Siegel, "Nothing in Moderation," *The Atlantic*, May 1990, pp. 108–110.
43. Paul Savoy, "Time for a Second Bill of Rights," *The Nation*, June 17, 1991, pp. 1, 814–816.
44. Quoted in Siegel, "Nothing in Moderation," p. 109.

Chapter 5

1. Quoted in Forrest McDonald, "A Nation Once Again?" *National Review,* July 11, 1994, p. 30.
2. See Donald J. Devine, *The Political Culture of the United States* (Boston: Little, Brown, 1972); and Gabriel Almond and Sidney Verba, *The Civic Culture* (Boston: Little, Brown, 1965).
3. Quoted in Arthur Schlesinger Jr., *The Disuniting of America* (New York: W. W. Norton, 1993), p. 12.
4. Alexis de Tocqueville, *Democracy in America,* edited and abridged by Richard D. Heffner (New York: New American Library, 1956).
5. Synthesized by the author from descriptions presented in Devine and in Almond and Verba.
6. Tocqueville, *Democracy in America,* p. 192.
7. Ibid.
8. Ibid., p. 198.
9. For a more elaborate analysis, see Peverill Squire, "Why the 1936 Literary Digest Poll Failed," *Public Opinion* 52 (1988): 125–132.
10. This discussion is adapted from Charles W. Roll and Albert H. Cantril, *Polls: Their Use and Misuse* (Cabin John, Md.: Seven Locks Press, 1980). See also Everett Carl Ladd, *The American Polity,* 5th ed. (New York: W. W. Norton, 1993), p. 295.
11. *Yick Wo v. Hopkins,* 118 U.S. 356 (1886).
12. *National Socialist Party v. Skokie,* 434 U.S. 1327 (1977).
13. *Coates v. Cincinnati,* 402 U.S. 611 (1971).
14. Polling data cited in James Davison Hunter, *Before the Shooting Begins: Searching for Democracy in America's Culture War* (New York: Free Press, 1994), pp. 86–87.
15. Ibid.
16. Ibid., p. 90.
17. John Courtney Murray, *We Hold These Truths* (New York: Sheed and Ward, 1960).
18. Hunter, *Before the Shooting Begins,* p. 5.
19. Diane Ravitch, "Multiculturalism: E Pluribus Plures," in *Debating PC,* ed. Paul Berman (New York: Bantam, 1992), p. 275.
20. Ibid.
21. Ibid., p. 276.
22. Ibid., p. 277.
23. Ibid., p. 278.
24. Schlesinger, *The Disuniting of America,* p. 76.
25. Ravitch, "Multiculturalism," p. 282.
26. Molefi Kete Asante, "Multiculturalism: An Exchange," in *Debating PC,* ed. Paul Berman (New York: Bantam, 1992), p. 175.
27. Schlesinger, *The Disuniting of America,* p. 45.

Chapter 6

1. This paraphrases a suggestion once made by columnist George Will to stress the significance of interest groups in contemporary Washington.
2. Jeffery M. Berry, *The Interest Group Society,* 2nd ed. (New York: HarperCollins, 1989), p. 4.
3. This paragraph relies heavily on Allan J. Cigler and Burdett A. Loomis, *Interest Group Politics,* 3rd ed. (Washington, D.C.: CQ Press, 1991).
4. Ibid.
5. This section draws heavily on the discussion in Berry, *Interest Group Society,* pp. 6–8.
6. *New York Times,* March 10, 1993, p. A10.
7. Robert Salisbury, "The Paradox of Interest Groups in Washington—More Groups, Less Clout," in *The New American Political System,* 2nd version (Washington, D.C.: American Enterprise Institute, 1990), p. 227.
8. William Lunch, *The Nationalization of American Politics* (Berkeley: University of California Press, 1987), p. 18.
9. Hugh Heclo, "Issue Networks and the Executive Establishment," in *The New American Political System,* pp. 87–124, ed. Anthony King (Washington, D.C.: American Enterprise Institute, 1987).
10. Salisbury, "Paradox of Interest Groups," p. 212.
11. Loomis and Cigler, *Interest Group Politics,* p. 26.
12. Ibid.

Chapter 7

1. *Cousins v. Wigoda,* 419 U.S. 477 (1975).
2. *Democratic Party v. LaFollette,* 450 U.S. 106 (1981).
3. Xandra Kayden, *Campaign Organization* (Lexington, Mass., Lexington Books, 1978), p. 61.
4. Gary Jacobson, *The Politics of Congressional Elections,* 3rd ed. (New York: HarperCollins, 1992), pp. 81–82.
5. Ryan J. Barilleaux and Randall E. Adkins, "The Nominations: Process and Patterns," in *The Elections of 1992,* ed. Michael Nelson (Washington, D.C.: CQ Press, 1993), pp. 21–56.
6. *Buckley v. Valeo,* 424 U.S. 1 (1976).
7. Frank Sorauf, *Inside Campaign Finance* (New Haven, Conn.: Yale University Press, 1992), p. 213.
8. Ibid., pp. 30–31.
9. Ibid., p. 30.
10. Ibid., p. 178.
11. Hendrick Smith, *The Power Game* (New York: Ballantine Books, 1988), p. 154.
12. Ibid., p. 157.
13. Ibid.
14. Mark Green, "Take the Money and Reform," *The New Republic,* May 14, 1990, p. 27.
15. Howard Penniman, "U.S. Elections: Really a Bargain?" *Public Opinion* (June/July 1984): 51.
16. Norman Ornstein, "Money in Politics: Campaign Finance Reform," *Current* (October 1992): 11.

17. Robert J. Samuelson, "The Campaign Reform Failure," reprinted in Annual Editions, *American Government 86/87,* ed. Bruce Steinbrinckner (Guiford, Conn.: Dushkin Publishing Group, 1986), p. 194.

18. Ibid.
19. Ibid.

Chapter 8

1. *The Federalist,* No. 48.
2. Quoted by Madison in ibid.
3. Edmund Burke, "Speech to Electors at Bristo," in *Burke's Politics,* ed. Ross J. S. Hoffman and Paul Levack (New York: Knopf, 1949), p. 116.
4. Ibid.
5. This story is related by Buckley in his memoir and reflections on the Senate. See James L. Buckley, *If Men Were Angels: A View from the Senate* (New York: Putnam, 1975).
6. Susan Webb Hammond, "Congressional Caucuses in the Policy Process," in *Congress Reconsidered,* 4th ed., ed. Lawrence C. Dodd and Bruce I. Oppenheimer (Washington, D.C.: CQ Press, 1989), p. 353.
7. David J. Vogler, *The Politics of Congress* (Madison, Wisc.: Brown & Benchmark, 1993), p. 208.
8. Adapted from ibid.
9. Norman Ornstein, Thomas E. Mann, and Michael J. Malbin, eds. *Vital Statistics on Congress, 1989–1990* (Washington, D.C.: CQ Press, 1990), pp. 56–57.
10. David Mayhew, *Congress: The Electoral Connection* (New Haven, Conn.: Yale University Press, 1974). The following discussion draws heavily from Mayhew.
11. Christopher Georges and Katherine Boo, "Capital Hill 20510," *Washington Monthly* (October 1992): 37.
12. Ibid., p. 41.
13. Ibid., p. 43.
14. Hedrick Smith, *The Power Game* (New York: Ballantine Books, 1988), p. 122.
15. Ibid., p. 149.
16. Roger Davidson and Walter Oleszek, *Congress and Its Members,* 3rd ed. (Washington, D.C.: CQ Press, 1990), p. 138.
17. Christopher Deering, "Congressional Politics: An Introduction and an Approach," in *Congressional Politics,* ed. Christopher Deering (Chicago: Dorsey Press, 1989), pp. 1–2.
18. *Wall Street Journal,* May 13, 1988, p. 17A.
19. These terms come from popular press stories on Congress in publications such as *Newsweek* and *The New Republic.*
20. Hendrik Hertzberg, "Twelve Is Enough," *The New Republic,* May 14, 1990, pp. 22–26. The following discussion draws heavily from Hertzberg.
21. Peter Kahn, "A Word in Defense of Incumbents," *Washington Post,* October 23, 1990, p. A-21.
22. Ibid.

Chapter 9

1. The "hats" metaphor for presidential roles originated with Clinton Rossiter, *The American Presidency,* revised (New York: Mentor Books, 1960).
2. See Thomas E. Cronin, ed., *Inventing the American Presidency* (Lawrence: University Press of Kansas, 1989).
3. See Donald L. Robinson, *To the Best of My Ability: The Presidency and the Constitution* (New York: W.W. Norton, 1987), especially ch. 4.
4. *The Federalist,* No. 70.
5. Ibid.
6. Robinson, *To the Best of My Ability,* p. 91.
7. Paraphrased from Rexford Tugwell, *The Enlargement of the Presidency* (Garden City, NY: Doubleday, 1960).
8. Discussion of the evolution of the office draws heavily on Ryan J. Barilleaux, *The Post-Modern Presidency* (New York: Praeger, 1988), especially ch. 2.
9. The postmodern presidency has been described in ibid. and Richard Rose, *The Postmodern President* (Chatham, N.J.: Chatham House, 1988). The two books describe the postmodern presidency in very different ways, but their arguments have been synthesized (and simplified) here.
10. Quoted in Samuel Kernell and Samuel Popkin, eds., *Chief of Staff* (Berkeley: University of California Press, 1987), p. 182.
11. Richard Neustadt, *Presidential Power and the Modern Presidents* (New York: Free Press, 1990), p. 3.
12. Samuel Kernell, *Going Public: New Strategies of Presidential Leadership,* 2nd ed. (Washington, D.C.: CQ Press, 1993).
13. Aaron Wildavsky, "The Two Presidencies," in *Perspectives on the Presidency,* ed. Aaron Wildavsky (Boston: Little, Brown, 1975), p. 449.
14. Quoted in Louis Fisher, *Constitutional Conflicts Between Congress* (Princeton: Princeton University Press, 1985), p. 23.
15. Quoted in ibid.
16. Adapted from Erwin Hargrove and Michael Nelson, *Presidents, Politics, and Policy* (New York: Alfred A. Knopf, 1984).
17. Daniel P. Franklin, "The President Is Too Powerful in Foreign Affairs," in *Point-Counterpoint: Readings in American Government,* 4th ed., ed. Herbert M. Levine (New York: St. Martin's Press, 1992), pp. 175–182.
18. R. Gordon Hoxie, "We Have a Constitutional Presidency: What We Need Is a Constitutional Congress," *Points of View,* 5th ed., ed. Robert E. DiClerico and Allan S. Hammock (New York: McGraw-Hill, 1992), pp. 206–214.

Chapter 10

1. The theoretical concepts in this paragraph are adapted from David Nachmias and David H. Rosenbloom, *Bureaucratic Government USA* (New York: St. Martin's Press, 1980), pp. 12–13. Nachmias and Rosenbloom add an additional feature—nonmarketable output—that I have discarded because I disagree that it is essential to defining bureaucracy. The examples from the USPS are drawn from U.S. government sources.
2. Anthony Downs, *Inside Bureaucracy* (Boston: Little, Brown, 1967), pp. 24–25.
3. Nachmias and Rosenbloom, *Bureaucratic Government USA,* p. 15.
4. *Washington Post,* July 21, 1993, p. A19.
5. Charles Peters, *How Washington Really Works,* 3rd ed. (Reading, Mass.: Addison-Wesley Publishing, 1992), pp. 56–57.
6. Michael Nelson, "The Irony of American Bureaucracy," in *Bureaucratic Power in National Policy Making,* ed. Francis E. Rourke (Boston: Little, Brown, 1986), pp. 164–166. See also James Q. Wilson, "The Rise of the Bureaucratic State," *The Public Interest* 41 (Fall 1975): 77–103.
7. Martin Shapiro, "The Supreme Court from Early Burger to Early Rehnquist," in *The New American Political System,* 2nd version, ed. Anthony King (Washington, D.C.: AEI Press, 1990), p. 77.
8. Kenneth F. Warren, *Administrative Law in the Political System,* 2nd ed. (St. Paul, Minn.: West Publishing Co., 1988), pp. 200–201.
9. Ibid., pp. 206–207.
10. This paragraph draws heavily on Martin Tolchin, "Are Judge and Agency Too Close for Justice?"
11. *Bowen v. City of New York,* 476 U.S. 467 (1986).
12. Thomas Cronin, *The State of the Presidency,* 2nd ed. (Boston: Little Brown, 1980), p. 274.
13. William Lunch, *The Nationalization of American Politics* (Berkeley, Calif.: University of California Press, 1987), p. 177.
14. *New York Times,* July 8, 1993, p. A1.
15. James Q. Wilson, *Bureaucracy* (New York: Basic Books, 1989), p. 245.
16. Nachmias and Rosenbloom, *Bureaucratic Government USA,* p. 31.
17. Peters, *How Washington Really Works,* p. 43.
18. Ibid., p. 62.
19. Ibid.
20. Ibid., p. 60.
21. John A. Rohr, *To Run a Constitution: The Legitimacy of the Administrative State* (Lawrence: University Press of Kansas, 1986), p. 39.
22. Ibid., p. 53.

Chapter 11

1. This paragraph draws from "Your Hamburger: 41,000 Regulations," *U.S. News and World Report,* February 11, 1980, p. 49. Although the citation is dated, the information is still essentially accurate.
2. David O'Brien, *Storm Center: The Supreme Court in American Politics* (New York: W.W. Norton, 1990); pp. 150–152.
3. Henry Abraham, *The Judicial Process,* 4th ed. (New York: Oxford University Press, 1980), p. 102.
4. Ibid., pp. 141–142.
5. Ibid.
6. This section draws heavily on ibid., pp. 143–145.
7. William Lunch, *The Nationalization of American Politics* (Berkeley: University of California Press, 1987), p. 148. The following discussion draws heavily from this source.
8. *The Supreme Court at Work* (Washington, D.C.: Congressional Quarterly, 1990), p. 66.
9. Ibid., pp. 157–158.
10. This process is most succinctly described in Bob Woodward and Scott Armstrong, *The Brethren: Inside the Supreme Court* (New York: Simon & Schuster, 1979), pp. xii–xiv. I have adopted the seven-step format outlined there.
11. *New York Times,* March 8, 1993, p. B9.
12. Ibid., p. A1.
13. This discussion is drawn from Martin Shapiro, "The Supreme Court from Early Burger to Early Rehnquist," *The New American Political System,* 2nd version, ed. Anthony King (Washington, D.C.: AEI Press, 1990), pp. 74–78.
14. Ibid., p. 47–48.
15. Ibid., p. 60.
16. Stephen L. Carter, "A Litmus Test For Judges? It Demeans the Court," *New York Times,* April 28, 1993, p. A13.
17. Paul Gewirtz, "Legal Views Do Matter," *New York Times,* April 28, 1993, p. A13.
18. Ibid.

Chapter 12

1. Quoted in Congressional Quarterly, *How Congress Works* (Washington, D.C.: Congressional Quarterly, 1991), p. 105.
2. Bradley Patterson, *The Ring of Power* (New York: Basic Books, 1989).
3. Ibid., p. 339.
4. "Counting Noses at the White House," *Washington Post National Weekly Edition,* April 26–May 2, 1993, p. 34.
5. Norman Ornstein, Thomas Mann, and Michael Malbin, eds., *Vital Statistics on Congress, 1991–1992* (Washington, D.C.: CQ Press, 1992), p. 125.

6. Richard A. Posner, *The Federal Courts: Crisis and Reform* (Cambridge, Mass.: Harvard University Press, 1985), pp. 102–103.
7. Austin Ranney, "Broadcasting, Narrowcasting, and Politics," in *The New American Political System,* 2nd version, ed. Anthony King (Washington, D.C.: AEI Press, 1990), p. 181.
8. Walter Karp, "All the Congressmen's Men," *Harper's Magazine* (July 1989), p. 56.
9. Quoted in ibid.
10. Ranney, "Broadcasting," p. 185.
11. From the Federal Communications Act, quoted in ibid., p. 186.
12. Ibid.
13. Quoted in ibid., p. 184.
14. Ibid.
15. Ibid., p. 185.
16. Alexis de Tocqueville, *Democracy in America,* edited and abridged by Richard D. Heffner (New York: Mentor Books, 1956), p. 91.
17. William Rusher, quoted in Karp, "All the Congressmen's Men," p. 56.
18. Michael Kelly, "David Gergen: Master of the Game," *New York Times Magazine,* October 31, 1993, p. 64.
19. Ibid., pp. 64–65 (emphasis on original).
20. Quoted in Samuel Kernell and Samuel L. Popkin, eds. *Chief of Staff* (Berkeley: University of California Press, 1986), p. 80.

21. Paul Light, *Forging Legislation* (New York: W. W. Norton & Co, 1992), pp. 48–49.
22. *New York Times,* January 5, 1995, p. A12.
23. Karp, "All the Congressmen's Men," p. 56.
24. Ibid., p. 57.
25. Michael Malbin, *Unelected Representatives: Congressional Staff and the Future of Representative Government* (New York: Basic Books, 1980), p. 243.
26. Posner, *The Federal Courts,* p. 107.
27. Ibid., p. 109.
28. Kelly, "David Gergen," p. 64.
29. Larry Sabato, quoted in Tony Case, "Covering Campaigns," *Editor and Publisher,* July 25, 1992, p. 12.
30. Carl Bernstein, "The Idiot Culture," *The New Republic,* June 8, 1992, pp. 22–28.
31. Michael Gartner, quoted ibid., p. 38.
32. Nelson W. Polsby, "Was Hart's Life Unfairly Probed?" *New York Times,* May 6, 1988, p. 35.
33. Hedrick Smith, *The Power Game* (New York: Ballantine, 1988) p. 282.
34. Ibid., p. 287.
35. Terry Eastland, "While Justice Sleeps," *National Review,* April 21, 1989, p. 25.
36. Ibid.
37. Quoted in Smith, *The Power Game,* pp. 282–283.
38. Harry T. Edwards, "The Rising Work Load and Perceived 'Bureaucracy' of the Federal Courts," *Iowa Law Review* 68:888.

Chapter 13

1. The following discussion of pizza labeling is drawn from Clyde H. Farnsworth, "Line-Item Pepperoni? Fiscally Sound Anchovies?" *New York Times,* June 22, 1987, p. 22; and U.S. General Accounting Office, *Food Marketing: Frozen Pizza Cheese—Representative of Broader Food Labeling Issues* (GAO/RCED-88-70), March 1988.
2. U.S. G.A.O., *Food Marketing,* p. 2.
3. Definition adapted from B. Guy Peters, *American Public Policy: Promise and Performance,* 3rd ed. (Chatham, N.J.: Chatham House, 1993), p. 4. The following discussion draws heavily on Peters's discussion on pp. 4–10.
4. Randall B. Ripley and Grace A. Franklin, *Congress, the Bureaucracy, and Public Policy,* 3rd ed. (Homewood, Ill.: Dorsey Press, 1984).
5. Ibid., p. 23.
6. Ibid., p. 27.
7. Ibid., p. 26.
8. Ibid., pp. 27–28.
9. Several different models have been developed to describe the policy-making process. Some have as few as three stages, others as many as eleven. The five-stage model employed here is adapted from Peters, *American Public Policy.*
10. Roger W. Cobb and Charles D. Elder, *Participation in American Politics,* 2nd ed. (Baltimore: The Johns Hopkins University Press, 1983), p. 85.

11. Ibid., p. 86.
12. Robert L. Lineberry, *American Public Policy: What Government Does and What Difference It Makes* (New York: Harper & Row, 1978), pp. 70–71.
13. Adapted from ibid., p. 70.
14. See Barbara Kellerman and Ryan J. Barilleaux, *The President as World Leader* (New York: St. Martin's Press, 1991), ch. 7.
15. Adapted from ibid., p. 70.
16. See Graham Allison, *Essence of Decision: Explaining the Cuban Missile Crisis* (Boston: Little Brown, 1971).
17. Adapted from ibid., pp. 70–71.
18. Jeffery Pressman and Aaron Wildavsky, *Implementation,* 2nd ed. (Berkeley: University of California Press, 1979). The following draws heavily from this source.
19. Lineberry, *American Public Policy,* p. 71.
20. Eugene Bardach, *The Implementation Game* (Cambridge, Mass.: MIT Press, 1977), p. 3.
21. Peters, *American Public Policy,* p. 350.
22. Nelson W. Polsby, *Political Innovation in America: The Politics of Policy Initiation* (New Haven, Conn.: Yale University Press, 1984). The interpretations of Professor Polsby's results presented here are my own.

Chapter 14

1. See John M. Rothgeb Jr., *Defining Power: Influence and Force in the Contemporary International System* (New York: St. Martin's Press, 1993).
2. See Hedley Bull, *The Anarchical Society* (New York: Columbia University Press, 1977).
3. See Ernest Gellner, *Nations and Nationalism* (Ithaca, N.Y.: Cornell University Press, 1983).
4. See Kellerman and Barilleaux, *The President as World Leader* (New York: St. Martin's Press, 1991).
5. Randall B. Ripley and Grace A. Franklin, *Congress, the Bureaucracy, and Public Policy,* 3rd ed. (Homewood, Ill.: Dorsey Press, 1984), p. 30.
6. This discussion expands upon Ryan J. Barilleaux, "George Bush and the Changing Context of Presidential Leadership," in *Leadership and the Bush Presidency,* ed. Ryan J. Barilleaux and Mary E. Stuckey (New York: Praeger, 1992), pp. 11–12.
7. E. S. Corwin, *The President: Office and Powers,* 5th ed. (New York: Cornell University Press, 1986), p. 201.
8. Quoted in Kellerman and Barilleaux, *The President as World Leader,* p. xiii.
9. W. Phillips Shively, *Power and Choice,* 3rd ed. (New York: McGraw-Hill, 1993), p. 144.
10. Ibid., p. 146.
11. On national constitutions, see Ivo D. Duchacek, *Power Maps: Comparative Politics of Constitutions* (Santa Barbara, Calif.: ABC-Clio, 1973).
12. On George Bush and the end of the cold war, see Ryan J. Barilleaux, "George Bush, Germany, and the New World Order," in *Shepherd of Democracy?* ed. Carl C. Hodge and Cathal J. Nolan, *Contributions in Political Science,* #305 (Westport, Conn.: Greenwood Press, 1992), pp. 161–172.

Chapter 15

1. *National Journal,* July 17, 1993, p. 1838.
2. This story may be apochryphal, but it is revealing of Franklin's view of things.
3. David Walls, *The Activist's Almanac* (New York: Simon & Schuster, 1993), p. 33.
4. This list drawn in part from Thomas E. Cronin, *Direct Democracy, The Twentieth Century Fund Book* (Cambridge, Mass.: Harvard University Press, 1989), p. 181.
5. James Sundquist, *Constitutional Reform and Effective Government* (Washington, D.C.: Bookings Institution, 1986), p. 111.
6. Committee on the Constitutional System, *Bicentennial Analysis of the American Political Structure* (Washington, D.C.: Committee on the Constitutional System, 1987), pp. 10–12.
7. Ibid.
8. James Q. Wilson, "Does the Separation of Powers Still Work? *The Public Interest* 86 (Winter 1987), pp. 36–52. To be accurate, Wilson was not directly answering the CCS, but an article written by one of that group's leaders (Washington attorney Lloyd Cutler); Wilson's essay has been widely reprinted, however, as a *de facto* response to the CCS.
9. Ibid., p. 39.
10. Ibid., p 44.
11. Ibid., p. 45.
12. Ibid., p. 45.
13. John Kincaid, "A Proposal to Strengthen Federalism," *The Journal of State Government* 62 (January/February 1989), pp. 36–45.
14. Griffin Bell, "Constitutional Convention: Oh, Stop the Hand-Wringing," *Washington Post,* April 14, 1984.
15. Melvin Laird, "James Madison Wouldn't Approve," *Washington Post,* February 13, 1984.
16. Ibid.

Photo Credits

Index